NO NAMES
NO PACK DRILL

An Oral History of
Canadians at War in Afghanistan

by

Steve MacBeth, MSC, MSM (w/Bar), CD

Library and Archives Canada Cataloguing in Publication
MacBeth, Steve, author
No Names No Pack Drill / Steve MacBeth

Issued in print and electronic formats.
ISBN: 978-1-998501-21-2 (paperback)
ISBN: 978-1-998501-22-9 (ebook)

Editor: Phil Halton
Cover Design: Pablo Javier Herrera
Interior Design: Winston S. Prescott

Double Dagger Books Ltd.
Toronto, Ontario, Canada
www.doubledagger.ca

DEDICATION

To my two families.

To my family, who carried the weight of my absence and lived through the many returns, giving me strength in ways that I could not have foreseen, your support and love are my buttresses against the hard days.

To my Regimental Family, my brothers and sisters who shared the dust, danger, and darkness with me in Afghanistan—we faced the challenges together, and many still fight their own battles today. Your courage, resilience, and unbreakable bond remind me daily that we are never truly alone, no matter where our paths take us. This work hopefully bears witness for all of us.

Pro Patria.

Kandahar Province

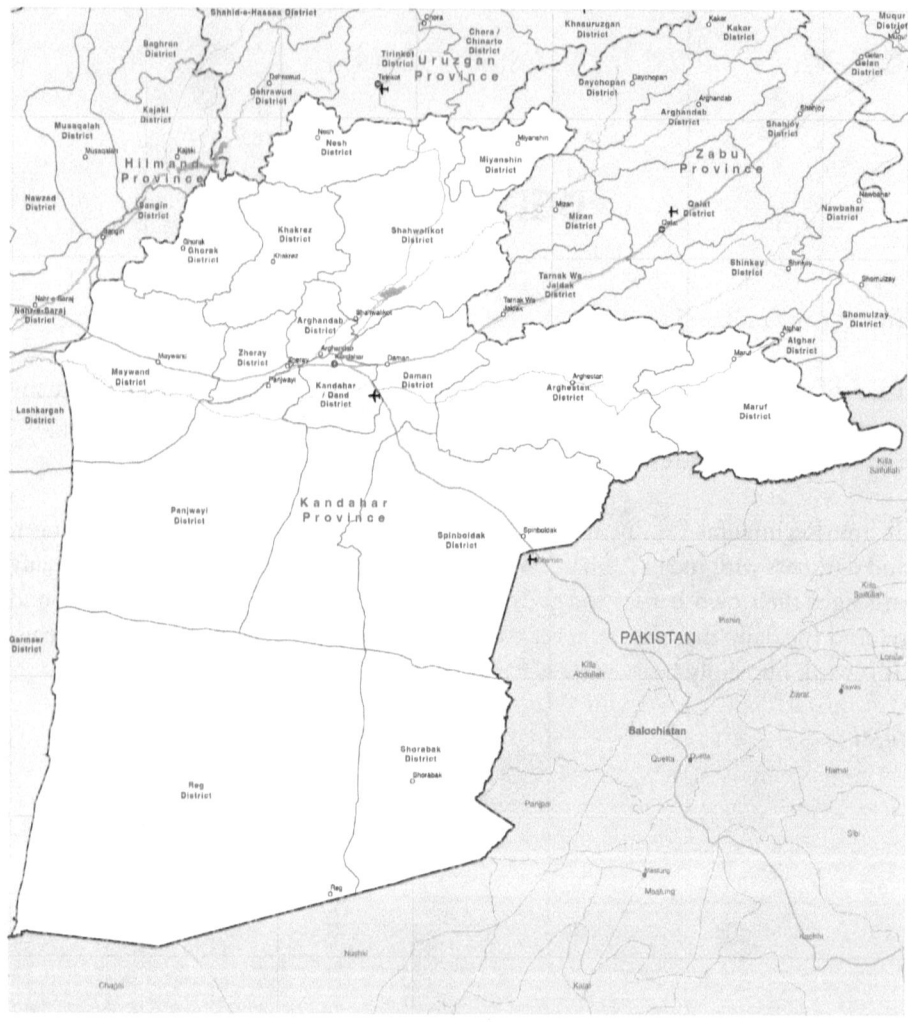

TABLE OF CONTENTS

GLOSSARY OF TERMS

A

Adjutant. The senior staff officer to the Battalion Commander. Usually, a Captain. On deployment, the Adjutant is responsible to the Commander for all administration and deals with all personnel issues. These can range from policy change to casualty tracking and the repatriation of the fallen.

ANA. Afghan National Army. The Afghan National Defence Security forces were partnered with the Canadian Army. They were mentored and advised by the Operational Mentor and Liaison Teams (OMLT)

ANP. Afghan National Police. This national police force, as a Para-military organization, partnered with the Canadian Army to bring the rule of law to the operations areas and interact directly with Afghan populations. The ANP were mentored and advised by the Police Operational Mentor and Liaison Teams (POMLT)

Aussie Peel Back. A section-level tactic for withdrawing under fire in canalizing terrain. It maximizes firepower forward and effectively breaks contact with the enemy so that the section may regroup and then manoeuvre to gain a tactical advantage. Made famous by Australians fighting in the jungles of Vietnam.

ARV. Armoured Recovery Vehicle. This vehicle is based on the Leopard tank chassis. It can move under enemy contact and recover friendly vehicles that have been destroyed or become stuck.

AAR. After Action Review. This post-operational debrief occurs as soon as possible after an event occurs. It is designed to allow soldiers to talk about incidents and learn internally what they could do better. It was also used to talk through events that saw the loss of comrades and served the emotional purpose of starting the healing process.

Audi 5000. Soldier slang for we are leaving. "We are Audi 5000".

Apache. The AH-64 Apache is an American twin turbo-shaft attack helicopter. This platform was utilized to escort Canadian Chinook Helicopters and provide ground forces close combat aviation support while in contact with Taliban elements. In addition to the US, the UK and Dutch Apaches supported Canadian elements in the Kandahar area of operations.

A-10. Single-seat, twin-engine, straight-wing subsonic US aircraft designed for close air support missions. This system was utilized heavily to support Canadian ground forces in contact.

AOR. Area of Responsibility. This is military jargon for the ground that a unit is responsible for securing.

B

Boat. Royal Canadian Regiment soldiers gave this nickname to the LAV III armoured vehicle. It is a handed-down tradition from when the regiment had armoured vehicles that swam. It is not practical, as the LAV III cannot swim, and so when the reader sees "the boats," the soldier is speaking about an LAV III.

BDA. Battle Damage Assessment. Required after indirect or air-based munitions were launched at a target, to determine effect, if there was any collateral damage, and to collect any intelligence that may be left in the target area. Often soldiers patrolled to the strike location to confirm and collect the dead.

BIP. Blow in Place. Engineers usually control an explosion on enemy equipment or explosive materials discovered during operations, which denies the enemy's use.

Badger. Armoured Engineer vehicle based on the Leopard 2 chassis. Primarily utilized for breaching obstacles so that the infantry could assault the enemy position. In Afghanistan, they were often used to create access roads through the grape fields and to knock down grape huts that were providing cover to enemy fighters.

BMP/BRDM. Two different types of Russian armoured personnel carriers could be found in Afghanistan. These were often remnants of the previous conflict, and in Kabul, thousands were left behind when the Russians withdrew.

Bison. Canadian armoured vehicle. Eight wheels, light armoured, armed with a 7.62 machine gun. Utilized for protected mobility (battle taxi through Kandahar), it was used as Command Posts, Electronic Warfare specialty vehicles, and was the primary armoured ambulance for the Canadian fighting elements.

Bn. Battalion. An Infantry Battalion is about 800 personnel and forms the basic building block of the Battle Groups in Afghanistan. Each Battalion has a Headquarters group, three rifle companies, a combat support company, and a combat service support company. There are three Battalions in each of the three Canadian Infantry Regiments. All nine Battalions deployed to Afghanistan between 2001 and 2014.

BG. A BG is custom-organized to address a specific task for a limited period and will be formed with sufficient combat power, combat service support, and other resources to allow it to operate relatively autonomously for the expected period. In Afghanistan, the Battle Groups were grouped for a six-month "workup period "and a seven-month tour. The BG had an Infantry Battalion as the initial building block and then added an engineer squadron, an artillery battery, a Leopard 2 tanks squadron, and an armoured reconnaissance squadron.

Bde. Brigade. A Brigade is an Army formation of approximately 5000 personnel.

Box Amb. Colloquial for the box shape of an ambulance on a utility truck chassis

C

Carl Gustav. 84mm anti-armour weapon. Shoulder fired used to destroy vehicles or to breach the thick mud walls of buildings in Kandahar.

Camp Julien. Canada's Base for the Battle Group in Kabul between 2003 and 2005.

Chest-Rig. Often called a "rig" in soldiers' narrative. These non-issued webbing carried ammunition, water, and other fighting necessities. The Canadian "tacvest" was not a popular item and there was a constant tension between leaders wanting soldiers to use issued equipment and soldiers purchasing preferred equipment off the economy.

COP. Combat Outpost. A small base for a platoon or less of soldiers. They are usually shared with Afghan Security Forces.

Cordon. This is the tactical action that soldiers take to control an area. This is usually done as an "inner" and "outer" cordon. This was often done on IED incidents and was an initial step to controlling the scene.

Company. This is the primary sub-unit of an Infantry Battalion. A Company size ranges between 120 and 160 infantry soldiers.

Combat team. A combat team is a sub-unit grouping based on an infantry company or tank squadron with elements of the other arm attached and supporting elements such as combat engineers and artillery. The combat team is the primary combined arms-building block in the Canadian Army.

CCP. Casualty collection point. This is a point where casualties that occur in battle are collected so that they can be triaged and then moved to the next level of care as necessary. It is in the CCP that their "priority of care is given." There is a chain of CCPs as each echelon collets their casualties and moves them rearward.

CO. Commanding Officer. The commanding Officer is usually a Lieutenant Colonel. Once training and preparation were complete, the infantry battalion CO would become the Battle Group CO.

CCA. Close Combat Attack (aircraft). The Canadian Battlegroup was usually supported by Apache or Kiowa helicopters, which provided close rotary-wing air support. The US, UK, and Dutch attack aviation elements also supported the Canadians.

CDA. Commander's Display Assembly. Located in the LAV III turret, this assembly provides the crew commander with the most up-to-date information about the vehicle's state and system functionality.

CIDA. Canadian International Development Agency.

CADPAT. Canadian Pattern Camouflage uniform. It is digitally generated to blend in with environmental surroundings. Canada developed three patterns for different environments: arid (desert), temperate(woodland), and Arctic (winter).

CIMIC. Civil-Military Coordination. This military specialty worked primarily out of the PRT and interacted with Afghan civil society to understand the environment and enable reconstruction and governance.

C/S 0. is the control station on the unit-level radio network. Call sign zero provides the voice of Headquarters control to the subunit (company) organizations. Subunits would be numbered C/S 1,2,3,4, etc.

Civvies. This is soldiers' vernacular for clothing that is not uniform: "I got into my civvies." It can also be used to describe the civilian population as separate from the military population: "There were a lot of civvies at the bar."

Category A, B, C, D, or 1,2,3,4. Category of casualty to prioritize the urgency of medical evacuation and care. The Categories evolved during the campaign, and so both (for example) Cat 1 or Cat A could be utilized to describe the type of casualty with the highest priority.

C130. Military Transport Aircraft that flew the replacement and resupply mission within Afghanistan. Commonly referred to as a "Hercules" or the "Herc".

C6. Canadian general-purpose machine gun. 7.62mm gas-operated, air-cooled disintegrating link. Usually, one per rifle platoon is the primary fire support weapon of dismounted infantry. It is also mounted as the Leopard and LAV III coaxial gun. It is also the pintle mount of the LAV, G-Wagon, Bison, and Leopard MBT.

C7. Primary service rifle of the Canadian Army. 5.56mm gas-operated air-cooled, semi-automatic, and capable of fully automatic fire.

C8. The carbine variant of the C7 utilizes the same rounds and operating chassis. A shortened 14.5-inch barrel made it a preferred weapon system for carriage for infantry soldiers in Afghanistan's built-up areas.

C9. Infantry section fire support weapon. A light machine gun, it is gas-operated, air-cooled, and belt-fed with 5.56mm 4B1T disintegrating link ammunition. Two C9s per rifle section (10 soldiers) provide immediate fire support when contact occurs.

Coax. These are C6 machine guns mounted parallel to the LAV III and Leopard MBT main armament. They are electronically fired from within the turret against unarmoured targets.

Chinook. The Canadian government purchased the CH-147 multi-mission twin-rotor medium-lift helicopter in Afghanistan to move people and supplies while avoiding the IED threat. It is armed with dual 7.62 GPMG for self-protection and has ballistic and other defensive suites. It can carry upwards of 30 soldiers and can sling load 12,000 kg.

CHAWLGOR. This is a contested suburb located southwest of Kandahar. It became a company forward operating base and was connected to the main access road by Route Nightmare. Soldiers named this route due to the high IED threat.

CQ. Company Quartermaster. At the company level, the Quartermaster is the senior Warrant officer responsible for all resupply and administration to the rifle company leadership. The CQ is accountable for all equipment accountability and replaces the Company Sergeant Major (CSM) should it be required.

CSM. Company Sergeant Major is the top Senior NCO in the rifle Company and is the soldier's representative to the Officer Commanding (OC). Usually, an NCO of great experience, the Sergeant Major, provides council to the OC and mentors the company's Senior NCOs. He is responsible for setting the company casualty collection point and conducting battlefield administration in concert with the company quartermaster.

CNS. Camp Nathan Smith. This was the Provincial Reconstruction Team camp located in Kandahar City. It was named after a Canadian soldier who was killed in a friendly fire incident in 2002.

CNR. Combat Net Radio is the primary communication network within the deployed forces on the ground. It provides encrypted voice communications across the Canadian and multi-national contingents.

CSAM. Crew Situational Awareness Monitor. Located in the back of the LAVIII, this monitor allowed soldiers in the back of the LAV to see what the gunner was seeing through their weapon optics.

CP. Command Post. This can represent the physical location of the headquarters from Company to Brigade. The Canadian Army utilizes the command post as the lexicon, whereas the US utilizes the "tactical operations centre."

CANCON. This was a Canadian entertainment group that provided live shows of Canadian entertainers to the troops at Christmas. This was primarily done in Kabul, not Kandahar.

D

D-Day. "Deployment Day" In military terminology, D-Day refers to the day on which a combat attack or operation is set to begin. The term is used to designate the specific day of an operation when the exact date is either not yet determined or needs to be kept secret for security reasons. The term "D-Day" often specifies the exact time an operation is to commence. For example, D+1 refers to one day after D-Day. In this instance, D-Day refers to the day that a Canadian soldier arrives in the Afghan theatre of operations.

DCO. Deputy Commanding Officer. Usually, a Major is the second command to the Commanding Officer of the battle group. Is responsible for overseeing the function of the headquarters, all BG administration, and, if necessary, taking over the battle group if the CO is a casualty.

DFAC. Dining Facility. This is a US acronym that Canadians adopted while on US bases. The Canadian army calls the kitchen and eating area a Mess Hall or Mess.

Down Range. This is a slang term for the operational area. Working "Down Range" means working outside the wire in the zone of operations.

E

Echo. Combat Engineers Radio Call Sign. This is a radio shorthand for any engineer call sign. Often used in soldier speak for their attached engineers.

ECM. Electronic Counter Measures. This could be man-portable or vehicle-mounted and send out a disruptive electronic signal to stop the Taliban from setting off their remote-controlled improvised explosive devices.

EOD. Explosive Ordinance Disposal. These teams were responsible for disabling or destroying improvised explosive devices.

F

FAM. Fighting Age Male. This was the approved coalition forces acronym for males between the ages of 18 and 40 who were suspected of being Taliban.

FOB. Forward operating Base. These bases were located outside of Kandahar Airfield and acted as staging areas for operations for the Battle Group. In the Canadian Context, FOBs were usually run by a combat team or company organization. These provided logistical nodes, a safe landing zone for helicopters, and a secure location for rest and refit for soldiers within the area of operations.

FOB Martello. Forward Operating Base located along the Tarin Khowt Highway. North of Kandahar City.

FOB Wilson. Forward Operating Base is located along Highway One, west of Kandahar City.

FOB MASUM GHAR(MSG). Forward Operating Base located at the base of the mountain Masum. Located adjacent to the town of Bazaari Panjawaii, Southwest of Kandahar City.

FOBBIT. A derogatory term for a member of the Canadian Forces that always resided within a forward operating base. This term was utilized to describe an attitude that reflected garrison discipline and a lack of understanding by the members of the activities that were happening outside the base.

FOLAD. A Combat Outpost that was located to the north of the town of Nakahonay. Nakahonay was a well-known Taliban transit centre and was located to the southwest of Kandahar City.

FFO. Full Fighting Order. This is the state of dress for moving on patrol or operations and included but was not limited to combat uniform, helmet, ballistic eyewear, hearing protection, flash-proof gloves, body armour, load carriage system, combat boots, personal role radio, and personal weapon. This could include a combat net radio if issued.

FOO. Forward Observer Officer. This was an artillery Officer who was attached to a combat team to control joint fires. They were responsible for a small team of technical experts that could direct artillery fire and combat aircraft that would drop ordnance in support of ground forces. They could operate mounted out of an LAV III or dismounted with the infantry.

Fragged. This is a verb to describe the use of a fragmentation grenade. "The soldier fragged the enemy in that building."

G

GAF Factor. Give a fuck factor. When a Soldier cares a lot or a little about a task, orders, duties, or instruction. "My GAF Factor is non-fucking-existent".

Gagetown. Town in New Brunswick, Canada. Home location of the 2nd Battalion, The Royal Canadian Regiment.

Gator. A light six-wheeled all-terrain vehicle manufactured by John Deere. Utilized by the Canadian Infantry to move ammunition, water, and rations to the fighting troops and to pull casualties back. Useful due to its rugged capability and the fact it could fit on narrow lanes in Afghanistan.

Golf (Artillery). "Golf" is the letter in a letter in the military phonetic alphabet that denotes the artillery corps on the radio. It is used as a short form of slang to denote that an artillery expert was in the group.

Grape fields. In the Kandahar region, grapes are a major crop. The vines are grown on large, hardened mud walls and have irrigation ditches between them. Each grape field is usually sunk below the height of the surrounding ground and encircled with a thick mud wall. This made movement and navigation in the region very difficult for vehicles and posed challenges for dismounted movement also. The walls created a "maze" "- effect and shortened the distances of engagements between the Taliban and Canadian elements.

Green Berets. The United States Army Special Forces (SF), colloquially known as the "Green Berets" due to their distinctive service headgear, is the special operations branch of the United States Army. The core mission set of Special Forces contains five doctrinal missions: unconventional warfare, foreign internal defence, direct action, counterterrorism, and special reconnaissance. The unit emphasizes language, cultural, and training skills in working with foreign troops; recruits are required to learn a foreign language as part of their training and must maintain knowledge of the political, economic, and cultural complexities of the regions in which they are deployed. Canadians often worked alongside or in the same area of operations as Green Beret Teams, known as Operational Detachment Alpha or ODA.

GSR. Gun Shot Residue. A test for GSR was applied to the hands of individuals suspected of having fought with Canadians and then put their guns downs down to escape as civilians. If GSR showed positive, they were screened for questioning by the Afghan National Police or the Afghan National Army.

GRIT. How a solider indicates a target. It is an acronym for Group (who), range (how far), Indication (main feature or clock indication) and type of fire (rapid, normal, etc). Section commanders or any soldier that spots the enemy use this method to direct the fire of their comrades towards a threat.

Gucci kit. Non-issued kit or equipment bought by the Soldier. The word "gucci" alone is also used to mean fancy, e.g. "that's a Gucci computer".

G-Wagon. Light Utility Vehicle Wheeled (LUVW) is used by Regular and Reserve field units and training establishments to provide tactical transport in the fields of command and control, liaison, reconnaissance and Military Police. It is powered by a 2.7-litre, 5-cylinder, turbocharged diesel engine. It can be outfitted with a tailored armour protection systems kit, and the turreted version mounted a 7.62mm or .50Cal machine gun. Originally utilized in Kabul and Kandahar, these were taken off the road by 2009 due to the catastrophic damage that IEDs and Taliban Anti-Armour weapons would inflict on them. They were replaced by the RG-31 armoured vehicle.

H

Handover. This is a term to denote the time taken to explain responsibilities, procedures and threat to units that are incoming or outgoing. The "handover" can be used by any level of unit and will result usually in the one element taking responsibility over from another.

Herc. CC-130 Hercules transport aircraft.

Highway 1. National Highway 01 or NH01, formally called the Ring Road, is a 2,200-kilometre (1,400 mi) two-lane road network circulating inside Afghanistan, linking the major economic centres. This Highway was the main artery of traffic for the coalition to move throughout the country.

Hwy 4. NH 04, was a tertiary Highway that routed SOUTH from HWY 1 past the Kandahar Airfield and travelled to the Spin Boldak and the Pakistan Border. Canadians patrolled this Highway in 2006 and were garrisoned in Spin Boldak in 2006 before being withdrawn and centralized in the Panjawaii region.

HUMINT. Human intelligence is intelligence-gathering using human sources and interpersonal communication.

Humping. Derogatory is the term for carrying your equipment in the infantry. The heavy kit forms a Hump on the soldier's back. It can be used as a verb Soldiers to describe walking. "We humped that hill."

Humvee. The High Mobility Multipurpose Wheeled Vehicle (HMMWV; colloquial: Humvee) is a family of light, four-wheel drive, military trucks and utility vehicles produced by AM General.

HLTA. Home Leave Travel Allowance. Canadian soldiers get 16 days off (including travel to and from Afghanistan) per 6 months of duty. This allowance paid for them to return to Canada, or an equal amount could be used to travel to a 3rd location.

HME. Insurgents in Afghanistan used potassium chlorate and fertilizer as the base for homemade explosives for the bombs responsible for two-thirds of casualties in Kandahar.

Howz E Madad. The town is located to the west of Kandahar which straddles Highway 1. A key node for Canadian operations and location of several critical events.

HQ. Head Quarters.

I

Iltis. The Volkswagen Type 183, more commonly known as the Iltis (German for polecat), is a military vehicle built by Volkswagen for use by the German military. The Iltis was formerly built under license in Canada by Bombardier Inc. The Iltis was initially deployed to Kabul and was removed from service in 2004 and replaced by the G-Wagon.

ICOM. Small handheld radio sets that scan frequencies to monitor traffic. These were held by Afghan translators to try to pick up Taliban elements speaking on open radio channels. Often, these intercepts would provide Canadian elements with a warning that Taliban elements were operating in the region. An "ICOM Hit" was the term used by soldiers for these intercepts.

ICS. Intercom system. In Armoured vehicles, the ICS is the system used for the crew, consisting of the driver, gunner and crew commander to communicate.

ISR. Intelligence, surveillance and reconnaissance. This is a system to gain information on the battlefield. The soldiers often use it as a noun to denote unmanned air vehicles that support ground forces. "we had ISR coverage".

IED. Improvised Explosive Device. is a bomb constructed and deployed in ways other than in conventional military action. It may be constructed of conventional military explosives, such as an artillery shell, attached to a detonating mechanism. IEDs are commonly used as roadside bombs or homemade bombs.

IMPs. The Canadian Armed Forces use a ration called the "Individual Meal Pack" or IMP. These were the rations consumed by soldiers who were out conducting operations in Afghanistan. Each meal pack comes with one main entree, a dessert, several types of beverages, a hard candy, and a package of cookies or a chocolate bar. The package may also include such accessories as instant soup mix, instant mashed potatoes or instant rice. A single IMP contains food for one meal — breakfast, lunch, or dinner — for one person. It is packaged in a way that makes it compact and lightweight. The main courses can be eaten cold or hot by placing the pouches in boiling water for five minutes.

ISAF. International Security Assistance Force (ISAF) was a multinational military mission in Afghanistan from 2001 to 2014. It was established by United Nations Security Council Resolution 1386 pursuant to the Bonn Agreement, which outlined the establishment of a permanent Afghan government following the U.S. invasion in October 2001. ISAF's primary goal was to train the Afghan National Security Forces (ANSF) and assist Afghanistan in rebuilding key government institutions; it gradually took part in the broader war in Afghanistan against the Taliban insurgency.

IRF. Immediate Reaction Force. This was a small element held to react to emergencies in the area of operations. It was a section of infantry with attachments of engineers and controlled at the company level.

ITW. Inside the wire. This was the slang for the actions and tasks that took place within the confines of Kandahar Airfield or inside larger camps and FOBs.

IR. An imposed restriction is a restriction of duty that may be imposed if the performance of a specific duty by a CAF member poses, or is likely to pose, a real and demonstrable risk to the operational effectiveness of the CAF or the safety of the CAF member, other CAF members or the public. Any restriction of duty must respect the Canadian Human Rights Act (CHRA). For example, an imposed restriction is an option that CAF members opt for if their dependents remain in their current location and don't choose to move. Soldiers use this as a descriptor of their living situation when away from family. "I was posted on IR".

J

JDAM. The Joint Direct Attack Munition is a guidance tail kit that converts existing unguided free-fall bombs into accurate, adverse weather "smart" munitions. With the addition of a new tail section that contains an inertial navigational system and a global positioning system guidance control unit, JDAM improves the accuracy of unguided, general-purpose bombs in any weather condition.

JPEL. The Joint Prioritized Effects List or JPEL is a list of individuals whom coalition forces in Afghanistan try to capture or kill. Coalition forces are authorized to kill or capture individuals named on the list.

JTAC. Joint Terminal Attack Controller (JTAC) is the term used in the United States Armed Forces and some other military forces for a qualified service member who directs the action of military aircraft engaged in close air support and other offensive air operations from a forward position.

JTF2. Joint Task Force 2 (JTF 2) is Canada's Tier 1 special operations force mandated to protect Canadian national interests and combat terrorism threats both domestically and abroad. JTF 2 serves under the Canadian Special Operations Forces Command of the Canadian Armed Forces.

K

KAF. Kandahar Airfield is located in the Daman District of Kandahar Province in

Afghanistan, about 17km southeast of the city of Kandahar. During the conflict, it was the second largest base in Afghanistan and, at its peak, housed over 24000 Coalition soldiers.

Kariz. A qanat or kārīz is a system for transporting water from an aquifer or water well to the surface through an underground aqueduct or large tunnel; the system originated approximately 3,000 years ago in Iran. These systems ran throughout Kandahar, and the Taliban used them to move undetected and lay IEDs under major roads.

KBR. Kellogg Brown and Root. A multinational US-based company that had a contract to run KAF.

KIA. Killed in Action. Acronym for a soldier who has been killed in combat.

Kit. It can describe anything that a soldier carries or uses. The personal kit is clothing, weapon, and load carriage, but a vehicle may be "a good piece of kit." It can be a single item or a collection of items in soldiers' vernacular.

Kill Box. This was a nickname for a control measure put on a map where a free fire zone had been designated as all civilians had been reported departed from the area, and all remaining individuals within the "box" were designated enemy, and when identified, clearance was given to engage.

KLE. Key Leader Engagement. This is a term used when a military leader is going to speak to a civilian leader from Afghanistan. This could be a low-level interaction or a strategic discussion. It was planned and had security and behavioural protocols attached. The desire was that increased communication with civilian leadership would reduce violence.

KMTC. Kabul Military Training Centre. The Kabul Military Training Centre (KMTC) was a basic training centre for the Afghan Armed Forces. Located about 8 miles to the east on the outskirts of Kabul, it offered basic courses, including 16-week basic infantry training. Kabul Military Training Centre was one of the biggest basic training centres in Afghanistan.

L

LAV. The LAV III is the third generation of the Light Armoured Vehicle (LAV) family of armoured personnel carriers built by General Dynamics Land Systems – Canada (GDLS-C), a London, Ontario, based subsidiary of General Dynamics. It first entered service in 1999, succeeding the LAV II. It is the primary mechanized infantry vehicle of both the Canadian Army and the New Zealand Army. Both countries deployed the LAVIII as their primary combat vehicle in the Afghan Theatre of Operations.

Laying arcs. The "arcs" of fire are established by leadership to control the fire of individual weapons systems within a zone of operations. Each weapon has a left and right arc of fire, and the gunner is responsible for the zone between these markers. Siting weapons this way is an example of the application of the defensive principle of mutual support. The advantage of siting weapons that mutually support one another is that it is difficult for an attacker to find a covered approach to any one defensive position.

LCA. Language and Cultural Assistant. These were Afghan Canadians who had enhanced security clearances. These individuals were partnered with Canadian Commanders and provided language and cultural insights when interacting with Afghan partners.

Laager. A laager, historically known as a wagon fort, is a mobile fortification made of wagons arranged into a rectangle, a circle, or other shape and possibly joined with each other, such as an improvised military camp. a laager is a formation of tanks or other armoured vehicles, used for quick resupply or refuelling. It is rather vulnerable to attack, especially from the air, so it is only maintained for a short period, in a relatively safe location.

Lt. Lieutenant is a Canadian Forces rank used by commissioned officers of the Canadian Army. It is a junior rank, and in the army, it is a platoon commander.

Loaded for Bear. This is an expression of carrying a heavy load with a lot of ammunition. A soldier is "loaded for Bear" when they are carrying extreme weight and moving into battle with a lot of ammunition on their body.

LZ. In military terminology, a landing zone (LZ) is an area where aircraft can land. It does not have runway capability. In the United States military, a landing zone is the actual point were aircraft, especially helicopters, land. Canada adopted this terminology and was utilized in Afghanistan for helicopter resupply, MEDEVAC and airmobile operations.

M

Mahr Ghar. Mountain located Northeast of Masum Ghar. Key terrain in the Panjawaii region.

Master Corporal. This is an appointment of a Corporal with a leadership qualification. Most often in the infantry the Master Corporal is a section second in command or the Lav III Crew Commander. Within most Canadian Army units, master corporals are commonly nicknamed "master jack" or "jack" by both superiors and subordinates. The nickname is derived from the former equivalent rank of Lance Corporal, or "Lance Jack." This is an informality and is only used within social context and never in formal proceedings. In general, only in closer working or socially comfortable units like rifle regiments or infantry units is this informal term commonly used.

MBITR. The AN/PRC-148 Multiband Inter/Intra Team Radio (MBITR) is the most widely fielded handheld multiband, tactical software-defined radio used by NATO forces around the world. Used by Canadian Infantry and special forces units in Afghanistan. Preferred by soldiers over the Canadian version.

Medevac. Medical evacuation, often shortened to medevac or medivac, is the timely and efficient movement and en route care provided by medical personnel to wounded being evacuated from a battlefield. MEDEVAC implies that the platform that is moving casualties has medical capability or personnel on board. CASEVAC is the expedient method of moving casualties when there is not medical vehicle or personnel available.

Mirage. Camp Mirage is the codename for a former Canadian Forces forward logistics facility located in Al Minhad Air Base located near Dubai, United Arab Emirates. The facility was established in late December 2001 and, though not officially acknowledged by the Canadian Forces, is considered an "open secret." It was established in December 2001 to support Canadian Forces operations in southwest Asia, primarily Afghanistan. The exact location of Camp Mirage and the nature of its mission(s) were not officially acknowledged by the Canadian Forces or the Government of Canada due to the sensitivities of the UAE government. Most soldiers who deployed to travel to Afghanistan utilized Camp Mirage.

MIR. In the Canadian Armed Forces (CAF), the term "MIR" stands for Medical

Inspection Room. These MIRs are medical facilities where CAF members receive health care services, including medical examinations, treatment, and preventive care.

MRE. Meal Ready to Eat. US ration packs. Favoured by Canadian troops for the jalapeño cheese and tabasco sauce. The US rations provided a change from the Canadian IMPs when eating them for weeks at a time.

M203. The M203 is a single-shot 40 mm under-barrel grenade launcher designed to attach to the C7 or C8 service rifle. Used by Canadians to attack Taliban positions or to mark targets with smoke.

Mushan. Village in the "Horn of Panjwaii" located southwest of Kandahar: Mushan, Nejat, Talokan, Sperwan Ghar and Zangabad. In addition to the villages in the southern parts of the Zhari district, these villages are considered the "Birthplace of the Taliban" and were seen as one of the most dangerous regions of Afghanistan for NATO forces. Canadians initially cleared this region in 2006, and the remainder of the Canadian commitment in Kandahar was stabilizing this region. It continued to see heavy fighting and was handed off to US forces in 2011. The Taliban recaptured the region in 2021.

Mullah. Mullah is an honorific title for Muslim clergy, and it is also an honorific title for a Muslim mosque leader. The term is also sometimes used for a person who has higher education in Islamic theology and sharia law. Often village elders in Kandahar were denoted as Mullah and were the initial point of contact for Canadian Forces if they were seeking to stabilise a village.

M72. The M72 LAW (light anti-tank weapon, also referred to as the light anti-armour weapon or LAW as well as LAWS: light anti-armour weapons system) is a portable one-shot 66 mm (2.6 in) unguided anti-tank weapon. Canadian Rifle sections used to carry two or three M72s in order to suppress Taliban positions located behind the thick mud walls or grape huts in Kandahar.

M777. The M777 howitzer is a towed 155 mm artillery piece in the howitzer class. It is used by the ground forces of Australia, Canada, Colombia, India, Saudi Arabia, Ukraine, and the United States. It was first used in combat during the War in Afghanistan.

MRAP. Mine-Resistant Ambush Protected is a term for United States military light tactical vehicles produced as part of the MRAP program that are designed specifically to withstand improvised explosive device (IED) attacks and ambushes. Employed in Afghanistan by US forces and Canadian route clearance packages.

N

NCO. In the Canadian Forces, the King's Regulations and Orders formally defined a non-commissioned officer as "A Canadian Forces member holding the rank of Sergeant or Corporal. The non-commissioned officer corps has been referred to as "the backbone" of the armed services, as they are the primary and most visible leaders for most military personnel. Additionally, they are the leaders primarily responsible for executing a military organization's mission and for training military personnel so they are prepared to execute their missions. NCO training and education typically includes leadership and management as well as service-specific and combat training. Senior NCOs are considered the primary link between enlisted personnel and the commissioned officers in a military organization. Their advice and guidance are considered particularly important for junior officers and, in many cases, to officers of all senior ranks.

NATO. The North Atlantic Treaty Organization, also called the North Atlantic Alliance, is an intergovernmental military alliance of 32 member states—30 European and 2 North American. Established in the aftermath of World War II, the organization implemented the North Atlantic Treaty, signed in Washington, D.C., on 4 April 1949. NATO is a collective security system: its independent member states agree to defend each other against attacks by third parties after the attacks of 9/11. NATO declared Article 5 on behalf of the United States and initiated the ISAF mission in Afghanistan in support of the global war on terror. (GWOT)

ND. A negligent discharge (ND) is a discharge of a firearm involving culpable carelessness. In judicial and military-technical terms, a negligent discharge is a chargeable offence. The Canadian armed forces automatically consider any accidental discharge to be negligent discharge, under the assumption that a trained soldier has control of his firearm at all times.

NVGs. NVG stands for Night Vision Goggles. These optoelectronic devices allow visualization of images in low levels of light, improving the user's night vision. Every Canadian soldier that was deployed outside the wire was issued an NVG.

O

OC. The officer commanding (OC), also known as the officer in command or officer in charge (OiC), is the commander of a sub-unit or minor unit (smaller than battalion size), principally used in the United Kingdom and Commonwealth. In Afghanistan an officer commanding was the rank of Major and in command of an infantry company, and armoured or engineer squadron or artillery battery.

'O' Dark Buffalo. A slang expression used in the Canadian army to designate late at night or really early in the morning.

ODA. Special Forces Operational Detachment Alpha (ODA, A-Team, SFOD-A) is the operational element of the U.S. Army Special Forces. These teams conducted operations in the Canadian Area of Operations and Canadians were often co located in FOBs with them or conducted operations in parallel with the teams.

OMLT. Operational Mentoring and Liaison Teams (OMLTs) were the NATO teams embedded with the ANA. OMLTs provide training and mentoring to the ANA. They also serve as a liaison capability between ANA and ISAF forces, co-ordinating the planning of operations and ensuring that the ANA units receive necessary enabling support (including close air support, casualty and medical evacuation). OMLTs are composed of 11-28 personnel (depending on the type and function of the ANA unit with which it is partnered) from one or several countries. Each OMLT is normally deployed with an Afghan unit for a minimum period of six months. Canadians were the OMLT for 205 Corps in Kandahar and provided support to training and fought embedded with their Afghan partners throughout the Canadian mission.

Oscar-Mike. In military terminology, Oscar Mike means "on the move". It comes from the NATO phonetic alphabet, where "Oscar" stands for the letter "O" and "Mike" stands for the letter "M". This term was commonly used in radio communications by US forces to indicate that a unit or individual is actively moving to a new location or objective. It was adopted by Canadian elements as they worked closely with he US and interacted on their radio networks.

OTW. Outside the Wire. This was a term for the activities that took place outside of Kandahar Airfield or outside of the FOB. It was also a way of describing a tour of duty. Individuals were either inside or outside the wire.

OP. An observation post (commonly abbreviated OP), temporary or fixed, is a position from which soldiers can watch enemy movements, warn of approaching soldiers (such as in trench warfare), or direct fire. In strict military terminology, an observation post is any preselected position from which observations are to be made - this may include very temporary installations such as a vehicle parked at a roadside checkpoint or even an airborne aircraft.

OP (operation). A military operation (op) is the coordinated military actions of a state or a non-state actor in response to a developing situation. These actions are designed as a military plan to resolve the situation in the state or actor's favour.

Ops O. The senior staff officer in the battalion or battlegroup. The Operations Officer is responsible for running the headquarters. The Ops O conducts the current operations to allocate resources and provide control functions on behalf of the commanding officer. This was a major part of the battle groups that deployed to Afghanistan.

OGrp. Orders Group. This is the meeting that leaders call with the subordinates to relay directions or "orders" to explain the conduct of the mission. The Orders group is the group invited to the meeting. In a BG, the Commanding Officers O Grp has the Rifle Company commanders, the engineer, the artillery commander, key advisors, staff and the Regimental Sergeant Major.

OP MEDUSA. Operation Medusa (September 2–17, 2006) was a Canadian-led offensive during the second Battle of Panjwaii of the War in Afghanistan. The operation was fought primarily by the 1st Battalion, The Royal Canadian Regiment Battle Group and other elements of the International Security Assistance Force, including A Co, 2-4 Infantry BN, 4th BDE, 10th Mtn Division, supported by the Afghan National Army and a team from the United States Army's 1st Battalion, 3rd Special Forces Group (Airborne) augmented by C Company, 2nd Battalion, 87th Infantry Regiment of the 10th Mountain Division. Its goal was to establish government control over an area of Kandahar Province centred in the district of Panjwaii some 30 kilometres (19 mi) west of Kandahar City. A tactical victory, it resulted in the deaths of 12 Canadian soldiers; five during the major combat operations, five in bombings, and two in a mortar/RPG attack during the reconstruction phase of the operation. Fourteen British military personnel were also killed when their plane crashed. Despite suffering a brutal battlefield defeat, the Taliban retained their presence in Kandahar province and did not lose their will to fight, leading to the subsequent Operation Falcon Summit.

Nonetheless, Operation Medusa was at the time the most significant land battle ever undertaken by NATO.

Operation Camel Spider. The camel spider continually moves to the shade during the day. When soldiers were caught in the sun they sought shade by their vehicles and as the sun moved, they would move around following the shade. This was termed by soldiers " Operation Camel Spider" as they moved ot the shade.

P

Patricia's. Princess Patricia's Canadian Light Infantry (PPCLI, generally referred to as the Patricia's) is one of the three Regular Force infantry regiments of the Canadian Army of the Canadian Armed Forces. Formed in 1914, it is named for Princess Patricia of Connaught, daughter of the then-Governor General of Canada. The regiment is composed of three battalions, for a total of 2,000 soldiers. The PPCLI is the main lodger unit of Canadian Forces Base (CFB) Edmonton in Alberta and CFB Shilo in Manitoba and is attached to the 3rd Canadian Division.

Panjawaii. also spelled Panjwaye, Panjwayi, Panjway, Panjawyi, Panjwa'i, or Panjwai) is a district in Kandahar Province, Afghanistan. It is located about 35 kilometres (22 mi) west of Kandahar. The district borders Helmand Province to the southwest, Maywand District to the west, Zhari District to the north, Arghandab, Kandahar and Daman districts to the east and Reg District to the south. Panjwaii was reduced in size in 2004 when Zhari District was created out of the northern part of it, on the northern side of the Arghandab River, which now forms the northern boundary.

Pashmul. A village and sub-district of Zhari district, west of Kandahar City. This is the village that is located north of the Arghandab River and the scene of heavy fighting during Op Medusa.

Petawawa. Is a town located in the eastern portion of Southern Ontario. Situated in the Ottawa Valley, with a population of 18,160. Today, it is one of Canada's largest ground forces base which is home to 2 Canadian Mechanized Brigade Group and 4 Canadian Division Support Group. Petawawa generated multiple rotations for Afghanistan based on the 1st and 3rd Battalion The Royal Canadian Regiment.

PID. Positive Identification. Refers to the process of positively identifying a military target, typically in combat situations. It involves confirming the identity of a potential threat or neutral/friendly forces. Soldiers would not shoot until they achieved "PID".

PRR. Personal Role Radio. These are small, unencrypted radios that allow soldiers to communicate across short distances within their sections. Due to terrain, high walls and narrow alleyways in Afghanistan, sections often were out of sight of one another, and these radios allowed for communication without yelling at one another.

Platoon. An infantry organization of 30 to 40 soldiers. It consists of three rifle sections of 10 soldiers and a headquarters of five to ten specialists and leadership. Platoons had 4 LAVIII vehicles for transportation, protection and fire support. There are three platoons per company.

PSP. Personnel Support Programs. There are Canadian civilians that are hired to work in these programs and reside in KAF. They fulfilled roles for fitness instructors for elements that reside in KAF, the running of the CANEX store, barbers and travel coordinators for leave to return Home.

PTT. Push to Talk. This is the button on the radio handset that is pressed to communicate on the radio network.

PPE. Personal Protective Equipment. Each soldier wore equipment to protect them from the effects of the environment and enemy weapons effects. The equipment included a helmet, ballistic eyewear, combat uniform, Kevlar flak vest with shoulder pads and neck protector, ballistic ceramic plates (inserted into the flak vest to stop rifle rounds), flashproof gloves, and combat boots. The total weight of the equipment is approximately thirty to thirty-five pounds (13-17kg)

PRT. Comprising experienced diplomats, development workers, police and corrections officers as well as military personnel, ISAF's Provincial Reconstruction Teams (PRTs) promote the policies and priorities of Afghanistan's national government with local authorities, encourage reform initiatives, and coordinate development projects. The Government of Canada formed the KPRT in August 2005 at Camp Nathan Smith in Kandahar City.

PA. Physician's Assistant. These were senior medical personnel who could perform emergency combat field surgery as necessary to sustain life. These individuals were forward deployed with Canadian elements and are accredited with saving the lives of many soldiers and ensuring that the casualties were able to survive until they reached the hospital in KAF.

PTSD. In earlier wars, it was called "soldier's heart," "shell shock," or "combat fatigue." Today, doctors recognize these issues as a distinct medical condition called posttraumatic stress disorder, or PTSD. It can occur after a traumatic event such as military combat, a physical assault, or a natural disaster. While stress is common after trauma, people with PTSD often relive a traumatic event in their minds.

POMLT. Police Operational and Mentoring Team. These teams are typically composed of military personnel who work alongside local police forces in conflict zones or areas where security and stability need improvement. Their mission involves training and mentoring local police officers, sharing security tactics, and supporting law enforcement efforts. Canadian POMLTs were half infantry soldiers and half military police. Their primary task was to live, fight, and mentor in the field amongst the Kandahar civilian population and counter Taliban activities.

Pogue. Adopted American pejorative military slang for non-infantry, staff, and other rear-echelon or support units.

Pintle. A pintle mount is a swivelling mount that allows the gun to be freely traversed or elevated, while the base of the mount is still fixed keeping the whole system in one stable position. Due to the stability offered by the mount, the gun typically does not need a shoulder stock, with many modern examples using two-handed spade grips. It is most commonly found on armoured LAVIII or G-Wagon vehicles.

PT. Physical Training. Soldiers slang: "doing PT" means exercising.

PZ. Pick-Up Zone (PZ) is a designated area where helicopters or other aircraft can land to pick up troops, equipment, or supplies. PZs serve as staging areas for loading troops and cargo onto aircraft before an air assault mission.

Q

Quik Clot. QuikClot is a brand of haemostatic wound dressing that contains an agent that promotes blood clotting. It is primarily used by militaries and law enforcement to treat haemorrhaging from trauma.

QM. Quartermaster. A quartermaster oversees logistics, requisitions, and manages stores or barracks. They distribute supplies, provisions, and equipment to troops.

QRF. Quick Reaction Force. A reserve force held at readiness within the Battle Group to Respond to emergency events. The size of QRF can vary depending on the task and threat in the environment. QRF usually comprises a command element, a security element and an engineering element.

R

Ramp Ceremony. A memorial ceremony, not an actual funeral, for a soldier killed in a war zone is held at an airfield near or in a location where an airplane is waiting nearby to take the deceased's remains to his or her home country. The term has been in use since at least 2003 and became common during the war in Afghanistan. The majority of Canadians killed in action were transitioned through a Kandahar Airfield ramp ceremony that was attended by all those Canadian personnel located in KAF and coalition nations serving.

Radio (521). Canadian Forces Low-Profile Secure Radio also labelled Lightweight Assault Hand-held Radio (LAHR). This radio is being designed under the TCCCS/IRIS (Tactical Command, Control and Communications System/Integrated Radio Intercommunication System) program by Computing Devices Canada (CDC). The design and technology of the AN/PRC-521 is supplied by Racal Radio and carries a Racal manufacturing number of PRM-4725TC which is a variant of the AN/PRC-139 Scope Shield II radio. The units are fully built-in Calgary and are strictly for hand-held use. It can operate in both non-secure and secure analog voice or data modes. This radio was not well-liked by the Canadian Infantry soldiers as it was unreliable. The US MBITR was often sought as an alternate radio.

Radio (117). Primary dismounted radio of Canadian land elements in Afghanistan. The AN/PRC-117 translates to "Army/Navy, Portable, Radio, Communication". It is a 12-pound, man-portable, tactical software-defined combat-net radio, manufactured by Harris Corporation.

RCR. The Royal Canadian Regiment (RCR) is an infantry regiment of the Canadian Army. The regiment consists of four battalions, three in the Regular Force and one in the primary reserve. All Regular Force Battalions deployed to Afghanistan and elements of the 4th Battalion deployed. The RCR is ranked first in the order of precedence amongst the Canadian Army.

RCD. The Royal Canadian Dragoons (RCD) is the senior armoured regiment of the Canadian Army by precedence. It is one of three armoured regiments in the Regular Force and forms part of the Royal Canadian Armoured Corps.

REMF. "Rear Echelon Mother Fucker" is the description for someone who does not work in the combat zone but stays on base. Interchangeable with POG (Personnel other than grunt) "Fobbit" (from forward operating base (FOB) and The Hobbit) are closely related terms, in that they are frequently intended as insults (although "fobbit" is to be taken as less a term of direct abuse and more a descriptive one).

Recce. Recce is an informal Canadian lexicon for reconnaissance. This is the process of getting information about an area for military purposes. It is also the name of the platoon that conducts reconnaissance. Soldiers can conduct a "recce" of an area to gain information or Recce Platoon is the specialty organization tasked with these missions.

Replacement Pool (10%). This was the element that underwent all work-up training and was designated as the first element to be deployed in case of casualties. The ten percent denoted the size of the element being supported. For example, if the Battle Group had 1000 personnel, there would be 100 soldiers of various specialties.

RIP. Relief in Place. Is a military operation whereby the relieving unit or formation replaces the force being relieved on a more or less one-for-one basis in situ and takes over its mission and assigned zone of operations. Once the relieving forces have been briefed on the situation and ground, the relieved troops then withdraw. It was used as a verb by the soldiers of Kandahar, "units were "Ripping" as they transitioned between rotations.

RSOM. Reception, Staging, and Onward Movement in military context. It refers to the process of receiving personnel and equipment, preparing them for deployment, and facilitating their movement to the next operational location. Soldiers were "RSOM'd" in KAF for preparation to move onto the battlefield in the Kandahar area of operations.

Rolexed. Soldier slang for being delayed. "Our Helicopter got Rolexed"

Roto 0. The first tour into a new mission. In the early 2000s, this usually referred to the 3 RCR mission to Kabul as the first Battle Group into the Kabul AOR.

ROUTE SUMMIT. Route Summit was a significant project in Afghanistan, specifically in the Kandahar province. It was a five-kilometre road that ran through the fiercely contested Arghandab River valley. The goal was to stabilize the area, but it came at a cost—eight Canadian soldiers lost their lives during its construction. The road was built as part of Canada's efforts to contribute to reconstruction and development in the region, even amidst ongoing conflict. Work was initiated on the road following Op MEDUSA and completed in 2007 by 23 Field Squadron (Engineers) of the 1 RCR Battle Group. This route connected Panjawaii through Zhari to Highway 1 and allowed residents to easily access markets.

ROUTE HYENA (Fosters). Route Hyena is a significant part of Canadian Afghan military history. It was formerly known as Route Fosters between 2006 -2008 and was renamed and built by Task Force Kandahar between 2008 and 2011 during the War in Afghanistan. This road played a crucial role in connecting various regions and supporting military operations from Panjawaii to Mushan. This line of communications assisted residents to easily access markets and security elements and supplies reach into historically held Taliban territory on the "Horn of Panjawaii".

ROUTE NIGHTMARE. Route Nightmare refers to a specific road in the Panjwaii District of Kandahar, Afghanistan located near Chawlgor. This narrow path was notorious for its challenging terrain, security risks, and frequent attacks by insurgents. Canadians faced intense combat situations, improvised explosive devices (IEDs), and ambushes along Route Nightmare.

ROE. Rules of Engagement (ROE) are the internal directives that govern military forces' use of force. These rules define the circumstances, conditions, degree, and manner in which force can be applied or actions that might be seen as provocative. They ensure that military actions align with civilian and military leadership's intentions.

RG-31. The RG-31 Nyala is a 4×4 multi-purpose mine-resistant ambush-protected infantry mobility vehicle. It provides excellent protection against small arms fire and mine blasts. It was purchased for the Canadian elements in Afghanistan when the G-Wagon was pulled off the roads and it was evident that IEDs would be a consistent threat to ground troops.

RPK. *Ruchnoy Pulemyot Kalashnikova*, "Kalashnikov's hand-held machine gun" is a Soviet 7.62×39mm light machine gun designed by Mikhail Kalashnikov in the early 1960s. Used by Taliban elements against Canadian Elements.

RPG. Rocket-propelled grenade (RPG) is a shoulder-fired, anti-tank weapon system that launches rockets equipped with an explosive warhead. It's robust, simple, and lethal, making it a popular choice for Taliban insurgent forces.

RSM. Regimental Sergeant Major (RSM) is an important appointment held by an army chief warrant officer. The RSM serves as the senior non-commissioned adviser to the unit's commanding officer. They maintain discipline, uphold standards, and act as parental figures to their subordinates. In the field, they are responsible, at the battalion level for battlefield administration (resupply of ammunition and casualties). This is the apex of a Senior NCO career and provides a voice for the soldiers to the Commanding Officer.

RV. Rendezvous. A designated point on the ground designated by the tactical leader that soldiers if scattered in action will collect act.

S

Shoja. Combat Outpost Shoja (often abbreviated as COP Shoja) was a military installation in the Panjawaii district, Kandahar Province, Afghanistan. It served as a forward operating base for coalition forces during the War in Afghanistan. It was established by the Canadian Army after a clearance operation in the town of Nakahonay in 2009 and in 2011 was passed to the US Army.

Sergeant. Sergeant (Sgt) is a non-commissioned officer rank in the Canadian Armed Forces. Sergeants led a section of soldiers, oversaw their training, and acted as one of three section Commanders within an infantry Battalion. They play a crucial role in maintaining discipline and cohesion within their unit.

Sergeant Major. Is the senior non-commissioned soldier of a company in the armies of many Commonwealth countries, responsible for administration, standards and discipline. In combat, their prime responsibility is the supply of ammunition and establishing the Company Casualty collection point for the company. The Canadian Company Sergeant Major (CSM) appointment is normally held by a master warrant officer. The CSM is the key advisor to the Officer Commanding (OC) of the company.

Section. This is the smallest infantry organization. It is comprised of ten soldiers and is led by a Sergeant. Three sections make a platoon. A Section can be mounted in a LAVIII or they can move dismounted.

SECFOR. Security Force. This can refer an element responsible for the security of a position or that escorted logistics convoys.

Spin Boldak. Is a border town and the headquarters of Spin Boldak District in the southern Kandahar province of Afghanistan. It's situated next to the border with Pakistan. Spin Boldak is linked by a highway with the city of Kandahar to the north and with Chaman and Quetta in Pakistan to the south. It hosts the Wesh-Chaman border crossing, which is the second major port of entry between Afghanistan and Pakistan. This crossing facilitates transportation, shipping, and receiving between the two neighbouring countries. Canadians were based in Spin Boldak from 2006 to 2008 to provide security to the region and the critical Highway 4 that leads north to Kandahar.

Sperwan Ghar. Is a hill located approximately 40 miles southwest of Kandahar. It sits between the Arghandab and Dowry rivers in Kandahar province. It was a historic location for the Mujahedeen during the Soviet War. During Op MEDUSA SPERWAN GHAR was secured by US Special Forces and Canadian Army. Following the battle it became a FOB for the Canadian Army and was the launch point for operations to the western edge of the Panjawaii Region.

Strathcona's. Lord Strathcona's Horse (Royal Canadians) (LdSH [RC]) is a regular armoured regiment of the Canadian Army. It holds the distinction of being Canada's only tank regiment. Starting in 2006, the Strathcona's generated a Tank Squadron to support every Battle Group that deployed to Afghanistan.

Sangesar. Is a Pashtun village located 40 km west of Kandahar, Afghanistan, in the Zhari district. The village's name originates from the phrase "sang-e-hisar", which means "stone fort". This name refers to an old fort in the area that was constructed by the British during the 19th century. Notably, Sangesar was the former home of Taliban leader Mullah Omar, who lived there between the end of the anti-Soviet jihad in 1989 and the launch of the Taliban movement in 1994. This gave the town special significance to the Taliban. It was the sight of many Canadian operations and battles during the Kandahar Operation.

SOF. Special Operations Forces. These forces are specifically selected, trained and equipped to carry out high-risk missions. In Afghanistan, they took on the role of Direct Action and killed or captured key Taliban leaders and destroyed IED facilities. These forces operated throughout the area of operations and were often collocated with Canadian Conventional Infantry elements during critical events.

Shura. Refers to consultation in Islamic contexts. It encourages Muslims to engage in articulate debates and reasoned discussions to form productive opinions and strategies for implementing important matters. Often, village leaders hold a Shura with Coalition forces to discuss ongoing issues and hopefully come to resolutions. These were large gatherings that Canadians and Afghans participated in to peaceably discuss security and reconstruction matters. These were targets for Taliban violence and required heavy security if they were held.

SPG9. Is a tripod-mounted, man-portable recoilless gun developed by the Soviet Union. It features a 73 mm smoothbore and fires fin-stabilized, rocket-assisted high explosive (HE) and high-explosive anti-tank (HEAT) shaped charge projectiles. Though an older weapon, the Taliban effectively utilized the SPG 9 to defeat LAVIII armour and kill or wound many Canadian soldiers.

2IC. Stands for "Second-in-Command". In military and organizational contexts, the 2IC is the individual who holds the second-highest position of authority or leadership within a unit, team, or department.

T

TACP. Tactical Air Control Party (TACP) is a specialized team of military personnel responsible for coordinating between aircraft and ground forces during close air support operations.

TACNAV. Refers to Tactical Navigation a system within the LAVIII. This system has a GPS antenna on the LAVIII vehicle and aids the crew in precision navigation.

TLAV. Tracked Light Armoured Vehicle is a tracked vehicle used by the Canadian Army. Built on a historic M113 chassis, the TLAV's improved armour and modern rubber band tracks provide superior cross-country mobility.

TAT. Theatre Activation Team. Deployed to Kabul prior to Roto 0 to build Camp Julian and establish the logistics for the Battle Group to arrive. Security was provided by a rifle Company from the 2nd Battalion of the RCR.

TB. An acronym used by Canadian elements for the Taliban.

Terp. Shortened slang for Interpreter. These Afghan individuals were critical to the Canadian mission. They accompanied all levels of forces into the field and shared the risks of the soldiers. They acted to connect the Afghan population to the Canadian operating elements.

TF Comd. This was the senior Officer that oversaw all the Canadian elements. (BG,PRT,OMLT etc). Initially, a national commander it evolved to a Brigade Comd position as US and other forces were added to the Canadian units on the ground. Initially a Colonel, it evolved to a Brigadier General position.

TCCC. Tactical Combat Casualty Care. Are the military guidelines for trauma life support in prehospital combat medicine? These guidelines are designed to reduce preventable deaths while maintaining operational success. TCCC emphasizes evidence-based, life-saving techniques and strategies for providing the best trauma care on the battlefield. This was an advanced course for 2 to 3 soldiers per rifle section. This system was credited with saving many Canadian lives with immediate aid at the point of injury.

TIC. Troops in Contact. This is was the term used for gaining in contact (fighting) with the Taliban. " Getting in a TIC" was how it was used.

Theatre (of War/Operations). Refers to a specific area where significant military events occur or are in progress. A theatre can encompass the entirety of the airspace, land, and sea that is—or may potentially become—involved in war operations. Within a theatre of war, a theatre of operations is a sub-area defined by the commander. It focuses on specific combat operations and their support.

TK Road. The Tarin Khowt (TK) Road played a crucial role in connecting two significant cities in Afghanistan: Kandahar and Tarin Khowt. The TK Road was constructed to link these cities, facilitating transportation, commerce, and communication. Before its construction, the journey from Tarin Khowt to Kandahar was arduous, taking 20 hours. Hospitals, schools, and humanitarian aid offices were inaccessible to the villagers of Tarin Khowt. Once finished, the travel time between Tarin Khowt and Kandahar was reduced significantly to just two and a half hours. The TK Road ended geographical seclusion for hundreds of thousands of people, fostering commerce and supporting the democratic process in Afghanistan.

Trigger Man. The Trigger Man is the person who activates the IED by either remote control (using a radio transmitter and receiver link) or through direct contact (such as stepping on a pressure plate or pulling a tripwire). There was usually a spotter and a triggerman. Coalition forces would look for these two individuals immediately if they found or struck an IED.

TOC. Tactical Operations Centre. This is the US term for the Command Post. This term was adopted by the Canadian forces in Kandahar to align with US doctrine. The terms can be used interchangeably s the headquarters that controls Battle Group operations.

U

UAV. Unmanned Aerial Vehicle. This was the first conflict in which Canada utilized UAVs or drones to observe the area of operations. These drones were essential to maintaining observation of the area and finding those Taliban elements that were operating and being an "unblinking eye" on the battlefield. These vehicles reduced the Taliban's freedom of movement and accounted for large numbers of IEDs and ambushes not occurring due to the warning or the fire effects that could be actioned from the drone.

V

VSA. Vital Signs Absent. This was the term that would come across the radio when describing casualties. Only a doctor can declare someone has been killed, and so the casualty report has "vital signs absent" and then once a doctor confirms the casualty becomes killed in action.

VBIED. Vehicle Borne Improvised Explosive Device. Vehicles are loaded with explosives and the driver is a suicide bomber and drives the vehicle into their target.

VPS. Vital Point Search. As the IED threat grew. Canadians began to realize that there were areas where IEDs were more likely. This then drove a series of standard procedures to search at these likely locations. Vehicles would stop, observe and dismounts would search around the area for disturbed earth, wires, antennae, or anything that may indicate a device. This slowed movement in the area of operations but increased the survivability of Canadian elements.

W

Warrant Officer. Warrant Officer (WO) holds a significant position. Warrant Officers are highly skilled specialists responsible for the administration, management, and training of soldiers within their area of expertise. They often serve as the go-to experts in their field, playing a vital role in the Army's effective functioning. In the Army, they are often the platoon second in command and the confidant/mentor of the junior officer (2LT/LT) who is the platoon commander. This relationship is formative in the Platoon Commanders development, and the Warrant Officer is an essential element in the smooth operation of the platoon.

Wilson (FOB). Military installation in Kandahar, Afghanistan. FOB Wilson served as a strategic hub for military operations during the War in Afghanistan. Located west of Kandahar along Highway One at the Zhari district center. Originally established by Canadian forces, it later became a joint base with contributions from other NATO forces. Named after a Canadian soldier killed in Kandahar. FOB Wilson supported various missions, including combat operations, logistics, and intelligence.

WIA. Wounded in Action. Acronym to describe those soldiers wounded in battle.

X

X-Ray. The phonetic alphabet represents the letter X

Y

Yankee. Phonetic Alphabet represents the letter y

Z

Zangabad (COP). Combat Outpost (COP) Zangabad was a military installation in Western Panjawaii occupied by the Canadian Army and the Afghan National Army. This was the "Horn of Panjawaii" located west of Sperwan Ghar and was a significant area of Taliban activity.

ZAP number. A ZAP number is used for secure communication. It allows for sending personal information over insecure channels without overtly revealing the individual's identity. This was used during the reporting of casualties so that the Company HQ could inform the Battalion HQ who had been wounded, without letting all elements on the radio network know who had been wounded or killed.

Zhari. Is a district in Kandahar Province, Afghanistan. It was created in 2004 from land that was formerly part of Maywand and Panjwai districts. The population is estimated at 80,000. The district lies on the north bank of the Arghandab River, and the general area is sometimes referred to as the Arghandab Valley. Most buildings are single-story mud structures, and the farmlands are irrigated by a complex system of wadis running parallel with the river. Grapes, opium poppies, and cannabis are common crops. The area north of Highway 1 is more desert-like with abrupt mountain ranges. The tribal nature of the district makes decision-making complex, and the district centre was the former NATO base (FOB WILSON). The majority of people in Zhari are ethnic Pashtuns, and several tribes, including Alizai, Achakzai, Noorzai, and Ghilzai, reside there. This was the birthplace of the Taliban. This was the scene of some of the heaviest fighting between the Canadian Forces and the Taliban.

Zulu. This is the term used for the LAV III vehicles once the infantry dismounts. These are "Zulu vehicles" where the crew can still manoeuvre and fire the weapon systems, but the dismounted infantry has been detached and is conducting operations in another area.

Zulu Tango. This is a preregistered artillery or mortar target. The letters identify which target is "owned" by which unit. Each target has a number. (i.e. ZT001) and is listed with the gun position officer. This allows the Guns or Mortars to lay the guns on a target called by the soldiers forward in contact quickly and to start firing without initial call for fire. Corrections are then called off the pre-registered targets.

FOREWORD

Steve MacBeth continues his impressive life of service to Canada and New Zealand, first as a battled hardened veteran, and now as an author. In this book, he has compiled the authentic first-hand accounts of soldiers who served valiantly as part of Canada's NATO-led, UN-backed mission in Afghanistan. This is a raw and real reflection though a soldier's eyes of the longest conflict in Canada's history. This book can be summed up as truth to Canadians about what soldiers did in our name. This is not a sanitized version of war. It is deeply personal, passionate, honest, and in some cases, uncomfortable to read. It is a unique window into what really happened in the theatre of operations, and what happened before and after.

Steve has collected the genuine, gritty facts. These are reflections from the dusty, dangerous places where Canadians, lived, patrolled, fought, bled, caused blood shed, and in some cases, died, on the hills of the never conquered Islamic State of Afghanistan. All who were there left a piece of themselves behind. Many took some form of injury and the battle back home.

This is a consequential book that all Canadians should read to gain a greater appreciation of the most significant mission yet in our lifetime. These pages do not describe the D-Day landing, or the heroic call "over the top" at Vimy Ridge. This book is presented in straight talk and in explicit, unapologetic language. The painful recitation of both the mission and the homecoming is a gut-wrenching reminder of the costs of war. Each individual experience is unique, but many of the perspectives offer a similar refrain: this war was unwinnable without a full, unequivocal, uncaveated commitment from all participants. Mind-bending frustration pours out in the often graphic, colourful and completely justifiable language. The hard truth reminds the reader of the relentless striving, the selfless-sacrifice, and the unbreakable determination of Canadian soldiers to "get it right."

These are the stories of Canada's son's and daughters: young men and women who took up arms, as previous generations did, and gave their all for a cause they believed in. They did what their country asked of them and more. The cost was high: fourteen years, 158 lives, and many thousand casualties, some physical and some psychological. It didn't end there. Even after they came home, much of that psychological pain resulted in more casualties for the soldiers and their families. The return was difficult, and the reception varied. There was no parade or hero's welcome for most. Instead, most received sympathetic platitudes, averted glances, and carefully couched language from the country that asked so much of them.

From the front end to the back end of the mission there were incredible challenges. Almost immediately after 9/11, the Canadian Army was required to spool up and roll out in outdated olive drab uniforms, and under-powered unarmoured Iltis jeeps. These equipment shortcomings were not nearly as challenging as the realization of how ferocious and unscrupulous the Taliban fought. From IEDs, to ambush and treachery, they hid among the local population. The Taliban were everywhere and nowhere. Many soldiers described it as "fighting evil ghosts". Their impact was felt even though they were never seen during an entire rotation, in spite of numerous fire fights. The home field advantage of the Taliban and their ability to slip across the fictitious border to Pakistan to rearm and recharge was among the biggest vulnerabilities of the mission. In a counterinsurgency you strive to isolate the battlefield, which was something that we could never do with the geography of Afghanistan. The result was chasing shadows.

The soldiers' words trace the delta between hope and despair. It goes some distance to explain why so many returned home broken from their service. Not only is this a book you cannot put down, it follows you as you process the experiences and the haunting memories that live on in the soldiers.

Unlike official histories, the main figures in this book are not the politicians, bureaucrats, commentators or international partners. They are those warriors closest to the sound of the guns, the danger and the hurt. Those at highest risk, the Canadian soldier, representing every corner of our country. This is their story.

This book makes it clear that professional and reserve soldiers served shoulder to shoulder. A respectable number had only recently enlisted while others had served for years. While some CAF members had been to Bosnia, Kosovo, and even Iraq while embedded with American troops, nothing truly compared or prepared them for what they would experience in Afghanistan.

Canadians are taught to remember the sacrifices of every generation, but somehow we always fail to include the current one. Those who served or continue to serve stepped into harm's way at great cost, just earlier generations did. There are, once again, lessons learned about the support and investments necessary for success, before, during and after the mission. The many ramp ceremonies and repatriations with flag draped coffins were a stark awakening for Canadians. Those harsh realities leave a searing mark on the reader, while digesting the comments from those at the sharp end who fought next to the fallen. Most fought with the knowledge that they stood on the shoulders of greatness, inspired by Canadians who deployed and distinguished themselves no less in previous wars. There is much for Canadians to be proud of. This book shines a light on what they gave, what they endured, and the burden the continue to carry.

What they fought for, remains a hard question for some. Most soldiers might answer "for each other", the unbreakable bonds forged in the fire of battle the brothers and sisters in arms. They also fought for freedom, human rights, liberty and a rule of law that did not exist in the dust bowl of a country few Canadians could find on map. They fought so little girls could go to school and so much more.

I highly recommend this book to all who wish to understand what it is like to go to war, the rigours of conflict with bullets flying and comrades falling. It is more than a historical account but delves deep into the truth about our contributions. In some cases, it tells of our failings, not of our soldiers but the governments they serve. What can be taken away is a better grasp of how we plan, execute, cooperate, and communicate the complexities of war, and how we may keep our citizens and soldiers safe in the future.

Hon. Peter Mackay PC KC
Minister of National Defence, Canada
2007-2013

PREFACE

"IMPROVISED EXPLOSIVE DEVICES ARE DESIGNED TO MAIM. Cheap, homemade weapons are hidden in the ground, full of whatever explosive can be found and ball bearings, scrap metal, nails, whatever can be included to kill you," the veteran sitting across from me explained. "These weapons don't kill cleanly, they buckle the steel of armoured vehicles and rip and tear apart flesh like some wild animal, causing jagged wounds from the irregular shrapnel and the force of the blast. Every war has its decisive weapon; in Afghanistan, it was the IED," he concluded.

He looked away from my direct stare, paused, and seemed transported back to that desert battlefield.

"It is the shock-the surprise that is the worst. One minute you are just walking or driving along and the next, chaos. Smoke, dust, your ears ringing, your head and chest pounding from the shock wave. You are disoriented and, if not injured, looking for the next threat. Are you receiving fire? Can you move? Are there secondary devices around you?"

He paused for a moment, lost in the reflection.

"You check yourself for wounds, there is a pause, like a moment of silence after the blast, where the world is very still, the dust is settling, and the carnage that has occurred has yet to reveal itself. Then, like someone turning up the volume quickly on a stereo from 0 to 10; the screams of the wounded, the calls for 'Medic!' The demands of the radio crackling for updates, and the yells of the surviving team, bringing order from the chaos. If you are a leader, you need to understand and act quickly. It is the difference between life and death. You need to suppress your shock, your horror, your emotion, and raw fear. You need to get on with the job. Establish security, understand how many casualties you have, and if anyone has been killed. Communicate your situation, control resources, and issue orders calmly and clearly so that you minimize any panic."

"It is basic, kill the enemy that has tried to kill you, try and save your casualty's lives, ensure that your dead's parts are collected, lifeless bodies treated with respect, and that the surviving members of your team are ready to fight again."

He was silent for a moment and then moved to his desk and opened his laptop. He showed me photos of his younger self, and mementos of his time down range. Short videos of smiling young men, tanned, thin faces etched with fatigue. He introduced me to his team and showed me a short video that they put together, action-shot photos, laughing at the inside jokes that were only funny to those who were there at that moment. You can see his face change when the images highlight vehicles destroyed by enemy action, his base scarred by mortar and rocket fire a reflection of the violence that sits just outside the frame of the camera. The music faded and the last image was a list of names, of friends, who were killed by his team. The silence hung for a moment between us, reflecting on the time that had passed and those who didn't return.

He returned to his desk and pulled out a letter. "This is a note from the family of one of my fallen soldiers. They wanted to know what happened to their son." He looked at me sadly. "What do I tell them? I have never answered this letter. Ten years. Do I tell them that we had a normal day, woke up, ate a ration, fucked around and joked with each other, planned an easy patrol, then as were just moving that the enemy was smarter than us that day? That their son was eviscerated by homemade explosives and some old artillery shells?"

I can't answer his question. I was there to listen, to find a path to deepen our collective understanding. Perhaps my bearing witness brought some clarity to how to answer his question or perhaps just being able to ask it brought comfort. We felt a long way from clarity, and so we just sat in silence in his living room, together but alone with our thoughts.

On a routine patrol, their platoon hit an IED, destroying their vehicle and killing most inside. Bodies torn apart, legs, and arms separated from their core, skulls shattered, or internal organs destroyed by the blast's overpressure. The armoured vehicle, the best that Western engineering could conceive, lay twisted and smoking, its promise of protection broken by the simple bomb devised in a mud hut by someone unlikely to have graduated high school. It was the most common way for a soldier to die in Afghanistan. The reaction at home was a programmed routine by that point in the war; a short news release, comments of regret and appreciation of sacrifice by political leaders, technical commentary by former senior soldiers who were unlikely to have experienced combat, and the return of closed caskets to Canada to be greeted by grieving families. In total, 158 caskets were delivered to graves all over Canada during the thirteen-year mission to Afghanistan. Since the nation's withdrawal in 2014, the detailed stories held within those caskets and those of the soldiers who carried them, have remained virtually undisturbed—not forgotten, but avoided, something to be moved past as quickly as possible. Like traffic bypassing a gruesome roadside accident, the nation moved forward, averting its collective gaze.

The lasting image of the Canadian war in Afghanistan is the picture of the "ramp ceremonies"; young Canadians taken before their time by violence in a foreign country, the images set to the haunting strains of a bagpiper, carried by grim-faced friends, survivors of the same event that took their friend. The casket was paraded along lines of saluting soldiers until finally being loaded into the backs of military cargo aircraft and flown into the darkness of the Afghan night to return to grieving families and a nation that seemed publicly grateful but was uncomfortable with the sacrifice. As time has passed, narratives have evolved from politicians, military leaders, diplomats, history professors, movie makers, authors, and media talking heads who have tried to tell the story of Afghanistan, establishing the reasons for the journey of those caskets. The stories follow two broad lines; the first, removes the human essence and individuality of the soldiers in the box, consigning them to the cooler of statistics, historical events, and political expediency. This story is one of senior leadership, why the sacrifice had to happen, and geopolitical reasons for Canada's involvement. The casket is the cost of a seat at the international table. It is the story that justifies the spending of national blood and treasure. The other storyline uses the cryptic nature of the casket to elevate those held within to mythical levels of heroic action. It tells of the necessary mythology of combat, the revelation of the value of the individual sacrifice.

Between these two extremes, there is a gap. This absence has become clear since we left that country. The missing story gave a broad understanding of the experience of a tour of duty in Afghanistan, as told by those most qualified to look inside that casket. Canadian society treats the war like an abstract idea: "Did it actually happen?" It is like some type of bad dream that happened to someone else. Details have been lost over time. The conversations that relay how soldiers lived are not shared outside the confines of the inner circle and those who were "there." Incredible first-person written accounts have sought to fill this space. Detailing personal events and the experience of combat, they recount both tragedies and victories. I am in awe of those efforts but felt that they too fell short of capturing the broad experience. I felt that we needed a recounting that was inclusive of more voices, spanning the entirety of the deployment and touching on all the experiences held within. I wanted to ensure that some of those stories were saved, that there was a historical record of the everyday details, without concern for the political discourse or judgment of different events.

These stories should be told using the soldier's vernacular, simple language, imperfectly perfect, sometimes laced with profanity, ensuring that the voices were genuine and answered basic questions for the record:

"What was Afghanistan like for you?"

"What tastes and smells do you remember?"

"How did you feel when you killed or when someone tried to kill you?"

"What did you carry?"

"What were the daily routines like?"

"Was it all worth it?"

Building discourse on Canada's strategy in Afghanistan is not what this book is about. It leaves complex discussions behind. It does not try to put the experiences into context or explain who was right or wrong, or whether decisions made were good or bad. It strips the events down to their rawest form and shares them in the words of those who lived in Canada's experience in Afghanistan.

Afghan vets know the stats, they know what events occurred. They rarely share their perspective with curious outsiders. The official story is usually told through documentary videos, by the same dozen or so subject matter experts and leaders who focus on the biggest operations and the most dramatic moments. I know, I have sat in that chair, and been asked to discuss my experiences under the lights and on film. It is nerve-wracking and, rarely, are the hard stories revealed. They are often avoided, and straight facts are substituted for fear of revealing too much to an audience. There is a fear of being judged by a nation that will use the benefit of hindsight to do so, with little understanding or context of the violence of combat. The minute details, those bits that bring the human elements forward, are rarely shared with a public who are transfixed on the largest, most easily digestible, and violent events.

The violence is central to the story of Canadian soldiers in Afghanistan, but it does not define the whole experience. The story that needs to be shared is not just what happened on the toughest days, but a translation of the environment, the boredom, alien culture, the practical jokes, the shenanigans of young people, the fear, the angry moments brought on by frustration, or days of happiness and beauty in that faraway place.

Canadian soldiers are humble to a fault, and as brave as they are on the battlefield, they are terrified of being accused of "self-promotion." Even worse, they hate the possibility of getting something wrong in their story, often not trusting their perspective and shaky memories of details that have been long suppressed.

It is easier to not talk about it, and so they reserve the stories for those moments behind closed doors with friends who can fill in gaps in their memories and, most importantly, who understand. The community is wary of "bullshit artists," and even when some act of incredible courage is publicly recognized, they downplay it. I had a Medal of Valour recipient explain his award as a matter of fact, "I stumbled into the situation and didn't realize how dangerous it was. I tried to do my best, kill the enemy, and keep my guys alive. I still don't see what is so special about that."

Usually, the request for further explanation is dismissed and the conversation closes with the avoidant statement, "It is what it is." This closes the conversation, accepting that much is left unsaid and outside the control of those who lived the experience.

I felt that this conclusion was not good enough and that the details of those days needed to be told. They needed to be preserved somewhere, an unreserved record of our commitment to Canada during this period of conflict. I hoped to capture these stories about our soldiers who deployed, their daily lives, their reflections, their good days, their bad days, and all those in between.

This book is my attempt to do so.

Steve MacBeth, MSC, MSM (with Bar), CD

INTRODUCTION

IN THE CANADIAN ARMY, we have an expression: "No Names, No Pack Drill."

This expression is used when you are speaking to a leader and want to articulate that something has happened below the threshold of requiring formal career counselling. It could also mean that an issue needs to be recognized, perhaps a lesson learned, but you do not want a punishment to be meted out (in this case "pack drill") or attention drawn to the individual involved. You just want the lesson passed on so that it can be learned from, and bad things not repeated or good things reinforced.

If a leader agrees to these conditions, they will receive an unvarnished version of events, what has been done to remedy the situation, and how the leader should consider this going forward. It's a way to create a safe space to cut the bullshit and tell the truth.

This is a collection of 150 Canadian infantry soldiers who privileged me with their stories—no names, no pack drill. The work follows the pattern of one of the seven-month deployments, or "tours," in Afghanistan. The reader follows the soldiers' choice to join the forces, the initial warning that they are deploying to Afghanistan, their training cycle, their departure from home, their arrival into the world of combat, and their eventual return to society.

Each of the stories is a snapshot in time, reflecting the reality of that soldier's perception of what occurred and what they remember feeling. They are simultaneously imperfect and accurate in a way that bears witness to their experiences. This book is for people who are interested in how we lived and at times how our friends died. It allows us a ground view of the average Canadian soldier's experience and connects with those who are now forever silent.

It is for those who seek the sounds, smells, emotions, and visceral experience that was our war in Afghanistan.

It should be read through the eyes of the 19 to 40-year-olds who fought the war day to day. It was our first experience of a "connected" war, where the soldiers could take and share live video and could communicate back to their families in almost real-time. News media further compressed this connection between the combat zone and homefront, with the ability to bring the war into the living rooms and mobile devices of every Canadian with such accuracy that each soldier who was killed was introduced individually to the nation and became a topic of national discussion.

Afghanistan represented the first generation of professional warfighters that Canada has ever deployed in the war, a departure from the historical citizen soldiers who reintegrated with society when the war was over. Livelihoods as professional soldiers were tied to this single violent conflict for a generation within the Canadian Army. Military careers and reputations could be "made" or "lost," and how one performed or what role they held in Afghanistan had career implications, which shifted the dynamics and motivations past simply winning or losing on the battlefield.

Winning was not defined by the government of Canada and so it had to be defined through the interpretation of the leaders on the ground.

Was it enough to just be there?

Was it a win for a leader to bring as many soldiers home as possible?

Was the defeat of the Taliban the end goal of the government and if not, how much risk should be assumed?

In the middle of all these questions was the average Canadian soldier. They had to put aside thoughts of political will and simply survive. The stories held within this book are short; some very benign, some funny, some happy, some sad, some violent. Each one is connected to a young Canadian: a man or woman of multiple races and ethnicities, from urban centres, small farming towns, First Nation reserves, and fishing villages. They are the kids you went to high school with, they are your neighbours, they are someone's family, and they are Canadian Veterans who fought in Afghanistan.

For many, this is the defining role of their life

Some have had a hard journey home, as mental and physical wounds linger long after the conflict is over and the country has moved on. These are their stories, told from one veteran to another. Permission has been given to share them with you, the only ask being "no names, no pack drill."

PART I
GEARING UP

FALL IN FOR BATTLE

"FALLING IN FOR A BATTLE" is a drill that the Canadian Army performs at the section level. It allows the Section Commander, usually a Sergeant, commanding ten young Canadians, to review the force that they will go into contact with. The section lines up for inspection and is prepared to explain why they are there, their mission, what they are tasked to do, who they will be working with, and how they will contribute to the success of that mission. Why Canadians "Fell in" for the War on Terror varied among the individuals - some sought challenges and opportunities for social mobility, those that were eager for adventure, those who were looking for an escape, and some were simply bored. Some were in the Army when the conflict started, surprised that they would face combat for the first time late in their careers, and later, many joined with the specific intent to serve in the grape fields of Afghanistan. The journey to joining or serving in an Army at war is the first step for soldiers in Canada's longest war. Over 40000 Canadians served in that country between 2001 and 2014, making it Canada's largest deployment since World War Two. For the first time in its history, Canada's war would be fought by an all-volunteer, professional force that was constituted from about one percent of the Canadian population. After the attacks of 9/11, however, many were motivated to serve, and the Canadian Armed Forces saw a significant increase in enrolments. From the moment our closest allies were attacked, and Canada declared its intention to fight, soldiers throughout the nation knew their lives were about to change.

There were many different paths for a soldier to find a seat on a Hercules C130 to Afghanistan. Initially, there was a feeling that they might miss "the show" and the government would withdraw before they had tested their mettle. That fear and motivation faded quickly with the realization that out of necessity and the limited human capital of an Army that had continually seen reductions in personnel since the end of the Cold War; many found themselves, deploying to theatre at regular 12-to-18-month intervals. Each soldier had a uniquely Canadian conduit of how and why they found themselves fighting in Canada's longest conflict. During this period, change *was the only constant. The Army not only had to shift rapidly from a peacetime to war footing for the deployment cycle but also had to adapt institutionally to tactical lessons that meant, for the first time in several generations, the difference between life and death for Canadian soldiers on the front lines. The window of time before a tour to Afghanistan- whether it was your first or your fourth was confronting. It was a time of constant pressure and adapting to previously unknown challenges. Before you even stepped on the plane, you were challenged with uncertainty in many different forms, deployment timelines, family, new training, career upheaval, and a newfound certainty of your mortality.*

I was a city kid from Toronto, and the military was a big change for me. From the first minute of my military career, Afghanistan was the focus. We were in an Army at war. I remember doing the first notifications of soldiers dying before I even really understood the army. Honestly, before I was a real Royal. I had just arrived in the Battalion. We are on PT, and I checked my work phone at the end of the session, I had to pull the platoon together, and time stood still, "I have bad news…" I remember telling guys that the first guys were killed in Kabul. It was surreal, like something out of a movie. There were Senior NCOs who had known these guys for years, it was a shock to them. To me they were just names, to the soldiers with experience, they were lifelong friends, they knew their families. The war had come home quickly. From my first minutes as an RCR leader, Afghanistan was the focus for the next decade. I learned that people matter, when the enemy wins, the losses are not just numbers and you had better have your shit together because the troops are counting on you. From the minute I started leading it was real.

I guess really for me, the whole defining moment of my adult life was September 11th. The interesting thing for me was September 11th, 2001. I was home sick from school in Edmonton, Alberta. I watched it all happen in real-time as events played out. But before that, I always wanted to be in the military after High School. So in between bouts of running back and forth the washroom, I'm watching this thing happen, you know, the first buildings hit, there's a big pall of smoke and it's like "Oh man, something big is happening." Then I remember watching the second plane hit the tower. I knew that we were going to go to war. I immediately felt that the world as we knew it changed after that, and at some point, I was going to be a part of it. So, I was in Grade 9, and from that day on I wanted to be in the military. The guys that went on the first mission were from Edmonton, I remember the news and watching them go. We did red Fridays and tied yellow ribbons and when they had a US bomb dropped on them, we stopped school, and all participated in the memorial by watching it as a class on TV. Everything I did in high school was shaped by Afghanistan and then the growing combat mission. By the time I was done in 2005, I was ready to go and the timing fit perfectly for a shift in Kandahar.

I'd been in the battalion maybe four or five months and didn't have anything in the way of experience, but I was all full of piss and vinegar. I was 19 years old and that 5 months was the first 5 months out of my mom's basement in our small town in Ontario. I wanted to get to Afghanistan. The Patricia's had gone to Kandahar in 2001, then there was a break in our deployments and there was a rumour that Canada would send a new mission, to Kabul, but no details were released. We were in Wainwright on exercise. Just doing normal army stuff, in the snow, nothing to do with Afghanistan, but you could feel the change in the air. There were senior people in Afghanistan and the rumour mill was going crazy. midway through the exercise, The Officer commanding Charles Company gathered the company together in the mess tent and explained to us that Charles Company would be augmenting the 3 RCR battalion group for Roto 0, which was to be in Kabul. I don't think I understood the significance at the time because I was 19 years old, but this would be the first of my four tours to Afghanistan, I would spend all my twenties, rotating in and out of that country.

I was a lobster fisherman in PEI, and I wanted something else. I joined after 9/11 to go fight in Afghanistan. I remember being in basic when Murphy was killed in Kabul by a suicide bomber and there was a guy that was staff on the course that knew him. If you ask me his name right now, I couldn't even remember. His reaction to Murphy dying kind of made you realize that it's pretty real. You can lose friends. The impact was very immediate on our course, and I knew then that I needed to dial in. I was 21 on Basic training and would deploy to Afghanistan 3 times, so by 27, I was salty. But what else was I going to do, I hate fucking lobster.

I came from a military family in Halifax, my Dad was in the Navy. I'd always wanted to join the army and deploy. I was in ninth grade when 9/11 happened and I was hoping to get on the tail end of Afghanistan. I did. I was super-stoked to be able to deploy to the fight. That feeling of elation lasted like 10 seconds once I was in it.

I think my family was more I was more nervous about it than I was about going to Kandahar. I think my family had a harder time with it. My mother immigrated to Canada in 1970. She'd been alive in Egypt with the Suez Canal, and she lived in Lebanon, with fighting. So, I think she had her own impression of how things were gonna go. Likely she understood war better than anyone in my Battalion who had never been in combat. She'd been a reservist in Canada, in Halifax in the late 70s and in the late 80s. As a woman and an immigrant, she was pretty tough and had a really good perspective. The actual departure, I think was emotional for all and I cried. Everybody cried. I cried, not because I was worried about myself, but because I didn't want what could happen to me, to hurt them. They cried, because they knew the losses that war could inflict, and had come to Canada to avoid them. They were also very proud of me, as a Canadian soldier. It was confusing but loving. lots of crying is what I remember and lots of support.

I had been an army cadet in Manitoba and had been influenced as a kid by the training officers who had been through the Balkans or Cyprus or even Egypt, some of the older guys. All peacekeeping missions. I always wanted to join thinking that that was the kind of mission I was going to go on. While I was going through Meaford, through the RCR Battle School, that's when Canada had deployed to Regional Command South in Kandahar. We were seeing everything in spring 2006 while in basic. I can distinctly remember being in the meal line for lunch in Meaford and having a CTV News or seeing CBC News being broadcast in the Kitchen of the fighting going on and then going to a weapons class and learning about the same weapons you just saw being used on the newscast. I think there's an acceptance of the legitimacy of the training that you're doing. So, the mindset, I think for the course was very different from what I see from some maybe some of the younger ones coming through today that we knew that this was real. I think it was a professional setting. Guys were dying and our instructors knew them. Some of our instructors had been downrange already, and when they weren't pushing us, they would mentor us on what Afghanistan was going to be like and why it was important to understand your weapons, navigate, and communicate clearly on the radio. It was all real. We were going to leave this course, join a battalion, and fight within a year of graduating. I was idealistic and couldn't wait to get into it.

My story is about not going at all. I hated watching other folks deploy and stay at home. I was part of a rifle company that was slated for an early tour to Kandahar. The Sergeant Major came to see me and let me know that it was time for me to be posted to do a training job and some newly promoted guys were going to take on my position. I wanted to stay with the rifle company as the tour was coming up, and this one seemed a lot different. But we are a professional army and career management does not adjust for your wants. So, I got moved and ended up training these guys for their workup that replaced me and then I was posted. The guy who replaced me was killed. And you're like, I wish I was there. Not to see these guys get killed or worse to be the one that was killed. But just because you like you felt that guilt that you're not there. It is not your fault, it is the system, it was luck, maybe it would have been different if I had been there. Who knows? But it sits with you, it is not rational, these people were your friends for years, it is just sad, and you carry that guilt, which is not yours to carry for a long time. For some guys never have it fade. It is weird.

We knew right away that this would be a difficult, challenging job. You watched the news and you read the books and you just know that this would be a much different game. I prepared myself for that mentally, and psychologically. And I knew that we wouldn't come back with all our soldiers. That's but that's the tough part of being a warrior. You know, for me, it's what we do. I don't get off on it or want anyone to die, but we sign the dotted line to take those risks for our country's interests. I think people forget that is what soldiers are for, we take the risks on behalf of the nation. Those guys who died in Afghanistan died as warriors.

We didn't know what was going on overseas, but we knew it was real. "Real" being that people were getting hurt and dying from enemy action. I was hypersensitive to the day-to-day operations and following what was going on closely. It impacted people in the Battalion, once people started to die, we had soldiers that, you know, suddenly became conscientious objectors. We had four cases of soldiers who requested their release before we deployed. I think that this showed that people need to understand the culture of an army. We are designed to fight wars; we need people who can do hard things and put it on the line. I hated those people who were just there for a pay cheque like they were working some civvie job. They have the freedom to choose to quit, and that is fine because there are people who don't quit and accept that they are the ones who will move into the darkness. I think we needed to remember that. Afghanistan reminded us of what we are there for. I hope we don't forget that before the next war.

I was supposed to go on the first tour to Kandahar. My husband and I had been together for a couple of years and had an "oops" baby. Of course, it was a blessing, but it did not feel that way at the time when I told the chain of command that I couldn't go to Kandahar. This moment that should have been happy, made me feel like I was letting the team down, or that I had done it on purpose to get out of the tour. My pills expired because the pharmacy in Pet didn't do their job. Try explaining that to your boss. I felt invisible, like as soon as I became pregnant, I was no longer useful as a soldier I was a burden. As a woman, the baby was supposed to be the big deal, but it was the tour. The whole town was focused on the guys heading off to war. I was supposed to be that team and the exact thing that makes people believe that women shouldn't be in the military happened to me. My husband was still deploying, and I was happy, scared, worried, and professionally jealous of his experience. I understood what they were getting into and the risks my husband would be facing. As a military couple, we did a great job compartmentalizing. But I think this is a part of the story that should be discussed because I think it is the first time in Canadian history that both sides of the couple could go. Our baby was born healthy and happy, and my husband left when she was 3 months old.

At the height of Afghanistan, if you were in an Infantry unit, you were deploying. I showed up from training sure that I had missed the boat. In like a week I went from not deploying to Afghanistan at all to turning 180 degrees and deploying. It was just thrown together. I was told in my first interview with the Commanding Officer that "you're not going to Afghanistan because the battalion is going to Afghanistan in 2010 and we need platoon commanders that are still around for 2010." The pressures being what they were on personnel and all the new tasks, I think I lasted about a week, we were down guys that could deploy and all of a sudden, I was going, as there were never enough guys to fill rotations. In the end, I went twice instead of one or the other.

———————————

It's funny. I deployed twice to Afghanistan but had been involved in the mission for a couple of years and saw it evolve. I think it was interesting to see the change in Canada from peacekeeping to combat. I'll go back to like two thousand-five. I was from Nova Scotia and had been posted down east so when I got posted to the Canadian Expeditionary Force has headquarters in Ottawa as a desk officer for Afghanistan, this was a big change for me in a lot of ways. I was there in Ottawa when the mission went from Kabul to Kandahar. I was not happy that I was going to have to fight the war from a desk, not very sexy but someone had to do it. And so, I was part of the Ottawa team that oversaw that transition piece. But it was fascinating to see the war from the Ottawa side, because we were I mean, at the beginning when warning shots were being fired, it was like national news. Canada was not prepared for the fight; a couple of warning shots would mean a significant incident report to the Chief of Defence staff. I remember thinking we're getting into war here and this is going to get pretty old pretty quickly. It was a problem that none of the bureaucrats nor senior leaders had combat experience. That changed pretty quickly when we started getting in pitched battles, I mean we went from counting ammunition and never shooting, to using thousands of rounds a week. It was a huge shift culturally for the Ottawa HQ. We used so much ammunition that I was responsible to try and find more 155mm and 25mm ammo because we didn't understand consumption rates in high-intensity combat. Everything changed around that time, how the Army saw itself, our relationship with the Canadian public, and the realization of the costs of war. Physical, material, and emotional.

———————————

I was working at our training centre when Afghanistan really kicked off in Kandahar. My buddy and I were watching the news, and it was all bad as the Patricia's were getting hit pretty hard and had just lost like their 20th guy on a tour. I thought, that is crazy, we are losing a platoon of people every tour. It is just a crap shoot. My buddy says," You know what? " in the next two or three months, some of those names are going to be people we know, people that were getting killed or injured that you and I have grown up with. You wouldn't hear about the injured on the news, you only heard about the dead, but there were always 2 or three injured, but you heard about them through your buddies that were over there. Sure enough, a couple of months later, I missed out on the first tour, I was sitting at home. All of a sudden, they pop up on the news, with no warning, and it's guys I know, good friends that I have known for the better part of 20 years. My wife and are just eating dinner, she had just seen their wives at a get-together, and everything was fine. We just stopped, we didn't know how to react, and then we called the families of the fallen to help. We went through the grief and saw the families at their worst moments. Then I got a call, and it was my time to go, I was a replacement for my friend. I think that was very tougher going over knowing what loss felt like at home. I did not hesitate, but I felt bad for my wife and how she had to be so tough after seeing the pain of her friends.

Things were changing in the army because of the war in Afghanistan. It impacted training and how we did business. That messed up a lot of preconceived notions of what was right, and you had to fight against people who just wanted to do things "the way things have always been done." It was sometimes slow for the people and institutions to follow the changes. Combat was different, we had to adjust, or we would die. I remember one example was using tourniquets. At the time, no one used tourniquets This is a big no-no in St John Ambulance as it could cost someone a limb, but in combat, it stopped the bleeding and could save their life. I had this reservist person who was a professional firefighter who was fighting the training that we were going to use tourniquets to sustain life. Every first aid lesson they would sound off, "You can't use a tourniquet. Blah blah blah." So, I printed off all these photos of IED injuries the timelines of when a person would bleed out, and the timelines of when a MEDEVAC helicopter may arrive in the best circumstances. Without a tourniquet, people would never survive to get on the bird I was like, "Are you fucking kidding me? Shut your mouth. Stop fucking with what we need to do to survive. You are impacting the troops in our section. They're young. Young troops that think you're good because you're a firefighter." I think his professional points were fair for what he knew and the norms of the day, but it was an example of all the things we needed to shift to get ready to operate in combat, instead of peacetime or peacekeeping. The change required of our teams was psychological, and not just physical.

Afghanistan made all the pretenders and Garrison troopers take stock. Time to pay the piper for the good pay, the pension, and all the training. Now you had to go do the business. For lots of people, this was a wake-up call. I mean, there is a lot of talk about "army culture." This goes back to first principles and understanding what it is you do for the nation. We fight wars to achieve the national interest. This is what we do. This is what the army is. It's about going to dangerous places and doing dangerous things. I get that sometimes you get what you don't ask for. That's fair. But we do it. Don't complain about it. We are a professional force. It was in the brochure. Just accept it and move on. I think I think many of us in the professional military in Canada, forgot what it was about, we got used to peacekeeping with limited violence, and we didn't expect to do what we trained and signed up for. Then people, especially senior people that have never put it on the line for the majority of their career complain about it when the mission orders come down or try to get posted out when it comes their way. If you're in a position where you're not comfortable knowing the government pays you to take the hit for the nation, then get out, because that's the nature of the job. That's our culture.

I found myself on my way to Kabul, Afghanistan. I was the only woman and mother in my unit. I didn't want to make an issue of childcare and be a burden to the chain of command. But it was an issue. Not just for the deployment, but for the 6 months of work-up training before leaving. My husband was posted to Ottawa and was trying to get posted back to Petawawa to take care of the kids, but when it came time to deploy, he was still dividing his time between the two locations. There was no system in place to account for two married service members and no consideration of the needs of the family. Just the needs of the service. We were OK with it, but our family had to step up big time to help. We flew my father-in-law from Edmonton to Petawawa to stay at the house so the boys would always be with a family member. They still went to the babysitter's every day to keep their normal routine so Grandpa could have a break. Before leaving, I made my parents promise they would spend Christmas in Pet so that my boys would have a piece of me with them over the holidays – I'm not sure why this was so important to me, but at the time I remember thinking that if my parents were there for Christmas, then everything would be okay. It's funny the things you focus on when you are getting ready to go overseas.

My story of getting warned to go to Kandahar is also my coming home story. I did my first tour in Kabul; we got off the plane after being deployed for 7 months and had to do 3 ½ days to reintegrate with the Battalion at work before going on leave. It lets us sort all our Admin. On the first day back the Commanding Officer brought us all into a classroom and told us to enjoy our leave because we would be getting right into work-up training when we got back to work 3 weeks later and would be deploying to Kandahar within the year. So, my leave was spent, negotiating with my wife about how yes, I had just been away for 7 months and yes I would only be home for 7 months before I was gone for another 7, but it was worth it. To be honest, leave was exhausting, and I was happy to get back to work and get focused to go.

I was a brand new Private just out of training and was placed in the 10% replacement pool up until two weeks before the deployment. This 10% pool were the replacements that would be the first to go if someone got hurt, killed, or could not deploy at the last second. In Petawawa, I was doing some administration for the leadership, building a spreadsheet of the qualifications of the 10 % pool so that, if needed they could be selected easily. This Master Warrant Officer came around the corner and said, "I need a guy qualified for this, this, this, and this". So, I started going through the paperwork as I hadn't finished my list yet. He says, "Well, aren't you qualified for all that? I said, "Yeah." And he goes, "Well, don't you want a tour?" I was dumbfounded, and I said, "Sure," He told me to load my name and just like that I was going to Afghanistan. I do know some people in the battalion at the time held a little animosity towards me because they think I put myself in there, but whatever, Fuck'em, right place, right time. I was heading to Afghanistan.

I was not supposed to deploy to Afghanistan again after being on two tours. But they had the Battalion drug piss test and that was always a sure bet that some of the boys were going to get busted. So, on the Friday before the test, Senior NCOs asked us to ask our wives if we could deploy again. Monday was the piss test and a bunch of dudes got busted. Then shortly thereafter, it was whether you wanted to go again or not you got assigned "You're clean. You're clean and you're clean. You're going to this Company. You're going to HQ, you are going to Recce." It was bad, as it meant a lot of guys had to rotate again back to Afghanistan quickly and the Battalion leadership didn't want to have to go to other units in the Brigade that had their own tasks because so many guys pissed hot. So, a bunch of us got thrown back in. Third tour in 4 years, maybe I should have smoked some dope.

We get back in 2007 and after a couple of months, the soldiers are saying, I want to go back. There was no shortage of opportunity because there were never enough people. As long as your head space and time were good you could go again. I got married after I got home, 10 days after us getting married, I was going out to Wainright to be an observer controller trainer, to train the platoons that we're getting ready to go over and they could benefit from our experience. I thought, this is great. My wife was not happy, I expressed disappointment that I wasn't gonna get a honeymoon AND that I was going to Wainwright but was secretly stoked to contribute back to the fight. So fast forward, I am deployed on the exercise, and it covers over Thanksgiving (also popular with my wife). I was having turkey dinner in the mess hall. I was eager to pass on what I thought was knowledge to the guys who had not been to Kandahar yet. I felt like maybe I could contribute to saving a life and wanted to stop them from repeating mistakes. While I was there, I got a call and was told there was an opportunity to deploy on the tour following the one we were training. About 7 months away, but training would start right after this task. I said absolutely. He let me know it was with a new team called the Operational Mentor and Liaison Team or OMLT. I said that sounds awesome. I want to do it. So, as I just got married, I forgot to discuss it with my wife. She was a little surprised when I got home. It was like you never left Afghanistan or the mindset. You rotated in, then you came home, you went away to train the next guys, then you did some more training and went again. It was like constant deployment for 4 or five years. My wife deserves a medal.

I remember getting a series of briefs from the PPCLI team that was currently in Kabul conducting the training. It was strange to me as they all seemed amped up. This was a training mission in Kabul, it seemed out of place. It was not Kandahar, for Canada, combat was over. So, that feeling of nervousness is kind of infectious, right? So, we turned up the volume of our training in response. Then, just before we went to Kabul, they had lost a soldier to an IED on the "safe" mission. Apparently, it wasn't all hype. That was kind of a sobering experience because at that point I was just freshly married, I was new to the army, and I had told my wife there was no danger. I never deployed to combat. I only did the training mission, but I would guess that the fear your family feels is the same when you are going to a place where Canadians have been killed.

I went to Afghanistan as a battlefield replacement when a senior NCO was killed. No warning. The RSM had brought me back to the Battalion that year in preparation for a tour to Afghanistan 12 months later. When I got back to Battalion the Afghan conflict was in full swing, and I was tasked to go to Cyprus as the Decompression NCO. "Decompression" was the Army's attempt to triage the shock of leaving combat and returning home. It was supposed to allow for initial psyche assessments and to allow troops to release some pressure prior to getting back home. So, my initial task was three weeks in sunny Cyprus babysitting troops that had been on tour for 7 months. Not the best task for someone who had not yet fought in Kandahar. One day my Major called me into the office, and she said, "You are not going to Cyprus- you will eventually get there because you are going to Afghanistan," I looked at her and said "Got it! I know we are deploying in the next year for our scheduled tour. "My Officer looked and me and said no.." you are deploying in 12 days." BAM! I asked if we could delay because I had just bought my wife tickets on a cruise for her fortieth birthday. The OC continued on her track, and said, "I hope you had Insurance, because you are not going on that cruise you need to go replace a Senior NCO who has been killed." I went home and told my wife, she wasn't happy, but then also couldn't get mad because I was leaving. 12 days later I was in Afghanistan, first tour in Kandahar, as a battlefield replacement for a great NCO who had been killed by an IED. The scheduled tour was a year out, so I went on that one also. In the end, I got two trips to Cyprus.

I remember feeling like I just wanted to get to Afghanistan. I had joined right out of high school in New Brunswick, was a new Private in the Battalion and I felt like you wanted to get into it, you were watching firefights involving people in your Regiment on CTV every night. I remember it hit home when I had to do a funeral party. Warrant Officer Mellish had been killed on Op MEDUSA and he was from PEI. I was on the firing party for that funeral. So, we were there for a week and we saw it all, we rehearsed and made sure that we were not going to screw it up, but it was just another task until the body came in a closed casket and I sat there and watched the family grieve and then knew what this was all about, the possible sacrifice and how it would impact the family. You know, it gave me pause, but only for a second, I was a soldier and I wanted to go face that challenge. Instead of deterring me, it kind of motivated me. Maybe that is fucked up, but as I stood over the grave, I knew that I wanted to be on the mission and serve.

TRAINING FOR WAR

THE ARMY IS A UNIQUE PROFESSION where you train for something for the entirety of your career, and if you are lucky, never actually do it for real. You spend countless hours, months, and years training - fighting simulated battles where the only consequence of mistakes are revived casualties and maybe a hit to your pride.

A tour to Afghanistan was seven months long, but the preparation, known as work-up training, was the equivalent amount of time of the tour or often even longer— sometimes up to a year. Professional soldiers who remained in the army would, in the end, deploy to combat on several occasions over the course of time between 2001 and 2014. For their families, this time commitment of seven months of deployed life would be compounded by months of training away from home. Their reality was not an abstract idea or simply part of the national debate about participation in the Afghan War. It was intensely personal - a daily pressure as soldiers left their families and people from the community were injured or killed.

Training was the perceived way to mitigate the risk of casualties and the cost was the absence from family and friends. Afghanistan became a focus of these communities, not just for the time that soldiers were in Afghanistan, but for the work-up training that would take soldiers away for months on end and which required absolute focus and dedication. It was the invisible bill of the professional soldier, paid for with missed time with loved ones.

Everything in their lives was subordinated to the Afghan mission.

Leaders trained to fight a determined enemy and to bring as many of their young Canadians home as possible. There is no greater responsibility. The military is the only organization that has "zero liability" to its people, meaning that a soldier can be ordered into dangerous situations, or even unto certain death, to accomplish the mission. It is accepted that you may lose life or limb to accomplish your mission on behalf of the nation.

The Canadian population does not understand this cost well; they seem disconnected from the sacrifice requested. Realistically, it is not always fully understood by the young men and women who volunteer to serve. Until they and their families are asked to pay the bill.

———————

The hard training before deploying was important. In the army things that suck bring you together. If you want to understand where your friendships are born? Not when the times are good. We were from all over Canada, and in a lot of cases had little in common. The suck brought us together. Dudes from the cities, little villages, the west, east, north, didn't matter when you were sucking wind through your ass. Our leadership put us through the paces before we went to Afghanistan. It was not even the formal assessment training that the army demanded. It was just hard, physical training that toughened our bodies and hardened our minds. My closest friendships were born by climbing this mountain in full kit in the driving rain and when we reached the bottom, our leader had us turn around and do the 4-hour haul again, I thought guys were going to shut down right there. But we turned around and drove back up that mountain, full kit, about 85 pounds in freezing November rain. But, you know, I think the worst times become the best memories in. No one walks into the room and talks about how easily accomplished things shaped them. That tough leadership, those bonds that formed, and that mental discipline helped our team get through some pretty tough times. I hated it at the time, but the further I get from it, the more I see it as necessary to prepare to do the things you need to do in war.

———————

I think a big change that came with Afghanistan was the idea of professionalized work-up training where you were measured on how you performed, and every aspect of your training was programmed to ensure that you were "ready". This took place in a camp in Wainwright Alberta. It was a huge endeavour. At its peak, we had close to 5000 people participating to train a task force of about 2500 people. Everyone who went to Afghanistan went through Wainwright. Wainwright is a big open prairie like NOTHING is there. It is bitterly cold, the weather changes every 5 min. If you were lucky, you got a tent, but if you were in the Battle Group or OMLT/POMLT it was more likely that you were living out of your vehicles and in various tactical positions. You would spend 4 to 6 weeks away for this training before departing for Afghanistan. Your family got used to you being away. Fake Afghan villages were constructed, actors were brought in to play civilians, and soldiers played the Taliban and the Afghan partners. There was so much different training for all the groups. There was Headquarters training for the Brigade HQ, there was mentor training for the Operational Mentor and Police Mentor teams that would spend 7 months living and fighting with the Afghans, a helicopter Squadron, the Provincial Reconstruction team that was responsible for integrating the other Canadian government organizations that were trying to rebuild Afghanistan. The big show was the Battle Group, the element that was tasked with providing security to the province and was supposed to conduct the majority of the combat operations. All of these pieces had very different tasks and they had to be generated every 6 months. At any one time, there was one of these Task Forces deployed to Afghanistan, one that had just returned and one that was preparing to go. It meant that you never really left the training or deployment cycle if you were in one of the Brigades. Usually, if you just returned, you got tapped to head out to Wainwright to help train the next group going over and so that happened just after you got home from your combat tour, by the time you got back from that training you would get the warning order for your next roto, so the clock in your head started. It is like you never really left theatre. You could guarantee at least 6 weeks away before and probably 4 weeks away after for the training bill, so a 7-month tour became a 9-month commitment. For those years I was either in Afghanistan, training for Afghanistan, or training someone else for Afghanistan. When I think about it now, it was a huge undertaking and it exhausted our Army and our people, but when you are in the middle of it you can't see the time costs. I totalled all the time I was away for tours or training between 2005 and 2010, and it was ridiculous, like 37 months.

Spring of 2006, our group was getting ready to go to Wainwright for Exercise Maple Resolve. This was the "confirmation" exercise where the army decided if individuals and the unit were ready to deploy. We were told that we were going to be the three duty officers in the BG headquarters. So, we'd go to Wainright and learn about that job. We're told about how critical it was and how much power we'd have within the TOC to help direct the battle. So, we, the three of us; Lts and myself, went out there and we never left the battalion, C.P. for the first 30 days of the exercises. 30 Days inside a 10 by 20 tent. We had no idea what Wainwright looked like outside of the concertina wire of the CP. We existed within a 400 square meter area for 30 days. It is high pressure as the army puts you under enough stress to "break" your system. Train hard, fight easy is the mantra. But the command post was a pressure cooker. I remember distinctly a "mass casualty event" where the designed training scenario was built to overload our medical system and chain of evacuation. It would be like a small town running out of ambulances so you need to triage effectively. One of the rifle companies, an organization of about 160 people had, in this scenario, maybe a dozen soldiers killed, and wounded another 30. I remember turning to one of the other duty officers and saying, this is retarded, I mean this would never actually happen. Everyone was losing their marbles, and we were not assessed well by the training team. I mean this had NEVER happened since Korea, why were we training like this? We dealt with that portion of the exercise, thinking how unrealistic it was, and deployed to Kandahar. As a footnote to the training, we got overseas and dealt with multiple mass casualty situations and things that you could not make up in a book. That same company that was assessed in Wainwright, had two mass casualty situations; it was eerie. It showed me that training and training hard were so important because facts are always strangers than fiction, and the chaos of battle cannot be replicated perfectly in training. It needs to be as hard and as challenging as possible so that young people who fight have an actual chance to succeed. I worry we are going forget that the farther we get away from combat and settle back into peacetime discussions and routines.

We did nine days in the mountains down in Texas to train to go to Afghanistan. I was pretty stoked as I was from a small Ontario town and Texas was my first time out of Canada. It sucked! We humped 98 kilometres in those nine days under about 75-120 pounds of kit on our backs. We had to carry all our shit to get us ready to fight dismounted in Afghanistan. The desert is so strange. It was hot during the day and then really cold at night. It snowed on us in the mountains. It was plus 30 and then minus ten, just standard army suck. Occasionally, we would do a simulated attack on an enemy-held village. This involved running behind armoured vehicles as they led into the attack. The first time running behind the LAVs, we were moving through this field of 6 to 8 ft cactus. As we advanced, the LAVs pressed the plants down as they drove over them, but did not snap them off, so they would be under tension and the LAVs commanders forgot that there were dismounts behind them. My Platoon Commander, a great guy, was moving along and was surprised when he got hit by a cactus that flopped up and hit him square in the chest, with these huge thorns. We're still running, he bounces back up, pulling thorns out of his chest and face. Then it is my turn and I get hit with a freakin full tree and get knocked on my ass, complete chaos! It taught us a little resilience and it was like taking losses in a fight, guys were going down everywhere as these trees would spring back and knock them out, but you had to keep moving forward and adapt your tactics on the fly to be successful. So, it all sucked, but it kind of has to if you want to prepare for combat. Those "Cactus IEDs" were a bitch though!

You need to practice hard things to do hard things. I remember that my platoon commander made us do extra physical training to prepare to go. We would march out to the ranges full kit when everyone else would take trucks, and on the way home, we would run back with weapons, flak jackets, plates, helmets, and vest combat loaded. I initially thought it was bullshit, but as I watched the news and saw what the Patricias were doing, no one complained. We didn't want our fitness to let us or our team down when we got into the fight. I remember all the platoons driving past us as we ran home, making fun of us. But it gave us confidence, and we were ready to fight. We figured out pretty quickly that fitness matters in combat and standards matter. I will never tell him, but all that bullshit fitness saved lives. I ran work-up training on my next two tours for my section and platoon, and it always involved slinging the PT cock to get them ready.

During training in Texas, we would sleep on dried riverbeds called wadis. We called this one "Snake Pite Lane" because one of the guys didn't know how to spell Pit. He wrote out pit and added an "E" at the end, so that's what we called it. That night, I woke up with a rattlesnake curled up beside me and the guys screaming at me, telling me, "Don't roll right, there is fucking snake next to you." I heard the rattle and rolled for my life the other way. Fuckin Snake Pit 'e' lane…I should remember more about work-up training, but mostly, I remember the fucked-up weather, the endless humping with 100 lbs on my back, and the fucking snake.

Work-up training before leaving became this marathon of time away from home before we deployed. The issue was that the Battalion leadership would rotate every two years, but the troops and the middle-level leaders would stay the same. So, when we first went in, everyone had the same experience. Whether you were the Colonel or a Private, neither of you had seen combat. By the time we got to the third and fourth rotations, the junior folks had a bunch of time down range, but the new leaders were fresh from staff postings or wherever they come from in the Army. Not their fault, but it forced us to start all over again every time. By my third tour, I could give grids in Kandahar without even looking at the map, but we had to build a new team. So, it meant we would get home from one tour, take a short break, do a course to get promoted or something, then come back, fit into the new team, train for six months, and maybe be away for 2-to three months of that and then deploy for another seven months. The training was exceptional; the army spared no expense to make sure that we had the best opportunity to succeed. We learned so much between 2003 and 2014, but I hated the preparing-to-go phase the most. It was so frustrating to be so close to my family but still not be at home, especially knowing I was going back to walk around in the sandbox and only luck would decide if I was coming back.

———————

The first tour to Kabul, the Theatre Assistance Team, was different from all my other tours to Afghanistan because there was very little warning and then no work-up training. By the end of the rotations in 2014, it felt that the workup was longer than the tours themselves. We didn't start that way. We had a good system. Our trained start state was pretty high. I was a section commander of ten dudes and felt we were ready to go. We got the call and were told we were going, then a week of getting passports, shots, and admin shit. In the second week, we did some ranges. In the third week, we did a three-day exercise that was considered enough to get into a theatre that no one had been to yet. We took about five days off and deployed. I think that was the favourite of my three deployments to Afghanistan because the pre-work-up drama was short, and we just went and did the job

———————

As the war developed and Canada wanted to develop capacity and not just kill the Taliban, there was an idea from leadership that the Afghan police could receive mentorship from leadership that the Afghan police could receive mentorship from small teams in the field and become a more professional force. I bring it up because I think it was the first of that type of unit for Canada and unique to Afghanistan. The issue was that the Afghan criminals were opium traders and Taliban and fought with heavy weapons. So, the mentor teams were built with half infantry and half military police. I was part of these teams and was an infantry NCO. I was responsible for the training and discipline of the team. They were called POMLT or Police Operational Mentor and Liaison Teams. Bringing these two groups together was not easy as their tasks and perspectives were very different, but both would count on the other to make the mission successful. The challenge at that time was bringing the M.P.s with infantry soldiers and just the biases that we all carried at the time. Because of our ignorance, not having worked with others other than our kind. We didn't even really speak the same language. There were some interesting transitions. I remember the Infantry Captain and I were running a range to get ready to go, and we just wanted to do a series of transition drills and movements to get the M.P.s battle-ready. The M.P.s could write tickets and traffic and make your life miserable, but they couldn't survive on the battlespace. They wanted to go through Canadian police escalations of force, as opposed to Afghanistan reaction to ambush drills. In the end, they adapted from Garrison policing to the realities of getting ready to police in Afghanistan, which looked a lot like fighting all the time. It was a constant tension between the desire to "police" and the realities of fighting an insurgency WITH police. I don't think we made one arrest, but we sure got into a lot of firefights. It was a good theory, but too early in the conflict, I think.

The training was super intense. It's the longest pre-deployment training I have ever done; it lasted the better part of a year. The most vivid memories I have of that training is we went down to Fort Bliss in Texas to live in a desert and manoeuvre in the desert terrain. I was in the Battalion Command Post. In modern war, there is a lot going on, and the CP is the "brain" of the battalion. You do all support for the teams fighting from there and provide all the support called "enablers." We built this team just months before we deployed, and so we had to learn all the new personalities and how they did things. We had coordination cells, like the engineer support coordination and fire support coordination. We got some new pieces we were not used to having, like a tactical air control party. We had never met these guys; they were all from the Air Force. It was not popular to bring the boys in blue into an Infantry Battalion! They had been off doing the Joint Terminal Air Controller courses. I will never forget the day that we heard they were showing up and that we were going to meet these guys. We're kind of having a really shitty day, just fucking like a busy day. So, these guys show up in a van, and they get out. And I remember my SGM saying, "who the fuck are these guys?" And they had their leader gets out and e was like he was in desert CADPAT which was weird because all the Army troops were still in green, and he had his fucking Airforce wedge on with desert combat uniform. He was like an aerospace controller from some radar squadron. He introduced himself using his "call sign" like he was "Maverick" from Top Gun. A fucking radar operator. "We are your TACP!" they were so smiley and bright and shiny. I was like, "What. The. Actual. Fuck." He's introducing the rest of the guys. An air weapons controller with a radar background. We had a Sea King helicopter navigator, an Aurora pilot and an F-18 pilot. I just remember thinking "Thanks armed forces. We're getting like a navigator and a radar operator who has never deployed who's gonna be responsible for, like, dropping bombs on people." It was a HARD clash of cultures between an infantry battalion and these air force dudes. But, man, never judge a book by its cover. These guys were lethal in action, and I think they were responsible for more Taliban deaths than our hardest SOF guys. But that first day was pretty funny, we just stared at each other and did not speak the same language at all!

I went down to the pre-deployment training in Texas as a spare. And I think the first day on the ground, they told me that I was going to Afghanistan. The situation changed, as always, and I was going as a part of the Police Operational Mentoring Liaison Team (POMLT) platoon commander, but I wasn't switching over to the POMLT until after the plead pre-employment training, which was which was perfect. we did all the training down there to support the Battle Group but none of my training. I acted as the Afghan National Army (ANA) to simulate the partners. I didn't know what the ANA was or how they worked, but I was I was an ANA commander for the exercise. When I got back, I took over the POMLT platoon. I remember I was very excited. I didn't know what it was or how it was going to work. No one at the time knew what the POMLT was. I think the first tour for POMLT was the one before us. All we knew is they get shot at a lot. What they did was kind of up in the air. So, as a platoon commander, I knew how to command a platoon in a conventional context. But to be a POMLT platoon commander, I knew sweet fuck all. The composition of the team was very different from that of a rifle platoon. Four teams each had ten each, and then I had a small headquarters of four folks. The idea was that they would both be at strong points in and amongst the population (read Taliban-held territory), and then all the reporting would go through me. That meant that there would be more Afghans than Canadians in each of the three locations. The ANP had a reputation of being two-faced with the Taliban, and half the team would be military police that were not combat soldiers. It was an interesting problem to deploy with few guidelines as to what we were going to do, little in the way of our training, and a not well-understood chain of command. What were advisors responsible for? You can't order the ANP to do anything; what happens when they disagree with the Canadians? It was dodgy but exciting.

The hardest thing I had to do in training was fire my Sergeant Major. I think guys were just too comfortable with the way things used to be done in the past. The training we had was hard and deliberately challenging to see if people could adapt, work under stress, and apply the lessons that had been hard-earned by previous rotations. Leadership is critical in combat, and if someone can't perform well, they shouldn't be in the position. Unfortunately, I had to go halfway through the workup and get rid of my sergeant major and bring in the new guy. I mean, the CO at the time left it to me to break the news to my Sergeant Major. So, it was probably one of the more difficult things I've had to do in my career. But at the end of the day, he was just like he was a guy who was very comfortable with the way things have been done in the past, and I don't think he was ready to take that that aggressive step that needed to be taken to fight a counterinsurgency. I think it just came down to when we started the work-up. During the initial phases, when it was still war fighting, you had to establish your standard procedures before doing theatre-specific training. It was the hardcore war fighting stuff that when the chips are down, and it's raining, and it just generally sucks; the sergeant major is the guy that takes the NCOs and kicks people in the ass to try to get things going. My guy wasn't like that; he would rather bundle himself up in the back of the LAV with a hot coffee. That is the truth. The more and more I saw it, the more I knew it was just causing dissension with the troops. The soldiers wanted that guy sometimes to be a hard ass. I had to fire him. It was an incredibly difficult choice, but it was proven correct. He ended up deploying to Afghanistan in a different role. One day he was tagging along on a patrol and foot patrol and master Corporal stepped on an IED and lost both of his legs. Another guy was seriously injured by the shrapnel. This sergeant major was close enough to see and feel but far enough away that he didn't get injured. When I showed up on the scene, he was borderline catatonic and not doing anything to help with the situation so that validated in my mind that performance in high-stress training did reflect reality and if people would shut down in training they would probably shut down during the real thing. His feelings may have been hurt, or his career negatively impacted but it served the mission and the soldiers better to have sorted it out before deploying.

––––––––––––

I remember going through, little vignettes for training. It was the first tour to Kabul and all our training was attached to the Bosnia experience as the frame of reference and I remember that all the leaders had that mindset. The battalion had gone through Bosnia in 2001 and now we're into 2003. These training vignettes sharpened our understanding of the rules of engagement for tactical use. We put each one of our sections through the scenario where they had a choice to escalate to deadly force legally. But even where someone had actually, pulled out an AK 47 there was there was hesitation, and on average the first time through the scenario no one fired. In order to get the sections to fire, we had to have the "belligerent" "fire" on them with blank rounds and then that got a reaction. That means our mindset was completely defensive and only after we had effective fire on us would we react. It was an immature mindset, in a place where seconds could save your life. It was because of this Bosnian peacekeeping mindset of only firing when fired upon, and even though the ROE was robust enough and we had the legal right to defend ourselves from hostile intent, it would take a while and some losses of people to get the leaders that had done multiple UN tours to understand that it was better to be judged by 12 than carried by 6. I think it was just maturing the army, after that first tour it was not an issue, but the transition was painful.

I was a LAV Crew Commander on my first tour in Kandahar. I think I realized that we were getting into something different when the Company Commander returned from his theatre reconnaissance and set the stage for us. He came back and gave us all a briefing about this patrol he had gone on with the Patricia's that were there. He said that they're walking through open country at night, and the FAC is on the radio with the Americans, and a fighter bomber is patrolling the night sky looking to drop its ordnance comes on the line and says, "I see a house over here," and the FAC dazzles it with his laser marker and says, "do you want me to bomb it?". The Patricia's that are on the patrol are like, "Nope, we're good, we're not in contact, we're alright". A few minutes later, the pilot comes back and says, "There's a compound over here," and he sparkles something on the right, "do you want me to bomb that?" The Patricia again says, "No, no, we're all right, nothing is happening." And that was the whole patrol. Fast air would come in; they would talk to the JTAC and say, "Ya, we see something over here; we can flatten that." The ground force commander would say, "No, we're fine, we're just walkin'" Like all these assets were lined up waiting for you to pull the trigger. So that sort of set the tone that we were gonna go over there, and we're gonna have all these assets, which is super cool and takes your confidence from, "we're gonna be ok" to, "we're gonna kick the shit out of this thing." The Company Commanders tone through the whole work up training was good, and it was about if you get hit, hit back hard, but do it right, follow the ROEs. In training, we were assaulting this mock village and drove by a piece of mod tent that had a burn barrel beside it, there were some actors there, and we knocked the burn barrel over into the mod tent and the mod tent burnt down. We paid no attention to it; we drove through it and reached our objective, but that set the tone. When you assault, destroy it, no half measure; the boss wasn't happy after that until something was on fire. So, the goal for every time we went out was to either pump enough tracer fire into something to light it on fire knock something over or blow something up. So that was the Coy's goal every time we went live. Folks may not understand it now, but that confidence was important; when it became a two-way range, you couldn't hesitate. I always appreciated my leaders training me like that; it helped me on bad days.

I was in the OMLT on my second tour. The Operational Mentor and Liaison Team (said OMLETTE). It was small groups of Canadians that would live and fight with the Afghans. We would act as mentors and ensure they had access to medevac and fires, and we only had four guys in a team. We were just infantry guys who went from being in a platoon to all of a sudden doing this unconventional task. There is nothing that really prepared us to be a mentor. I formed some pretty strong opinions about how we should train. I made up all these Dari and Pashtun language sheets, then gave geography lessons to the troops. So, we'd go into like the shacks at night after the day's training and the Kandak team. I would instruct my team, and every day, we do a little bit of geography and history and language. We were gonna be immersed in this culture. We went to the hills with reservists who played the ANA, and we had to "mentor them." I don't think they know what they're getting into because we need these massive hikes with all of our equipment, like all the light infantry stuff in these hills. We would make one of these reservists, the Afghan company commander, like a young reservist. And then we would mentor them. I thought it was it was excellent. They brought back guys that had already been on OMLT rotos to help us out and he basically mentored us and said the only right track. It was a really good exercise. We came out, I think, a really strong team and were as prepared as we could be to do this task.

By my third tour the ground had not changed, the enemy had changed but we were still learning and sending in fresh troops. Not many in my platoon had any experience. M senior sergeant, he was seasoned in the military but not with Kandahar experience. My number two sergeant had his roots in Kandahar at the height of violence in 2006-2007. He was the most vocal about doing certain operations and what the leaders should be thinking. But the enemy and the mission had changed in the two years since he had been in theatre. It was a challenging leadership environment, and by this point, a lot of the senior officers were also on their first tour so there maybe was some imbalance between the SNR NCO experience and the Officers. That said, the troops were eager to get in and were focused. Everyone always had a good sense of humour, which was essential if you were going to be successful as a unit in Kandahar during this time. We felt our platoon used to always get chosen to lead because our platoon leadership was strong; even in Canada, during work-up training we would do more, which translated to theatre, where we joked that we were the "tip of the spear" because we always seemed to up first for every task, which is a compliment, but fatigues the soldiers in a high IED environment. The relationship between the platoon commander and warrant officer was so important. The CO of the Battalion recognized this and asked the Majors to involve the Warrants in the selection of the Platoon Commanders so that the senior soldiers would have some voice in who their partner would be for the tour. This built strong bonds between the platoon leadership, which paid dividends when we got down range.

We were all close friends in the Battalion. But at the end of the day, there has to be one person in there who maintains discipline amongst the Officers, and that person is the DCO. This was important to establish as we got ready to deploy into a combat situation where there would be disagreements and high emotions. I used the terminology "bend in the road." I said, "If someone has to be the bend in the road, it will be me. So, you know, the HQs work for the companies and do what they need, But if someone has to say no to the Commanding Officer, it's me who does it. I am the bend in the road that is navigated by all the groups. This creates space for everyone to voice opinions and not break relationships.

We did this giant parade in the field right after the final exercise was over. This was like the end of 6 weeks in the field, and we were exhausted. This Colonel, who was the TF Commander, tried to get us fired up, and he was like, "Let me hear your HOOAH." Canadians aren't good at that shit. We like quiet professionals. So, this Colonel was a bit flabbergasted that there was no shouting. Then all of a sudden, the crowd goes crazy, and troops are clapping and yelling, and the Colonel thinks he has inspired us. What he doesn't see is that some crazy engineer was driving a 4-wheeler behind the Colonel's platform butt naked except for the helmet to protect his head and identity. He peeled out, and we saw the MPs head to chase him. I hope he got away. He had gotten into the beer before us! Awesome! Time to go.

PURGATORY

AT THE CULMINATION OF TRAINING, soldiers took a couple of weeks of leave to spend with family before their deployment. It was a pregnant pause between the intensity of the work-up training and their arrival in the theatre.

Families tried to fit in as much as possible during these leave periods - visits, weddings, travel, celebrating milestones that would be missed - attempting to cram a lifetime into a couple of weeks. All this was done while trying to avoid the reality of the situation. Death and injury would undoubtedly find many. It is an emotionally exhausting time - families focused on spending every possible moment with their loved ones while the soldiers themselves were torn between providing that connection and reassurance while simultaneously being distracted by their own worries and concentrating on their upcoming deployment.

The tension between the present and the near future is unbearable. It is impossible for those deploying to stay perfectly in the present moment and avoid focusing on the challenges ahead. News channels are avoided by the family as no one wants a reminder of the realities of combat that are shared on everyone's television through the 24-hour news loop. There is a polarity within those deploying; the safety of home with all its warmth, and the required mental hardening as they prepare for the combat to come. There is a point when it is just time to go. Strangely, the final departure is often a relief to everyone - one step closer to returning home and freedom for soldiers to focus solely on the mission.

I was a section commander, and I remember the day I realized that I was responsible for the lives of my section. You always talk about it but maybe don't realize it. We had a Base Family Day for the families, and everybody's families came for the BBQ and send-off. I had a great private in my section, a young guy, a light machine gunner. I remember his father coming to me in the base gym when things had started to quiet down and everyone was leaving. He comes right up to me and looks me in the eye, grabs my hands, and says, "Make sure he comes home." Those words and responsibility just landed on me, heavy. It was real; this parent was holding me accountable for his kid. It was like getting hit by a freight train.

———————

We'd gone down to Myrtle Beach as part of leave before deployment and, every night went out to party. And it was it was a bit surreal because, being in Myrtle Beach, the states had troops dying all the time. The News would report daily numbers that seemed shocking as we were at the height of the Iraq and Afghan wars. I remember watching TV and seeing all the faces of the dead soldiers, and outside, there was this sort of carnival festival atmosphere; there was no understanding of sort of what was happening overseas. It kind of smacked me in the face that dying was a possibility, and whether I lived or died, it really wouldn't matter except to my family. The world would just keep partying in Myrtle Beach. It sunk in with our group that was down there after the newscast. We had a little talk and acknowledged that not everyone was coming back from this one; that was the job, but it just got real.

———————

Before I left on my first tour in combat, I wrote a "death letter." I got up in the morning, probably around five o'clock, and then went downstairs; I put on a pot of coffee and took out my laptop. It was a four-page document, and I called it my "last gig." I just fucking laid it out. I wrote to all my family. I wrote to my kid, my brother's kids. You know, you get this; this is how I feel about you, etc. It was overwhelming to sit down and emotionally connect with everyone you love on paper to say goodbye. I tucked it away in my kit; it sat there waiting and staring at me every time I opened my Barrack box. I hated it. Like I acknowledged my death, or worse, I was already dead, but no one had been told yet. When I went back a couple of years later, I didn't repeat the effort; I vowed never to do that again because I was very hard.

———————

My dad had a hard time saying goodbye. He and my sister came to Petawawa to say goodbye to me. They got stuck behind one of the Highway of Hero's convoys on Highway 401. They had just left Petawawa after saying goodbye before my tour, and now they were following the coffin of someone who, in their minds, could be me in a couple of weeks. Later, my Dad told me that it was a terrible feeling. My sister was bawling, and it was so slow, all the way into Toronto from Trenton, 3 hours; neither of them said a word; they knew that they never wanted to do that drive again. That would have been hard; sometimes, I wonder if going was easier than being left behind.

I think about it all the time. I remember when the Patricias first went in there into the white school in 2006. They lost 4 guys and had a bunch wounded. We were deploying like three days later. I remember sitting in the shacks in Petawawa with the boys and one of the guys, one who ended up getting killed overseas by an IED. We're all sitting down drinking beer and watching Afghanistan on the news, and nobody is saying anything, but everybody's glued to the TV set. Then, finally, somebody broke the silence. "Well, I guess this is going to be pretty real." And then we all kind of laughed and just continued drinking. But I remember it was a feeling that we all kind of wanted to talk about it more, but nobody wanted to say, "I'm going to be scared. How am I going to deal with this?" I guess "this is gonna be pretty fucking real." was all we could manage and be comfortable with.

I went on a Tac Recce in June to understand the situation before getting into theatre and taking those last insights back to my soldiers. We started deploying at the end of August. When I got back, I decided to brief the entire company about my one-week experience over there. When I was over there, I was out with the rifle company we were going to replace. On the convoy out, the LAV ahead of me was hit by a suicide bomber, and that was a wake-up call for me. We didn't have any direct firefights during the week, but certainly some IED events, which is probably enough for one week. What struck me was how many things happened in a week all over the area of operations. It did not feel like we were in control; it felt like the enemy was dictating the tempo, and we did not have enough forces to deal with all the threats. However, I only experienced a week, so I held my opinion and just focused on the tactical situation we would be in. I got a bit of a taste of it there. When I got back to the company, I had everyone come to the junior NCO's mess in jeans and T-shirts for an afternoon. We ordered pizza, we had some beers, and I just got up and gave a very informal briefing about what I learned over there. What are some of the things that the guys can expect, how we would be living, and some tactical tricks that were new to me for finding IEDs in the ground? I think it was at that moment, and we kind of rolled over and spent a good relaxed five- or six-hours kind of drinking beers and talking about things over there. It dawned on me after I had done the briefing, and everybody kind of broke off; the platoons were all together, talking in small groups about how they were going to do things. Professional conversations were earnest, and I hoped they had the answers and were focused on the mission. As we surveyed the Company interacting, young men and women with a Molson Canadian in hand, sunglasses on top of their heads, talking about their next seven months in a conflict zone, the anticipation was heavy in the air. I remember looking at the sergeant major and saying, "This is when it feels real and like we're leaving. We've been talking and training for it for so long." It all fell away that day, and I knew that we were in for a big challenge. That afternoon was perfect; I hoped that everyone that I was looking at would be back in 7 months to do it again.

I wanted my wife to get flowers every month that I was gone. So, I went down to the flower store and ordered flowers for the whole tour. Different days and different times of delivery, so it would always be a bit of a surprise. I wrote seven notes each to be put with the flowers so she would see my handwriting. Once I was overseas, I realized what a shock it would be if something happened to me, and the flowers still came for the next couple of months. I think she liked it, though.

Here's a story for you, classic bullshit as we were getting ready to go. We had a send-off party in the Battalion lines. There was this guy who was a regimental patron, some business guy who donated money to the Regiment. I am sure he was a good dude; I can't remember his name ... But he wanted to do the send-off. There was a stage set up so he could address the outgoing troops. The troops are pissed off because they have to wait around for this guy, and they have to change their uniforms so they can escort him. Then he is late; he lands in a helicopter and is brought in and fed really good food and booze and then gets up on stage to give us a Hooorah speech and announces that he is going to award a trip to Costa Rica to the soldiers or some shit, I am pretty sure he is loaded. So, his wife intervenes so that he doesn't make any crazy promises, and he is bundled off stage. The troops now are confused and standing around like what the fuck is this? It was like an episode of the office, not the way we would have chosen to be sent off... but funny as shit.

My daughter was three and so didn't quite understand that I was going away for so long. She was really worried about not getting her bedtime stories from me. So, my wife and I spent two days in front of a video camera. Recorded me reading stories that my wife would play my daughter at Night-Time over the next eight months. She loved it, and in some ways, I felt that if the worst thing happened, I would be there reading her stories forever; she would at least have that connection with me.

We're leaving in early August. I came in one morning, and the sergeants from the platoon were waiting for me. They tell me, "The guy you're replacing is wounded." The Battle Group we were replacing fucking took a bunch of hits in that first week in August. 4 guys were killed, a bunch wounded, and the guy I was replacing got hit. That brings it right home; this handover will be different. I needed to adjust mentally. It is not easy to have a conversation at home. I didn't tell my wife; she would have just worried, so I just kept it in. Probably the start of lots of things I didn't share, but I didn't want to start the deployment with, "The guy in my position just got shot." And so, I just went along like nothing happened. But my platoon knew, I knew, we were getting into it and would be lucky to come through without getting hurt. It dialled us right into the problem, but I was nervous as hell. I felt like there was a target on me.

I think where it probably hit home a little bit more was when my dad had a going-away barbecue for me, and my sister was there. Towards the end of the night, there was lots of drinking, and people certainly got emotional. A news flash came up on the TV. A soldier had been killed in an IED strike. I remember my sister just losing it. I remember telling her like, yes, people can die, but my job is in a secure airfield. You don't have to worry. I think for my family, it was kind of understood that I was going over. But I had this staff job in the airfield, and I'd be somewhat buffered from the violence. Little did I know that I would be deployed outside the wire almost immediately and then take a platoon leadership role due to casualties. I am glad that initially, it made my wife and family feel better and made them think I would not be in harm's way. After a week in KAF, I was outside the wire, but at least they felt better before I left.

My son was born on the work-up training for my third tour, OTW. I was able to get back for the birth, and I was glad to be there because we almost lost him. He and my wife came through amazingly well. My Mother-in-law came out to help, and I went back to the field. By this point, we were experts, having done this routine every 12-18 months over those four years. It was just a conveyor belt counting down to the flight to Dubai and the C130 flight into the suck. I remember getting out of the field and heading home, getting no sleep because we had a 3-year-old, a 2-year-old, and a new baby. I think they all sensed the stress, so we tried our best to keep it light, but we knew what was coming and the separation that was coming. I tried to be invested every day, but I was thinking about Kandahar; I was worried about what I was walking into, what had changed from the last time, and I wasn't present at a time when I should have been enjoying my new son. The one time I treasured was the middle of the night when he was restless. I would wake up and put him on my chest and try to give his mom some sleep. It was the only time I felt connected. I took a picture one night of his whole hand around my finger; it was incredible to me. Something so small, entirely dependent on me, and I was going to leave him behind. By the time I got back, he would be eight months old and moving around, and time moved on and could not be recreated. In the morning, I was back to being detached and thinking of what was coming up; I had to work hard to separate myself to get on with the job. On the day I left, my family took a picture with him in my arms; I hated that because I knew that would be on the news if I was killed.

I remember beforehand, we had the big Red Friday rallies. These were popular at the peak of Afghanistan. Everyone would wear a red shirt on Fridays to remind everyone of the soldiers fighting overseas. So here they had become a big thing for all the families down at the base. My mum came up from Nova Scotia. a few days out from deployment. So, they had a little concert and an event in the gym. All the families were out in the field, and they had to hold up these big red and white pieces of Bristol board over their heads to make the Canadian flag. They took a picture from a cherry picker to give to everyone to keep. It was almost like a carnival, forgetting what we were going over to do or that we could get hurt. Reminding us that we were doing something bigger than ourselves. We were citizens, and fighting for what our nation needed was part of the package. It was cool; you could tell that Afghanistan was different from other deployments. Everyone's family was getting involved and were supporting each other. But behind all the smiles, you could feel this tension. I felt it after we got home from the sendoff party. That was the last step. Now, as I leave this place, I am not sure if I will be back. It was a weird feeling.

Saying goodbye before the tour is the worst. You get to a point where you have nothing else to say. It is just time to go. You are together with your family, but you are in your thoughts and have already moved on. So right off the hop, we were supposed to deploy March 1st, but New Brunswick being New Brunswick, the weather closed in. So, I said goodbye to my wife and called my parents. You know, we're getting ready to go. We're all in the two RCR buildings, and the flight has been rolled to the next day. So, we're like, what do I do? I made the conscious choice not to call my wife again and go through the emotions of saying goodbye again. We just stayed in the barracks and had a lousy night's sleep. Then, the next morning, we hopped on the Airbus and started the journey. I wonder if I should have gone home. Somehow, in my mind, it made more sense not to have to do the goodbye again. Maybe I was wrong. She will never know, or I would be in big trouble.

When it came time to leave, I refused to let my family come to the departure point. The last thing I wanted to do was get emotional in front of my peers, superiors, and subordinates. So, we said goodbye at home. I had my husband drive me to 3 RCR, and then I hopped out without so much of a hug in the parking lot. Probably a bit extreme, but at that moment, it was what I needed to do to box that piece of my life up and tuck it away for the next six months. By this point in my life, I was an expert in compartmentalizing– I harnessed that skill with all my might as I left my three and 5-year-old boys at home with their dad, who was also serving and a grandpa who loved them dearly but who they barely knew. This seems absurd to me now.

I felt like I was ready to go. I felt like I was ready to do the business. Say goodbye to family, you know, get on the buses. Switch On. Let's get real again. Here we go. We're driving to the airport. Like I was getting emotional. There're fucking people everywhere, holding up signs as we drove past like, "We love you." "come home safe." "Best of luck," "We'll see you in six months," I still get goosebumps when I think of it now; the community knew this was different, like we're getting into it. Like this is war.

Being a private soldier, I was tasked with the baggage party duty. I had to show up early, load all the baggage on the trucks in Petawawa, then go to Trenton and help load all the bags on the Aircraft to fly to Dubai. We stopped off in Tweed Ontario and I took a picture of all of us seeing our last greenery and lake. At the time, I hadn't thought about it. When I got into Afghanistan and everything was Brown and shitty in Afghanistan, just a dustbowl I don't know how many times during that deployment I looked at that picture and thought of the cool green. I still actually take that picture out picture 20 years later. Still makes me feel good.

What is winning in Afghanistan? How long is this war going to last? We're a victim of our own experience. But at the same time, I think we're the beneficiaries of that, too. And I think we all realize those of us who've gone through the Bosnia years and had done multiple tours already leading up to this point, that this was an enduring thing. There was no finish line, I don't think, in Afghanistan the way I think a lot of us would like to project. It wasn't going to be a ticker tape parade, I don't think. So, going into this, one of the things I told our soldiers is that we joined to do this type of job. I still remember the whole company in a couple of classrooms. We've ripped down the walls and had them all stacked in there. I said, "I want everyone to take out a piece of paper and write down what your personal mission is." I said, "Because I can tell you what the mission is. I can tell you what the strategic mission is. The operational mission is on any given day; I can tell you the tactical mission." If I want you to know what your mission is, I want you to write down your personal mission. I don't want you to share it with anyone unless you want to, so write it down. And if your personal mission is something as crass as you want to be, I want to be one of the first people on my, you know, to use a bad line, the first kid in my block to have a confirmed kill, if that's what it is, I don't care. Write it down because the day's going to come when something bad is going to happen, and you're going to ask yourself, why am I here? And I won't tell you why you're here from a Canadian perspective. And I can tell you why you're here from a company's perspective. But I won't be able to tell you why you're here. And so, you're going to be able to reconcile that yourself. If you can't figure it out now, you're going to be grasping for straws when bad things happen. So, take a moment, write it down, and be prepared to accept the good and the bad to come on this mission based on what it is that's personally motivating." Everyone did it, and I'd like to believe that helped in the long run. I do know that people came back to me afterward and showed me the slip of paper, sometimes years later, and said, I'm glad we did that exercise because there were bad days.

On pre-deployment leave before Kandahar, my wife and I had a long, hard chat. We felt that it was important that she move back to Newfoundland for this deployment so that she would have a little bit more family support because, at this point, the kids are young. They're only three. The oldest is five. That age timeframe where, you know, you want all hands on deck. There was a lot of news and a lot of, you know, media coverage on what was going on there. There were a lot of casualties. Everyone saw those that were killed but the wounded weren't reported. We knew about them from internal reports. We kind of knew that we were gonna lose some soldiers there, and if that happened or if I was wounded, I wanted my family taken care of. So, we moved them back to Newfoundland. We packed up the car with three kids and we went. I got them settled, said goodbye there, and left all of my family back in Newfoundland. I flew back to Petawawa for a few days before deploying, and it was an empty household, so I cleaned it all up and down and put everything in its place. I made sure that any important documents were easy to find, and when I locked that door for the last time when I left for Afghanistan, I accepted that I was not coming back. My family was safe and with people who loved them, my admin was done and if someone had to come to my place to sort out my shit if I died, it was sorted, and it would not be a nightmare for them. I was ready to go and maybe not come back.

Part II
WELCOME TO THE SUCK

OSCAR MIKE

IT IS A LONG JOURNEY INTO THE AFGHAN THEATRE.

Transported from the normalcy of family, hockey night in Canada, Tim Hortons, lush green forests, cool breezes, deep lakes, and wide rivers, you are pushed into one of the most ancient, desolate, deadly, and beautiful environments on earth.

The two countries could not be more different.

One with all the advantages of geography, climate, natural wealth, political stability, and personal freedom, the other, seemingly trapped in a cycle of violence and constantly pulled to the brink due to its location and intersection with history.

This teleportation between worlds happens in just 24 hours. The emotional and mental shift within this short period is astounding. In the early hours of the morning, you gather at your unit drill hall - children quietly being held by their parents, partners, and families saying tearful goodbyes. Squeezing out final seconds before the inevitable call to get on the bus, goodbyes are said, soldiers are organized and loaded onto buses and finally depart for the drill hall. Everyone tries to be cool, and hide tears and worries, as they watch their family disappear in the distance.

The bus to the airfield is quiet as most are consumed by personal reflection, occasionally interrupted by nervous small talk and laughter. Getting on the plane for the first leg to Dubai, the crowd relaxes, and the majority rest and chill out, maybe talk a little while settling into the first leg of the flight. You're finally on your way and some degree of normalcy returns, some sleep, some fucking around with each other, but the focus is still on Canada, your family, events you will miss, and normal bullshit about the mission.

When you land in Dubai there is a noticeable shift in the focus of the group. You open the door and feel the heat wave and the initial smell. It hits you that this is different. This is the last step before Afghanistan. The mood of the group shifts to one of business; shit starts to get real, you take out all the combat kit and put it on, and you are given your initial load of ammunition for weapons, as you load the C130 you see the guys that are coming out of theatre as they get off the plane.

As you load, you pass them. You are segregated but can catch a glimpse.

They look tired and skinny, combat uniforms worn through. There is an air of relief and exhaustion. They're so happy to be leaving the place you're headed.

If you haven't already left home behind, now is the time to do it. You start thinking about what you need to do to accomplish the mission, to stay alive, to keep your team alive, and to do a good job. There's no choice but to dial in. Within 24 hours you have shifted from the warm embrace of a loved one to entering a war zone. You are fully consumed in the present, in the now. From this moment, you stop thinking about what you left behind, what you may never see again, and focus on what's about to come.

The acronym in the early 2000s for Kabul International Airport was "K. I. A" like the military acronym KILLED IN ACTION. I don't think it was great flying in there or seeing it on the map. I know in later years it got adjusted to K A I A or Kabul Afghanistan International Airport. I always wondered if it was because didn't want that acronym to be to be kind of synonymous with the place you were coming into.

I was posted to Gagetown, but they needed senior NCOs in the 3rd Battalion, so I went IR for my tour to Petawawa. I went home to NB for leave prior to departure and then went to Pet to depart to Afghanistan. I'll say my goodbyes at home. It is easier. This was like my 6th overseas tour, and we found it easier to be emotional at home and then she would drop me off and I would just go. I think it's better that way. So I get to Pet, we get on the bus, we take the bus to Trenton and stop in Tweed for a coffee and we get to the plane and get briefed on our route. Our first stop was New Brunswick! To pick up some dudes from other elements. Our first stop, Fredericton, took me 3 days to get back to where I started. Only in the Army. I felt so bad for my wife and our first phone call was explaining what had happened.

We got to Trenton, and everyone was nervous and thinking about the dudes that they were going to replace. There had been casualties in the days leading up to our going in and so we knew we were heading into a fight. The Air Force didn't seem to know that. As I was getting on the plane in Trenton, I was one of those guys that had my issued Gerber utility knife on me, I mean Fuck, I was heading to war and I was a new Private, you always have a knife a compass and pencil and paper, those are the rules. Well, the Airforce saw fit to take away my multitool before I go on the plane and did not even hold it until I got back, they just were dicks and took it away. So, I landed in KAF, and I don't have my multi-tool and the CQ won't give me a new one, because it was my fault and there was paperwork that had to be filled out. I go to the PX and buy one for 135 USD. Fucking Airforce. Like I was going to Hijack the fucking plane or something. Fuck those guys. I still have that multi-tool. 18 years later. Never made that mistake again. Fucking Air Canada wannabees.

The reality of what we were about to do first hit home was when we drove from Petawawa to Trenton to fly out to Afghanistan, after saying goodbye to our families in Petawawa. It was our first real quiet moment in several months. We stopped in Tweed on the way down, the Tim Horton's, I think. I think it was like a CAF appreciation thing. The busses drove through, and they said they were gonna stop, and they wanted us to get out and shake hands and everything. And so, people were lining up in the streets and I remember getting off the bus and people waving flags and stuff, and, you know, I cried after, no shit, I was like, holy shit. We're going to war. And, you know, I was like, fuck me. And that's when it first sunk in. And, yeah, it was then I guess it was just because I had not had time to think, we had been so busy before we left. And that's what good training does for you; it focuses you. But when then you stop and have time to think of what is going on, it is different. I'd done four tours before that. I always kind of just go out the door. We often get so caught up in our own stories that I think this was a reflection on the communities and families and the reality that you may not come back. Tweed was a central part of the story of any RCR soldier who went to Afghanistan. Everyone who went had to stop and was wished well on the way out but was not necessarily there on the bus ride way back to Petawawa seven months later.

We had to fly in during the night. The Air Force was concerned that the Taliban may have a shot at us. About an hour out, the internal cabin went to red light, just like the movies and we got the order to put helmets and flak jackets on. I thought

" What the Fuck, I thought the airfield was secure…why all the drama?" It was hot in the back, the old C130s were not climate controlled, you are jammed together like sardines in a tin can, you are tired and thinking about landing and what you were about to get into, it is like they did it on purpose; the heat, making you sleep fucked right off the bat by coming in at night, cramped and then they start evasive manoeuvres as they approach the airfield, precautions against ground fire. Troops start throwing up around you, your uniform is soaked in sweat, the smell of AV gas, transmission fluid, and vomit filling your nostrils as you descend in the darkness, everyone trying to act cool like it is no big deal, and then you land, NCO's start barking directions, you look out of the aircraft at your first look at Afghanistan it is pitch black and you are stepping into that darkness. What the Fuck have I gotten into?

Camp Mirage in Dubai lets you feel the heat of the desert. When you open the door, you feel like you're in the exhaust of a jet engine and it takes your breath away. I had a unique reunion in Dubai, one of my friend's mother was there. She's a military traffic tech, sorting out our kit and ensuring it all gets into Afghanistan. I think that was unique, but I am not sure there was ever a time when a mom was also serving and watching her son get on the plane to war. Like if there was a mom loading paratroopers before D-day. Crazy shit. I think unique to modern war and modern militaries. Not sure we understand the impact that has on people. My thought was that traffic techs sort out all loads, including when coffins with our fallen come back from Kandahar. If something happened to me or her son, she would be strapping the coffin down. How fucked is that?

So, we flew from Dubai. We were only there for maybe eight hours or so and we jumped on the Hercules brought us in and I remember them doing contour flying. That was my first experience with that joy, which involves the plane sticking to the "contours" of the earth and involves violent pitches and rolls as the plane manoeuvres to ensure it is difficult for anyone on the ground to fire weapons at it effectively. Fortunately, I don't get airsick, but several guys made a great deal of vomit that went into their helmets and onto the floor so that it was all over the uniforms and boots. I guess it sort of helped to make things a bit more real in terms of getting us mentally shifting into theatre. I was 19 and brand new in the Army, frankly, probably didn't understand why we were doing it. I attributed it to the pilots being assholes. As I got off the plane, I thought that perhaps I'd gone about going about this whole adulthood thing all wrong. It occurred to me that all my friends who, you know, at that time, the year prior, I'd been in high school with, were getting drunk and chasing tail in university. Here I was I was like an idiot, covered in other people's vomit and freezing my ass off on the cold tarmac in January in Kabul. I looked out and could see no lights in the city of 3 million. That smell of Av gas, cold fresh air, vomit, and the burning braziers of Kabul is set in my mind as a lasting memory.

I remember there were weird things during travel with the Canadian Air Force that people had you do. The Air Force had to follow civilian air rules while we were in Canada, but I think they took it to extremes sometimes and I remember you had to pass your weapons through the metal detectors, lock away your knives, and pass through like bags in which you, had your bombed-up mags full of ammo and it seemed administrative and detached from military activity. I am sure it is normal for every army; you know to treat your soldiers like criminals before they go to combat. "Was this rifle with ammunition that he was given by the government of Canada to exact violence on the enemy, well I don't trust you put it through the metal detector... Yes, it was" ...box ticked...now get on the plane to go to combat... Well done, Chair force. You know how to make sure that even an infil into a combat zone is the most uncool thing ever.

We flew to Kabul for the very first rotation on civilian airlines. It was insane. It added so much time to the deployment and extra headaches because of connections and it is difficult to move a 45-person platoon on a single civilian aircraft. We overloaded the ticket and baggage people in Halifax. Weapons, we met them in the UAE as they had to be shipped separately. We travelled commercially with kit bags, barrack boxes, and rucksacks. Hundreds of pounds. The flight out of Halifax took us to Toronto. We had like a twelve-hour stopover in the city. I had been asked early on whether I was going to confine the confined guys to the airport. My answer was no. I'll treat everybody like adults. Seemed to make sense, I thought I was exhibiting trust-based leadership. I was feeling pretty good about myself, and I met my parents I went out for lunch and then came back to the airport. Then I learned what young soldiers do when they have lots of time off and no tasks. I found a couple of the guys in a state where one of them was so drunk, that he had passed out before flight, on the chairs in the lounge. A second was almost incapable of walking. We got everybody on the aircraft including the guys that couldn't walk without lots of help and a forgiving staff. The next flight was from Toronto to Amsterdam, before the final leg into Dubai. When we arrived in Amsterdam, we had a seven-hour layover. I learned quickly and based on my experiences in Toronto that Amsterdam had likely even more opportunities for young soldier "activities", I said nobody leaves the airport and nobody drinks. I acknowledge that we have a responsibility, and I learned some good leadership lessons but what the hell, even if we just had a proper military aircraft to get into Afghanistan, we wouldn't have to play trains planes, and automobiles all over the world and my troops would have the feel of being deployed into a conflict zone instead of a vacation feel.

The stopover was in Scotland at that little airport we always stop at. I say that because I deployed 4 times and it began to feel routine. It was closed when we got there. So, we landed there, and we carried on to Dubai and when we got off in Dubai it felt like you were standing behind the jet, there must be fire blowing on my face right now. But you weren't, you were in front of the jet, and it was just so bloody hot, like holy Jesus! Heat's coming off the tarmac, heat's coming off the plane, heat's coming off the sun which feels a million times more powerful than it is. And then uh, we're in this weird little paradise, this little camp. Everyone is logistics, and they have great food and a great gym. This is their tour! They called it Camp Mirage, like an oasis in the middle of the desert. I remember signing for my ammo, I signed for 150 rounds from this supply tech, and she made me sign a 638 card as though, I had to be accountable for it. I mean, we're not handing this back, right? We are going to fight for fucks sake. She looks at me with this weird perplexed like, "What do you mean you're not handing it back?" I turned around and walked out with my ammo. That night we were there and a Sergeant in the Battle Group already in the country was killed. He had only a week left in theatre before he headed home. He used to live across the street from me. So, a bit of a sober moment there while we were in Dubai. Then you got on the Herc the next day and flew into Kandahar. That Herc we were on would carry his body out, so they prepared it for the ramp ceremony after we got off. It was my first ramp ceremony and the first thing I did when I arrived. That made you pay attention.

Forty or so of us were sitting in the cargo net seats that ran along the length of the

Herc. There wasn't much room since the centre of the aircraft was fully laden with palletized loads. We all shifted in our kit, trying to find a comfortable position for the long trip ahead. The Herc's engines began spinning up when I heard somebody call for my attention from a couple of spots down. One of my former reconnaissance section commanders, who had been moved to the rifle company with me leaned forward.

"It hasn't been a year." He smiled and sunk back into the cargo net.

I did a quick bit of mental math. He was right, it had been 350 days since we had flown out of our last mission in Kabul. In a few hours we'd be in Kandahar.

There was this dude that was a big "tough guy" And so sure enough, as we were on the flight from Dubai to Kandahar we started the combat flying. We start banking and diving at one point into the final approach. He's sitting right across from me on the other side. We're in our FFO, with his helmet and all his gear on. I just saw I saw him go wide-eyed the whole time, starting to sweat. The plane is creaking and moaning in protest to the high Gs and he's nervously shifting left to right. Then he finally calms down after 20 minutes or so. Suddenly there is some unexpected turbulence and I think he just shit his pants right there on the spot. I liked the look on his face. Part of his brain imploded or something because his eyes went wide, and he didn't know how to react. This was just the flight in. I laughed out loud, and it was lost in the noise of the aircraft. I wondered if he was going shit himself the first time he was in contact. Sometimes the guys that seem the toughest aren't.

I remember being on the Herc, you know, getting ready to go and how fucking hot it was in that fucking plane. And I was sitting where the wheel was. So, you know, you're fuckin jammed in there like sardines. I remember lifting the lid from the box lunch and fanning my face. It was so hot, and I was so sweaty the cardboard just literally disintegrated in my hand. This is fucking miserable. I don't ever remember being nervous or anything like that. I just feel a little alone in the darkness. I heard so many people puking in their helmets as we started to descend into Kandahar. I think the thing I remember most about that whole thing though was waiting to get off, as the darkness, the manoeuvres coming in and the smell was terrible. Just get this fucking plane on the ground and let us off before I fucking lose my mind.

After you arrive in Kandahar, you wake up early the next morning and have a series of tasks that have to be done before you deploy out to the area of operations. You spend the first day zeroing your weapons and doing induction before you head out to the field and, it starts hot, like 30 degrees by six am before the sun gets up in the sky. I remember coming out in the morning and thinking that the heat was already oppressive, like a weight on your chest that created difficulty breathing. I fucking hate the heat, I'm just in combat fatigues, with no body armour, and am already sweating my bag off. It was fucking miserable. How the fuck am I gonna fight if I can't even walk 50 m without sweating out all my body's water? The logistics team tried to make it better by moving us around the giant camp on buses. Those stupid buses were hotter because they were old shitty Afghan buses there's no ac. The drivers would turn on the AC but it was just hot air and hadn't been cleaned so you got a face full of hot air and dust in your face. Once weapons are set, you go to your classes and the common theme was " outside the wire, this shit can kill you." I know the one that threw me off was the IED class. It was a series of pictures of IED casualties to drive home to us that the threat was real. We know the threat was real, they made it seem like everything was an IED. This slide show was brutal, "This is a blown-up leg and this is a blown-off leg and this is a blown-up vehicle." Made me think, "What the fuck are you doing here?" It was super demotivating, there were no briefings on what had been accomplished. All I was getting was that the troops were getting IED'd everywhere. The pictures were pretty scary, to be honest, legs shattered by explosives, split like over-boiled hotdogs. Missing feet, bodies not identifiable due to the burns, and loss of identifying limbs. Just charred meat. I got a message: "This is what you look like at the end if you aren't careful." The message was you're gonna fucking die. To bring the point home, they take us to the "boneyard" in Kandahar, where all the destroyed Canadian vehicles are. I remember seeing the vehicles in there. There must have been ten to twenty. All different types. Burnt, melted down, large holes in them where soldiers had sat. Where people I had known from other Battalions had sat before, they died or were hurt. There was one that had been blown in place by the previous battlegroup. They had to abandon it after an ambush and dropped a 500-pound bomb on it. There was no turret, the tires were shredded, the paint was all peeled off and what I thought was my protection, showed how weak it was. It made me think that all the stuff they told me about the protection was bullshit. I remember that sticking out my head because I'm like, man, if we're just blowing up a fuckin vehicle, and not recovering it, what kind of problems are we having? When you see the IED strikes where the armoured hull is penetrated by a ground-laid IED or where a vehicle a suicide bomber fucking hit the driver's side and penetrated the hull right where I was going to be sitting. So not a great first 24 hours. Shitty flight in, super-hot and can't breathe, briefings on how everything is going to kill you and then a tour of the vehicles that you are going to use but didn't protect their last occupants. Awesome. Time to Cowboy the fuck up and get out to the field to get after the work. I think too much time in KAF would fuck with your head.

When I arrived in KAF, I had a day or two to sort myself out before heading to the field. I looked up a buddy of mine who was the Assistant Operations officer and let him know I was going out with the operational mentoring and Liaison team or OMLT. Our job was to work in a small team of 4 Canadians and live and fight with the Afghan National Army. It was a little dodgy because the Afghans had various levels of training, we had to move in a single vehicle and our security was guaranteed by the Afghans, not fellow Canadians. It was the end of a long tour for my friend, and I was fresh in the country. They had seen some serious fighting and had taken the first round of losses and high casualties. He had seemed to change so much, he was jumpy, always seemed tired, and was a bit cynical. I remember that I caught up with him and another guy I knew who was a LAV Captain and they both pulled out cigarettes- neither of them had been smokers 7 months before. So, they pulled out their smokes, lit them up, and took a big drag. A memorable scene to this day for me. He said, "Oh, you're going with the Afghan army". And I said, "Yeah." He goes on, "I hope you got your life insurance sorted out." I was dumbstruck and I remember sitting back at that time thinking to myself, well, that's quite the thing to say. I shrugged it off, but it did not fill me with confidence before I departed for the field.

When deploying one of the first things we did when we got in the theatre, was attend a ramp ceremony for some guys that were killed. So that set the tone. We weren't watching this on TV anymore, we were in it. We may be the headline if we fucked up.

Kandahar itself reminded me of stories my parents told me of their time in the old country. I grew up like any immigrant kid. It's ingrained in my brain about my mother growing up in Egypt and Lebanon in the heat and her stories of making the asphalt soft from the heat and different types of trees and people and bartering of people in the markets. When I was a kid, I had this illustrated kid's Bible. When we pushed out of the camp and into the area of operations, the mud walls and the mud huts and livestock were just like pictures out of this Bible. I remember the stories told me stories about sandstorms that she grew up with and how they dealt with them around the house. So, it was really interesting to call back and tell my mother about Afghanistan on this deployment that is linked to her childhood, something that she could never do more than tell us stories about. It was a shitty way to learn about it, but I felt closer to my mom after living in a desert environment on my tours and those first days really connected me to my past and culture, I realized for the first time where I had come from.

We took civilian airlines into Kabul on the first rotation, and they lost my luggage. All my fucking kit for 6 months in theatre. What kind of chickenshit organization flies Civilian Air Lines to war? One that doesn't know what it is getting into. There have been big changes in the CAF since Afghanistan, but the biggest, I think, is being serious about serious things.

I remember we had bad weather both in Dubai and again in Afghanistan on the flights in. We had rain, which was a head fuck as it never rains there. We got to Dubai. It pissed rain on us for a straight day, like the old fat thunderous downpour of rains. I thought I was supposed to be hot and dry. Our flight out would get rained out a few times. Once we got into Kandahar, we were hopping on Helos to head out to the strong points. They got rained out a couple of times. I remember sitting in the back of a truck on the tarmac waiting to see if we'd have to go or not. It was like a movie; the canvas cover of the truck was belted by rain, and we would sit around in the section and bullshit until it was decided if we were going to fly or not. When we got Rolexed we would drive back to our sleeping area and wait for the next window. I remember one talk in the back of the truck, I was pretty quiet when I was a Private soldier, I didn't want to say anything stupid. I'm sitting there and I remember all the boys sitting in the back of the truck and they're just talking about hypotheticals like, "Man, if I step on an IED and my balls get blown off, I want somebody just shoot me." And all the guys are just like, "Yeah, yeah, life would be over." It was just a big echo chamber. "I don't wanna live without my balls" is the general consensus. Everybody seems to agree on this. I remember speaking up, "Boys just because you guys are in the majority. I want everybody to know specifically my wishes if my balls get blown off. Please don't shoot me. I'll give it a try, and if I don't like life with no balls, I'll just wheelchair myself off a fucking pier or something." The things you talk about sometimes. Crazy shit.

My first impression of Afghanistan was being a little overwhelmed. I had never travelled anywhere outside my small town in Saskatchewan until I went on basic training. This was another planet. When I think back, it is the smell that sits with me. If I think about it. It's almost like you can still smell it. That combination of heat, diesel, AV gas, burning garbage, and cooking smells all blended. It's like nostalgic, maybe triggering like it can bring me right back there. I remember how excited I was to be in Afghanistan and to get to do this shit for real. Be a part of something that not everybody gets to do. I know it sounds cheesy, but to be a part of some part of history, something bigger than me was real. One of the big things that pushed me over the edge to join was watching the TV show 'Band of Brothers.' I remember talking about it with people, who asked, "Why would you ever want to do that?" You know, to be a part of something that not everybody can do. It was overwhelming. It's something bigger than yourself. No one can ever take it away from you; you are a small part of history. I remember getting off the plane and thinking, this is crazy, the whole western world was there, and I was a part of it.

The idea of sacrifice and service are sometimes used as punch lines. The idea of war. War on drugs. War on obesity, war on whatever is trending. That's not war. I got off the plane, all disoriented, and went into that old hangar. I looked up moonlight streaming through the roof with all the shrapnel holes, and it seemed like hundreds of fucking pigeons. There were also old helicopters in pieces left over from the Russian times in Afghanistan, like a marker from those that had been here before us. I remember having to try to find our Kit in the dark and we couldn't turn any lights on lights on due to the rocket attacks and we couldn't find our fucking kit. There was a kit all over the place. Then this is Patricia comes out and he says, "This is not a relief in place. This is a relief in contact." I thought who the fuck is this guy? Fuck you budz, stop with the melodrama bullshit. Then as you finally grab your kit, you slowly realize, that this reception machine has one purpose, to prepare you to go outside the gate and fight. This is it; you are going to take that next step into the darkness and experience war.

As soon as we arrived, we did a ramp ceremony for the Patricia's. It may have even been the same Herc that we arrived on. What a way to start, it hit you right in the face, seeing that flag-draped coffin get loaded into the bird to get sent home. Pretty sobering. When we drove out to the AOR, we lost the Sergeant who escorted us out to Sperwan Ghar. His last duty on the tour was to bring us to Sperwan Ghar and go home, drop us off, and go on his way home. He hit an IED on the way back to KAF. I felt terrible, did we need him to come with us? I felt like it was our fault and he died in the last week of his tour. Then you realize that it is game on until the minute you get on that plane home to Canada, to the very last second, there is always a ticket waiting for you if you are not careful and you don't want to collect it.

I mean the C-130 was awesome. It was rock and roll. This is what soldiering is all about. Night insert into a dangerous country, contour flying and loaded up for bear. When you get off the plane and finally see the base, you see all the aircraft and realize the scale. I think Kandahar was one of the busiest airfields in the world at the time. You start respecting the power that was resident on that base. Nothing had prepared me for the size of Kandahar. There were thousands of people and billions of dollars of equipment. I really didn't understand how big it was until my CQ told me how many people were unaccountable in the camp. So, they had brought people in to work as civilian contractors from places like Indonesia. And they've lost them on camp. They just disappeared. So, they could keep working under the table when their contract was up. I remember cycling in, and feeling like I couldn't wait to get out into the field. I felt like with all this shit, there is no way we could lose. This was gonna be awesome.

We all arrived in-country, and it was a lot of joking, a lot of false bravado. Hanging around in KAF everybody thought we were ready. With the amount of training we had and the leadership we had, I just felt like we were the "killiest" guys alive and nobody could ever beat us. Once we deployed out, like once we landed and once, we got into the "boats" and out to the strong points and replacing the other guys, and seeing what, you know, Kandahar looked like and what the area looked like. That feeling of awesomeness got shaken pretty fast. You see all the burned-out cars and remnants of a hundred firefights, highways are cratered from IEDs, and big black grease marks from where vehicles got hit. We are all RCR, and we got that Boy Scout thing going on; all properly dressed, boots bloused and we've all just been issued our desert stuff so it's all still starchy. So, we're coming out looking like G.I. Joe is fresh out of the package and the guys we are replacing look nothing like what we expected RCRs to look like, big old fucking beards, long hair, just scruffy. I think when we got to the strong point, there was a guy in a puffy jacket, his hands in his pockets in a set of flip-flops with like a hillbilly beard. What happened that made RCRs, the best parade troops in Canada, whose Regimental expression is "never pass a fault"[1] look like this? When we first got in there, our leadership denigrated the in-place force, this look will NOT be us, "guys will shave every day and we'll send out a set of clippers and you guys can have haircuts in the field." The medics kiboshed that. You are not sharing one set of non-disinfected clippers among 35 people. That's disgusting. So, it became clear that we were pretty isolated, barbers were not coming out to our COP and as the cycle would turn, our hair would get longer, our combat uniform would get dirty and as we ran short on water, we wouldn't shave, saving it for drinking. I am sure the next tour felt the same way about us when they showed up. Taught me a valuable lesson of not judging anyone until you have walked a mile in their shoes.

———————

Have you been to KIA? There is a fuckin metal detector there, at the airport that receives and is the hub for combat troops going all over Afghanistan. They made us X-ray our bags. This renta cop is working security and tells me, "We are looking for weapons." Dude, look at me. I am a walking explosion. I have just come out of combat in Kandahar. This was the dumbest bullshit bureaucracy. So, I throw my bag on, throw my weapon on the conveyor belt, which makes me super nervous, because I have not been without my weapon for 5 months, and I am still in the fucking country that loves to try and kill me. So, we go through this process, and I am agitated. What the fuck are you looking for? Drugs in my weapon? He then lets me know that he is just doing his job, I ask him if he has ever stopped anyone and he says no, so this is all such bullshit. Then he decided that my purple smoke grenade was unsafe, and he tried to take a smoke grenade. I'm like, you're not taking my smoke grenade. Fuck you. I thought I was going to shoot this guy. That's the one thing we couldn't get, purple smoke, it was great to mark Landing Zones. The Taliban had green and red smoke that they would pop to try and

---

[1] "Never Pass a Fault" is the motto of the Royal Canadian Regiment. A focus on detail and excellence, in all aspects of soldiering, including dress and deportment which seemed detached from the battle-hardened soldiers that replacements interacted with during the handover period.

confuse the MEDEVAC pilots to land in the wrong spot, but they could not copy purple smoke. Eventually, a US supervisor came over and de-escalated the Mexican standoff. I just kind of walked away and onto my military flight to head back out to the fight.

First time out, I don't think I've ever done so much in my life. Just taking it all in was exhausting. Looking around and it's funny now, everything was a threat. Everything you looked at was a threat or possibility. Your senses are so high. I remember being overwhelmed by the number of inputs the traffic, the smells, and then on this hill outside of KAF, in GIANT letters in English, someone had arranged rocks to say, "no drugs," on the side of the mountain. The guy I was with was like "Yeah, that is " no Drug Hill" what the actual fuck is this place! Who takes the time to write 40-foot-high letters in English on white rocks on the side of a hill? It was surreal. The speed of movement was dizzying. At the time, IEDs were being constructed using these big yellow jugs that were filled with homemade explosives or HME, but they were EVERYWHERE. As you drove into Kandahar, nothing around but these yellow jugs. Jugs everywhere. water, cooking oil rice, everything was held in them. It was a mind fuck because in training they had just been IEDs. Once we get Kandahar City itself and the congestion and where the arches are, there was absolute chaos. You may slow down, but we never stopped. Kept the same sort of movement, moving the target is harder to hit. Kandahar has unique smells. I still cannot stand the smell cannot smell of burning garbage. I had a tough time getting used to it, but I'd say the worst thing for me was going out at night and smelling whatever type of tree they burnt to stay warm. It still sticks with me; Kandahar hits all the senses. It is a LOT, and you have to adjust fast until you learn to filter that shit.

I had already had two tours in Kabul when I went to Kandahar. I felt like a grizzled vet, but I had no fucking clue. When we landed in Kandahar, it was surreal, just the fucking scale of place. I remember thinking as I saw it while we were deplaning from the Herc. There is a grim efficiency, a sort of grey pall that overhangs the entirety of the camp. What an undertaking it must be logistically to have created this fucking place and then to sustain all this. This is bonkers. It was like running a city. There were various levels of governance and formal lines of authority and national lines of authority and then a shit ton of unofficial lines to get things done. I think at the time KAF was one of the busiest airports in the world, with the most planes in and out. I am not sure if it is true, but it never seemed to stop. Transport planes, fighters, bombers, little creepy private planes that were VIPs or three letter agencies, all sorts of helicopters and so many different nations. I remember being very thankful at the time that it wasn't a logistician for the 24000 people that called KAF home, all their interests, all of them armed to the fucking teeth. Half of those people who are armed to the fucking teeth have no concept of how to employ that weapon system should they need to. I did not spend much time in KAF but when I did, I found it overwhelming and a parallel wally world to what was going on in Afghanistan. I think there were people there who could have gone a whole tour and never seen outside the wire. Bed, gym, office, mess hall, bed. Crazy shit. I am glad someone did it. And I am glad it wasn't me.

There were a few Patricia's on the ground when I got into KAF. It was humbling talking to these guys. Some of these guys were in tears, hugging, and so happy. They had tough contacts up until the last day they were supposed to fly out. I remember overhearing them say "We fucking made it, man." That struck me, they were not being dramatic. They were very happy to be alive. Oh, no. What the fuck have I stumbled into? Perhaps I wasn't prepared for this. I started to regret not buying a chest rig. They talked about the gunfights; ammo water carriage and sustaining the fight. Our issued vest was designed for peacekeeping and getting in and out of vehicles for Bosnia, it carried 5 mags and a useless Vietnam-era water bottle. It sucked, it also had a zipper that if it got dirty would stick and was hard to get off if you needed to treat a casualty. It was shit and so I decided to buy a rig from the outgoing guys, imagine soldiers paying for their kit, well most of us did. Weirdly, it brought me confidence.

The inflow to the theatre was good because the planes were all contracted planes from the states. I remember thinking that this was gonna be a problem because all the stewardesses on the plane looked a lot like Britney Spears. They all seemed to have a southern twang and short skirts. I thought that this was going to go wrong. Many troops fancied themselves Lotharios and would try for the mile-high club. Those ladies were experts at warding off unwanted advances and deflecting the "but I could die" logic of young boys heading to war. We made it into Dubai. I remember landing on the tarmac at Mirage grabbing all the kit and unloading it ourselves. Plane leaves. We're standing there in the 40-plus-degree heat in our civvies with all our kit piled around us, sweating from having done the mad dash to unload the plane. And then we changed out of our travel clothes to our combat uniforms. Put on your game face because now you're getting ready and you're flying into theatre. On the C130 flight, there was a point where they told us to put on our armour as you're coming in case the Taliban engaged us. We landed without incident and got our first taste of KAF. Taste is the right word because the air is full of various smells like you can chew it. It stays not in your nose but settles into your mouth and your consciousness. It smells like shit. It's dusty. It's loud. Thousands of people milling around. Quickly moved off the tarmac to sequester into your tent to get your mandatory briefs, only to have someone else coming, grab you, and say, yeah, no time for that. You're launching out the door without the full indoctrination period. We were in KAF for like 6 hours and then got loaded up and started the RIP.

Before heading out to the field, We had to stay in Kandahar Airfield for a couple of days to get used to the 55-degree heat and RSOM (stands for I don't know something onward movement) Waking up, the airfield was a city under construction, most of us woke up early and took our first look. The heat was suffocating, you were immediately soaked in sweat, and thought" How the hell am I going to move and fight in 60 pds of gear when I can't even walk from my room to the shitter without almost passing out." The base was spread out, kilometres separated classes, operational briefings, confirm your administration (Your Will) weapons/ammunition draw, and confirmatory ranges to test your weapons function. Every platoon had a schedule and a bus, the bus was from the 60's the "air-conditioning" blew hot dust on you and the Afghan driver was as likely to get lost as the new arrivals were. We consumed a litre of water an hour, when we were active in those first couple of days it was normal to consume between 12 and 13 litres of water and still piss yellow. After 2 days we were "acclimatized" and ready to head out, I just hoped I didn't pass out from the heat-- that would be embarrassing—maybe worse than contact with the Taliban.

In 2006, the IED threat was still relatively new to us; we had lost a couple of guys in Kabul to a suicide bomber and a dug-in bomb, but nothing of the numbers and size we saw in Kandahar. With those numbers came injuries. We exited the plane and hit with our first class from the outgoing medical group. First Aid in an IED environment. The first half of the class was just a Master Corporal Medic telling us how many IEDs were out there and then showing us what seemed to be hundreds of pictures on PowerPoint slides of smashed feet, hands, amputations, and destroyed vehicles…awareness is one thing…this presentation took it to a whole new level. It was fucking real…dudes made jokes and fucked around, but everyone was nervous. It seemed an unfair weapon, we didn't mind getting shot at, and that was cool, but a bomb hidden in the ground, on a person, in a vehicle…attached to a goddam donkey…that was fucked.

So, it's hot, you get on the Herc, and it's boiling. There's no bathroom, there's a million of you in there, like…the worst flight ever. Think of like coach level on an Eastern European airline and then take away all the niceties of it. You're just jammed in there, elbow to elbow, and it's uh, I forgot how long the flight was. It was not long but not short. It's a couple of hours anyway. Then they come over the line, ok we're gonna do our approach to Kandahar airfield, and you look out the window, and this thing goes down to like the nape of the earth. You're looking out the window, and there's a camel, and there's a cactus, and there's a mountain, and you're like, what the fuck are we doing? He's banking hard right and banking hard left; people are throwing up. Some people are cheering, some people are praying, it's this weird like, what the fuck is going on, and they're like, well, they're avoiding anti-aircraft. We're like, what! Nobody told us about anti-aircraft. Is there anti-aircraft fire that was not in the intelligence brief? And then we land, and we all get out, and again, it's a blast of heat. You're in a completely different environment; it's NOT Dubai. Like, you're looking at hangars, and they're bombed-out hangars. The first night there, we got off the plane, and we got this little bus ride to go to the shacks and to get our stuff and everything, and then we're sitting in our rooms; we don't have any beds at this point, so it's air mattresses on the floor. We're sitting in our rooms, and then we hear this rumbly noise, and we all sort of look at each other. We had been briefed about rocket attacks, so we looked at each other, and we're like, no, I don't think…that must have been somebody with a sea can or like, maybe it's outgoing, who knows. And then the sirens go off, and now we're all pie-eyed, staring at each other like, now what do we do? And somebody comes in, and they're like, "Get the fuck out, like go into the bunker." Oh shit, ya, and so we grab our stuff and go out to the bunker, and we're just like stunned. That was probably the scariest rocket attack I had ever experienced because, in every rocket attack after that, we didn't flinch. If the rockets had already landed, no more were coming in. We were rarely in KAF, but when we were, we never went to the bunkers; that was for the FOBBITTs. But that first one. Scary as shit.

I remember when we arrived, there was an Ops Warrant Officer from the in-place battlegroup we were replacing. He gave us an intelligence brief on the area of operations. I remember thinking this guy's commentary was repulsing me. He said things like, "We went up here, and there's some good fighting, some good killing up here, and we went down here. Good fighting. Good killing." I remember thinking like, I bet this guy has not fucking ever left this base, and he's telling everybody else's stories; I remember being so annoyed thinking there are soldiers in this briefing that are about to deploy out. And he's talking about the fights as if he's commenting on a boxing match. It was total bravado, and it was gross. It was the start of "us and them," the KAFites ...FOBBITS, and the folks that were 'Outside the wire." It likely wasn't fair, but it was real; everyone has a job, but I couldn't help but hate them right from the start.

I remember seeing the hangar at Kandahar near the airfield that was beaten to shit, with bullet holes and shrapnel tears; the moon just shone through it, giving it an eerie feel. It was like, oh, man, I am at the front. Then we walked through the hangar to the rest of Kandahar airfield, which is like a modern city. Never mind that this one banged-up hangar was like a gate with the memories of war to welcome newcomers with that sobering realization and to remind everyone who never leaves the camp that violence is still happening in this country. KAF is a fucking city like it's a metropolis. I could get lost on this damn base. It's ridiculous. There were about 25,000 people, and most never left! So, we got to our shacks and settled in, and I remember specifically the company, Sergeant Major, when we were loading all our stuff, getting ready to go out, saying," Don't bring anything useless." We're gonna be fighting all the time. So, we are delayed and leave the tarmac with our kit piled neatly. And I remember walking past Canada house, and there was a chalkboard for the folks in KAF to have guitar lessons on Tuesdays. So, thinking that I would have time, I bought a guitar. And I thought, well, I'll give the guitar a go in my downtime. I need to get a how-to-play guitar book, and I have to teach myself. I even snuck it onto the helicopter to get it out to the FOB. The SGM was right; we fought all the time. I was not in KAF, and I did not learn the guitar. It is 15 years later; I still have the guitar. I still don't know how to play it.

I remember the video that played as we landed in Dubai. The task force commander, who was already in Afghanistan, made a video message to the troops. The video talked about the present challenges and what was going on. It was virtual; he was sitting there in the theatre with a million things to do, responsible for 3000 Canadians and many other countries, and he took the time to speak to us. There was no effort wasted; he was clear about the seriousness of the challenges. It was amazing that he took the time to record a video; it was like he was talking to me. It was very impressive. It also accomplished his goal. It was probably the first time I considered the things we would be doing, the dangers I would face, and the responsibility to my section. It was the first time that I felt a little bit of fear. Like, holy fuck, it was like a lightbulb went on, and I needed to get into it. I was to get shot at, and at some point in the coming months, people were going to try and kill me, and my life was the cost that our country was willing to pay for the mission. All the thoughts of being protected were stripped away. I was fine heading in, but that was the first time that I had any fear of what I was about to do.

We were supposed to still be in issued chest rigs for our tour, "No cowboy Shit," was the Sergeant Majors Mantra. I figured that once we got in the ground and everyone saw how shit the kit was, we would be able to wear non-issued tactical vests. There was a reason why no other army wore these vests. We were stuck in the 1990s Bosnian designs. We didn't need to be issued vests. We could buy them for 600 dollars online as lots of companies were producing better kit. Tactical Tailor was a favourite, but it didn't matter; it was how the ammo was accessible, how you could carry more, and how it was more comfortable. The issue was that the army wanted us to wear the issued stuff as it looked terrible that we were buying our own, and it seemed like Sergeant Majors loved uniformity over capability. So, we were always packing "illegal" kit away to pull out when the fight started, and they relaxed the rules. It was total bullshit, but it is the army. I tried to order a vest at the last minute, but being a private and not having the extra funds to throw around, I couldn't afford it. Luckily, this older soldier we called Creep Show had already been to Kandahar once and lent me his off-the-shelf rig. It at least made me look like I was the real deal because it was all beaten up from a previous tour. A small thing, but having that rig gave me great comfort as I went into theatre. Like I had an advantage and could fight better, it gave me a little pride and, let's face it, made me feel "tacti- cool," but for a young kid going into his first fight, any little bit of confidence is good. When I got on the plan, I felt good to have that packed away.

———————

We flew the Herc into KAF. Contour flying. It's my first time doing that. Looking at the guy across from me, hoping he doesn't puke. It was even worse when you started to hear some people puke just because of the angles that the Herc was flying at. The risk of the Taliban shooting down a C130 was like 0. Other countries flew in jetliners, and civilian flights flew in, but not Canada. I wondered if it was so the pilots could get danger pay. I figured it was to get us to switch on, "like, okay, you're going to do something hard, so we'll start it off hard. Welcome to the terror dome." It was so fucking hot in the aircraft as Air conditioning did not work. It was just fucking hot; your chest plates compressed your chest, and your helmet strap fucks with your breathing, and all those bodies pressed together; I am not even sure the guy's puking was from the manoeuvres, but nerves and the heat. I benefited from this little iPod Nano. I just sat back, closed my eyes, and could not wait for it to end. Those pilots were brutal.

———————

I'm going to get off the plane in Dubai. It's so hot that you think you're in the backwash of the aircraft engine. Then you realize you're ahead of the engine, and actually, that's just the climate. I remember thinking Christ, that's hot. There was no real anticipation. I was not that stoked. I had an office job. For everyone else, it was like they were going to war, and I was the guy who didn't get to go but would listen to everyone else's stories. It would not be that hard; I knew I was going to go into it. I would sleep on a mattress daily, do twelve-hour shifts in the CP, and not get out into the fight. That changed when we took casualties, and all of a sudden, I was out of the office and into the shit. Once I did get out, I sure would have liked that mattress!

———————

When we arrived in Kandahar, we couldn't sleep and went down to Canada house to hang out. We ran into some Patricias who were rotating out, and they told us some stories. I don't know how many of these stories are true or how many of them were there just to fuck around with us. Still, they told us about encountering Chechens when they were out. They said they don't look like Taliban cause some of them will have red hair and some of their blonde hair, and they're wearing body armour and proper kit, and they're doing proper fire and movement and communication and stuff. You're in trouble if you get into with those guys they told us. The rest of the home-grown low-end fighters just run around like idiots, and you shoot them. So, the Chechens are the ones to look out for. One of the guys was telling us he had been shot or hit by shrapnel, and then we asked, well then, how come you're still here? He said, "Well if your wound scabs if your wound heals over within two weeks, you get to stay in Kandahar." he continued, "But if it's still open, well, then you have to go back home cause then they'll send a replacement." I don't know if it's true, but I know I paid attention, and we realized that we were in a different situation than we had ever been before. It was a total change from other tours.

My introduction to theatre. It's funny because we ass long flight, and we got there in the middle of the night, and you know, your jetlagged and all fucked up. My MP3 player had broken, for the volume was cranked on max, so I was pissed off and like got there, had no music, and then we got off the plane. As we were disembarking, my first kind of like contact with any other Canadian was the outgoing battlegroup getting on the Herc to head home. I can see the guys getting on the plane, and they were fucking done. And I remember thinking, hey, these guys do not look good. They are saying shit like "welcome to fucking hell," and some of the comments and shit shocking to us a little bit, and it kind of pissed me off. I shrugged it off; whatever, it is what it is. I remember we got trucked over to the big ass tents and were sorting our shit out. All of a sudden, I looked at my sergeant major and said, "I think I fucking lost my pistol. What fuck. I think I left it on the plane when I was like jet lag and all fucked up." He told me to stay put and continue with the handover as we only had 24 hours before the in-place guys left. So, he grabbed the vehicle and returned to the runway; I was beside myself when the guy I was replacing showed up. "Like, dude, I am fucked. The first day of war, and I fucking lost my gun." He looks at me and says, "What The fuck are you talking about?" I repeat myself, "I fucking lost my pistol on the plane. The plane probably took off. My sergeant majors over there, like looking for it right now. He looks at me strangely and Grabs my shoulders, "What the fuck are you talking about. It's like right there!" pointing to my tack vest and pistol holstered safely in the top mag pouch. I was ecstatic but also super embarrassed. This story gets better; my Sergeant Major, I had not seen him since I discovered I was a numpty, comes up to me like 45 minutes later and says "Sir I stopped the plane, and I and the loadies ripped it apart and they kicked everyone off the plane. Everyone, like, searched for checked. We couldn't find your pistol." I had fucked the departure of the outgoing troops. I am in full self-loathing mode at this point. I looked him in the eye, begging for understanding and forgiveness, "SGM, I got found it; it was in my Tac vest" I went and apologized to everyone; they knew we were sleep fucked, but no excuses. I shit the bed. But the cool thing about that was my sergeant major's care, and it just goes to show you, like, the kind of man he was; he held me accountable but was also super professional and kind. So that was my introduction to war; after that, it could only get better…right?

I remember it being underwhelming when we landed like it was very army administrative when we landed at night. And it was a logistics officer who came, grabbed us, was kind of condescending, and continually talked down to us, like, "Oh, I know, I know the score. "It seemed to me that was kind of the tone of the whole 2-day package in KAF. All the dudes we were replacing were OTW; folks who didn't live it daily were our first introduction. Not their fault, but their attitude was. As I learned later, they were all KAF FOBBITS, people who had never been outside the wire. They did not know who we were; for all they knew, we were also log folks who would spend the tour sipping Timmie's coffee and going to the gym. They seemed to speak down to us, and they were not necessarily knowledgeable but acted like they were the real deal. I am not trying to chuck shit, but everyone was making out like they were a war hero when we wouldn't even meet the dudes that had been out for another 48-72 hours. Just say what you did and do your job well. Don't put on airs. I hated the KAF part of the handover.

Between 2003 and 2007 I did two other deployments. Three in 4 years, plus work-up training. So, everything was all just starting to mush together. I remember getting off at Kandahar Airfield and what stands out most was I remember getting bombed up with ammo. The CQ of the in-place force was just throwing it at us. "here's your grenades, smoke, here's your unlimited rounds of ammo. Don't worry about colouring in the fucking top round because if you lose ammo like it's no big deal. I could just remember the difference in mindset between my first two tours, Bosnia and Africa, compared to this one. All the discussion was focused on surviving and killing the enemy. We never said the word "enemy" on other tours. We were neutral. Now we had one. The combat was the focus, and the ammo was just fucking crazy, the amount of ammo that they gave to me, because we were going to use it and not just hand it back in 6 months later. Then we had to carry it all. It is something that can never be replicated. I don't think I've ever felt that much weight in my life with the helmet, body armour, weapon, radio, ammo, water, rations, and first aid supplies. That was just what we had to carry; if we were heading out for longer periods, we would try and squeeze in something warm for the nights, a change of socks, and a ranger blanket or something when we crashed. But those were niceties. As soon as you get over 75 pounds, you become less useful in the fight. The ammo and the weight, those two things were shocking when we first got in.

I don't remember much of arriving in KAF, but the one thing I do remember is I thought it was ridiculous that we were carrying our weapons in KAF. So, you didn't have to carry a weapon if you were doing ablutions. Much to my Sergeant Major's chagrin, I decided to carry a toothbrush around with me. So, whenever somebody asked and stopped and asked me, the first couple of days were like, Where's your fucking weapon? I would answer that I'm going to brush my teeth.

We landed in Kandahar and turned in all our green stuff. We had desert (brown) combat uniforms, but there was not enough combat kit to outfit us in Canada, so we had to get the flak jacket covers from the outgoing BG. We get stuff we have never used before and now have to set it up. New tac vests, ballistic plate carriers, and stuff like that. So, we got kit issued, and then we got a bunch of briefs that the things that I remember about the briefs, like one thing, just how condescending it was, just how we were getting talked down to like we're idiots. That's what sticks out of me. I remember this young reservist captain. He's like the visits officer or the duty officer or something. He was super condescending; shit, it drove me crazy. He was postured," I have all this knowledge, and you guys are like super green, and you don't know anything. I just fought a war. And you didn't. "My warrant came up to me as we received this brief. He is a shit-disturber. So, he was a chalk commander, and there were very few BG people on the ground yet. We're walking through KAF, and everyone here is supposed to be armed. All the infantry dudes have long guns, as we have only been issued the bare amount of 5.56mm ammunition to this point. He says to me, "We haven't been given any nine mil, so all those guys that just have their pistols walking around have no rounds and are too lazy to carry their rifles. We should probably remind them." So, we said fuck it and ripped into everybody.

We would stop and ask folks what they were carrying and the state of their weapon, fair game, we had to carry these fucking rifles around. It was all REMF majors and Senior NCOs that would KAF bound for the tour walking around with a pistol with no ammo. I figured that maybe the Captain, who was condescending, saw that kind of crowd who had flown in and assumed that it was going to be " KAF people," and he could tell other people's war stories during that time and be all badass. It was a bad way to start; new senior guys walking around with no ammo and outgoing guys talking to us like we were idiots. Maybe we were idiots. I could not wait to get the fuck out of KAF and get in with a rifle platoon in the outposts. That time in camp was like a day and a half and seemed like forever.

So, we get in and are bagged. We had been rerouted and delayed for something mechanical for about 5 hours on the tarmac. It sucked, and we couldn't leave the airplane. It was so hot on the tarmac. We are starting dehydrated and fucked up. So, we finally get into Kandahar; we are all a little fucked and don't know which way is up. I just remember the heat and the stale air. KAF smelled of AV gas, diesel, and burning plastic. The welcome crew took us into some kind of up armoured sprung shelter type thing. We got into this thing and were not even in there for five minutes, and we heard the sirens going off, and rockets were incoming; there were some blasts, but they were nowhere near us. No one reacted; it was fine except for this one guy who listened to the drill as briefed; he's grabbing people off their bunks and throwing them onto the deck and saying, we're all gonna die. I was like, this dude is panicked; this is going to be a good tour.

The flight into Kandahar was different. Everyone was acting cool, but when we started getting close we got the word to put all our combat gear on and to strap in for the contour flying in for final approach. It was different atmosphere, you know, and everybody's looking at each other. And, you know, you can see there's a little uncertainty in people's faces. But at the same time, you're like, this is exciting. The pilots were rough, and dudes hurled; the smell was bad, a mix of body odour in 55-degree heat, vomit, AV gas, and hydraulic fluid. When you finally land, you don't think anything can smell worse, and you are so thankful when that ramp comes down on the KAF tarmac, and you can't wait for fresh air. But it actually gets worse; the smell hits you like a smack in the face, the burn pits and the poop lake where 24000 people shit goes. I remember getting off is like, wow, what is that smell? Kandahar Airfield. No other smell in the world like it. Like the world's Asshole. When the sun came up, you realized how big KAF really was. Multinational armies spread out through this huge base. You know, and then and see choppers, jets, and stuff on the tarmac, and that's a good experience; it gives you some confidence. On our first day, there was a ramp ceremony for some Patricias who got killed, which negated our confidence and brought us back to the reality that we were leaving this heavily protected area, and we knew we knew that we might come back in a box if we didn't take it seriously.

I remember being in the Hercules flying in from Dubai, and it was uncomfortable and hot, I was taking pictures because I had never been inside a Herc before, and it was a big adventure for a 20-year-old. The old dogs made fun of me for being keen, but I pretended not to care. (I became those guys on my second and third tours and was a dick to the new guys.) I remember feeling very clever when I realized that I could pick up my seat belt and just go to sleep on the rucksacks piled on pallets at the back of the HERC. It is hard to get to Kabul it is a pretty remote place. I remember getting to Kabul in February, and it was COLD. I remember the smell. The smell is probably what first hit me, just the open sewage. I remember being dizzy in the first couple of days due to the altitude. It's like stone and mud buildings, open sewers, and camels in that city of three million. It doesn't really have all the qualities of a city of 3 million that we're used to. I felt like I was at the crossroads of history, right? Like, Afghanistan has been strategic geographically for thousands of years. Our camp, Camp Julian, was situated between the King's and Queen's palaces, part of hundreds if not thousands of years of history, going back to Alexander the Great. But instead of it having a vibe, it was like the city was on life support it just kind of destroyed. We felt like we were providing oxygen to help it regain its feet and recover. Our job was to give it space and time and not take any more hits. It was ISAF in the early days, and we were fighting hearts and minds; we really believed that the world wanted to see Afghanistan get on its feet. We were idealistic. That idealism was tested and even when we lost three Royal Canadians in Kabul to enemy action, the threat didn't feel particularly high. Like the enemy was grasping at straws but could not really land a counterpunch. I think we did not understand the environment, or perhaps there was still a sense of hope in Kabul in those early days.

The trip to Afghanistan has so many different inputs. Canada, Dubai, Kandahar. Three different environments with different emotions and mental gymnastics attached. I can remember that the movement to Afghanistan was just sort of surreal. I didn't know what to think... I just kind of remember almost being outside myself like a movie, like watching myself travel through these gateways, feeling the heat of Dubai and how that base was set up like a resort. For some reason my head, I remember a chocolate fountain, like one of those at a wedding, and a table of fresh fruit. Everything there was perfect, and people were so happy and calm, their tour was in this awesome vacation spot, and then it was your time to leave the oasis and get ready to head to Afghanistan. You get your taste, and then it starts getting real; you grab ammunition and fitting combat gear; you get on the Herc, and you just jam in like sardines and don't see anything. The Herc flight is terrible; the tactical flying into KAF and the Herc would just drop in these random manoeuvres. I remember looking across, and a guy had a water bottle in his hand, just an empty water bottle. He was trying to throw it out of his hand. But it was just stuck to his hand because of the G's or whatever we're doing coming down. Then you land at night, and it is just chaos. CQ's yelling at you. The base is industrial; everything has a purpose: to make war. It's sea cans everywhere. A stark contrast to Camp Mirage, which was this calm oasis with good food, the vacation staff, and the tours to downtown Dubai. It's 2:00 in the morning by the time you get in. Your next timing is at 06:00 so maybe 4 hours of rack. So, quick turnaround. I was rooming with this guy Murphy, and he found out that he was leaving that night for the field. He didn't even get orientation. He was on the OMLT to get a handover because the guys he is replacing are leaving Kandahar in the next 24. Someone fucked up the Relief in Place. I helped him repack his kit and get ready as I had a day or two in KAF. I put on music, and on my playlist, it's playing random on shuffle. The Song "The Night Paddy Murphy Dies" by Great Big Sea comes on. Well, I'm just like working on kit, singing along. I feel the heat on my neck. I look around. He says, "Hey, are you fucking kidding me? turn it fucking off" He didn't like that as a send-off song...I don't blame him. I didn't think of the fact that he was named the same, and he was thinking about dying. I didn't have to face going out for a couple of more days, so I was not in that headspace. He headed out an hour later. You must be ready to turn your mind fast when all these changes in the environment are happening, and situations are coming at you.

You fly into Kandahar at night. It is pitch black except for the necessary light to land planes and the security lights facing out. Outside the camp, there are no lights;

the whole country is black. I remember getting off into Kandahar, getting off the plane, and moving through the terminal at the same time as the departing chalk of the outgoing soldiers was leaving. There is a metal fence that separates you, and I've never once in my life felt more like a new guy. Then at that moment, maybe if there was any moment like, holy shit, am I ready for this? these guys who had had a tough tour looked very battle-hardened and were losing guys up to the moment we arrived, literally on one of the last days their BG was in theatre and were ready to go home. You're walking in the other direction in the middle of the night. Two groups on two different journeys. You can't see anything of the camp as it is just pitch black. Get on the bus. No one tells you the schedule; you've no idea what's going on or what is next, and as you sit there on the bus in the dark, you realize it is your turn to pay the piper, and soon enough you will be heading out into that vast darkness beyond the security lights that those guys leaving just came from.

WTF AM I DOING?

AFGHANISTAN WAS AN ALIEN ENVIRONMENT. Nothing that could be fully explained without experiencing it first-hand.

New rules of life were established by the "in-place force" that was completing its seven-month tour of duty.

Lessons learned. Actions had consequences.

People died, even when you did everything right, so you paid attention. There was an order to things, a hierarchy of knowledge that had to be quickly assimilated. Lessons were passed on from the outgoing veterans to the new guys fresh off the plane - how to pack your equipment, which items were necessary to carry and which could be dropped, the warning signs of ambush, how to spot IEDs, what mistakes had been made, and what limited successes had occurred.

Those that were on the ground seemed larger than life, so confident in this environment. Even after a year of training, those who were new immediately felt out of place and unsure of their skills. The only way to gain confidence was by doing.

It was time to step into the darkness

The outgoing platoon had lost a lot of guys to IEDs. Their perspective on what getting killed looked like and how easy it was stood out from the handover conversation. One of their most painful stories was about a guy they had lost when he was coming in to go on his mid-tour leave. There was no helicopter landing spot at their strongpoint in Western Panjawaii with too much contact to land a helicopter, so the platoon Commander in the outpost got ordered to foot patrol back with this guy to get him on the helicopter, they were contacted enroute, and he died on that patrol. So, they were hammering home the point, "Don't ever go out without a mission; ensure the troops have something to aim for and something that's contributing to some kind of tactical advantage over the enemy. I took that to heart and lived by that for my tour. But right after he tells this story as if by some perverse reality, we have to do a "handover patrol" mandated by our higher headquarters. We do a patrol that's like a total joke patrol, just sort of a last little walk to get us out in the environment, and they do not want to lose someone on the last day, so it's my platoon that is the unit to go, and we're all super keyed up. I've got the heavy 117 Foxtrot radio to do, like the two Klick patrol and extra batteries, seven litres of water, and boatloads of ammo. It was ridiculous. It was it was like the heaviest load I feel like I have ever carried. But as we go out, we use a big conga line going up route brown. Loose file. Or "ack ack" with elements offset along the road. You can see our brand new kit; we're all super heavily laden and small packs on. Then you contrast it with the outgoing guys, and they have a Camelback, an MBITR, a couple of grenades, and a couple of mags. I remember that they just looked very comfortable in that environment. It's Ramadan. So, the locals are agitated, and we are super keyed up on our first patrol. You could feel the tension less with the outgoing guys, and then an RPG gets fired; we aren't sure if it is the enemy or where it came from. The FOO is in overwatch on the radio and calls in stuff, and it just turns into him trying to find these guys who are potentially dicking in the patrol. So, we have decided it is an enemy RPG and think we've got them cornered in this grape hut. So, the OMLT comes out with his company of ANA to respond to the contact. They were super unhappy because it was Ramadan, and it was still daylight, but it was getting later in the day, and we were now potentially getting in the way of mealtime. This simple patrol kept on escalating and escalating. It was out of control. The shot was way off, obviously miles away. But it's our first patrol... Even the OC, who was super awesome, is on the net. Everyone was fired up, the folks were manoeuvring, the ANA breached the grape hut and there was no one in there... nothing. Nada. Totally not cool. and so, it was a ridiculous first patrol, and we turned around and walked back to the patrol base, all dehydrated because we had too much crap on, and then we did an AAR with the outgoing force. They kind of were gentle but laid it out that it was a little bit ridiculous. They were not too harsh on us, not a big deal; the difference was that we saw what it meant to "be" combat experienced, and we weren't. We learned, we got calmer, understood the environment, what to carry, how to build a mission, and how to survive, but it showed me that there is no replacement for experience. I appreciate that first patrol, it was a shitshow, and no one was hurt, but they could have been. I am thankful for that, but it was still a total shit show, though!

Looking back at my time at Camp Julien, I'm struck by how naïve we were. This was before the fighting in Kandahar. Although the Theatre Activation Team had gone in ahead of us, the camp was still pretty austere. There were no Hesco Bastien barriers around the camp, nor were there any bunkers. For those of us not assigned to camp security, when the rocket attack siren sounded, our drill was to put on our PPE and lie on our cots. That seemed absurd then and is now – the canvas modular tentage we slept under and my XL Cold War era frag vest would surely not protect me from much. In the early mornings or evenings, we would jog around the perimeter of the camp – a simple barbed wire fence separating us from the friendly locals tending to their animals in the field. They had to be friendly, right? After all, we were Canadians, and everyone likes us. I think that was the naivete, we still had a Peacekeeping mindset. When we lost Sergeant Short and Corporal Beerenfenger to a roadside bomb and later Corporal Murphy, it was a huge shock. Suddenly the lack of armoured vehicles, PPE, and our overall naivety hit home. I'll never forget scrambling to find body bags and figure out casualty administration – this was not something we had talked about, and it wasn't part of our training. This shit was real, and we were not ready in terms of equipment or mindset.

I was part of the Theatre Activation Team for Kabul, so one of the first Canadians on the ground. We had to build a new camp for the mission between these old Palaces known as the King and Queen's Palace. We were settling in, with no real protection up and just a strand of wire and canvas tents and a loud explosion going off. It just really didn't register. We figured it was some local thing and we would figure it out tomorrow. There was a patrol sent out the next day, and it was somebody trying to set up rockets to shoot at us from the king's palace. Some dude trying to set up rockets and blew himself up. I think that's when it kind of hit me like, This is the real shit. On our Peacekeeping tours, we did not have this type of activity in Bosnia, Haiti, or Africa. I think it resonated with a lot of guys because we had trained for years and you scan your arcs but there's nothing out there and no threat. Like it was real shit and people want to kill us.

I think the speed at which you adapted to things was crazy. You arrive from Canada, and you have three environments in 4 days. Canada, Dubai, Kandahar.

Huge changes. We got to Kandahar and did our little training there, whatever the briefings and explosives training in KAF, which is a giant and miserable beast. Then fly by helicopter right to the FOB and all of a sudden, we are on this hill called Sperwan Ghar. It was an eventful couple of days, it just becomes real, and the dudes in place are ready to get home, and you are heading out into it. When I first got there because we were sitting there getting briefed about how this camp has never been attacked the whole time they've been there, and then you hear some gunshot, and the front gate is under attack, literally while he is saying that shit. Surreal. Other than that incident, it was pretty mellow. They took care of business and were very professional, but you are hyped up. I have never been in contact before and you can't stop that inevitable feeling of something is coming, like the big test. Everyone is on edge. The next day, I heard bam--bam-bam. Inside the building, I open the door, and there is a guy, white ass in the air and this guy's pants are down. Another guy had a three-round burst negligent discharge with a light machine gun, and it fucking hit this guy in the ass. What a way to start. I attribute it to nerves. I was there a couple of days and then they sent us right to Zangabad, a little COP in the middle of nowhere, because they wanted their guys out of there. It was well built - Hesco Bastion walls, armoured sea cans pockmarked by strikes from enemy mortar rounds and bullets, concertina wire, and towers. That team had been in contact every day and was right in the middle of the Taliban territory. We get choppered in and told if shit goes down, no one is coming to get us by road, because you can't drive in due to all the IEDs that have been laid. We were on a fucking island. What a change in like 120 hours- I have gone from Trenton to Zangabad, and now I am in it...and no one is coming to get me out.

I remember when we first arrived in Kabul on the set-up mission, we had no armoured vehicles and so drove around in these little minibuses. Think of that, with all the money we spent on LAVs and new armour during Afghanistan, the first part of the mission we were in Toyotas! Downtown Kabul was chaos, to make ourselves feel better, we threw a C6 MMG in the back and I guess would throw it down should something happen. Whoever was navigating, it was one of one of the guys from the crew out of Kingston JHQ was in the lead vehicle and they'd been on the ground for a few days sorting out some of the contracting issues. Because the contracts team was put into the country before the security elements! They were leading us back to the multi-national engineer camp. We came around the corner and we were just in the middle of a street market and people everywhere. We weren't going anywhere, fast. I remember the press of people being like a wall. I recall moving very, very slowly through the crowd as the crowd parted and thinking, you know, moving slowly through the market, waiting to get shot. If we did there was almost nothing we would have been able to do, I remember that people were inches from the van. They weren't tinted windows or curtains or anything. So, you know, you were just these white guys driving minibuses with helmets on all kitted out, so, you know, flak vests, helmets, weapons in the back of a Toyota. I remember being overwhelmed by the crowds in Kabul, you learn like you look at hands. They will tell you more than eyes, more than posture because where their hands were that was the threat... It certainly was like an uneasy feeling, I think, particularly being in that mass crowd, not knowing what the threat might be, and there had already been a couple of NATO fatalities. Thankfully, the next day we went and retrieved the platoon's LAVs off of an Antonov aircraft. That was funny also because Russians are helping deploy us to Afghanistan in a plane that likely helped them leave when they invaded. It was a strange place.

So, we went through Kandahar, and it was like you could close your eyes, take in the smells, and be in Africa, Haiti, or any of those other countries. It wasn't that different. The terrain was beautiful. I'd been to the desert many times before. So it wasn't that much of a culture shock. What was a culture shock was driving over places, and I could see the crater where someone I knew was killed. That was different than all the other missions. You have got sandbags under your feet, you are staying low in the turret, and you are actively scanning for threats. The culture shock was knowing that someone was trying to kill you

---

I have 4 tours in Afghanistan: Two in Kabul and two in Kandahar. On my 3rd tour, 1st in Kandahar I knew something had changed. I was like a fish out of water. I showed up, and these dudes had been fighting for 6 months; they were skinny and edgy, But I remember looking at them like he's a fucking dude but looks like really tired. I knew these guys, but they were not helpful because I didn't understand the reality of the fight. The last time I had been in Afghanistan we didn't even put a round up the spout and had very restrictive ROE. Now we were engaging by day and night- killing or being killed. Trying to get something out of these guys, they just gave the facts; they didn't say much. Not many times have I felt like an absolute new guy. But this time- I'm a fucking new guy.

So, we rolled into Camp Nathan Smith. I think on the second day, they had this interesting little ceremony. They fixed up this building within the camp for Popeye, the local caretaker. He was an Afghan local, and Hamid was his son. The Taliban caught him and tied him to a tree, heated up a piece of angle Iron with a blowtorch, and sodomized him to death. Like those were the fucking people. This was a super nice guy, just his friend, the old dude who used to fix things and make our camp nice. It wasn't hard to hate the enemy after that.

First day on the ground in Kabul, in what would become Camp Julien. It was that first night that we occupied the position and our relative immaturity in understanding threats in comparison to a peacekeeping experience. So, we're living on the ground. We don't have a complete perimeter around us. We're living in canvas mod tents. No ballistic protection around the tents at all. There was a huge explosion that night, and we weren't sure what it was. I certainly wasn't sure what it was. It was kind of that evening, early morning, and I wasn't sure. But whoever wasn't up on shift was woken by the explosion. I was off checking on the security patrols at the time. I was walking around and doing my rounds with the warrant. And I said to the warrant, I said," it must be a bad day for somebody that must have been like in like a mine or something like that." And I kind of just left it because I didn't know I had no frame reference. His reply was, "Sir, I wouldn't be so sure." Let's get to "stand To." Which meant waking everyone up and getting them to their fighting positions. This was "crazy" at the time; no one had "stood to" on Peacekeeping tours and could be seen as being "flinchy". So that's what we did. We stood, too, and, you know, observed, and nothing else happened. Later that day, we found out that it was an IED maker that had attempted to fuse a couple of rockets right near the base of the king's palace. And the IED maker had functioned the device and blown himself up. So initially, you know, the indication was that it was one person. Weeks later, there was we had a visit from a bunch of people in civilian clothes, who identified themselves as being from the FBI as being an investigator. They had taken DNA swabs of the site and found that there were two people there who were killed by the explosion, so it was a deliberate cell that was targeting us. On your first day getting settled into a new mission, one that is supposed to be stability, you find out the enemy is already watching you and already seeing where they can test or strike you. I felt like we were just lucky that they blew themselves up. I also felt lucky for my Warrant's instincts. When in doubt, be ready. I remember thinking welcome to Afghanistan.

_____

One of the first things we do is report to our Company Quartermaster to sign for our vehicles. He came early and had already taken the stores over from the outgoing guy. This means he is our CQ, but as long as there are soldiers from the other BG, he is their CQ also. As soon as he took over, a bunch of guys from the outgoing BG were killed. Tough start, and he has to do all the administration for soldiers from another unit. One of the things that you do not think about is accounting for all the stuff of the guys that were killed. As rough as it sounds, the army needs to use it again, and so it has to be confirmed and that it is working and then will be reissued. So my platoon arrived at the CQ to get vehicles, and he was processing all the guys that had been killed kit. All making sure it was there, what was damaged, what could be used again. Just the mechanical activities that have to occur when a guy is killed. While his team is doing this, they still have to issue us our equipment before we head out to the field. Invariably, we need to take a piece or two from the pile of those that have been killed. My guy stuff was mixed in with the guy's stuff that had been killed, all the "serialized" (means it has a serial number and is tracked closely), things like night vision gear and radios, if it was serviceable, were accounted for and then issued to us. Often, a soldier will put the first three letters of his last name and the last three numbers of his service number on the kit. So, it's like, oh shit, we recognized the names, and it was an eerie feeling to be issued someone's kit who had been killed. This was a view into how real the mission was and was a terrible way to get your kit issued and for the CQ to start his mission.

_____

The platoon I was taking over from was a divided unit; the platoon commander had been wounded, and the 2IC was not well respected by the other leaders because he had not been out in the shit with them but had taken on more administrative roles in camp. When the Platoon Commander was wounded with 3 weeks left in the tour, he was thrust into a leadership role. So, it was a difficult start; it seemed that everything I got told by this leader then led to a quiet sidebar from another outgoing leader who would tell me the opposite. So, I just tried to find the middle ground and figure my way through this mess so my platoon could get these guys on a plane and we could start our tour. I felt sympathy for both sides. I started my tour in a place called FOB Martello, which was a nod to the old towers that defended the St Lawrence Seaway that Canada built. This place was insane. It was in a valley with high grey mountain walls on all sides, there was only one way in and out, and the hills were so close that a rifle shot was only 300 to 400 m away from the centre of camp. I am not sure who sited it, but it was shit tactically. The enemy took full advantage and constantly harassed us with indirect and direct fire. We get in for the night and immediately mortared in Martello. I had no clue what to do, really. I just reacted like the in-place guys. It was crazy shit, and the guys I was handing off from the last tour told me, "It is like this all the time." It got my attention when someone was shooting at you on your first day; I had never had anyone try to kill me before. The next day we have to go patrol the area, and it's like an IED textbook. We are going down this fucking valley. There are two blown-up ANP cars on our side of the road, indicating an IED or ambush site. There's a puddle in the middle of the road. There's only one road. We had to go through the puddle and this was before we had developed the tactic of doing vital point searches. Our tactic was to drive and hope for the best. I was lead vehicle, and we were in G-Wagons, which are just up armoured Mercedes SUVs. I look at my driver I grab my handle above the seat and lift my feet off the ground as he drives through the danger area with a half-smile and says, "It's all about standoff." My feet not being on the floor means that maybe if an explosion happens it saves a foot or a life. He must keep his feet on the controls. Weird humour. We held our breath, waiting for the explosion. It is all micro-stress. He tells me to eat shit and drives hard through the puddle, no IED. We carry on with the patrol. We get to this beautiful plateau and up in the mountains now, and there's this little fucking trail that goes off to the Mianishin District Centre. There is a corporal from the last tour who knows his business and is not keen to head to the district centre. He's the guy who told me all about the mortar attacks and how to dig in and gave me all good advice. I developed a good relationship with him and trusted his no-BS approach. He said, ". This NCO that is leading has not been out of camp before; he stayed in all tours until the platoon commander got wounded. So, he doesn't know shit; I'm two days from going home; if we go down this fucking track, it's not if we get in contact; it's when we get in contact. "He looks at me and says, "I got two days, man." It struck me that I didn't want to be in contact the first time with a unit I didn't know, and they didn't trust each other. Right or wrong, I made a snap to get them back to KAF. I had never been in a position where guys counted days so they didn't get killed. I could see how that was stressful, and I got shot at like 3 times in 2 days on my first time out, so I knew they weren't BSing. The best thing was to get them in to get home, they had done their job, and it was time to pass it on. They had great knowledge, and I appreciated it, but they were a little bad for our fucking morale. We still had 7months to go and were standing at the bottom of the mountain looking up. I didn't want my soldiers to start with the attitude that this mission was fucked.

———————

From KAF to the Panjawaii you need to drive through Kandahar city. It is about an hour of driving on a good day, but the first time you do the trip, it is stressful, and you have to learn about the different environments. Kandahar is a city, it's a dirty city, a smelly city, a city of a thousand smells. Every white Corolla is an SVBIED, and of course, that's all you get from the INTREP, "watch out for a white Corolla" with a license plate, but you can't read the numbers, so as you are cruising through traffic with a thousand Corollas around you, you're like well, there it is, there it is and there it is. But they're all taxis, and you can't shoot them all. Eventually, the city starts to thin out and you get to the western side suburbs called Panjawaii, the birthplace of Mullah Omar. It will be flat, perfectly flat, and then there will be a mountain out of nowhere, intersecting the mountains are a couple of big rivers, and it is all connected by this "green belt" of farmland. The farmland has all these wadi systems for irrigation and the grape fields are built with heavy mud and are all walled off. Really difficult terrain is full of natural obstacles. In the afternoon, you could drive in a dense urban environment, head south and into the open desert, go through a mountain pass, and then navigate the narrow alleyways and rivers of the farmland. There was no "one" environment. It was overwhelming because it was all new, so different than Canada, and each area you transited had different problems that required different tactical considerations. On that first drive out, I wondered how I was going to do this for 7 months; I was exhausted mentally by the end of the day.

———————

When we left KAF, we were headed right to FOB Martello. So we headed up the TK road (Tarin Khowt Highway), and going through Kandahar City was stressful. I think that's probably where my grey hair started because your head is on a swivel. Before we even left the gate, we had another soldier who was in our BG killed in action. You could hear the contact on the radio as you were waiting for your time to leave. Then, you had to follow them down that same road. The apprehension of leaving the wire was enhanced, your team can feel the stress, like sitting in the locker room and not being able to get out on the field before a big game. First trip out, someone was killed, the other team got a quick score, and now you are playing catch up. It plays on your mind. You need to shut it out and decide that it's game on. You know that the two-way range started; those targets are shooting back.

My first home in Afghanistan was a little "strong point." This was a collection of mud huts and walls that had been brought together to house a platoon and was a spot to defend and patrol from. It was very austere. No running water, a small generator for electricity; it was essentially living in trenches. These guys had been getting hit every couple of days as the Taliban tried to move them out of the neighbourhood. I was just a new private and so had zero experience. So, this is what it's like in Afghanistan. You're like, holy shit. Weapons were ready to go, grenades were taped and without a safety clip, and they used the local 60mm mortar to fire illumination and high explosives into the wadis around the strongpoint to disrupt the Taliban approaches. Shit and garbage were burned, food was hard rations and water was for drinking. It was hard living. Even to this day now, the smell of burning garbage or plastic takes me back to that spot. We slept in this Afghan building made of mud and had 6 to 8 guys in the room. Wooden shutter doors that looked like they were from another century and had been used by whoever had occupied this structure before the fighting. At that point was January, the night to dip down almost freezing, and there was no heater. There was like a rusty bird cage where I was sleeping or some kind of animal cage; it was big, and one of the guys set up his bunk in it. So strange. It was a huge shock to shift to living full time in the dirt, surrounded by sandbags, and immediately get into the fight. You had to learn fast.

I was part of the training mission at the end of the Canadian commitment to Afghanistan. I had just been in the army for a year when I went. It was a massive culture shock from my small town in Newfoundland. We first got there right after the Koran burning by US troops at Bagram. For us, the roads were black, which means that the threat was too high to travel. So, we couldn't leave the camp, because the Canadian government was taking no chances with casualties. We never really did a full handover of all the routes from the outgoing guys. When we did get out, it was like we were beginners because of that lack of handover. Bit of a shock on the traffic around Kabul. Absolute chaos. On the outskirts of the city, wasn't too bad. But as you get into Masood Circle and Camp Eggers (NATO HQ) traffic becomes ridiculous. One thing that always struck me was the infrastructure. The roads are complete shit, but people are always in a rush to get nowhere. So, I remember one day we were doing a convoy towards Camp Phoenix, which was like the main ISAF camp in Kabul. There's a beggar just sitting in a pothole in the middle of the road and cars swerving around him at high speeds. It was my first exposure to real poverty. For someone to sit in the middle of the road in a pothole. What are they thinking? if they were even rational? I wondered if they were begging for money or are they begging for their life to be over.

As a POMLT we were very light on the ground, maybe three Canadians on each patrol. For perspective, the BG was patrolling at Platoon level. Our security and ability to fight were all tied to the Afghans. It made you feel vulnerable. During the handover, I was loaded for bear. On that first trip, I carried 16 grenades for my M203, 13 magazines of 5.56mm, and two belts for the 7.62mm C6 because in our patrol, we always had a C6 GPMG with us and an M72. I carried four litres of water plus two bottles of Gatorade. At the start, I felt like I still needed more. I was too heavy, but you need to learn that. It was a sensory overload initially. Everything's an IED. There are IEDs everywhere when you are out walking around for the first time. Add to that trying to work with the Afghans that don't speak English. So a lot going on. It's pretty crazy working in an environment like that, and over half your team doesn't speak the same language! Looking back on it, I adapted pretty quickly. I mean, I went in as mentally prepped as humanly possible. But still, it was a lot, smells, language, threat, heat, weight, and violence. I had never been out of my hometown in backwoods Ontario, so all these inputs were pretty crazy.

When I first got in the country, I was embedded with the rifle section that I would be taking over from. I was the one guy there that was rotating in. Everyone else would be following over the coming days. I wish they could have had that experience of working within the team that had been doing it tough for 7 months. The handover is always a bit false. The section I was taking over from and embedded with was a bunch of Royals that had been through the shit. They knew their business, I felt like a TV show, like a rookie cop shows up for their first shift and gets a wake-up call from the old vet that this is the real deal. I am, the incoming section commander, but I'm filling in as a private; just a dude tagging along with their section. We are out patrolling, there's a drone overhead that the section is coordinating with to get vectored not a suspected Taliban position. When you halt at night, you set out claymores, go to 50 % percent on shift, and then patrol out to set ambushes, with no hook privates leading the patrol. Patrolling, aggressive patrolling to own the space. I'm like, this is night one of my tour, I have to match what this team is doing for the next seven months. I'm in this place that has been rubbled, everything was blown to fuck in the fighting, IEDS on every path, ambushes being set by both sides. These guys moved around like it was their backyard.

My first time out of KAF was spent in the back of a Bison. We ramped up at KAF was all of a sudden, I was at Masum Ghar, my camp. Even then, we didn't see much because it was all behind Hesco barriers. There was a last-second change, and I was told to get back in the bison and that I would be going to a new COP. I climbed back in, and they ramped down in the little COP of Pashmul North and said, "Welcome home." My bags got thrown off the truck, and that was it. Home sweet home. Combat outpost Pashmul North was a little shit compound surrounded by people that would prefer that we were not there. This had been ground 0 for MEDUSA and was Mucho bad Taliban country. It had about 15-foot mud walls two Hesco towers surrounded by barbed wire, and a TLAV blocking the main entry. I remember walking in, and the gravel that was laid to keep down the dust was this big, crushed stone. It was still new, so you rolled your ankles and tripped under the weight of your kit. I was met by the in-place force and they took me to the "living room". The living room was a "MOD" tent behind ten-foot concrete barriers, known as "Texas barriers". They were placed around to stop the mortar fire shrapnel. "What about the fucking canvas roof I asked, "they said that you couldn't account for everything. We slept in armoured sea cans. As the new guy, I got the bunk next to the door. There are bunks bolted to each side of it. There's a total of 6 to 8 bunks. We had a team of 7, so pretty close quarters. With our 7 Canadians, there were 30 Afghan Police. These guys were crazy. We rotated out of the fighting. They did not. So, they were set up in a mod tent, supplied by us. They had two tents, four sections apiece. About 20 to 30 feet long. They had mattresses strewn on either side and dry rugs in the centre for them to sleep. Then they had one open kitchen and ablutions where they prep their meals and showered. A few times, you will see the gentleman prepping your meal, and when you go to eat with them while somebody else is showering and helping them clean vegetables while they shower! I knew I was in for something pretty crazy, but this was like being in another world!

I think the most memorable class when I arrived in Kandahar was the environmental class where they told you about the snakes and the scorpions and we were told, if there's a hole in the ground, don't sleep in the hole in the ground. I'm like what the fuck, why would you tell us this, we have to sleep in holes at night to avoid Mortar and direct fire? Someone on the last tour crawled into this little hole in the ground because it would be a good cover to sleep in and it happened to be a scorpion nest and he got stung by a bunch of scorpions and had to be medevac'd out. Then we got told about camel spiders and spider bites and I, I don't like spiders at all. So the camel spider, like I was dreading seeing a camel spider. I never saw one, but even with getting shot at and IEDs and all the other shit, the camel spider scared the fuck out of me. Welcome to Afghanistan

---

Before the other BG RIP'd out, they were letting us call in some fire missions near the graveyard by the giant anthill near our combat outpost. There had been some contact, but nothing serious, and so we were looking to shake off the rust and disrupt any Taliban elements that were patrolling near us. One of the other sections called in an airburst fire mission. I still remember lasing where the rounds impacted, and it was 650 meters, and the FOO said we were good. That Section was further behind us, so it was 850 to 1000m. So, we unnecessarily called a danger close fire mission. We almost killed two guys. One new guy and one guy leaving were standing up talking when the rounds came in. They were handing off a DAGR GPS between them as an exchange of gifts, and a piece of shrapnel hit the DAGR, knocking it out of the hand of one of the dudes. He showed us later the busted DAGR and the chunk of shrapnel. So incredibly lucky and stupid.

The guys that were on the ground were only there for, like, that first day. It was a fairly quick handoff as they wanted to get out of dodge. They took us all up the C6 GPMG position, which was the best-made C6 position I'd ever seen. Heavily reinforced sandbags with just a firing slip, a full-on panoramic drawing of the machine gun range card on old ration boxes that look like you could have framed it and put it in a museum. This hand-drawn picture of the rolling mountain ranges and all the compounds in the field in front with all the target indications on it. I hope it survived the war because it needs to be somewhere. So as we are getting briefed on the defences, we learn from them that they have laid a lot of claymores. They have them all registered and show us the clackers, and I can't even remember, but it seemed like 8 to 10. Then they explained how they employed trip flares because Taliban recce would come in close. They were employing trip flares in a new fashion; some buildings had like thatched roof huts. So, they rigged up trip flares to set the roofs on fire. If you see this building catch fire somebody moved into it because the roof catches fire. If the hut catches fire, lase it with rounds because someone is coming for you. There were no civilians in the area at the time, and so the platoon wasn't fucking around after being in contact almost every day for the last couple of months.

The platoon has to drive back from the field to get us, which is super dodgy as there are so many IEDs. We go down to the CQ and think it will be a handover like in Canada, but we show up, see that the vehicle is there and sign for it. There is no time for fucking around; these guys have a plane to catch and two more drives on the roads before they are done for good. They are hard tickets, and you can see the impact of firefights and soldiers who are comfortable in the field and with their weapons. In the back, it's just loose ammo and grenades ready to go. The ramp goes down, and we load our stuff and depart to the FOBs. It was this massive convoy to a PBSG. I most vividly remember the drive out. It was like afternoon, super-hot. As we're driving, we're stopping to do Vital Point Searches all on Foster's, like all those culverts and everything and everyone's on edge. No one knows what normal is, and the outgoing guys just want to be done. I was I was crew commanding, and my Gunner was one of the guys from the outgoing Battalion. I mean, he's kind of just talking on the ICS. So, kind of what things are like. And there's a guy out of the air sentry hatch who is like freaking out about every little thing that he sees. I think he was a kid; he was just along for the ride to MSG; he wasn't one of my guys; maybe he was one of those guys who was in KAF all tour and just wanted to get out, but he was freaked out. This guy next to me, a Master Corporal from the outgoing team, was just dismissing all these concerns; he knew the environment and knew what was going on. I remember we stopped in MSG and the Bazaari Panjwaii. I remember coming out of there, and as we looked around, the paving project was going on at the time, and they weren't working and had not gotten far towards the west... They were still at Masum Ghar, basically. So, we start driving on fosters towards PBSG. it's all dirt road now. I think it was the paving crew, but it could have been someone else, they had an ARV, and there was a guy ground guiding it, which was super weird, was basically they were doing VPS is all it was, and you could see the smear on the ARV from an IED that was fresh and was either earlier that day or the day before. At the dirt road, the Master Corporal, that knew his shit got quiet and serious; he pointed out the blast on the ARV and let me know that there was shit in the road here all the time. So, then we get to route brown and there's like blown up robot, and some combat engineers and a big hole in the ground. We get into PBSG and get the story that they've seen the guys putting the IED in the night before. For the snipers, it was just a shit show like this is what we now call extended long-range shooting. It was pretty far and at night. So the optics were kind of garbage, and they could not confirm the target or kill it. So you had this situation where you could use a LAV or a TOW ITAS, But no one could be really effective in shooting at the distance. So, the dudes got away, and in the last 2 days of their rotation, it was understandable they didn't want to send out a clearance patrol into a known IED location. They knew something had been in place, and the next day they sent out the robot and the robot got blown up. So that was kind of his job. The robot did his job. It was quite the introduction to the environment. Game on.

I landed and was sent down to Spin Boldak. A camp on the Pakistani border. we employed civilian, civilian contracted security. It was really interesting. It was my first interaction with Afghans of the tour were these guards. They didn't have uniforms. They didn't have weapons. They had their own weapons. But their weapons were decrepit and not very effective. So, what we did, is we worked with NATO to try and get them new weapons. We made a deal that we would essentially send them to the policing school that was run by the Germans up the north, and we would rotate them through. This would increase their pay and professionalism. Then I went to get them uniforms. So we went we purchased uniforms. No problem there. They were now essentially dressed like a policeman. That was because we made this agreement with the Germans, and then the weapons were the next big thing. They didn't have good weapons and so couldn't protect our camp effectively. So, I bought weapons from a Pakistani arms market across the border. I was involved in the first arms transaction to support the new police in Afghanistan. I am sure I did the contract all wrong, but I was trying to solve the tactical problem. It was kind of funny because then, all of a sudden, the CIDA or Global Affairs Canada, was called, and they were not happy. I basically sent an interpreter along with the leader of the unit over the border. They bought a case of AK47s. They came back with it. I got the receipt. So, I thought I was golden. This is why I was in trouble, because they're like, why are you buying weapons? I explain but it was still apparently an international disaster. So, I'm like, hey, I'm just trying to be pragmatic. there's no point in having guards if they're not armed in Afghanistan. So, anyway, the guards loved us. In the end, it got sorted; I was a new guy trying to do the right thing. It should have also been a warning. If I could buy a case of AK47s in Pakistan, then really, the border is not doing its job, but perhaps we have bigger problems. I was probably wrong, but our camp was super well-protected.

I think about how little we knew when we first went to Kandahar. None of us had fought a determined insurgent enemy before, and everyone was in the "we are here to help, and if we are nice, people will be nice to use mindset." When we first got in, I remember we had set up a VCP at a Y junction outside of Kandahar, and the people were not friendly at all. I was on the initial contact point and traffic started getting very, very backed up. I remember halfway or three-quarters of the way down the line maybe eight or nine cars in there was an SUV, which was a bit strange. I remember thinking that's a bit odd. It had four male occupants in it. A month later, the alarm bells would have gone off, but it only registered as slightly strange at the time. We're apologetic to them... and want to get the traffic moving. So basically, I tell the line of cars, if you guys want to go like fucking back out of town and around, you get around it. No problem. In retrospect, it was potentially the stupidest fucking thing that I have ever done. Shortly thereafter, the LCA was talking to the platoon commanders who got ICOM hit. A group of four dudes in an SUV reported how they almost got nabbed at a checkpoint. The same guys that I just fucked off, and the Taliban leader saying how to avoid coalition fucking traffic. The exact directions I had given! I felt terrible and felt like I had to explain myself to my section commander and platoon commander. We kind of looked at each other, and both realized that I was an idiot. They let me down softly as they were in a similar mindset and none of us were attuned to the realities of Kandahar yet. Early days in the tour, my first "contact with the enemy," and I was a helpful fucking tour guide! I just sent the enemy that we are here to fight on a shortcut around us. Lesson learned, but bad drills on my part. I defined the stereotype of a fucking new guy.

It was really quiet for about two weeks, and I had my first kind of "almost contact," but it wasn't a contact... we were we were driving to rotate security. So, I rotated off of MSG security and into another little combat outpost and on the way there, the lead vehicle there was a warning shot. I'd never been that close to 25 going off without being on a range. I thought it was an IED. I thought for sure. This was like my first move outside the wire, like 20 minutes into the move right in the market, "BAM" 25mm is used. I had to generate a whole bunch of new reporting on it because it was probably the wrong thing to do. No one was hurt. But it's weird. I came out of that with actually more confidence. Like it was like, I don't know. I think we felt safer because we knew that, you know, I knew that they weren't afraid to react that way. So, you felt it was like a safety blanket. Later on, I had some guilt, the guy was still moving after being told to stop. He got a round through the engine block. I had some guilt like maybe he was hurt, you know. The reality was that VBIEDs had been striking with regularity, people had lost their lives and so at that point, guilt wasn't a factor. it's an interesting first day and first engagement for the platoon. Was the car driving erratically in Afghanistan or was he driving normally.? We didn't even know, we had barely been out of the camp. Fact is you have seconds to judge, and it was a confidence booster knowing we could make the call.

My arrival in Kandahar put me right into the largest land battle that NATO had fought to that point. I was a LAV crew Commander. When we arrived, we immediately rolled into this brewing problem in Panjawaii. The last Battlegroup had attempted to clear and hold an area called Pashmul, which the Taliban had declared as their territory and it was going to be our job to fight it out with them. It was so eye-opening when we received orders. There were 700(+) fighters in this area, dug in and holding terrain. The most memorable part of Op MEDUSA orders about it is talking about "the kill box. "I remember the leadership saying, anything in the box is fair game. We were told that we've dropped leaflets, we've done this we've done that to warn people and there should be nobody in the box. Therefore, anybody in the box is a bad guy. So, if you see a grape hut and you don't like that grape hut or think that Taliban is hiding in there and, get on the radio, call somebody and they'll put a hellfire missile into it and we'll see what it does. If you see a thing, you don't like, and you wanna call an indirect fire thing on it, go ahead and call for fire artillery on that thing. The Rules of Engagement were adjusted to allow for Spec fire and so there was an understanding that these fighters had dug in, and it was our job to get them out. It was a bit old school, we sadly found out later that we did not use prep fores as effectively as we could have, which gave the enemy an advantage over us. That is another story though.

Once your replacements arrive the ones heading home want to get out of the field and the ones that have just arrived want to get in. No one wants to die on their last day. We arrived just a little late. My time in KAF got cut short because the team we were replacing lost three guys. We were out on the range at KAF doing the confirm zeroing of our rifles before going out and I remember being told to shut it down and come in. I came in to get briefed and went down to the airhead to see if I could help out, not knowing what that help would be. Helicopters were coming in to evacuate the VSA and the injured. There were a lot of them. I kind of had to wait at the gate and watch the dead and wounded arrive. It struck me immediately that there are consequences to being here. The Battalion Ops Officer that I'm standing next to says that the platoon was supposed to go home in a couple of days, and he was going to bring them in. I should grab my team and kit and get ready to RIP them out. The next day we were in the routine and we were on our own doing overwatch on HWY 1 to stop IED emplacement, no real handoff as the Platoon had taken those hits went in to do the Ramp ceremony, and then had to depart for Canada. I understand it, but less than ideal. All the corporate knowledge stopped with that outgoing platoon. We started over again. Not good for anyone.

So, the big focus at that point of arrival was just like information collection. I still had a pretty big delta in knowledge. I mean, I missed the work-up training because I got put on tour at the last second. I don't think anyone was as prepared probably as they would like to have been but I was a last-second replacement so it was just soaking up as much information from the guys that were there as we could. My biggest memory at the start was that guys were kind of itching to get in a fight I never felt that way. Now, from the start, I was like, if it comes, I will be ready it comes but I'm in no hurry.

We found out after we arrived in Kandahar that we weren't going to do Zhari, we're going to Panjwaii. And I'm like, OK I guess all the prep is out the window. I didn't even look at the map. Sure, let's do this. The HQ launched me first, by myself to link up with the former team that were located just at the end of Masum Ghar while the rest of my team was still rolling in. I jumped in the back of a Bison and you could see out that one little one, little peep hole on the back of the ramp, through cloudy armoured glass. It was just like being on the moon as I looked out, the window, it looked so different. I was crapping and myself because I knew Bison could not take an IED worth a shit and looking through that little window Kandahar seemed crazy. Bikes and little tuk tuks and everything going flashing by.

Radio crackling, the crew talking on the intercom about threats, a warning shot to cars that got so close. I was just like, my God, what am I doing? This is insane. We hit the ground in MSG and got a quick introduction to the guys, and then we climbed into the RG. We were immediately tasked to respond as the guys had just hit an IED on Hyena. First day, first hour on the ground. A Patricia Sargent died out there, and we rolled out, and then I remember the dudes yelling on the radio. The dudes are fighting with the CP " So what you want me to do is ping pong this road from the IED strike back to Masum Ghar and be IED Bait. Yeah, no." I had never heard a junior element speak to a CP like that, but the POMLT didn't work for the Battlegroup. They were both Canadian but had different chains of command. So, this is my first day, a Sergeant was killed and the dudes I am replacing are arguing with the CP with the armoured corps, as the Armor Squadron that owned that part of Panjwaii. Quite an introduction. I mean, an IED strike, head out to respond; the team on the ground thinks the plan from the CP is stupid and kind of says Fuck you. What a wake-up call. I was like, this is real. All these guys were the Patricia stereotype, like total cowboys. They just got back from a strong point called Hadjii Beach. So, they closed down all the stuff out in the horn of Panjawaii. They were at Hadjii Beach which had more contacts than anyone else combined in the battle group. Their little six-man detachment. So these dudes were like people out of the movie "Platoon", the thousand-yard stares and talking about how the logistics resupply runs wouldn't go all the way down to Hadjii Beach, to their strong point due to the risk to the logistics convoys. So, they'd have to get the rucksack frames, hump out to where they would drop all the food and ammo and water, Two k's out and then hump back in. Just to get resupplied, so they're not very happy and feel pretty bitter and to top it off they just lost their terp to a suicide bomber. So, these guys these guys were pretty hard. And I remember thinking. These guys are cool. Well, everything they did was not perfect. I started realizing that maybe they weren't halfway through the tour. But initially, you are so overwhelmed and impressed that these guys lived through this; I thought they were pretty cool. When I got on the ground, and they were leaving, it was probably a better choice to stick with what they did than try to change everything after that without knowing anything. We did a few patrols with them. First patrol, the next day, we hit an IED and found an IED. It was quite an introduction. No one does everything perfectly, but my advice is don't be the new guy who tries to change everything right off the bat; respect the fact these folks fought hard for 7 months, learn what you can, and get them home. I think those crazy motherfuckers helped me stay alive, and I will be forever grateful.

———————

So we get into FOB Wilson and get told by the Patricia's, "There are mortar attacks now and then. And we're living in those tents outside the building. If the mortars come in, get up and go to the G-Wagons as at least the glass is armoured." that night we got mortared, and then the next morning we got mortared. And that afternoon, we got Mortared. What a welcome! But no one was hurt, one of the rounds even embedded itself in a G-Wagon hood and didn't go off. Imagine that: dudes sitting there get rocked by a round and see the fins sticking out of the hood! That afternoon we went out with a platoon, and I was gonna just get a feel for the place. 400 meters down the road. We got lit up by an ambush. The group we were replacing had done this before. I expected that we would " punch" and get out of the kill zone to get off the X. but no, not at all, it was just small arms they slowed right the fuck down absorbed the RPGs and small arms on the armour of the LAVs, cool as ice, and they turned their guns over the deck from where the fire was coming from. They identified where the fire was coming from and they let it rip. It was surreal for me; in 24 hours I had been mortared three times and was exposed to my first direct fire. Like this shit was effective fire, impacts on the car and you could see the return fire, I realized that this was a different ball game and that we were going to be in deep. I hoped we were ready.

Arriving on my second tour was different. You're so focused on the mission, you're over there, and you don't think about the impact. Like, I certainly underestimate the impact on my immediate family. So, you know, we left as a very small group, and the departure was much different for. So, half of our little Kandak team was flying over in the back with C-17s rather than the journey through Dubai. We're going to be a cargo plane this time, and that's two small teams going in first. Then, it was just very different. All of us had already been there and were already combat vets. I think we were a little bit probably cocky when we got in there. And it was everything like where drills were down so well. Once we got in, we stored the shit we wouldn't need. Barrack Boxes are going into storage on top of your bare box; you will place your beret and make sure it's accessible because if there is a ramp ceremony, you need to wear it, and if you are killed, it is carried behind the coffin. Very quickly, we got pushed out to Panjawaii via convoy, and we got held up because the Patricia's got hit by a recoilless rifle or SPG-9. Three young Patricia soldiers were killed in the back of a LAV. I remember from MSG that I could see very clearly the LAV ablaze; we held in the spot until the situation was sorted out. We were talking about how it was September 3rd, 2008, two years to the day that light armoured vehicles were being destroyed on the exact same ground during the first days of Op MEDUSA. That was when that cockiness was just like stripped right away from like, this is not where I thought I thought we were in the mission, I thought we were winning. Soldiers are dying two years later in the same spot where I had fought last time. It hit me hard, and I remember that I was brought back to the feelings of losing soldiers two years prior, and I don't wanna lose soldiers ever again. It started becoming the dominant theme in all my thoughts. As September became a very violent month and we were way too cautious in our approach. I started to see that my lack of aggressiveness was emboldening the enemy. I recognized that to keep my soldiers alive for the next seven months it was necessary to risk more. We had to rethink it as a team. We shifted after 20 days, we made ourselves "hard targets," we patrolled continuously when we came under contact, and we used every resource available to win. We did all the little things well. Luckily, we got over that first couple of weeks. That whole fall in that little outpost, there were only three days during that time that we weren't under contact of some sort. Welcome to the suck.

CONTACT WAIT OUT

A YOUNG SOLDIER STOOD NEXT TO ME IN A LINEUP IN KAF.

He spoke, not to anyone in particular, almost thinking aloud, "I can't wait to get into a gunfight. I mean, I just want to get the first one out of the way so that I can stop thinking about it."

Another soldier answered, "I don't care about the gunfight, that's a fair fight, I just don't want to get blown up by an IED, that's bullshit. If I am going to be in contact, I want to get my gun on; just getting blown up would suck."

I nodded to them both but didn't respond, and they seemed happy with the exchange. We returned to a comfortable silence waiting in line for whatever piece of kit was being issued. I remember that I wasn't sure I wanted to be in a gunfight, but I was pretty sure it was going to happen.

First contact with the enemy weighed on everyone's mind.

It was a scary prospect, someone deliberately trying to kill you. It did not seem real. Conceptually, you practiced for the moment a thousand times. The foundation of your training is focused on that exact event - responding to contact. The fear of dying or being hurt is real, but the fear of failing publicly seemed like the bigger issue for the average soldier. You just didn't want to screw it up, you didn't want to let anyone down, you didn't want to be known as the guy who "froze" when the bullets started to fly. Personal safety didn't initially enter the equation, neither did understanding how to seek the enemy and gain the advantage of being the attacker and not being attacked.

Both of those realizations would come with time.

Not being a liability to your unit was first and foremost in mind.

Most Canadians had no combat experience before the Afghan deployments. Everyone was in the same blender of chaos the first time. Training kicks in, you respond, and when it is over, most wonder what happened. You take the first step, you continue to move forward, and there is no time to think. You just keep moving. The first contact is just that—the first.

It is a starting point, not the finish.

Once you accept the possibility that you might not make it, you can relax and do your job. That was a really powerful thing. If you accept that you are already dead, then it is easier to live in that environment. It is like you have nothing to lose.

After extended contacts where we lost dudes and the enemy lost dudes, fuck me, the feelings are so raw; afterwards my hands couldn't stop shaking. Just the flash of adrenaline running into the system. I can see why guys like this, it pumps you up at the beginning of it, and like nothing else, you feel so good. Then when it is done, and you have survived, coming down sucks. Hands shaking, some guys would throw up, and most of us smoked or dipped chewing tobacco. Everyone likes to be in a gunfight once, and if they survive it, you don't enjoy it again. You get good at it, though; everything slows down, and you learn to handle that adrenaline; the rush becomes less, and so does the dump, but the first one is crazy. I can see why some guys miss it; I don't; I will be happy never to feel it again. The worst is when you know you are getting into contact, and it is deliberate. It is one thing to be surprised by a kick in the nuts; walking forward and keeping your legs spread to receive that frozen boot to the junk is another. Maybe that is what being a professional soldier is, knowing there is a kick in the nuts coming, and you move forward anyway.

For me, the whole experience was dreamlike because now I'm in Afghanistan. I didn't create the conditions that brought me here, but I'm touching on a part of history that will be a part of our national consciousness, and I'm creating a little piece of the unit and my regiment's history. The whole thing was rather bizarre. Even the first firefights there was a sense of numbness and surrealism. You know, it's like an out-of-body experience, like watching someone else doing it, but then you realize it is you pulling the trigger, trying to kill and avoid being killed. This ain't happening, you think. Whenever I see it on TV, there's rock music. When is the big explosion going to happen? But it doesn't… just leaves falling off trees as the enemies' rounds scatter around you like angry bees, cracking around you and impacting them on the cover to your front or on a wall backstop behind you. You barely hear the sounds of your weapon, smoothly working through the actions that you have done thousands of times in training. You are just so focused, and then it is done. Silence falls immediately, the calls for ammunition, or the moans of the casualties, ours, or theirs. You don't know, you have to snap out of the state quick; there is shit to do. You survived.

I was 21 years old in Afghanistan. Just a private in a rifle section. Didn't know much and really had not done much. High school graduation from my small town was still fresh. I was a C9 gunner. That is the light machine gun, fed by a self-disintegrating link, powered by cycling gas from the rounds expended and air-cooled. It provides the section with immediate fire support and volume of fire to suppress the enemy. It only fires on automatic, so you fire it in 3-5 round bursts. Controlled chaos but it can fire up to 1000 rounds in a minute if you can feed it that fast. It is a lot of power in a young person's hand. It was heavier, and so often, the "new guys" got the guns, and I learned to pack that thing all over Afghanistan. I lived with it day in and day out. I carried 4 boxes of ammunition, at 200 rounds a piece. Each weighing between 4 to 6 pds. Then our marching order would have water 2-3 litres, body armour, a helmet, and all the other things a soldier needed. It was like 65 pds of shit in 55-degree heat. At the time, I couldn't feel it; I had lived in it, and now I think the weight would kill me. At 3 months into our tour, we were living in little outposts in the TB territory and were often in running gun battles with them. My job was to respond when we came under contact and suppress the enemy, but we didn't often see them; they would ambush us, or we would respond to an IED, but never a pitched fight, and after three months, I had still not fired my weapon in anger. The enemy seemed to always have the advantage and we realized that if we were ever going to get the drop on them, it meant we were going to have to change tack. So instead of being predictable, we started working like them, off hours and hitting them where they least expected it, when they thought they were safe. For the rest of the tour, we would go out late at fucking night between 2300 and zero dark buffalo, and we move in under the cover of darkness into an area. We would set up observation positions in known areas where we figured the Taliban fighters lived. The TB didn't do much at night as they liked their rest and did not have much in the way of night fighting capability or training, so we would get into position, go to ground, and wait for the sun to come up. So, they just pop out of houses in the morning with the RPG to do a stretch. Morning prayers are called, and there they are, carrying weapons, going for water, stretching in the morning sun, normal shit, just like when they IED us or ambush us on the road or mortar us when we are chilling out in the COP. We caught them by surprise. It worked well to the point where we just kept doing it as a rope-a-dope. They didn't seem to catch on. The secret was to exfiltrate out of the area after you hammer them and before they could flank you on your exfil when you were vulnerable. Because in that terrain, they had the advantage and the population. So, to keep them honest, we had to adopt the insurgent tactics of ambush, hit hard, make them take losses, and not have the opportunity to engage us decisively. Our company loved these tactics and we felt like we were securing our area by being on the offence rather than waiting to get hit. This one time, we went out, and we were rolling through a bunch of villages, and we got to a place, I think it was Hadjii Berm Al-Hamad. We got there a little later in the day, and there were a bunch of farmers sitting around; the platoon commander decided to do a snap interaction with the locals to see if he could figure out what had been going on in that area and get some intelligence. So, he sat down with these farmers, and we pushed out the sections for a sort of perimeter security so that the boss didn't get hit while he was in a relaxed state trying to get info. I'm facing down a path on our axis of advance, like I'm the number one C9 gunner in the lead section. So that means I was the farthest the Platoon had advanced, and no one was in front of me. I'm looking down this path. I've got my section commander right next to me. They train you for combat indicators, things that are off, and your alert should be up. I felt, not sure what, but something was not right. So, I'm looking down this path, it was kind of a curvy path following a wadi with like buildings on either side. You get into the closed country in Afghanistan. It's all those sorts of compounds, like a Tetris game, all piled onto each other. A nightmare of ten-foot mud walls and narrow alleyways with lots of 90-degree corners. So, it's almost like an interior close-quarter battle, but it's not interior and it's just this maze that gives you the feeling that there is danger around every corner, and if you do bump into someone it is like a western quick draw. Your observation lanes and fire arcs are very short and it would be easy to get surprised. So anyway, I was observing down this trail and there was sort of low overhanging foliage about 12 to 20 feet out. I could see the path, but I couldn't see people on it. Then all of a sudden, I see feet. At one point I saw a set of women's feet, bright-coloured pants, like the sort of dainty footwear that is associated with women's feet. I don't think I've seen a woman outdoors since I've been in the country. You never saw them. After 3 months, this was weird and got my awareness up. I saw a woman's and children's feet and I saw the feet run in the opposite direction. I was like, hey, I just saw women and children take the fuck off, get out of here. At the same time, the platoon commanders talked to these farmers and they were mysterious and avoidant saying that we shouldn't be there. They repeat that we should not be here. We should go away. And all this over the radio. I'm just like, oh, it is fucking on, something is happening, and I remember looking at those trees because there were the trees and there was a corner of a building. So, you could kind of see the approach through the trees. There's a blind spot behind the building and I saw somebody coming. And I saw a big tube, too, but there are also guys carrying out big plastic tubes for fucking constructing Wadis all the time so I let my Section Commander know,

"Movement to our front looks like FAMs with tubes, can't confirm weapons." He calls in the movement over the radio to the platoon leadership.

I follow up with, "The guy's got something. It looks like an eighty-two".

Then the first guy rounds the corner and he's like 20 meters out like I saw him clear as day. Little fucking tac vests, AK at the trail, and in my mind, the biggest fucking turban I've ever seen. Like I just sort of fixate on that. It was black too. I've never seen someone with a black turban, but he came around the corner, and I didn't think I just aimed and fired like I was on the instinctive shooting range. We talked about the quick game shooting range; I think it saved my life that day. It's twenty meters like we saw each other at the same time. I remember just quickly queuing up, getting a site picture, and letting fly. It's the weirdest fucking thing. I don't remember the Shot like I have a mental blackout of every shot I took. I remember site pictures, but I don't remember shooting like I remember site pictures, trigger control, follow through, and reset onto the target. I remember drawing up a side picture on the first guy let fly and I sort of blacked out. I remember the second guy, the guy with the tube was turning to take cover. I got a site picture of him, and there are three of them in total. I remember aiming shots at the first two and the third one. At that point, it was pretty fast. It was like C9 in the suppression role left to right, knocking down targets on a range. The rest of the section opened up by that point, and we advanced through the contact. When we finally got up to those guys we contacted, they looked like fuckin Swiss cheese. Every weapon we had zeroed in on them. I remember I was just there in the open, and there was no thought of taking cover like they were right there, kind of frozen. I had to shoot. There's no running away from it, and you must deal with it. So, after that first little burst, my section Commander started bounding back down the track and withdrawing to a position of cover. There was still fire coming at us from what seemed to be everywhere, and shit was popping up next to us in the trees, branches were snapping, and leaves were falling off. There's still fire coming from somewhere down that path. Once we got back to a corner, my section commander dived into the water on one side in a wadi. I tucked into the fuckin corner behind the wall, and there are a couple of our other dudes there, so from that corner, I was laying some fire, and I noticed the section commander was isolated by himself, and without fucking thinking, I just stood up run and sort of baseball Slide into the wadi, fucking threw down the gun, kept firing down range. The section got over the initial shock and started to control fire, we had 3x C9s, the platoon C6, and the snipers came up to us. At one point, I just observed my fire and had to reload. Like everywhere I looked, shit was just getting wrecked and it was a hell of a feeling. You know, I was like, whoa! A lot of firepower and it was brought into action as it was supposed to. On a range, you're always open firing in like an open area. There's nothing in it. Your paper targets in a blank field but when there are buildings and plants and shit like that, shit is getting fucked up. Like things were just coming apart. There's mud flying off the walls. Windows breaking, it is pretty nuts. Holy fuck. I was going to keep shooting Until they are gone and we're all safe. I'm just gonna keep on doing this. You don't think, you just need to act right now. And I did it. Like, I didn't think about my safety. I didn't think about anything. It was just like we were in contact, I had to do my job. Here are the things that I need to do in contact. Now I'm doing them. And then I kept doing them. And I didn't have time to think until after the check fire was called. It seemed like hours, but it was like 15 or 20 min. We continued the advance and we bounded forward and stepped over the fucking bodies, That in itself was a fucked-up situation too, I'm walking over guys that I shot and I'm seeing the effects that a light machine gun has and this dudes head was like, you know, inverted, just seeing blood bubbling out of people and just walking over them and realizing that I did that. That was a hard one to shake. When they got hit, they started pulling back to pull back into an open area at some point. They got hit by air artillery or something. At that point, we sort of went firm. A badger smashed a route to us and the LAVs came right to us. The Platoon behind us bagged the bodies and put them on the badger. We looked to exfil out and return to the patrol Base and the other platoon stood that ground. But then at the end of the day, at patrol base, Wilson, we rolled through to hand the bodies over to the ANP and there were no other platoons available. So, we had to take those body bags off the badger, the police opened them up so that they could get the intelligence photographs of the dead guys. I carried those bags out and I was the one who had killed them and then I was there when we opened them back up and all the impact of taking a human life is right there for you to see when your blood is not up and your brain is no longer protecting you. That really sucked. After that, they established an S.O.P. That if you're the ones that hit a group and do the shooting, you're not the ones that bag them. And you're definitely not the ones that do the admin with the bodies afterward because it is really hard on the team, and you need them to kill the next time; they need to do the job.

This was the first war where the CP could decide if we dropped bombs. I mean people who were not in the fight directly but could bring weapons to bear directly. Remote air systems crisscrossed the Kandahar airspace with "loiter time". Meaning they would fly to our area and hang out in our airspace on call, strapped with bombs and missiles to bring death "on demand." The hardest thing I had to do was say no to that service when troops were in contact or had had a hard day and the blood is up. Remote killing is cold; it is distant; it is done with data and enmeshed in your nation's legal parameters of targeting and killing when you do not face immediate danger yourself. The second hardest part of learning how to kill remotely was the first-ever decision to strike for the very first time. To drop a bomb or a missile on someone and take life while viewing their activity from miles away through a camera and at a thousand feet above them. I wanted to make sure, and I was very deliberate. I realize that after we did it, the first time- we became very proficient. We became the human component within the killing machine. It is a drill. Step one confirm the contact and enemy location. Is it a target? Can confirm where everyone is on our side? You get the asset lined up, and then you go through the steps to drop the bomb. I was lucky at the time in the TOC, I had all the right people, professional and capable. The biggest job is translating the situation as it is described by those on the ground or the Commanding Officer wanting to strike. They were in the fight and more emotionally connected to the decision. It was my job to know the big picture. Temper the emotion and increase the clarity that we needed to shorten the cycle so that we could get it done correctly and kill the people who needed it without harming those who didn't. That balance was probably the most difficult. We became- I think- quite good at it. I deliberately separated myself psychologically and emotionally. I have been passionate throughout my whole career, but in this instance, dispassion was required to be effective. What we're doing is not personal. You just need to follow the trail. We've got friends at the other end. From a personal perspective, everyone just wanted to drop whenever the guys forward asked for it. I remember a couple of times where, you know, the artillery officer would say, "We got people in contact. We need to drop." and I'd have to be the one to say, "Calm the fuck down." I think like everyone else, as casualties mounted, you got frustrated. But you are not about vengeance; you are about killing the bad guys doing bad things. How do you know that person is not a farmer, just taking care of his family? You have this "hand of god" ability and are essentially able to kill without risk. You had better respect that power. The most frustrating was one of the times I remember was one of the Companies suffered five incidents IED incidents in one day. They took both KIA and WIA. It was tough as there was no accountability in the fight. There was an opportunity to strike as we found what looked to be IED emplacers in their area. I was on the horn with the

CO at the time, he was fired up, and you got to hit it. Wait a minute, you know, like calling me on the phone to pressure the decision. I know you want to see it get done, but we have controls in place for a reason. This was my second tour in Kandahar; I had already been the guy under fire; I knew what that felt like, and it made it even harder for me not to just say yes. I'm like, hey, I'm trying to go through our process, confirmation, friendly force, lawyer, etc. The dots did not line up that day, and we could not strike. There were too many civilians around the targets, and the targets did not continue to demonstrate hostile intent. We all wanted to, but it was not within our legal ability. There is nothing harder than not giving that feeling of getting back at the enemy when they hit you hard. Of showing restraint. That's hard. That's hard for the guys on the ground, especially when you've had five IED incidents. There are times I felt like striking because I was pissed off and seeing what the enemy was doing. But when it's all said and done, and you see the weapons effect, and you see the BDA, and you see people lying around dead and in pieces, you realize that it is more important to be sure about the thing you did. I would do it all again.

There were several IED strikes. We were blown up in December. Escorting Niner out to Sperwan Ghar. The commanding officer was in the vehicle behind us, and my vehicle rolled over a double-stacked anti-tank mine, not HME, thankfully. That would have gotten hull penetration and killed me or my guys. The IED blew off four of the eight wheels on my LAV. To put it in perspective, each tire has a solid steel hub weighing a couple hundred pounds. So, we are all very lucky. One soldier knocked me out, and I was all fucked up with my ears, and I smashed my back from the blast. I still get cortisone shots today, 15 years later, as my back is all fucked up. It is hard for the Doctors to put it together, and it will stay with me with limited mobility for life. But we're very, very lucky because a couple of months later, the Taliban adapted their IED tactics and learned how to build bombs that were going to kill most people inside them.

At the time, I think that it was easy to make the right decision not to shoot people right away, which presented a threat. When you are calm and gain an understanding of your environment, go through your progressions to engage rationally. But then, the next day after you lose friends because of a suicide bomber or a VBIED or an IED in the ground is set off by someone not carrying a weapon, the day after is where it becomes more difficult to make the right decision. The beast awakens once you start to let yourself feel something. Loss, anger, sadness, frustration, it's an issue. Emotion is best reserved for back home or not at all; if you let emotion in during a tour, you will drive yourself crazy or make bad calls.

I was a junior Battle Group Ops Duty Officer. There was a friendly fire incident; a US aircraft shot up one of our companies. I was on shift in the TOC and a panicked report came over that they'd just been strafed by the aircraft. I didn't understand. It didn't register. I spoke into the radio, "This is Zero, say again, confirm 'strafed by an aircraft,' over." They confirmed, ongoing assessment, multiple casualties on the ground, the company was ineffective, and a US A-10 Warthog had become disoriented and had used its 30mm canon on the South side of the river instead of the north side where the enemy was located. I turned to the fire control centre that was responsible for all fire effects between aircraft and artillery and said "Check all fire. Check all fire." Then we start going into the motion of navigating a hostile enemy situation, mass casualties on the ground, and a rifle company that, for the moment, was combat-ineffective. What was eerie was that this exact scenario, less friendly fire, had occurred to this company in Wainright during work-up training, and it was now occurring for real. In these situations, there is a lot that happens at once; there is a balance to zeroing in on the major incident while, at the same time, other things are going on in the AOR. You are managing casualties, ammunition resupply, resetting the plan to attack the enemy position, managing information requests from the various media organizations, and a thousand small things that make the machine work. You need everyone on, and there are never enough people. Just as we are starting to get into the management of the scene a Warrant Officer from the Company that got hit came into the TOC. A few days earlier, he'd been wounded at Patrol Base Wilson by indirect fire and mortar rounds and received shrapnel across his whole back, back of his legs and ass. Due to his recovery, he was not out on the ground with the Company. We had been in the battalion together, but I'd never met him. I'd never spoken to him. He came in there and said, "Sir, you're probably telling me to leave because I am in your way, but that's my company that just got hit. I need to I need to be here, and I need to help somehow." I did not question it. It was my first introduction to him, thinking like, well, here's this Warrant Officer; the look of concern on his face was so real, and it stuck with me for the first time: the human cost of what was going on out there. We weren't exposed to what was going on; it was voices on the radio, pins on the map, and problems to solve. It became real because there was somebody attached to the force on the ground, someone who had troops they were directly responsible for, and someone who had lost two of their peers within the last two days, and now the Company they had served in for much of their adult life was hurt badly. We sat there for hours over that day. Managing big things and small things, anything we could do to make the day better for everyone on the ground. I think we did 16 hours straight without taking a break. It was hard emotionally to listen to the reporting, to deal with all the casualties, and the feeling of helplessness was very real. I will never forget the human connection with that Warrant Officer, who had to be out of the fight because he was hurt, and how hard it must have been for him. It taught me a lot about our responsibility to the soldiers on the ground. As an epilogue to this story, this was an introduction for us and we would go on to work together on multiple occasions over our respective careers. I will never forget the lesson.

Every professional soldier wants to test themselves in combat. I know it sounds fucked up, but the first contact was super fun; you know, we're doing what we trained to do since we joined the army. I got into the army in ninety-five, and twelve years later, I'm doing what I've been trained to do. I remember that it was not that close; some rounds travelled close enough to give us the feeling of danger, and we saw some enemy teams setting up RPKs and RPGs. They shot at us, we shot at them, and then we brought in Apaches to attack Helos, and they were done. High five's all around. I can't remember the second time. Kind of fun but not so much fun. Then, the third time, it was just starting to get annoying, and frankly, you realize that those rounds coming in are serious, and as you bag the enemy, you realize that could be you, with one day of bad luck. The cycle of operations was a three-day cycle; we did battle prep, inserted at night, made contact, shoot and scoot and then had a day of rest and regrouping. No holding ground or staying static. We were fighting like they did, which meant nothing decisive. We're getting into quite a bit of contact, and as we're getting more and more contact, it just wasn't fun anymore. You knew it was only a matter of time before the bad guys got one over on you. And they did, and you realize it is just blind luck it wasn't you going home to your family in a box. The excitement of the first TIC wore off quickly. I tell that to the young troops now. Careful what you wish for, that excitement wears off really, really quick when it is a two-way range.

Sometimes you learn a lot about people from how they respond to their first contact. I was LAV gunner and we were the QRF in Wilson and were just shooting the shit and smoking cigarettes. Our sigs Master Corporal yells, " CONTACT!". I run over to the LAV, start the weapons system, fire up the engine, and sit quickly on the top of the vehicle, waiting to get into the TIC. We knew we would get a call if a strong point was under contact. We sat on top of the turret, looking over the wall, watching RPGs explode on the strongpoint and wanting to get into the fight. By this point, we had gotten through the initial shakiness of first contact jitters and felt like- let's do it. We just had to wait for the command to release us. I remember hearing the Platoon Commander who was under contact on the radio. He was a great leader, but you could tell he was adjusting to his first time in Combat. On the radio, he was saying, "I need artillery laid down here and here and over there." The fire mission just wasn't making sense.

The Company 2IC was calm and spoke to him on the radio, "Stop, Send your fire mission." That calming voice on the radio of the 2 IC made all the difference. It calmed down the platoon commander and stopped the panic spiral, giving that young leader confidence. The tone brings things into focus when things are chaotic. Imagine your first day on the job; shit starts to blow up everywhere, two of your guys are hurt, perhaps killed, and everything seems to be coming your way at once. The calm voice must've flipped a switch in the platoon commander's head, and like the drill just kicked in and he sent in a textbook fire mission. Exactly what he needed to do in that moment. I sat there ready to go, listening, and knew it at that moment these guys got it. We didn't need to deploy to break the enemy attack; the platoon did it on their own, and the platoon commander led and established himself as a combat leader. Everyone has a job, and that day, the Officers did theirs.

You always think that your first contact, you will be awesome and react exactly like you have been trained. The first time I got shot at, I did not realize it, and I was just lucky not to get hurt. We had gone static in a location in Panjawaii, and there had been regular contact with the Taliban, but my section had not been into anything yet. It was my turn to get into the turret of the LAV to take on the gunning responsibilities for a sentry shift. In a moment of stupidity, instead of coming up through the LAV, I treated it like a Sunday on the range at home and was standing on top of the boat silhouetted against the sky, with no cover. I'm standing on top of the turret, waiting for the gunner on shift to vacate, so I can climb down and do the job. I heard a sound, and then it started to pick up volume and tempo, but nothing registered. I just stood there. The gunner looks up and is all of a sudden moving the turret, throwing me off balance, shouting at me. "They're shooting at you. You need to get down. "I was like in slow motion, I heard the crack, then I put two and two together. What the Fuck, someone is deliberately trying to kill me! But I still didn't move. Then I hear, "Hey, man, they're shooting at YOU. You may want to get the fuck down! Something clicked, Oh yeah, sweet, I'll do that. I turned around and hopped back down into the boat, and the LAV opened up on where the fire was coming. 2 seconds later, we got rocked by an RPG slammed right next to us, sending shrapnel all over the vehicle. Had I been up there like an idiot still, I would have been hit for sure. Everyone else has these stories of how awesome they were under fire the first time, I was not. I got better, but I was stupid and lucky.

I remember the first time we struck using a UAV from the TOC. Everyone was on edge. It's interesting because anyone who says it's like a video game has never done it. I can tell you there's a high level of stress because you get trapped into looking at things through the soda straw of the system's camera. There's a whole checklist, like a technical checklist of everything from blue positional awareness or where your own forces are, where the enemy is, clearing airspace, looking at collateral damage, and cross-referencing against rules of engagement- is a hostile act or hostile intent which needs to be confirmed by a lawyer. Then, probably the biggest issue is it's like positive I.D. or PID. Is that person carrying a weapon? Are they planting something? Is that just a farmer? It's extremely stressful, and it's a team effort. But, we trained for this. It had become a drill. The interesting thing is, once you hand off to the pilot, once you give them cleared hot, whether it is manned or unmanned aircraft, it's their call. They own the bomb once it's off the rails. Even if all of a sudden, a family or a child or something walks into the picture, it's not your call anymore. You place that trust in the pilot. This time, we launched a hellfire, and you have to put it in the narrow field of view. We were chasing the motorcycle that was an IED layer. The missile is inbound and tracked, but it is not instantaneous; the time of flight of the missile has a delay, and that guy takes a left turn and ends up in a village. We're like, abort, abort, abort! The pilot states, no, we got three seconds. Fortunately, we hit this guy in an alleyway, and the blast was contained by the heavy mud walls. No collateral damage. It's an extremely like stressful and very emotive process. You're always wondering what's going to happen, and you don't have the same pictures as the guys on the ground. So, reconciling those two with the ground force commander is a matter of reconciling them. During the whole time I was in theatre we did probably over 70 strikes or so, all of them successful. There is never a time we hit a target that was not warranted. We had a couple sort of close calls with collateral damage. In fact, I think there are many times when we didn't strike, where we should have, and we were exercising restraint to default on the side of caution. That was probably the hardest thing. I know that through our actions, we killed 70 people at a minimum. Those enemy pieces were taken off the battlefield; I have never been in a gunfight, and so I had to learn how to kill without passion, without the feeling of my life being in jeopardy, and without remorse.

I was a Master Corporal in a rifle section, and after we got in our first big firefight, we had lost some guys; I can remember sitting out on the back of the ramp of the LAV and just breathing. I couldn't stop breathing- heavy, heavy breathing. The adrenalin was coming down, and that's when I realized that Holy Jesus, I could hear the bullets going past, but I never really thought about it like now we're getting shot up. We're gonna shoot back to try and get them to stop shooting at us and to take that piece of ground they are on. After it was done, there was just a flood of emotion. You could see the combat stress in some guys. We were helping get some casualties and they weren't wounded in a physical sense. This one dude was as white as a sheet and was completely incoherent. He didn't know where he was. He didn't know who he was. He is one of the more experienced guys. If that can happen to him, that can happen to any of us. I used to believe that the reaction was being a coward or being weak. After that eye-opening experience, I never question anybody. Up to that point, it's like, if you break, it's just that you weren't able to act irrationally, suppress your need for self-preservation and be "brave". Every part of you wants to live, and it is so irrational to run towards explosions and into machine gun fire. We are surprised when the human mind rejects that a little and shuts the body down to protect it. The dissonance is huge. I was lucky that I was able to function in those situations; perhaps if I had kept in constant contact, there would have been a point I would have failed to function. I don't know, and maybe the dam would have burst. You have to question who is fucked up, the guy whose brain shuts him down so he lives, or the guy that runs into the hail of machine gun bullets and dies or is wounded but is brave? Maybe we need to keep the shame of cowardice alive to make sure that we still have people to run into the fire; if not, who would choose that?

We were patrolling west of Sperwan Ghar. There had been some issues due to a bomb striking a home that may have had children in it, so the locals were not in a friendly mood. The observation group relayed a grid to me that there was a movement to my front and an armed team manoeuvring to hit us. I took out my map to confirm the grid and realized it was like 20 to 50 m away to our front. I stopped and set up on a wall to observe for the threat. I can hear my breathing in my ears and my site is moving up and down as I catch my breath so I can fire effectively if I need to. As I look through my weapons site, a Taliban RPG team emerges, and the next thing I remember is the weapons signature of a rocket launcher firing. That's the last thing I remember. I came to, and I was upside down and on the ground. I felt a burning sensation in my right shoulder. I saw blood, and for some reason, my arm was behind me, I couldn't see my arm, and I started yelling, "My arm, my arm." I know I am hurt; I think I hear bees, then realize those aren't bees; they are incoming machine gun rounds all around us and yell, "CONTACT." Then I heard this voice, "It's behind you." I was so disorientated. My fire team partner is also injured, and he repeats, "Your hand is behind you." I thought I lost it. I close my eyes for one second and I know I want to walk off the plane and hug my wife with my two hands. That was my prayer. I open, my eyes. I see them, the guys that shot us. I started firing back with one arm. I was so angry; you guys tried killing me; I yelled, "You tried to kill me," and at the same time, I was calling for the medic, "Doc, my arm!" he answered, "I can't help you. My ass is burning. I think I'm hit." I'm like, OK. I am angry. Then there is a third voice: "It's OK! You are ALIVE!" And then this guy grabs me and sits me up, and I recognize him; he is this reservist who I left with the LAV, and I say, "Hey, you are supposed to be in the LAV," and he says, "Stop jacking me up! I'm here trying to help you guys. You are wounded!" He thought we were dead due to the size of the blast we took, I'm still talking and all fucked up. He moves my arm to my front and tells me, "Your arm is still attached." Which raises my morale. We are still under a lot of contact. The Platoon Commander is still confused as to who is hurt and why we can't send a grid, so I say into the radio, "It is ME, and I can't get to my map because my arm doesn't work and my Starlight (medic) is also down." The radio goes quiet, and the soldier with me says, "Sorry, man." He takes over, and I had no business being on the radio. Then he tries my 521, and the radio dies; I hate that radio; it is a piece of shit. The young reservist grips the situation and tells the other section commanders to stop listening to me because I keep giving directions, like to clear my weapon, and things are just flowing because the adrenalin is pumping, and I feel like I am not really hurt, and generally I am doing more harm than help. The reservist clears the weapon just to get me to stop talking. He says, "You guys are out of the fight, but we're still under contact out here. So, wait and shut the fuck up." So now the other platoon shows up as the QRF. I can hear them yelling and telling us to move to the Bison Ambulance. We have to move through a big open field. And it seems both sides are engaging across this space that we must move through. This young guy who came to our aid is at it again and moves us back, and we are under fire through this open field the whole time. He got us back to the armoured Ambulance with rounds bouncing up all around us, I was awake all the way back to Sper, and they cut off my shirt, my military ID was in that sleeve and so I asked them not to cut it half, the medic was looked at me and said, "you're injured, let me do my thing." I think I was a big pain in the ass, and I was obviously in shock. I get strapped into the chopper, and we start to take ground fire; the helo starts moving quickly and doing evasive manoeuvres. Then my shoulder starts burning more. As soon as I got to KAF, I was done, tired. I want to sleep. The next thing I know, I wake up in a room. This Nurse, who is a friend of my wife, asks, "How are you feeling?" "I'm good," I say. "I'm sorry, but you have to call your wife." That was a very hard and emotional phone call. I then had to talk to the doctor and get told I was going home. Right away, I was angry, "I need to get back to my platoon." The Doc was like, "So you're a very lucky man." I said, "No, I'm not lucky. I believe in God. So, I'm blessed." He continues, "You may be blessed, but you are not going back to your platoon. You need to go home to Canada." I was ready to break down and cry because all I could think about was the guys still out there. So, he said, "Let me explain something to you: you have a ball and socket; it is like the size of a fastball; it is shattered and needs to be completely rebuilt. We will need to rebuild the shoulder, and there is no guarantee that the arm will ever work again." That got my attention. That's when I realized how badly I had been hit. It was all business after that. The next day, my replacement, a good guy, we went through the handover. The medic had shrapnel in his ass but was able to stay in the theatre and finished his tour.

My interpreter had stayed with me the whole deployment and we always did an early morning patrol and an afternoon or evening patrol. This guy was always with me and as a part of our routine, I would stop short of the entrance into our COP and count the patrol through and then he and I would be the last ones in. There was this open area that we had to cross over to get back into the COP, and this one day as we did cross, we got lit up by an RPK off to a flank that caught us in the open. I and another Canadian Corporal, the interpreter, and an Afghan soldier all had to decide to move across the open area to the COP or return to the grape fields for cover and see how to sort out this contact. We decided to head to get back into the grape fields for cover, and the Corporal yelled over to me that the Terp was hit.

I kept trying to get up to move and the fire was intense. The radio was on my back and the antennae was fully extended for range, this was attracting a lot of attention as the enemy knew that meant I was a leader, and the rounds were focused on me. They were splashing around me, so freaking close. I couldn't get my head up and was burying myself behind the cover of a low mud wall. I yell that we will try and suppress the enemy fire to win the firefight, gain some space, and we'll go back and get the interpreter who was lying prostrate in the field. My Corporal said, "I can go now," and I said, "No, wait for more support." He completely ignores me and says, "I'm going." I couldn't see him as my head was down behind the wall, and the enemy rounds were spitting up around us. I put my rifle above my head, peek my head out, and start trying to return some fire to give him some support. I don't think it did much, but it certainly attracted a lot of fire in my direction. The Canadian sprinted 50 meters into the open field under fire, grabbed onto the interpreter, and pulled him back undercover to safety from the enemy assault. Behind the safety of the grape field walls, he did some medical interventions on the wounded Afghan. Eventually, the fire subsided when some Attack helicopters came to the station, and the enemy decided to survive to fight another day. We move to collect the interpreter and bring him back. Shot through the spine, the round just missed the ballistic plate positioned on the back of his vest. It went low by about a centimetre. I later recovered the round from the front of his ballistic chest plate. He died from an infection in an Afghan hospital. That Corporal was incredible. On the day, right after my patrol report and I got the medevac all sorted, I wrote his citation for valour in the face of the enemy. I transmitted it back to headquarters. The Corporal left about a week later to go over to another OMLT team and was sadly killed in the IED strike. About 6 months later, he was awarded a Medal of Valour posthumously. I think his actions were in the highest traditions of the Canadian Army, and moving out under fire to rescue a wounded comrade is consistent with historical Victoria Cross winners. I think we undervalue what our young Canadian soldiers did in this conflict, but it does not lessen the memory of the man or his valour when it counted most.

We were under contact from a compound at night. My platoon was dismounted and had nothing heavier than M72 rockets and the C6 machine gun. Nothing that could breach the walls of the compound. There were some assets in the airspace, and the TOC suggested using one of them to breach the wall or destroy the enemy that had engaged us. I did not have a JTAC, so dropping ordnance close to your own unit is a bit nerve-wracking. We were in contact, and I was talking to

TOC and the Reaper that was circling above in the dark night sky. Fuck. I don't wanna get this wrong. I describe the target it is building. The TOC and the pilot were great, walking me through all the steps, knowing I was under pressure and nighttime made clarity even worse. Launch in 5,4,3,2,1. "Can you see it?" they asked. I remember that specifically. It's gonna drop, and those couple of seconds seem forever; where is it? Did I fuck this up? Then the rocket kicks in. I confirm, I see the trail of the rocket. It's in the air now and heading towards those assholes that were shooting at us. Bam, it just drops the compound. No more fire. We asked to breach a wall, and they dropped the compound. Awesome. Suck on the long dick of freedom, you fuckers.

I was getting some rack near the LAV as I had been on a shift in overwatch for hours before. I am tired as fuck, and even though there is constant shelling going downrange and LAVs lighting up dudes across the Arghandab River, I was crashed out hard. I'm sleeping, and I get kicked awake that we are crossing the River now, and we got in our vehicles. We formed up and named the Order of March. We were front left in the Company formation and depth in the Platoon, we crossed the Arghandab, and our objective was the white schoolhouse. We crossed the Arghandab without incident, and then we started to get into the marijuana fields on the north side. That's when all hell broke loose. RPG or an SPG9 hit the G-Wagon that was following us. The G-Wagon had our electronic countermeasures, which seemed less important when under vicious direct fire. We did not have time to address the G-Wagon. We started taking fire from that arc, from our front, from our left; it seemed like we had rolled right into the TB Kill Zone. I just heard the explosions, a lot of confusion on the radio, and a lot of yelling until we got our bearings and identified where the fire was coming from. We settled down and moved up to deal with the vehicle that had been struck and deal with the casualties. The anti-armour round hit pretty much the passenger side of the light-skinned jeep. It hit the front windshield passenger killing the passenger instantly. The medic was in the backseat with the Terp. They were both wounded and, after the initial shock, knew that the vehicle was inoperable. We dismounted our LAV, providing covering fire while trying to do first aid and trying to get the medic to do first aid on themselves. They were all locked down, and we were having trouble extracting them, and they were all fucked up inside. The medic also tried administering first aid until the platoon extracted them. We provided covering fire while the extraction was going and finally, when we got them out, we all piled them back into the LAV. I mean, you could hear the tempo of the enemy fire increasing, and the marijuana plants were so high you couldn't see the white schoolhouse. All you could hear was the rifle rounds going by. You never saw the enemy, but you could feel the weight of fire coming down on you. Our job was to extract the casualties, which we did. The next step is to get back in the fight. There was a danger of getting bogged down.

We have to move forward.

Or we have to move back.

But we cannot stay here.

All our training was to leave the wounded and take the objective, but we did not have a good picture of what was going on across the Company. Just our little piece of the fight. That "fog of war" shit is real, so as we were deciding our next step, we got called to make a tactical withdrawal so the Battalion could smash the objective with fires, and then we could have another run at it once it had been softened up. Lesson learned, enact a fire plan and use artillery to enable manoeuvre on a deliberate river crossing. Who would have guessed? So we moved to return to the south side of the river. The ride back across the river was crazy, and our LAV was like a clown car with people piled in it from various vehicles that had been destroyed or damaged. Wounded, dead, and survivors all mixed in. I had to ride back on top of the vehicle because there were 2 sections of people loaded into one LAV. That was a crazy day.

The first contact was strange. I guess I gotta be honest; I barely reacted at all. I didn't even know what was going on. In training you never really get a feel for what the sounds are of rounds coming at you. RPGs were coming in over to my right. I was just kind of like, what is that? What's that sound? You know, I never immediately thought my life was in danger. I'm an inquisitive idiot. I mean, like, "Oh, what's that." Then people started yelling RPG, and then I was like, oh yeah, that's right. This is a war. I immediately got down and I remember thinking like, Jesus, what do I do now? oh yeah. Crawl onto the cover side and crawl up over the wall. Then it all came back. I guess what you got to do is it came back; I came out of the initial fog, started communicating, all that stuff and directing fire. That first one is a blur. When we advanced to where the enemy had been firing at us, we found some blood trails and some enemy rounds and weapons but no bodies. We had to learn how to be faster to catch them or gather those we killed. Contacts were always crazy, but that first one sits there in my mind. It is not really memorable because my mind wasn't conditioned to even recognize what was happening.

My first contact was all fucked up, and I was pretty lucky to get through it, as it was a crazy day. The Bazaar I Panjawaii was completely abandoned. The downtown was eerie, like a ghost town, we were pushed back from the fight on the River because there was something wrong with our CDA. Techs have to come from KAF so we're hanging out until then. It is my birthday, so everybody's like, Happy birthday, so I'm eating a shitty ration for breakfast; we're at war; it's pretty cool. I had myself, the driver, and the gunner, and I had two guys in the back: my reservist from Ottawa and a C9 gunner. All of a sudden, the CQ comes running up, and he's like, shit is going down; once your CDA's fixed, you're going to take that Bison Amb, parked next to us up to the front line, and you are going to bring up a full battle load of ammo to the Company. The company is in heavy contact. I didn't know the company was in contact. The radio had been really quiet because the power was off for the CDA, so we had no knowledge the Company was in a giant fight; nothing was on.

Fuck.

We get ramped up to go. The CQ is all over the place. I let the CQ know that I know where I am going and he corrects me. He's like, no, different route due to enemy activity. Different route, cool. So CDA gets fixed, we power everything up, do a quick test, and yep, CDA works. Turn on the radios, and it's fucking chaos on the radios. The world has gone crazy. I'm like, holy shit, what's going on? We're following the bison and link up with the LAV from the Company, that's escorting us, and we take a right instead of a left; we go exactly the opposite direction of what the CQ told us. We are immediately in the riverbed. I look around. What the fuck is happening? A lot has changed in a couple of hours since we were getting our CDA fixed. I don't know who's across the river, I don't know what's happening, I don't know anything. I just know that we're following this Bison Amb, we're being escorted by this other crew and I have a company's worth of ammo shoved in the back of my LAV. We get across the River, and by this time, the Company had taken a bunch of casualties, and the Company was preparing for a withdrawal so that fires could be brought onto the objective. We get across, and I see that there's a LAV stuck in a ditch, and there's a few other LAVs scattered around. We pull our LAV up in a firing position sort of to the left to see if there is any support we can provide, and I yell at a guy on the ground. I'm like, hey, where's the bad guys? He looks up at me and he looks at this big grape field and he just goes like this, spreads his arms nice and wide and lays out arcs for me. The left of the arc is 180 degrees that way, and the right of the arc is 180 degrees that way. I'm like, holy fuck, we're in a situation here. Just as he did that, the air became alive with enemy rounds, like they were welcoming the new guys who had not been into anything yet. So, I think I gave the worst fire control order I have ever given, but I basically laid my gunner on the left of the arc and said put it on 100 rounds a minute, traverse over to the right of the arc, go. No friendlies to your front, just give 'er. So, he pumped all the way across the arc with HE and pumped all the way back again. By this time, due to casualties and the need to bring in close fires, the bosses were on the horn giving instructions about pulling back across to the other side of the river. I yell at this crew commander of this other vehicle like, hey, when you move back, radio me when you're set and then I'll move back, I'll take a bound back and then we'll continue to bound back together. He gives me the thumbs up. Then he left and I was still firing away at this giant arc they had given me to try and suppress all the small arms coming our way... He left and his bound took him back to the other side of the river and I never got a radio call. So now I'm the lone LAV on the other side of the river. Last man. Again, nothing on the radio, the LAV Captain rolls up maybe 100 meters away, and he gets out of the back of his LAV and runs over to us. There's a scene in Band of Brothers where, like, Lieutenant Spears runs through the German town to link up with the other unit; that's exactly what this dude is doing. He's sprinting across this field, and there's shit-kicking up from small arms all around him, and mortars are landing near him, and I just watch, amazed. He jumps in the back and he's like, "What are you doing?" I'm like, "I don't know. I was told I was to stay until I got a radio call, no radio call so I keep fighting." "We're leaving!" he says. He asks, "Give me your headset" so I go to give him my headset that is on my head. He says, "No, not your headset, give me A headset." So, somebody hands him a headset, but it's not plugged into anything, so he's like, "Not what I wanted...fuck, never mind!" and he throws it back down; it would be a comedy scene if it wasn't in the middle of a firefight. He gets out of our LAV, and he runs Lieutenant Spears back to his LAV, going back through the gauntlet of fire. He got in, and then we both left. When I got back to the other side of the river, I found out that we had senior NCOs killed, and the other guys were killed, and we had taken all of these casualties. We were in the fucking in the hurt locker. I still didn't understand what we were doing across the river or any of that until we got back to the rest of the platoon. It's all starting to come together, and I'm thinking, why the fuck didn't I hear any of this. We start looking at my radio and we figure out that the antenna cable that plugs into the front had been cut and the antennae itself looks like it has taken a round or two. So, when I'm within 100 meters of someone, I can talk to them and they can talk to me so of course, you do a radio check with the first guy you can see. Ya, you're loud and clear but when anybody gets more than 100 meters away from me, I can't hear anything and they can't hear me. I had no situational awareness at all for that whole day. It was crazy. I had no clue what was going on, I was just following the last order I received and, in the end, I was the last LAV all by myself on that day covering the withdrawal of the

Company, it was just a comedy of errors for me and we were lucky were not killed.

We were short some guys from our section, but we went out anyway; maybe 5 guys dismounted, and the LAV. Maybe it was because we looked smaller, but the enemy decided to hit us. We were in this village, and a couple of dudes popped up with RPG us and hit our guys. Volley firing the RPG, hitting the LAV and the walls around us, and people were hurt, but they weren't killed. It happened in slow motion. I saw the RPG gunner raise the RPG, aim it at me, and then turn and hit the LAV. I fired at him and winged him, but he took off; I think the only reason why the guy didn't fire the RPG at me because I had an Afghan kid standing next to me. The guy got up, and his buddy fired another RPG at the wall, and the shrapnel hit all our guys. That was the first time that my platoon had any casualties. The team got picked up by a REAPER in orbit and got smoked by a hellfire. think our weakened state gave the Taliban confidence to unmask themselves. After that first contact, we realized this shit was real. We medevac'd our wounded and advanced to do the BDA on the hellfire strike. We found the smoking hole and put all the pieces of the dudes in a garbage bag for intel. Apparently, the IED lab guys would see if the biomaterial matched any IEDs that had been found, and then we would know if we killed IED guys or just a plain old RPG team. Hauling those garbage bags back was terrible. There was not much left of them. It is crazy that we used a missile for like two dudes.

Everyone has these joe cool "the first time I was in contact" stories. I think, for the most part, they are bullshit. I think there is a bit of chaos until you are conditioned to work with someone shooting at you. You will fuck up because you will rush a little bit. Like little kids trying to play hockey, they are good in practice but the game gets the better of them until they settle down. In my case, there was a reporter with us and that added to the fuckery. I got in my first TIC as the C6 machine gunner so we've been doing a lot of bounding from rooftop to rooftop to C6 and then covering junctions as the boys cleared through the compounds. We were loaded for bear, and I carried far too much ammo and water. I was probably carrying about 80 pounds of shit on top of my normal kit. As I was moving across one of the roofs, construction obviously was not up to North American standards, and because I was heavy as fuck, one of my legs had punched a hole through the roof, which is just made of mud and hay. So, I'm sort of stuck now in this L-shaped split, and I can't pull myself out. To add to this, we had a Globe and Mail reporter with us, and he got to witness this no-so-cool act of being caught in a roof. So, I am struggling and feeling pretty lucky as it would have been a 10 to 14-foot drop should I have punched through completely. My partner rushes over and pulls me out, and we are a bit fucked off and not feeling too cool. Just as we are sorting ourselves out, I get a nice surprise and learn what an RPG in-flight actually sounds like. And I remember thinking to myself immediately, what the fuck was that? And then want to put two and two together. Oh, yeah, RPG sound. So, know that these things have been terribly misrepresented in Hollywood because they just scream at you like maybe fuckin 500 angry children, and it smacked into the wall right below us. Looking at this dude in my section, a great Asian Canadian guy, we freeze for just a second behind the wall and wonder, like, what the fuck do we do. Then the Master Corporal does what he is supposed to do and starts giving us direction, laying arcs, and sending GRITs for us to engage. My partner and I take the gun on that treacherous roof and climb this rickety fucking ladder to get to this second roof that will give us a better vantage point, and we start engaging in the direction the enemy fire is coming from. It was all happening so fast; I could have died falling through a roof, I could have died when the RPGs hit, and I could still die with the bullets coming at me; I am not feeling cool and calm. I am just mechanical, following the direction of the Master Corporal and engaging targets. The Taliban Fighters had climbed the trees and were firing at us on the roof from the trees. My cone of fire must have gone from something very, very small to something very, very much in a big hurry. They are quite literally up in the trees... so I would extend my bursts and shift fire across the middle of the trees until I would see an AK47 or RPK drop, meaning I had hit someone or you would see a body drop. It came down to a system. The fight didn't last terribly long because the other two boats rolled up, and then the 25mm cannons just went to town and made short work with their coax, and the firing stopped from the treeline. It was incredible to have survived. That was the first feeling I had. As ridiculous as everything was, that feeling of survival was real. The globe and mail reporter is right there and starts snapping photos of me as I'm firing. I remember stopping what I was doing and putting my fucking machine gun on safe. Looking at a reporter and saying, don't print that asshole. My wife thinks I'm a cook! I don't tell her what I do. From the roof to the reporter to the dudes in the trees, that is my first contact.

———————

My first contact was weird. This ANP station got hit near our COP. We responded as the QRF, and after the shooting was done, we helped evacuate the Afghan casualties; I had to find a fire position and settled near the spot where the SPG 9 rounds had hit; the Hesco was all burnt and black and fucked up. The sun starts to go down, and we have been there for about 4 hours and nothing, so we start loading up to head back to our spot, and WHAM! SPG 9 comes in and drops short. We see the signature and just start lighting the area up. C6 opens up, and the 84mm opens up in the direction of the contact. Rounds were coming back at us, so we had to clear the area. The Company brought in the Badger; this crazy engineering machine built on a Leopard 2 chassis. Unstoppable, they smashed down a wall, and then two leopard tanks started punching through behind it. We went up in intimate support behind the leopards into the compound we were taking fire from. We smashed into the compound with the armour, and then we started clearing room to room. We still weren't shooting without targets so we came around this corner and we found this old man and his son. Really, he's an old guy and a small teenage kid; maybe it was his grandson. After we sorted out that they had not been firing weapons by GSRing them, we talked to them and figured out that the Taliban came into their house and held them hostage while they set up the SPG 9 and machine guns. He showed us where they had come in, where they fired from. Then they fucked off after the contact got hot. They told us that the Taliban would fucking kill them if they didn't let them do what they wanted to fucking do. The Taliban were pretty brutal bastards. I mean, they threw acid in women's faces, strapping kids with bombs, using people with mental handicaps who could not understand orders to test the security protocols of bases; it was easy to conjure up a dislike for this enemy. This family just got caught in their web. We had used artillery before the armour went in, and the old man had survived. I was glad we didn't hit them. I don't know if the old man and son were some type of sympathizers or just people trying to live. Maybe they weren't. Maybe they were-I think that the normal people just had to let both sides do whatever they wanted or risk getting killed. Pretty fucked up first contact though.

You have to respect the adversary. They really got the drop on us whenever we got lazy or rushed in the environment. We were finishing a Company patrol for 36 or 48 hours and had no contact, and an American Sniper team was in Overwatch. The US team was an isolated element and came under contact at the end of the patrol. An American sniper took a round through both legs. My platoon was tasked to turn around and go get these guys out and provide security for the MEDEVAC. End of the day, we were tired, and we made a classic mistake. And what did I do? I followed lines of drift through the grape fields and compounds; we took the easy way, well, the fastest to get to the wounded soldier, which you shouldn't do it. As soon as we crossed the bend where overwatch was no longer effective as the snipers were pinned down, we got hit with very effective heavy weapons fire. I happened to be behind the building. I remember looking forward, and my lead section Commander was down in a wadi but had a wall behind the wall raised on the top part of the Wadi; I could see the splashes hitting the wall and taking the mud wall apart behind his head, and I was yelling at him to get his head down. He didn't feel the fire initially, and I could see the rounds being walked onto him, like in slow motion, by the grace of god or just bad shooting on the TBs part they missed him. I turned around and saw my middle section commander huddled behind a little wall that was being chipped away around him as rounds pounded all around us and I thought Jesus Christ, they had us dead to rights and we were pinned down. This was going to shit. We were caught in a perfect ambush and had to break out. Out of nowhere these little Kiowa Helicopters, they came in fast and low, could see us and immediately identified the enemy heavy weapons det that had ambushed us. It was over minutes after that. The Kiowas did what they did best and killed the Taliban heavy weapons team. We were able to create space and evacuate the US sniper; he was medevac'd. It seems like a non-event but until you are under pounding heavy weapons fire it was pretty clear we were lucky rather than good and taught me that one lazy day could get your whole team killed. I never took the easy way again.

We were driving along Hwy 1 at night and taking a Dutch Lieutenant Colonel and RSM to another base after a planning conference. I was observing out of the family hatch for rear security. My NVG was flipped down, but it was a replacement from the last Battlegroup and the inside lens was all scratched and so nearly useless to aid me at night. I remember saying to myself, fuck this, this is dumb. I turned it off and I put it up because there's some illumination from the moon. I figure I'll be fine and I have not been in contact at this point. Then everything explodes in the span of a couple of seconds. I heard a burst of machine gun fire and I thought it was from one of our turrets in another vehicle that had malfunctioned. I dropped down there and essentially had to look at the Dutch guys that were there. I said, "What the fuck was that?" The Colonel and RSM looked back at me blankly and then they said something to me. I didn't know what they said, but I remember just thinking that makes no sense. But what they said was, I don't know, RPG, but I didn't hear an RPG. I didn't even process that. I had just heard this burst. But that's the dumbest thing I've ever done, how the fuck are these guys down below going to know what is going on up top? So I look up again, and all I can see is green

STEVE MACBETH | 109

tracer and red going the other way. The Convoy was in contact. I saw that and kind of clicked it. So, I hopped up and I couldn't see anything out of it. So, I just did the old battle-school thing of aiming at the muzzle flashes that were on the side of the road. Just like a quick aim firing. I don't know if I hit them or not. It's never bothered me if I did or not… I dropped down. I did a quick little mag check. I still had what seemed like a lot of rounds, but slapped in a fresh mag, popped back the backup, and back in the fight, making myself feel good by engaging the muzzle flashes that were getting farther and farther away. I just feel this pat me on the back of the leg. And it was the Dutch Lieutenant Colonel with a big smile; he gave me a thumbs up from the bowels of the LAV, "You did great." I remember looking back at him and saying, "Thanks. It's my first time!"

———————

It was a bad day, but the sergeant turned it into a funny thing because this is the type of guy that he was. Our section is moving through a routine patrol when they come into contact. The Sergeant gets hit in the chest, and one of the Corporals runs over to him, starting to first aid. The rest of the section is with the 2IC winning the firefight and suppressing the enemy. The Sergeant sees that the young corporal is in a state of panic, and he's trying to do first aid on his section commander. And the sergeant decides, like, this is a good time for a practical joke when he is shot through his chest! He missed his heart; it went up and out his side, in the lower rib cage thing right below the heart. So, he's lying there, and he looks at the corporal, and he's like, "You're losing me, man. You are going to lose to me. It was great working with you." The kid is flustered and says, "Sarge, don't die…" "Shut up, patch me up, and watch your arcs" the Sarge barked. Hilarious, I mean a little crazy, but hilarious. The section cleared the area, brought in MEDEVAC and the Sergeant survived. Toughest man in NATO.

———————

So, we came back from HLTA and guys are already on the line, they had been living hard and had not had showers in weeks and we were coming in all sweet smelling from leave. We pull out to PBW and we get the ground brief and we take our LAV out to the strong point, we pull up into our parking spot, we hang out and uh, we meet the new platoon commander. He had changed out over leave due to casualties. The new guy was a good dude. We were happy to have him. We get the warning order that we're gonna do a joint ANA, Canadian patrol in the morning. We're just gonna go down the road, and into the compounds on the west side, check'em out and come back, no big deal. So, we wake up in the morning, get our stuff ready, we're now on the road with the ANA and the Pl leaves the LAVs on the side of the road as kind of an overwatch, and so I am up in the turret as a Crew Commander and we watch the platoon patrol into the fields and compounds. They do a little patrol, they come back, no issues. No issues, no contact, no incidents and then as uh we're leaving, the lead LAV hits an IED on the way back to the strong point. He hits on the drivers side, first road wheel. The driver gets knocked unconscious; a couple other guys get knocked unconscious. So, we hang out there and wait and secure the site, we don't wanna move much now, because it seemed like every day someone was getting blown up on those little tracks. The counter-IED guys come out, sweep the road, give the ok Clear. We pull all of the guys out of the back and its protocol now that, if you got hit by an IED, you had to go back to PBW to get checked out Docs and then you can go back on the line, very generous given that we didn't know much about concussions at the time. The radio crackles, movement to the west. Three to four groups of Taliban. The ICOM says they're planning a simultaneous strike on the route and we're like, cool, well, we're here so bring it on. Then around, two o'clock, between two and two thirty, we're hanging out, some dudes are napping, playing Operation Camel Spider and there's dudes in the back of the LAV. It starts, it kicks off and it kicks off with RPG's fired into the position. The first RPG hits the building near us, but maybe the third or fourth, hits our vehicle and it hits the TACNAV antenna, at the back. The little stubby guy, it's maybe two feet tall and it's got a little cube shaped base at the bottom. It hits that cube shaped base and sprays shrapnel through the open-air sentry hatches in the back and then straight down at the back of the ramp. It hits one of our young dudes who takes shrapnel all down the neck and bleeds out almost instantly. The shrapnel that came straight down on the ramp, hit the Sergeant that was standing straight at the back so he took shrapnel straight down in his back and his upper chest and everything, so he's down. I took a piece of shrapnel in my side. My gunner took a little piece of shrapnel in his pelvis and a little piece of shrapnel here that nicked his temporal artery so he's bleeding a lot. He's all fucked up, I'm all fucked up, we're all fucked up. The guys on the outside, they're a little bit fucked up but they're right back in the fight. It's a weird thing that like, I remember Lieutenant Colonel Grossman telling a story in one of his talks, that you're conditioned by the media that you consume. So, you've watched war movies before and every time somebody gets hurt, they yell medic. It happened to me, I crawl out of the back of the LAV, it's all dusty and smoky and I'm screaming for the medic, MEDIC!! I also needed a medic, so I am not sure if Grossman was right there. I am on auto pilot and my mind comes back to me, I realize that, well that's me, I'm the TCCC guy! I grab my little bag and I go back into the LAV and my gunner is making noise, I go to him first. I do a check, he is fucked up, but not that fucked up, so I go to the young dude that got hit with shrapnel and sort of sit him up to see how he's doing, and we see the wound, we see the blood, ok well, he's gone. We need to triage now so go over to the Sergeant and start pulling kit off. He's got no pulse, he's not breathing, turn him over, and he's got shrapnel all through the back, and well, he's not with us anymore, so put him down. But now, back to my gunner, ok, he's alive, he's kicking, so we can do something with him. We put an Israeli bandage on his head, wrap him up nice and neat, put his helmet on and tell him, ok, get out, get your shit, and get in the fight. He gets out, puts on his shit and now he's in the fight. As he gets out, I'm getting my shit, cause now I'm gonna get in the fight. I'm putting on my cool tactical tailor stuff that I just bought on HLTA and I'm starting to give out arcs. At this point, the turret is still working. In the turret is my reservist and big gorilla corporal. They're in there and they're shooting things with the coax and the main gun. We're on the ground, I'm issuing arcs, we're redistributing ammo, we're bombing up mags and then in comes the platoon commander. He comes over, sees what's going on, and I'm like, I got this; I got two guys down, I got one wounded, plus me, I'm wounded. I'm like, my gun's still working. My guys need more ammo. He nods and gets after what I need; he goes up to the observation post where this other guy in our platoon was single-handedly fighting off a Taliban group with a Separated vertebrae in his neck. This dude in the OP had been knocked unconscious at some point. He used up all the C6 ammo, was firing M72's, he cracked open like a half dozen M72's and was just firing them into the Taliban. Then shifted to using up his C9 ammo. It was insane. So, the Platoon Commander went up there to see how he was doing, and this dude smiled and gave him a thumbs up like it was just another day at the office. The QRF arrives, and the commander asks what I need. I got these two guys down, and I need more ammo. we are still hammering away, and the TB are applying fire heavily. He resups us and moves onto take on flank security as there are more TB inbound. At that point, the turret stopped working, and the 25mm cannon jammed. Then the coax jammed, the gunner gets out, and he comes and gets me, and he says, "The guns are not working; you need to fix it." I am kind of busy, but I'm the crew commander so I'll go fix it. I took off my stuff, and I crawl back in there, and yep, the 25 is jammed all to hell. It's all fucked up, and then the coax, there's no reason for the coax to be jammed, so I'm trying to open it up, and it's not opening up. We eventually get that unjammed, load it back up, it's working again. We get told that the bison ambulance that was coming to get the wounded and the dead had one of the wheels fall off en route; no shit, a wheel fell off, so it's not coming. The action was starting to slow down a little, and we had managed to put our two fallen into body bags. We're gathering up the wounded. I wouldn't say we're not in direct contact, and I would say that the firing has slowed down. We're not taking as much incoming fire, and we've slowed our outgoing. I look at my gunner, and he's bled through his Israeli bandage. It's an arterial bleed so we'll have to fix this quick. I pulled out the QuikClot, and it says right on the directions: do not use on head and face. Well, I got nothing else, so I will use it on his head and face. I lay him down, a sandbag for a pillow, and I put my hand by his eye to make like a seal, and I pour the quick clot on him and I brush it away. All that's left is the stuff sticking to his wound, so I put the Israeli on, and I kneel on his head, and he's like, OW! I'm like "you go ahead and scream like no one can hear you there's so much gun fire". He screams, "It burns," and I'm like ya, well it's supposed to, you'll be alright. So that fixes him and we put another Israeli on him just to keep it clean. He's back in the fight. I get on the radio and I tell them, my vehicle is down. The turret doesn't work anymore, it's all fucked up. I can load the wounded in my vehicle and I can take them back to PBW. Then you can put a new vehicle in here with a turret that works. The TOC agreed, good idea, do that. So we load up two dead and one wounded in the back in the back, and I'm in the crew commanders seat and I got this awesome driver and he gets us back quick. We drive to patrol base Wilson and fuckin drop the ramp. I don't know where the VSA go as a whole bunch of people swarmed the vehicle at this point but it's me and my gunner are at the back and the medics are on us to check us out our wounds and stuff. They put us on a MEDEVAC helicopter and off we go. So that was that. Funny story about the helicopter. My gunner has blood below the waist on his pants. He was sitting up when they took the quick clot out of his wound at PBW. So, he had bled down his face and then onto the crotch of his pants. When they put him on the chopper, he's lying on the stretcher, the medic that's on the chopper, the American medic, does the full body scan and then he sees the blood on the crotch of his pants. He undoes his pants, pulls them down, pulls out my Gunner's junk and is l all over the junk like up and down and around, inspecting it closely to see if there is a bleed. Everywhere he was lifting it and shifting it, and it was all slippery with blood, and because where I was in the helicopter, lying on a stretcher, it was right next to my face. Staring at it and I'm like, this is gross. I don't wanna see this right now. I've just gone through this fucking afternoon and now this guy is molesting my gunner in a helicopter, I mean this is surreal. And when he's done the medic just looks up at me and is like, thumbs up. I'm like ok man, cool and he puts everything back. What a crazy day. Like 24 hours after getting back from leave. Welcome back to Afghanistan.

———————

A guy walked into the patrol and a dude comes at us " Allah Akbar" hit his button to blow himself and it failed, battery failure or something. He got strafed across the hips and went down and obviously didn't die for quite a long time. EOD showed up; they sent the robot to try and pull the vest off; we can't go give aid because we can't go near the guy. He's got a bomb on. The robot approaches this guy and tries to shake the IED off, and the guy is screaming his head off because he's in a lot of pain as he's taking four rounds through the hips and eventually, he expires or bleeds out, and they're able to get the vest off with the robot and disarm the bomb. It was kind of fucked up listening to that guy die. I mean, a couple of minutes before he was trying to blow himself up and take us with him, I felt no sympathy, but I took no joy in his pain. I wished we had gotten the vest off and treated him, but it just was not possible. We were lucky that day. Our team wasn't that lucky throughout the tour, there were other days the bomb didn't malfunction.

A burst of machine gun fires goes off, maybe at head level, between myself and the guy ahead of me. Then, an RPG came crashing in; the sound made us move. We all hit the deck. There's a wall by myself and some other guys. I hopped over. The adrenaline kicked in, and we took a breath behind the wall; the medic piled over the wall also and like fumble fucked as he got over and crashed into us. We rolled like a bag of hammers to our feet; the Warrant let out some dad joke cheese humour and looked over; the medic said, "Hey, doc, that's what an RPG sounds like," as they continued smashing into the other side of the wall. I stick my head up over the wall to try and find the enemy, and I remember the poppies being in full bloom. As I scanned, I could see green tracer coming at us, and it was like everything slowed down and I took in the contrast of colours, the deep green of the fields, the blossoming poppies, the bright blue sky and the contrast of the brown walls and tracks, I remember not having a deliberate train of thought, and thinking, you know, of all the places to die, this would be a pretty beautiful place to die. How fucked is that?

The first time we were under sustained contact, it was surreal and made me reflect on our training. The contact was actually a simple case of a meeting engagement where the soldiers were walking down the road, and the Taliban came around the corner with RPGs just kind of slung over their shoulders and their AKs at the trail. And next thing you know, they were ten feet away, and it was kind of people pulling their weapons, shooting at each other and running in the opposite direction. Nothing cool about it at all. I had three platoons with me at the time, so it was very close contact for the snipers. Who bumped the enemy? Right away, it erupted all around us. There was an RPK up on the rooftop. Within 5 minutes, this was bringing fire down on us. It was the first time that I actually felt I really kind of manoeuvred my company in a traditional style. So, I had a platoon already down there to set up a firebase. I got my Platoon Comds in and decided to do a left flanking along a Wadi that was a couple hundred meters away, which was clearly what the Taliban was using to move up and down to get to us. It was kind of a little tunnel system through there, too. We wanted to clear that avenue, So we managed to get a UAV up that finally took out the RPK with a hellfire. I took the other two platoons. We did a fighting roll up the wadi from there and cleared the objective. It was amazing how close the actions were to training. Sometimes, even though it was real, that we were in a scenario, and it was like we had done it a hundred times before. I guess that means training works.

––––––––––––

Our first contact was a bit of a mess on the radio and figuring out who was in charge, when, and what exactly was going on. Artillery was coming down, which was actually enough to keep the enemy fire down and allowed me to manoeuvre to get into the attack position. Then the decision was made by our higher headquarters to stop the Artillery, from back in KAF! That has to be new to war when a Commander about to cross the Line of Departure loses fires and someone else makes that call due to safety. They were uncomfortable with how close the artillery fire was coming down near us. So, it was ordered stopped. And as soon as the artillery fire lifted, all hell broke loose again, and we started eating a ton of AK and RPG fire. Luckily, they were shit shots, and we were down in a wadi. We basically had to fight into the attack position, and I lost my shit on the radio. I don't know how it got sorted out, but the artillery fire started again. Then we were notified by the eye in the sky that another group of Taliban, all armed, were reinforcing, and they were going to fire another hellfire missile at the group. The missile dropped and as it was in flight at the last minute, they called it off because there were some unknown guys that may have been civilians in the group and they took the missile off, but it actually came towards the attack position and dropped 50 meters in front of us, again we were lucky that we were undercover and we had one guy get some minor shrapnel wounds. I kind of wish KAF HQ would stop helping. Holy fuck, that rocket was close. The first contact was at 0730. By 0930 we had been under contact for 2 hours. It was taking too long, and we lost momentum. After the missile struck, we started the attack, but right before we rolled up the objective, they had some Dutch aircraft come in and start to strafe the wadi around the enemy, and so then we managed to push through but didn't find any enemy. The Taliban must have taken away the bodies as we had confirmed a couple killed by UAV video and found blood trails. They must have taken them away after everything consolidated, and then, just as we thought it was calming down, we came into contact again. We fight through some more minor contacts that are just delay tactics, and they do not want to be decisively engaged. By this time, we were actually running low on small arms, and guys were out of water, so we went into consolidation and brought the LAVs up for resupply; it was all over in about 4 hours but seemed like a lifetime. As a company commander that was my first contact. Lots of lessons learned and felt very lucky there were only a couple of light wounds and no killed. We wouldn't always be so lucky.

My first contact ruined my breakfast and started me smoking again. We were overwatching this poppy field and things had been quiet for a couple of weeks, it lulls you into being a bit complacent and we had not had any action yet. Afghanistan is beautiful when it is quiet and green. I was sitting in the turret and was hungry, I asked my gunner and he said that I could eat first. You eat in shifts so there is always one guy ready to go, on the weapon system and head in the sites. You do everything in shifts; eat, sleep, shit, everything, one man covers while the other does his thing. My gunner tells me to go down into the hull and eat. So, I pop down, and I am talking to one of the guys in my section; we were shooting the shit, and I'm just grabbing my fucking Beans and wieners, and we step out of the back ramp of the LAV, all of a sudden we hear an unfamiliar sound and BAM! An RPG round lands between this dude and myself. All I wanted was my fucking beans and wieners, and now it was all over me, it was warm and wet, and I thought I had been hit, but I was OK... Sons of bitches. I jump up into the turret. Gunner is scanning but can't see anything. I pop up out of the turret and see them running through a little poppy field in front of us. I reach down and bring the cannon onto the four forms with the RPG running through the field. I ask my gunner if he sees them, is he " on" and he says no! I ask again can you see him now? No is the answer. I am pretty pissed, they're fuckin running away and then an RPK opens up to cover the RPG withdraw so we get our heads down in the turret. I look through the sites and can't find them either so my gunner was not fucking with me, I jump up on the Pintle mounted C6 7.62mm and let off a fucking third of a belt like 40 rounds. It is too late; they are gone, and the RPK has stopped firing; there is no big war story here. They shot at us, almost killed me and the other guy, covered me in beans and wieners, and we did not get them. Some good learning for my section, about staying undercover when you eat and how to better bring the gunner on in shorter range obscured shoots. I wouldn't make those mistakes again. I looked down after and I was covered in beans and wieners, just gross and I only had one set of combats and would not wash for another 8 days as we were out on a n Op, we shit the bed on reacting to the enemy, the adrenaline dump was crazy but we had to laugh, we lived and it was a bit of a comedy of errors. I asked one of the guys in my section for a cigarette to calm my nerves, he said " I thought you quit?" "Not today, buds; today, I am a smoker." So that was the end of that. I started smoking again. I smoked for the entire tour and still sneak the occasional one. Funny first contact, the TB go the better of us, ruined my Breakfast and got me smoking again.

When you are scanning the terrain in a LAV the optics let you get up close to your targets. You have the option of the day site, which is like a really powerful scope, the image intensifying site, which allows you to see in low light conditions and then the thermal site. We primarily used the thermal site because heat signatures would stand out. Sometimes with how hot the ground was, it is hard to see detail with the thermal site. Everything blends in the heat of the day. I remember seeing what I thought was muzzle flash coming out of a corner of a building. I opened up and I got the guy. I remember, you know, seeing the rounds impact and then the thermal change as the dude's body exploded from 25mm hitting him and the thermal image changed colour. I will never forget that impact. Usually, it was not too clear. Rocks heat up and look like heads, or when someone else rounds ricochet it looks like a muzzle blast coming at you. Who knows how many times I shot at someone else's splash, not being sure if it's like Taliban or if it's someone else's splash. Well, you know, better safe than sorry.

Our first contact is kind of a funny story, actually, because so we were on patrol with a platoon, and we had broken off with the section. It was probably 2 Klicks out of FOLAD, near Nakahonay. We came upon what we thought was a cache, an IED cache. So, it would be a busy day. All of a sudden feel the need to shit. I never shit, I had to shit so badly. So, I moved off to an area to do my business, and one of the guys came with me for security. I go up this little hillside type thing, and I'm in behind the building and having the shit. This guy's like watching my six while

I have a shit. The OC asks, "Where are you? I am almost done here so I call back to him. He lets me know we are going to be moving soon. Then BOOM, we get opened up on. The OC dives into cover and at the same time hits his chin, cutting it open it. I didn't see the cut happen. I never got my pants up, I didn't even wipe, and we rush down; I see blood and think, holy shit, the OC is hit. I go into my sergeant major mode. You know, perform first aid on him, mostly he's like, "No, no, I'm okay, I'm okay. I Just cut my chin. "Oh" I am standing there dumbfounded, I have all my First Aid stuff out for nothing, we weren't paying attention and we're not even worried about rounds flying, as rounds are hitting the wall beside us. He's like, "SGM, get down." I'm like, oh yeah, I should probably get down and do that. Then I thought, " You motherfuckers". They got the nerve to shoot at us. We start shooting back like it was just kind of crazy, I never thought about us getting shot or getting hit. It was naïve, it isn't like the Taliban care about rank. We had the ÁNA with us and they, they were just lighting everything up at the and firing their rocket launchers into the direction of where the enemy was. High explosive rounds going everywhere! High over the trees, over buildings. We were not sure where those rounds are exploding. The guys were returning fire and then we get hit again from the trees at a couple of hundred meters. We had the airburst rounds for the 84mm Carl Gustav. You could set the timer or the distance on the nose at to do an airburst. We set it for 250m and it explodes spraying the area with shrapnel. You see leaves fall off the tree. I'm set for 350, and we are about to fire again. Two American choppers show up, and my 84mm gunner fires his round set for 350m. We watch the trail and see the explosion, and all you see is all these leaves falling off the tree, and then you see one guy drop out of the tree. Then this US chopper comes out of nowhere and lights up the area. That finishes the Taliban; we patched up the OC as good as new. What a strange first contact, from taking a shit to knocking guys out trees with the Carl G.

We were moving into deliberate contact with an established enemy and honestly, I'm mad as we were rolling in. We went into it with no direct prep fire and no indirect fire. The choice was made that we would open up when we were opened up. So were vulnerable in the open because we chose to be. For some high idealism and bullshit ROE. I couldn't even speak when the first shots were fired. Like fuck, fuck-you, we should have been shooting first. We should have opened up as soon as the first rounds start coming in. I was like, fuck. I just knew it. My heart just sank. We've been shooting these people and killing without orders the night before, but for most of us, this is our first direct contact. We killed bad guys at twenty-two hundred meters. You see a threat and locate the target, and like you fucking kill the guy. Watch the guy's head and body explode in the thermal, then for some reason, here we are, less than 24 hrs later, they are dropping us at range with SPG and machine guns because we didn't do a proper firebase and preparatory fire. Like how the fuck could we allow that? I remember … I was so frustrated. What are we doing? We learned and never made that mistake again, but it cost us good people that day.

There was excitement going into the Roto Zero, but we weren't sure. Well, I wasn't sure what we were getting into. To be honest, like, I was like, OK, we know the Taliban are there. We know that. There will be there will be some contact. But to say exactly that, we're gonna get into a gunfight. I couldn't connect with it. It seemed unreal. It was odd because you're like, OK, there is an enemy out there. They have killed some of our dudes with IEDs. Yet we're simply following rules that are from Bosnia. Like no bullets up the Spout, chambering a round is a deliberate escalation of force. Stuff like that was a bit confusing because as a leader at that time, we used everything that was peacekeeping because of Bosnia, Rwanda, and ROE. And weapons states and stuff had been. The weapon states for a roto 0 was particularly interesting because, in camp, we carried weapons. However, there were no mags on them, and there were no rounds in the chamber. One specific story is one that one of the towers was being manned to guard the base and this shift wasn't just infantry. So, we had clerks or maintainers, but they were admin personnel. Both these two people are in the bunker, and a white van pulled up along the wall and started shooting. They had a C6 in the bunker, but nobody shot back. They actually left the bunker to go back to headquarters to let them know they were being shot at. It was crazy. People lost their minds; shoot back! After that. It was only combat arms that manned, the towers. It was a shift in mental state. The difference between Kandahar and Kabul was that in Kabul, people were not in the mindset that we were in a war, and from leadership down, they were hesitant to pull the trigger.

We are in this giant Convoy to head out to our COP kind of scanning and guys in the back of the LAV are throwing up. The vehicle was bouncing and rolling and everyone was hatches down. The Battalion that had trained us had lost guys from being too far out of the sentry hatch, so I was sticking to the lessons that had been passed on. As the crew commander, I was the only one I could see what was going on. The same thing for the tank in front of me. I had one guy who was really sick, and not much was happening around us as we snaked our way slowly out towards Mushan. He was begging, like, can we please pop the hatch? We stopped at one point for a short halt, and l said okay, like pop the hatch, and a dude got up and dumped a pop tart box full of puke out the side. I felt kind of bad. But better sick than dead from shrapnel. We're moving along the Arghandab, scanning the Zahri side. We're pretty close to the riverbank and it starts getting a bit built up. There's this kid playing with a kite. As I slew the turret back, I see this flash. In front of us, the tank in front of me explodes. These guys with an SPG nine come out shooting at the tank. I'm watching this; pretty cool. The tank just slews its turret and vaporizes them. The Leopard 2 did not miss a beat, no damage from the attack. As I was looking at this really cool show, there was an explosion in front of my vehicle. I look over and there's an RPG team and a couple of guys with an RPK I'm not even sure if I saw it, but the guys were looking through the screen, and confirmed it. They missed with the RPG and then followed with a high rate of fire from the RPK. I just looked down at the joystick, and it looked massive, and I was slow, and I realized we were going to have to engage these dudes. Fuck you, like all drills are gone. I hit it and told the gunner, "You gotta fucking see that guy, fucking shoot! It's HEIT (high explosive incendiary trace) 25mm, like at 350 meters or whatever. We obliterated them. It was shocking what weapons do to the human body, and it doesn't sink in that you have just done that. That you have just killed someone that was trying to kill you. What the fuck were they thinking opening up on a LAV and a tank? That was the first time getting shot at.

———————

The 25mm cannon is awesome, but it is not easy to load and unload. 120 rounds of ammunition is heavy and the feed shoots have a lot of tension on them when the canon is loaded. If there is a jam you must be deliberate in how to clear it and ensure the feed shoots are sorted out. You need to use ratchets and mechanical levers to lower the ammo and "ratchet them down" This is called downloading. Then when the canon is clear and ready to go you need to "ratchet" them up" this is called an upload. So, this one day, we had been in and out of contact, and the gun had been jamming. Things went quiet and so we decided to do some maintenance and my LAV was halfway through the middle of a download and then re-upload. And of course, that is the time that we start taking fire. We're taking mortar, RPG and small arms. I'm in the turret trying to get the gun back in action. The 2IC jumps in the escape hatch ripping the ammo. We're trying to get this thing back in action. The section is out to the side starting to lay down small arms fire as we try and get the turret back up. The section to the left of us started taking casualties They had a bunch of shrapnel from the mortar rounds And of course, the shrapnel basically sprayed into the back of a vehicle, The casualties were being dealt with and we could not get this thing going, everything is jammed. A rifleman, our number one rifleman, actually got up on top of the LAV and start fucking laying some fire down with the Pintle mount on top of the turret. Good. He is basically straddling over the top of me in the crew commander's hatch with his feet like Audy Murphy, you know, and I am jammed below trying to fix the turret. The hot casings falling down my neck burning me, I didn't even feel it at the time, as we try and get the cannon up. So finally, we get it back in order. He jumps down and we start engaging with the canon and then all of a sudden just out of nowhere the roof lifts off of yellow school where the fire was coming from. "Holy Shit did we hit something with the Cannon and hit a secondary?" Nope. It was a JDAM that hit that called in by the TOC from a bomber flying overhead. Scared the shit out of us. We weren't really that far away from that building, within a couple of hundred meters and the roof lifted up this building, it was quite a boom. And then you realize, alright, is everybody okay? We went through our Ammo Cas, the other section medevac'd their dudes. Pretty fortunate that we never took any shrapnel or anything from the bomb but that ended the fight. We didn't receive any more fire after that. It was like a 30-minute fight but seemed like hours.

The POMLT team was attached to my platoon as we did partnered patrols in Zhari with them and the ANP. The POMLT team and the ANP were getting ready to enter into this building. We had a ton of indicators and were pretty sure there were bad guys in the area. As the team is going in, the fourth man hits the pressure plate. A huge explosion, and there is a wounded soldier with multiple amputations. This was followed immediately by an ambush. The enemy flooded a wadi we were in to flush us out of cover, this was brilliant by them, as it trapped us. It is my very first contact. And we've got three priority bravos and one pri-alpha which are all separated from our Med chain. We're fighting in this chest deep water, being overwhelmed with incoming fire. I remember thinking holy shit, this could go badly. I sent the medic into a building with a couple of guys, like in one of these movies where rounds were splashing at their feet as they covered the open ground to get over to it. Not one of them got hit. There was an open field, kind of a fight between us. It split us into two groups. I made the call for the 9 liner and medevac due to where the explosion and casualties happened and where the Warrant Officer was. He controlled the fight which is the opposite to what should happen. But it's all situational. Especially in that type of terrain and when your element gets split by an IED and then hit from unexpected directions. I realize my GPS isn't working as I have to call in the 9 liner and contact report. Fuck nothing is easy. So, we get that stuff sorted, my medic is stabilizing the casualties, so I crawl forward to with my Warrant Officer, as I am crawling into the wadi a troop fires an M72 rocket without checking his backblast, I get blown backwards by the backblast, the fight is still on and I am kind of knocked out… I hear my machine gunner yell… I think the Platoon Commanders dead… I come to and give him a smart-ass answer but link up with my Warrant Officer. We called in 155 smoke and as soon as the guns come online the enemy fucked off. We moved on to clear out our casualties. A bit of a bright spot, our casualty had lost both his legs and had a mangled hand, our medic had done some amazing work to stabilize him. I went to see him before he got on the helicopter and he asked for a cigarette with his one good hand. He was a triple amputee that made it off the battlefield. Big lesson for me, is that once shit starts to happen, things will always go wrong, and you just have to adapt and get it done.

We're getting mortared. It's pretty effective enough that they haven't hit us, but it's close. The artillery direction-finding radar, guys I didn't even know were with me, come up on the radio and give me the bearing and distance of the tubes that are firing at us. Awesome. We are launching a quick attack or hasty attack on the position. Just move in the direction and orders to follow. The Badger leads the clearance towards the position just smashing through shit to make a road for us. We dismount and we started clearing compounds and shit, which was friggin pretty cool. We were going through, h and then we got to the one spot and we couldn't get into it. We tell the tanks and they fucking blast a hole the wall with their 120mm cannon. The guys go through the holes, you know, the dust clears, they go through and catch the Taliban by complete surprise. We end up capturing these five mortars. We get these mortars. It was awesome, they were still warm from firing. The guys just fucked off in their little white van or truck, whatever they had, because you see going off in the distance. Then other Taliban fired at us for getting the mortars. There was this big explosion, and we thought, What the fuck was that? The engineer, Master Corporal, goes and finds whatever it was. He comes back walking down the street with this fucking thing in his arms. So, they shot out this big Chinese rocket. No one got hurt. We're gonna get the fuck out of here. Then a tank gets stuck as we are exfil off the position, the badger goes to recover it, and then the Badger gets stuck. Now we're staying for the night; it's getting dark, and the enemy knows where we are, and we have their mortars. Now these fucking retards are trying to surround us again and start probing our perimeter. We were able to fight through the night, a series of small actions, because they forgot that we can see in the dark, and we ended up getting a bunch of them and extracting with no further casualties. It was an awesome day, but we got tripped up by vehicles getting stuck. It goes to show the simplest thing is hard in war.

The jeep is 4-seater each seat has responsibilities. Driver, commander, signaller, security. The Sergeant asked the question the guys every morning: Where do you want to sit? This guy asks the other young guy if he minds being the signaller because he had never been rear security to that point in the tour, and you get to sit backwards and see the world from a different vantage point. Just by virtue of that question and that decision, this young guy was in that seat. We got hit by a suicide bomber that day and he died in that seat that he chose. Just bad luck, if it wasn't him, it would have been someone else. But I always remember him asking for that seat.

This is kind of a "no contact day" story. There was talk of getting that combat action badge. This means you get to wear a badge on your uniform if you were in combat and were in a gunfight. There was a bunch of criteria. It was trying to mimic the US Combat infantryman's badge. Terrible idea that never happened in the end. But now that there was a rumour, everyone wanted one, so people started trying to get in TICs; it was ridiculous. Folks that had no business doing it. The CIMIC teams had talked about going on a patrol with us. We said, okay, we're going to this village over here. Would you come? We know that they could benefit from you guys. Would you come out with us? And they said yes. So that we've set it up for the next day. And we got ready. We did our usual stuff. They showed up, and we noticed they showed up heavy. They brought C6s with them. They had two sections of SECFOR with them. C6 gunners had their C7s also. That's a lot more heavily armed than the battlegroup. These guys are the hearts and minds guys; why are they loaded for Bear? I can't even remember the village name. We just called it Fuck Town. We couldn't get near it We would come under heavy contact before we would get. Within 500 meters of it, and they said they wanted to go there. We reacted poorly; we didn't think they needed wells, and if we went there, we are in a fight. It was obvious the CIMIC guys wanted to get their guns on to get their badges before the end of the tour. The Officer said, OK, if there is a mission that CIMIC thinks there is and people need aid, we will go with them. We're all looking at each other, and we're grabbing more ammo; we know we're going out there and think this mission is bullshit. Our captain comes out, looks at us, and goes, "All right, boys. This is one of those days that brings us closer together," and then walks away. Those words are ingrained in my mind because we all stared at each other, and we started ditching water, ironically, and going with more ammo. We just knew it. So we started walking out, and I was third in order in March because I had decent control over the Afghans. There are two Afghans in front of me. We got within probably about five, 600 meters of the village and we heard that the CIMIC hadn't even fully left the camp yet… And they were already coming down with heat casualties, as they didn't do many dismounted patrols. I set up on one side behind this kind of little mud outcropping. My fire team partner set up on the other side. We were just kind of looking down. Next thing you know, we just see people on top of buildings waving flags. I look to the south and see vans, women, and children running away. Oh, no. We see about 5 to 6 heavy vans flying into the village, just full tilt. And we look at the captain and he goes, "Nope, let's get out of here." This is BG stuff, not OMLT and CIMIC. Yeah, thank fuck… And he's radioing back to confirm his call. No badges for CIMIC guys today.

We were in an extended TIC, and my Afghan fire team partner was not firing. I finally got the Afghan firing, then he stopped, and I told him to reload. Then I see he's reloading the only magazine he is issued, with a Ziploc bag full of ammo. Shit, Rounds started coming our way, another teammate bounded up to me, laid down the C6 and fired a belt, and then it just stopped. "Guys, I think I'm hit." There is still a firefight going on. We just all stopped and looked. What do you mean? Do you think you're hit? Something just doesn't feel right. He puts his hand down his plate and comes out with nothing on it. He goes, "Dude, I don't see anything. Feels all wet, though." And I'm like, Okay. I took off my gloves and put them down his chest. I go, "Dude, you're clear." And he looks at me and nods, "Okay, cool." So, he gets back up on the mound and just starts hammer at the enemy with a C6 down the way again. And we found out a little bit later that he took a PKM round straight to the centre of his plate. He just kept in the fight. He just needed to be sure that he wasn't going to die. His vest was all fucked up, and that is what "felt weird. "Crazy. How lucky is that? It is why we wear body armour.

The guys used to call me "bullet catcher" because I was always on point for our night patrols. I remember this patrol; we would bound as the Alpha security of the platoon. The platoon commander would have the UAV scan ahead of us, then the Sergeant would scan with the thermal weapon site, and we're talking the like, I don't know those Gen 1, it looks like a fucking camcorder on the top of his weapon but works phenomenal in Afghanistan. Just the atmosphere, the environment or whatever. It just it worked well. Then I would scan using the IR site so we covered the spectrum. Then we would move forward. I would step off into the dark night, and we get our spacing, and away we go. I remember getting up, getting out of the wadi, and moving into the open area, basically getting the spacing at about 5m. The moon was bright, so our NVGs were less useful, and then immediately, some rounds started kicking up around me. They seem so much louder in the stillness of the night. I hit the fucking dirt. I fucking didn't respond with a double top or anything like that because I could not locate the enemy, and I did not want to spray and pray. We had just passed through a rifle company and if we started a big fight, it is likely they would open up behind us we'd been in the middle of a goddamn crossfire. I remember hitting the ground and the guys thought that I got shot because I dropped so fast. I was basically down but was fine. I was in the open, so didn't want to draw more fire. There was a compound, and I just lay there, and every once in a while, the fucking Taliban would shoot a couple of rounds. That let my guys and the JTAC locate the enemy. But it sucked lying out there. I was a dark form on that white sand in the bright moonlight. After the target was identified, they eventually dropped hellfire on it. So, this is why they call me the bullet catcher. It was so strange, my first contact. I didn't fire back, but we still got the guy. I got up, and we went back to our routine and we carried on with the patrol towards our objective, like no big deal.

So, there were no buildings in the new strong point I was assigned, just a mound. The mound was just the obliterated Grape Hut, piled rubble that had been a Taliban position that had been dropped by a bomb and an assault from the company clearing; the coup de gras was the engineers loading up the structure with a bunch of C4 and blowing it up, so it could not be used again. Now it was my position to defend. The ground dominated approaches in the area and we would use it to control the territory. Whoever we had taken over from had already filled, I'm sure, thousands of sandbags. We got there, we did a quick handover with the outgoing guys. I immediately gave tasks for improving the position. With how poorly the protection was on the ground, I recognized that if we did get hit here, we're essentially just fighting from our LAVs, which was not ideal as it doesn't maximise the Platoon's firepower. I wanted to improve each section's position on the greater position. I gave tasks for improving the position. One of the lines in my orders though was that we wear PPE during the construction of the position. This is a normal part of Defensive routine in training, but the reality is that we hadn't been in this type of situation since Korea. We had been under lots of direct and indirect fire. So, I wasn't going to fuck around. A master corporal disagreed with me on the dress state. I was not prepared for a master corporal to actually challenge me on the protective dress. But people under stress, physical and psychological will react in different ways. I didn't blow up, I just got on with it. He said, "It's so hot. We're not going be able to fill as many sandbags." I said, "I'll have a pretty good idea because I'll be I'll be doing it with you." We all got to work. If you weren't behind the sights of a gun, you were sandbagging. We built sandbag walls to cover from fire. And we built a hump of sand underneath the LAV because we recognized that as I looked back at our position from the enemy vantage points that there were vulnerabilities. Something that stood out was the slanted belly of the LAV. If I was going to fire an RPG. I'd aim it right at that front of the belly and hopefully have it ricochet right underneath the LAV and into where the sections are sleeping or doing admin behind. We built a speed bump and sandbags underneath the LAV. So LAV sat on top of the little platform so that if somebody did fire, it would run into the sandbags underneath the LAV. Clearance patrols. Non predictable clearance patrols at different times, both east and West of the position. Our north and south approaches were covered off by other platoons. I figured the West was where the biggest threat was. We actually found what I believe to be aiming markers to the east of the position. I remember one of the soldiers saying, I'm going to go and knock those sticks down. I said, don't knock those sticks down. Leave those sticks there. We'll shoot a bearing back to the position. I will go lay the guns on that bearing, and as soon as we are in contact, we should know exactly where they're firing from. We settled into a routine, the bitching became less, and the soldiers grew in confidence with the work. It was hard and hot. The first few days were kind of uneventful. We had to do our first patrol with the Afghan army. We went in one night to the location, and it turned out to be a mosque. I didn't realize what the building was, I thought it was their HQ. I offered the Commander a backwoods cigar. Because I had seen him smoking. He was a little bit insulted that I was gonna smoke within the mosque. I apologized profusely, and we got back on track; he took the cigar later outside as a peace offering. So, once we got that issue out of the way, then we took the Russian series topo map turned it over and used it to sketch out how I thought we should conduct a patrol the next day together. We're going to push for about a kilometre max out to a group of buildings and we're going to search it. It was hard going; the units did not know each other, this was new territory at the time, and there was limited trust. So, there was a lot of back and forth. No surprise, we didn't speak the same language, we had not fought together before, and if something did happen, we would have to count on each other and hopefully not shoot one another by mistake. In the end, we managed to hash out a plan that was agreeable to all. It was basically a show to demonstrate that we can work together. The Afghans drove off and then we loaded up in our LAVs. As my lead section reverses back out onto the trail, there is a massive explosion. And I was maybe 100 meters from them. The force of it was incredible, and I was surprised the LAV was still there. Lots of dust. IED contact. Fuck. One soldier was knocked down and was pretty shaken, but there was no penetration on the hull of the LAV. Everybody essentially walked away. It was a big blast. The medic wanted everybody in the section to go back up to Wilson for observation. I was down a section for the next 24 hours. We headed back to the strong point, and the CO, the district leader, and the Regimental Historian were out to see what we were up to. I had been asked to do an interview with the historian. This is my number one regret, maybe in my career. I did that interview. This would not normally have been a problem because my platoon 2IC could have taken over to do all the necessary things the platoon needed while they re-occupied the position. He was in the vehicle that had been hit and was up at Wilson getting checked out medically. So, no one was doing the walk around, confirming dress states, who was watching what guns, schedule etc, just coordinate that defensive position. I wasn't doing any of that as I was in the interview. We had just come back to the position we'd been out all morning. The guys were tired probably really hot. Over the radio came a warning about the potential for an attack. There was always a warning, and so this did not seem out of place, but the district chief, who had just been on his cell phone, was really eager to leave. What he kept saying, "must go now. I must go now." He's telling the CO like go, go…They get back in their vehicles and they left. I was about to get back to the business of platoon commanding and checking out the position. We then got a more detailed internal report stating that our position was going to be attacked. It was two minutes too late. One of the soldiers handing me the headset so I could listen to the report come in. That's when kind of all hell broke loose. There was not much noise, but the ground seemed to be like popping everywhere as the rounds hit the road right in front of us. All that dust was being thrown up. Fine dust spreading over everything like, talcum powder, it was obscuring our observation. I immediately wanted to get some fire back. I think we paused because we were in a little bit of shock. It didn't take long for the guys to switch on and the turret to start returning fire with twenty-five and COAX. A brand-new corporal and his partner ran forward with the C6, I remember placing them behind this small sandbag wall to return fire to the West and immediately the volume of fire returning at the three of us was increasing and showed us that this is bigger and the enemy is closer than we thought. I ran to my LAV. The route there was pretty much all under cover because of all the sandbagging that we had done. I jumped in the back and we tried to get some sort of fire support going. I tried to get the best target indication I could but it was rushed and it was terrible. The battery commander happened to be just up the road and corrected my shitty call for fire... Lucky for us. When asked for more precise grids, I said just hit everything west of us. In retrospect, I knew at the time, as soon as it came out of my mouth that that was not going to work. It was how I felt, not what I should have been doing. The Company 2IC talked me down, I got the fire mission sorted and be good for three seconds later the Battery Commander came over the net and said that he was going to control all fires. Thank fuck. It was one less thing I had to worry about. Reports from the sections started to come in, I got the word that a section had just been hit by an RPG and they had two VSA and a number of wounded. I immediately thought, how do you know? How do they know their VSA? we don't have a doc and that they needed more medical supplies, they needed resupply: fuck I realised my 2ICs not here. All the Sgts are now fighting their sections and they are saying that they had lost comms with the OP. I needed to get out of my HQ LAV, get to the sections and get an appreciation of what was going on. As the 2 IC wasn't on the ground, I would resupply them while I gained awareness of where I needed to be in the fight. I just assumed that there was a casualty in the OPs. So I took the medic. I forget her name, I remember she seemed really small, but was awesome and gave great care to the guys. We had not finished sandbagging to protect the mortar position and the OP so we had to cross open ground. I remember looking up over at the O.P. and thinking like there is no way whoever is in there is alive. it is just shredded. You know, there was a little bit of sun protection on top that had been ripped off. You could tell the blast had ripped apart many of the sandbags. I just assumed whoever it was dead. I yelled out a few times, as we're still under a significant amount of fire. I remember thinking eventually the fucking Taliban gotta fuckin run out of bullets because they have been firing for a minute and a half at this point. I called out to the OP and nothing and first, and then somebody responded and it was a 21 year old Private, from the inside of this destroyed position. He had been in the OP. I asked, "Are you all right?" And he said, Yeah, I'm fine. Then he just had popped up and he fired a C6 to the west. He was still in the fight. I need to go through that OP to get to the other side, that position in order to get the medic there and the extra rounds of ammunition. The enemy is still like raking the position. I knew I was going to have to run. I looked at the medic and I said, I can't really, spare you right now or afford you to get hit because as we went open across open ground, so give me your medical bag. Later I would I got chewed out by senior medic as I took the medics bag instead of taking the medic. But to me, I thought to keep the medic central and alive, I only had one. Regardless I made that call. I asked the Private in the OP to provide me some supporting fire. And he did. He popped up firing until I was in the OP to give him ammo and med support. I mad eit, it is something to sprint out under fire and do it consciously, I was scared shitless. I looked around and the place was a mess. There were three M 72 tubes that he had fired. He was keeping his arcs both east and west. He had a C 9 setup facing to the east and then firing back to the west with the C6 that was in the O.P. at all times. I remember thinking like, this kid's impressive. I said, "you're doing great, but I need you to keep going." He said something to the effect, "then you need to bring me more ammo." My 2 IC had decided to self-deploy back down to get into the fight. The section up in Wilson punched out and my 2IC was making his way down to do resupply and got hit enroute from an Enemy cut off team about 200 to 300 meters north. He had the vehicle drop the ramp, ran out and then covered the rest of the distance on foot. He is probably not going to be the fastest mover and he was coming from the north, running through what was left of some of the grape fields, where we had set up trip flares, he managed to set off every single trip flare we had set and did not use the running password. He just said, "it's the Warrant. Don't shoot. It's the Warrant. Don't shoot!" I was glad to have him back, it was incredibly brave. That would have been the first time I'd ever seen our soldiers, dead. It was a bit of a shock, like I could not believe it. I even quickly checked one of them for my own sake and it was clear that he was gone and the other soldier was slumped in the back of the LAV. I remember slipping in his blood because he'd been hit in the neck by the same shrapnel from the same. RPG, that hit the LAV and then we're thinking Why are these air sentry hatches not closed? That probably could've saved at least one of their lives. That's when I go back to doing the interview, I think that had I been doing my job, I would have gone around and probably seen air sentry hatches because it had been something we've been harping about. I get snapped back into reality. The Master Corporal that took over indicated that he needed more ammo. I remember. Saying that they get the casualties out of the way cover them up and then just keep what's left of the section fighting at the wall. I ran back up through the OP where the Private kept firing, got a couple cans of C6. The 2IC was back on the position and he said he wanted to go and do his job o the resupply. The enemy fire was subsiding but had not stopped. I remember thinking like, I know the way, I'm gonna be fastest. I'm going to go, give me two soldier soldiers to carry the ammo my perspective, that was the critical point of influence. That's where I need to be. Retrospectively That wasn't the case. I was dead wrong. It was something he was not happy with and he's right. That was his job. Ammo resupply, casualty handling, all that right. I knew he was close with one of the members that had been killed, and I also didn't want him to see that. No excuses, I was wrong. Regardless we delivered ammo to OP, and back to the section. I told them to cover up the casualties. What they had available to do that were air mattresses, those self-inflatable air mattresses. So, they had thrown their mattresses over them, when I got back, it was really ridiculous seeing these two dead soldiers with these air mattresses balancing on top of them. So, we--- myself and the two soldiers, two young reservists, loaded up the casualties in body bags and we would evacuate the casualties in a LAV that was enroute with the QRF. The Bison Amb had some type of issue and the wheel had fallen off. Other than two killed, we had four wounded so that we knew at that time, we didn't really have a choice. I had to evacuate the dead in the back of the LAV with the wounded, which is something you don't want to do. And I can't imagine what a terrible ride up it was for those guys to back to Wilson. A dead buddy next to them. And then I ran back over to the other side. There was a moment where a soldier manning a gun watched us load the bodies and the wounded into the LAV. He asked who it was, I told him. It was his best friend; they had done all their training together and were roommates back in Canada. He just found out that his best friend was killed. He just went back to work. The professionalism of the guys was humbling. The firing stopped, the enemy withdrew, and we had to send out clearance patrols; I was exhausted. I was emotional, the leaders were amazing with me. My Warrant Officer was pissed, but he understood why I had made the calls I did, and we worked to put the platoon together again. I learned that time improving a position is never wasted, I learned you stand firm on protective dress states, I learned you needed to be accurate when calling for fire, I learned that you take the medic and not the med bag, I learned that you let the Warrant Officer do his job, I learned that my soldiers are professional and when the fight is on they will respond. I learned a lot in my first contact.

We were patrolling through this area that had well-known Taliban activity. I looked back and I remember telling everybody to watch their spacing. As I turned around, there was a long burst of machine gun fire, and it kicked up dirt by my feet. I was like, holy shit. I just reacted. To me, everything, time and space, like, slow down. Weapon up. Yell to move to the left, my fire team partner shifts, and I just started firing. As we were stretched out in loose file the platoon behind me had no concept of what was going on. because they had no fucking concept of what the hell was going on. I started firing, and I just remember thinking, like in the fucking open, and I can't stay here as I could feel the rounds going by my head. I am frozen, with the smallest bit of cover, and I can feel the rounds being walked onto me. Dirt and rock bouncing up around my feet. I'm going to fucking die here, and there's no fucking cover. I remember firing. I remember stopping and looking back and I didn't see anybody. When I yelled "contact," and they all took cover. We were canalized by the terrain so no one could move up. I was isolated. I had the radio on, and I was yelling like a motherfucker; I couldn't fight my way to the wadis, so I just fucking "hail Mary'd" it. I just turned and ran into the fucking wadi. I jump in there and in water past my knees in this fucking mud rand rounds are still coming in, fuck. I'm down, and I'm like, OK, like, what are we going to fucking do here? I can't fucking cower here and fucking like die. I am sure the troops are all looking at me and thinking He's cowering in this fucking ditch. We got to fucking fight back. So, I remember fucking sticking my head up and just start fucking returning fire. We're gonna overrun them with superior firepower. It's not a brilliant plan, but winning the firefight is a step we are supposed to take, so I am comfortable with my choice. I could feel the rounds going by my head, and I remember looking back, and I finally started to see the guys get into this action. "Get the fuck up here." I'm like, start laying down the law. Look where you're going, and don't Shoot me!" They are bounding up, and I finally get a C9 LMG in the trench next to me. Then we just started laying down good fire. That seemed to quieten the Enemy for a bit; they weren't too keen on bullets coming at them. Now we need to extract; I couldn't get the platoon commander on the fucking 521 radio; we had to get back to the platoon. Because it was a canalizing alleyway, we did an Aussie peel back to break contact back. When you let loose on that it is a lot of firepower. We linked up with the platoon and the Platoon Commander had brought forward the Leo's. Those beasts rolled forward and decimated that Taliban section. All fucking good with me, don't fuck with a 120mm gun! What remember most was trying to get the troops to fire the first time. Like they were going to get in trouble and I remember yelling at people, I was literally like pushing people, kicking people in the ass to fire. Once they realised, I was firing because I was getting shot it, it all came together but that first time young troops are nervous. The adrenaline was so strong I felt sick. I did get sick but I felt like, oh my God, I am exhausted. You need to figure out the adrenaline dump. We were all like gelatine when it was over. There's nothing to us, just limp.

Here's a story for you. This is this is one that's been kind of sticks with me, and it's taken me a long time to be able to discuss it. I continue to process and it's not I'm not sure I want to attribute it. I think those guys who were there know and I think it is important for other soldiers to know that this happens.

I was a LAV gunner and I couldn't fire the first time I was in contact. I didn't fire the cannon. My first time in combat, I froze under pressure. That kind of stuck with me for a while. August 26, the first time I got shot at. I was a last-second replacement due to someone getting in an accident. I did not do any work up training or integration due to other tasks that needed to be filled but had the right qualifications. The company had already deployed, and I caught up with them when they had a couple of weeks in theatre. I literally had not been in a LAV Turret since the course, two months prior. I show up at PBW and we first come across one of the maintainers and this guy has fucking thousand-yard stare and is just scary, like he just like so fucked up and he is telling me that we get hit in the evening and he is saying "hey...you know we usually get mortared in the evening and in the morning most days but not all days."

It's the evening and I'm thinking, fuck… what are you doing here?" We settle in and are waiting for it but we do not get mortared that evening. And then the next morning woke up to getting mortared... And this is fucking real...someone just shot at us. So, I am ramped up a little, this is a big change and I still do not have a unit yet, I am kind of bouncing around trying to find a slot as a replacement. A Master Corporal grabs me and says that I am joining this platoon for a patrol later that day. I can't remember the turret drills and before we go out, sit in a LAV turret and go through the drills. I had not touched the system in a couple of months because I was a replacement, and I needed to get confident now that I thought I was actually going to have to shoot the cannon. The last time I was in Afghanistan in Kabul, there was no shooting the cannon, this was different and I knew it after we got mortared. After I kind of went through just the basic drills with the Master Corporal and a 15-minute refresh on how the cannon works, I get told that we are going on patrol.

So, you got to do it the first time sometime. It figures that for the first time I'm a gunner since the course, I'm getting shot at. I remember, going through and kind of scanning. It's kind of like you really fall back on the training like, you know, crew commander puts you onto whatever target there is. You fucking shoot the guy, you know. Next target, next target. Whereas the expectation was that I was authorized to be wasting people that are shooting at us. The Crew Commander is on top of the turret with the Pintle-mounted machine. He can shoot bad guys that are closer than what the cannon can see or depress onto. We are driving, and all of a sudden, there is a whole lot of yelling on the radio, and things are bouncing off the turret, and we are under effective fire in an ambush. He's telling me to shoot. I am telling him to put me on the target. (place the gun on the target as per training). I am too slow in following the drills as per the textbook. I don't even know what I am doing here. I think I remember seeing the Taliban through the thermal site. You know, I remember seeing thinking I saw some muzzle flash, but not really knowing if there was a muzzle flash. I was just really hesitating about taking a life. This whole thing is playing out in real-time for the dudes in the back on CSAM. So, they know I did not fire. We got through the ambush, and when we got back to camp, people were on me for not having not fired a shot.

"Why the fuck didn't you shoot, man?"

I was defensive and said I was waiting for orders. I wanted the crew commander to put me onto targets, like they did on the course. I think that first time I needed the shared responsibility. That's not how I did it on the course. There was some trust lost immediately in the team. People were saying, fuck…first time I froze in combat. That kind of weighed on me. It bothered me for a few days because, especially, guys talk, right? We had to go back in Kandahar Airfield. I got moved out of that platoon and into the Company HQ; the LAV Captain talked to me about freezing under fire and asked if I could be good to go next time out. If I could do what was needed. I said yes, and he trusted me.

We rolled out again and we got "bumped" by the Taliban along the highway and I had to kill a couple of guys there. The guys in the back saw me acquire targets and fire without hesitation. Then you realize you are a killer. You have taken human life. It is such an odd feeling, and for me the motivations were that I had failed, I was angry because people were trying to kill me, and I needed to not fail my team again. You know, so I had the validation from everyone around me and I was like, OK, you know what? I can do this. I needed to hear that I was good to go, that my reputation as a soldier and a man was intact.

In the end, I ended up getting a lot of combat experience. But that first "failure" was hard to shake. The whole thing, it took me some time to process it. The moment of truth. Well, we are 15 years down the road. You know, it's taken it's taking quite a bit of time to process. Well, what do you expect? You take a 21-year-old soldier, put him in a crazy situation and he considers the process of killing? You know, if it's like if the worst if the worst anyone's got say about me is that I hesitated taking human life, that I thought about it and followed the commands we had been given?

Well, that's OK. Maybe that's not a bad thing. I think it would have been different if someone on that patrol had gotten hurt. I think that would have stuck with me more, but just by luck of the draw, we kind of made it through that TIC without any of our own guys getting hurt. Combat is actually a learned skill. It's not one of those things where you have it or you don't. Having dealt with the shame and embarrassment of "freezing" and then over the course of the tour becoming quite confident in my ability through a large number of TICS, I can honestly say that by the end of it I was settled and very, very effective in combat. Shaky off the start but I got good at it. Which in of itself is odd as that means that I became better at engaging and killing humans. Odd what a positive is in that world.

I think it is important to tell this type of story; "I've been frozen up before, I got through it and was able to do my job." Or "Leaders demonstrated a bit of compassion and a bit of respect, and it allowed me to stay in the fight." As I developed as a leader, I would use my failing as a teaching point, an important perspective of reflection for the next generation and I think it is important to demonstrate vulnerability and that you can be resilient and persevere through adversity.

The first time we came under contact, we didn't even know we were being shot at. How could that happen? Well, it is possible. We were moving in a small convoy of two LAVS with skeleton crews. Moving down the Highway in Kandahar, the LAV behind us got hit by a VBIED. I remember watching movies and thinking, bullshit, that's not what an explosion looks like. That proved wrong in that particular moment because I remember, like some cheesy actual an action movie, this massive, like 2-story high fireball. The LAV just pushed through it like something out of Terminator 2 or Mad Max. I was like 75 m away in the family hatch looking back at it, I felt the overpressure and the extreme heat. The feeling of my ceramic plate compressing on my chest and taking my breath away. I was worried at that point because once they came through, you heard screaming, and it sounded like somebody had died. But really, when it happens, all the guys in the back, they're temporarily deaf. So, you had these 10 guys in this vehicle all yelling back and forth to each other. Are you OK? Are you OK? All yelling at the same time. As they came up to us, it sounded like there was one person yelling like he was dying. It's funny- afterward. The Crew Commander took a piece of shrapnel through his right forearm because he had it up outside the hatch. I hopped out to help with first aid… So he took care of that as he was doing that. The wounded Crew Commander came on the radio he was very calm. "0 this is XX. We have been hit by a VBIED, and I have a piece of shrapnel in my arm; we're punching through; we will not secure the scene as we do not have the forces, and we will require medical attention, over." Like there's this is calm. We just punched out of there. We linked up with guys from the PRT and went into CNS. We did a quick after-action and got the attention that we needed. When we looked around the vehicle, there were two chunks of human flesh on the LAV from the suicide bomber. Seven of the eight tires were blown. Some of the upper panelling was blown off. The driver had some soft tissue injury to his right shoulder from the blast. We looked at the LAVs. There were bullet holes and different markings that were the strikes. Were there some strange scratches on it, too, that we later found out were from the fins of an RPG spinning along the side. We were so focused on the SVBIED that we didn't even realize we were under contract; it must have all happened simultaneously. How could we have missed it? ignorance was definitely bliss at that point. Then we crashed just on the crushed gravel of CNS. The adrenaline dump was huge.

All of a sudden, I heard "RPG!" but it was actually an 82-millimetre recoilless that went through the side of the carrier behind the crew commander's legs, through the ammo bin, ricocheted off the wall, bounced by my head, and the round itself didn't actually go off. It embedded itself in the hull behind the signaller that I had just been leaning towards, half asleep. I just happened to sit up at that point time and it hit right beside me. Then, in the darkness of the LAV, I hear, "I'm hit," "I got it in the legs." My legs are soaked and warm; they are all gooey. I turned on my light. Buddy, you're good. It's shaving cream; it exploded on you and covered you; you are fine. Stop fucking around. Pretty lucky that night.

We were near Nakahonay, working with the tank squadron and living out for about the first month away from our company, where the platoon had its first incident. One of our drivers lost his leg. When the blast occurred, you heard it and then could feel the concussion of the blast in your chest. You could see the tire of the vehicle, which weighs a couple of hundred pounds, go airborne. I was immediately into the action with the wounded and the vehicle; the adrenaline kicks in, and you want your drills to be correct. And you're also thinking about other threats right after the blast, siting the PZ. You need to ensure that the situation doesn't get worse because of secondary devices in the area or if the enemy hits you with an ambush simultaneously. You hear your wounded, you know there is trauma, but you need to slow down, right at that moment. Even though everything is telling you to speed up. Rushing could take a bad situation and make it catastrophic. That's what the platoon grew up. The drills were not just a routine, they were going to save lives. Siting the Casualty Collection Point (CCP), we established security, ensuring recovery of the vehicle and clear the space for the MEDEVAC chopper could land, ensuring there was no more devices that would hit the chopper. While we were doing this doing that, we secured the casualty and provided treatment, including initial pain meds. The injured driver was lying on a stretcher in the CCP under the watchful eye of our medic. There were people coming and going out of the scene and this dude on the stretcher reached into the pouch of an NCO and got a hold of a satellite phone, that was present for emergency communications should radios fail! He called his mom to tell her that he was injured. We were so busy that we didn't notice and here is this guy missing a leg, high on pain killers calling his mom while we are still in the situation! I look over and he is on the phone. So I took the phone away as he was speaking to his family, I had to talk to them, explain he is OK and then hang up so we could treat him properly. This was not something that had been in the drills, and was something new, who would have thought that once the drugs hit and he was waiting for the chopper with his injury so bad that he would try and call home! The war was different, technology brought it so much closer. I finally got a chance to pause, and I looked at the wounded soldier on the stretcher, and he looked me in the eyes, and that's when I got a little bit emotional. He looks up and says, "Hey, Warrant Officer, I made it!" Then he said again, "I made it. I didn't die." When I looked at him, I knew he was going to lose his leg, I knew that because of the way it was twisted, but his adrenaline was going and the drugs had kicked in. Incredible, like he was releasing me from any guilt of him being hurt. In that moment he knew he had lived and he was happy.

––––––––––

We pulled into a Laager, and after we were set, I wanted to see what had happened on an IED strike we had had that day. The UAV had caught video of the blast, and so we could review what had happened and what we did and learn from it. I don't think that has happened in any other war. We got called over to the Golf (Artillery) call sign to look at the footage, and the way her vehicle was positioned, she asked us, myself, the platoon commander, and section commanders, to get down into a foxhole instead of standing at the back of an LAV. Just as we got settled to watch the footage and learn from the incident, a rocket-propelled grenade came in, and BAM hit right where we had been standing. One of my sergeants immediately said, "I think I shit my pants" We started laughing, and just about died; a guy shits his pants, all funny stuff. It was a pretty full first patrol between the IED strike that day and then the RPG. All you can do is laugh at it. We would be back into it tomorrow.

––––––––––

I went into the TOC, the tactical operation centre in this place; it's like a theatre, all the big screens and maps and everything up there. I think it was my first full day there, and the relief in place was going on with the other Battle Group. One of the Patricia Callsigns hit an IED. These guys were on their way back to Canada within a day or two, and one of them died. The Sergeant who died was from my hometown, and we had been on a course together about 7 months before. When I met him, I was in the back of his career. He was a good dude, and he was telling us about his previous tours in Afghanistan. How he caught shrapnel in his hand from a grenade he had thrown in a room while clearing it. I mean, this guy died on his last day in theatre. I saw the effects of the war. Then I just saw the amount of shit that the Ops O and the Ops team did, everything from coordinating airstrikes to managing troops under contact. I thought, my God, how am I going to learn all this stuff? It was overwhelmingly, just overwhelming. The stress of being in theatre and being a new guy was a rough start when we had to manage the death right away. Everything was sensory overload. You don't have time to think or feel nervous. You don't really have time to adjust. You just adjust, or you fail, and people could get hurt or killed.

I was a LAV gunner. I know for everybody that first time, that first contact it was still surreal. We were moving past this Village, one that had never had any incident and had been quiet for months, according to the outgoing BG and all of a sudden, they were shooting RPGs at us. It had been very quiet in March, and it was just like one day, they hit the switch. and it was game on, and it was game on until the end of September, like 4 months later. We turned South off Hwy 1, and it was like we hit their OP Screen. They observed us, and then they fucking hit us with RPG fire. We'd gotten maybe half the combat team off the highway. Yeah. And that's when the RPGs start coming in and they start firing them in volleys, think they were kind of outside of their effective range and I think they were ineffective. But it was a wake-up call. That first time, we could not identify any targets in the green belt or amongst all the buildings; it kind of just surprised us, you know, like someone is trying to kill you, it is not just training. The rounds were harmless, but the message wasn't. After that time, we started making ourselves a hard target and got real serious about identifying teams that could do us harm. It is a real mind-shift to go from "riding" in the turret to truly scanning for targets and going through the engagement process.

Sometimes you just get surprised and run into the Taliban. I was a new Afghan mentor and had only been in the country for a couple of weeks. I was part of an ANP team patrolling through compounds. I hopped over some walls and turned hard left, then turned right to confuse anyone watching us, and we stumbled onto the Taliban setting up a linear ambush. Total surprise to both sides. Things are immediately chaotic. Rounds are popping off everywhere; the sound is close, but I don't feel or see the impact. There are high walls surrounding so my line of sight is limited. I move forward, trying to figure out what is going on. We're in a gunfight, so it is just a reaction; I am not thinking clearly now. I take cover by a little tree around me; branches start to get snapped off by bullets. That's inbound, time to move or figure out how to stop the shooting coming at me. There are five to eight fighters that are engaging us. We have a whole platoon worth of Afghans and six Canadians rolling up on them. The Afghans are moving fast and are starting to converge. There is a real danger that they will shoot each other if we don't get a grip on them. I need to get his guys to stop firing on one flank and hold so we can push forward. I can't find my terp. I went forward when we came under contact, and he went sideways. We are split by the walls and channelled by terrain. I move up, start drawing the problem in the dirt, and motion toward his troops. The platoon commander is a smart guy and gets it pretty quickly. He holds up the guys. We rolled through the objective, and the Afghans killed the Taliban. It was amazing that after working together for a short period, two organizations that do not speak the same language, have never worked together and have different training were able to respond to a chance enemy ambush so effectively. There are lots of stories of the Afghans not responding well, I think we need to reflect on what they did well, how hard it actually is and the level of trust required to do it.

———————

We were still in the block position. As we're peeling off, I was last in the order of march and had one guy with an AK come around the corner, like 5-10m away. I let loose almost the whole box of my C9 down that roadway. Nobody else popped their head around the corner. But we didn't go see if we killed him. We just moved back to the platoon.

———————

My first real contact was a day long. It was a shitshow. We were told the Taliban had aggregated in an area of Pashmul, which is across the River in Zhari, North of Bazaari Panjawaii and had dug in and that there were 600 to 800 fighters in the area. All the locals had left, and so the zone that we were attacking was a kill box. We had done prep fire and had engaged Taliban elements at a distance, but this was different; this was us closing in on them and engaging in a close fight. It was a deliberate movement to contact and a clearance of an objective.

At the last second, we decided to lift preparatory fires as higher ISR saw no enemy movement. I think the thought of our HQ was that our show of force was enough and they had left for Helmand. I remember the plan was we had to cross the Arghandab River, and the engineers were going to make a breach for us at the riverbank. The engineers were going to lead us, but the whole fucking road to the east of our objective, which was an old UN-built schoolhouse, was full of fucking IEDs.

We had no breaching equipment, just an engineer section in a LAV and a Zettlemeyer bulldozer thing. During the prep, we realized my fuckin HQ LAV was down with mechanical problems, and so my platoon was down to 3 LAVs and an electronic countermeasures (ECM) G-Wagon, a light-skinned jeep that was supposed to protect us by disrupting the channels that could set off the electronic detonation of IEDs. Funny we considered that, as most IEDs were pressure plates at the time and in an assault that wasn't even the biggest threat. Getting shot was. In hindsight, it was fucking stupid. But we didn't know, and hindsight fucks with us.

The ECM was mandated to be with us and seemed more important than direct fire protection and armour. We had built the IED bogeyman up in our heads, and this was our first time heading into this type of fight against an entrenched enemy, and we didn't know anything. We learned a lot really quickly. We didn't roll across with our guns suppressing the enemy - like doctrine would have told us to do, because we had orders that we had to see the enemy before we fired. We knew they were there, and we knew they were dug in.

It was silent as we crossed the river, except for the low growl of the diesel engines. It was fucking relaxed; maybe they had left? Nobody had seen fuck all, and because Recce was on the NIMROD crash, we had no ground recce assets forward. One of the platoon commanders had mentioned that he saw a kite flying across the river. It was taken in stride; perhaps that could be a warning, as the Taliban used kites to signal. Over the radio, somebody else mentioned they saw mirrors reflecting, another signal the Taliban used, but still so quiet. No confirmed enemy, so we didn't fire. We rolled forward, scanning for the threat, silently anticipating the next action, and hoping we were right.

On the riverbanks, the fucking marijuana fields and grass were so thick that we could not see anything at all. The marijuana was warm, and the thermals were shit and couldn't separate human heat signatures from the warm plants. We shook out in formation, and all of a sudden, I fucking heard a loud bang; not sure what it was, but I hadn't heard it before. It was not an RPG, and it was not an

IED. Then I heard some rounds go off, and you're trying to look out, and you're trying to get your fucking bearings, but you can't because the grass is so high and thick, and you realize that fire is just pouring out of that green mess at us.

We still can't see the enemy; we just feel the impact of rounds on our hulls, we start returning fire you and now I am trying to give a sitrep, a contact report. But the fucking comms went out, just dropped. No voice comms. I can't get anyone, and it is like a bad war movie, where the comms fail at a critical juncture and I can't talk to anyone, just when you need them, to create shared awareness so we can win this fight.

More explosions go off and there is a high volume of fire coming at us. It is disorienting, but the dudes are starting to respond and are starting to give as good as they were getting. Comms are out; a runner shows up from one of my sections to tell me the G-Wagons have been hit, and there are a couple of our guys down. We can't get a response from the engineer call sign because they are hit also. That bang was an SPG 9 that had penetrated the hull.

I was fucking frustrated. You know, everyone's just trying to default to their training. But the training wasn't this, right? The training was in open fields and pretty controlled. We were trying to fucking locate the enemy and right now that seems impossible. All the engineers were reported dead as the vehicle was a K-kill from the recoilless rifle and nobody was coming back from it. First reports are always wrong, and we figured out that the round went in through the neck ring and killed the sergeant. At this point, I knew I had a G-Wagon down. One of my LAVs was moving around and engaging the enemy and then they got hung up in a deep wadi, and so were trapped and immobile. Now things are looking pretty grim. My Warrant Officer's dead. The G-Wagon is blown up, medic is down wounded, the terps are down. My Engineer callsign is out of the fight and I still fucking can't see shit. I am really in a blender at this point. We're engaging to the front and to the flank. So that point, honestly, my thoughts were like, we need to pull back, we don't know the size of the enemy force we have hit, and I've got no comms with my HQ to get a picture of what's going on. Before this gets bad, we need to reset and retake the initiative.

We finally got a fucking separate radio going, my man pack. I just fucking threw it on and used that. I got comms with the boss and my assessment of the situation was, yeah, we could try and fight through whatever the fuck this is. But I was pretty sure if we did that, more people were going to get killed. I was 100 percent on that. They took the initiative and drew us into a knife fight. Because we just weren't able to meaningfully locate the enemy, to kill the enemy, essentially, we were just in a fucking grinder. I lost vehicles and the situation was deteriorating.

The Boss acknowledged. "Yep. Pullback."

So, you know, in some way, shape or form, how did you extract those vehicles? The engineer vehicle, the crew recovered from the strike and got it going, it comes limping back with its turret out of commission. We just start to pull vehicles off and bound back across the river… My other LAV that had been fighting hard, just smashing the enemy with cannon and coax fire, was still stuck and it wasn't going fucking anywhere. It was like a pillbox. The wheels were sunk into the gap and because we had no armoured breaching equipment, recovery, or tanks, complex recovery under fire was impossible. We would just lose the lives of our maintainers and their vehicles.

We ended up having to leave both a G-Wagon and a fucking LAV on position. The G-Wagon was a fucking catastrophic kill, and the LAV was a mobility kill. We did the drills to destroy the shit in the vehicles. The next part I remember quite well. We had to extract the bodies of our dead. It was shitty. We couldn't get to them until we secured the area and fight through the enemy to do so. At the same time, we needed to pull back to bring in artillery fire. I just wanted one fucking thing to get better because it was really going bad. I sent a rifle section back to where the Company was aggregating. It was just my signaller and myself left on the position.

"You go take a cover position and then once you're set off, I can join you."

Initially, we left the fallen in the vehicle. I made the decision. We would have to go get them once we had consolidated. So, I just fucking ran back and was essentially the last dude. I roll into the casualty collection point and started to count up what and who we had left. Our plan was to reattack, bring fire upon the position, kill what needs killing, take the position and recover our dead. We're still under direct contact in the consolidation position and firing with the enemy that seemed like forever. My sense of time. I don't know if it was 15 minutes or five hours. I just wanted to fucking get my guys in a position where they can take advantage of the situation, because up until that point, we didn't have one.

We were not in a position of advantage. We didn't follow doctrine and we are paying the price and the job is to get back in as quick as we can to take it to them. So, I run up to run up to the Boss's LAV, but fires were still coming in and just as I am approaching a 500 pounder fucking tumbled right in front of the fucking LAV!

Thank Fuck it was a fucking dud. If a five hundred pounder went off, we would have been fucked. I report, "the fucking CCP is set up. My platoon is presently off the objective. We're set up here and here. We're down to this many vehicles. Comms is intermittent. What are we doing?"

The call was to bring down as much fire on the objective and then reengage.

I start moving back to the CCP. As I'm running back, there was this fucking flash of heat. Slow motion. I was just standing there, and it was like a blow dryer. Just a plume of heat hit my face, but it did not push me down. I looked at the CCP and there was smoke and I was like, oh, Fuck no. The casualty collection point is where we took all the casualties for triage and the Sergeant Major and Platoon 2ICs administer the wounded to get them out and get resupply. It is a vulnerable spot and it getting hit by the Taliban was bad news. I went and everybody was down. I was like, fuck. What the fuck? A whole bunch of casualties at that point.

It had gone from bad to worse, obviously. Remember that simultaneous to this, other platoons are engaging the enemy and there is a fight outside of what I am doing. There is a lot going on. Now my task was to get the fucking hurt people somewhere to get care. American medics came out of nowhere. I don't know where the fuck the LAV Captain found them, but they are on the scene, it seemed immediately. Simultaneously with my arrival, these fucking US dudes showed up. I mean, they're checking bodies. I went to assist, and the Doc said he's dead. I was like, fuck. That was my first dead friend.

Simultaneously, the other platoon has found a route to our destroyed G-Wagon. The other platoon commander is taking his platoon to retrieve the bodies of my guys forward. So, me and this other dude that survived the strike on the CCP, grab the fallen to extract them and the wounded.

I say, "Help me, grab him, We're going to bring him to the bison over there and load him the LAV." The troop is teary eyed, like, fuck, he survived, and he just watched people die. He did the job I asked and moved the bodies. It's fucking hard to drag a dead body under fire. Then pick it up and put it onto the back of a vehicle. It is not like how we practice, because a guy that's alive will help you a little so he doesn't get hurt, but a dead body is well, just different.

Then we go back for the second K.I.A. He looked white because of all the blood he had lost and his face seemed to change shape. I didn't recognize him, though I had known him for years. Second body, dragging him back was fucking hard. Like it was the hardest fucking PT you have ever done. Like the adrenalin was there, but moving those bodies exhausted me. By this point, we've been running all day. I don't know if I ever fucking had any water. I've been just bouncing around trying to do the right thing. Whatever the fuck that is.

As we were organising to get people off the position, I put my rifle on the bench of the vehicle, the walking wounded are getting in and we are fitting as many people as you can. We load it and want to get them out of there. Then I see my rifle. I had had a mind fuck and left it under some wounded guy fucking lying down on a stretcher. You know, I know there's always that mantra, you know, never, never leave your rifle. The LAV was a clown car of wounded. It was impossible to unload, and the enemy fire was not going away. I was wrong, but I didn't give a fuck. I had other shit to do. I just wanted those guys to ramp up, get the fuck out. So that's exactly what happened.

I told the crew commander: "Fucking head out." So, there I am and all I have is my fucking pistol. That's all I got. It's all good. The other platoon has made its way back, covering fire is going down range and we figured out the Sergeant Major was wounded when the CCP was hit and had been evacuated. People just stood up and took over without being told. This one NCO had a reputation for being a real negative guy. Sometimes he is. But I tell you what. Like when push comes to shove, when you need that guy, he's fucking incredible. If there was anything that I learned on this day, it was that like our NCO corps is incredibly professional and when things go to shit, they get the job done.

We moved off of the fighting area into the into the Arghandab riverbed in an all round defence. I remember planes were coming in, and attack 'copters. They were just fucking levelling the place. Just everything we could throw at it, just hitting it. Explosions, plumes of smoke were going out. We had a moment to breathe and have a smoke. There were piles of rifles near where the wounded were evacuated. You know what I was doing in the all-around defence? I was looking for my fucking rifle, I felt ashamed I had let it go. One of the NCO's said, don't sweat it, just pick up a fucking random rifle, we will sort it later.

Everything slowed down. I saw the body bags. The other platoon had brought my guys back to me. I had bagged and loaded their guys. So fucked up. I wanted to see, I wanted to see the people that had been my friends. I remember going to unzip the bag and the acting Sergeant Major said, "you don't need to do that."

So, I didn't. I would have time to say good-bye to him later. We had to get ready to go back to re-hit the objective. We learned a lot in one day, the time to mourn wasn't now, it would come, I was so mad. For the first time in my life, I knew I wanted to kill those people that had done this to my friends.

Generation Kill, the book, had just come out. I remember the quote that combat is like "petting a burning dog." I remember writing in the margins that I agreed; going out, getting in contact, and then coming back without a scratch on us was like we were petting a burning dog. Eventually, we're going to get burned or bitten. So, we were on this Op as the POMLT. We did all the searches as we were police, and by this point in the War, the BG needed to have an "Afghan Face," so that meant we went in first. We were searching buildings. I was located in a cut-off position and heard a huge explosion; all I saw was smoke, which I knew was not good. My buddy had stepped in the doorway and triggered a pressure plate IED. The rudimentary device, a sawblade, was buried and connected to the explosive; when he stepped on it, the pressure touched the blades together and completed the circuit. I moved to the location, and he and the other casualties were getting packaged up; he had lost three limbs. I think he was the first triple amputee to survive. As I got him on the chopper, he asked for a cigarette with his only good working hand. Seeing his ability to joke around was amazing like he was making us feel better about what had happened. After we loaded him, I went to a position of overwatch and got ready for the expected probing that seemed to always occur after a strike. We could see motorcycles with men coming into the area and cars full of dudes. But we could not confirm weapons. We didn't have a proper PID and so could not engage. We knew who they were. It was very difficult for us, given the emotion of the day and the very real desire to make someone pay for what they did to our friend. We even talked about engaging but decided against it. Cooler heads prevailed. Our rules of engagement did not allow us to engage; it was legally the right thing to do, but morally, it hurt.

I remember there were some dudes digging in an IED. I was just into theatre and in the Command Post prior to a patrol, and the officers and operators in the CP did their thing and lined up CAS to strike the IED emplacement team. Super slick and calm. They maintained PID on the guys digging in with the camera from the observation balloon. The next thing you know, a jet flies over and drops its load, and there is a big explosion. The guy is still alive; we see it on the camera. We actually got to watch their evacuation procedure. There were three of them digging in two, were killed. This one guy stood up and was all messed up, he's still alive. Out of nowhere, other people come out. They grab him, they bring him to a school, very deliberate act because we're not gonna hit a school if we reattack. The next thing you know, a taxicab shows up. We're tracking this on the balloon. They throw the guy in a cab, and they're starting to do casualty evacuation, and they bring him to their hospital. En route, they were stopped by the POMLT and ANP because we were tracking on the radio and feeding the movements on it. We got the guy. It was interesting to watch the CP prosecute a target, follow on, then make a call not to shoot again and to observe how the TB did medevac and how they used a building that everyone knew we would not strike. The unblinking eye was able to track them and caught the guy who was laying IEDs. I was out doing the patrols, it was interesting to see how calculated this was, how hard it was to hide and how we could strike with great precision. The professional machine of humans, sensors and airborne strike platforms was impressive.

I was placed in a blocking position on the outer cordon to stop any Taliban from escaping the operational zone. I had only been in the theatre for about 2 weeks. So, we set up, and I remember seeing my first Taliban through the scope of my rifle. This is funny. I didn't shoot. We knew they were coming down the trail, and I remember going to the sergeant who was in charge of us and saying, "Hey, I see five guys with AK. They don't look like the Afghan army." He's trying to tell me. "No, no, no. They're Afghans. They're the army. They're the army. They're coming down." And I'm like, I don't think so they just don't give me that feel. I'm watching them the whole way. This is funny because you go through the things in your mind. I'm looking at them, I'm ranging them, I've clicked my scope in the right spot for the range. And I'm like, this is it. I just need the Sergeant to understand these dudes aren't ANA. Ironically, we never got a chance to engage because the enemy had moved outside of my observation and got opened up on by a couple of heavy machine guns that just started hammering the rooftop that we were on. We were not being able to identify the target properly, they got the drop on us. The training of double tapping some rounds dash down is not a thing when heavy fire is coming in. We just got down and couldn't get our head over the edge to observe; the volume of fire was so high. I remember taking cover behind this little wall and getting up and trying to find where the fire was coming from. I got tunnel vision. Another private saw that there was a threat and that the roof we were on was in the line of fire and so we had to get down. We get off the roof and the wall just gets pummelled by fire. I leapt down and end up doing the splits, just narrowly missing my nether regions with these big thorns and falling to the ground. We are under fire and my partner starts laughing out loud. He hops down and we are out of the direct line of fire. These Americans roll up, call sign Cowboy Five; they rolled up with their Humvees and formed a firing line so that we can pull off. We had to run through an open field and I was the last one to run through that field. It was like a frickin movie, with the rounds spitting up dust around me and the Americans yelling at us to hurry up so they could engage, because we were obviously in the line of fire. I was so pissed off that I hadn't shot a single round and all these guys were shooting at me. My dudes yell, "Get your fucking ass moving" and like, Fuck, I just want to fucking check out these enemy guys because they're coming pretty frickin close. It was pure adrenaline. I ran across the field and jumped in the wadi. This was dangerous as the enemy had IED'd the shit out of the Wadis. But we were lucky.

The US teams and the ANA suppressed the enemy and broke the contact. Our day was done; we didn't do much; we observed, misidentified, and ran away but at the end of the day, we felt like we were the cock of the roost, we SURVIVED… but we also did not fire a shot. We were a shit show tactically, but really it was two privates and a Master Corporal. We got better and quick! That first contact within the first week and then we had a contact every day after that. We learned how to shoot and move and survive by taking it to the enemy instead of letting him take it to us.

––––––––––––

There was no waste of time of us getting into TICs. Less than a week in the enemy was testing us. We lived in area in Western Panjawaii called Zangabad and were nicknamed TIC Platoon. It seemed every time we went out we got in some kind of firefight or got engaged by something. Nine times out of ten we were engaged, but very rarely would we get engaged when we went out at night. They liked to sleep and did not have good night vision, so we were pretty good at night, less the IED threat. They finally decided to hit our strong point in force; they hit us from three sides all at once. They shot two 82mm recoilless rifles and another RPG to open the attack, using HE to wake us up. No one got killed because we had reinforced the COPs defensive works. This RPG hit the tower. It was just a fluke. The way that RPG hit the shrapnel came straight down. Just shit luck and hit this kid, who's a reservist, in the back and the shoulder. We had a little medical thing set up in there, and they were the medic was taking care of him. The medic called the Nine Line. He thought it was a punctured lung. Holy fuck. I'm trying to call the 9liner in, and 400m to the North, the enemy was gathering at Rich Man's Compound. They were hitting us from two sides, East and west, and, in fact, setting us up for an assault. After I called 9 Liner, I started calling fire missions with artillery. It's all good. All preregistered targets. So, I call them whatever Zulu tango, whatever the nomenclature was. The rounds dropped a little short. So I gave my ad because it's very close, only 400m, danger close, so I made them like add one hundred meters, and the rounds and you feel the shrapnel from the 155mm hit the Hesco and the blast. Awfully loud and way too close. Well, the Fires Control Officer at the other end queries my original grids, and I realize, Fuck, the registered targets don't get passed on did not get passed on between the Battle Groups. I scrubbed the mission and started from scratch; I was lucky that I didn't kill us all! The enemy kept on pouring the fire into the COP and we are now getting approval for the fire mission. So, I'm firing the 60mm to try and keep the enemy back. I fired 68 rounds of 60 millimetres before they frigging would give authorization for artillery. We were continuing to be hit from three sides but were just doing enough that the enemy that was aggregating did not want to attack our position. The fight went on for an hour and 13 minutes. I remember that specifically. It felt like 5. The enemy decided that it was not worth the assault. Our casualty was stabilized, and we got a chopper in to evacuate him. It was a memorable start to the tour. They tested us right away.

During my first contact, a LAV had to be abandoned because it got caught up in a Grape field. The Platoon had taken a lot of casualties and had orders to withdraw. We were in an overwatch position with our LAV. When they moved out of the way, we started putting rounds into the area as the Taliban was trying to get in there to get stuff out of the vehicle. We just sat and picketed that vehicle all night long. Because the Taliban were coming out trying to get stuff out of it. They would climb up on the side or in the back; we just pump some more rounds into it and clean them off. They didn't know we could see them with thermal and hit them at 1600-1800m. We ensured they didn't get anything from the vehicle or could use anything as a trophy. When we went back in the next day to secure the vehicle and recover it, we could guarantee the enemy had not benefitted from anything inside, and they had lost about 6 dudes trying to get into it.

My first contact was quite violent and a long day. Oddly enough, I don't remember the morning. Not in detail. This is it's fucking weird. I don't remember waking up that day. I don't remember talking to anybody, having a cigarette or taking a shit or any of the routine things that happen in a day. What I do remember is being right in the centre of the fight. I remember the first rounds coming our way, the SPG 9s slamming into vehicles near us and all the near misses of RPGs and rounds sparking off the hull. Machine guns going, The LAVs finally opened up in response to the enemy fire and the radio crackling with direction. I am immediately transported to those moments of violence, but everything that surrounds those events is hazy. I don't know what happened. That's just something I've always sort of struggled with. What do I say to people about that morning?

"What the fuck happened?" they ask? I nod knowingly, but I have no idea.

People died; people were injured. People that I was close to. We killed people that were trying to kill us. It's hard to explain because people will tell me what I did. They are respectful and seem to believe that things I did under pressure were right and that I led well. But I just- I cannot for the fucking life of me remember what happened that morning. It's very frustrating. Something that I'm always trying to just remember. But there is nothing there. It's a void.

PART III
THE DAILY GRIND

SAND, SUICIDE BOMBERS, SPIDERS AND
SUCK-O-METERS

THE TOUR HAD THREE TIME MARKERS: the date of arrival, the home leave dates, and the final departure date. Between these signposts, the routine must reign. In developed camps, there was usually a gym, showers, and good food; later in the conflict, there was Wi-Fi. This allowed daily interaction with home, which was impossible during previous operations when communication was done through "snail mail" and the odd phone call if one was lucky.

Despite the best attempts to develop a routine, however, there was enough going on, that every day was anything but routine.

The environment was harsh, and the "crud," a common stomach ailment, ran rampant through soldiers out in the field. There were snakes, spiders, and scorpions to share space with. The human population was alien in both their appearance and their customs. Soldiers were told to connect with the Afghans but found it difficult to decipher friend from foe. When they did succeed at making a true connection, it was fleeting as the soldiers would move on, and the civilian populace would be left behind to face the Taliban on their own.

Once the excitement and lessons of the first month were complete, the necessary grind settled in.

The day-in and day-out routine of patrolling with 75 pounds strapped to your body, walking down that same road that needed to be secured every day. Dealing with an elusive enemy that at times seemed just a shadow. Finding or striking IEDs, saying goodbye to friends who got hurt or died, rapidly refocusing to get back in the fight, engaging in combat, sleeping, digging in and improving your camp, completing logistics tasks, endless conversations with village elders and the creation of whatever little traditions and routines allowed an escape from the dangerous monotony of month two to month six.

Soldiers outside the wire lived in close quarters—a section often lived in or around their vehicle, slept in shell scrapes, and did everything in pairs: ate, defecated, and cleaned weapons. Whenever you moved, you were never alone. The story of Afghanistan is not the headline-grabbing activities vaunted in the press; it is living the grind.

Understand the grind, and you will understand the soldier's experience in Afghanistan.

Afghanistan is the only place where I have shit my pants as an adult.

We created a suck-o-meter when we had to go live way out in west Panjawaii with the ANP to build checkpoints as a section. It wasn't bad for morale; it just acknowledged how we were feeling and the level of suck at the time. It was constructed from a ration box, with an arrow pinned to it like a kid's craft, that could be spun and indicate easy suck to terrible suck, but the starting point of understanding being that it all sucks. We used locations that we hated being in or areas that were dodgy to articulate our level of suck. It started with Wainwright suck as the lowest level, then Kabul suck, then Panjawaii suck, and then Nalgham suck, which is where we had our most TICs. The red line for the worst was Montreal Canadians suck, so when things were terrible, the arrow got pushed to point at Montreal Canadians suck, as we were all Maple Leaf fans, it made sense to us.

We received a contact call over the radio, and a team had shot a dude who was wearing a suicide vest. I am not sure if the team lead saw it or the guy went to attack and the device failed but regardless, he had popped him in the market square. The outer cordon was established, and the guy was assumed dead but with a device, so no one approached him. We got there quickly, and when we showed up, he was still moving and was not dead, so we had to put some more rounds into him until he was dead. I called ceasefire, and then all of a sudden, you realize your team has just killed someone; you just want to be right. It is very public, in the middle of a market in Zhari. We can't see the vest from that distance. We send in the robot to see if there is a device. The robot is shaking the body and using an arm to try and confirm the vest, so if it blows, we only lose the robot. The whole time I am thinking. Please let there be a vest. . . The brutality of the killing and then a robot bending limbs of the body, the sound of bones breaking was something I will never forget. Eventually, on the cameras of the robot, there it was a suicide vest. We had been right. I did not feel better about the kill, but I felt like the team(s) had responded to their training, and we had taken out a threat that was meant for us. The IED teams cleared the device; then, we needed to package the body for biometrics and return it to the community. That was the first dead body I had ever seen.

We roll into Kandahar as the first Canadian group since 2002. The convoys between Kabul and Kandahar were a big deal as Canada was leaving behind peacekeeping and getting involved in the war. I go into the TOC in Kandahar Airfield to check in. It is located in the TB Last Stand, a building that has a JDAM hole in the roof and was the HQ of the TB before the invasion. It looked impressive, there are huge wall maps of the area of operations, screens showing the locations of troops and feeds of drones scanning the desert for enemy activity. It was quiet, calm, and professional. These two US Army captains are throwing around a football in this big open space. They are reclined in office chairs, one eye on the screens, ears to the crackling radios and just throwing this football back and forth. Neither knows who I am nor why a guy with a Canadian flag on his shoulder is in their headquarters. For us the move Kandahar was a major thing, we had just driven 380 Kms from Kabul and they didn't even know we were coming or who we were! As I am explaining, this Lieutenant walks into the TOC and gets orders from one of the two captains who had been throwing the football moments before. The collegial atmosphere shifted to one of serious intent as they discussed the Lts' tasks. The Lt looks at the giant wall map, takes some notes, and then leaves the TOC. I asked what he was heading out to, assuming it was some type of patrol or village engagement. I was surprised when I was told that he was going to raid a target that was suspected Taliban. It was said matter of fact and was so chill. No senior officers, no panic, task issued, junior folks fighting their war. It was so foreign to me; I left Kabul and was Peacekeeping, lots of top brass control, concern over any engagement, no thought of seeking and killing the enemy and now 400km to the south, they are doing raids to capture/kill targets. We are taking over this area. I knew at that point we were going to be in the hurt locker initially. Our army had not been fighting in a long time, we loved ensuring that Ottawa knew everything that was going on, and I found it difficult to believe that Canada was going to be able to replicate the activities that I was seeing and the necessary diffusion of responsibility and decision making. I had just done a convoy from Kabul to Kandahar that required me to check in with Ottawa HQ every 2 hours. Not even Kabul but Ottawa! How the fuck were we going to adjust to actually fighting? The captains go on to tell me that most of the US troops are in Iraq, and activity has been reduced as NATO is coming down to Kandahar, so it has to look like there are fewer TICs, so NATO will come to do stabilization. They said that they were just mowing the grass to make it an acceptable level of violence so that NATO would take on the task and free up US troops. Looking back, it was probably just young officer bullshit, but I always wondered. It was a different world down there, and when I went back a year later, I found out how different. Maybe those US Captains knew something.

You had this bubble around Zangabad that nothing living or moving. You just get a free fire zone around the COP. There was this bazaar across the road, a couple of compounds. they're basically just fighting positions for the Taliban. There was almost this line in the ground; if we crossed that line, it was game on. We've been attacked a bunch of times but had done well. I attribute that to good advice that I got from the last platoon commander that had occupied this position, which was don't ever move as a single element. We would move in "multiples" so that the Taliban could not track where all the elements were, and if something happened, these small groups could aggregate on the fight so they never they could never get a complete fix on us. So, to allow for control, I think they waited until they saw the last guy go in the COP and then hit us; this was OK as we would get better cover. But took away any initiative we could build. This one attack stands out to me; they were hitting the towers. I was outside, and you could hear a bunch of booms. SPG9, some PKM fire crack overhead. I ran up into the tower when I got that map of the range, and everything was laid out to call in Artillery fire. They hit the other tower. I look up and see it get smashed; just lucky for me, it wasn't my tower. One of my guys got hit; the shrapnel smashed into the weapon he was firing, went through the butt of the medium machine gun, which is solid wood, through the steel butt plate, and then embedded in his shoulder. His soft body armour stopped the round. But he had a severe laceration. We didn't know that at the time. His section commander dumped quick clot into the wound, which impeded his recovery. In three weeks or whatever it was, that was our only casualty. It was just this constant game of cat and mouse.

Our lifeline was the satellite phone. Guys could call home and we did not monitor it, but just made sure it stayed charged and that guys took care of it. The thing was that you couldn't tell when the enemy would attack, and there were a couple of times that I was talking to my wife when shit started to go off. One time, I was on the phone, and mortar bombs came in. They exploded off to the side, but I knew I had to open the line up in case we needed to call using the phone. So, I was like "Got to go" but in my rush, I did not disconnect the call. She could hear the machine guns going and incoming mortar rounds going off, like war in real-time. I think that was the difference, not sure that happened in other wars, Communication arrived as letters months later in the old days. In Afghanistan, you family was right there with you sometimes. When there is a pause, I see the phone on the ground and pick it up. I hang up again and this time it disconnects. The last thing she hears is all that shit going down. I forgot to call after because there was a lot of shit ongoing; I eventually called her, and she was not impressed.

The TOC was a plywood box. It was built for one job. To enable the battle group to conduct operations. It was in KAF, and so there was this weird "in the fight but living in KAF atmosphere." We're able to run over to the mess to grab meals and stuff. I think they'd have a late meal at night. So well-fed, and you could live quite comfortably there. There also is a little bit of a mental shift because you go back from, I mean, doing airstrikes, type two strikes where we controlled the assets and the BDA. We would see in high-resolution people getting blown apart. I actually remember we did a strike; we hit this guy and blew his leg off. You can see it quite graphically, and then, for half an hour, we could see him through the optics of the drone. He was still moving there, obviously suffering. We saw someone come along with a wheelbarrow, put him in a wheelbarrow and carted him off. You can't unsee that. I think some people had a hard time going from that type of intensity to back to the room and being able to Skype with their wives; there is a mental dissonance. I think, for us in the TOC we treated it like this was our war. Our contribution to the fight. This is how we do our combat, just with a different weapons system. I think so for me personally; I can go to sleep knowing that we never took revenge for the guys they killed, but in the long term, we hit back and made the enemy pay the piper.

A buddy of mine and I found ourselves in Afghanistan at the same time. We had been friends for 20 years. We had to do some planning down route FOSTERS, and at the time, the IED situation was bad. Because we both had responsibilities, and we couldn't afford to lose both of us we had to travel in different vehicles. There hadn't been a strike in a couple of weeks and so we knew, through the law of averages that someone would hit something soon. As we were debriefing, he looked right at me and, with a wry smile, said, "You should lead; my wife would never forgive you if something happened to me; I have kids, you don't . Your wife, if she loses you just gets a big payout and can find a replacement pretty quick." I laughed and told him to Fuck off and he took his position in the lead vehicle. In no other circumstances is that funny, but soldiers need black humour to keep it light.

We headed into KAF to receive orders. We spent the night, and the next day, we were heading out and needed to grab our interpreters. The interpreters were living outside the main KAF gate, and they had their own little compound. I'm sitting there waiting and I'm trying to write orders as we're getting ready to go. I'm just sitting in the carrier. We're less than 100 meters from the front of KAF, the most heavily defended position probably in all of Afghanistan. A whole bunch of Afghans are waiting in line seeking jobs or making a claim for a field that had been destroyed. Regardless, there was a big line of humanity there. I look over, and I can see this kid. He must have been about ten years old. Then another kid who was just a toddler, nothing more than a baby, and then a bunch of men. This little kid is pushing this toddler. The toddler is trying to stand up and the other kid just keeps pushing down on his shoulder. Just an act of aggression, just mean. We're sitting there and like, I'm in this country to help provide peace and security for the people of Afghanistan. I yell out to tell him to stop pushing this baby around. The kid stops and looks at me; he kind of has a devilish smile and steps away as I watch him. Our interpreter jumped in the carrier, and we took off; as we were leaving, I looked back and saw the older kid come back and clock the two-year-old right in the side of the head. I have no idea why anyone would administer that kind of violence to someone else that age. The men standing around did nothing. I thought, Isn't this ironic? Here we are. We're in the heart of the location where the protection for the people of Afghanistan is supposed to be emanating. The bottom line is I still can't stop one kid from hurting another kid and can't have the adults see that the behaviour is not acceptable. It is an inherently violent society. Perhaps we can't judge, but we need to recognize that how we view right and wrong and fair play may not be the same. I don't struggle with that dissonance. It's the irony that we couldn't see it. You have all this power and mandate, but you're powerless in this very simple thing.

———————

The Dutch had left these pouches of tobacco when they departed FOB Martello. They had these big boxes and their pouches of tobacco with rolling papers. This was the beginning of me smoking because I had nothing else to do. I could only read and smoke when we were not patrolling or securing the base. Initially, I didn't smoke, but the action of rolling was relaxing. I would get bored, and I would just roll cigarettes; I got a lot better, and then I had this massive pile of cigarettes. So, I guess I had to smoke them! The other thing the Dutch left behind was paté from their rations. It was it was biscuits and regular liver pâté. So I would be on shift, have my hot cup of tea, watch through the spotting scope, have a little bit of paté and then a hand-rolled cigarette. Pretty cushy deal. Sounds like a spa instead of an observation post routine. The Dutch knew how to live.

———————

We rolled up to Sperwan Ghar; it was this hill in the middle of nowhere; the Taliban liked it because you could see for miles around, and it controlled the approaches into Panjawaii. The earth on the hill this really fine powdered dust that got on and into everything. It would create huge dust clouds, and you were always covered in it as you moved. There were no showers; other than pouring water bottles on ourselves, there was no cleaning for weeks. There were no bunkers or gravel or anything like that. We just set up LAVs all around the hill to make sure the arcs of fire made sense… As a new platoon commander and a replacement, I was trying to figure out how am I getting to know these guys. We got dispatched to the north side of the Arghandab River for an extended patrol and it was our mission to do some local patrolling there to troll north during the day to try and find contact. At night we would settle into a spot that provided us stand off, and we could use our optics from our turrets to maintain security. We didn't have a full complement of soldiers because of HLTA and casualties; we would always need two soldiers in each turret for an hour at a time at night. You would rotate through, and so you're only getting like maybe 2 hours of sleep, if you were lucky, at a time. I would use the opportunity to just talk to the different soldiers as we were doing shifts, even if they don't want to, I can't fucking go anywhere, and they're not going anywhere because they are stuck in a turret with you. I did not have to do security shifts as the platoon commander, but I felt it was important as we were short people, and it gave me an opportunity for one-on-one. I got to know the soldiers really rapidly.

Which was good. They were a little bit surprised that I was doing the sentry shift... So that really helped. I started to know these guys, and once the walls were down, they started telling me stories about all the different characters in the platoon. All these characters were in the same section, the section that was on Leave. I would get told, "You have to meet so and so". He's crazy, these guys from such and such provinces on the East Coast. He said he was in a relationship with his first cousin. He didn't grow up with her. They didn't know when they met as there had been a big family breakup. So, there is no relative stigma that he's actually having an affair with his cousin, and so this kid was trying to figure out this problem. It was crazy, but everyone was open and honest. I'm just starting to learn about these guys. I certainly learned some of the dynamics. I felt like I was less of a platoon commander and more of an anthropologist, trying to figure out relations and make the official hierarchies and unofficial hierarchies understood clearly enough. Then there's the unofficial hierarchy. It was really good. I remember the Warrant Officer was old school and was getting annoyed that I was injecting myself into the sentry shift and maybe not getting enough sleep. I said I had to do the turret engagements, but I understood his point: no sleep can lead to bad decisions. So, after I had been through the whole platoon, I reduced the amount of time I was in the turrets. It made the Warrant Officer happy I had listened. I think if I was going to tell a new leader anything, it would be to take the time to get to know your people, and the more open and transparent you are, without judgment, you will benefit ten-fold when things get tough. Too often, we get caught in the hierarchy and forget to understand these young Canadians who are putting it all on the line, and the more we understand them, the better we can operate.

On my third tour, there was almost no direct contact with the enemy. They seemed to decide it wasn't worth it. Just lay out as many IEDs as possible. It was all just booby-trap stuff. So frustrating. When people ask me about like, what's the most difficult thing you've ever done as a leader? Wake up every day and walk down the same road where, you know, there's something buried there, and no one's going to shoot at you. You would take losses daily for the Afghans and weekly/ monthly for the Canadians, or you would find devices and clear them. But they were always present, if not physically, in your mind and your soldiers' minds. A high IED environment plays with your mind. It seemed so insane. Like a version of " going over the top" -just keep walking forward, keep the route clear. The enemy is invisible. The toughest thing is keeping people motivated and focused when it's an unseen enemy, which is incredibly difficult. IEDs are a terror weapon. take your legs or an arm, or your face or balls. This was even harder when the Government announced we were leaving Afghanistan. Why get injured now? The government doesn't care, so why not just sit in the FOB and wait for the time to rotate out? Humans are humans; they get lazy. You can't look under every rock, you know. And it's incredibly taxing and mentally fatiguing, I think we under we underestimate that side of it. It's hard to translate it as a leader and make the daily grind matter to the soldiers. That was easily the hardest thing.

———————

I remember the whole company decided to go out on our first company-level fighting patrol. Full combat reconnaissance patrol. We'd go out, walk, see if somebody shoots at us, and then annihilate them. That first patrol, we were testing out some stuff. We went out, dismounted. I think we planned to get it done in like two days. But the first day we're hauling extra ammo. And how do we haul all this ammo we're gonna need to sustain ourselves in a protracted firefight? We had the John Deere gators. We decided the gators would follow along with local security, and they'd be chock full of water and ammo interactions. That was good until we hit the first wadi where they had to fjord, and water got into them, and they died in the middle of fucking nowhere. We ended up busting our cargo straps, and I remember pulling these fucking things like pulling a fucking sled and traces through the middle of Afghanistan. Finally, the OC says, just this ain't going to fucking work. Spots an Afghan with a tractor. He ends up paying him to tow the fuckin gators to our next spot where we can link up with LAVs. We spent a night on this bombed-out hill that the ANA told us used to be like a Taliban fucking stronghold or something. But at this point, it just ruins on a hill. We settled in for the night, and then everybody started getting gastro. Like in this little patrol base, guys are throwing up and shitting their pants. It was rough. We lost so many guys that we had to stop the patrol. I remember going to ground at night in the middle of night, I get woken up by fuckin like these little explosions going off. I was like, oh shit, we are under attack, and I'm trapped in my sleeping bag and trying to fight my way out of my sleeping bag and thrashing around, not smooth at all; my section 2IC kicks me and asks, "What the fuck are you doing?" I am sleep fucked and say we are under attack! He's like, "No, it's a Blackhawk coming in to evacuate the guys that are fucked up from gastro, and it fired flares or some shit on its approach. That is what you heard. Settle the Fuck down. "The numbers were so high, and it was so fucking bad that they had to shut it down. So, on our first big patrol, we had our gators towed by an Afghan, we all got sick, and half the company got medevac'd. Fucking embarrassing. Chalk it up to experience. We got better, but that first one sucked.

Everyone had been getting smashed by vehicle suicide bombers, and we had taken losses. So, we were told to own the road and that the civilian traffic needed to get out of the way. I remember this jingle truck. We pulled up in our LAV, and this jingle truck was taking up possibly all two and a half lanes of this highway. It was moving left and right and all over the place. It is super erratic and is an indicator of an SVBIED. We were the lead call sign at the time. We pulled up beside this jingle truck, and I told my driver just to push him into the ditch, like a light bump, to clear the way for the convoy and reduce the potential threat. Let's just nudge him; I don't wanna roll or scare him. Then he just hit that truck; we underestimated an armoured vehicle travelling at 80km per hour. WHAM, the mirror came off, and the side of the truck got caved in, and I was like, holy fuck, that's not...not what I wanted. I wanted you to give him a little kiss, but you gave him a good smack. But he pulled off the road and stopped, so, mission accomplished, and we kept on truckin'. I am not sure it was the right thing, but neither was getting suicide-bombed.

I was giving Convoy orders in KAF before we headed out on Op MEDUSA. Our first task was to escort artillery ammunition to the guns. As I was going around the team for questions on the missions, one of my Sergeants passed out! We immediately got him to the hospital and then had to depart on the task without him. We did not go back in, and about a week later, he showed up in Wilson; he looked terrible. He had contracted malaria and had lost about 25 pounds in the week since I had seen him. I asked him if he was good to go, and he said that he was, and I thought nothing more of it. We were at the height of the operation by that point in time, and I needed every dude I could scrounge up. We carried on with our mission, and he did great. Nothing further was discussed. About 2 weeks later, I had to go see the CO for an Orders group. After orders were done, he asked me if I had Sgt_____ in the platoon. I said yes, he had been in location for two weeks since he was released from the hospital. The CO looked at me and let me know that the Hospital had never released him, and they had been looking for him for two weeks! He had still been sick with Malaria. When all the wounded and killed came into the hospital, this Senior NCO could not stand to be in the hospital while the fight was on. He apparently pulled the IV out of his arms and walked out of the hospital. He grabbed his kit and weapon and hopped on a CLP (Combat Logistics Patrol) out to Wilson and never let me know he was AWOL from the hospital. Because everyone was so busy with the casualties from September 3rd and the A10 strike on the 4th, they were just realising their mistake now! I groaned and wondered if the Sgt was in trouble. The CO said he would take care of it and that, at this point, we needed every NCO to get out doing the business. Though the Sgt did the wrong thing, it fit the need and we could address it later. I went back to the platoon, and the Sgt came clean. It was pretty impressive, to be honest.

The best mission in Kabul was when went out to Sarobi with the Germans. At the time, there was a threat to the electrical power in Kabul. So, we went out there to observe and secure it. I think we had a recce troop, and we were providing sniper support. OPs during the day, for overwatch and then we would we patrol. I remember patrolling on foot, and we had a young sniper come upon this little Afghan guy who seemed to be moving erratically and the young soldier just drew his gun on him because he perceived a threat based on indicators that we had been told. Our unit had been hit by suicide bombers, we had lost some friends, and everyone was a bit squirrelly. The old man was carrying a bag, and the young troop was freaking out. I thought this was not going well, and I spent my time de-escalating him to go through the process and understand the threat picture. I got off to the side of him, not in his line of fire, and talked him through the situation and why he needed to lower his weapon and relax. All I could think was, he's going to he's going to cap this guy and it's just an old man. You never know; maybe the old guy was a threat. It had happened before. In the end, he lowered his weapon, and we went through the proper search procedures; no bomb. My guys were 19-20-21 and were scared of this threat, suicide bombing was new and no one understood as a soldier how to identify it. If all you have is a hammer, everything looks like a nail. They don't have that experience of shoot/ no shoot training like a police officer. That one's kind of stuck in my head. We were just one second away from someone pulling the trigger. It was a pretty crazy time; I was 24, and this young dude was 20. I mean, what does the average Canadian 20-year-old make decisions on?

So, night, morning, and afternoon, we would get harassed by mortar fire. The mortars in the afternoon were most accurate. Pretty quickly, we would get the drill down pat. The first mortar would usually come outside of the camp, and we put on our vests and got to the vehicle to take cover as there were no bunkers at the time. We sit there and wait. What can you do? By the third time, though, I mean complacency happens fast. So whoomph! first mortar comes in, we get up and put on our vests. The second one is closer, vests on, and we get in the vehicle as it is the only cover. I have one guy that is slow and still in the tent putting on his boots. We have a G-Wagon and nothing else, and it fits 4 people, and we have 6 in the diet. I count 5. Where the fuck is the last guy. As he comes out of the tent, there's an impact in the camp from accurate enemy rounds, and that hustles him along. They are getting closer and more accurate. So now he's pulling on the back door, and it is stuck. More mortars. He is getting antsy, and we watch him. He just opens the trunk and piles in. Just as he got in, another impacted closer the shrapnel flattened the tires of the G-Wagons. Holy shit. Just sitting on our jeep because it seemed ridiculous. We figured we could spot the enemy observer as the fire was too accurate to be unobserved. We went up on the roofs. The camp Sergeant Major (SGM) was more worried about the fact that we were on the roof and not following the "sit in your vehicle drill" rather than trying to find the enemy that was trying to kill us. We weren't wearing helmets because we couldn't get behind the scope with a helmet. The brim is too low, and it is impossible to get a site picture with body armour. Bad design by the Army, who I guess didn't need soldiers to shoot and wear helmets…The SGM is losing his mind over helmets AND the get-in-your-car drill. Even with this distraction, we got our heads into the spotting scopes and were able to identify a guy with a phone. Talking as the mortar rounds came in and looking at the camp. He was obviously directing fire. But was not holding a weapon himself, just a phone. No one else around, just him. We couldn't shoot that guy and did not receive permission from the TOC. A couple of months later, that would change as we learned about the enemy, but we had to eat it. We sent out a patrol, but he got away. I think it was sad but funny, learning about being under fire and what was important- Helmets, defensive drills or finding the enemy and stopping the attack. We got there eventually and needed to flip the script from passively being shelled like a Peacekeeping tour. Those were crazy times.

Like anything you do in the military, I think it is all about the people. I would've been fucking terrible if it wasn't for good people, you know. Some of it is so funny and ridiculous that you must remember that you are dealing with a bunch of 19- to 25-year-old kids. I can look back at the hard times and, holy shit, like there is random shit that pops up. We had the "cock" bandit in the HQ. Someone that would tag dicks everywhere with a marker. There's this little bathroom outside the TOC. This bathroom was the favourite target of the bandit because it would drive the Ops Sergeant Major crazy. He was in a death struggle to stop the bandit tagging this bathroom. We get word that the Regimental Colonel is coming over for a visit. The Sergeant Major will not have the cock bandit branding his bathroom and sullying the good reputation of the deployed Battalion. He painted the whole bathroom on his own time, and it was his pride. He let everyone know not to fuck with it. It's all painted and looks good. The Colonel is an older gentleman who has a lot of time in the army, is now retired, and has to use the bathroom when he arrives. I escort him into the now pristine bathroom. As I am waiting, I look up and, on the ceiling, see big, crossed cocks stencilled on the ceiling. It was like it was the biggest fuck you to the SGM, and it's funny. I couldn't help but laugh out loud. The Colonel looks back at me as he is washing his hands, hears me laughing out loud looks at me quizzically and asks, "What's so funny?" I pointed up, and I told him the story about the mysterious cock bandit, the SGM's sworn enemy, and he laughed. Then he realizes that the bathroom was painted because of him. He feels terrible.

"Should I tell the sergeant major about the Bandits' dastardly deeds?" he asks.

I tell him no, it would break his heart if the cock bandit had won this round and had exposed the Regimental Colonel to the seedy happenings. Discretion was the better part of valour in this case, and we kept the cock bandit's victory a secret from the Sergeant Major, and when he did find out, I lied through my teeth and said the Regimental Colonel did not see those giant cocks on the ceiling. So funny.

We had to link up with some US forces on a clearance Op. There had been a lot of fighting, and TB seemed to be in every building. I was with this US Colonel, and he was sitting, taking a breather as we were advancing and clearing buildings, and he saw a hole the size of a rabbit hole.

He asks, "Has someone checked this hole?"

He looks around, and no one says anything; he says, "I'll ask again. Has someone fragged this hole?"

No answer; why would you frag a little hole like that? No human can get down there. Maybe an air vent for a tunnel? But unlikely.

He looks up at his Command Chief and says, "Command Chief, frag this hole!" So, the Command Chief comes out, pulls out a grenade, and puts a grenade in the hole. Meanwhile, I am like, what the fuck is going on? There is no person in that hole? No person is getting in there, and the grenade goes down. Nothing happens. Oh Shit, this is awesome, now there is a dud grenade below our feet. So, they put another grenade down there. Let's see what happens. I decide I'm gonna like to cuddle up to this armoured vehicle here because I'm not sure who knows what's down there. The second grenade goes off, and then there is a secondary explosion…likely the first grenade (maybe he did not pull the pin?). The Colonel seems happy with the result: a random hole and two grenades. I was like, what the fuck is this. Is this how we win?

———————

I was the first person to receive military discipline charges in Afghanistan, at least in the 2003 to 2014 period, but I am not sure about the 2002 mission. It's not really a point of pride to hang my hat on, but the story is interesting because it shows how garrison-focused we were in those early days in Kabul. I got a task to pick up a lighting kit as we were just building the camp and lived in our little corner. So, another corporal and I got tasked to go down and pick up this lighting kit. We're in an Iltis, so we drive through the chicane and there's a bunch of locals sweeping the road. So instead of hitting the locals, I drive around them, and I hit the dust that's on the side that they have piled up, and I send a big cloud of dust into where they're building the main gate. Unbeknownst to me, there was a tour, and the headquarters contingent of ISAF was in there. And I sent a big cloud of dust in through it, covering everyone in this fine silt that likely had a lot of human feces in it. There were fairly high-ranking people inside who got upset anyway; we went down, picked up the lighting kit, and then were asked to report to the CP. The people inside the gate determined that I was driving too fast. They put the charge of reckless driving. I tried to defend myself. I was a new private. I just paid the piper and ate the charge. There was no there winning. And that was back in the day when it was just "march the guilty bastard in." It's numbing, though. It was a $400 fine and confined to barracks. I am in Afghanistan? Where I am I going to go? They basically paid the fine. My platoon all knew it was garbage. Old school senior leaders who were upset they got dusty thought that it was worth a 400-dollar lesson to a Private soldier. We have come a long way. Maybe if I am not the first to get charged, I can win the award for the stupidest charge.

———————

I didn't see any camel spiders, but I did have an incident where I saw l a big hairy tarantula looking thing. I was on a welfare phone at Spin Boldak, and I was looking out the door; then I looked up at the door and saw this huge thing as big as my fist in the doorway. It is moving towards me, and frankly, I am freaked out. I have my weapon and can shoot it but probably not a good idea in the FOB. I'm looking for something to throw at this spider to make it go away, I look away for a second to grab something and I look back and it's gone, which makes it even scarier because now you don't even know where it is but you know it is there. It's up there in the ceiling, it could be on your shoulder, who knows. I hate spiders.

We were moving back to KAF with a number of slow-moving ammo trucks and our platoon as the escort. Senjary market, just on the west side of Kandahar city is a comms dead zone and so if anything happens it is hard to let anyone know, you had to move to regain communications. On this trip we got ambushed. One of the reasons why was so my memorable is because the response was so effective. It was so different from when we first got there and guys were not used to coming under fire, they would speed up and it would be a dislocated response and you could hear the stress on the radio net. This time there were a couple of our RPGs went over and by the time I knew what was happening. The LAVs slowed down, gain the target and were engaging, the enemy never had a chance. They were on the bald ass open field and that was it, fuck you guys. Don't shoot at us anymore. It was awesome. I felt good. When we got to our next stop the troops were smoking and joking like nothing happened. Just another day at the office.

It was like 45-55 degrees most days in August and September. We were intensifying our operations and assaulting into known Taliban positions. It came at the cost of rest, food and comfort. Combat is an endurance game. We had this fucking crazy heat rash on our thighs and backs because we couldn't change our uniforms, wash our bodies and the constant rub from the body armour. Blisters would develop and turn to calluses quickly from the amount of walking with weight. It was just a constant blur. Maybe you eat, maybe you don't. Continuous combat is a 24/7 game when you are trying to pressurize the enemy. That was actually when I started to drink coffee. I never drank coffee before that. The water was so fucking warm in the 500ml plastic bottles that I would just dump the instant ration coffee unit and just drink it because I needed the caffeine.

As soon as we start to get into June, we were facing between 50 and 60 degrees. Our patrols were generally between three to twelve hours, depending on what you're trying to achieve. The conditions were so hot that we were going through like nine litres of water, in five hours and not pissing. So that's takes a toll on the amount of weight you are carrying. Water was huge consideration and all the guys always carried more ammo than they needed to at the first couple months because they just didn't know what to expect. "Have and not need is better than need and not have." I think with the radio on my back I was carrying probably around 120 to 130 pounds. We had load bearing chest rigs that we bought because the army wouldn't buy us any. But the only way you could carry that rig is if you had a good backpack on your back. Otherwise, you were walking all hunched over because the amount of weight that you had in your chest. So, it actually works when you balance it out with the backpack and radio, like a counterweight. I remember thinking the first time I got all geared up to go and you think, how the fuck am I going to be on the move with all this shit on? And then it just all disappears when shit happens. You are light as a feather and do whatever you need to do.

I was eating a lot of salmon rations, which were not popular, as preserved fish in a bag in the desert is pretty gross. For some reason I seemed to always get them. I was new and thought that I was taking a hit for the vehicle crew so that the troops did not have to eat them. Turns out, later in the tour, I lost a vehicle to an IED strike, and when that vehicle crew was recovering in KAF, I did not get any salmon. I discovered that when we were out when we would get resupplied, that crew would volunteer to collect the goods, and they were collecting all the salmons from the platoon, filling a box, then at night sneaking over and packing them on the headquarters vehicle, and so all HQ were eating was this disgusting salmon meal, for weeks. Funny shit.

The later tours were so tough because of the IED threat. They were everywhere, and we had lots of guys lose feet and legs or get lucky and just get shrapnel. It became a game of cat and mouse. It was nerve-wracking because you know that you are always walking in a mine belt. The locals would tell you that the Taliban hook them up only at night or at the last light. Of course, there you are at last light walking through. There's no more locals, and you know; you know, that means that they have all sorts of things hooked up and live all around you. So, we had to be pretty innovative, I guess, on the way we would travel. The second they flooded the fields, we were in the shit ditches patrolling through the water because they flooded the fields for agriculture, which would've forced you out of the paths. And so instead of walking in the paths, you walked in this shit water that was the slough from the houses and the fields. Better wet and terrible smell than lose your feet. When we needed access to the laneways, we avoided the paths, we would use sledgehammers to bust through the grape field walls and make new paths. So, we got pretty good at avoiding the IEDs and could get through a wall in about 15 minutes. Each square foot of wall had a calculation that we would pay the farmer if they wanted to claim it. I think 10 to 15 dollars per square foot. Money was well spent, and the walls were made of mud and straw and rocks that baked. Good investment from my perspective, though I am not sure the locals saw it this way. We essentially created an industry. It was trying, sensitive and stressful work, but we were able to surprise them with our movements often and keep our guys safe.

For Christmas dinner, I made a Christmas IMP. Somebody showed me taking the chicken a la king ration and then you mix the stuffing, dried mashed potatoes and the cranberry sauce right in with it all heated up and then you have like, Christmas dinner in a pouch. I took the ration bits and my personal stove up on the hill and Masum Ghar after it had gotten dark. I was all alone and it was nice to have some space. The guys were great but I was missing home and my family. I took the time to do all the steps to prepare the different parts of the ration and actually warmed it up. Usually, I would eat it cold as it was warm enough from being in the sun. After I had eaten, I relit my stove put on some water and made a 3 in one coffee. It was these Nescafe packs that were very rich because the sugar was already in them. It was a real treat. Then I just sat there, sipped on that coffee, enjoyed the silence, watching the lights of the UAVs above me, blinking on Christmas Day and the lights down in the camp as the troops enjoyed a bit of Christmas break. I reflected on our time there and how far away I was from home. It was nice to have that little break. I packed up my stuff and walked back down the hill, and joined the team for some Christmas cheer. There were patrols the next day to plan for. Merry Christmas.

I remember when the battlegroup lost its first casualty. I guess it would be on a convoy through Kandahar City from a suicide bomber. He was a popular member of the Regiment that had been killed. We took that personally. My fellow Duty Officer took it really personally because he gave the Convoy the recommended route through the city. He couldn't have fucking known there was a goddamn suicide bomber. It became very, very real, and I connected the purpose of my being in the HQ with the mission. Now…. now Canadians on our deployment are actually dying. It was just started getting ramped up. There would be more and it was our job to not have bravado or ego, but to provide resources and solve problems in the background. There is nothing "cool" about being a staff officer, you won't get it right every time, and you can't take the blame when the enemy wins on any given day, but you can put in the hours to make sure that to the most extent possible everything is set for the guys forward to achieve success.

You have to get back on the horse after you take losses; you can't just stop. It is a hard leadership position to be in. No one tells you what to do. I came in as a replacement leader in a platoon that had taken losses. I told my guys, "I didn't have the privilege of knowing the fallen. But from what you've told me of them, it's clear to me that if fortunes were different, they would be the ones telling us to carry on and get after the mission. So that's what we're going to do. We're going to take a little rest here. I can go get orders, and I'll see where we go next." I was essentially down a section of about 12 soldiers between dead and wounded. We got sent down to Spin Boldak, a quiet outpost on the Afghan-Pakistan border, to recover and integrate replacements. It was just this weird little world, like an old French foreign legion fort, with mud walls in the centre of the Reg desert. I remember hating it because it was too quiet. There was nothing to do. I was told not even to leave the base. No local patrolling, nothing. The Battalion wanted my platoon not to take more hits; they wanted "in theatre reconstitution." So, we had wide-open arcs. Nobody was attacking us unless a car drove up with a bomb or something. But we needed to stay engaged and maintain discipline of soldiering. I had been in charge during our last contact and so had earned a level of respect from the soldiers. I recognized that operating at full throttle in combat ops to doing nothing was not ideal either because there is just way too much downtime for everybody. Like going from 5th gear to first and wrecking the transmission because the revs are too high. So, we got into a routine even though we didn't need to. We did a lot of maintenance. I became super unpopular because we ripped apart LAVs. I wanted to stop everybody from being by themselves and those soldiers and to being together; it was hard and so necessary because when the call came to get back out and get mixed in, we were ready. It is something leaders need to understand, work is good for soldiers and togetherness fights those dark moments that can be destructive.

I found working with people in KAF super frustrating. One of our guys got rocked by an RPG Volley and bunker collapsed on him, so when he was in the hospital and I was in to help him navigate the medical system. I was back in camp because I had caught some shrapnel in the same event. It was like they didn't treat him like he was wounded, but he was there for some type of sick chit for a sore throat. We're sitting in the waiting room for a good 45 minutes. They told him not to leave. We had just lost two friends killed, and four of us had been wounded. We're like, what the fuck, he's got a headache. Can we just go and come back when you are ready, or at least get him to lie down? Then they come out, and they slap a neck brace on him and tell him that they looked at the X-ray. All of the vertebrae in his neck are separated right now from the blast, and the bunker collapses, and his head could flop off at any moment. Like a dandelion, pop right off. Probably not exactly right, but that is how it was described. I'm like, holy fuck, I told him, you're going home, you're done. We had to get him on a flight back to Dubai and then a flight back to Canada. As we were going through the process, one of the questions asked was, does he have a credit card because he'll have to book his own hotel room in Turkey because the flight doesn't go straight back to Canada? This made me so angry. He was a 21-year-old kid who had just been rocked, got a neck brace on like his head's gonna fall off, and didn't bring a credit card to the theatre. Why the fuck would a medical repat need a credit card! Then they're like, well, ok, we'll see if we can get him a direct flight. What the fuck, I am getting riled up. No, not "we'll see", like, you will get him a direct flight. They were not happy with me, and they got him a flight and no fucking visa required. He was not going to have to be out of pocket on top of having a fractured neck! Amazing! We went to put him on the Herc, and we're walking up to the Herc, and he can't wear any PPE, so he can't sit in the back; he's got to sit up where the pilots sit, Dr's orders. We get there, and I tell the ladies, hey, this is a medical guy, he can't wear PPE, he can't wear a helmet or anything, he's got to sit up front with the pilots. The guy blocks it and tells me that somebody else is already sitting there so he can't travel. Again, I am like, what the fuck is wrong with these people? This is a wounded soldier; shake your fucking Fobbit head! I'm like, "No, they're not. Is he a medical?" Well no is the answer "Well then he's going to sit up with the pilots because he's got a neck brace on and he can't wear a helmet, this is a medical repat." "I'll see what I can do says the loadies." So, he goes up, you see him go up to where the pilots are and he comes down and this MP officer comes down. He goes in the back and sits down and he gives us the thumbs up like he just did us a huge favour and our wounded dude and goes up there. I'm like, whatever man, it's not a favour. It's what you're going to do because you were told to do it. I was so pissed off with everyone. We had just come out of a bunch of TICs and had lost dudes and had a bunch wounded. This kid that everyone was passing around had killed like 10 TB fighters that were trying to flank us and was actually a goddamn hero, but the minute we get back to the system, he is just another Private. I hated KAF. It wasn't their fault, but I still hated it.

I had this funny troop under me, a real character. I had taken him through his basic training and then we ended up on a small team in Afghanistan together. He went on leave in Bali and had a pretty crazy time, so much so that he got a tattoo of a hooker on his shoulder when he came back from Bali. We thought this was pretty crazy and gave him a hard time. But her name became a type of talisman in our group. So much so that when we had to name a new piece of Tactical infrastructure that we were in, a " COP", we tried to name it after her. We put the name up for approvals, and we actually got through the initial approvals; this name would go on maps and be officially used by the mission! If there was an event by it, the name of the COP would be in the news. Hilarious. Loose lips sink ships and when someone in HQ heard that It was actually the name of a Balinese hooker and the idea was kyboshed by command. Proper thing likely, but it was funny as shit.

We were doing satellite patrols and pushing through the green space, where the Taliban was always hanging out. Our point man is this skinny kid is climbing a wall and he is turned sideways. The TB opened up on him. He is up on the wall, and the rounds pepper all around him; all of a sudden, you hear the PRR. "Sarge." "Sarge. I'm hit, Sarge. I'm hit. I'm a hit." So, the Sergeant jumps over the wall to check him. Under-fire grabs him and pulls him back down to the safe side of the wall. He starts doing an initial check, and he feels warm liquid. there is a red stain all over the troop, spreading over his tan combat uniform. The medic comes up, and they start ripping this shit off and find the bullet holes; the rounds go through the plates on each side. But it wasn't blood, this kid was so skinny, the rounds missed him and went through a red Gatorade bottle he was carrying and his water bottle creating a red warm liquid. You could see the bullet tracks on the plates. Lucky as fuck. We were engaging, and the enemy broke contact; we lost track of them; just a quick meeting engagement. Afterwards, it was funny, him yelling, like a little squeal, " Sarge I'm hit I'm hit, I'm hit Sarge. They got me. He got me." Like a little kid playing guns, He could feel the warm fluid and saw it was red. He was just in shock. That is a close call. I am glad we could laugh about it and we never stopped busting his balls about his drama queen moment.

_____

I love the Badgers. That engineer vehicle helped us get to the hard dug-in positions and avoid IEDs. The thing is giant, a Leo 2 tank chassis, with no turret, but a big bucket arm that can dig or smash and a big bulldozer blade on the front that can make a road through anything. We were out in Western Panjawaii and advancing on these Taliban positions, the Badger smashed through the grape field walls, pushes them in in and then everyone follows. There was this mud villa that had enemy fighters in it, we wanted the Badger to plow a lane to get us in there. He starts ploughing, he suddenly stops and they lift a wire with the dozer blades. This is not good news; it means there is a device somewhere close. They all stop and the combat engineers start to exploit it. They see it goes right into the compound that we were all going to assault into. They follow it in clear the compound and find a massive Chinese rocket that was all rigged to blow. They made it safe and took away the danger. A bomb that size would have collapsed the whole villa and killed or hurt everyone in it. Likely a platoon would have gone in there. This was very lucky; looking the other way or not paying attention, we would have missed it, and when the platoon went in, the enemy could have easily detonated it and maybe killed a full section. That equipment saved lives, and the engineers were our best friends dealing with all the explosive shit in the ground. They really saved a lot of lives. We were just lucky that day. We were not always that lucky.

_____

We were going out on our first-night patrol against enemy-held positions. I was walking point. We were concerned about dogs compromising our approach positions, so I asked the snipers for a suppressor for my C8. They gave it to me, giving me confidence as I prepared for the patrol. The Sergeant and I had to plan primary and alternate routes. We also had to plan RVs enroute and crash RVs if we were compromised and needed to fight our way out. We were a small element walking into an area where Rifle Companies had been smashed within the last couple of days. I remember using satellite imagery to help plan these routes. It was great to have the imagery, but it was lower quality, and sometimes walls looked like trails, and the spacing was off. It was good to visualize, though, and I was glad to have them. I was nervous being Alpha security and the point man, I really didn't want to fuck this up. I also remember being very happy and glad that it was me.

Just because one of the things for me sounds kind of stupid, but I was happy to be the person up front taking that risk. So, we were getting ready for the patrol, and all of a sudden, an LAV came screaming in with a bunch of wounded from the Rifle Company that we were going to pass through. I remember watching the guys get carried into the building, and I remember seeing their combat uniforms all stained with blood, and they were all fucked up. Blood everywhere. I remember being pissed off just because we weren't into the fight yet. Guys are getting fucking wounded, and I just want to go out and do your part. The platoon commander came in with the contact report from where the dudes got hit and let us know that we had our starting point. We would start to hunt the enemy from their last known location. That woke me up. We were going to hunt them. It was time to leave; final orders complete, we left Wilson, and we used our G-Wagons to get across the highway and vicinity of the company that had just been in contact. We are going to link up with them and "pass-through" them and operate into the enemy territory that they haven't been to yet. I don't ever remember having time to be stressed, going over my routes, making sure I have all my shit squared away. And I remember kind of getting ready to move and talking to the guys in the Company, and they were like, "Better you than me". I also remember kind of being like fucking rights, we had taken a lot of hits at that point, and it felt good to take the initiative against the enemy. We departed and headed south into the grape fields. We didn't get very, very far, and I don't know who reported it, but there were dogs chained on stakes, it must have been the Taliban's early warning. It is dark, the moon is just starting to come up, and we start hearing the dogs. I peeked across the open ground and asked if I could engage, and the platoon commander was like, "Yep, that is why you have the suppressor, giver." So, I looked over the wall, and it was probably 150 m. there were two dogs chained up, one fucking chance, I didn't want to miss. I took aim and let loose three shots. The dogs went down, and there was no more barking. First kills in Afghanistan, fucking dogs. But necessary. The patrol started, and we stepped off in the platoon order of march, moving down the wadi. We were set up in a classic fighting patrol organization and had 2 C6, but the wadi was a good cover but restricted us from bounding, so we spread out and walked slowly along this trench. I remember having my fucking gun up. Oddly enough, it's funny how your patrol discipline is just fine whenever there's a real threat out there. Gun up, head up, me and the Sarge move through this wadi. The walls had been widened by shovels and scraped out for their fighters to hide in. There was human faeces where their fighters had shit, there were cigarette packs and there were all these footprints. As we looked back, we could make out shapes where the rifle company was located. It was creepy, like we were sharing space with the enemy in their lines, and that they would be around the corner. The moon was fully up now and the sand seemed to be gleaming, my NVG was not useful as it was so bright. I looked down and I noticed that there was a X drawn in the sand on the ground, which kind of freaked me out, I don't know, stupid now but at the time we were freaked out about IEDs. I passed it on the radio, there was a fucking X on the ground. The platoon Commander thanked me for being observant and then says, "look up do you think a fucking anvil is gonna fall on you?". It was nothing and that was good to break the tension, I remember kind of like laughing at myself, but I did NOT step on that fucking X. As we moved past the initial enemy defensive position, we moved into a field that was open and leading into the target compound. Let's get on the fucking objective to set the objective rendezvous (ORV). We crawled through this fucking grass and dope field. The only thing on my mind is that I'm going a bit in the face by a fucking snake. We set the ORV, and the sections went out to do the close target recce on the compounds. There was a dude on the roof of one of them and one of the sections got close and asked if they should shoot him or if we should do a raid. The platoon commander asked the HQ and we were told not to do a raid, but just observe and report. We confirmed enemy locations, and they ended up dropping bombs on it, and the next day, the rifle company cleared it. They dropped a JDAM on that fucker. We made our way back to friendly lines, and it was super stressful because the rifle company had contact with the Taliban while we were out, and now we were walking back towards them, and the Taliban were obviously moving around us. It was like a shadowy game of hide and seek. Like we could feel them out there. We got back to the lines, cleared through patrol reports learned the company limit of exploitation for the next day and then started planning for the next night's patrol. It just became a cycle of us applying pressure at night and the rifle companies attacking during the day.

I had some interactions with this senior leader in KAF. My platoon had gotten pulled out of Panjawaii to guard the chai house in KAF for a meeting with the Pakistanis. We didn't really know why we were there. Maybe show that they had enough security; KAF had like 24000 people! We made the dangerous road move to come back to KAF, which we hated. I got there. We were just there to show that Canada was taking the meeting seriously. We weren't actually there for force protection. This senior clown says to me, because I am a "new" platoon commander, she says "to be clear, if anyone dies during this thing, it's got to be your guys." I look at him and say, "is that funny? you know, that's a real thing for us, right?" That's something like it might be a punchline for you." We are out in it every day, and even the stupid drive back to KAF makes dudes think about whether this is their day. He had a fucking coffee mug in his hand. I still remember it to this day. Coffee mug, wandering around telling me what's what. Like you, piece of shit. The troops are seething after that. Dying was just bad luck; no one deserved it any more than anyone else. I know he was trying to be funny, but I wanted to smash his face with that coffee cup. It still bugs me to this day that, like a senior officer, thought that this this war was that much of an abstraction that he could make comments like that in front of troops that had lost friends. People talk about the divide between KAF and being out; there were a lot of these guys that didn't think the fight was real like it was a video game. They would see it through ISR feeds and Commander Update Briefs. I know it wasn't everyone, but some of the ignorance really pissed me off.

I found within the army, there was a discussion of fighting season and non-fighting season. It made your tour "hard or not." I can tell you that I've never experienced a non-fighting season. So, generally speaking, the fighting season was the summer months when it was dry and then the winter months, when it was cold, miserable, and rainy, with a little bit of snow. A lot of the insurgents in Kandahar province had tended to regroup and go back across the Pakistan border. What I found during our rotation is I wouldn't classify it as fighting, or a non-fighting season. I would classify it as just a change in tactics because, I mean, a lot of soldiers on my tour died. Every single one of them was an IED. Our first soldiers were not killed, I think, until December. It was early December, an IED. A big fucking IED. It was the first one. So, we kind of said tongue in cheek, you know, this is harder than the traditional fighting season. When we were under Contact, we could shoot back and fight. With IEDs. It's a different kind of fight. You actually got to go and hunt them and you've got to be deliberate. It is just a grind, every day, patrolling and never seeing the enemy with a weapon but always seeing them with cell phones and either finding or getting hit by IEDs. I think the wounded were worse sometimes than the killed; I mean the impact on the troops. When you see your buddy lose a leg or legs, it is really hard on morale. His life is changed forever. For what? The government was leaving Afghanistan. It takes so much personal and professional discipline to restrict firing on people you know are spotters or triggermen and try to outsmart them and so much leadership to motivate troops to get out and walk every day down those paths and roads that we were responsible for keeping open that every step they took could be their last.

We were inserting Recce platoon one night for one of their dismounted patrols onto Taliban positions. They loaded up in our LAVs, and we drove down to the drop point. On the way we had to go through a rifle company that had been fighting during the day and now was at the forward edge of the line. The guys were resting and preparing for the next day. It was dark, and we were driving under goggles. We were driving down the road, and you could see the lead vehicle sort of doing a little shimmy, so he didn't do something, but the dust kicked up, and we lost all visibility. So, the other vehicles just go straight through. We do the drop Recce, and they move off into the darkness towards the enemy. The engines get turned off as we wait for them to return the next morning. We hear screaming from where we just came from; we are not sure what it is. We found out later that there was a guy, he went and lay down on the road. He didn't know that and the light dust completely covered his bivy bag. He did not mark his bag with an IR glowstick. Three vehicles in the platoon all ran over this guy. We were going so slow he probably felt each tire go over his fucking pelvis, 12 LAV tires, and he's screaming and trying to crawl away, then the next vehicle comes, and the next vehicle comes. And nobody knew it. There's not supposed to be a guy sleeping in the middle of the road; you're not supposed to sleep on the road! Rule #1 don't sleep on the road. I guess he was a big snorer, so the platoon sort of kicked him out of their sleeping area, so he was like, fine, I'm gonna take my stuff and go sleep on this flat piece of ground. Which happens to be the road. Six inches of moon dust and this guy in a CADPAT bivy bag, and then we come along and ruined his whole night. He lived, by the way, and was so lucky. I am being an asshole; we felt bad, but there was nothing we could do about it. Don't sleep where armoured vehicles move.

I was an OMLT team leader and loved operating at night. The next day, when the Taliban realized that we had been operating at night, we would hear about it on the ICOM. I always enjoyed the feeling that they were worried about us. So, in between patrols, we would rest and eat good meals because we had these freezers full of meat, but we had all of these bootleg DVDs that we would buy in the local market. Yes, the money was probably going back to supporting our enemy, but the pirated DVD did more for my morale than for IED builders. For us, Deadwood was the series that we watched. I would tell the guys that, like, if you do, everything goes well. We'll come back. Watch one episode. It was like the old rum ration. It was a good day! We're going to watch two episodes. There was this one time we needed to build a ramp to get the RG 31 to see over the HESCO walls with the remote weapons system... So, you'd have to drive it outside the COP to do observation at night. We couldn't get any engineer assets down to help us build a ramp and needed about three feet built up. So, at night, my soldiers and my team of four started building like filling sandbags and lugging them inside. We had to do it under darkness because the enemy was less likely to attack. So, we had to measure everything, like basic engineering, but none of us were engineers. It was just that ingenuity. It is what Canadian soldiers do. The Afghans would help us. Once they saw what we were doing, they started pitching in and after. Finally, we had this run-up position. It's a force multiplier. We had this .50 calibre machine gun attached to an amazing optic and could see 360 degrees around the strongpoint. That was awesome that really helped out with confidence. We always leave one soldier behind in the RG when we go on patrol to man the gun because comms was really poor on the man pack. One day, in their eagerness to go and watch an episode of Deadwood or play video games or something, somebody left all the electronics on in the RPG. So, it died out. Battery very quickly. The only way to get it going again was to call our neighbouring closest callsigns to drive down the most dangerous road in the world at that time and come in and give us a boost to recharge the batteries. I was serious because it was sloppy and needlessly risk the lives of another team. The other team got a good laugh at us, but I was pissed. It was embarrassing. I didn't see a need for a charge. I grounded the team. The Warrant was super pissed So we cut off everything except for the satellite phone. So, no Deadwood, no TV. It was interesting, they started doing letter writing and stuff like that and just found other things to occupy themselves. After a week there was another significant incident. I'm not sure what it was, but it was something kinetic, and the guys did a great job. And when they got back, they said," We all did pretty good, I think, today. Can we not be grounded anymore?" For the rest of the deployment, that was a joke. We were all like we're all on a first-name basis in a small team, and I loved them; I also didn't watch Deadwood, so I kind of grounded myself, too! In the end we learned our lesson together and it was all good. Funny shit though.

We had our own shower in this compound we occupied after the fighting was done. It was really ghetto. It had a tank and worked off of gravity. You had to pump it a bunch of times. Most times, it was hot as long as guys had quick showers. It was just a pipe coming out of a wall. It was put there by whomever the Afghan was that owned the house beforehand. It was probably a fancy compound because it had hand-pumped running water. But it was great. You could get a hot shower every day. That's good for morale.

I found I became a little bit emboldened and felt bulletproof. We didn't have any casualties in the first three months and guys started to take more risk than we probably should have. It wasn't until we started to have injuries later in the tour that the guys realized the costs. I found that we were looking to get into firefights. Guys were missing that adrenaline rush. We go a couple of days without one. It was almost like guys were rushing forward again, and we would reach for it, and they would get hurt, and then all of a sudden, they would not wish for it. Through the winter months, the direct fire stuff toned down. You kind of wanted to get a shot at and manoeuvre and engage the enemy. I know I was missing it. I hated the fucking routine of patrolling and finding or striking IEDs; it was not the same as the gunfights.

There was a schedule in the COP. Two weeks patrolling. Then, you're off on the Quick Reaction Force (QRF) one week. The two weeks patrolling, you're high. You were taking it to the enemy for that two weeks. You owned your schedule, headed out, and you got the TICs and the interesting missions. The troops looked forward to it. I mean, they were looking forward to fucking engaging with the enemy. But as the days got closer to QRF, things changed, and then the section spirit changed. As the section commander, I had to be careful with this. They knew they were going back on a week of QRF, and they got difficult jobs because they were cleaning it up when the mess happened. Bagging bodies, pulling out vehicles that gone blown up, enabling medevac. You're always moving your vehicles into other people's AOR, where they won't dare take their own vehicles. We're pushing vehicles into there because if we get called, it will be bad. It's a whole different fuckin ballgame. And I always say that to the guys, if you ever want to eat shit, there was one experience in Afghanistan that is that. Being on that fucking QRF is a hard fucking pill to swallow. It's all mental stress. It's a hard ticket. I'm the lead vehicle into high IED environments where there has just been a strike, where you know that the risks are extraordinarily high. The section's atmosphere changed. I mean physically. You could see it change, and all the boys and everyone would internalize and deal with it differently. You knew you were starting that first day of QRF. Everyone was tense and on each other, and then by the end of a week, we were almost done. You know, one day left and then you're like high-five and tagging in the next the next section that's got to do it. It is their turn to clean up. Funny, the patrolling and fighting should have been the hard part, but it was the stress of QRF that was the worst.

The easiest things in war are hard; You get humbled quickly if you don't pay attention to the small things and keep focus. There is a mystique around SOF, and it is deserved, but screw-ups happen, and when they do, the consequences can be high. As a young leader, I learned a good lesson about taking care of the small things and how quickly a situation can turn on you even when everything seems to be going right.

I was part of an element operating in Kandahar and was conducting a Capture-or-kill operation on a suspected enemy commander and IED facilitator who had killed Canadians and other coalition force members. My Task Force had been watching this network's activities to determine points of maximum value, vulnerability, and accessibility, and on this particular evening, everything lined up for a mission. The target was positively identified and fixed through multiple corroborating intelligence sources, his entourage and materiel where in location, and with these conditions met, the mission was triggered earlier that night. The target was in rural Kandahar City in a location appropriate for a ground insert to minimize my force's signature and achieve surprise.

The ground assault force moved up on a rural compound in the middle of the night after a foot infill from our vehicle drop-off point about 2 kilometres from the target. With air cover from a predator drone that provided persistent intelligence surveillance reconnaissance (ISR) and contingency fire support, we dispersed and silently made our way to the compound's perimeter to prepare fighting positions for blocking, observation, fire support, and explosive breaching. Our approach was deliberately slow to ensure stealth and surprise, maximizing our advantage.

It was all going smooth, all positions reported in with no activity of collateral damage concerns, and with explosive breaches set, after a short period of calm, I gave the order to initiate over the radio net. With no delay, two near-simultaneous explosions, designed to punch man-sized holes in the outer compound wall, went off shaking the ground and marking the start of the interior combat. Detachments immediately flowed into the compound from multiple entries while snipers covered our movement and provided commentary from elevated positions on any activity. As we progressed through the complex series of rooms and outbuildings, flowing through a deliberately rehearsed plan designed to rapidly saturate and control the situation, fighting-aged males (FAMs) were rounded up while ensuring that all women and children were protected, safely controlled, and brought to a pre-determined location making use of our basic language skills.

As I moved through the compound with the team, I entered a room and came upon a sleeping infant just lying on the dirt floor, sound asleep a few meters away from a woman who was sitting silently in a bed searching the dark for the source of the commotion. With no threats in the room identified, I lowered my weapon and while covered by a teammate, picked up the child as carefully as I could, swaddling it in a nearby blanket, and handed it to the woman trying to reassure her in the calmest voice I could produce that we meant her and the child no harm; a difficult thing to communicate in this dynamic moment with no light. She seemed to respond calmly and offered no resistance. I understood how terrifying the situation must have been for her and as a father of young children, and I did my best to not allow the emotion of the situation distract me from the complex and dangerous task at hand.

After a few minutes, with the compound mostly secured, a yell came from the perimeter as one of the FAMs scaled the outer wall, dropped to the ground, and proceeded to run down the road. Though weapons were found on target, in many cases next to sleeping fighters, this individual appeared to be unarmed. Making a snap decision, one of the sniper positions did not engage as the individual did not pose an immediate threat to the force, and it was thought that our blocking position would interdict before he was able to escape. Calculations of this nature were routinely made; our job was to destroy the network and gain valuable intelligence while minimizing unnecessary collateral damage and death.

Action in the compound was slowing down at this point, with only sporadic interior combat noises being heard in addition to barking dogs and distant voices from the local area breaking the silence of the late night. Commentary from the ISR platform described the unknown FAM's progress into an adjacent cornfield losing contact with him in the dark foliage. As everything was going according to plan in the compound, I determined that we could spare some capacity to handle the squirter. This is where things began to unravel…

I gathered a team of operators who had completed their tasks, and we made our way to his last known location, setting ourselves up in a spaced-out extended line on the perimeter of the cornfield. This is where we went from having control to stepping into the unknown. We made a quick plan to move into the dense field and search for him as he could have been the targeted individual or a member of his entourage. This seemed like a good idea, drawing on my understanding of Canadian cornfields; however, it would turn out cornfields in Afghanistan are more jungle than crop. As soon as we entered the field of thick, intertwined, and mature stocks that towered over us, we lost visual contact with each other, and the ISR platform was unable to track our progress.

Trying to maintain direction with bearings on wrist compasses, we made our way further into the field, cracking our IR glowsticks to keep track of the location of all friendlies, we crashed through the brush, all noise discipline having gone out the window at this point. After a few minutes, it became clear that we were literally in over our heads as we became completely disoriented with my team moving in multiple directions lost in this thick bush. With every step, the long flat leaves clung to our gear, tied nots around our legs and arms, and in some cases even removed night vision goggles, knives, and anything else exposed.

Growing concerned over potential threats and increasing blue-on-blue risk in this mess, I made the decision to stop the search and consolidate back where we started our walk into the field. The only problem was that not one of us could determine what direction to travel! We had lost our focus on the basics! Now it was no longer a search for the bad guy that skipped out, I needed my unit to reset itself safely before we wandered into each other or worse, had a chance contact with the enemy resulting in rounds flying around without us knowing where everyone was. It was just a simple mistake right now, but add one more issue and it would become a dangerously uncontrolled situation.

Calling everyone back to my position in the corn forest, guys fought their way back. I even caught a few guys smiling sheepishly and laughing under the faint green light of NVG tubes; It was a pretty ridiculous situation. It was all good now that we were back together, but those initial moments of feeling disoriented were dodgy. I was ready to put this night to bed asking if anyone had any ideas. With no good ideas materializing, I tasked the predator to help us navigate by pointing its infra-red (IR) indicator on the location we had started from, and using our NVGs, we looked up and followed the beam of light out of the field, thoroughly embarrassed at our agricultural defeat.

This situation was bad enough, but I had also made a significant error in judgement in the hasty planning; I left the main effort and did not leave a clear command structure to deal with contingencies. SOF operations often make use of a significant stack of lethal enablers that require coordination, and I got tunnel vision. This could have been catastrophic had enemy reinforcements moved in. The team would have been expecting to receive coordinating direction from me while I was lost in a cornfield with zero situational awareness. I have every faith that my men would have done the right thing and repelled any attack, but to maximize combat power and minimize unnecessary risk, I needed to keep my eyes on the whole mission, not get sucked into a tactical task.

In the end, we accomplished our mission, and my ego was hurt, but it could have been worse; we didn't understand the terrain and didn't do the basics brilliantly. Worse, I made a terrible mistake as a leader, and I am glad that I learned the lesson without causing terrible consequences.

It was a very hot day. We were clearing western Panjawaii towards Mushan (Again). I'm bringing my section up on the advance, and there is a maze of trails, grape fields and high mud walls. We are the depth platoon and the reserve section, so we are responsible for doing all the Joe jobs, like medevac if required, security and anything that needs doing. Coming down the trail towards us is a soldier pushing an old shitty wheelbarrow with a flat tire. In the wheelbarrow is a Canadian soldier who does not look in the best shape. This guy is extracting a soldier who went down with a heat stress case by himself. No security other than the incoherent guy half holding his C7 in the wheelbarrow. The guy pushing is extracting this casualty back all by himself. Between us and the lead elements are between 500m and 1000m. With the complex terrain, it is easy to get isolated away from other teams and these two had no working radio. There may not be Taliban around here, but we are clearing these grape fields for a reason, and Western Panjawaii is a historic hot spot. A flat wheelbarrow tire, pushing a one-hundred-and-eighty-pound guy plus 60 pounds of kit through territory that is known to be seeded with IEDs and the Taliban constantly had small patrols out that we would contact. We grabbed the dude to give him aid and set up MEDEVAC. We help him, and I ask what is going on; he explains that these two guys were on a two-person flank security task, and one of them drops from the heat. The guy behind the wheelbarrow panics because he can't get anyone on the radio, can't find anyone in the maze of Alleys, finds the wheelbarrow and, without telling anyone, heads back by himself through bad guy country. I had four tours and been in a lot of stuff, and that kid was one of the stupidest, bravest things I ever saw. I didn't know whether to jack him up or tell him good job. A fine line between hard and stupid.

We were on hard rations for a couple of months. We got some fresh meals, but it was a diet of "boil in a bag" Meals Ready to Eat (MRE). This just meant you left the silver packs out in the sun to heat up your meal, or, if you had time, you would boil water and do all the extras like powdered mashed potatoes or the rice. Dessert could be chunky pudding or some weird cake thing that stayed moist for months. Hot sauce became man's best friend, and the ration did not matter; hot sauce went into it to give it some fire. The other thing that we ate all the time was pop-tarts. At some point, the army must have bulk-ordered pop tarts, and they were pushed out with the resupply. These were so popular that I think troops went into a calorie deficit because Pop-Tarts were basically what we'd lived off. We were sick of rations at that point in time, you know? The rations are good but they all kind of taste the same. We would eat Pop-Tarts to the point of getting sick. Often, they would get crushed in the resupply trip out or in our kit when we were moving around, so we would just pour the crumbs into our mouths, and that would be our meal. When I got home, I couldn't look at a pop tart. I still can't.

I think the stress of combat is really hard for those people at home. I know that sounds strange because, of course, it is hard on us, but the news of what was happening to us travelled so fast back home, and I think all the live newscasts brought them into our reality. It wasn't abstract; their spouses were in this fight and could be hurt or killed, and it played on their minds. I did 4 tours over there, and my wife lived through every minute. She actually dislocated a rib by watching a movie while I was overseas. She was watching "For the Boys" (I think it is called), starring Bette Midler. It's about the U.S.O show. They're entertainers, and they go to the battlefields through World War 2, to Korea, and then they go to Vietnam and entertain the troops. In Vietnam, she has a son. He's a platoon commander in Vietnam. They're performing for the Vietnam guys; in one of the firebases, an attack goes off. Everybody scrambles. The son gets shrapnel in the back or whatever. When that happened, my wife said that at that instant she saw me, she had been reading about rocket attacks and knew that I was out with the infantry. She cried so much that she popped a rib. I immediately felt terrible. I was fine. It also amazed me. Somebody that concerned about, Someone who loves actually to love you back that much? We laughed about it after, but it really upset her at the time. That is when I realized how they lived in a state of constant stress at home, and the tour for us was a tour for them also.

I rolled out to the field from KAF on one set of combats. We were supposed to be out for 4 days and we were out for over 35 days with no resupply of uniforms. I tried washing my shit every day. We would draw water from whatever compound we were in and use the old washboard and a galvanized steel tub. I had some socks and underwear spares, but I had saved room in my ruck for ammo and water, so the extra combats went. I learned that lesson and always ensured I had a spare pair of pants afterward.

We were a rifle section working in Zhari and Panjawaii. There were a ton of IEDs.

They seemed to be everywhere. We were very aggressive about counter-IED drills and avoiding known routes. The grape fields are set up to canalize along these narrow routes and trails. There are 6-foot walls on either side of the trail. If someone put an IED in the trail, you were going to hit it. To not get caught in choke points, we avoided the trails, made our own routes and never took the easy way twice. We had an axe and sledgehammer that we used to make our pathways by smashing through these mud walls. We called them " the keys to Panjwaii". It was hard to smash down walls and hop over walls through the fields. it was worth it because we also didn't lose our legs.

———————————

Things were getting real. When the orders were given, the O.C. said his piece because there were so many moving pieces, he wanted to simplify what the tasks and scheme were so that we could get after it . Holy fuck it woke us up. He let us know the threat, and there were dug-in enemies all over the location. He laid out his scheme and what we were supposed to be doing over the next couple of days. It was clear that once we got there, anything moved over on the other side of the River, even a guy moving on a bike; it was enemy forces moving between positions. It filled us with confidence; it was such a change for Canadians. We had not come over with this type of action in mind, but it was what we had to do now. He said, if they surrender, use these little cards, you will behave like a Canadian soldier in accordance with the Laws of Armed Conflict. We will do it all by the book but we will get our job done. I had not had that type of experience before, and I thought the OC did a great job prepping us for a shit task.

———————————

One of the things we had to do in Kabul was count burqas. The higher-ups wanted to make a city count of burqa-clad women and use a reduction of burqas as a measure of the success of NATO presence. I'm not sure it was helpful or useful, but there was a requirement for metrics, so they wanted to know which zones there appeared to be a reduction of burqas. Why are there certain zones where people still wear burqas more? And where there were burqas, could we lessen the influence of non-Western perspectives in those zones? I think it was all fake metrics. Count Burqas! Try counting baseball caps in Toronto as an indicator of something ..how useful is that? Fucking weak…but I counted burkas to make sure the patrol report was full. Stupid and pretty elitist. Not up to us to decide what people wear. Seems like we had this democratic freedom thing all wrong, like it was only our version that was right.

We got detached to the guns north of PBW and did security for the guns. They were happy to see us because they were doing their own security and getting worn out. All day and all-night fire missions and then security as well so, no sleep for them. They were happy to see us, and we were happy to be there cause it's a big open desert, your arcs are clear, and there's nowhere for anyone to hide. Then they told us one day, like, if you guys wanna come run the gun, you can do that. We'll just show you how to run it, and then you fire a fire mission, and it'd be cool. Ya, cool. They come over and get us one day, and the Master Bombardier is like, alright, and he divvies up the jobs for firing the M777. Ok, so you're the guy on the curvy stick, you're going to put the bullet on the cradle, you place the charge bag, you're gonna close the door, you pump the handle, you get to pull the string. I, as the Master Bombardier, will look through the sight. Do what you're supposed to do when I tell you to do it. Cool. He's listening to the radio, and he's like, alright, show time, and he gives directions, put a bullet on the cradle. He puts a bullet in the cradle. Curvy stick, go! He pushes the curvy stick up and pushes the bullet into the gun. Bag! Puts the bag in. Door! Closes the door. Pump the handle! Pump, pump, pump. Pull the string! BOOM. And we're all like YAAA we did it!! And he's like, alright, 15 more, let's go, and we're all like, oh shit! Bullet on the cradle, curvy stick, bag in, door, pump, pump, pump, pull the string, BOOM, YEAH!! The enthusiasm waned as the fire mission was going on, but it was a lot of fun for the first few.

Human waste needs to be disposed of. We did it by burning shit in 45-gallon barrels cut in half. Part of our daily routine. Corporals and Privates, whichever one happened to draw the short straw that day for tasks. It's not fun. You need to mix fuel, diesel and gas, pour it over the shit barrels and light it, then stir it until it all burns off, inhaling that smell the whole time. One day, one of the guys mixed up the ratio of gas to diesel. It's supposed to be two diesel and one gas. You know, if you do two gas and one diesel, it pops and explodes. Well, he did like 3 to one gas to diesel and had a massive blowout, covering him and his partners in shit. It's bad for morale but funny.

Maybe I was lucky because my wife wasn't engaged in the news, so she wasn't aware of how violent things were overseas. I liked it that way. My platoon Commander blew that up. He really fucked me on this one. She didn't really follow the news there were rumours on the wife network of what was going on, but I always downplayed it when I called back home and did not really let her know what I was doing. I remember we had an embed reporter with us, and we were travelling from KAF. It was a fucking downpour. We're returning from a patrol, and this reporter is with us, beside my LAV; a huge flash went off. So, we called in, you know, the reports and all that. We came to find out later that it was an IED that went off and missed us. A few days later, we're doing an operation, and we drive over a double-stack anti-tank mine with a pressure plate. But the guy never attached one of the wires, so it never went off. I saw it as we rolled over it. The engineers dug it up, took a picture, and the embed reporter reported this in a newspaper. My platoon commander was a great guy who was giving the interview and told the story, "This happened. It was no big deal. Blah, blah, blah." The same day I told my wife that, nothing's going on. We're just in the camp. The fucking Pl Comd does this big interview that highlights me by name, and it gets back to my wife through the network and Facebook. She reads the report, I tell her nothing is going on the phone that nothing's going on. When she found out, I felt like I would have rather faced the IED, to be honest!

The FOBs were pretty safe, save the occasional bad luck rocket or mortar round. We got back one night and were getting ready for a shower when a rocket hit it. It had to be the only time a Canadian was not in the shower trailer late at night. Sadly, It actually ripped an interpreter right in half. Think of the odds of an artillery round through a fucking human being. We had to clean that up. It was terrible; I had been talking to my aunt when it happened, she heard the explosion, and then the line went dead. That was not good for morale. When I finally got to call her back, it was like I had to calm her down. Funny I was the one doing the business and I was responsible to calm her down.

We had to go to KAF to add new armour to the LAV cupola. We drove back in. It was an opportunity to chill out, buy some shit and just have a break. As soon as I got out of the vehicle, I realized I didn't have my beret or bush cap. I have my helmet. I have nothing else. I think fucking whatever, who cares, it is a non-saluting zone, and it is just a hat. I bloused my pants. I put rank on and I'm walking toward the boardwalk in KAF to grab a burger. I should have remembered how important hats are to the Army. As I'm walking down, this SUV does a U-turn. This total Fobber Master Warrant Officer hops out. He sees my rank and says, "Hey sir, you know, like the uniform, you need to wear a hat. Right. So, you could tell a KAF guy versus a non-KAF guy. Cause they have like clean uniforms. It's just a different look; they don't have that black-like grossness you get from wearing it constantly in the field. So, he knows automatically, like where I'm where I'm coming from. But he keeps pushing, "Where's your headdress?". I try, ", oh yeah. You know, I left it in Sperwan Ghar. I don't have it. Just a mistake. He could not get over it, "but you need to have a headdress on!" I answer, "it's a no saluting area. I made a mistake; I'm just going to get a coffee." "I am not going to take the 2 hours to go sign for a headdress at stores. I'm not going to go spend my time off getting a fucking headdress, man. I'm here for like three hours. I don't know how you think this will end, but I know I'm gonna be gone back to the field and in Zangabad before you get someone up the chain of command to jack me up." I kept walking and left him there, all pissed off. These interactions were so frustrating; I always found that there were two personalities in KAF. There were people that were uncomfortably sycophantic to anyone who was outside the wire, which is super awkward as well, and then you had people who were really complete douchebags that there was no just normal. I hated KAF and always felt that if I had these types of problems, how were my privates and corporals treated? Like just use common sense and have some empathy.

Getting sick was something that accounted for a good number of soldiers being left out of battle over the years. One of my first tours was terrible. We had a task out by Poli-Charki prison to guard the ammunition compound, and we lived in these open tents. The prison shitters were not of a high standard, and the human fecal matter would dry and then blow in the wind. Our camp was in the plume, and all our food and the air was full of microscopic grossness. Everybody got the fucking krunk. I got so sick and a bunch of dudes had to be medevac'd back to Julian for gut medicine and IVs to keep us hydrated. We packed all the sick guys into a couple of LAVs. We went back in the LAV, a very small, tight compartment, and as the vehicle was moving, everyone was throwing up in this one garbage bag. One of the guys puked so hard that he cracked ribs. It was like a mass casualty. Just disgusting. I never got sick, ever. That was the only time I got sick in Afghanistan over 3 tours. I think I lost like 14 pounds in a day… I will never forget the back of that LAV. One of the guys is shitting and puking at the same time into two different buckets as we are rolling back to Julian. It was insanity; It was terrible. It was just terrible.

I remember we finally got some showers when setting up Julien. It had been a couple of weeks. You had to walk by our tent to get to the new showers. The Kabul crunch, our name for a violent type of gastro, kicked in around the same time. It was terrible, and no one was immune. I remember we could sit there we'd just watch the guys walk in the shower after a shift and then they would get like halfway back to their tent and just shit themselves as they are walking. They could just turn around, walk back, and then they process again with all the shower kit on. So miserable to be a grown man and be shitting yourself. We all got it, but it was terrible.

This reporter was in Masum Ghar and came to see me about coming out on patrol with my OMLT team. I let her know that we were doing a big sweep through the grape fields South of three tank hill like from Panjawaii to Sperwan Ghar. We were probably going to be out for three or four days and we were going to find the guys that had laid an IED and killed one of our POMLT guys. She says that seems pretty dangerous. and was going to go out with the PRT to do a village outreach patrol. I let her know that I thought driving on the roads was way more dangerous than walking in the grape fields, but up to her. She thought the PRT was a better story. I said goodbye and wished her luck. The next day we were on our Op and there was a huge explosion, a PRT LAV had hit a massive IED and killed a number of people in the back, including a Canadian reporter. I thought it was sad and so odd; it also showed that that things that people thought were more dangerous weren't; the most dangerous thing was transiting roads; it took a while for people to figure that out; those roads were the kill zones. I will never forget that discussion or her choice. I don't feel guilty, but I feel sad for her and those troops, and sometimes I wonder if I should have insisted.

There was a threat of rockets and mortars against Camp Julien, so they would darken the camp at night. I'm walking back from the company headquarters and it's pitch-black dark. There was a massive shit ditch that cut the camp in half, and there were only three spots to cross at this point, they weren't proper bridges, and they weren't marked. So, you'd have to kind of gage and feel your way across. It was probably about four or four and a half, five feet ditch. I misjudged, and I went headfirst into it; I got up and got over the ditch, and no one saw because it was pitch black. But I had lost my wedding ring. I was just newly married then, just married before that tour. I was more concerned about my new wife (my second and I did not want a third) losing it on me than I was about being covered in shit. So, I went back into the ditch because I was already covered in shit looking for this ring. I went shit water diving until I found it. It was disgusting I am surprised I didn't die from some rare disease. I never told my wife that story. Still have the same ring today.

We're on a foot patrol, and we stop somewhere, and there's this fucking emaciated fucking Afghan chicken that is chasing us is clucking and being annoying. It's an Afghan chicken like, fuck, she's got a horrible life as it is. One of the troops decides that he's going to toss a rock at this fucking chicken. I was like, hey, what the fuck are you doing? Leave the fucking chicken alone. Like, She's got it bad enough. She's an Afghan fucking chicken. Leave her alone. How would you like me to throw rocks at you? You had to make sure that the troops stayed centred and didn't get cruel or do something stupid because they were bored or pissed off, and you had to watch that they were not just becoming cruel as they got more used to death and violence. The chicken is small, but you need to watch the small things and protect their humanity.

Spin Boldak is kind of a crazy forward operating base in the middle of nowhere near the border with Pakistan, surrounded by the red sands of the Reg Desert. It was like something out of a movie. It originally housed the French Foreign Legion. It was fitting because it looked like something out of a French Foreign Legion movie from the 30's. It had big mud walls like a castle and a big gate. It had a massive tower in the centre, and within the structure, all the walkways were covered with ratan woven coverings, so you always walked in the shade. It had all these little tiki bars on the inside. The French had buried empty bottles of wine everywhere and they would work their way to the surface. Basically, the French would just dig a whole with their foot and then bury the bottle where they finished it. It had its own Afghan security force with a couple of real characters leading it. You know that book by Dr Seuss that had the characters "thing one and thing two". Instead, the local leaders were just called commander number one and commander number two, nobody understood any English. So, it was always awesome to try and articulate what we needed. To their credit, they did a great job of protecting that camp. We didn't stay down there that long, but it was like this weird world, we shared the camp with an ODA, whose leaders looked like Billy Bob Thornton. They would just get up and hurl shells into Pakistan with their 120mm mortar and hang out with the Afghans. It was a pretty jammy go down there, but I was happy when we left. It felt like something out of Apocalypse Now.

I had bad experiences going back to the main camp, KAF. It's not an us or them thing, but the issues are different for those that live out and those that live in. There's a stark contrast to how you're living in your everyday existence. You are hit in the face with the difference when you go to the boardwalk. This one time we came back in and it had been a bit of a bad day. I came back in for a ramp ceremony because we had lost a guy and went to grab a coffee at the Green Beans. After I went for a walk with my coffee to see people and check out the camp, there was a four-string quartet boardwalk. No shit... a four-string quartet and there seemed to be "couples" enjoying the warm evening air and listening to classical music. It was such a dissonance, the music would be interrupted by the occasional fighter jet taking off, and I had to really think about where I was, 6 hours prior I had been tip toing through grapefields, getting shot at and had put one of my friends into a body bag. This is such a different world. Folks in KAF are so separated from what we are doing that they almost have a kind of a real life. I just felt if I didn't fit in and I didn't want to be there, If this is what we're doing here, that just doesn't seem right. After that, I tried to avoid KAF and just stayed in the field. KAF fucked with my head.

My biggest fear was not in terms of being shot and losing a limb or when my biggest fear was screwing up so badly that, you know, I caused the mission to fail or possibly getting troops killed or injured. We had lost some guys to an IED. There was intelligence that said that the bombmaker was in our area or the facilitator. We were able to train to do a raid on this place to capture him. We trained, and as part of it, my platoon was supposed to set the outer cordon. This was a very personal raid, and we wanted everything to go well. It was in the city's centre, a mess of alleyways, compound walls and obstacles. It is a mess. It was also the first time we had used SPERWER as overwatch, so everyone could see the whole raid in real-time. We go through orders; the SF guys help us with CQB and how to grab detainees and teach the engineers to do SSE. I need to get set first and then my guys will get " eyes on" and be the recce element that will lead the strike team into the objective area. You don't want the assault force bumbling around in the city at night, and you want them led to the right door and do the hit. Well, my team got disoriented in the city, and they got lost. The Recce team got fucking lost! And so now, I am sweating because I have to sort this out, and the bosses are watching through the UAV and most importantly, I could fuck up the whole mission, and we lose the opportunity to smash the guys that killed our dudes. But we're lost in a maze of alleyways and compounds. I would say this is a great vignette for young platoon commanders. This is one you got to earn you've got to earn your pay because everybody is looking at you saying, what do we do, sir? It was about pausing for a moment and THINKING, and I was able to navigate to a known point and start again. We totally had to drop the ego, acknowledge the mistake and then get through the alleyways; we managed to reorient everybody and bring them through to successfully do the hit. When they breached and found information and carted that guy out with a bag over his head, I was so relieved that I had not fucked it up.

The OC had a negligent discharge. There were no witnesses; he self-reported. He was outside his vehicle, and he decided to clear his weapon. He was not paying attention, messed up the drill and put the round in the ground. No one saw it. No one heard it. He got back into the LAV, told the dudes, and then reported it to the HQ. The general charged him, and it was essentially a self-charge. The guys asked, why did you tell us that? He didn't want to get away with something that a soldier would get charged for. It was an amazing example of self-discipline and respecting the rules. The soldiers loved him more after.

We're going to escort the guns because they're moving the guns to a new position. We went down to their position with a platoon and got ready to bring the guns back. We get into the camp, get linked up and get ready to move. The interpreter with the ICOM hears chatter and explains that they're waiting for you to come back to hit us. They referred to the LAVs as tanks and stated, "The tanks are coming back; we will hit them when they come back." OK, so now we know, At some point along our route back, we're going to come into contact. We're prepared for that. Without us knowing, an American patrol left before us. It wasn't planned, and we couldn't warn them because they were on a different radio channel. We were maybe ten-fifteen minutes behind them. We heard explosions and shooting. When we rolled up, the Americans were decimated; they paid the price, and they lost six guys. Where they got hit and how the ambush was set up would not work out well for anybody in that area because the TB locked down the position. What added insult to injury is that the American first sergeant, or whomever the platoon 2IC was, said they were waiting for the casualty collection point to get set up, and when he set it, they moved the casualties in the CCP. The Taliban knew the collection of casualties would occur, and they focused on striking that and killed six guys in the CCP by direct fire. An American Apache attack helicopter team showed up and killed the Taliban as they retreated across open fields. But it was a bad day, and though I was glad we didn't get hit, I felt guilty that they took on an ambush that was meant for us.

I responded as part of the QRF when one of our patrols had been hit by a suicide bomber. A suicide bombing is an incredibly shocking and violent event. The blast not only causes casualties but tears the bomber apart. There is a requirement to find all the parts and ensure the bomb is defused. The pieces are used as evidence and are assessed to see if anything can be understood by the lab as to who made the bomb and if we can attack the bomb maker later. This is called "attack the network" and leads to slow collection of the evidence and it is treated more like a crime scene rather than a military operation. By the time we arrived, the wounded had been Medevac'd, and our fallen was still on scene but had been covered up by a blanket. We set the outer cordon and a civilian bus was within the scene. There were civilian fatalities and casualties that had been moved away as well. Some bikes were resting in bloodstains, and a couple of bicycles were hanging in trees. People have obviously been hit by this bomber. This dude walked up to my teammates' jeep and initiated the explosion. The bomber's legs were resting in the middle of the road, having been thrown by the explosion, and the side of the bus was splattered with human remains, hair and blood. He had 2x82 millimetre mortar bombs strapped to him. The upper torso was flung another hundred meters away, and outer cordon troops had found the torso. Only one of the bombs had gone off; the other was still lodged in his torso. I called everybody over, and the IED team and engineer that was going to have to diffuse it. In that sense, the patrol was lucky. It was gruesome but necessary work. The suicide bomber had killed one Canadian and wounded two others but had killed and wounded many more Afghans. It is a terrible weapon and tactic. I will never understand it.

Afghanistan taught us to use some new equipment, but the most important was not what you would expect. There are some things we could've used. We begged, borrowed and stole from the Americans' smoke grenades and Infrared para flares for very good reasons. Locals were told not to dig at night as it was perceived as hostile intent. Some of them chose to because it's cooler. Usually, they're digging irrigation ditches. We would pop an IR para flare that we got from the Americans and observe with our night vision. The folks on the ground are none the wiser. We could see if these guys are digging in an IED or an irrigation ditch. Because quite frankly, we didn't have to, but we didn't want to shoot innocent people. So those IR paraflares helped us determine the intent and observe more clearly. The M203 smoke we didn't have it issued to us. Just the Yanks did. It was so helpful if you had top cover from the attack helicopters; you could mark a target reference. Shoot the M203, Red smoke. That's the target. You kill it. But one of the most useful pieces of equipment we had there, much to the chagrin of the locals, was a sledgehammer and an axe. You're fixed on your COP. There are only two ways into the zone to patrol. The Taliban can guess where you will go and can lay IEDs on either route. Once you get a little separation from the base, you can make your own trails through the mud walls. We'll make a hole in that. What we're going this way. No, we're not going to go down where they expect. We're gonna go where they don't expect, and they don't know we're gonna put these holes in these walls. We put a lot of holes in a lot of walls. There are bad people out here trying to kill us, and we need to do everything possible to survive and take the fight to them.

We had a ground intelligence of TB movements about 6km from our base. The BG TOC called in artillery fire on it. We also received intelligence on enemy movement from aircraft. I said, OK, you know what? We're going to launch on it. We'll try and figure it out on the ground and we'll mount a patrol. Let's stop trying to do this from 20000 feet. We'll do our BDA quickly and see what comes out of it. Well, we didn't have to do the BDA because the Taliban drove all the wounded fighters up to us. The guys that came up were all wearing these black turbans and had huge beards and looked fierce but had no weapons, so we couldn't do anything. All the wounded were kids, like older teens and younger, but that fit as the Taliban had been using kids to dig in IEDs. "Fighting Aged Males" or FAMs is how they are described in reports. Seemed to range from 9 to 40 years old. We started doing first aid and we're evacuating them. I think that all takes its toll on you. What is a " fighting age male"? They all seemed to be fighting. 14? 17? 21? I consciously knew they were using kids, but it was so fucked up that rounds would go in on targets and then the enemy would bring us their wounded, but just the young ones. So, our soldiers just saw the kids and their handlers and local commanders watched us care for them. On patrols we found TB hospitals, where older fighters went. I think they did it as a form of psychological warfare, on purpose or not; it was effective; constantly seeing kids hit runs you down and sticks with you.

This reservist replacement guy just came in to replace somebody in our section who had gotten hurt. He was a great big fucking guy. Not an easy task for anyone as a replacement. Harder on a reservist. One of the things the section loved was these Spunkmeyer muffins. We had like a fucking pallet of fucking Spunkmeyer muffins on a 6 ft-by-6 ft pallet of yummy goodness. The Spunkmeyers were a high calorie treat, US I think, I am sure not good for you. They would stay moist and soft for weeks in their cellophane wrappers. So many preservatives, and they were 460 calories in each muffin! This pallet had to last until resupply, and so these fuckers needed last. The rationing was serious business. We come back from patrol this one day. The new guy was left in overwatch in the turret, and when we got back, there was a serious dent in the Muffin ratio. The section is not happy; equilibrium has been upended because these fucking muffins are gone. So much anger at this new kid. We are going you kill you, motherfucker. Why the fuck would you eat so many fucking muffins? Troops were mad. I am trying to keep the peace. I say, slow your roll, folks; he didn't know. He doesn't know anything yet. Not a good start to his war. Now we have to integrate this guy. We took him on his first patrol. He's all pasty white, just out of Canada. No sun on his skin. He is having a hard time with the heat and likely sweating out the load of Spunkmeyer he consumed. I get him as my partner. So, we have the 84mm, and I give him two eighty-four rounds. All he had to do was put them in a small pack. We went on a small patrol. Panjwai, that village that runs along the river. At the base of the tall mountains in the area. We head out, and the snipers engage someone in the distance. This kid reacts to the outgoing fire, and with the weight in his backpack, he rolls his ankle. He can't walk it back. So, we need to MEDEVAC him. Bad start. In the first three days, he eats all the Spunkmeyer muffins; troops want to kill him, and he can't last on his first patrol. Life's a bitch in the infantry.

The whole tour went by, and we never saw clouds in the sky, fucking sunny every day, clear skies, and 50 degrees every day. All of a sudden, this monsoon or big storm came over India and Pakistan, and it reached all the way into Afghanistan. The temperature dropped, the skies went black, and the temperature dropped from fifty-two to thirty-two. It sounds crazy, but that 20-degree drop makes it feel so cold! We're in the middle of this open desert, miles away from anything, watching this village because the governor of Kandahar province was coming in to do a little bit of outreach in the community. It starts pouring rain. This monsoon comes in. There was thunder and lightning. It's just raining sideways. This young guy was new. This new fella in our section just starts kind of crying. And we're under the LAVs to get protection from the rain because it is so hard it hurts and hail pellets and I think dust. It really sucked. This kid is crying, and I'm like, what the fuck is going on? Why is someone crying? It was super annoying; he was like hyperventilating like a little kid. Maybe he was still a little kid, like 18 or 19 but he was supposed to be in the fucking infantry. He was a replacement and so had not lived out for extended periods or grown resilient. It annoyed me. We needed to get him to shut the fuck up. It was bad for morale to hear this crying. I mean everyone could cry right? What went wrong in your life that you are huddled under an armoured vehicle sheltering from crazy weather in a country where everyone wants to kill you? Maybe there was reason, but I didn't want to hear it. Eventually, the rain stopped, and so did the crying. Maybe it was just a release and he didn't know we could hear because the wind was so high. We didn't say anything, and neither did he. We just carried on like nothing happened. I do think that when people talk about simulation being the same as training, I laugh. I think that this is a good example. You can't simulate the suck; you have to live it to get resilient.

––––––––––––––

The shit we carried. It's a huge weight, and I can't remember it being heavy at the time, and I don't remember ever being incapable of carrying it. But it is difficult. I mean, memory pain is dulled, but it didn't seem like that big physical feat. But consider the load. The CQ just loaded you up. Here are your ceramic plates and body armour, like 25 pounds. C9 LMG 16.5 pounds, Here is your M 72-4lbs, 4 boxes of C9 25 pounds, here are your grenades and all the little stuff. So just your personal kit is like 70 pounds. Then you need to Carry platoon water and platoon ammo. Then advanced to contact all day in temperatures between 35 and 50 degrees… I tried to kind of put that shit on recently, and I went blind in one eye. I had this massive searing pain in my neck, and I'm just like, how the fuck did I do this in Afghanistan? Like, I know I was younger, but I mean, shit, we humped a lot of kit.

It was the stupidest thing I had ever seen. I think it might have been actually a flashmob. We went to one of the camps for the day, and the people in the camp there broke out of flash mob. In Afghanistan at one of the big HQs. It was a combination of Americans and British and just a bunch of people around the green beans. Just people doing this stupid dance that they must have had time to rehearse because they never left camp. I remember we had just returned from patrols and looking at my section 2IC. Where the fuck are we?

We definitely had close calls. We were lucky. We had a close call with a friendly fire from the Artillery. We were doing a joint dismounted operation with the ANA. We had light contact and were just moving from one position to another position. We could hear the artillery coming in, we hadn't called it, which is a scary, scary sound. There was a big ravine just off to our left, and as we heard the rounds we decided to wait it out there. As the bombs landed, we hunkered down in this wadi, which provided us with shelter. The triple seven round landed right by us. It was so loud and I thought we were fucked for sure. The only person that got injured was our signaller who got hit by a little piece of shrapnel in his ass. He was screaming like a bitch. Our TCCC went over, and remembered like he did the whole checking everything to make sure he was alive, and we couldn't find anything just to find out it was the tiniest piece of shrapnel in the ass; it was all psychological. Once he knew he wasn't going to die, he carried on. The initial reaction to that incoming Artillery was that we're all fucking dead. To have one guy was just a little injured, not even like a Band-Aid. We were pretty lucky. Sometimes, it pays to slow down and just see what is going on if something feels off. The choice to go to the wadi was key, it saved lives, sometimes it is better to be lucky than good.

One thing that struck me was the detainee issues. It was frustrating because we used ANP to take the detainees because we weren't taking them ourselves. I was a little conflicted on, you know, what's the difference if we're if we take the detainee and hand him over? Or if they just take them? If we're concerned about handing him over. Why are we not concerned about them taking them? You know, what's the difference? It was political. If we took a detainee, we were responsible for their welfare, so we just "screened them," and the Afghans took all the detainees. Lawyer tricks to keep the government out of trouble. When I was with the ANP, sometimes they saw stuff I didn't, so maybe they were right, and if I interfered, I was wrong. The answer was, you know, it's their country. They want to take a dude; it is their country, you know? We're not concerned about these things in general; we are concerned about our equities. Kind of a vague thing that's interesting. Like now all that history interesting to me, when they had all those discussions in Ottawa. We sat at that that crossroad of strategic policy as tactical soldiers. There's the legal and ethical guides and we were walking the line. I didn't see any abuses, The politics of detainees was something I was aware of and considered. Though I was powerless, they had autonomy in their country, and we did not take detainees.

I have had lots of great leaders to work with. But it is also important to talk about the ones that are not so great. I was a warrant and 2IC of a platoon. The warrant's job is to help new platoon commanders as their number two and to mentor them to smooth the edges between training as a 2 LT and the real world. The relationship is usually symbiotic, and the platoon commander grows, and eventually, the "training wheels" come off, and they lead on their own. Sometimes they know everything and listen to no one and are dangerous. My platoon commander in Kabul had zero experience, zero experience, and trying to get him to understand at the end of the day that when he passes on orders, we're going to carry him out. But you'd be smart to talk to your Sgts and your platoon warrant, who all already had tours in different places and get their opinion. You don't have to listen, but engagement is helpful to create understanding. In the end, when the decision is made, we're going to support it. But to do it blindly and then give orders is a perfect example of bad leadership. We were going out on a deliberate clearance mission as a platoon within a Company construct with. The platoon commander wrote up his orders and he gave the warning order. I did the platoon Warrant Officer thing and we had the map model built in the area and all this stuff using the ammo cans and that. I asked him the night before if he wanted me to look over his orders and give some thoughts before he gave them… He's like, no, I got this. OK, but if you let me, I can tell you, just by reading your orders, what questions the NCOs are going to ask. He says, "Remember Warrant, I'm a small unit tactical genius." I think he was kidding, but he also didn't let me see his orders, like it was a big reveal or some shit. The next morning, orders were zero 6, we were leaving at ten, and his orders were horrible. He got torn up by the section commanders. They had one fair question, "what's the mission?" He went through orders and never mentioned mission once! Rule number one…tell us the mission…that is why we say it twice! I wanted to help him, to ensure that we were stronger. I found him to be very childish. He was one of these young RMC guys and very immature as a platoon commander for his first tour in Afghanistan. It was very exhausting because two of the Sgts did not want anything to do with him. I was always trying to buffer between them and the platoon Commander, like, "Hey, guys, Roger, I know he said this, but he means this, and this is how we're going to do it and blah, blah, blah". Just like a bad war movie script. It was hard balancing between the Platoon Commander and the NCOs. I will admit it was hard to keep the peace. And sometimes, they would just blow up. There was one Sergeant. He just had enough. It was a lack of trust. This is the most important thing in a unit. Trust. This Pl Comd never allowed it to develop, he wanted to do it all his own way and did not understand that we were connected and wanted him to succeed, because then we succeeded. It was a good thing that this was Kabul, in the early days, and not Kandahar with the heavy fighting. We could absorb this type of leadership. Later on in the mission, not so much. When you have a platoon commander who thinks he's a small unit tactical genius it is hard on everyone.

Some days it was just so crazy. We would have weeks of nothing, and then BAM, everything at once. We were on QRF for probably the craziest three days of my life. The Afghans found a friggin I.E.D. We go to the site, secure the perimeter, and the engineers who deal with this while we control the bypass route. We watch one of these big trucks, the Afghan version of an 18-wheeler, driving by and watch it blow sky high on the bypass "safe route." We watch it happen. Not my problem. The route is cleared, and the truck is dragged off. Another platoon came by and asked how the route was. I let them know the routes clear from here to this intersection as that's where we came from. Anyway, they kept going; they went off-road and hit an IED, and the LAV driver was killed. So, we had to move from the first IED we were just finishing to the new scene. It was pretty messy. That was our first big LAV IED cleanup strike. I mean, the engine block was thrown 100m away from the scene. The LAV was all fucked up. There was shit everywhere. We were there for a while, cleaning up all that stuff until about midnight. Instead of heading back to base went to ground in a local compound. In the police station down the street, the cops fell asleep. The Taliban came and killed them all. When we woke up in the morning, the HQ wanted us to go there because they believed it was booby-trapped and it needed engineer clearance. So, after a busy 24 hours, 3 IED strikes, and two clean-ups, we head straight to the scene. We set the perimeter and send in search teams. The team lead comes out. I'm talking to him in the back of the

LAV on the hard pack going into the compound. He let me know they are almost done and actually just need to give the Afghans the body bags for their team that got killed, and it should be GTG to depart. Then BOOM. An IED goes off right near us. It throws me and my Master Corporal 10, 15 feet in the air and onto the ground, with shrapnel and dirt and rocks and pieces raining down on our heads. What the hell just happened? I am all fucked up. Then I heard a voice saying, We got a casualty. your instinct kicks in again. I checked out my partner; he was knocked out but good. The IED had been laid just off the track; when they went to hand out the body bags, someone had stepped off the track and had set it off. 4 guys were around the blast. Afghans and a Canadian. Those four are everywhere. One of their upper torso flew over top of us and literally landed right next to my C9 gunner's head. So, we need to grip this scene and confirm casualties. We still have the bodies from the night before, and now we know the area is boobytrapped. I'm runarounds. I am trying to sort it and send reports. It is a bit of chaos. "four VSA, one pri alpha, etc etc." We get our guy into the ambulance. At that point, He's still alive, and we medevac him. Now we have to do our thing. We're trying to clean up now. We are trying to clean up all the body parts and try to put them into body bags. It's a lot of body parts. So, I am trying to think about who I think is mentally strong enough to do this. No one wants to do this. Who do I think can handle this and get through this. I think some guys that I think over the training over the last year are pretty mentally strong. I give them the task of going around picking up the bodies. While this happened, one of the Cpls said, "We got a problem." He's behind a bit of a berm. In front of him, one of the KIA's kits had a grenade with no spoon on it, and it didn't explode. My engineers are all fucked up. They have done 2 IED sites in 24 hours, and now this third one with all the casualties. Now I need them to figure out this grenade that is in a KIA's kit. It is dirty work, and they got it done. Although I had been in the army a long time, no one had trained me for all those events. It was the worst three days I have ever had. The guys were awesome to come through it like they did.

Three million people in Kabul. No sewage system. Just these big ditches where people duck into to do their business or the house systems run into them. Sometimes they get full. It is really gross. We would patrol the street in these open topped jeeps and so were exposed to all the sights and smells. Pretty raw. We had this one driver who drove like he was vying for the F1 pole position. I tell him to always slow down, and he has this like lead foot. This one time he is cruising, he hits a patch of something, and the vehicle dips down quickly and starts to sink. He has broken the crust on something. The smell is getting more and more intense. We slowly realize what's going on; we're in a shit ditch, but not just a normal shit ditch. Like a massive ditch filled with excrement that the vehicle is sinking into like its quicksand. I have enough time to get up, run off the back and jump. I land on the edge of the pit and I pull myself up. The jeep was becoming completely submerged. In a couple of minutes, we wouldn't be able to see it. The other three guys did not move so quickly. This one big guy had his night vision goggle fall off when the jeep started sinking so he had to find it. So, he's up to is armpits trying to get his night vision and all the stuff is covering him and even got in his beard. He is wretching and swearing, and he finally finds his MNVG. We had a manpack radio, and we called recovery. We got him to get the vehicle back. The vehicle is towed back to Camp Julian, and it is put in the maintenance area. Camp June was big. When the wind shifted, you could smell that Iltis through the whole freakin camp. It was so disgusting. I was amazed we didn't catch something.

———————

We could have been a little bit more honest with our AO and how we fought in our AO. We kind of inherited the previous rotation's structure and we didn't do anything about it. In Afghanistan, if you weren't physically on the terrain or didn't have eyes on it, you put yourself at risk. The enemy would find those seams and IED them. The first IED that we had was on a route we had travelled regularly. The second one we hit, we actually watched them plant the IED. We were talking to a bomber the night before. The Overhead feed was a bit fuzzy, so there was a reluctance to drop a bomb on it because the only option was a 2000-pound JDAM. But when you put all the things together, like at 2:00 in the morning, someone digging on the road we are on all the time, it's not the fucking Kandahar road crew fixing the culvert. But the boss said no. The next day, guys drove all over it and were killed. That one broke our hearts. The fight was always like that, every day, trying to determine intent from 20000 feet through a soda straw, and most times, we got it right, but when we didn't, people paid. That was hard to live with. The counter-IED fight is a slow, hard slog that is hard on morale.

———————

I ended up on an I.V. for a couple of days. It was a super-hot out. I was passing out and losing my lunch. I had the crud hard. As soon as it hit, I went into role 1 for observation and treatment. I passed out. I woke up, and the IV had gone wrong; my hand was all puffed out..." Is this normal?" I asked the medic; her eyes widened.

"Oh god, no!" They sorted it and put me to bed, and I was shivering in my winter sleeping bag. And I've got every puffy jacket and cap on. It's still super-hot outside, but I was shivering and cold. You're so miserable. I came out of it after 48 hours and went back to my platoon 9 pounds lighter!

———————

There's this random memory. I remember the first time I was driving outside of Kandahar and realized, holy fuck, the people here do not like me, and some are trying to kill me. We were on an Op. We dropped the plow, and the Badger made the road fucking through grape fields. We're just ploughing through farmer's fields and whatnot. I remember looking over, I saw this this Afghan guy with his son. We probably looked like eight to ten, and as I was driving by, I waved to him like we did in Bosnia or Africa. In return, he made the gesture like he was going to cut my throat. And so, it's like, holy fuck. It was like a little bit like a little bit scary because it's very personal. Then I thought, I guess we're being kind of a dick because we're driving through your fields and making roads. But it opened my eyes that we were not always seen as helping and the next generation already didn't like us. I may have been naïve, but I don't think that I was the only Canadian to feel that surprise when I first got into theatre. We weren't used to being seen as the enemy.

———————

We got hit in our strongpoint by SPG9s, and RPGs volleyed fire, and they hit our tower. I worried that we had lost the guys up there. I see the person from the tower comes out and he's covered in talcum powder. He is pure white. But he is not a white individual. He's a black guy. He's white and covered in talcum powder. He's just saying sorry. I'm sorry. I'm so sorry. I'm sorry. I was so confused by that but I figure he is in shock. I find out later, he had a claymore clacker in his hand. He thought he blew himself up by hitting the clacker at the wrong time. He thought he blew it into the Camp. Of course, a claymore is not going to blow up the camp, but his mind could not connect that he had been on the receiving end of a lot of rockets. In his mind, this whole contact, he's coming out covered in Talcum powder that was placed in front of him in a bottle for foot care and blew back on him when the rocket hit, blinding him. He just caused the whole thing. He's still apologizing. We had to be a bit gentle before he was medevac'd to explain that it wasn't him and he had been attacked and probably had a concussion. It was the craziest thing what your mind will convince you of.

The PRT was fucking amazing. You go out and do the job. You always came back to the showers in the bathroom and the gym. I did three tours. Battle Group, OMLT and PRT. The BG and OMLT suck for living and eating, so if you are going to risk IEDs and ambushes why not have great food, a good gym and a bed to sleep in! Everyone else can tell the "I was hard as fuck" stories. I loved the PRT.

I was a Liaison Officer with the US forces on an Operation. We used the same route out that we used going in. Never a good idea. There's a little bit of a choke point, but we didn't go find an alternate route. It was kind of a cool, cloudy day. I was I was riding in a Humvee, which I wasn't supposed to as national rules said I needed to be in the most armoured vehicle. But I wasn't gonna kick an American out of a more armoured vehicles so that I could be more safe. I'm riding in the Humvee, the vehicle in front of us is an MRAP and an IED detonates. We stop and start scanning, there's only one motherfucker on the field because everyone else is gone inside because it is raining and he's out there hoeing like nobody's business, with this big explosion, it is like nothing happened near him. Head down, Hoe, and Hoe, He's building a garden. I'm like, that fucker, I am pretty sure he is the trigger man. Dust is settling guys are in the vehicle. We can see some movement we're just starting to come to because of the shockwave that came back and hit the Humvee because it's an open turret for the gunner, transferred inside, and we're all dazed and confused and stupid. Stagger out of the Humvee and start trying to organize stuff. The Afghans that are with us are just star bursting everywhere. All of a sudden Rocket comes flying in at us, but doesn't explode, just augers in like, okay, good, we can make this work. We're hunkered down in the dirt. We're waiting for the gunfire. But that was it. Then this one guy, sitting out there still hoeing. What the Fuck. Vehicles have exploded. Rockets have come in. He's still going away like nothing at all. So, we launch guys down. We grab him up. Grab his phone. Find the phone. Check the phone for calls made. No calls in the last two weeks except for the one that was dialled like 30 seconds ago. So, he's the detonator. They started doing other data collection, thumb printing. We started recovery, and The vehicle was dragging it off the X. As they were pulling it off, it exposed this secondary device. It is a big bomb with lots of HME. It's now been exposed, and it didn't explode. Everyone in the first vehicle is fine. We were lucky as fuck. Think of that. Choose one seat or another; go in the heavily armoured vehicle or don't; the rocket is accurate but doesn't go off, and secondary goes off or doesn't. All the permutations of what could have happened can fuck with your head. It is all luck.

So, we're all on Highway 1, and we're making our way back to KAF. We get hit by a fuckin VBIED. It struck us just underneath the driver's hatch sort of along the side of the boat. I was up in the air sentry hatch on that side with the C6. The week before, I'd strapped some containers to the side of the LAV to carry extra Jerry Cans and rucksacks to the side of the LAV. That box ended up being a godsend, eating a great deal of shrapnel that otherwise would have impacted my hands and face. When the car hit, I remember very, very vividly this column of fucking fire that came from this IED strike. It looked like it came from the fucking sky and was massive. I had enough time to think to myself, oh, my God, that's fucking hot. And then the next thing I know, I'm coming to the floor of the boat. Just had a bit of a glass jaw, I guess. I got knocked out. I'm on the floor of the boat, and there was a guy who was a paramedic before he joined the army, and he was in his element. He's all over it and is checking me out. He's like, I think I think you're OK. I can hear him shouting to the platoon commander up in the turret. Because I dropped so fast the platoon commander obviously had called me in as a casualty. Reasonable assumption: I was not dead, so that was good. Then I was up, moving and talking. We're okay. I was downgraded to priority Charlie or something to that effect which is good. We didn't know nearly as much about TBI or concussion as we do now. I had my bell rung hard. The LAV was all fucked up, and I just wanted out of it. I couldn't open the back door. The boat had been fucking twisted by the blast. We pile out of the top of the boat and just collapse into a fucking yard sale on the ground. I managed to get myself up, and I'm looking around in this fucking terrible daze like I know what's happening, but I can't verbalize it, and I know I'm fucked up. But I'm too fucked up to know that I'm too fucked up if that makes any sense. I'm looking around and looking for a job to do. I see the platoon medic and he's running around and he's working on some civilian casualties from the blast, and it is like one of those movies where there is lots going on but no sound and my eyes are in and out of focus. I remember looking down the line, and a buddy of mine who I deployed with several times had found a length of the human spinal column, likely from the suicide bomber, looked over, and he goes, "Look at this, I'm the Predator." He was fucked up from the blast also; the Medic comes over and gently takes the spinal column from him and moves him to the casualty collection point, and then he comes to see me. Apparently, my eyes were all fucked up, and he wanted me to go sit down and let someone else do security; I didn't even have my rifle; I was just standing there like an idiot. We were lucky, just a bit of shrapnel and a blast; we needed to get treated in KAF. The bomber died, and all he did was kill himself and hurt some of his own people. I was glad we all lived.

***

I was in Kabul, and the routine was pretty set unless there was something big going on. I was in snipers, and if there was a fastball, we didn't really know what was happening 'til the day of or a couple hours before the Operation. It was a pretty quick flash-to-bang kind of thing. What I remember is get up at whatever time in the morning. Usually, the mornings were relaxing as we patrolled at night. The afternoon we're getting briefings. Then we would do prep and head out late afternoon or the evenings. It was really just presence patrolling, in Kabul during this point of the conflict we were stabilising and the threat was present but direct contacts were not. Especially in Kabul. All of NATO was there and we really just locked the city down. We did do a deliberate operation called "Operation Octopus" where we operated with the German battlegroup, the French and with the Gurkhas. And then I think we're with the Gurkhas for two weeks and then two weeks with the French Foreign Legion. These operations pushed outside of the city proper and to the edges and approaches of Kabul, where the Taliban were still operating. We never gained any contact. It was just kind of dull, the presence patrolling. It was to be visible. Based on European peacekeeping templates. It was hard because we did not understand the enemy, and even on that boring tour, we lost a couple of guys to enemy IED action. People often forget that the first Canadian casualties to enemy action were in Kabul. It kind of just gets forgotten because it was not the big show that the combat mission in Kandahar was. The routine was what it was. There were risks, but they were muted. I learned a lot, but on a day-to-day basis, I often wondered if what we were doing made a difference.

***

I went through orientation and received my med brief, and I just didn't know what to think about the malaria medication. I did a bunch of research on the mefloquine pills they gave me. I was like, I'm not taking the medication; that stuff makes you crazy. The docs said no. We recommend Mefloquine. I nodded; great, and I took the other one that didn't have all the write-ups about making soldiers nuts. They didn't recommend the alternative cause it was one day every day, and they knew soldiers would not stick to the habit. They were right. I took it at one o'clock for the first two days, and I had the shits every day. I stopped taking them a day three. I never got malaria, and I wasn't crazy from mefloquine.

I saw this big airplane go down in Kandahar in 2006. It was surreal. I mean, I have never seen anything like it. We are out in the desert waiting to go onto an attack, and we look up at the sky, and somebody's like, oh man, look at that plane; I think it is crashing. We all look at this plane and it's a fireball, a fireball flying over and we're like oh fuck, that's crazy, how did that happen? And then you hear this plane crashed and Recce is going to go and check it out. We were supposed to go attack an enemy position and then we had to stop because all the aircover went to secure the crash site. I'm sure the recce platoon had another task other than waiting for the plane to crash. So, when the plane crashes and the recce gets re-tasked to do that, it upsets everything else. We had a pause and then found out that the Operation would kick off 24 hours later once the crash was dealt with. It was sad; it was the largest loss of UK life in one day in the theatre. All I remember is this giant ball of flame and then the radio going crazy. You don't see that every day.

I did the first couple of months of my tour at a strong point in Zangabad. We were in firefights every day. After a while, I think they wanted to rotate us out due to the level of violence, and we got a task to go help with security at the Provincial reconstruction team. Camp Nathan Smith in Kandahar City had a completely different vibe. We were a combat-focused rifle platoon; our reality was digging in, patrolling, living on hard rats, the odd shower dodging IEDs and ambushes. Then you go into the city, and it's got good infrastructure to live in, and the focus is on reconstruction. Academically, it was possible to shift your thinking like that; I mean, doing reconstruction while fighting was hard. In Zangabad, we were living in armoured sea containers that were pockmarked with shell holes, and in CNS, we had sheets on beds, a kitchen and a gym, and instead of heating hard rations, we ate fresh every day. I mean, you get French fries there! It was just a totally different vibe. The PRT were on a schedule; they had a blend of civilian aid staff and other governmental departments for engagement and so worked during the day, dealing with their Afghan counterparts and had nights off. I remember we would watch movies in the evenings with the civil/military teams or CIMIC people. You know, there were also civilian women from foreign affairs or other governmental departments. It was like this parallel universe where Afghanistan was rational inside the protected envelope of this Canadian base in downtown Kandahar. We did not adjust quickly or well. It is hard to go from fighting every day in a high IED environment to one that is more permissive. Hard to wrap our minds around. I always felt like we were kind of like the knuckle-dragging outsiders that, like, you know, kept on reminding everyone that it was not Shangri la and that the moment you let your guard down, the enemy wouldn't hesitate to take your life. We had a high number of "use of force" incidents in the city. Meaning we used non-lethal force to get our point across. It caused some stress with the CNS folks. Neither group was wrong, but neither had been conditioned to deal with the other nor trained to interact in these ways. I was happy to get back to the Battle Group and Sperwan Ghar, where things made sense; we understood our role and felt like we were doing what was needed to fight and win.

We lived in our vehicles for weeks on end, just moving to keep the Taliban guessing and then leaguer in the desert so that we could gain security from stand-off and let our presence be known. I remember how I was totally amazed by how harsh the landscape was. It was just flat and looked like the surface of the moon with all the big rocks and white sand. It was barren and hot during the day and cold at night. There was no protection from the elements and so we constantly were in a game to find shade. I slept on the ground, just with a Therma rest. It's kind of cool because I remember looking at my Therma rest and thinking this looks like it's been used because it's starting to get torn up. I am not a fucking new guy anymore. It is funny that that's something I'd even think of. I would usually try to find a piece of shade from the vehicle and generally try to be on the inside of the vehicle as we had no armour. We were in G-Wagons for the most part… The G-Wagon was kind of like your home. We had three six-man sections, two G-Wagons per section and three dudes per car. So, I was your driver and then your section commander or 2IC. You have all your rucksacks and all your extra ammo, water and rations. I remember any time we'd have an interpreter with us like, there'd be no room for him to sit because everything would be stocked up so high. I mean, three rucksacks in that vehicle and, plus, like, all your other stuff. Basically, it is a small Mercedes SUV with three people living in it. Because there was no armour on these things, we blast blankets, layering the floors and seats Kevlar blankets that would catch shrapnel and hopefully mute blast if we ran over something. That was the safety; psychologically, it was good. It was good emotionally. Having seen 30-ton armoured vehicles ripped in half it was hard to consider that you were going to be OK in a jeep. It was funny how those blast blankets made it better. We were extra careful with our routes, and walked as much as we could. You just had to trust. It made me feel safer.

We took over a strong point at our handover, and you could see the scars of battle on all the walls and the bullet holes from the fights. The briefing that we got from the guys was like, "There's the graveyard that was here when this was a village. They attacked from there all the time and they'll open up with volleys of RPG. Then they'll hit you with MG till they reload their RPG and they'll keep doing that till they're out of RPG and then they fuck off or they die." It happens once about every twenty-five days, and you are due for one- have a good tour, fellas; we are Audi 5000. They left to head to KAF, and I was like, "FUCK". We're just like fuck, fuck. We were totally on edge and basically, I don't think we slept much initially. It was. We are going to get hit any second now, any second now. But it never happened. I think just as we arrived, the Taliban's money had dried up, so they went into their winter vacation. We're all keyed up, and nothing happened for the better part of three months. We got there expecting to be in a constant high-intensity gunfight at the start of the tour, and we had three months of nothing. But one day, 3 months in ...we ate it…it was like a light switch was flipped, and we fighting every day until the end of Sept.

I got burnt quite badly in an IED strike and was in the med centre in KAF to be treated. They were worried about inhalation from the smoke itself. So, they had to keep me awake. I was coherent. I was having a good conversation with them. They wanted me to self-notify my family that I had been hurt but was OK. I had a really hard time breaking bad news to my wife. I got on the phone with her, and her friend was visiting. They both had a yard sale the day before. My wife is eight and a half months pregnant. I called her in New Brunswick, the wrong time for normal calls, and so I knew she would pick up. This is different. So right away I ask, "How did the yard sale go." That's my that's my first question. She's like." It went fine." I mean what? How was the yard sale? That was my opener. She was onto me, "What the fuck's going on, you could care less about yard sales?" I got really choked up calling home and just mumbled. I explained to her like, I'm OK. I'm alive. Everything is still where it is supposed to be and I have some burn on my face. I'll be alright. Then I had to stay in KAF for a bit and recover. But the hardest part was letting her know that I would be going back out. It is a necessary but terrible process of calling home when you are wounded. After I hung up, I felt better, and I was allowed to go for a walk. My head was all bandaged up and I went to the Tim Hortons. When they saw the bandages and new I was wounded in an IED I could no longer buy coffee, it was free. Pretty sweet deal. Silver linings, I guess. You got to look at the upside. Burns on my face but I lived and got free coffee.

We had a big IED strike right under the driver. The blast had created a massive hole, and the driver was trapped in his hatch. He was wounded quite badly. This soldier climbed down into the hole and was initially underneath the vehicle, a very dangerous spot, and he was coaching one of the other guys who survived the blast on how to deliver first aid. They were trapped in that dark hull of the LAV, all wounded, and here was this guy talking through how to care for each other. Nothing flashy, but he was at risk physically, as there could have been secondaries, or the vehicle could have shifted onto him. Those guys in the vehicle must have felt so alone during those moments, and I think this guy kept them alive through his coaching and presence. When we got everyone out eventually, they were alive; one soldier would likely lose a leg, but not his life. I checked on him, I checked on him when he was in the Ambulance on the way to getting picked up by the MEDEVAC chopper. And when I went in to see him and he asked me how I was doing. He was worried about the other members of the platoon and that we were OK. Not to worry about him. It's crazy. it hard to describe in those moments and the intensity. Seeing these kids, really just kids performing so incredibly well in impossible circumstances.

The strong points were austere, but there were some good living accommodations. I mean relative to living in bunkers and our vehicles like we were before. We lived in this old sea can. It was surrounded by sandbags and there was no OHP (overhead protection) so the sandbag weight was bowing the roof of the sea can. It was cool to see how innovative everybody was and willing to make life better instead of bitching. In some ways I think we liked it better the more austere it was. It was simpler. I remember when our food got ruined. It is a good example of how the team came together. We would get resupplied every couple of weeks and when the convoy came in this one time, they had been hit by the Taliban and were all shot up. So those are rations, water, fuel. Well, we didn't realize at the time was like they had all that packed together. So- diesel, water, rations, they all mixed and each was ruined once they got shot up. When they opened the can to get to the new fresh rations, there were maggots all over them, and they were all wrecked by diesel. We lost all our fresh rations. We had hard rations; they had been pretty picked through. All that was left was clam chowder and salmon. Ever tried to eat those IMPS warm? Disgusting. We remembered there were these freezers that we had not opened. It was like Geraldo opening Capones grave or whatever, and we found that they were full of bacon and shit like that. Still not enough to feed a whole platoon for a month, but it was a start to supplement the gross, hard rats. We rationed it. That was like a big morale boost, and bacon is good at any time. There was some pancake mix and some cans of beans and stuff like that. And one of the guys like, was kind of the platoon cook. It sucked, but we made it work. The important part to remember was that it could always suck more, and when things did suck, it was not helpful to bitch; it was better to try and make the best of it. No one gets better from "I remember this time it was easy."

So, there was this guy, he was killed on a later tour, but on this day, he found a 500-pound bomb rigged as an IED... We were moving to the objective area and when we got to this choke point. We dismounted and I said, OK, this doesn't feel right, you know, pattern life, there is no one around or anything. So, we are going to bring up the Badger, a heavily armoured engineering vehicle, to gently scrape the ground in this area. As the scrape was happening, it lifted an IED command wire; we got the Badger to stop, and, there was a movement about 100m away, flushed out the Trigger man; a section gave chase and dropped him. We followed the command wire; it led to a 500lb aviation bomb. That would have easily destroyed any armoured vehicle that we had and killed or wounded everyone inside. It was just instinct and a brave Badger driver. I loved those moments. Afghanistan was a collection of small moments and people doing micro skills well. I think they saved a lot of lives.

We had a unique battalion command team. The CO is a story unto himself and not a good one. But the ridiculousness of these two individuals was something we rallied around. The OCs and Battalion HQ sometimes felt they got things done despite him. To maintain morale, we would highlight ridiculous things that we would get on with. This is "Pre Memes" online, so we made a little slide deck because we are going to get jacked up by the CO for some random shit that we can't control. It was l like a pie chart of times getting jacked up for things that our leadership would get frustrated by, like the weather, the enemy and things like Ottawa policy all things we got yelled at for constantly. We made up these little pie charts and would brief them to the whole staff about the potential for getting jacked up the next day. Like a risk analysis. It was just a little way to start the day to get the job done and support the teams forward. I am not trying to throw shade; it was in spite of our command team that the show ran. It was frustrating but we made the best of it.

———————

We were patrolling in the early morning between the strongpoints and Nalgham. I was walking point. I took great pride in this. I knew the responsibility that held; if I missed something or didn't see movement, my section could step on something, or we could be walked into an ambush. The light in the early morning is this deep, rich purple as day takes away the veil of darkness; it is cold, we can see our breath, there is no sound, and we hope to find the Taliban waking up this morning. The birds are just starting to stir, there is a dog barking in the distance and around the area the calls for prayer begin as the Mullahs wake up and call on the faithful to start their day. Suddenly, behind me, the engineer hisses at me to stop. I freeze. When those guys say something, you listen. I look down and don't see anything, and it's kind of like, holy fuck, how do I not see it? What is it? My heart is racing. He tells me to stop moving and points behind my heels, there is the smallest bit of orange showing. It is det chord, peeking out of the hard-packed dirt- I walked right over it. All of a sudden, the silence is amplified. I am standing on a goddamn IED. He prods around himself and then gets down on his gut. He finds the pressure plate, It's like a box. Everything in my mind was screaming to move, but oddly enough, we did our drills, and I stayed still, shitting my pants. It was the same setup that another guy in our platoon had stepped on, taking both his legs from the knees down. This one wasn't set up correctly. This is one of those moments that you just breathe; the engineer finished his work and allowed me to step off. Then I had to carry on. This is still happening; the patrol still needs to go. I think at that point you just man up to get through it. It is like when a mortar round or rocket lands near you: you are OK; it didn't hit you; keep moving forward. But FUCK, that was terrifying. I was so lucky to have an engineer with that patrol and one who was an IED expert. Maybe it would never have gone off, but who knows? I owe that guy my life or at least my legs.

———————

Night patrol is really, really quiet. It's like a creepy quiet as you infiltrate towards a Taliban position in the early morning. It gave me the heebie jeebies. We do the infil and everything would be totally quiet except the odd dog barking in the distance. No talking, kit squared away, nothing rattles, choosing each step with incredible concentration. As soon as the sun come up, you know the snipers would be in place, and you could start smelling the fires as the locals rose, and then prayers would start. It was loud through these shitty speakers. The call for prayer was both haunting and beautiful and scary. That's when we'd start hearing the snipers engage Taliban who were coming out for their morning routine and got caught with weapons in their hands. That's when we knew that it was showtime. But it went from very quiet to like immediate action. I just remember the smell of the fires, and the quiet and the fact that the Taliban didn't know what was about to hit them.

Guys nickname stuff makes it easier to identify quickly. We would nickname compounds around our little outpost so we could put fire on it quickly. We had Rich Man's Compound because it was all built up and nice, which I called RMC. So when we took contact from that area we dropped fire missions on RMC . I thought was super funny. All the ring knockers (Royal Military College Grads) did not know it was for Rich Mans compound rather than the college. There was a field south of the outpost called RPG Field due to the number of RPGs that we had received from that direction. We put the helicopter landing spot inside some wire for the appearance of security. We'd been hit with so many mortar rounds that the landing site was all beaten to shit and someone way in the past had decided that they were going to use Hesco like sort of like, you know, just straight out of the package, and laid it flat to try and keep the dust down. Yeah, except as mortar bombs hit it, these prongs would come up as the steel bars got smashed. Eventually, Black Hawk landed, and the Hesco started peeling up and rolling toward the rotor blade. We were all out there like holding the HESCO sections down, so they wouldn't get caught in the wash and crash the bird. The aviation guys after that let us know, we can't land there anymore. It's not safe. So, we needed to have the discussion on no aviation support, we may have to abandon the COP. But how? FOSTERS ROUTE was so full of IEDs that you couldn't drive it. We would have to go down the riverbed. Do we really want a lone vehicle with dismounts walking? That is a recipe for disaster. They could jam us tactically; the Riverbed is a great kill zone they had used effectively against us. I changed the Helicopter Landing site to RPG field. We set it all up, and the LZ/PZ was approved. With one caveat. Change the name. RPG field gave pilots no confidence and once we articulated why we called it that, we needed to reinforce security. This is kind of just a daily routine and how we named things with a bit of dark humour. It was indicative of how isolated we were out in the combat outposts and how the daily risks of attacks and IEDs were normal to us but were above the threshold of risk for almost everyone else.

It was like playing hide and seek with the Taliban. I can specifically remember some of the night patrols. At times we would come across armed guys and look to bypass and pass off to higher ISR so we could get to our objective. It usually meant the TOC would drop something on those dudes we bypassed if they confirmed weapons. It was crazy to move like that, almost completely silent and then have shit being struck by artillery and higher assets on timings in the same space we were moving. This one time, we hear maybe five seconds of talk in a foreign language on our PRR. Holy fuck, that's not us. The Taliban were on a similar channel, and our unsecured personal role radio was mixing with theirs. We were that close. And that was it. Of course, you're like, okay, I take my weapon off safely now. These assholes will be on the losing end if we bump into each other.

We had a couple of tough days in September and a hard fight to cross the Arghandab River. Once we got across and into the Taliban positions, we advanced, looking east to west along the river. It was a blended force with the Afghan Army, Canadians and lots of Americans walking and driving through. No one seemed to be on the same radio net and we were lucky rather than good that we didn't have any accidents while we were clearing compounds. All the higher Headquarters, like the Division level, seemed to show up after we got across, and the fighting died down. I see a group of Humvee jeeps that seem out of place and I head over to make sure that we don't shoot each other, and I know where they will be as we advance. Who was there? Harjiit Sajjan is in the HUMVEE! Future MND! The fucking "Architect"[2] of this shit show that was MEDUSA! Back then, he was just a fucking dude, and he's nothing to me, but I go over to them, see what they're doing. He's talking about how we had enemy all over the place and what had happened over these last couple of days. We had we had a look at this map he had and it indicated

[2] Harjiit Sajjan was a Canadian Army Reserve Lieutenant-Colonel who served as an intelligence expert to the Division Commander during Operation Medusa. He later became the Minister of National Defence of Canada. "The Architect" is a reference to a 2017 misstep that the Minister made during a speech, where he claimed to be the architect and central to the execution of Op Medusa. He later apologised for misleading the group he was speaking to as to his role. This has led soldiers in the rank and file to call him, without malice, the "architect".

all the enemy positions. I was super pissed like what the fuck are you saying? What do you mean we had all the positions? That never got passed down to us, it never came to the BG. They had all the positions, and we found them by getting shot at. Trenches, enemy HQs, logistics everything, they had it all, but we didn't have that detail. Fucken not helpful 2 days after we cleared the position. The fucking "Architect" had the plans, but they didn't get passed to us, the builders!

We were down in Spin Boldak with an American SOF team and some Afghan dudes who seemed shady. We were away from the Battle Group and disconnected. There was nobody telling us what to do. These guys had a camel in the camp and, after that, I think, a monkey. It was a little weird, and they were building a zoo. That was my first exposure to an American SF team. I think maybe they were in Spin Boldak because they got in trouble or something.

In the OMLT, we received some US logistical support. It was it was headed up by this giant black guy, and he had played football for Alabama. I played Canadian University football and we had won a national championship, so he liked to visit and shoot the breeze. He was a captain, and he had a super high voice for a giant man. We used to joke because the US was always paying for things, so we called him the American wallet. If he was being stingy, I would say, "That is not your money," And would fire back, " Goddamn, It is not my money. It is the money of the US Taxpayer. That's the United States of America's money. I have to use it wisely." All the graft in Afghanistan, and I get the responsible American. We had nowhere to do laundry because we were just living in this old mud compound. He actually brought in an old washer with his US dollars. He had a washer, and we had a well in our compound. So, we used his washer in our compound. It was like a secret luxury, wash your clothes and then hang dry them. I found it was some of the best times to decompress. I looked forward to doing laundry, either by myself or by my new American friend, who would reflect, "God Damn, this is good." Funny how simple things took on deep meaning.

The town was so full of IEDs that the kids would make fake IEDs to fuck with us. I watched them do it. Little kids would look at us, and they would build and lay "toy"

IEDs. This is not an abstract thing, right? I know members of their families have been killed by this shit. They're laughing and they look at us and callout, "Ha-ha. Canada. Boom, boom, boom." They'd run away. Like, these are not ignorant Western children who didn't get what they were doing. They've seen this, and they think it's funny because fuck us, it is fun to play "find the IED." This was made worse because the Taliban used children to actually lay real IEDs. So now we had a problem of whether it was a game or real. It fucks with you, using kids as soldiers. Fucking cruel.

We went out there to the area called Bandi Timor, south of how made. We suspected there was some badness going on through there. They're moving IED stuff through there. Our task was to interdict a couple of cordons and searches. We were living in leaguers out of our boats at that point. You're living in the boat for we were there for like a month straight. You're living really tight. Every day is a patrol, every night security shift, but the annual personnel evaluation reports for Canadian career management had to be written had to be written. So, these would be compared to people doing stuff in Canada. So weird. "Sergeant so and so risked his life and destroyed an enemy position, etc..... While in Canada, folks were doing normal career stuff. I wonder if any other war had to do that? It was important because those reports resulted in promotions and postings when guys got home. Has anyone looked at how a professional army at war is different? How do you even compare it? How is it a professional comparable for who is better at their job? The guy in combat or the guy doing the training job in Canada. Both necessary. How do we value them? Regardless they had to get done. I was so terrified of the company 2IC that I would get them in on time regardless of sleep. I come back from a patrol. I will probably do a 10-page patrol report. Photos everything, run out to the C.P. with a memory stick and then get into the PERs. As a leader, you generally try to take one of the worst security shifts, which does not allow me to sleep very much. I wasn't getting a whole lot of sleep, I was getting, you know, 4 hours or less for sure. So, this imposition of Career Administration for professional career advancement impacted my effectiveness while serving in combat. It was crazy, but if you didn't do it, the guys that were putting it on the line would have the tour as a neutral report and fall behind their peers in Canada. I am not sure the career system was ready for a war.

A stand to is done at first and last light or anytime that you think there may be a threat. This meant that regardless of patrol schedule or their security shift timings, everyone had to get up, go to their fighting positions, and wait for the call to stand down. Often this meant spending an hour or so staring at nothing over an open desert. Our officer at the time felt strongly about doing stand to's and it was a big point of contention in the company. Not everyone was convinced that it was useful. I didn't care. Perhaps it was good. Maybe it wasn't. Maybe it is why our leaguers didn't get attacked and everyone else's did. I think he knew it wasn't popular, but he stuck to his guns and that is all you can ask for a leader. Sometimes doing the right thing isn't easy. We used to have an MP3 player in our boat and liked to listen to music. When we were sitting on the stand to staring at the desert, we would put music over ICS so we'd all be less miserable. I was happy to stand to. I used to call it the seventh-inning stretch, like the Red Sox have at Fenway. Where everyone has to get out of their seat and get the blood going. I used to pipe over Sweet Caroline on the ICS and the whole the whole boat would sing Sweet Caroline on stand to. It was pretty funny stuff, but we always felt better after, and something that was unpopular became something we looked forward to. We had our seventh inning stretch and for that time we could just be in the moment and be together and get the blood flowing and do something positive. It was nerdy but fun. You need that sometimes.

I had American EOD attached to me for my QRF rotation. Good guys. One of the guys had been in various theatres a lot, like Hurt locker shit and was on his last day of this rotation before going home. We got an IED call out. It did not seem that difficult, but maybe that was the issue; it seemed easy. He got out a grappling hook and was hooking it up so he could walk back to pull it from behind armour, and he was standing over it looking right at it- the fucking thing was in water and low ordered. Sending up a small blast, smoke and water spray. It was his last day in theatre. He was going home the next day. You can't make this shit up. He was OK. He was alive, he had some small cuts, but he had just missed taking an IED full in the face, and he knew it. He sat there with the medics for a good half hour and had the most textbook case of combat stress reaction I've ever seen. He was non-verbal. Just rocking and rolling back and forth. Like you took an IED in the face and lived. He had been doing this for too long. His cup was full. Time to go home and stop dancing with the devil in the pale of the moonlight.

We parked the LAV right on top of an IED. The Sergeant felt like something was wrong, and we were lucky because our wheels were on either side of it. We dismounted and saw it and so slowly moved off it, and then we parked like 50m from it to mark it until IED teams could come out to it. They couldn't come out until the next day and so when they showed up, some US call signs came also. They also parked about 25 to 50m away from the device, and then both of those vehicles found new IEDs right around their vehicles. IEDs were littered everywhere. There was a lot of stuff sticking out of the ground. We were pretty lucky, so weird how fast you become confident in an environment. We just went through the drills carefully and pulled them out one after the other. I remember the first time we did the first real battle group operation in an area called Nakahonay. I decided, for whatever reason that I did not like using I used the LAVs to get from point A to point B. I did everything dismounted. We would leaguer to up each side of the town. And I decided that I was not going to take the road or the highway, and I was going to go up and over all the grape fields and walls to gain access to the town. I wanted to stay off the road due to the IED threat that we had seen was so prevalent in the area. After a kilometre of jumping over these grape walls and moving through very difficult terrain, we had to stop and take a 30-minute break. The platoon was exhausted, and because it was just exhausting, I don't know if it was a good lesson or a bad lesson. You can't always stay on that level; try to switch it up all the time. But the terrain was so challenging, and you had to take it into account every time visibility was 25 to 50 m. The ground was canalizing, and the greenery and tight lanes obscured movement and slowed you down. The movement was very slow. If you rushed, you would likely step on something or walk into an ambush. It is tough going in tight terrain where optics and weapons range matter less; in a knife fight, you must surely move and try to get the drop on the Taliban. It was their terrain, so you needed to negate that advantage wherever possible. It was mentally and physically exhausting.

———————

Going in at night or early morning was our best bet for taking the Taliban by surprise. I would take out a group of snipers, with an American POMLT, ANP with some engineers and the JTAC team. They would go out hours before the main company group, under cover of darkness, set up in overwatch positions and cover the company infill at night. You had to have a long haul into the operational area if you hoped to surprise the Taliban. That worked quite well, but the one sound I always remember was the fucking dogs barking and letting everyone know that you were coming. It seemed that it did not matter how early or quiet you were trying to be, to get from point A to point B, the dogs were always there. The sounds of those early in the mornings; all the dogs barking, then the call for prayer, eerie, like a movie, silence broken by these loudspeakers that seemed to just appear from ancient mud huts. The low wail of the local mullah finding his voice to wake the villages from their slumber. I would shivering cold, and with the sun coming up and those sounds initiating the day, I would be suddenly warm. I could feel the tension of the silence before the first contact reports to see if we had surprised them or if they were going to surprise us. The dogs just kept barking until the first shot was fired.

I remember freezing in the desert north of Wilson. It's freezing, freezing… why is it so cold in a country that is so hot? I asked my driver if he could check the temperature with the G-Wagon. It was 29 degrees…What the fuck.. That can't be right. I can't be gyrating at 29 degrees! It was 55 degrees during the day. Such a big drop in temp was difficult for our bodies to adjust to and we learned that we needed some snivel kit for the night. It felt like you were just gyrating, but you were OK if you put on a puffy and a toque in 29 above the weather. Imagine doing that in Canada. People would think you are insane.

We were in contact and called for CCA. The chopper showed up, and a medic chopper showed up at the same time but wouldn't land because we were still in contact. So, they were looking to get the casualties out, but the fire was too intense, and the CCA hadn't effectively suppressed the enemy. This voice comes on the radio, and it is a female pilot; it shouldn't matter, but it did. It was surprising and comforting all at the same time. She was confident and kick ass and gave directions as to where she thought she could land. She landed in a grape field, just a quick touch and go and the walking wounded went to meet her. It was awesome. Our officer did up a letter to the American chain of command, explaining what she'd done and wanted her to get a commendation. We found out later that she actually got grounded for endangering the aircraft. What was meant to turn out to be a good thing because she saved a Canadian life while under contract ended up being negative because she ended up getting grounded for endangering the aircraft. I'm like, wow, total bullshit. Can't ever assume the bureaucrats won't figure out how to make something awesome suck.

The front gate was a super interesting task in Kabul. It was absolute chaos. Hundreds of LEPS (locally employed people) came through every day to make the camp run. We figured that giving locals jobs enhanced our local security and lifted the local economy. We had a routine of searching all of them; it was hard on the guys and draining. It was my least favourite task. The Platoon Commanders did a draw every week to give a soldier the day off, and the Platoon Commander would eat the shift on Sundays. This would help the young commander learn what the gate was like and be able to interact with the platoon in a fairly static environment. It raised morale, shared some hardship in a small way and they could see how execution was done, like that show undercover boss. I was doing that one Sunday and the RCD were coming back from patrol as the KMNB Recce Sqn. They were approaching the camp and not properly doing their cannon and machine gun clearance drills. They were driving through with basically their weapons pointed at us. And so when they pulled through the chicanes, they pulled up beside me. I yelled at them to not be an ass, but I needed to be heard over the engines before one of these idiots had negligent discharge and hurt my troops. They had a history of it; when they had been doing maintenance on their cannons a couple of weeks before, they fired rounds out of the camp and into Kabul. We had to trace where those rounds landed, and thank goodness no one was hurt, but the short story was I did not appreciate them not doing their drills properly and having their weapon systems pointed at my soldiers. So anyway, I yelled up, and I guess some captain took offence, not knowing the guy on the ground was an officer speaking disrespectfully to him. The duty Sergeant received the now irate RCD officer, who was offended that a soldier at the gate had corrected his weapons drills. This Sergeant liked to stir up shit and was an aggressive dude. So he baited the RCD officer and invited him down to discuss it face-to-face. He said, "Hey, Sarge, tell your fucking soldier up there that if he ever talks to me again, I am going to pistol whip him." The Sergeant looked at him and said, perfect, you can tell him yourself. He radioed me, and I came down hot under the collar. I was a lot bigger than this guy, and I had a reputation at the time for being pretty aggressive; it was pretty unprofessional as I went right after him. The Sergeant knew it was coming and was ready to hold me back and make sure no weapons were involved. I wanted to throttle this guy. It led to bad blood between us and the RCD, and the Captain was surprised an officer was out front with his troops, and it goes to show some dudes are just assholes. Imagine saying that? His surprise was that there was an officer out there not that I will " pistol whip" you for correcting gun drills is a completely insane way to speak about a soldier. Was this guy from the 1800's. I wish I had been allowed to kick his ass. He and his troops were unsafe, what a dickhead.

———————

When we were out in the field, my priority for water was for friggin drinking. Not shaving. Ablutions were difficult, and haircuts were impossible. We had a little homemade shower, and there was a well, it was local, and so you had to have armed security to get washing water. The guys just let it all grow and looked like Wolverine because they were young, and their beards couldn't connect. We were out in this little outpost getting smashed by the Taliban every day; who cares if you had a beard? It was all good. Until senior leadership saw you, then you would think that shaving was the only thing on the agenda, not that there was no water being delivered, we were short on the nature of ammo, medevac was questionable, and the enemy had us isolated by fire and IEDs. I think those dinosaurs in the senior had no clue what we were doing every day, so they defaulted to what they knew. Shaving and bloused boots made good soldiers. I think they came out with the best of intentions, but most often, they lowered morale with their constant focus on shit that didn't matter. Stay in KAF, or don't leave Ottawa if you aren't going to help.

———————

I think the kids were the hardest part. On that tour, I saw three kids killed, one through a firefight, which is terrible but has happened in war forever, and the TB did not discriminate with their rounds. But there were two that were just hit by cars. These little limp bodies that impacted me. The cars just kept driving. That country is fucked, that would have happened if we were there or not.

———————

Being in the turret was exactly like training except the focus was next level. You knew you were the eyes of the company, and if you let your guard down and the enemy got the drop on you, that is when people got hurt. I think that shooting at the enemy from the LAV turret is different, and there was just a disconnect from the human side of killing. Looking through a gunsight lining someone up and pulling the trigger. It didn't bother me. It wasn't like when I had to fire my rifle at shapes in a tree line. That seemed somehow more personal. The LAV was like being at the range. I think it was because looking through that optical site connects you differently to your target. Your drills are mechanical and you share it the killing with the other guy in the turret. It is air conditioned in the LAV turret, you're in your own little world and feel separated. You can do lots of things and fire the cannon. I hated rations. So, I'd bring out as much cans of beef ravioli and I'd throw it up top on the turret to heat up, in the sun. I would eat like my dinner, traverse and look for targets. You hold a water bottle in one hand and traverse, and if you see something, you can engage. I could take a piss in a bottle and traverse, arm the gun and fire the gun. It was like weird how casual it could be.

There were more things flying around the skies in Afghanistan than airliners above a major city. Each one of these platforms, helicopters, UAVs, Jets, Bombers, and whatever else was up there had one mission. Look for bad guys through an unblinking electronic eye and if you can confirm that that someone is up to no good, drop ordnance and kill them. The process was strict, I did not really know anything about it as I was junior, but I assumed that when I saw rockets at night and heard about a strike on the radio that the system had worked and some asshole that was trying to kill us had got his just desserts. But invariably, there are two sides to this story. I remember having a conversation with village elders from Senjary, the town just west of Kandahar, and the night before, the leadership was not in the FOB as they were out for orders in KAF. The night before, the battle group conducted a strike on two guys who were presumably planning a legitimate IED strike. It got the locals fired up that it was an inaccurate killing of young men out farming at o dark buffalo. The crowd were basically coming down Highway One in classic protest style, yelling and cursing NATO. ANP were out there trying to calm them down. The ANP were firing rounds in the air. I thought, fuck, this could be a disaster, and there's nobody here but me. The ANP may shoot all these people if they get pissed off enough. So I went out, I was shitting bricks and I asked to speak to the leadership. I was super junior with no authority. I was young, like 22 years old and looked younger as I had always had a babyface. I listened to their grievance and then laid it out. I showed them a recording of the UAV feed, that we could see at night you know, we can see from the sky and implied that omnipresence and explained to them why it happened. I showed them the dudes digging in the bomb. Then I shamed them a little bit as to their responsibilities as leaders. "If they weren't doing that, they would be alive; we have lost people at that spot from bombs in the past. You guys know by now that your young man shouldn't be doing that at that time and that even if they were fixing the culvert, which I don't believe you should know, it's your fault for not stopping them. Tell your young men not to do that." I thought they were going to explode, but they backed down, and it kind of ended. The IEDs didn't end, and so now, at least, we knew where everyone stood.

They were going to try and kill us, and if we caught them, we would kill them in accordance with the rules. No more crocodile tears. But it was a more stressful engagement than any firefight; I don't know where I got the courage; I think it was just because no one else was there; pretty crazy for a young guy to stand up to a crowd of (most likely) TB leaders and have them back down.

By my 4th tour in Afghanistan, things had changed a little. Each combat outpost had its own wifi hotspot. It did not have a lot of bandwidth but considering that we were in the middle of Afghanistan with limited communications architecture, it was pretty sweet. My team loved watching Sons of Anarchy, and we would rip an episode every time a new one came out. To do this, you had to coordinate the bandwidth, or you would never be able to download anything. So, like everything else, it was a drill, whoever was doing the download, somebody would come out and yell, "OK, from like ten thirty to fifteen-thirty. Nobody is allowed on the internet. Everyone turns your Wi-Fi off." This would give us the bandwidth to download episodes of Sons of Anarchy because it was so fucking slow; anybody checking their e-mail would fuck it up. It was a small thing, but it meant the world to us. You would be in a world of hurt if you checked your email and fucked up the download.

We are coming back from a patrol, and there's this one culvert between MSG that we have to cross. And this is the only way to get from full that out onto the main route. So, we VPS that every time. We stop, there is a grape fields with access, and there's a grape hut within 200m that someone could hide in. It is like a ready-made IED spot. It's too convenient. As we VPS, my partner leans over to check to make sure there are no wires going up to the culvert, and then boom, he disappears in a cloud of smoke. The officer calls in contact IED, and I immediately grab my nine-liner. I was pretty sure he was dead. Smoke kind of clears and there he is standing there. "They missed me!" My heart stopped. I was so happy. He was grinning so I said Fuck you and watch your arcs. They are still out there. Our crew commander swings the turret and just starts putting 25 mm into this grape hut. We figured that was where the trigger man but there was no movement; when we cleared it, there was a depression that you could crawl out of the back of the grape hut, so we figured he left immediately after he set it off. Our guy was so lucky he needed to go buy a lottery ticket. It was a shaped charge, and it was just low-ordered, just enough to create a dust ball and no shrapnel. When the IED guys came out, they had to dismantle it. There was a crazy shrapnel packed in the bomb. A pair of scissors, forks, nuts and bolts, etc. After they were done with the investigation, I went and got the stuff, and I gave them to the troop in a bag, which he actually brought home. A bag of shit that was supposed to kill him. I heard he let his kids use the scissors to do school crafts. Hilarious. A reminder of how delicate life is and how he got away with one. He was so lucky.

We had these self-contained poop bags easy to use, and when in the field, they sealed up nicely to carry out. We had this one guy. He always went for a shit in the field. He went to do his thing, and we had to rush out of there, and he dropped his shitter bag by mistake. It was aluminum cellophane when it was all wrapped up, shiny and clean. Later that day, we put our eyes on where we were to see if the TB were coming to IED, the position they had a habit of doing, and we saw two kids screaming around the spot, snooping around where we were. They pick up the shit bag and hold it up like they just got a prize, and they're fighting over it, and then we observe them bringing it back to the village. You open that up to your elders and get quite a surprise.

The enemy always tried new things and so we tried to mix it up as well. We tried new things. How do we outsmart the bomb layers? It was a game of cat and mouse. We found a lot, but sometimes they won. One day we hit an IED. The driver of the RG 31 knew we were about to hit a bump which could rock us in the back; the habit was to yell " BUMP" so people could brace themselves and just after he called BUMP, we hit an IED. It blew a wheel off. The RG31 did its anti-mine thing well that day. Everyone's good. The insurgents clearly got our tactics, so it was time to switch it up again. The troops hated losing and were superstitious, so they no longer liked calling out BUMP. The warning word when you were a driver, when you're about to hit a bump, was "chocolate." After that scene, yelling that a bump was bad luck and connected to hitting an IED. Drivers would yell, " CHOCOLATE!" troops are so funny. Of course, it made no difference, but it was the rule.

We were the IRF and sitting in the COP when we heard a massive explosion; I got my dudes kitted up and ready to go; we knew that we would go secure the scene, stabilize casualties and then help EOD IED teams do their business. The threats in this type of situation were secondary devices that the Taliban laid out to wound or kill the first responders who were sent to deal with the first incident. So, this task was not popular and was tough on soldiers as you did not trust the ground underfoot. So the call-out started terribly, we rolled out in our vehicles, and the lead vehicle's driver got confused and took a wrong turn and put the vehicle into a ditch, making it stuck and making the section useless, I remember driving by and the Sergeant was up on the top of the LAV over the drivers' hatch yelling at the Driver, shaking his fist, about what the fuck was he doing…it was like out of a movie, like a dark comedy, we just kept rolling and left that drama to sort itself out. We get on the scene, and our job is the security of the perimeter; another section has the casualties. We dismount and push out, we are probably 200m to 300 m away from the blast site. Like a couple of football fields, you know to ensure an "outer cordon" or security perimeter. Suddenly, one of my troops suddenly comes on the radio and says, "You should come over here; I have something and don't know what to do with it." I walk up, and there is a leg, from just below the hip in with a boot on it ..so a leg and a foot, US camouflage, stained dark red with blood, covered in these wasps or bees that were in the area, We just stared at it, not knowing what to do, the weirdest thing was there was a small plastic water bottle in the cargo pocket of the pant that had survived the blast and the leg being thrown a couple of hundred meters. After moving the wasps off the leg, we pulled out a body bag and placed it in the bag. I remember we didn't talk, and the leg was heavy. It kind of shook the guys, I think if we had been closer, they would have been ready for it, but to see something like that so far out from the scene, the destruction on the human body and how far it was thrown, it makes you take stock of what you are doing and what can happen if you step wrong.

———————————

Getting up at 4:30 every morning and do my laundry made me happy. We had to do our laundry in wash tubs, and I knew that the guys would come right off patrol would do their laundry. So I got up every morning at 4:30 like clockwork, and I'd go do my laundry and hang on the line that we made between two six ft pickets and. Yeah. By like eight o'clock in the morning my laundry dry and put it away. Then the troops had access to the laundry at night. That was my morning routine, and it made me feel relaxed that time in the morning on my own let me take stock of the day. It was quiet. I would have a smoke and coffee and scrub my laundry. Good for the soul.

Christmas in Kandahar. We just wanted a day down. It had been a hard Sept-Dec slog and the team wanted to just chill. We also didn't really want anyone to die on Christmas Day. The issue was that the Battalion had prepared a Christmas meal for us. That was a good thought by the leadership, as we had been on mostly hard rations for months; it would definitely hit the spot. But the catch was we had to patrol out of our position to go back to the larger FOB to get the meal. I got the task to pick up the Turkey and bring it back to Sperwan Ghar. I have never been so opposed to anything in my life. We had been getting smashed by IEDs daily, and I knew the Taliban would love to get one of us on the Christian holiday. What I hated worse was that I couldn't just leave all my troops in the camp. I was irrationally livid and got rightfully lit up by my boss and told to get on with it. I had no issue patrolling or taking it to the enemy, but if one of my troops died picking up Turkey, I am not sure I could forgive myself. We left as many troops behind as we could; in the military Christmas tradition, SNR NCOs and Officers serve their troops Christmas dinner to thank them for their service throughout the year. We took it one step further and did the patrol to pick it up, leaving all the most junior soldiers in camp so they didn't have to take the risk on Christmas Day.. In the end, no harm was done, and everyone had Turkey. Within 48 hours, there would be several IED strikes on that route; sometimes, it is better to be lucky than good.

My one-section LAV driver was a Red Seal chef. My LAV likes to cook. The two of them would get together once a week to go into the town and, as a platoon, do a patrol, usually bartering five to ten dollars US to buy a goat. We would slaughter and clean it, and then they would create whatever we had for rations and mix it into a stew. It's just, you know, the oil drum cut in half a charcoal barbecue that we made and then cooked whatever we could scrounge. It was pretty amazing what the dudes could come up with, and even though we were on hard rats (less Goat and Naan), we were never hungry.

We went through a gap in a wall. Tanks went by and boom, hit an IED. It was it was surreal because it was just like a movie. It's like slow motion. The LAV went up in the air and came back down; in my mind, it was like us being deliberate, like almost like everything slowed down. It hits the ground. I tried to contact the radio nothing. I was up in the family hatch. I bent down and checked everybody in the back. Everybody OK? I Get nods. There was coughing, dust, and smoke, and no word from the turret. So, I jumped on the LAV top to check out my turret crew. they're all banged up, but the least are giving me the thumbs up. So, I'm yelling for the driver. He's not answering. The IED hit on the right-hand side of the vehicle. So, I went up on top of the vehicle, you know, or banging on his hatch, yelling at him. He's not responding. I open up the hatch, and then I see this kid looking up, and he's just covered in oil and boiling hot engine oil. I'm thinking that, my God, it doesn't look like he's burning. I ask, "Are you okay? Like, are you okay?" He answers, "I think so, Sarge." Right. I said, "OK, hang on". The medic came in and now my driver, is just he's sucking on one of those lollipops. One of those morphine law lollipops. He Just looks up and says "Sarge my I'm gonna lose my LDA (hardship allowance) A 19-year-old guy. His foot is just hanging on by a thread and he's worried about his hardship allowance. His danger pay. The rule was that at the time if you weren't in theatre, you stopped getting the tax-free allowance, so if you got wounded, you might also miss out on an extra 50k tax-free. This is the stupidest thing. They say the strangest things. He lost the foot. He lived. I think he got to keep his danger pay but the fact that was top of mind is crazy.

I remember dealing with the bodies after contact. We had to collect the bodies for intelligence, and I think there were biometrics and photos taken in case there was a senior leader or someone important who just happened to get killed in a firefight with the line troops. The lead platoon got into a TIC and passed one body back to us. We were in depth and they passed back a guy who's wrapped in garbage bags. For some reason, I don't think we had enough body bags due to the number of contacts. The dude was in garbage bags, and I taped him up. There was another one that we went into as we advanced, and they dropped a bomb on a compound, and when we went in, they were already dead. Somebody else had bagged them up, but we had to carry them out. The guy that we had was just fucked up and was in a bag sloshing around, and we couldn't carry the bag because of how it moved, and we put the bag on a stick, and we walked it out like it was a deer. I remember they hadn't taken the kit off with him. So, we're in the midst of putting him onto the aviation to take the bodies to KAF for the lab assessment, and someone is like, where's his weapon? He had an RPG. where's the RPG? We put the bag down very gently. We unzipped it. We very carefully pulled out all of the RPG rounds, and at that point, they were like swimming in fucking soup. It was fucked up. Other than burning shit, dealing with bodies was the worst task.

Beef jerky came in little packages, and Tabasco was in tiny bottles. It was super simple: open up the pack of jerky just a little, pour the Tabasco, and shake it out into the beef jerky. Tabasco Beef Jerky! It was super spicy, which was good for morale and kept us awake on colder nights.

One thing I will tell you, sometimes I would sing to the crew on the radio, on the ICS. If we had a pause, especially just before a mission kicked off. We kind of chatted for a bit, and then I would leave the ICS on and just chat, and then I would sing John Denver songs and things like that. Kind of for me, I was trying to lighten to lighten the load a bit and make them all laugh. Everyone would be smiling and I would just try and make it seem like I was a cool, cool cucumber. I was probably just trying to convince myself that everything was going to be okay because, once again, we were in that spot where you're like, okay, it's game time.

We ended up finding an IED, and there were tons of explosives. The IED team coming up to deal with it. This American guy comes to do the blow-in-place (BIP). He asks if we can just provide some security for overwatch. We say, no problem; where do you want us? He said, "Not too far, just a hundred metres or so." I ask, "Is that safe?" He replies, "If you blow it in water. It's pretty safe." I ask, "If you are going to blow it in the water, What about that stream right there?" He asks, "Why?" I reply, "Just go with me on it." The stream is about 30 meters from the left side of my vehicle. And then for another 25, 30 meters for some extra space. So, he gets it all set up. He puts all the shit in the stream fucking and gives us fire in the hole. There is a giant geyser. Now there is a giant hole filling with water. I tell my partner that he is on shift in the turret. I go to the back of my boat. Grab my shave kit. I haven't fucking shower to clean myself in a month and a half. I am going to use the hole the US guys just blew in the stream. We had a ready-made bath! The Americans just shook their heads and called after me as I got naked in the tub. "You fucking Canadians are crazy."

I come out of Zangabad. We've been there for over a month by month and a half now. Senior people are worried about haircuts. I'm all about getting my haircut. I understand hygiene and stuff, and I always have. Everyone had been back to KAF except for us. We've been out in a COP. We've been there for almost two months. I would always hear about haircuts. There was no one with clean clippers and I thought it was so crazy that people cared so deeply. It was emotive. I do not get my hair cut either. I know my guys will get in trouble when they get into KAF. Two and a half months later we get to go into friggin KAF. The guys had time to go to the Canex to get haircuts and all that shit. They showed up, and they didn't have appointments, so no haircuts. We head back out to the field. I'm on patrol the next day, and we've gotten into a TIC; we're fucking hot, tired… You just get back and have that adrenaline rush coming down . Fucking first thing, the RSM says to me, Where's your fucking boot bands and why don't you guys have haircuts? I fucking almost snapped. I lost it. I said, "fuckin really?" I said, "we just came back from patrol getting shot at and shooting people and you are worried about my fucking boot bands and hair" "I'm not talking to you right now." I walked right away from him. It could have been bad for me but it never got mentioned again.

My troops go on back into KAF because we're going back to Canada, and this big fat Jabba the Hutt freakin whatever trade came up and scolded them saying my guys are being overly aggressive and telling their war stories to each other at Canada house. You can't use the term "outside the wire here," he said. It created divisions and made those inside the wire feel "less". Well, if you're so bothered by the fact, then get a job that puts you outside the wire! It fucking pissed me off. You know, I was going to make up T-shirts. O.T.W. I was I was incensed, like, you know, these kids are putting their life on the line. They have their stories, and they earned them. They could tell because they have been there, are you going to say no, you guys can't tell your stories in Canada house? Because it insults your what? Does your legitimacy as a soldier hurt your feelings? What the fuck is this place! KAF should have been the first step to normalizing their experiences in combat, but it was the first stage of "don't talk about it. Makes us feel bad." This is the same thing that happens when you get home, talk to a therapist, but don't talk about it in society. How about talking to your friends and family about what happened outside the wire? No one really wants to know or really wants to care; it is too ugly. I understand civvies, but some fucking fat FOBBIT making my troops feel bad is totally unacceptable.

From my perspective, the inside and the outside of the wire were normal, and we exacerbated it by making KAF like a luxury hotel. Everyone has this perception that, like inside the wire, everyone is sipping coffee at the boardwalk. To be honest, there was a lot of that with some elements that were there. Being in the battlegroup in KAF, my room and the TOC were my life. Without a word of a lie. My average working there was like 18 hours. It's always on the go. It's always busy. So, to be honest, I didn't feel like I was in this bastion or the city. There were times when you could come up for air and get over to Tim's or the Green Beans to get a coffee or something. You were just completely immersed in that little bunker that was the TOC. I understood both sides of the argument. I felt like the guys that were out deserved to be cut some slack and I understood that the NCOs in camp didn't quite understand how people needed to relax in what was their place of work. It didn't lower their job, but it may have felt that way to those in camp. It was not ideal. I wouldn't make it so cushy if we were going to do it again. I would put the genie back in the bottle. No PSP, no civilian gym instructors. No fitness classes, no boardwalk. No civilian restaurants. Make it more spartan, and it will balance out the us and them.

The POMLT teams were made up of Infantry and MPs. A lot of the MPs were ex Infantry as there was little police work to do as the checkpoints were fighting almost every day. Initially, I was at MSG with our headquarters, and then one of the other NCOs didn't want to be out on the checkpoints anymore, so I changed with him. I was now out and was security on the routes. Our morning routine was to wake up and be the first on the road to do the route sweep looking for IEDs. Walking the road first thing in the morning for anything that had been planted the night before. It was scary. I felt bad because there were so many IEDs. Every morning, we were responsible for the IED sweep of Route FOSTERS. If you think it is hard to wake up for work on a normal day, think of how hard it is knowing that the first thing you are going to do in the morning is walk along one of the most heavily IED roads in Afghanistan. You will be the first one to find or hit something, fucking sucks. We found IEDs almost every day. Motivating troops, ANP and Canadians to get up and go is hard. It seemed like an endless cycle where we were expendable.

When you're going out dismounted you had to put a guy up on point. That's the part I didn't like, and I'd have to rotate the task. Though IEDs hit people throughout the order of March, the point man dealt with IED stress first, contact stress on close contact in the grape fields and needed to communicate effectively. It was slow, painful work that took a lot of effort and was exhausting. As the section commander, I knew that some guys were better than others. It wasn't a punishment, but it was hard on those individuals. In fact, some guys took huge pride in leading the section. If they missed something, one of us could die. As the section commander, I liked the guys with the quiet confidence. It's like if something happens, I think you're going to survive, and you are going to help the section win. One of the issues that came up was that I never walked point. There was a guy that I used the most, and it stressed him out over the months. I had to have that talk with him and was just like, hey we all have our job to do. We never train with the section Commander leading. But at the same time, I'd always put myself number two. Instead of 3 or 4. I think if anything happens. I'm right there with you. So that part I didn't like was if someone got hurt because of decisions I made for others. It happened, and I live with it, but it was necessary, it was bad luck, and it sucks.

I never had all my personal protective equipment on (PPE.) It is 45 pounds before ammo and water, and you are like a robot with a neck protector and shoulder pads. I got to shed weight wherever I could. Think of that load and then try to move and fight against an enemy with nothing on. I think that's one of the discussions that should have come out of Afghanistan, but we never did because we got to the point where that triangle was all out of balance. Protection, mobility and firepower. We are all about protection. We limited mobility and had good firepower. Had I hit an IED or been shot in the shoulder, I would've been in big trouble from the chain of command because I made my PPE as small as possible. On my third tour, I got into the habit of stripping those shoulder pads off because I needed to be able to climb up the walls. I felt like mobility was more important. I hated all the focus on protection. I always kept my plates, but the external stuff drove me nuts. I had an experience where I couldn't actually open the thermal site on my rifle to confirm a target for an Apache. It was activated by putting my eye into the sight, but my helmet berm was too low, so I took it off in contact to confirm it. Well, fuck it. Had I just had a higher-profile helmet, I would have been able to activate that site, and I wouldn't have had to take my helmet off. They bring the helmet down so low that it's great for protection, but it's not great for what you need to do, which is fight, communicate, and move.

I remember one of my buddies who was hurt from a blast; he had some shrapnel and maybe a fracture, being stoned on morphine, and he was hitting the medic while waiting for the MEDEVAC chopper. He was asking the medic to marry him. She was holding his hand and keeping him calm...and he was so happy to be cared for; he kept saying, " Thank you for saving me. Will you marry me..."

I remember coming back from patrol and getting jacked up by the "environmental" NCO. There was like an environmental person on camp in Afghanistan. To make sure we kept everything green. We'd left a couple of batteries in our parking spot even though we had just come back from patrol that day. This dickhead was pretty sure that we going to destroy Afghanistan environmentally by having those batteries there. Give me a fucking break. You need a real job, dude. Where the fuck do you think you are? We were patrolling along the river. The Afghans were dumping engine oil into the river, like doing the oil changes, and we were coming back and getting jacked up for even some garbage in our parking spot. You know? That's what was really weird. I feel like there was a disconnect somehow. You have people that deploy for governance and bring bullshit rules into a war zone. Like it's Canada. Then you're out patrolling and it's a gong show out there. The risk is real, always so easily getting jacked up for haircuts all the time. But a lot of FOBBIT leaders didn't care that we were out in that crazy environment. They didn't know how to lead in combat. They had been peacekeeping as troops and were leaders because they understood dress, deportment, and drill. Now, they needed to know their tactical job and couldn't switch. I remember specifically pushing back on me to do something to get a haircut. We were out patrolling for days. We get back, it's like a three or four-day waiting list to get into the barber, and then if you had to wait, you would get jacked up. It was like one of those crazy army movies, and this a really weird dynamic where people who only operated inside the camps saw that type of discipline as their priority and did not understand the transition or issues of those who operated outside. I hated going back. We couldn't seem to do anything right, mostly because we were never in and so did not know the unwritten rules... it was terrible.

I did not have a glorious job; I was a duty officer in the TOC, but there were times I was super proud of what I did. I recognize that if people don't do their job throughout the system, it can fail with spectacular results. I remember just having the discipline to double-check stuff when things were stressful. We're trying to bring in a medevac and the company had given the wrong grid. They were pressuring the CP because the bird was in the air. "Just go with it" was their message. Sometimes slower is faster in the long run; everyone is yelling at me to get on with it, So I double-check. If I hadn't, they would have landed the helicopter on the exact spot between where the enemy was firing and between the rifle company who was firing back. Nothing sexy, but important.

Burning your own shit is the worst task. We were in Sperwan right after the big fights and dug in because we were getting mortared every day. There were no showers or toilets, so we had to build thunderboxes, just wood platforms with holes cut in them and a 45-gallon drum cut in half underneath. With about 60 dudes on the hill, they would get full pretty quickly, and with the heat, it would get pretty ripe. To make sure we didn't get disease and could maintain some cleanliness we had to dispose of our waste. That meant burning shit. There is an art to it; it doesn't just go up. You have to blend diesel and gas at a certain rate to keep a constant burn and stir it…it is disgusting; you are breathing in the shit of everyone on rations; I cannot think of a worse thing to have to do. So, this task would rotate, we would patrol, dig our holes to fight and live in, get mortared, eat, drink lots of water, get in a gunfight and do camp routine chores. That meant burning shit. It was hard living, and I don't think many people can understand both the extreme fear and being uncomfortable from not washing, living in a hole in the ground and fighting. Believe it or not, you get bored! So anyway, my section had this task, and by this point, there were like 6 thunderboxes, hours of work to burn them and the terrible smell. We were done with it. So, we thought, what if we made a pyramid of shit barrels and tried burning them all at once, like one of those fancy chocolate or champagne fountains you see at a party, where the chocolate or champagne flows from glass to glass, but we were doing it with human feces. So, we drag out these barrels, sloshing with their contents and mix in the diesel and LOTS of gas. Then we started to stack, 4 barrels on the bottom, then three, then two, and then one on top; it was over 6 feet high and pretty disgusting to lift, and some spilled out the side and onto the guys. It's funny, though, in only a way that someone in that situation could find it funny. We just climbed up and dumped gallons of fuel into these barrels and lots of diesel… they are brimming, and then we started throwing matches in… NOT a good idea. The whole pyramid explodes into a ball of shit fire six feet hire, belching acrid black smoke and huge orange flames, and the smell of burning fuel and shit hung in the air. No one got burned, one guy got singed, and it was in the middle of a desert, so nothing could get burned down; we just stood back in awe of our masterpiece, a burning pyramid of shit, which seemed a fitting picture for Afghanistan.

I got dumped by my wife. We only had satphone communications, and so were lucky to talk home once a week, and then it may be odd hours because of the time difference. So, I finally got on the satphone and tried to call like three times in a row. Finally, my wife answers and just comes out with it after a couple of minutes. We are done, and she has already moved on. She was pretty straight up about it. She basically waited until I was overseas, moved out of our house, took everything she wanted, knew that I was in combat and couldn't do anything about it, and left. No answers, no explanations. Just done. So that was awesome. You can't really freak out; you just need to get on with it. So not a lot of room for human emotion, especially when you can't do anything about it. Just control what you can control. And I could not control that my wife left me. I got off the phone and walked into the strongpoint CP. I was upfront with it. I'm like, guys, my wife just left me; I'm probably going to be bitchy for the next few days. This is why. I don't really have anything else to talk about. Nothing I could do about it. She started divorce proceedings while I was over there, and I just had a good cry that night and then woke up and went on patrol the next day. Shit happens, and you just have to roll with it.

I was a 21-year-old Duty O in the BG HQ working night shifts. There was one time when we couldn't find anyone to authorize a drop on what was a clear IED target. There are only like 4 people authorized to use force ROE, and I could not get any of them on the phone for various reasons. I finally get the most junior one, the Assistant Ops O; he doesn't believe it is a big deal and heads back to bed. A month earlier, we had lost a bunch of guys because we didn't drop on an IED emplacement. I thought this is fucked up. So I passed the contact to the US TOC to kind of scope it out. They came back and said yeah, looks like an IED. There was a B1 bomber in the air, and they asked if they could drop in our AOR. You're authorized a 500-pound bomb. So, we dropped that. We killed a bunch of guys, and we brought in more air, and we could have dropped some more. Then the Assistant Ops O, who had gone back to bed, rolls in, and he is like, what the fuck is going on? I was sure the US authorization dropping was OK, but apparently not true. The authority had to come from our HQ. That's when the shit hit the fan. I've never been so scared in my fucking life because people were willing to tell me I was guilty of war crimes. The Operations Officer came in and was great; he got everyone to settle down and check the facts before stringing me up. He sent me back to my rack and told me not to talk to anyone. The next morning when they found the crater, there was the biggest IED in it that they had found to date. So, the action was judged to be correct and the process was wrong. The officers were like, you did the right thing. But that in-between period, I've never been so scared; I am glad I took the IED off the street so that no one would get hurt, but I learned a valuable lesson about authority that night. Faced with the same circumstance, would I do the same thing? I don't know. Does that mean the IED would have been out there? Not sure of the right answer on this one.

We had a big IED incident and had to use all the Body bags in my platoon. It was busy with all the wounded and we were undermanned on the position. There was another body that had to be cared for, so I gave my bivy bag to the guys so that our fallen could be covered and transported off the site. We finished the scene and got back into Wilson. I went to see the small logistics node there to see if I could get a replacement bag. When I went in, the guy behind the counter asked for my bag to exchange; I wasn't in the mood to explain; I did not want to talk about it. I said I didn't have one. He looked at me dumbfounded, "Nothing to exchange; you can't have one without exchange. When you get your other bag, you can get a new one". I didn't know what to say; I was immediately furious; he was following the garrison rules, but here I was standing with the blood of our soldiers on my combat uniform, and I didn't want to talk about it; I just wanted a fucking bivy bag so I could get some sleep. I started to get angry, and luckily my Warrant was walking by; he interdicted and pulled me out before I went over the counter. He went back in and explained the situation and came back with a new Bivy bag and a clean set of combats. He was super gentle; he talked me down, I changed my kit, and then just let me let it out. He took care of me like a son and helped me get through the day and back in the fight.

I think it's a combination of my radio being fucked up and the Patricia's being Patricia's, with the regimental motto being, "fuck you; I'm ok." Of course, I love them, but that is what we say. So, they would send snacks forward, like chips and pops, Gatorades, and, you know, the Spunkmeyer muffins and pop tarts and everything. All of that stuff would come forward, and it would come through the CQs. When it got the Patricia's CQ, he would always forget that we were attached to his company. He would redistribute the snackies to the other three platoons, and then we'd pull up and get nothing. I remember being on the net and watching us not getting snacks, I am getting pissed off and mumbling, and my gunner is scanning. He's scanning his arcs, and he sees this motorbike, and we got told that anything crossing the river from south to north is bad. There's no reason for anyone to go into this box unless they're bad guys. He's tracking these two motorcycles, and they're about to cross the river. He can't even talk. He's so excited; he's pulling on my pant leg like, "OH OHOHOH," and I sit down, and I'm like, WHAT, fully focused on no snacks. Fine motorbikes, cool, let's shoot them. So, he's not a qualified gunner, he's just looking through the sights, so I grabbed the stick, and I gave them a lase, and it's 2385m. Max effective range is 2400. Ok, so I pull the stick up, put the aiming dot on them, and give them a healthy lead 'cause they're motorbikes moving fast. I squeeze three rounds, and there's such an arc on them that they go up and out of sight, so you can't see them. The Gunner wondered where the rounds went. So, I say, just wait, they're comin' back. And they come back down and they meet these motorcycles like perfectly. It was so good; it was the best shot ever. The motorcycles disappear in this cloud of dust and smoke, and the young gunner is cheering like YAAA, and then I fire like maybe twelve more rounds into that area just to make sure. I have a friend at JTF 2, and he was actually on the hill behind us that night doing his thing, and he was watching these motorcycles, and he watched these rounds hit'em. He said the whole day, they were up there like golf clapping like, very nice, well done. Great shot, but still no snacks.

I was an Ops O. It is hard because you are always "on" and friends with the Officers commanding the companies in the fight. But you are back in the Battalion CP and not out doing the business. There's always that fight for resources. I remember one OC being quite upset once about why the other OC got all the assets, like Fires and ISR platforms. The fact was, the OC getting the resources was in contact far more often and needed them. But it does not make it any easier. We are all friends, but it was hard to balance. We were on our last battle group operation. One company went in by foot, and one company went in by air assaulting out of helicopters. The other company that walked out from the leaguer walked into a substantial firefight, the fight was done, and they were making their way back to the rendezvous. It was around 6 in the morning, there was a large explosion to the north, and we thought it was an RPG attack because it was so loud. Not ten seconds later, I heard one of the callsigns," IED Contact wait out." That's when I kind of like went numb, and my vision kind of got blurry because I was relaying this back to the HQ main. First, IED attack. Second, and it was one of my friend's C/S and third, because it was a dismounted IED, that's not good. I waited for the casualties; one of the platoon commanders took command and did a good job. Everyone was calm. The terp died. I wondered if the OC and the CSM are dead. Waiting is the worst part. I mean, dismounted IEDs are the worst, but waiting is hard. The ZAP numbers come across none of them are my friend, but they are people I know well. Two times cat B, two times cat C 3 VSA. Fuck. We can medevac and deal with that. Then, at eight thirty-seven, another explosion. IED strike two times VSA two times Cat B. I remember being there was like, holy shit. Now we're managing the contacts and multiple VSA. Then Bam, another explosion, a tank, also hit an IED. It's just a fucking shit show. The hardest part is doing your job and thinking your friends are dead or hurt, and you have to do this task of control. It is necessary, but it is very hard.

I can't remember the full details, but a warlord was coming in and meeting with Canadians. It was to transfer weapons as we initially looked to stabilize the Kabul region. I guess it was kind of working on both sides. I remember this was crucial, so we started planning to do an observation task on him and his team. We got the map checking out, you know, minefields. IED threats. We have the spot. We want to go in to do the job and we get told there are other "agencies on the ground" WTF. So, we don't have all the information but go do this observation task. There's just three of us. We got dropped off in a vehicle and worked our way into the OP location, so we're in an old crater. Nice spot. And then these guys we are watching start moving around, and they're, and they're shooting their weapons in the air. So we're laying the threat state there, like it's increasing. Something's going on. We never want to get detected. We knew we were going to fucking have to haul all this gear if we were going to get compromised. They circle around, and this guy is 20 meters from us and never sees us. You could see his eyeballs, and you're sitting in that one spot. They've been firing their weapons. At the time, we had about a section of these guys walking around this location. What do we do? And we just sat there and just let them walk by. We got lots of good information, but it was pretty scary. Next time we didn't go out with more information and an understanding of what we were going onto.

Like when you're a young dude, you go out drinking, you have 3 beers and say, "Oh, I'm so wasted." Some of these guys are like those "3 beer guys" when it comes to combat trauma. "Somebody shot at me. I'm so wasted." This one dude was a fucking disaster. He wanted to put on a show. He wanted to be in Vietnam. He talked himself into PTSD and a bunch of his fucking troops also. I'm sure of it. Like I watched him talk while we were still in Afghanistan about how terrible everything was, over and over again. Instead of being a real leader and saying like, yes, things were rough. Let's talk about it. Now let's dial it back. Like, let's just chill now. He was the leader that made everyone wound tighter and focus on the darkness. One day we lost a soldier to an IED, and we got back to the strong point, and I said to him, "Here, give your guys some water and check on them." He threw his helmet in front of the troops and threw it across the COP. He screamed. I can't believe he fucking went into our CP and started to cry. He left all these dudes sitting out there. I could not fucking believe it. Deal with your own shit on your own time. Take care of the troops first. How fucking selfish was that guy? Guys like that ruin it for the dudes that really have psychological injuries.

There was a day when our Sergeant came, and he sat down; he was low. "I just talked to my ex-wife, and she says, you know, my kid hasn't seen me in so long, and my kids asked if I was dead. All he knew was that I was in Afghanistan and like he hadn't seen me for a long time and people died here. He kept asking her if I was dead. I had to call him just to let him know that I was alive. Actually alive." And at the time, I remember being like shit, that is so sad. I didn't have any kids. That's hard to say to explain you're not dead just cause you're in Afghanistan, and that is all that is on the news. I think that we don't appreciate that type of thing with families. I remembered this conversation when that NCO was killed on a later tour, it was like his kid knew something. So incredibly sad.

I had just gotten off the Chinook. We were on the ring route, and I was getting dropped off after a recce of all the tactical infrastructure. As I got off, the Chinook powered up and took off; I watched it rise into the sky; it was such a great thing not to have to always dodge IEDs and sometimes get a ride as I watched it fly off ..all of a sudden it seemed to stutter and then seemed to explode into a ball of flames,

I thought oh fuck there are at least 18 Canadians on that Helo. Even though I had just gotten back, I hopped on a truck that was going out to secure the crash site; it was incredible, no casualties , and everyone was OK. The chinook had been hit by and RPG or a lucky enemy 7.62mm round that hit the fuel tank. We stayed on the scene for hours as the aircraft burnt and cooled. When we finally cleaned it up, all that remained fit into the back of a single dump truck. The pilots were awesome, but everyone was lucky. It shook us. The Chinooks getting shot down weren't part of the deal. It reminded us that we were always vulnerable.

I think one of the best examples of leadership I ever saw was this Master Corporal who was in our stores. There was this group called contract management. They would manage big projects, like paving routes, building dams and stuff like that. They were a bunch of this kind of airfield construction engineers. They went out south, a massive growing repaving some roads. They want a force protection element full-time because the Taliban saw the routes as a major threat. But we really couldn't carve out anything. So we put together this section from headquarters and the stores. I see this master corporal, solid dude. I'm like, hey, man, we need an infantry section commander out there. We kind of threw him out there, not willy-nilly, but basically, you're gonna go take all these broken toys and build a road during a war. He went out and was in like fucking contacts all the time and just had to be a small unit-like a leader. He was just thrown in, and he kind of became a go-to guy. I remember it became a little bit of a joke; the contacts kept getting bigger, and there were F18s that came in to support. He was trying to coordinate as best he could. He had a platoon minus out there and was deployed to count socks in stores. He kept keep going every day and they built that road. He took it with this dark sense of humour and was just a great example of a junior leader who was just a grinder. Doing the job in the face of all sorts of adversity and excelling. Our Army needs to know stories like that.

This engineer had thought he had disarmed an IED. He was over the top of it. There was the secondary, and he was lying on the ground, and it just exploded from underneath him and took his head off. He had done the drill so many times. It finally got him.

There was a road that was IED'd all the time. They seeded it with explosives. And it has already caused the injury of three sergeants, two of which two lost limbs. You know, the only way you get around it is to bring in your ground-penetrating radar from your ROC suite, which conveniently didn't work for this operation, of course. We had done an earlier operation south of Panjawaii. It was a sweep and clear. You know, we would go door to door and just basically clear the whole area, whatever that means in a counterinsurgency context. We realized that this was a significant piece of ground, and we couldn't service it with our LAVs. We would have to go with a completely dismounted option with a dismounted supply system. So, the best option was donkey support. I said I basically said to my guys, I want a donkey. Let's buy a donkey and let's see what we can do with this for resupply and everything we can think of. Someone from the platoon went downtown within a day, and they purchased the donkey and came back, and we had talks with the guys in our maintenance group. They cut a John Deere gator in half, and it was a trailer for the donkey, we would build a harness, and the donkey would pull all of our rations over water and place radios in it like a mobile command post. It worked out famously. It didn't destroy anything when we moved, and it was easily accessible. The troops loved the donkey and kept it at their FOB. They named it Jenny. Jenny the Donkey. She became a social media darling, and Jenny had a Facebook page. She saved lives and interacted with soldiers worldwide.

We came into KAF like stupid early in the morning. You want cash because we hadn't been in in like a month. So, we went to try to find the clerk. she's like, oh, I'm on Sunday routine. Come back at 13:00. We're like we're rolling out again at 12:00. We want smokes. Pizza. Red Bull. We need cash. She shut us down. So, as we were leaving, we ran into the Company 2IC. He said he could tell that we were pissed off. We told him, and he was livid. He went and told her; you go give these guys cash, or I'm going to put you on the next thing with wings back to Canada. When they're in from the field, you work. So, we got our cash, and the Sunday routine didn't exist for her when we were into KAF anymore.

Sometimes, it is worse to NOT be to be there when an incident happens; I remember this was the only time I've never I never went out with my platoon because I was backfilling the LAV captain who was on leave; I was at the ops meeting. The platoon headed to Senjary, where the OMLT guys lost three personnel in an IED strike a few days before. I spoke to the Sergeant leading the patrol; all was good; the boys were loose. A thumbs up or a green check across the board and everyone is good. They head out and I go into the coord meeting in a room adjacent to CS0. We got into the coord, and the radio crackles, "IED contact-wait out." I immediately left the meeting. I just went to the other room. What's going on? The duty staff was Confirming that there was VSA in the strike and trying to paint the picture. My heart sank. Obviously, I can do nothing. I waited, and I listened to the reports. I heard them come back in the camp. I went over and met them by the boats. I feel like they looked at me differently. We just lost three guys and I wasn't there. I know there is no way I could have known---I had another task, but I hated that this was the one time I didn't go out. They hit a huge IED, and I lost 3 of my soldiers. I have had a hard time getting over it. Super hard on myself for fucking years. For years. Even now, it is just manageable.

I called it the 4Bs-bombs, bullets, boredom, and bullshit. Mostly it's boredom in bullshit. And, like, that's a good thing. As the war dragged on and guys were going on multiple tours, I think NCO leadership became harder and harder. I remember that there was one time we were having a huge bitch session, bad food, no showers, blah blah, and out of nowhere, there was this voice, "I want everybody fucking to be at the mortar pit in 5 min." He called us all in. He lines us up. I don't remember all of his exact words, but he said he essentially said, "Listen, you motherfuckers are here, and you gotta do the business the right way, or you will get yourselves or someone else killed. You guys were bitching, and none of it is helpful. Cowboy, the fuck up." he did not. He didn't hold back. He fucking lit us up super hard and tore a strip off of us. He walked away, and I sat next to the C6 Gunner. He looked at me in the dark. I'll never forget it. He said, "You know what-we deserve that". Could fucking imagine, we are living in the shit, and we are fucking miserable, some sergeant jacks you up so perfectly that you go, yeah, he was right. You can't teach that level of leadership.

We had a terrible leader. When we would get cut away from our unit, it was like a vacation. We enjoyed our two weeks in Pashmul. Imagine that it was better to be in a place where folks were dying almost every other day than to be in a PRT camp with that guy. Fucking free from bullshit.

The first time I experienced an IED strike on the on to the Engineer OC's vehicle. Some of the engineers were wounded, It could have been so much worse. This is where JNCO leadership was so important. If not for one of my master corporals, I'm sure we would've had three killed from the platoon because they'd just been standing on the side of the route, you know, during the construction of an Op, and my Master Corporal walked by, saw three of the guys standing close to where one of the vehicles was moving and said "get away from the vehicle. You know better." Basically, there's a vehicle moving around and had just got them out of kind of that danger radius because the LAVs attracted RPGs, and we had guys killed by the sprawl from ricochet or LAVs hit IEDS and caused big hunks of steel to fly around. You were either in the LAV or got the fuck away from it. When the LAV hit an IED, the area where those three soldiers had been standing was destroyed from shrapnel. So very small details, no one would notice a junior leader applying skills that were drilled into them during training that saved three lives. Troops hate when the NCOs remind them of the right way to do things. There is a reason. It saves lives.

We stopped and set a leaguer and dug shell scrapes for the night. The company leaguer is a group of armoured vehicles set in a circle, almost like a wagon train from the wild west. Then all administration happens in the centre in a protected area. It does not leave much for privacy. Especially in a desert. I really needed to go and take a shit. It was early in the tour and I was a bit shy. In order to have some creature comfort, We had this steel fold up office chair that we cut a hole into that was strapped to the side of the LAV. So, I take this chair out and like, I go like 50 m away from my vehicle, but not in the middle of the leaguer. I'm trying to get as much privacy as you can. I'm sitting there. So, my body armour was still on, and my pants were down. I'm, like, leaning on my rifle doing my business. All of a sudden, there is these there's two Afghan dudes staring. They're looking at me with a cell phone, and I'm taking a shit, and I have never felt so vulnerable in my whole life. These Afghan dudes could shoot me, and I'm gonna be that guy who dies with his pants down, taking a shit, and breaking SOP. In the end, nothing happened, but a lesson was learned. Stay in the Leaguer. I always wondered if I was on Afghan Facebook, "Canadian Shitting in the Desert".

There are always frustrations, and the inside the wire, outside the wire was just this War's leading discussion. We created this weird dynamic. It's like if you're out in your grape hut that you occupied on patrol, you are living so much harder than the soft bastards in the COP. The boys in the COP think the teams in the FOB have it easy. The guys in the FOB think the guys in KAF have it easy. The guys in KAF think the guys in Dubai are soft. It is never-ending and pretty annoying. I did all my tours outside the wire, but I think this conversation is not helpful. No one part works without the other. I understand the frustrations, and we can learn from it, but it is not useful to devalue other people's roles.

I remember a guy who made a comment about, you know, the KAFites. He commented to one of the CLPs, which was very disrespectful. His punishment was he had to go back to KAF to learn how the other half lived and gain some respect. He had to do some kind of gate duty for ten days. I think it backfired. He got back, and he told all of us that's a fuckin best time ever over. Regular schedule, gym, good food, women. No bullshit IEDs, patrols, TICs. You got a shower. I am not sure exposing field soldiers to KAF did anything to improve relations ITW with those OTW.

Funny story about the Minister of National Defence's visit when he did come over. He flew in on a Herc. The ambassador had a team of close protection people. RCMP, and they might have been RCMP. He was with us for a bit, but spent a lot of time with the Afghans and at the embassy and dealing with kind of higher-level ministerial things. We were tasked to provide some additional security for the party as it moved around. We had a couple of LAVs moving with the man. I was at the airport the day he was leaving, and his entourage was travelling in an armoured suburban. His entourage pulled in, and they pulled the suburban right in front of the nose wheel of the Herc. Blocking the nose wheel, they hopped out. The Close Protection Party hopped out. Everybody hopped out. They left the vehicle running, and the minister got out. Everybody was doing their thing, shaking hands, saying goodbye, and he was getting loaded on the Herc. In the interim, they had closed the doors on this armoured vehicle. I don't know how or why whether it was like the old technology but the doors closed and it automatically locked. The keys were in the car with the vehicle running, the doors were locked and this armoured SUV was right in front of the nose wheel of the Herc that was supposed to fly the minister. These guys were running around looking for something or somebody who could move the SUV because they were pretty embarrassed. The plane was on like a siding. So, it couldn't like it couldn't taxi or back up. It was gonna have to wait until this armoured SUV could be moved. The Germans were kind enough to bring in a massive forklift, and they just slid the forks of the forklift under the belly of the suburban, picked it up and moved it out of the way, like off of the side, put it down and left it there. Now the ambassador who had arrived in the suburban now needed a ride. We ended up giving the ambassador a ride back-to-back to his car. I sent one of my section commanders to run that convoy to take the ambassador back to his place. I didn't go personally because we were still waiting for another task I had been given. The Suburban sat there running for hours. The Close Protection guys were gone because, of course, they had to go back. The vehicle's just sitting there running, and another German came over, and he said, You need to get in this vehicle out of here. I agreed but didn't know how. He says, I used to steal cars before I joined the army, and I should be able to get you into the vehicle. He had like a slim a Slim Jim device. He just walked over and, within about fifteen seconds, had had the driver's side door open. We could turn the vehicle off, move it off to the compound we had at the Airport and put it there with the keys. What a funny day. I am not even sure the Minister would have known about the delay or why it happened.

Off Route Foster's, there's like a blue-painted United Way or UNICEF Village built in the '80s. So, one day, the OMLT was going in there, and we were meeting for support. It was quite an important meeting of Afghans, and many people and children were around. And there was a Kiowa "Azriel" callsign flying over top of this compound, kept going and then came back and dropped a soccer ball into the crowd… And they dropped this ball, and the fuckin place erupted. The chaos from the kids. Right, because of the ball now. All they wanted was the ball. We are trying to grab the attention of the local leaders; it was just comical. The meeting was ruined, and senior individuals were getting frustrated. C'est la vie. Just another day in Afghanistan. Random shit always happens. You can't take it personally.

That was a thing like the only thing that had ever really run through my mind in any of the TICs that we had, was how similar to training it was, which is a huge credit to the training system because it all seemed familiar. Even my first contact, I was like, okay, I know what to do here. That was the only time I ever really felt fear. I could hear the RPGs coming in and striking the wall I was taking cover behind. And I remember thinking to myself, like, well, if it makes it through, I'm fucking toast. I was scared, but I did my job, which meant the training worked.

The camp commandant that we had for the training mission was a total Dickhead. I was frustrated because this guy was such a shit leader. He was a Major who had "missed" the combat missions and was trying to prove something on the advisory mission in Kabul. On this one day, I received more incredibly ridiculous, bureaucratic and self-aggrandizing direction from him. So instead of arguing with him, I went outside and I was chain smoking. The CO of the mission, who was not from my Regiment, had seen the interaction come down, and he could see that I was not myself that day. He asks, what's up? We had a quick chat, and he told me something has stuck with me to this day. "The problem with a CAF is that the intelligent officers see issues and know they can't fix them because those that love the bureaucracy will use the rules to ensure it doesn't change and stay in power, so the good ones jump ship. Leaving too many promotions to senior levels through attrition. What we need is the people who want to make changes to stay and help make the necessary changes. But it's just frustrating for too many.

HOLDING HANDS WITH A WARLORD

AFGHANS: WE WERE SUPPOSED TO BE THERE FOR THEM.

Read any mission description and Canada was in Afghanistan to "secure the population and support the government of Afghanistan".

Most Afghans had known nothing but war in their lives. They are incredibly resilient, tough people.

In the previous forty years, the Russians came, then the warlords, then the Taliban, and now NATO and the US[3] had come with promises of stability and a better life. The Canadian rotational deployment cycle created a feeling of Canadians being in a continuous sprint. The Afghans, however, were in a marathon. We were running two different races.

Afghans were a mystery to the Canadians. Living a spartan existence in thick-walled mud huts, fiercely tied to religion, deep-seated and complex cultural and tribal norms, and existing in one of the harshest environments in the world, the two groups couldn't be more different.

Afghans live a tribal life. There are between 30 and 59 officially recognized languages, including 40 minor languages and approximately 200 dialects. Fourteen major ethnic groups reside in Afghanistan, and hundreds of major tribal affiliations exist. Each group is geographically centred and has little connection with other parts of Afghanistan. Being regionally and tribally focused, the push for a national agenda was difficult to put into practice.

The Canadian soldier was placed into direct contact with the Afghan population and, not surprisingly, often found themselves at a loss when it came to the "right" approach.

---

[3] During this period of the mission in Afghanistan, there were two ongoing missions in Afghanistan - The NATO-led ISAF (International Stabilization Force Afghanistan), the US-led Operation Enduring Freedom.

The Provincial Reconstruction Team (PRT), the Police Operational Mentor and Liaison Teams (POMLT), and the Operational Mentor and Liaison Teams (OMLT) were the main thrusts of these integration efforts. This meant living with them day to day and building deep trust that is difficult to comprehend. The Afghans they came to know had been fighting battles their entire lives. Their Canadian "advisors" were on their first or second rotation to Afghanistan, and what they lacked in combat experience they made up for in access to weapons and equipment that would enable the Afghans to take the fight to the Taliban.

The Canadians lived in small four-person teams with thirty to sixty Afghans in little outposts that were their only security. Trust was not nice to have; it was implicit in the survival of these small teams. They lived in small outposts, often surrounded by Taliban elements, and could not communicate directly except through an interpreter.

This incredible demonstration of professional and personal trust should be considered an example of the spirit of the bond between Afghan and Canadian fighting elements. This does not mean there were no frictions or points of failure between the Afghans and their partners. These could often be attributed to differing views on societal norms and the constant need for Afghans to adapt to rotating Canadian units while they remained in the location throughout the conflict. Despite the differences in language, experience, and customs, Canadians formed deep connections with the Afghans whom they lived, fought, built, and governed. Young Canadians formed very human bonds with the Afghan security forces that they were partnered with, often creating lifelong friendships. After multiple tours, they identified with the towns and villages that they had patrolled over multiple months. They ate Afghan food, participated in Afghan festivals, observed religious holidays, and were deeply invested in Afghan success

---

Afghans are the people; Afghanis are the national currency. It is an important distinction. My first interaction with an Afghan was with my linguist, who was Pakistani. It was good. I remember having a strong positive impression of my linguists. Mostly, guys who'd been there before had automatic distrust of everyone. I think they were shielding themselves and not connecting with the people and culture too closely. They listened to the rumours and stories of reporting to the Taliban and had an automatic distrust of everyone. I was aware of the pressures our Aghan partners were under, the fact the Taliban threatened their families, and that members of their communities applied pressure to stop helping us. I didn't feel mistrust. We needed to be more open to make them feel like the risks they were taking were worth it.

I had to hold hands with a warlord. Afghan men show their connection and trust in public by holding hands so that their community can see that they should provide the individual they are connected with the same respect that they afford their leader. I was on a position in Kandahar, and a local leader who held great sway in the local area came to visit me with his huge entourage. He had been mujahadeen during the war against the Russians and was still a pirate as far as I was concerned. I was sure he played both sides, the Taliban and us, to his advantage. I can't really blame him. On this visit, he was keen to demonstrate that he and I were partners in security against the Taliban threat, so we had to hold hands and visit his team and all of my team. I consciously knew that it was cultural and that nothing was wrong with it, but it did not make it any more comfortable. This old guy grabbed my hand tight and led me around to visit all of the Afghans and all of my soldiers, publicly declaring our intentions as partners. The troops thought it was hilarious. They couldn't get enough of it, and there was no shortage of ball-busting at my expense after the Afghan leader had departed. It is a small thing but a departure from what we knew to be "normal." Just another day. We held hands every time he came, went through the motions, and played it up. It was probably good for me; it added some levity to the team at my expense; walking in the sunshine holding hands with an Afghan warlord wasn't in the briefing before we deployed.

———————

Afghanistan does not have the Western niceties of paved streets, lighting, water systems, power, etc. However, they did have a social fabric reminiscent of the Victorian era, a kind of etiquette: formal greetings and sitting down to tea. The discussion of the family occurred before anything else. Even if it was someone later in subsequent tours in Kandahar, where the relationship with locals was often tense. If you were slighting somebody in conversation or calling taking them to task, there was an excellent way to do it and a means to do it that we don't observe here in the West. We are much more confrontational. When you have an aggressive discussion with them, certainly you get into an argument, and they may shout or wave a slipper at you. But before that happened, there were a lot of social niceties observed, whether there was the most hated person sitting across from me or their best friend. There was a way that you conducted yourself in the civil society, which seemed out of place for the poverty and violence that we experienced. These two things seemed to be at odds. If we thought we were dealing with a Stone Age group of people living hard in the desert, it would not have been the case. There's an old culture that exists here. There are things here that we don't understand and probably never will understand unless we spend excessive time in the environment and learn to speak the language. I think this was one of our biggest mistakes in Afghanistan. We could not take the time to learn and help society in the way it needed. Right from the top down, we decided what it was supposed to look like, and then we tried to shoehorn that vision into the situation. That vision looked a lot like a Western democracy. I am not sure that was the right starting point for discussion.

I have such a poignant memory of Kabul. It is not a human story but about a horse. We were out on patrol with our platoon leadership and driving along about to return to the camp. There was one white woman without a head covering and a few other men on horses just outside the gate in our secure zone. As it was so close to the camp and in our security 'bubble" we stopped to see what was happening as this was out of the norm for behaviour. The white woman is also an indicator of something strange, so it seemed like a good opportunity to understand if something was wrong. When we stopped to speak to her, we realized that they were gathered around the ditch that surrounded our camp and that a horse in the ditch had fallen in and was trapped by the fencing. No barrier was next to our trench, and the horse had fallen and broken its leg. It was the first time I had seen a horse hurt like that; it was alive and in great pain. The woman was down in the hole with the horse, and there were a bunch of Afghan dudes around them with blades out, and it was obvious that they wanted to kill and butcher the horse. She looked up at me and said hello in English, and I asked her who she was and what was happening. She explained that she had lived in Kabul for about four years, was an author and journalist and worked in humanitarian aid and support for the time after 9/11. She lived in downtown Kabul. She was a bit eccentric; she had horses and rode around the city. One of the horses has fallen in the ditch and broken its leg. Horses, to me, have always been noble beasts. You're seeing these other ones that are beautiful standing on the road beside you. They were nice horses. And then there's this one, like writhing in pain, making all kinds of terrible noises. I asked, "What do you do with this horse?" She replies, "Well, nothing to be done." As she is speaking, there's an Afghan down in the pit, and he grabs the head of the horse and pulls it back, making the massive neck taught. The horse's eyes bulge, but it can't move; in a single deft movement, he cuts the horse's throat. The blood explodes from the wound, and we witness the death of this beautiful horse. Its life drains out of it into this trench by the side of the road. No one in the crowd flinched; the woman calmly observed and provided commentary while this was going on. This was a shock to us, just the casual violence and the killing. In Canada, there would be a vet, euthanasia, some distance from the killing and space from the death. It was a wake-up call that death was a part of everyday life in Afghanistan. We were insulated in our camp. What a fucking misfortune for this beautiful animal. It was transformative for me. We'd stroll out from our exquisitely resourced camp, and you would see the poverty and how decrepit the buildings were; you understand people are impoverished, but it is hard to relate on the level of understanding what it meant to be that poor. There was a distance there. We departed on task and left the lady and her crowd to their business. About an hour later, the lady, the other horses, and most of the crowd are gone, but there are dudes down there butchering this horse, cutting in the steaks, and stacking those steaks on wax paper on this cart. Yeah, those motherfuckers are going to eat the horse, and it was now dinner. I think it was a metaphor for Afghanistan. Do what you need to do to survive; the weak need not apply. It just brought home that you are in a really poor place, and survival trumps idealism. I figured we needed to understand this poverty level better and not assume that they think like us. This was my first realization in Kabul, a fucking horse that broke his leg and became dinner. There were many examples to follow over my multiple tours. The West tried to make Afghanistan a fucking democracy; who cares about democracy when you are tearing into a horse that broke its leg for survival. I think we may have had it wrong. We probably needed to start lower on Maslow's hierarchy of fuckin needs if we wanted to help the Afghans.

I remember the children. They stand out to me. Always dirty, big eyes looking up at you. We would stop by and give them candies from our rations. They were constantly filthy. They didn't have jackets. I had experienced poverty in Bosnia. It was my only frame of reference was that Afghanistan was worse than Bosnia. "I'm in a spot worse than Bosnia" was sobering. I remember how tough the kids were. They used to play this game; I think they called them "chicken" fights. I remember we would be driving up these narrow roads up the mountains, and in between the houses on the hill, these kids were holding one leg behind their back, thus standing like a chicken scratching and trying to knock the other kid down, who was also holding one leg. I'd never seen kids wrestle like that. They were all in to win, and it got violent between them. They are just trying to knock the other guy off the path down to the side of a mountain with old Russian minefields all around them. What a uniquely Afghan Game.

One day, my Afghan partner came to me and asked me to buy large audio speakers for the ANA's Mullah. I did not understand why. He insisted that it was imperative to help secure the local area and was not just a frivolous purchase. I was doubtful. He asked me to wake up the following day and come down to his location in Masum Ghar during the morning prayer, which was about 0430. I went down the following day with my translator. Before he prayed, my partner asked the translator to tell me what was heard coming from the loudspeakers from the mosque across the river. As the morning call floated across the river, I got a live update: the Mullah in Pashmul was calling for the local population to resist cooperating with the ANA and the ANP. To not work with the "invaders" (us). This was an eye-opener; the Afghan CO wanted the speakers to provide another means of communication to the local population. He believed this was where many of the locals got their truth, and we were missing it. Like advertising on TV when everyone listened to the radio. He was one hundred percent right. I got him the speakers and started the "prayer battle." Whenever one side started, the other would start yelling into their loudspeaker like some prayer rap battle. Crazy stuff: we spent so much money on "influence," and probably a lot was accomplished with a couple of hundred-dollar speakers.

All the locals left the area of operations. It was a stream of misery leaving their homes to avoid fighting. In the morning, we departed PBW and sped down the Hwy. I noticed a lot of local people seemed to be leaving. Their vehicles were loaded to the ground with their belongings, and their entire families were crammed into small Toyota Corollas. The one image that will be etched in my memory forever is a woman and her child standing on the edge of the highway in a parking lot at a gas station. The woman stood there in her body-length burkha, and her head followed every military vehicle that passed by. Her child stood by her side, and their belongings lay on the ground beside them, mostly bundled in blankets. Although I could not see the woman's face, I could feel her staring at me as we drove. It was as if we were in slow motion as we passed her. I wondered what she was thinking and what she may have been through. Where was her husband? Was he coming to get her? Did the Taliban kill him? Then, I had a thought that troubled me. Could her husband have stayed behind to fight us? Was he Taliban? Was he not Taliban but felt it necessary to stay and protect his home? Did she hate me? Did she wish I was dead? Our armoured convoy passed without incident, getting into position for the next assault. I still think about those people impacted by the fighting. The costs to the average person are so high, and I am not sure those who have not experienced war can understand the utter helplessness of those caught in the middle.

———————

We didn't have a lot of KLEs as our area was pretty remote. It was hard to balance the demands of interacting with the local population and maintaining our security. We had to keep a hard line with the suicide bomber threat. There had been a lot of guys hit with suicide bombers, and this made getting close to people difficult. I just felt like kind of a dick moving through those areas that people would roll up on you, and they're just trying to get their day-to-day done. You have to tell them to stop- back up, lift your shirt-turn around so you can confirm that they didn't have a suicide vest hidden. I remember one. It happened later in the tour, but I felt terrible about it. The little Pashtu we learned were these orders, "stop, lift your shirt, lift your hands." They were similar-sounding words and quickly mixed up. We were out on patrol, and this guy and his little boy came around the corner. I give the order to stop- he stops. I try to get them to lift their shirts, and they put their hands up. I get a bit frustrated because I want them to comply, and the Taliban had used kids as suicide bombers just before this incident. It was getting tense fast because they weren't listening. I am shouting, he is shouting back, and tempers are getting hot in this alleyway in Zhari; it is fucking ridiculous. Thank fuck, the Terp comes out, and he gets the words of command right. The man and his boy comply immediately. The terp let me know what I had done wrong. As a private, I did not always have an interpreter with me, but I was the most likely to encounter people. Thank god he was there. I got scared, and I was scaring the shit out of those people. I felt terrible about it as well. I always wondered how often that happened, and there was no terp. So much was just misinterpretation between people that had no clue what the other was saying. Scary, I still think about that. My son is about the age of that kid now, and I would hate to think that a guy with a machine gun stops him and tells him to lift his shirt because some other asshole would be willing to strap a bomb to him and sacrifice him for the cause. How fucked up is that? There is no winning in that scenario.

———————

I remember clearing through a compound and finding a grown older guy in one of the rooms. His legs were hurting. The backstory was that the Taliban holed up fighters in his compound and held him hostage. He didn't want them there. So, they beat him up until they broke his legs. They had healed, but he was having a hard time moving. His legs were in a bad way. All the medics could do was give him some pills for pain. We moved on, and as we moved into another compound, I came across one of those old Disney viewfinders with a cartridge of slides from the 70s and early 80s. It's like a red pair of binoculars. So, I picked it up and looked through it. Much to my surprise, it was not a children's story. It was instructions, photographic instructions on how to assemble IEDs and how to place them. Those two experiences demonstrated to me that unless we were in neighbourhoods all the time, we would never beat the Taliban. Guys would keep getting their legs broken, and kids would keep getting taught how to make IEDs with children's toys.

Sometimes, the motivations for joining the Taliban were super simple and human. I remember we responded to an IED on Highway 1. It had hit two US support trucks. We arrived, and the guys were knocked out inside, and the trucks were on fire. We set security, and then I was lucky because I had a Sergeant who had been a firefighter; he figured out how to extract the casualties from the trucks. While security was out, they found the cable and ran it back to the compound where it seemed to originate. They kept eyes on, and once we extracted the trucks and casualties, we set security on the compound and did a hasty raid on the firing point. When we went through the door, there was livestock and chickens and kids and women, and it seemed out of place; the guys were awesome and quietly moved the families out without firing a shot, then they went to the last cold door and called out the three males in there, they came out with their hands up, they knew that they were nabbed. Initially, I thought a TB bomber had just held up on the farm, but then we questioned the Dad and his two twenty-something sons and found traces of explosives on their hands. They said that they had blown up the trucks on the road and that the TB had provided them with training and equipment. I knew that we had to pass them off to the National Police. While waiting to hand them off, I asked the Dad why he decided to blow up the trucks. He said he had lived there a long time, but since NATO had come, the trucks went all night on Highway 1. It kept everyone up and kept the kids awake, and no one got any sleep. All the trucks used to be off the road by 7 pm. Eventually, it seemed like the most significant issue, and he felt he had no other recourse. The TB were happy to help. I was blown away; this guy was willing to kill to dissuade us from using the highway, and also, we made the locals feel so helpless that they had to turn to the TB to solve a traffic problem.

The Afghans would bring all the injured people to the medic to get treated. We have a picture at home of our medic treating a 12 to 18-month-old girl who had yellowish-like infected skin that was completely falling off her body. The medic treated the child; I am unsure if it was an infection, but the parents were grateful, and we got closer to the population. I remember a kid in that town who had given some bread to the ANP. People supported the ANP around there, so we were building bridges. The Taliban in the area didn't like this. They killed the boy and beheaded him. The boy was like ten years old. The locals reported, and we had to try and do something about it, but it sent a clear message. The ANP and Canadians may provide care and security, but the Taliban are always watching, and you are never safe. To drive their point home, they killed the father also for not raising an exemplary Muslim. His crime, on top of having a son who gave bread to the police, was that he supported girls going to school. Then they hit the town or the district centre a day or two later. They were raining RPGs and machine gun fire down and burning some trucks. Due to the isolated nature of the area, we could only stay up there for weeks at a time, as we had several villages to patrol and try and protect. The Taliban could be there all the time. It is not a wonder that the Taliban controlled the population. It was very frustrating. I think about that little boy and his father a lot.

We responded to a suicide IED incident that caused a mass casualty situation. There were more casualties than any of us to do security and first aid on the scene. We were moving from casualty to casualty and ensuring we didn't miss anyone. I noticed two small girls on the side of the road, only ten meters from me. One of them was injured in the attack, and the other, the younger of the two, was kneeling beside what I assume was her older sister. I went over to the two girls, and they both looked at me. Neither one of them was making a sound or shedding a tear. Another soldier and I knelt with them, and an interpreter joined us. I asked the interpreter to tell her we would help her because she was bleeding a little bit, and she said it was okay. Right away, we noticed that she had an intense cut over her left eye and that her right foot was in danger of being lost. I put a field dressing on her forehead and secured it while the other soldier tended her leg. I offered my assistance to him, and once we had done all we could, we began to do a secondary search for other wounds. I put my hand under her left thigh and brought it back out, dripping with blood. I looked at the interpreter and told him he needed to tell her we had to cut her pants slightly. Another interpreter stepped in and was enraged that we even suggested cutting away the clothing as if the requirement to be covered was more important than the requirement to live. We argued with them a little bit, and then one of them understood that it was in her best interest, so we did it. The amount of blood suggested that she could have bled out as a result of this injury, so, in my eyes, this little girl's life was in our hands. It turned out that she had a clean hole in the front of her thigh caused by a ball bearing from the bomber's explosives. I could have fit my index finger in the entrance wound. The exit wound wasn't so clean. We patched her up, and I could hear the MEDEVAC choppers from in the distance. We would get her and her sister onto one. She was six years old.

The boss was out of the vehicle doing a KLE; I was standing up in the back of the LAV doing security, watching from the back hatch. The Bazaar was busy, and so was passively observing the crowd for threats. There was a commotion, and the police descended on the area; I watched this guy get taken by the police. I hadn't seen what he had done. I watched them beat him every time he would talk. They would give directions, he would start to speak and, bam! They would smack him with these rubber truncheons or with their fists. They apprehended him and pushed him towards their car. They squished him in a small box in the back of the station wagon and kept smacking him with these rubber truncheons until he bent himself into this box in the back of the car. I assume it was to secure a person in a cage. It was small and seemed like it was built to fit the vehicle, so this guy was all crushed up in the back, and I watched him get taken away. I was sure this was not how to act as police, but we were prohibited from getting involved in their business. I felt like this is wally world, what the fuck is this place. We will lose if we are aligned with people who treat their population like that.

During those first days in Kabul, some kids played games with us. We were a new playgroup, and it was a game for them. It was annoying and dangerous for us. There was this OP at the Queen's Palace, and we had our little area wired off. The local kids would get up into the palace and up one of the balconies and then throw boulders at us because it was an entertaining game for them. So, you try to ignore them, but you get these giant boulders, probably about four or five inches, coming down. We threw them back to the kids. They Loved it. It was a fun game for them. You try to ignore them, and they just come back and start throwing shit. You just ended up playing this crazy game with these kids that had so little in the world that throwing a game of "catch" with a rock made for a day of entertainment. I can't confirm, but I feel that in a fucked-up way, it helped us with the community; we made the kids laugh and kept their kids entertained in a safe (relatively) way. What parent doesn't like that? In the end, we called that OP a daycare shift. Crazy stuff, imagine that in Canada, "go play with the heavily armed soldiers, be home when the streetlights come on…oh wait, there are no streetlights." Crazy.

I remember a crazy day with a life-and-death game of tug of war. I was on patrol with one of my OMLT teams doing the morning IED sweep on ROUTE Fosters with the ANA weapons Company from 2/1/205 Kandak. Everything was pretty chill on a crisp morning, and though everyone was intent and focused, there was a relaxed atmosphere of professionals who were comfortable in a dangerous environment. Suddenly, there was a commotion and shooting ahead and out of view of my fire team. My Captain, team leader, moved up, and he saw an Afghan soldier grabbing onto a cable on the ground and leaning back with all his weight; two other Afghans ran over and helped out. The Captain had no clue what was happening but could see that the line they were attached to was lifting out of the sand and running about 150m back to a compound. He went to see what was up and discovered that they had spotted the line moving and that it was a "pull" IED; the trigger man was at the other end of the line, trying to pull to connect the metal to complete the circuit to set off the IED. They were pulling in the opposite direction in a serious game of tug of war to stop the device from being triggered. The Captain got the remnants of the patrol and started firing at the compound, advancing towards the likely trigger location. The cable went slack, and the trigger man was long gone by the time they covered the 150m. The reaction of the ANA infantry was incredible; they saw movement in the sand and immediately knew something was up; they were fast enough to stop the IED from being triggered. I am not sure Canadians would have been so in tune with the environment. It was impressive. They stopped what could have been a terrible day for my team.

We had to go out on a patrol on Ramadan. This is super hard on the ANA because they don't eat or drink water, and if you get into a fight, they are already fatigued. We figure that we will be done by 11 am. We're leapfrogging through the grape fields, and then BANG, BANG, BANG, a couple of RPKs open up on us. We're spread out, and we're, you know, firing back and forth with the TB. They are shooting at us, we are shooting at them, but we can't get the Afghan platoon moving. I am trying to coordinate that on the radio. I think we can flank the enemy. I'm talking on the radio, and I see this ANA guy get up with his RPG to fire toward the enemy. That very morning, their trainers had said, never get behind them with an RPG because they don't look back, and you can get burned by the rocket blast out the back of the tube. I'm right behind him. FUCK. I stand up, and before he fires, the troops think, "Why is the Warrant running away in the middle of a fight?" I'm running, and my handset is dragging on the ground. I'm trying to get out of the backblast area because this guy will fire his RPG. Sure enough, he does; he lets it fly. He stood up to look back and said, "Rocket!" you know, in Afghanistan. I make it out of the way and get knocked on my ass by the backblast. Everyone else sees a cloud of smoke, and they thought a round came in, and then the dust cleared. I am all dust-covered and look all fucked up, and I let them know, "Yeah, I'm fine." So that was funny. After the rocket, the firing back and forth stopped. We were going to clear the objective, but the Afghans said it was time to go home. They were not interested in the close fight that day. They thought it was a pretty good day, and it was Ramadan. As advisors, we could not do much about that. After that, the guys never stopped yelling "rocket" in Afghan at me; they thought that was funny as shit.

We had a significant IED incident in Panjawaii. It killed four Canadians and wounded most of the platoon. Caught in the chaos was Mom and two little girls. The bomber had used them and took advantage of our understanding that the Taliban wouldn't hurt women and children to get close to our soldiers and set off his device. My platoon responded to the scene and did the casualty evacuations and scene management. It was chaos; they patched up those little girls and the Mom who had been smashed by the ball bearings that were the shrapnel from the suicide device. Because we were in triage mode, we got them onto Helicopters and off to coalition medical care, and once the casualties and investigation were complete, we moved off the position. The next day, we understood that the Taliban had reported that we had kidnapped the mother and daughters. It was insane. We sought out the village leadership and the girls' father. When we found him, he was beside himself, and once we assured him that they were being cared for and would be transferred to the Kandahar hospital, he could visit. I spoke to him at length and explained why we needed to extract his family; I had a daughter at home, so I understood his concern. We had some tea and talked at length about family and daughters, and then we ensured he was given the contact information to visit his family. About a week later, he showed up at the FOB. The girls were still touch and go and may not live. He had brought with him a small hand-sewn linen stuffed doll. Strings of yarn had been sewn on as hair, and the eyes and heart were lovingly hand embroidered on this treasured child's toy. He thanked me for helping his family and presented the doll to me for my daughter in Canada. I was utterly overwhelmed. It was an incredible offering from a family that had so little. He left after he gave it to me, and I never saw him again. My family still has that doll, and the memory of those young girls lives with us.

We stayed at the Panjawaii District Centre. It was supposed to be a one-stop shopping for the government for the locals, but really, it became another security outpost. It was terrible, and we had to live closely with the Afghan Police. We were not mentors, so we kept them at arm's length. You could always hear them; they were loud, and there was always some incident happening or brewing. This one time, we could listen to the chief of police arguing back and forth, and then the chief smashed this guy with his coffee pot full of boiling coffee and scalded him. The dude took offence and pulled his pistol on the chief. They started having a whole out gunfight in the district centre! They were shooting back and forth, and we left to get into our armoured vehicle because we were unsure if round ricochets would catch someone by just bad luck. It was a bit of a crazy environment to live in because when you were "safe," there was shit going on with your "roommates" that could hurt you.

I am in this key leader engagement, and we're making small talk. We had only met for the first time, so we felt each other out. To help communicate, we had this card with old pictographs. It was all to imply our intent, but there are no words. You'd have a picture of a wounded person with an ambulance to show that we could help hurt people; several scenarios were on the card. They thought it was hilarious. During this interaction, they kept feeding me tea. I do not want to say no, as I understand that isn't polite. I always found them very aggressive with their hospitality. They have very little to offer, but they'll offer; you better take it. If I were to refuse the tea, it would hurt our communications. Relationships don't start until your third or fourth tea in Afghanistan. So we're looking at this card, laughing, and I'm getting tea, and I must be on my fifth or 6. It's funny. But now, for whatever reason, I'm finding it REALLY funny. They're finding it funny. They're all laughing, and everyone's laughing. Everyone's having a good time. So, the Platoon Commander comes out. His thing is done; we return to the Iltis and return to camp. I'm pointing out mountains. I think the mountains are funny. I think he's funny. I think everything in the world is funny. He asks me, "Are you alright?" And like, I'm, like, not feeling any pain. I know everything in the world, and everything's got a glow around it. Shit. My little hamster brain starts running. I have enough cognizance to recognize that something is not correct. Why is everything so funny, and why am I so numb? The only thing I can conclude was that there was some local concoction that they had found some way of putting in the six teas I had with them. I was as high as a kite, and the platoon Commander secured my weapon. We got back to camp, and it was just surreal. The whole experience was intense, walking through the camp and being high on something. I have never, ever in my life tried drugs, and to be drugged from the Tea was a big wake-up call. I would have been in the hurt locker if it had gone badly. Luckily, nothing wrong happened. I don't think they were trying anything malicious; I think they thought it would be cool to give the tea a little opiate "kick." After that, my terp tried all the food and drinks before I consumed them.

I was on my first of three tours to Afghanistan. We were pretty fresh on that first tour in Kabul. We had a massive area of operations and were trying to connect with the locals to bring security. The fighting didn't happen until we were down south in Kandahar a few years later. So, one of the patrols we did on a somewhat regular basis was in the Southern operations area. It was a police station, just on the fringe of the border of the no man's land. We went further into the hills, knowing that you were running into the belligerents after this outpost. We've been down there many times to talk to the police chief and see how things were going. During one of our trips down there, the platoon commander went in to speak, and I was outside, providing us with a security cordon. The ANP were there, and we talked, and they offered me some Nazur. We didn't know what this was and had been told to accept goodwill from the local constabulary. I learned a lesson that day. Nazur is snuff. It's got a lot of opiates in it, and it's been mixed with little pieces of cut glass so that when you snort, it cuts your nose, and you get quicker absorption of the opiates. I tried some, and I was all fucked up and had to be taken care of by the medics when I got back to camp. Fucking Opiates. So, we learned our lesson, no Nazur.

We are on patrol and enter the ANP HQ, where the usual suspects are. And there's a guy in a corner, and I don't know who he was. This guy was death incarnate. Honest to God, he sat there. He had a stare. He made me feel very uneasy. You got the impression that he did not like you for some reason; you thought it was tangible. This person had been killing people since he was twelve. Didn't say a damn thing during the meeting. Nothing. He was sizing us up. And I knew this. I wanted to, you know, let him know that if push comes to shove, we're not to be fucked with. But, man, this guy was scary. So, by the end of the meeting, the police chief said he would invite us to lunch. They have very little to offer. So you take the offer when they offer unless it's against the rules, and you can make it work. The Captain says, no, we have to go, and we have timing to meet. We can't. The chief insists Oh, no, no. You're staying for lunch. Second offer, no, no… we couldn't really. Well, you're staying for lunch as the third offer, and now we're looking like assholes. I kick him under the table, which is like, you know, to let him know that he was not getting it. We're staying for lunch. And if we don't, we might be the lunch cause that guy in the corner. He's bad news. We stayed for lunch, and the food was good. Very spicy. Colourful. The same smells you get in India and Pakistan. They spread out on the floor with a big hunk of cooked meat and a bed of rice. My mind immediately flashed back to the meat markets we passed coming to this location. Some were freshly slaughtered, still dripping blood, having hung on the hook for days, and maggot eaten and still on display to be sold. The Captain remembers those meat shops also and quickly avoids the meat. I wanted to stay, so the Captain took the rice, and I ate the meat. He's eating the rice because he doesn't know what the meat is. So, I dive in, and I'm eating the meat, and I'm a bit of a chilli head, to begin with. And there's a plate of jalapeño type peppers, so I grab a coupe to cover the taste. I didn't know that these were the Commander's Chili Peppers; I am just hoping there's enough punch in these peppers to kill whatever I'm eating. I take one of the peppers, and everyone goes silent and looks at me, including freakin Mister Death. What the hell is this? Oh, you like the commander's pepper? I think there will be an incident, and I have offended someone. So, then I play it up and pretend I do not know what this is, but it's very hot. And I'm waving air into my mouth and gulping water, and the silence breaks, and they all laugh. It was like one of those moments in a movie that could be a joke or a gunfight. Now they want to force-feed me the peppers, no issues. I'm just hoping it kills whatever bug will be inside me from eating a plate of mystery meat. I broke the ice by eating the peppers, and we started a relationship with the rotation, and I had more standing than the platoon commander. I will spare you the gory details of how my insides reacted to that sacrifice I made for the mission. I should have gotten a wound stripe from how it tore me apart later.

In our first introduction, we took over security, which I believe was the queen's or king's palace. We have to do the security as we have OPs in there. It was very odd because there were kids everywhere. We learned quickly, is that like if there are no kids, that's when you need to worry. That's when you need to be more alert. We had kids who would come up to us. And they had these bricks of what looked like shit to me. It was bricks of hash, and they were trying to get us to buy them for a dollar, a brick., A DOLLAR A BRICK. There are so many temptations not to do the drugs, but what is the street value of Hash and that size of brick in Canada? I would be lying if I said it did not cross my mind. But common sense prevailed. No, I was not getting into that.

Relationships and daily living are meaningful in Afghanistan and essential to understand if you want to understand Afghans. Shirin Shah was a Kandak commander. That meant he was an Afghan Battalion Commander of about 600 soldiers. He had been fighting the Taliban for the better part of 10 years when I met him, and he had been on every tour the Canadians had been on. I think people forget that. They saw us as we rotated in and out of their country, but they stayed. In the operational mentor and liaison team (OMLT) we had guys with three or four tours, but the Afghans were in it all the time. He had a good relationship with the Canadian army. It was an adaption for us to live with the Afghans and for them to have us along in the fight. This is not a standard way for Armies to fight. There is no definition of how to "partner" or how to "mentor." Getting to know them and building relationships was significant if you wanted to be successful. You would not have gotten very far if you tried to be "all business" with these guys. You could tell he was a good leader right from the get-go. He's a big, big man and a big imposing sing man, with a massive black beard and booming voice. A smile could light up a room, or a deadly stare that could chill you to the bone. He was brilliant and was very charismatic. The dinner meal was central to our relationship. We would see each other have chai during the day, but it is the supper meals where we would sit down to talk. That's where we would do most of the planning or the discussion about stuff because he wanted to know how we interacted and how we thought and discussed things that weren't operations. He had an intuition about people, and I saw many commanders fail the test. If they were too busy, rushed, or wouldn't eat with him, the ANA were less likely to do the operation. Before dinner, we would play volleyball. He loved volleyball, and it took nothing to set up a net. We'd play volleyball back and forth. After volleyball, it was time to pray. He would wash his feet. He'd pray. I would wait. And then we would go in to eat. I remember he would take the naan (bread), rip a big chunk off, and share it with me. Soldiers would come in. They'd serve him, then serve me. And then we'd sit in his room. He had a TV in his room. He had his planning area and his bed. I brought in a table and some chairs for us to plan. He used to laugh because every time I had to sit on the floor, he knew I always found it uncomfortable because I wasn't used to it; I was forever shifting and making faces. So he was nice enough to have chairs, and we'd sit there if I wanted to plan an operation. We always had to eat and watch a Bollywood movie, and then we would get in to discuss business. Okra was my favourite. He called them ladyfingers but always ensured I would get some okra. Usually, it would be the ordinary sheep and rice. I totally enjoyed it. The bread was excellent. He always offered me the opportunity to suck the marrow out of the bones, and I said that I wasn't a big fan. I said, no, you go ahead. It's a lot of nutrients. So he would always do it. I had no issues with the food until I saw where they prepared it. The Afghans had very rudimentary infrastructure, but it worked. The local mud fashioned the ovens and stoves and hardened them by fire. They heated them with firewood; it was inefficient but worked for them. These big pots would fit in on top of the hardened mud oven and have fires underneath. They would kill the goats or sheep right in the kitchen. They hack it all up and then scoop everything into the big pots, spice it, add rice, and serve. It was not the most hygienic, but it was fast, and it worked. Let's just say it would not have passed a health and safety inspection. I am here, and so it must have been OK.

The Afghan Commander had a dog and he didn't even have a name for his dog. So we started calling him Spike and he kept him in the ANAN/OMLT area. My wife liked that we had a dog and would always send over care packages and there would be dog treats for the dog. I would be shaking my head at these gifts but loved that my wife cared so deeply. The Afghan Battalion Commander would be shaking his head as he couldn't understand the concept of sending over treats to feed the dog. It was a perfect example of how the two worlds would look at a problem. I think the Battalion Commander liked the dog, but not enough to name him and it was the dogs' job to survive. My wife, saw the dog as a living entity to be cared for like a pet. To the Commander, think of how rich you had to be to take care of a pet and give it treats!

Love eating food with the Afghans, I ate a lot with them. I worked hard at the language and I was able to have decent conversations with that. I would get invited quite a bit. Yeah. The food is what we would call one-pot wonders. Everything got put into one pot and cooked on a fire. Then it would get spread out into a communal place. We think the Afghans are dirty kind of dirty, but they all wash their hands. Anybody that would come up to the eating area had to wash your hands with the bowl of water at the entrance. Somebody watched and freshened the water Soap wasn't really a thing, but every time I came, I made sure to bring a bar of soap. They'd use it then. Then the communal plate came out heaped with food. You sit on the carpets, cross legged. There's no plates. No individual plates. You would grab the piece bread, grab the rice with your hand, and. The biggest thing was that they only eat with their right hand, The left was the "dirty" hand. I wanted to make sure I maintained that, which was hard for me as I was left-handed! You had to make sure the water for tea was prepared properly and making sure that they boil it enough. Yeah, we did try and always keep them stocked for drinking water with our bottled water. We would play volleyball with them after or soccer. The weirdest things probably was being invited for a dance party. It's probably the first dance party I've ever been in, with no women. Dancing for them was always all men and was an expression of different things in the seasons and comradeship but was very awkward dancing with other men. I usually tried to be a bit of a wallflower and just enjoyed the bread.

I took an Afghan cab out of a village in Kandahar to do a Recce. Likely a pretty stupid thing to do, and though not explicitly stated, I don't think Canadian leadership wanted us in Afghan vehicles. I figure the statute of limitations is up. I was on the NIMROD crash site in 2006. It was a UK aircraft that crashed in a big fireball and was the single day largest loss of UK life in the War in Afghanistan. Our task was to secure the crash site, collect the bodies, and recover some top-secret kits that could not be left in the field. It was a difficult task, made more difficult by the fact that the plane had come down in a populated area, and the Taliban were not only interested in the plane but now knew that we would be on the scene. Eventually, we would have to leave, and my concern was that they would be able to template our movement and lay IEDs or an ambush. While we were working in the debris field, an old guy would continue to come to a nearby wall and hang out. I was unsure of his intention and so went over; he identified himself as a village elder for the area. I asked him to keep kids away as the crash site could be dangerous, and I was worried that at nighttime, they could be mistaken for the Taliban. He agreed and moved all the kids out of the area immediately. He came back with some questions and then let me know he was also a Taxi driver and wanted to know how to avoid getting warning shots placed in his direction when he was driving his cab. He had been shot at a couple of times by coalition forces and wanted to avoid it. I talked him through the dangers of suicide bombers to our vehicles and the instructions to avoid escalation; finally, I showed him the signs on the Canadian vehicles that gave warnings. We built up a good rapport. We had hit a bunch of dead ends coming to try and get to the crash site, and with all the high walls and close compounds and small bridges that may not support the weight of our vehicles, it was a labyrinth that I did not want to get trapped in on the way out. I realized that I did not know the various paths to get out of this very congested area and that it would be wise to understand all the routes out so that we could make a plan before departing. We were needed back with the Battalion as Medusa was kicking off for real, and I did not want to be delayed by the urban obstacle. I also figured that as a local, I suspected he may have some contacts who would tell him about IEDs being laid. I figured that if the Taliban were watching us, they would be watching for the Army vehicles to depart, indicating that security was lower on the position. So, a bit reflexively, I asked him if he could give me a ride in his taxi. I did not expect him to say yes. It seems benign, but it was pretty crazy at the time. Most locals had left Pashmul, and it seemed that everyone who stayed was an enemy or was affiliated with the Taliban. It was a risk, but the payoff was worth it. I agreed to a price, and my signaller acted as security and my interpreter hopped in his white Toyota Corolla, me riding shotgun. With one Canadian vehicle trailing us at a distance, recording the routes, we took a cab on the reconnaissance. I did not tell my boss, and now, looking back on it, it was probably pretty stupid, but it made sense at the time, and most importantly, it worked. We confirmed primary and alternate routes; he gave us local knowledge of the area, and all was done for about 40 US Dollars. I know it was a bit crazy, and I got away with one there; I think I felt comfortable because of our human interactions and the building of rapport and trust. I think that was one of the only times that I had that type of interaction with a civilian, where there was mutual vulnerability-perhaps we needed more of that as the mission progressed.

In Kabul there was this massive hill in the centre of the city known as "TV Tower Hill." In order to extend radio range for the teams working in Kabul we put a radio rebroadcast (RRB) site on top of that hill. This was a small group of signals or radio technicians and me. I was not the most senior soldier but was responsible for making sure everyone on this site was secure and the area was protected. Everyone has their role, let's just say these radio guys knew radios, but had no clue about the risk they were in or how to defend a position. This was before Kandahar, no one had died, and everyone was still under Bosnia rules. This meant in the old days these RRBs were a good time, not much to do, limited chain of command oversight and all you had to do was keep the radios running. I was a sniper and the thought was that by putting me on this feature I could also, if necessary, provide arcs of observation into the city. But frankly, it was a shit show. My job was to be the security element for the RRB. I was essentially alone on that hill, and as the only infantry guy I often felt like I was a pain in their ass to talk about security and good drills rather than everyone dialling in and just doing their shit. To them, the threat was not real. I had my C-3sniper rifle, my C 8 with a M two–o–three and pistol. All sorts of stuff to observe people with but no authority to do anything if I did observe anything going down. ROE was held much higher in those days. The only way I could secure the area was to ensure that we had a good relationship with the new Afghan Militia Forces (AMF). This was very early days, and so these dudes were really just militia and likely had been Muj (Mujahedeen) before NATO came. Not professional, but tough. I spent a lot of time building a relationship with them because I was junior, but responsible for security but had no authority or resources. So I ate a lot of goats and drank a lot of tea. Anyway, they seemed to trust me and then we had an incident. The last thing we want as it breaks trust and I need these guys to protect us. A survey crew came up to do some work, to put up some more permanent antennas, not just for us, but the coalition. And one of the surveyors had a very nice camera. It was sitting on his truck seat and when he came back The guy came in, and said "I don't make a big deal of this, but it's very you know, it's very expensive and it's not mine, My camera's missing." I need to be accountable for it. So now how do I deal with this? So first I go see the AMF commander and let him know that we are looking for this. He assures me that none of his people would know anything about it and that likely it was misplaced or it was picked up by a German or a Canadian. I take him at face value, so as to not offend him and go see the other groups. I check with the Canadians. Anybody see this? Check with the Germans. Nothing. Now I have to go deal with the AMF. I'm basically now telling them that one of their people stole something and I want it back. I thought of how to how do I approach this? Do I approach it as a question? I go to the commander and bring it to them like I have exhausted all my options and I gave him an out. I said," In the next couple of days, those guys will be back. If the camera could just be left somewhere and somebody tells me where it is and I'll go get it." Everything will be good, no issues as I am sure it was just a mistake." The next day, the little guy that's on shift at the top of the hill comes over and he points at the wall where they had a lot of buildings. And there was the camera sitting on the wall. So, we went and got it. BUT. The commander who was down in Kabul heard this. He initially said there's no way any of these people would do this, he came up and then he beat that kid. Beat that kid hard. In front of me and I was like, this is just a camera, stop it! Our rules of engagement did not allow us to interfere with domestic violence or the disciplinary actions of the forces of Afghanistan. I just watched this kid get beaten bloody, the Commander was satisfied that his unit would not do it again, but I had another problem, that kid was responsible for my security. I didn't want him beaten; I just wanted the camera. That was my first lesson as a young Master Corporal on a hill by myself on "ethics" and cultural understanding. I had tried to do everything right and still had got it wrong. Afghanistan is different and is a steep learning curve. I am not sure I have forgiven myself for how that kid got hurt over a camera.

We had to go do BDA. Three bad guys, plane dropped a 500 pounder on them. Go do a BDA. We get out there and we think, our chain is being yanked because there's nothing in the area. We look closely. You see little piles of ants. You look a little closer, like a little piece of rag, piece of bone and then look up in in the trees and there are clothes are in the trees, like ragged clothes, bloody clothes. The bomb struck and blew them up into the trees. We have a cordon and then a Sergeant comes over the means and reports that he has found what appears to be a head. The head had money in the mouth. They dug back and found a body underneath. Somebody had caught this guy. They put him near the road. They buried him up to his head and put money in his mouth and then left him to die. It was a warning to anyone coming from Pakistan. I was never sure if it was the TB, the local villagers, the ANA, or the ANP. But someone was sending a message. we've got to take this guy out of the ground. We called lots of engineers to make sure the body is not booby-trapped. The BDA was complete, there was always something else going on in Afghanistan. The Afghans have their own ways and you learn something new every day.

We have our own values as Canadians and sometimes it was hard to watch and not impose those values on the population. This one time I was the tail vehicle, and we're convoying and there was a guy behind us on a motorcycle. There was a little boy or girl, on the front of the motorcycle. waving at the convoy. Then as the convoys passing, I'm going to assume it's the father, is takes them off the motorcycle and beats the shit out of the kid who was waving. The impression I had is that our mission was that we're there to help. But the culture is different and we're there to support, like we can tell them democracy is good and capitalism but not to beat the shit out of their kids and wives… You see that kind of stuff and you're like, no wonder why their violence begets violence. The kids grow up in violent households, there is violence on the street and it normalizes. So, the next generation is violent.

We're doing a shura and I had my interpreter next to me. I made a habit of not eating the meat. I would eat the rice and the stuff but not the meat. One time I got these massive meatballs. What the fuck is this? "Just a big a big meatball boss," says my terp. "It's good, its beef," so I actually bit into one and it was almost hollow and it squirted out. As soon as I did that, the interpreter said, "Actually, it's a bull testicle." Now, I don't know to this day. I don't know if it's true or not, I don't know what it was as I have never eaten a testicle. After the shura, he went running out and told everybody that I loved eating the cow's balls. Like it was the funniest thing ever. It did not encourage me to eat meat when invited to dinner.

When we first got to Afghanistan the ANA didn't look very professional to me. We had to go on these partnered patrols and it was hard to have guys along that seemed to not care. They'd have their weapons slung over their shoulder. While out they'd stop, be in the green fields and seemed to focus on picking and eating grapes… And then one day, one day we go to pick them up to depart and it was like something was different. They were dressed to the nines. Their helmets on, body armour and weapons at the ready. And the interpreter says, "now we fight," like, holy shit. And that was our first TIC. These guys actually know when fighting season is, like they have they got it marked on their calendar. There was a six-week period where every day within 600 meters of leaving their camp, they got hit. That went on for like six weeks. Those ANA guys knew the environment so well that they rested when they could and then fought when they had to. We were on a 6-month sprint, they were on a decade long marathon.

We ate a lot of goat. They hosted big meals for us every once in a while. Which were like Medieval feasts. It was pretty amazing to be sitting on a large carpet in the middle of the desert, eating naan and goat and rice like Lawrence of frickin Arabia. One of the most interesting things was the Afghan wine. It's sour. goat milk, creamy and white and warm with chopped up cucumber. Pretty gnarly. They had us into this big meal and it's pretty safe because, I saw the meat on the fire and it went right from the fire to the plate. So I feel pretty good about the meat. The bread, I was a bit suspect but got over it. So this guy, I think he was like the district judge. he was an influential guy in the district. He sat next to me. We were talking. I don't remember these off-topic discussion, but I was trying to convince him to stay in Ghundey Ghar. So the meals went good. Then they start passing the bowl of sour milk because I didn't know it was sour milk. I just thought it was milk. He kind of set me up like there is a little. They're all drinking from the same ladle as this guy who had the crustiest most disgusting tobacco stained beard and moustache. I remember he takes the ladle and takes a big slurp of it and the milk running down his beard. He turns to me and says it is Afghan wine. I took it out, took a sip, and it was all I could do to not throw up and just spray it, warm curdled goat milk with chunks just floating down my throat. I held it together. It's just because you weren't expecting the spoiled taste of fermentation. The old guy looked and was laughing at me, but he would keep talking business and so perhaps it was worth it.

We are just chilling out in the COP when all of a sudden we hear this couple at God awful kaboom, and we get ready to go, not smooth, we're like bumping up against each other, trying to get to our fighting positions, probably looked like a comedy routine. I've just throw my boots on, I'm in shorts. I put my frag vest, my tac vest on. I put on my helmet; I got my rifle. I look ridiculous. Not how I thought I would fight. Then hear a call for "medic, medic" from the guy just round the corner. So go around the corner and somebody is already attended to casualty. Then there's another kaboom. But from another direction. They hit us with eighty two millimetre recoilless rifles. They might be a little bit dated, but those things are freakin deadly. They went through the Hesco and so one guys walk around, he's got a scalpel wound, he's bleeding, he's in shock. They're tending to this other guy this guy. I think tension pneumothorax, and now this was a prolonged engagement. They caught us napping but now we are starting to give as good as we received. This engagement lasts for two hours. I was running ammo to the ramparts for the machine guns and mortar bombs to the mortar pit. Thank god we had mortar qualified guys in the Infantry. The Taliban are not fazed by machine gun fire. But when things start exploding around them. That's when they will start withdrawing. They hate rockets and artillery. So I'm running ammo. I'm running mortar bombs to the mortar pit. Just a constant cycle and hoping I don't get hit by incoming. The ANA is kind of frozen There's a there's an interpreter sitting there next to the ANA section we have attached into the COP. He's very scared and wants to help. We need more mortar bombs, "help me bring mortar bombs," I say. I bring on a mortar bomb case. I show him the case and show him the marking SMK. It's smoke. I need "H-E" High Explosives. He goes back, brings back ILLUM or illumination. No, no, no, I say I need H-E and I show him the marking again. He runs away again like a jack rabbit. He kept coming back with the wrong stuff. Probably three or four cans worth. I said "listen, stop helping, go sit down and get the ANA up on the wall to fight and locate the Enemy. But stop helping me with ammo!"

We're just up and down the Arghandab River using the riverbed as our primary route for movement and then picking different points to enter into the Horn of Panjawaii or the South of Zhari. We're doing one of the tasks of surveying various crossing points, collecting information, comparing it to the information on the map, like different routes, what we could push vehicles up, and trying to gather local information. Going into towns, I remember, you know, we're starting to get exposed to locals who had not fled. We had little contact with locals and realized how tough it would be because these people were unhappy seeing us. So, we go into the villages to speak to the local people. When was the last time Western soldiers were in this village? They informed us that it had been the Russians in the 1980s. I was like, WTF are we doing? It was so random, just bouncing in and out with little impact; we were spread so thin we could not "own" an AOR like folks had in the Balkans or even Kabul. The locals would not talk to me because I was so young. I was 23 years old. Baby-faced as a clean-shaven Westerner, I looked very, very young. They were more prone to talking to one of my bearded soldiers than talking to me because he was in charge with his beard, and I wasn't. That prompted the Major to order me to stop shaving so I could grow a beard and look like I was actually in charge. I tried for a little bit, but it did not work out…my beard was shit. Eventually, we had a new mission, and the beard became less critical in the new area. But think of that: Russians and beards…if you aren't going to stay and build actual relationships, not much will move forward. The Taliban lived with them every day.

———————

To avoid IEDs, we had to travel cross country and off the roads. Our LAVs are heavy and would often do damage. We destroyed this farmer's irrigation, and I could tell it wasn't good. I got out, and he was just livid. By this point, we had an interpreter, and we were still trying to make things better. I told him that getting a claim is going to Kandahar City, putting a claim in the provincial reconstruction team, and helping pay for the damage. You can imagine a farmer with no vehicle is not interested in that explanation. He was so angry with me; I don't think I'd ever been exposed to anyone so angry with me. I just took out my wallet and all my American cash. I just gave it to the farmer and said I was sorry; we mounted up and left. Then I remember thinking, this is so stupid. I could be distributing funds everywhere, and I have no money to give to anybody. I could have done something there and then officially… I can fire as many 25mm rounds as I want out of these LAVs. I don't have a single dime that I can spend or help people. Financial risk was a "real" risk, and Canada and Foreign Affairs could not figure out how to use cash to make an actual difference. That farmer was right; I remember being put off and angry about that.

———————

We used to take pictures of kids and show them. It's one of the ways that we just learned to develop relationships with local people. They would have no images of their children. So, we would take pictures of their kids in the street. Then we'd go back to that same area, and we'd give it to the kids or give it to the parent. The parent was overwhelmed as they had no way of having a picture of their child. People cared about it. We take it for granted. And yet, for them, that was the biggest gift. That little initiative really brought us some good rapport with people for something as small as a picture printed and given to them. All of a sudden, we had like best friends for life, and they would start telling us everything happening in their area.

———————

Don't kick a chicken. It was hot, the patrol had been extended, and for some reason, my medic launched this chicken that was following the patrol. He just kicked it out of the way, and then some kids were yelling at us about it from on top of a wall, and then they jumped down behind it. Then all of a sudden, from the other side of the wall, they chuck a fucking grenade. Holy shit, holy shit! Everyone hits the deck, and it explodes; some guys caught a little shrapnel, but no one hurt. Kids were long gone. Lesson: don't kick the livestock, and don't fuck with kids that have access to grenades!

The ANSF would go out on patrol and go into town, and their favourite thing to do was go into town and beat up the police chief. Allegedly, the police chief was a bad guy; he was Taliban. So they would go to town, rough him up and come back in. Then, they would tell us stories about it. So sometimes, a corporal would pull camp duty. He'd be hanging out with the ANSF guys, and they would go into town and come back and tell him all about their stories…" We went into town and beat up this guy." They were really good, though, other than this habit of beating up the police chief. If any locals came near the camp, we would point them out to the ANSF, and they would load up in pickup trucks and go out and shoo them away. I was never sure if they beat anyone up as it was not our task at the time to patrol with them, but their stories were crazy. "Partnering" is a strange term. Each side is just in a location with each other. With no command relationship. So, whatever they did, we could report it, but if their chain of command approved, well, good enough.

So, company headquarters had this pet mongoose with a leash-like collar, which was super tame. Then they let it off the leash so it could start running around the camp. Knuckles the Mongoose. Troops loved him, and he kept the snakes down. Then the Afghans ate him! That pissed everybody off. Can't blame the Afghans, who has a pet mongoose? I am sure old knuckles was good eating, but it really pissed off the Canadians.

We had been on an operation with the ANA for two or three days. They patrolled without returning to the FOB, gaining contact and keeping the enemy off balance. It was grinding, patrolling, walking all day, moving slowly, IED finds, small contacts, hard rations and sleeping wherever we finished for the night. The Afghans indicated that they needed to resupply and switch up the routine. Two of them left on foot to go back to link up with their Ford tan painted Rangers (the truck of the ANA for combat). They take the car into town and bring back a big bag of rice, and we are told to meet them at the canal. We go back to the canal, and the Afghans are gathered by the side and are aiming their under-mounted grenade launcher into the canal. As I approach, I can't see any threat. Still, all of a sudden, the soldier with the weapon opens up into the canal, smoothly firing, extracting the grenade, reloading and firing again and firing a total of three grenades in quick succession into the water. He then grabbed a burlap bag and waded into the water to pick up the fish that had been killed by the concussion of the grenade and then floated to the surface. The ANA is not interested in patrolling anymore. It's been quiet for most of the day. We are supposed to keep patrolling, but this day has gone in a different direction. I let the CP know we were establishing our patrol base for the night. We've got a wall around us. We are still pulling security. But the rest are feeling like a party. They want to play shot-put games or games of strength. They want to arm wrestle me. You know, things like that. So, it's just soldiers being soldiers. So, in the middle of this operation, we have a fun night, a fire and a fish fry, play some games and sleep. No harm, no foul. No names, no pack drill.

———————

My favourite meal was goat. Whenever we ate fresh, it was goat. Daily we ate the Afghan Bread or "Naan". The bread was amazing. Once we did our patrols in town, I saw they made it or kneaded the bread with their feet, so I stopped eating it for a little while. I don't care if they washed their feet five times a day, just like, no, I am not eating any more bread, no more "foot" bread, for this guy. But it was delicious; there is no denying that. I wish I had not seen that; perhaps I was being too sensitive, but I just can't unsee it, and it ruined the bread for me.

———————

The ANP are often described as corrupt, unprofessional and untrustworthy. At times, they might have been. The ANP also took way more casualties than we ever did. I remember they would do some good work but seemed not to get public credit because they weren't directly in the NATO reporting chain. Because they didn't get credit in the NATO reports, it was hard for us to shift the narrative on the organization. There was this one giant IED that had been built into a culvert under a road; the Taliban had stood in the water for hours and chipped out the inside of the Culvert and planted a giant pot inside the culvert cement and then lightly cemented back over it. When you glanced through the culvert, it looked completely clear. It was massive and easily would have been one of those catastrophic destructions of a LAV if it had been set off. All the BG patrols had completely missed it. On this one day, nobody was with the ANP at all. They were coming back from Kandahar City, and they checked the culvert on their way back and found the device all by themselves... They called the police chief, and the chief would call us. We would go out, confirm the device and then call the BG QRF to deal with it. Canadians would respond, defuse the device, or BIP it, which would go into the Canadian SITREP and stats. There is no shortage of people willing to take credit if it's a good news story. We should have given more credit to ANP, but the original find and securing would get lost in the handovers. To us, as Advisors and mentors, the independent finding, searching and reporting was the win. The technical stuff the engineers did was awesome, but if we wanted to win in Afghanistan, we needed to pump the tires of the Afghan forces, not our own. The ANP did the dangerous work on many of these and got no credit. I just think we need to acknowledge them sometimes.

We had been told that women in Afghanistan had been liberated when the US had invaded. We discovered this was not the case when we arrived in Kabul. We never saw women; they were not part of any power structure, in any meetings, nor present in any decision-making circles. One day, a woman was introduced to us at a meeting, and it threw us for a loop. We had just started this, and there was a knock on the door; I opened the door, and standing there was this beautiful Afghan woman who walked in. She has a hair covering but is not fully covered and is dressed in stylish Western clothes. All the Afghans acted very much in deference to this woman. She came in, and she was very apologetic. She spoke to all of us, stated her points, and said she had to leave for another meeting. She went, and we were dumbstruck. It was so outside of the norm. It turns out that her father was a very prominent doctor and very embedded in the region's power structure. So there was this deference to her parents, and as there were no sons, the family being represented was more important than her gender. Whenever you think you have Afghanistan figured out, some new layer will be pulled back, reminding you of how little you actually knew.

As we became more confident and familiar with the locals in Kandahar, there were times that we were invited into their homes. The hospitality was amazing, and we did not realize then that these people could be risking a lot by visiting with us. The structures were simple: backed clay and bricks with dirt floors covered by carpets. Windows were open and shuttered with steel shutters. The heat was usually a fire. It was like being transported back in time. The houses themselves are very simple. In most cases, they'll be one long building with several different doors, but none of the rooms are necessarily adjoining. A compound could be a bunch of individual rooms or huts. Generally, there is at least one large gathering area, mostly devoid of furniture. All visiting was done on these six-foot-long cushions and carpets, and you are relaxed on the floor. Generally, the youngest male member of the family would get tasked with producing the tea and providing sweets for the guests. We would sort of circle around and drink tea and shoot the breeze by and large. As we were a rifle section of 10 big dudes, most of the section was left outside for security. The Sergeant felt I understood the people well and could use a bit of Pashto. It was hard to be relaxed and comfortable in all our combat kit. There had been a Patricia in the tour before us who had been wounded because he took off his helmet in a friendly situation and had been hit in the head with an axe. We would stay partially geared up. The tac vest and body armour would stay on just for no other reason than it's a pain in the ass to take off and put on. But I would put my weapon down on the ground next to me. Generally, I'd set the C9 down. It would be within arm's reach of me. I was a light machine gunner, and I just deployed the bipod legs and set them down right next to me. How crazy must it have been for these families to have dudes in full battle rattle with machine guns placed around them at the family house? Then we would sit there. People from different worlds speak different languages and have tea in the afternoon in Afghanistan. It was bizarre, but it was probably my favourite thing to do because I felt like I connected with the Afghan people, and it connected me better with my mission than the fighting.

What will I tell these guys about warfighting that they don't already know? I was an LT with no combat experience tasked with mentoring ANA leadership. I had reservations about how the ANA was structured and our role. At a larger scale, the US structures and system had been imposed on Afghans; things like personal weapons and their doctrine were also just US. There wasn't any actual Afghan-generated doctrine; they just translated American doctrine into Dari, saying, here you go. By 2012-2013, the Afghans were fatigued with the rotations of personnel, meeting and learning new faces and mentoring on a system that was not of their design. So, I had to speak to the Afghan Commander and say, "We're not politically connected. We're here to soldier." He seemed to appreciate that, and then I told him, "I'm here to help you in whatever way you need to get the job done.". So, we had that professional rapport. I treated him as a lieutenant colonel. Irrespective of being an Afghan. I'd walk the room, and I'd salute. I'd leave. I'd salute. I always called him sir and provided that degree of professional respect. I resisted imposing my Western ideals or values or thinking I was any better than him. At the end of the day, we're both soldiers. We are both interested in the same things; I found that we were more similar than we were different. My guys in the North were educated professional soldiers. So, we had common ground right there, and by showing respect and trust, I could allow him some freedom to deviate from the" system" imposed and introduce Afghan rather than Western initiatives. I believe this would have served well had we done it on a larger scale, but we didn't, and I think the final collapse was an example of a lack of ownership. The Afghans didn't own their army; it was imposed on them to be the army we wanted, not the one they wanted or would have designed.

We had this amazing Afghan police officer we used to call "Afghan Rambo." He used to run towards Firefights. It didn't matter where they were; he was going in full tilt. He'd be in the truck as soon as the bullets were flying. Whoever he could get to go with him, it didn't matter. It was just him or his driver, and they would roll that because he was such a figure in the town that this aura of invincibility existed around him. It was impressive and a bit crazy. He always called out the Taliban publicly and pointed out locals he thought were aligned with them. I think they were out to get him. One day, there was a contact at the district centre. Which was pretty common, you know, every couple of weeks. They fire up potshots at night, which would be over in 10 seconds. Afghan Rambo heads to the contact. The only guy ready to go is this ANP soldier and driver with one eye. They take off into the night and drive full speed down through Bazaari Panjwaii, headed towards the district centre so he could save the day. There was a checkpoint before the district centre, which was the dirty part of Bazaari Panjwaii. This is where people weren't nice and threw rocks at you. It was like the scariest part of the town. There was a one-speed bump there for the checkpoint. The speed bump was aligned perfectly to an alley. So you knew, if you're ever going to get ambushed in the town, that would be the spot. You have to slow down; there's a perfect aiming point down the alley. So he slows down at the speed bump, looks to his right and sees a dude with a PKM down the alley. He tells his one-eyed driver to stop so you can roll down his window and shoot this guy. So just as he gives the order, these guys down the alley open up. There's more than just that one dude. Afghan Rambo had missed that.

The one-eyed driver receives rounds through the windshield and blinds the other eye. So now he's the no-eyed driver. He panics, turns and turns the truck. Afghan Rambo is firing out of the window while rounds are coming in. A round hits his AK and puts it out of commission. So, he has one choice: to get out of the vehicle. He is shot four times, opens the door, pulls a sidearm, and starts firing back. He hears holy shit in Pashto, and the assailants recognize him and that he is still alive. They run away. He collapses. The rest of the ANP catch up with us and grab him. They bring him back. The ANP trucks always came into our little parking lot first with all their wounded. We would jump in the truck and then go to the front gate of Masum Ghar reporting on the radio to get him up to the role One aid station. He's been shot to hell. He's got four rounds in his chest, like a partial evisceration. He's got guts coming out, a few rounds through his legs. He's lying on the back. He's still conscious, and I jump in the back of the truck, and I figure he's going to die. So, I started going through my TCCC bag and trying to patch him up. We go up to the role one and get him all patched up. He is in and out of consciousness, and I wait with him while the helo is inbound. It will be about 30 min. He looks at my boots and says, "Where'd you get those boots?" I answered, "I bought them with my own money. "He jokes, "Oh my, nice boots, can I have them?" I let him know my boots were not available. He jokes around that when he gets back, he is going to steal my boots. The helicopter is now in sight, and I am ready to move him. As we get him onto the PZ and put him on the helicopter. He's still conscious. I yell, "Listen, brother, you pull through this, I'll buy a new pair of boots.!" He's all fucked up. I am sure he'll never remember and with that he is taken off by the helicopter and brought to the role 3. A month to the day later, he walks back to the strong point. He is hobbling in, and he pulls up his shirt. he's got staples from the top of his chest to his belly; the holes are still seeping. He looks right at me, and he first says, "You owe me some boots." I did not even know that he was alive until he walked in. I'm like, you're the toughest motherfucker. Yes, I will get you some boots! I called my wife and ordered a size nine SWAT boots from Valley Workwear. They arrived two weeks later, and he was over the moon. Sad thing. A week after he got the boots, the Taliban finally got him- he hit an IED and was gone.

One of the tasks we had with the PRT was escorting the Canadian Corrections officials to the Afghan prison. We would assist the prison mentors from Canada and give them security. I am not sure it was understood all the other things that Canada was doing to help Afghanistan. Professionalizing the prisons was one line of effort. We're doing a prison walk-through one night. There were two sides to the prison: political prisoners and criminal prisoners. We were on the criminal side, and we're just moving through. We see this kid in the prison. When I say kid, I'm talking about maybe five or six years old locked up with his old man. I remember this Corrections Canada kind of guy losing his fucking mind. So, we see the Afghan warden, and he asks the Prison mentor what they should do. There's no one to look after the kid outside. Families were locked up if the males were locked up. The families are all in the jail! So where is a kid better off? I am not sure; they had family support and protection in the prison, there was even a small playground, and they ran a little school. But I don't know, it was like something from the 1800s. There might sometimes have been overly high expectations of how fast a country can progress under Western "mentorship" when a whole culture is not focused on change. I hated those prison visits, but they taught me suitable lessons, patience, and the ability to try and listen and understand, not just judge.

The CO asked if he could accompany us on patrol one day, and something funny happened. We would mix the patrol up, drive the city, and then, at intervals, stop and dismount out of sight. The LAV would carry on so that two elements were patrolling: the LAV crew and the dismounted section. Anyone in the area would not necessarily know the dismounts had been dropped. On this particular patrol, there was a police substation we would go to check in with and see how the new police force was doing. We would stop in and have Tea with the night duty staff. I always take my helmet off because we're inside, but I keep my headset on with my PRR (personal role radio.) I was also a radio man. While inside, One of my soldiers hops on the radio and asks.
" Hey, you guys having tea?"
I answer," Yeah, why?"
He told me that he observed them pulling water out of a drum outside. He said, "I hope they boil that water!" I asked what he was worried about. He told me a dead rat was floating in it. That was the CO's introduction to how we were living!

We visited with the governor of Kandahar, who had come in with his entourage. In his support group, there was a woman. All I remember was a big group all standing around and just kind, being on the back part of the inner circle; officials were saying their pieces, and someone came sneaking out of the audience and threw gas on this woman and lit her on fire. Holy Shit... She's burned quite severely. We wrap her in blankets, put out the flames, and start doing first aid. I will never forget the smell of her burning flesh. This guy's grabbed up, flex-cuffed. He's on his knees. There's lots of yelling. ANAs got a grip on him. And this big guy from the US part of the Human Terrain team unholsters his 9mm and looks like he is going to blow the guy away; we all froze; everyone would be glad this piece of shit is dead, but you can't shoot him while he is flex cuffed. This US guy got talked off the ledge, and the dude that set the woman on fire was handed off to the Governor's guys, as per the agreements with the Afghans: their crime, their prisoner. I wouldn't bet a lot of money he is around today.

This guy from the community was a source for us. He approached our CIMIC guy and said, "Hey, the Taliban killed my cousins." "I'll tell you guys what they're up to around PBSG." He gave us intelligence and saved people's lives. Things like IEDs being laid in certain places, ambushes, that type of thing. So, based on his intelligence, we caught and detained a guy who was JPEL. He was a local facilitator. This was important stuff, and we didn't know anything about handling sources, and we fucked it up somehow. The Taliban compromised that guy, and he was beaten to death. We found his body, and on it was this photo of him with two young boys, the cousins that the Taliban had killed. I have kept it as a reminder that you shouldn't do tasks you are not trained or equipped to do; we should have handed that off to HUMINT or SOF. Being an informant in an insurgency is dangerous, like someone reporting on the Mob. It takes training to deal with those people. We cut corners and approached things amateurishly to solve our immediate needs. The result was good; people got killed.

So early in the tour, we were forced to abandon an RG-31 vehicle in an area with restricted access and lots of enemy activity. It had come around a corner too fast and had slid into a wadi. We were told to abandon it and carry on with our task, but due to collateral damage, we could not bomb it. So we had to strip out all of the kit and then come back for it after our big operation was over. We returned to the site a month later to find the RG31 stripped to nothing. Those motherfuckers that live in that area are so intelligent. They had used a donkey or something to flip it out of the wadi, and that vehicle was stripped down to the bare bones, stripped to nothing but an armoured carcass. I knew I couldn't recover any pieces, but I was shocked to discover what had happened. I went to find a local elder, and as

I approached, I noticed an RG31 Armoured door built into his mud house. The armoured windshield from the vehicle was in the fucking mud hut! So they got a front bay window and an armoured front door. So, I asked him where he got his house upgrades, and he looked me right in the face and said," I don't know anything." He's lying straight to my face. He's like, I don't know anything about an armoured vehicle or who would have taken all that stuff. You must appreciate the balls on this guy and the ability to survive and improve their life. There is no Home Depot, but there is an abandoned armoured vehicle down the road.

We found a heroin lab. In Panjwaii, East in Nakahonay. There was a truck bomb in the area, also in another compound we searched. It was odd to be in Taliban infrastructure, like a bad guy museum; it made you feel like you never knew what was going on and seeing what they did when we weren't looking. These are bad dudes, Heroin, and Truck Bombs. They were not happy we found that shit. ANP truck got ambushed right after leaving our position, and a couple of police guys got killed.

We were out on this Operation, and it was so hot. I'm drinking from my Camelbak, which is like drinking hot water. And I'm suffering from "water boredom." Just so much water consumed, lukewarm water, necessary, but boring. My terp brings me these grapes. They're so refreshing. I'm eating these grapes. Cool. You know, they've got water on them, and I was just going' got town and having another hundred of these grapes because they are just so good. I made the mistake of asking where he washed the grapes; I assumed that it was our bottled water. My terp said, "No, I just washed them in the canal near where we are resting." Then, our patrol route takes us near that canal. He tells me, "This is the canal I washed them in; he was pleased as punch that he had made me happy. I'm walking beside it, and I look down in the river and see this murky green water and bloated dead animals floating in the fucking river. I didn't say anything to my terp because he would have been devastated that it upset me, but I wondered how many parasites I contracted for the joy of eating those grapes.

We were POMLT and so different than a rifle platoon in the BG. There were only like 4-6 of us with this ANP crew. People felt we were at a disadvantage because we didn't have big armour or heavy weapons. But we had our minds, the Afghans, and lived in the terrain. I had the mentality that it was my AO. This was my first tour, and I was a "mentor." I didn't know much more about how to be anything but a regular infantry platoon commander. So I treated it like a learning experience but defaulted to aggressive manoeuvring, much to the chagrin of my MPs and Warrant Officer. I really felt it kept us safer than sitting at our base. We just took it as it came and tried to improve the ANP. For example, we would get told that this road is loaded with IEDs and we can't use it anymore. We would go VPS, find some, pull them out of the ground and then find a cache. That would slow things, and we would not see any IEDs for the next month. I never never thought of myself as a victim. We chose to be there, and the ANP had to be there, so we might as well take it to the enemy. I always went out there and thought, fuck you, Taliban, not today.

I was out between Helmand and Kandahar on New Year's Eve. It was our job to spot Taliban moving between Helmand and Kandahar or from the Reg Desert. We went into a position, but if I am totally honest, it was a little half-assed. We had fifty percent of our vehicles up on their thermals, watching for enemy movement, but my driver and I lay on the hood of my Jeep and watched one of the rifle Companies launch flares and illumination into the sky at Midnight to bring in the New Year. We were about 25km West of their positions on Route SUMMIT, but it was pretty impressive in the darkness of the Afghan night. Not disciplined, but amazing. Suddenly, my Driver sees movement and has his weapon up; a dude emerges from the edge of our view. This little Afghan guy. Scared the shit out of us. We went through the drill, and he was clear. He lived in a little mud compound that we had thought was abandoned. He invited us back. I accepted just after midnight on New Year's Eve. So, my signaller and I go in. My signaller stays at the door all kitted up, and I leave my PRR depressed and go into the house with just my pistol and my translator. The house was immaculate, with all dirt and mud walls but freshly swept with carpets and evident care. His wife brought tea, and we saw his daughters. It was a big eye-opener as we had not had this type of interaction before. On the walls were pictures of foreign capitals, such as Paris and Rome, and works of art. He wanted his family to know there was something else other than Kandahar. As we began to talk, he said he had come back from Pakistan, as he had heard there was an opportunity with the West in Afghanistan. But he could not even get power to his home. He pointed to the power lines that ran along Highway One and wondered aloud why so much money was coming into Afghanistan, but he could not get running water or power. Good point. We had this weird conversation and drank a lot of tea. It was very social and lasted a couple of hours, and then he asked me to go before the sun came up as he didn't want the Taliban to know that he had hosted me. This type of action, with one security guy and I having no body armour or actual security, was not how things were done. I am sure we broke all sorts of rules, but if we could help this guy somehow, it would be the incremental move forward we should be making. It is just this human connection. I promised to return the following day to fix a well, and we did, demonstrating that when we say something, we do it. As I was leaving the next day, he asked for "English lessons." This was a way for us to meet and not arouse suspicion. He handed me this Pashto /English textbook. Inside were notes on Taliban movements and IED emplacements. It was Incredible. I delivered it in my report, and he was handed off to HUMINT. I was sad to stop contact, but we don't do that kind of work. It was a pretty wild night, where we were just people in a situation; we broke the rules and let down barriers, which was very human. He was the first Afghan I spoke to, not a Talib or government official. He put a very human face on the problem. A guy with a wife and two daughters who wanted more for them, the same as I wanted for my family in Canada. As an epilogue, I returned to that area on my next tour to try and find him. The house was gone, and he was nowhere to be found.

I was a POMLT lead in Panjawaii, and when I arrived, there was a new Police Chief who had just been brought in. The previous chief had been a political appointee and was corrupt. Naim was his name, and it was like he was a new sheriff in an old western town who would clean up the streets. He hated the Taliban and needed to try and fight corruption. His first step was to clean out the old cops, and he needed to "pick his team." These fuckers were tough. They had been fighting this battle for a long time; they were supposed to be Police, but they rarely arrested the Taliban. They drove around in green Ford Rangers with no armour and had limited combat training, but were armed with AK 47s, RPKs and RPGs and got in more TICs than anyone else. As much to do with their aggressive patrolling as the fact, they were the softest target for the Taliban to strike. Naim brought in this character; we used to call him Afghan Rambo. He's like the second in command or the sergeant major of the police in Panjwai. He was legendary for his bravery and his ability to motivate the ANP to get after the Taliban. As the POMLT, we lived and worked with them. They became our friends and our comrades in arms. We likely understood the war from the Afghan perspective differently than the BG. Not better, just differently. Being with Naim and Afghan Rambo was quite a journey as they tried to clean up Panjawaii and build a police force. I know the Afghans had a lot of issues; corruption is present in every police force, but I hope the message gets out that there were Afghans who were dedicated to a better life, that they put their lives on the line and knew what it meant to have Taliban control of their country.

I had young translators attached to my team. At one point, one of them was getting married. I said congratulations. He was 18, and he could afford to get married because he had a job. He came to see me and asked to talk. Bashfully, he asked about his wedding night. I asked what? What do you mean? He said that he did not know anything about the female body, and so did not know how babies were made or anything to do with physical interactions with a woman. It is not covered by any school, media, or family. So, he was at a total loss. I told him I was no expert but could go through the basics. I researched sex ed from the Canadian School Curriculum, and I did a sex ed class; it was unbelievable, but that is where society was. He told me it was super helpful and that his wedding night was a "success."

I was a mentor with the ANP. We had this one Afghan dude; he hated the Taliban and was a super-aggressive fighter. Best I have ever seen. One day, we are patrolling into a town, and we start getting shot at from the edge of the city, and the RPGs start coming at us. So, the idea, the drill, was that as we were Police, we would form the outer security ring and the Canadian infantry platoon that we were with would conduct the fight. They would take care of any of the contacts outside of the town. The police would just hunker down, take cover and then flow into the village to make arrests or maintain security once the heavy fighting was over. As the attack started, this dude was pacing around, impatient to get into it. He had no weapon on him; he had a "gun bearer." Another ANP soldier would carry his gun until it was time to fight. To occupy himself, he finds some locals with gunfire in the background, and he sits down and drinks tea with the locals as if the contact is no big deal. I'm trying to see where the enemy is coming from. Fire was coming from the southeast, and I was hunkered down behind this wall, trying to pass the information.

The Canadian Platoon Commander is doing his thing, trying to get LAVs sorted out and organized to attack, but it was very canalized in an area called the Dragon's Back. So, it took a little time to get the cannons into action and return fire effectively. Our aggressive Afghan stands up and has lost patience, and he sprints past me toward the contact, now holding an AK47 with an underslung Grenade launcher. I hadn't seen him with a weapon all day, so he must have called his weapons guy up, and he decided it was time to fight. He's running full speed by himself down towards where the contact is; I'm yelling at him like hell, hoping he doesn't get shot by our guys. The terp is screaming all the stuff I am yelling. I see him like 150 meters down the track, and he yells back, "You're not going to kill any of them. You're too slow!"

The LAVs get turned around and start laying 25mm fire onto the enemy locations; he realizes that he is likely to be killed by the Canadians. He walks slowly back towards us." He is now dragging his rifle dejectedly, and I lose sight of him momentarily. By the time he arrives, the rifle has disappeared again. You could feel his disdain and frustration due to the slower response. He sits right in the middle of the town. Cross-legged and stares at his teacup. He looked up at us like we were losers.

"You can't do anything if you are going to be slow. The enemy hits and moves. They do not stay still. They are like a boxer; you Canadians are trying to wrestle." He wasn't wrong; we were too slow initially and didn't understand the speed of combat. Man, I loved that guy. Hard as Chinese rock candy.

The Afghans loved to garden. Not just food, which made sense as vegetables were hard to come by, but flowers and plants. The Afghan Commander I worked with made a beautiful little garden in Masum Ghar near his barracks room. His troops would help maintain it. It is good to be all business on tour, but these guys lived in the environment for years. Forever, when we went home, they stayed. Our 3 or 4 tours are like a drop in a bucket compared to everyday living the life and constant grind of deployed life and fighting. My Afghan partner had been in Kandahar since 2003, when I met him six years ago. His Family was in Kabul. He had served with Russians and with Massoud before this war. He had a life of conflict. I always wondered if all the officers loved to garden a little bit as it was given such a desolate country, and there's a lot of violence. The garden was an aspect of peace, something alive that he could grow and care for, something beautiful in an otherwise bleak and desolate desert environment. Maybe there is a metaphor there. I don't know, but I know they loved to garden.

Many people say to keep the kids away. Kids are going to get hurt. We started realizing that No one would be shooting at us if the kids were there. Like you, you don't get away with killing kids, even if you're the Taliban. So there was one part of the town, like the north part of the town, where the kids were. We called it the good side and the wrong side across the street. Everyone's grumpy on the south Side. Then, the north side, the schools are up there with playgrounds, and you do a north patrol, and you're like, nothing is going to happen. The only thing on the north side is the IED dog. This one dog would be chained up somewhere on our patrol route; we knew the area but never exactly where, like his owner did it on purpose to fuck with us. The dog would stay quiet and then lunge, biting and snarling at us. It would surprise and scare the shit out of us, so we called it IED Dog. When we had battlefield tourists (VIP visitors) and stuff rolled down, we'd always take them in North Central and loop them around. To give a "feel," we would take them by IED Dog. There was this doorway with a sheet hanging over an entrance. The visitors would get spaced as we approached, and the dog would bust through that door and start barking at you. It would never attack you. Just bust through and stop and bark. It scared the shit out of everybody. So we'd take, like, battlefield tourists on the IED dog route, and you'd see everyone get the spacing a little wider so they wouldn't notice. And then they come by, and this thing would bust out the door. I think their heart stopped, but maybe it was good they felt like they understood a little of what we did daily. Regardless, everyone would laugh and point and think haha, You thought you would die, right?

I feel like the training and the workup cultural training made the initial interaction with the Aghan population worse. They gave us all these bullshit rules and a script that didn't exist except in our minds. They tell you in our cultural training. Don't talk about this. Don't talk about that. It is offensive; it will upset the people, it is impolite. The issue was that the Afghans who taught in Canada had not been in their old country in years and had no clue. What I found is that people are just people. I started realizing, like, you know what? In Canada, if I just went up to somebody I did not know, I just met like, hey, I'm so and so, Pleased to meet you. How's your wife feeling? Yeah, that would be super weird and inappropriate. So I realized that they're just people. They're good people or bad people. Many of them had differing priorities. They all survived, Right? For most, their main priority was survival. How they decided to get that done was very different from how we would understand life. Their last concern was social niceties. They knew what men with guns do; they usually just wanted to ensure you were there to help and not hurt them.

You can only live on the edge for so long in Afghanistan. That edge was a razorblade for the Afghans. All the Afghans that were making a difference died because they had to push too hard for too long. The work that the Afghans did to secure their own nation was also not recognized. Everything was about the Western coalition to keep support at home. An example of this was the routes being freed of IEDs. Route "Foster's" and later Route "Hyena" was the main artery through Panjawaii and out to Mushan. It was one of the most heavily IED routes in Afghanistan. There were an incredible number of Afghans and Western Allies killed on that road. Ultimately, I don't think it became safe because of Canadian efforts. Fosters became safe because the Police Chief of Panjawaii, Hadjii Naim, went to all the towns that were complaining to him because of the Canadian tanks. The tanks ran through those towns to get further south towards Nakahonay. They would constantly plow over everyone's fields to avoid the roads and the IEDs that were embedded in them. The locals were mad at the Canadians running over their stuff and wrecking their farmland. They went to the chief of police, and he said, " I will get the Canadians to stop running over your stuff if you tell me who is laying IEDs and where they are." He came to me one day and told me about this, and he had a contract with all the leaders, all the way along the road in Foster's, out to Dand with their thumbprints. The agreement said they would now report anything happening on the road after that day. Not one IED was found on that road without us knowing about it. The ANP found every IED after that, and they would call the chief. Those ANP officers were targeted and killed by the Taliban for this kind of work. It was far more effective than whack a mole on Taliban fighters. I know we were there to mentor them, but sometimes we could have also learned something or celebrated their victories.

We hosted a large KLE at our district centre and ensured there was food for the local leaders. The Afghans took care of the food and protocols. A small basin of water was left in front of the centre to wash up before lunch. The first guy came out and took his dentures out; he rinsed them off in the bucket of water, then took a stiff drink to rinse his mouth and Spit it back in the bucket. He put his dentures back in, and the next guy came out and did the same thing, no dentures. But he took a swig rinse in and eventually got to a point where everyone was coming out either rinsing the dentures or taking a drink of this water, spitting it back in there. There was no thought of hygiene, and it was just accepted. I didn't use the water.

There was this old guy and a donkey that used to come down through our Checkpoint. The old dude and the donkey carried dried grapes from the fields and all this other stuff for farming. Every day, we would search for him, and I remember we got a complaint saying we were stealing grapes and we were checking the donkey, checking the old man, that it was rude and unnecessary. Every day, you know, we checked, and then for a week, we had to shift tasks away from that checkpoint. The choice was made as a part of COIN doctrine to lessen the searches on civilians, and when we rotated out, that is when the changes happened. Later that week, just outside our outpost, a patrol was coming in the gate just as the donkey guy was coming by the gate, and BOOM, donkey guts everywhere; it was a fucking DBIED (donkey-borne IED). Luckily, everyone was undercover; there were some blast and concussion injuries, and one of the guys lost his ring finger. The funny thing is that during the sweep, they found the finger, and the ring was still on it. So the guys gave him back his ring. Crazy, that old guy got checked every day, and the minute the team didn't check him he tried to kill us with a fucking donkey.

Afghans have lived with violence for a long time. They are not impressed with disruptions to their lives that can be avoided. I remember we had to secure an IED scene in Kabul. The Canadian Ambassadors team had eaten a blast and everyone was OK, but an investigation had to occur, which means that you have to hold up traffic on the one working highway in a city of 3 million. We found controlled chaos at the scene. The bomb had gone off on Kabul's major highway. The charge had been concealed to the side of the road. It left a small crater in the side of the road and had peppered the ambassador's armoured SUV with shrapnel. No one had been injured, but the vehicle wasn't driving anywhere on its own. Traffic stretched out as far as the eye could see in both directions. A team worked to load the truck onto a military flatbed while the infantry platoon on site worked to hold the inner cordon. It was not just angry drivers; an IED had just gone off, and the guys that had laid it could be watching and looking for another opportunity to strike. The traffic jam was annoying, but there were other reasons to get this task moving.
We quickly spread out and assumed the outer cordon. Cars honked and tried to creep forward in the vain hope of making it past us. One of my guys kicked the bumper of a white Corolla that refused to stay in its place and made it clear that they needed to stop. I couldn't blame the driver for trying. They all had places they wanted to be instead of watching a bunch of Canadians tell them they had to stay put.

A very well-dressed man stepped out of a fancy car that looked very much out of place in the sea of weathered Corollas and Jingle Trucks. He looked like a power player: jet black hair greased back, black mock turtleneck sweater, purple business suit, and spit-shined black leather shoes. He stormed up and pointed at me, seething.

"You people are worse than the Russians!" He shouted.

"Why's that?" I replied.

"When the Russians got bombed, they would clear the road and let everybody get home. You? You keep us all here hostage while you play CSI Kabul!"

I decided not to remind him of all the other things that the Russians had done. Just as he looked to escalate, we got word to break the cordon and wind up the task. I let him believe his intervention had some impact and thanked him for his perspective, leaving him dumbfounded. Sometimes, discretion is the better part of valour.

We had a parade for a local warlord. This was the early days in Afghanistan before the government was really on its feet. We had an honour guard for a local warlord to try to, I guess, schmooze him a little bit because his compound was less than a kilometre away from us. He had Soviet-era tanks, BMPs, and BRDMS all parked and being maintained by his force. We could see it all from the Queen's Palace. I guess as part of the disarmament of the warring warlord factions, they could have caused us problems and so we treated him like a leader. But somebody decided, hey, let's invite him over, and as he arrived, have honour guard for a warlord. It is probably lucky this was before mass digital media. Who knows what this guy had done? Lots of these guys had killed lots of people to gain power. A picture of Canadian troops saluting him may have had the best intentions for local relationships but could have been pretty bad in the long run. It just showed how immature we were in our worldview.

I think the most important thing I did over there was get toiletries for the Afghans. In four tours, I think the best, the biggest battle I won and probably the most satisfying experience of that whole tour, was my small victory in terms of dealing with the ANA; their bureaucracy was getting basic toiletries for the troops. My Kandak wasn't issued their Sundri packs, which were their soap and stuff, so they're getting like really rank. It was weeks of unwashed bodies. It was pretty bad. So,

I thought, fuck this, I'm going to solve this. I went to the brigade commander, who sent me to another group of guys. I basically harassed these guys all day until finally, they said, "OK, fine, we'll give you the stuff. They took us through the camp through this weird, surreptitious route until like a piece of dead ground. And I was like, this is different. So I started walking slowly as I was not sure if they were taking me out of the way place because I had pissed people in power off, and I was about to get jumped. No, it was just that they had stored all the goods in this really remote area that no one would know about it, and when we went into this little building, it was packed ceiling to floor with the goods. The leadership didn't want people stealing it! But they had hidden it so well no one could gain access! I got these Sundry packs, and it was so satisfying to just show up to the Kandak lines with boxes of soap and towels and toothpaste. I showed my kandak commander and showed him a look; this stuff was in your system; I got it for you guys. This is the process, so we never have to go through this again. It was awesome. I mean, it's all small battles. It felt really good to solve something tangible. I know it sounds stupid, but after 4 tours, that sticks with me. There's nobody there's nobody in Afghanistan that won big battles, man. Everybody fought little small battles, whether it be getting sundries for the troops, fuckin avoiding IEDs, or getting a bit of a road built; it was all small shit that was supposed to add up to change.

The ANA viewed death very differently than we did. Perhaps it was the Muslim religion and "Insha Allah" fatalism, but I think it was also just the number of casualties they took and that they became conditioned to carry on after loss quickly. We were out on this Operation and were moving back towards the River. The ANA's Ford Rangers were loaded with troops, usually 3 in the cab and 6 to 8 in the bed. We egressed a Ford Ranger and hit a landmine right on the north side of the Arghandab River. Holy fuck, it was a mess; there were nine injuries. The company commander had his legs blown off. We went through the MEDEVAC procedures and then carried on. We get to the Arghandab River. It is a hot day, and we have been on ops for a couple of days. We have just had this major incident and all the troops start swimming, jumping in the water, and having fun. I suggest to my Afghan Partner, let's get across this river to the fucking camp because this area is a perfect opportunity for the enemy to attack. This specific area was by the old white schoolhouse in Pashmul and had been a Killzone against two different Battle Groups before. The Afghan looks at me and acknowledges the loss of his soldiers and then says he must let his soldiers have fun now because who knows if they will ever have the opportunity again? Right now, the sun is shining, the area is quiet, and there is an opportunity that may never come again. Let my soldiers enjoy the day. Tomorrow may not come. I didn't agree with it militarily, but I had to respect it.

The top US general in all of Afghanistan came to visit us. Afghanistan's doing this, Afghanistan's doing that, and he's doing this to enable victory. This is what winning looks like and the most important thing was cultural understanding. . Well, I remember he came there about six months before he did that speech. He came to visit my Kandak and we were told to keep the Kandak on parade to wait for him to visit. It was overlapping afternoon prayers. You could just see them seething, like the Afghans who want to go and pray. You could hear the mosque up on the hill doing the call to prayer. I want to cut them loose, so I call in and say I got to let these guys go to pray. I was told no, hold them, He was late. So, they missed prayers, and when he arrived, he stayed for about five minutes. You know, shook hands. Gave us the great work you're doing. This training is nice. Then he Beatled off with his entourage of 20 people. That's where you lose the war right there. Like that. Cultural ignorance. I reflected on that when he gave his speech, never releasing that likely, he had broken this mantra a hundred times, due to how Western leadership interacts and what we value. I am sure the general did not know. I am sure all those staff offices were just trying to keep the schedule. You know, and it's just because just fundamental not knowing the country or the people. The General visit is not more important than prayer and the connection with Allah. Nothing is. Basic shit.

I remember before this big operation there was this sea of humanity that was coming out of the area. There were already strikes ongoing and bombs being dropped in the area. All the women and children and old men pushing kids in wheelbarrows and farm animals were walking north over highway one and into the desert. The line of people just stretched on for kilometres and kilometres. I understand, obviously, that we put leaflets over ahead of time saying, hey, we are coming in, and if you want to be safe, you should probably get the fuck out of your village. But I guess it didn't really become real for me until I saw them all and it was just this incredible fucking line of misery. Like just beat up, caught between the Taliban who have decided that their particular area is the right spot to make a stand and fight. Then there are these Canadian motherfuckers on the other side who are going to wreck what little property they have. I remember very sheepishly waving at them from the fucking air sentry hatch of the LAV, like, sorry, you're here to fucking blow your house up, smile and wave, really I am a nice guy; it is the Taliban's fault we have to do this. I felt like an asshole and it was the first time I felt conflicted. I knew we had to clear the TB out, but I had underestimated the cost on the normal people.

———————

The ANA brigade training lead was a major. He was a very tough old guy. To be honest he kind of scared me. He was trained in Russia and switched sides at the end. A lot of Afghans told me that he killed his Russian handlers and joined the Mujahadeen. I was not unaware that I'm now in the same seat as the Russians were 20 years prior.

———————

I was on my Op Attention tour in Kabul at the end of Canada's time in Afghanistan. The US was responsible for catering. It was the worst greasiest food every day. By the mid-tour, I was just so sick of eating fries and burgers and all the DFAC food. Mid-tour was fruit season in the North; training would slow down, and troops would want to pick fruit. Then, around lunch, we would see these Afghans pull out a big slow cooker with chicken and long rice and chop up the watermelon they had picked. I let them take a break on training. It was pretty unprofessional, but their lunch was way better than heading back into camp and eating a shitty burger.

———————

After intense combat it was hard to understand that people live in this environment. As people started to trickle back into Pashmul, we had to start to get used to normal patterns of life and not everyone was bad. It was good to observe kids in the area and parents caring for their children and playing. A lot of people, including myself took a long time to realize that there's no difference between them and us. Up to the point that the constant fighting stopped, I saw everyone as a threat, only later did I start seeing them as people. If you were born there and raised in that environment, I would guess that you would develop along the same lines with the same values. If they were raised here in Canada, they would be the same as you and I. It was slow learning and the habit was to go to the guns first and figure out what was going on later. This one night, I was just getting my head down at the strong point when I heard para flares go off. I rang the observation post on the field phone

What the fuck just happened? The guys were looking through the thermal sites and they saw a man walking over in the open field with a bag. It's pretty strange to have anybody walking in the field in the middle of the night. So, they radioed down to the CP to ask us what to do. They fired this para flare to see how he reacted. If he reacted "tactically", we could engage him as the bag may contain explosives. If he did not, it would mean more investigation. The man just stopped and stared at it floating and burning in the sky. He did not react tactically, so we continued to observe. Once the flare went out, he put his bag down and these little heat signatures and started walking out. He had a bag full of kittens and that was it. He was just letting these cats go. Maybe he was doing it at night so his kids would not get upset. That was it, we could have killed him. He never knew that he was under observation and there were fingers on the trigger.

At Camp Julian, the guys screened every worker coming in. The day would start with us screening all the local employed people that were building the camp like and we would wear these leather gloves to protect our hands. And every day, the guys would go through a set of these gloves because they pat down all the local workers. They would become disgusting by the end of the day. We would just end up burning them. I think we would screen about 250 local workers a day to build the camp. We had to have a ration box at the entry point for all the stuff they would confiscate daily. Take the knives, take the drugs and just fill out these ration boxes. We did it going in and going out. There was this one guy that would get an erection every time he was searched. It was always with the same guy regardless of who was searching him. He would lift his arms, spread his legs, and encourage the search with a big smile. So, I don't know what was going on there, but we all hated that duty.

There are two seasons in Afghanistan: Winter and Fighting season. I did all my tours during that period of time, and it is a real fucking thing. On my first tour, during the first couple of weeks, we could drive Highway 1, through Howz e madad and all the way down through Sangesar and across the Arghandab river and then drive from the tip of the horn of the Panjawaii, Mushan on Route Fosters back to MSG and always, always smiling and waving children, chilled adults and we felt good. Then, one day, with no big indicators, it all just changed. By the end of the roto, you couldn't go 10 feet on Fosters without getting blown up. Hwy 1 was all contacts, and Sangesar was a deliberate operation to get into. It's interesting that we went from complete freedom of movement and no issues to having full-on fights all the time and not seeing any of those folks with that we made relationships at the beginning. I was told that it was a summer/winter thing. But it seemed to be two different groups of people, as the bad guys leave in the winter and then come back in the summer, and the people that live in the winter get out of dodge until the fighting is done. Maybe we should have figured out how to stop those guys from coming back every year. North of my pay grade but it was such a big change. I felt bad for us, but I felt worse for the people that had to live through it. I can't believe those kids who were smiling and playing with me at the start of the tour were faking it. It wasn't a surprise that when the tours were aligned to Afghan winter and summer you would get two different reports. Winter tours would report successes and summer tours would report fighting. No one had context. Maybe we should have stayed for a year to get a real perspective. So, it looked like someone had a good tour and the next one fucked it up. Not the case, just no understanding of the Afghan cycle.

I worked with the Police Chief of Panjawaii. His name was Bismullah Jan., The local district leader, Hadjii Baran, used him as a muscle. It was less about policing and more about enforcing Hajii Barans vision. Bismillah Jan was very soft-spoken; he didn't really want to do anything. I started looking into some of the corruption. There are levels of corruption in this type of environment; there is outright corruption, and then there is just getting by. Afghans don't pay taxes. When you're an ANP officer, you've decided to come be an officer of police and you'll get paid because the dude, three or four people above you, filter the money down and not an electronic system. Everyone skims off the top. So, your pay is a buck when it should be 10 bucks. I started looking at this. You'd see them take pomegranates at checkpoints. Why? The Afghans would come up to the checkpoint. ANP would look in the back, grab half a box of pomegranates, give the thumbs up and the driver would carry on. Why is the driver not pissed off? If I was in Canada, and the cop came in and took a bag of groceries I would be pissed. I started realizing this was pretty much their tax, instead of a fine, they took an extra bag of groceries. The locals realized that this guy was in there providing security right next to their house, so they saw it as valuable to keep them fed. Then there was other corruption. They had a whole ring of sections of ANP that would never talk to us. They were local Kandahar guys and used the uniform to gain advantage and were just another gang. They would stay away. There were sections that hung out with us all the time, wanted to learn and wanted to get better and loved working with us. We benefited greatly. On our first patrol, we didn't hit IEDS because the ANP dude saw it first and halted the patrol. On the first day, my life was possibly saved by an Afghan whom I didn't even know yet. The ones that stayed away from us were as far away from Masum Ghar as possible. We eventually realized there was a civilian police officer who was looking into all the stuff, too. He was from the Ottawa police force and I ended up building a good relationship with him. And we started realizing that they had a ring of supply, any supply that came down to the road projects and was cut off by the ANP. Then a protection task was laid on them. And it was like 200 bucks American to get a load of gravel down Fosters. So, we started leveraging this, and we eventually got Bismillah Jan out of there. The next guy they brought in was the complete opposite. Hadjii Naim was not one of one of Hadji Baran's lackeys. Naim was one of the Muj (Mujahadeen) during the Russian Conflict. He was part of a faction that did not like Baran, so they hated each other. There is a long history in Afghanistan, but we immediately saw a change with a change of leadership.

One of my interpreters, Hami Abraham, was a young guy, I think was 19 years old. We're on a hillside somewhere hanging out. I was interested in the marriage culture and how this works. I remember looking up at all these buildings and how tightly packed and everybody was living on top of each other. Electricity just started coming back in, but it was still the generators at night. I wanted to understand culturally, you know, how it all worked because he was making about 400 bucks a month, which is pretty good compared to the average Afghan. They were very shy, so I was teasing him and asked him what he was doing with all his money? Are you going to move out? He looked at me with this look of horror. "Oh, no, no, no, no." "That would be an insult to my parents." Basically, what he said was that his money was being earned on behalf of his family. So when he gets paid, he gives his money to his father. His father would use it and distribute it among the family to pay for things the family required and then give him a cut of the money, whatever, was necessary. Very much a family-oriented culture. Even when he got married, he did not move out. In fact, when you get married, you move in, you move your wife in with the family, and you get your own room. Then when you can afford it, you buy your own house. But guess what? You still maintain residence at your primary family location. You have two residences so as to not disadvantage your parents when you move out. It was all about the family unit and very different than how we understood life.

When we first got there, Medusa had just ended and there was no one in the environment. Everyone had left and there had just been the BG and the bad guys. Eventually, people needed to come back to their farms, and our fighting positions were right smack dab in the middle of their neighbourhoods or what had used to be their homes in some cases. They were walking, checking out everything after the fighting, which made us really nervous but was in line with our task of securing the population so they could have a better way of life. They come into their neighbourhood and all of a sudden, this Castle Grayskull with Canadians living in it, right where, you know, "Abdullah's" house used to be. For them, it was a shock, just, well, that's fucking weird. They wanted their house back. They were rightly a bit perturbed, but they also knew they were caught between groups who had guns, so they just got on with their business of surviving. So you'd have farmers out in your Killzone fucking starting to put in crops because it is not a Killzone to them; it is their field so they can feed their family. Right away this made the job hard. We went from a secure environment with relatively clear ideas of "good guys" and "bad guys" to a returned population that now was butted right up against us. The enemy could use it to cover their approach to attack us or lay IEDs.

———————

We had suffered multiple attacks on our strong points. The Taliban started using people with mental disabilities to test our responses. In particular on individuals that could be suicide bombers. This one time, this guy with obvious mental issues approached the strong point. The boys went through the escalation of force and gave clear directions to stop, lift his shirt, and we would approach to talk. He just kept coming. He had all the same indicators of a suicide bomber, not listening, acting nervous, keep approaching regardless of warning shots and indicators. So, the guys dropped him with the remote weapons system from an RG31. No suicide vest. Fuck. We found later he had been coopted by the Taliban to test us; now they know they have sewn doubt in our minds, so the next time we may approach and not follow protocol, they will get us with a suicide bomb. It sucked; the population suffered.

———————

I was a mentor with the Afghan National Army. I had a four-man team, and we were attached to an Afghan Company that would average between 80 and one hundred dudes. You learned to live and fight with these guys, but sometimes it was strange and funny if it wasn't so serious. My company commander was a guy named Shafiq. He was very good at what he did, and he had good leadership. His men wanted to follow him. I had seen him perform bravely under fire on several occasions. This one time we were crossing the Arghandab to head to Shia Choy or some other village that is west and just north of the Arghandab river. As we are walking across, we come under contact. Small arms and some RPGs. Nothing too heavy but enough that we should be moving off the river and into cover of the built-up area. For some reason, we are stalled. I am positioned about halfway back in the company. So about 20 or 30 dudes back. I move forward to do my mentoring thing and try and get this going. As I move up rounds are going both ways. I see Shafiq sitting up and he's got his socks and his boots off. I try and keep calm and speak slowly, "Hey man, What's up? We are in the middle of the kill zone. What are you doing?" Without a pause, he looks at me and says "Look at the water between us and the area with the enemy. I don't want to get my boots wet." The reason we are stopped is that he is changing out of his boots, into some canvas sneakers to cross the water.' He hated getting his feet wet and then walking in wet boots. It was crazy because it was so hot that the boots would dry in 30 minutes. We had a conversation and he got the company moving. It was just one of those things you work through. In the end, the Mentors took the lead in this case and waded through the water with them crossed the river, got under cover and then attacked the enemy position. The Afghans were probably very unhappy with me and felt like I had shown them up a bit. I found that the Afghans had a great gift for reading combat fear, some of them fearless. All of them were conditioned not to demonstrate fear in the face of the enemy when bullets were whipping past them. Of course, they still suffer fear, obviously. It manifests itself in actions like delaying the contact by not "wanting to step" in water. A lot of being a "mentor" in combat is being a hack psychologist. Getting the best out of your folks and understanding them in a way that perhaps no one else does.

I became pretty good friends with my Afghan partner. We had fought together twice across three of my tours. We actually knew each other on a personal level. He lived in Kabul, and when he would leave and talk about getting home to see his wife, he had to eat lots of almonds as they gave him " the power" to have a lot of sex. He would talk about what was coming up and was pretty excited; he had this habit of saying that he could not wait to be with his wife and her "special places." I was laughing and I asked if he kissed her special places. He looked dumbfounded.

What do you mean? I went on to explain oral sex. He was taken aback. He shook his head "No way. No one does that." I was like, "Yep, and it is awesome." He took off for his weekend, and he came back on Monday to Kandahar with a big shit-eating grin, he stated, "I kissed her special places; she was so happy!" I think that is the best piece of mentoring I ever did in Afghanistan.

––––––––––––––

 I got a miserable spot with the ANP. They were high all the time and, I think, connected to the local Taliban. I was actually nervous. To be honest, I slept with my pistol under my pillow with it readied. All the time. I lived that way for six months it was terrible.

––––––––––––––

There were these local police district headquarters as well as the larger headquarters, which were the Kabul headquarters. Which was also their police college, where they were training everybody. At the district headquarters, we would go into these on a weekly basis and sit with the police. And I remember thinking you know, what if we can't trust these guys, like who's trustworthy? We would meet, and it would not lead to much. I remember there was one particular guy, then two weeks later, like, he was gone. Then there was somebody else there, and he would tell us that the other guy was crooked and ran away with the money. We're hunting that guy now. It just seemed to me to be a very difficult environment, and you couldn't really tell who was going to be good from our perspective. We just had to assume that everybody was friendly to the cause if you wanted to have any chance of moving the ball forward.

––––––––––––––

We had Smiley, an ANP guy that seemed high all the time. Maybe he got hit in the head when I was a kid. Regardless, he was always smiling. He was our main breacher. At the time we were getting smashed by IEDs in buildings. I had lost a member of my team to this tactic, and so we were very aware of the risk. They would boobytrap full buildings, the walls the doors, the windows, everything could be wired. To get into compounds, we stopped going through doors because they were booby-trapped. We started putting guys over the wall. Smiley would go and clear the door from the inside out, looking for wires, or any indicators. We came up to this one abandoned building. We drive the RG up and he would "surf" on the top. He had an uncanny balance. We would pull up, and the momentum and his jump would launch him over the wall as he'd jump off. We had this ladder we could throw up but he would always leap over the wall and thunder in. We would stack outside the door ready to breach, and you'd hear him fall and grunt as he hit the ground from ten feet. The next 60 seconds seem to take forever. We are exposed, he is separated and trapped if something happens. You would hear shuffling and scuffling as he cleared the door and then the door would open. His big smiling face would pop out and he seemed to say, "I did I did GOOD!" You sure did bro! better you than me Smiley! These characters like Smiley were needed, they were in it all the time, and it was their life. We were in it for 7-8 months. I always wondered if they were already messed up, if Smiley just was the way he was because death was inevitable. He was in it for the duration, with no rest. So he may as well go out on his terms. They lived in war their whole life; their humour was crazy, but it seemed to fit.

The Sergeant Major of the ANP comes storming into the shelter. He is PISSED. He's been beaten up. He's got bruises on his face and is cut. He's yelling at us. I get the interpreter and he tells his story. He was just out and there was a contact. He knew where the Taliban were, so he went after them. The issue was that the ANA were also out there and they figured it was their job. He was going to kill the Taliban in a grape hut. There was no coordination. He just went right past the ANA. They stop him and say, we got this. We're gonna go assault this. He said it was a police issue, and so he took his guys out to go assault. They're yelling get back as there was an Apache gunship that was about to level the Grapehut and the ANP didn't know the plan. The ANA grabbed him and beat him and his team for getting involved. I asked, "Did you fight back?" He's like, no. The chief of police told us we weren't allowed to fight with the ANA we had to make friends with the ANA. "But I don't care that I got beat up.; I care that they called me Taliban." He was livid. The ANA did not trust the ANP because the ANP were mostly from Panjawaii, so when Afghan Rambo went out to assault, the ANA was suspicious that they were stopping the Apaches on purpose to let the Taliban escape. There were only a few of them from the north, and all the ANA were from the north. The ANP were Taliban in the Anas's eyes. So, he was super angry that they'd call him an insurgent. There was a Dari/Pashto split and so the ANA and ANP often did not even speak the same language. Just, you're southern Afghan and I am northern Afghan, so fuck you; I'm Hazara or Tajik, and you're a fuckin Pashto. We hate each other. I don't know why, but we do. It was so hard to navigate the battlefield and the enemy while at the same time navigating tribal and national rivalries that you may or may not know about. The senior leaders also did not understand that it was a BIG deal when they wanted joint ANA/ANP patrols; they were not friends. We tried to navigate it the best we could, but these rivalries are hundreds if not thousands of years old.

————————

The ANA loved their TV. They would even bring it with them on operations. I was a Kandak mentor, and I remember sitting in a big leaguer in the desert in the back of a Ford Ranger, huddled under a blanket to block the light while watching a TV on old rabbit ears with the HQ of the Kandak. 6 grown men huddled under a blanket, in a war zone in the back of an American pick up seemed a bit like a scene out of a movie to me. Other than old Bollywood movies, the Afghans loved this show called Afghan Star. It was a crazy singing competition like American Idol. There were judges, all old guys with beards, judging these other old, greasy guys who would be singing and stomping their feet. I guess the music was an acquired taste. But it was interesting that there were no women, and really nothing other than very traditional acapella music. The big winner received $5000 of bath products, and they all looked like they could use it. But you had to have a favourite, and there would be much debate as the winner was chosen. No matter what was happening what plan was ongoing, or what operations, I planned around Afghan Star.

————————

There was this one Afghan guy who was just, just a character who's really touchy and loved making the Canadians uncomfortable and exposing their Canadian homophobia. Lots of Canadians thought the Afghans were always having "man love Thursday". The thought was Thursday was party nights and in societies where women can't marry women until they are rich enough and they only get exposed to men, that they would pair off together. Maybe there were higher rates of homosexual behaviour; I lived with those dudes for 8 months and never saw it. Anyway, it was a thing, and if you ask any Afghan Vet about Man Love Thursday, they will laugh uncomfortably. There was this one young, really young Canadian guy in the rifle company. We're all on this patrol, and this funny ANP guy always went and sat next to him every time he took up a fire position. This guy would sit down. close and then start looking at him. Just freaking this kid out. Eventually, I'm like, hey, get away from him, stop teasing and let's focus on the job. And he's like, come on, then he pulls out his wallet and he starts pulling off Afghan money, like Afghanis (dollars) give to me. I laugh out loud and say, "he's not for sale! And if he was, you would need more than that." Having found an audience and a joke the Joker starts to petition all his buddies for money and he comes up with his big stack of cash and like, now we're talking business. The kid asks, " Are you selling me? " He laughs it off. Negates the offer, and everyone carries on with the mission. The same Afghan guy used to run into the room we slept in in this mud hut that we shared with the ANP, and every morning, he'd wake you up by jumping in bed with you. Just like jokers in your Canadian Platoon. No real difference. You had to fight a common enemy with people whom you could not even speak a common language, all the jokes were exaggerated, it was crazy. I will never forget that young kid-he really did think I was selling him… those characters were so required to make those crazy teams work well and stay chilled in that environment.

When we were doing roadblocks to stop Taliban movements, the worst thing was fast-approaching vehicles. Suicide bombers were a threat we had suffered and lost soldiers to. There had been an increasing use of vehicles, so it was a hard environment. There were only seconds to choose what to do; go through your escalation of force protocols, which were placing signs as far out so that approaching vehicles could be warned to slow down, then signal a warning by waving your arms, giving a verbal warning, then warning shots and then engage the vehicle. It seemed that this system was reasonable, but it happened fast. There was this one night when we were out at a checkpoint, and there was a fast-approaching motorcycle. There had been a rash of suicide bombers in Kandahar city, and we had lost soldiers and vehicles to this tactic from the enemy. This motorcycle blows through the signs, and he doesn't stop. The ANP forward of us didn't get their guns off their shoulders and didn't get their guns up fast enough. He's coming down the road at the section. My fire team partner recognized the threat and levelled his rifle at the oncoming motorcycle. The driver is increasing speed and coming hard. There are shouts to stop and arm signals. My buddy fires one single round. One single round, the exact centre of mass. It hits the guy and passes directly through his chest and drops the bike, but two people come off the bike. We only saw one not two. We run up to deal with the issue not knowing if they are just wounded. We didn't see two people. We got to the bike, and there was an eight-year-old boy holding onto the driver from behind; the round passed through the driver and smashed into the child's face, killing him instantly. We applied first aid, and the driver lived. It was a legit shoot in accordance with the ROE. The next day we took the body to the family. We had to take photos for proof of everything, for the investigation. The higher-ups gave it to our section. I fucking carried the body bag and had to interact with the grieving family. How does a family deal with that? How many Taliban did we make that day? I carried the body bag, and I will never forget how light it felt to carry a child. I just kept telling myself we did everything we could and acted like we were supposed to; that was just the thing; it was legit, it was sad, and it really crushed me, and my buddy never got over it. That place is fucked up. I am not sure how we could have done anything differently.

I always wondered about the connection between the ANA and the Taliban's local elements. Many had fought together before during the civil war and the war against the Soviets. Being in the OMLT I always felt that we had some weird protection that I didn't understand. When we left an area in Western Panjawaii, another company replaced us. An Afghan company, day after we left about a kilometre down the road that company was ambushed and eight guys were killed. So, it's like I'm pretty sure they had that ambush sited for a while. Pretty sure they're waiting for a target of opportunity. It could have just been luck, but Shafiq, my ANA company commander, was well-liked by the community that was around that part of Panjawaii, and he knew all the players. He had also been Muj during the Soviet occupation, which brought great credit to him, even from the Taliban. We always missed getting catastrophically hit by days or hours. I always wondered if the fights we were in were unavoidable but that the Taliban and Shafiq knew each other, like they had some kind of unwritten rules. Kill guys new to Panjawaii, but not the teams that will always live there and not "their Canadians".

Every morning my team would wake up and walk the route along Fosters between the checkpoints. With the ANA. It was the shittiest task, and it was the Weapons Company 2/1/205s task to do it. These guys take the brunt of their casualties. It just happens to be a small thing for Canadians all the time. The Afghan Company Commander had a big job to keep the troops motivated and to keep those roads open. How do you motivate guys to live in this shithole and walk down a road that every morning is seeded with new IEDs that will take your limbs or your life? The Company Commander was a Pirate. I loved him. He had super high morale and always had more troops than he needed. Why? Because he took care of them. I knew he had a series of schemes that paid the soldier bonuses that I did not pay close attention to. I cared about the tactical results and the road being open. I equated the new ANA army to being more like a series of Medieval armies where soldiers needed to pay in spoils, and the various warlords were still competing for the best soldiers. All the Company Commanders had been Muj before, and so it was how their army ran until the Army outgrew it. This guy would run a scheme, like black-market diesel, then would redistribute that wealth to his community on an organized scale, and the best warriors got a little bit more. But there was a flat rate bonus and then families could receive a little more should someone die or need help. The ANA system was fucked, so although I know it was wrong by our standards, I chose the positive treatment of soldiers and the open roads over an investigation that would go nowhere and likely give me a non-effective combat leader. Interesting ethical debate, perhaps. Hindsight is 20/20 but there were no deaths on the road in our 6 months.

The Afghans know how to survive. They always knew that we were going to leave and that they would need to fend for themselves. My Afghan partner's life could be a movie or a book. He had been a trained artillery officer under the Russians in the 1980s, and when they left, he signed up with Massoud; during that fighting, he got captured by the Taliban and was put in Pol-e-charki prison. He was sure that he was going to be executed. But he was released from prison if he would teach the Taliban about indirect fire. So, he grew his beard and was the Artillery Advisor to the Taliban Army. He even showed me his Taliban ID Card. He did not like the Taliban, so he escaped with his family to Pakistan to a refugee camp. When the US invaded, he joined up with the Warlord Dostum to help with the freeing of Kabul and, in 2003, was one of the first sign-ups to the new ANA. He was attached to the US Special Forces and then had been down in Kandahar since 2003. He shifted from the USSF to the Canadians as partners in 2006, which is where I had met him on an earlier tour, fighting during MEDUSA. When I came back, and he was my partner we already had a good relationship. He was up one rank, and so was I; it was like we were moving through our armies together and taking on our next positions in Parallel in Kabul. He knew we were leaving. He did not hold it against us, but he had to look out for himself. He would ask me to take pictures of him with all the important guys that came to Kandahar. Petraeus, McCrystal, Allen, General Fraser, the Canadian Ambassador, RC South British

Division Commander. It did not matter, US, UK, Canadian, whoever showed. I asked him what was with the scrapbook. He said it was his safety net. When we left, and the Taliban were resurgent, he would go to these embassies and countries and show that he had fought with us for years against the Taliban. That he could be trusted and would surely be killed by the Taliban when they regained power. He was sure that this would convince governments of their moral obligation to him as a human and a warrior who had served loyally. He could not have been more wrong. When his vision proved true in 2021, and the Taliban retook Kabul, no government opened their door to him. He was not recognized as a Canadian Employee and therefore offered no seat to come to Canada. There was no quarter given. He survived the first assassination attempt by the Taliban with a bullet in his ribs and is presently in hiding somewhere in Kabul, hoping for respite and continuing to survive. I still talk to him on WhatsApp. It kills me; sometimes, I don't want to speak to him as it makes me so sad. He is hiding like a dog, his daughters can't go out on the street and the future does not look good for him or his family. I know the Canadian government has its reasons, but I can't help but think that we let them down, and worse, he knew we would.

———————

When we pulled out of Afghanistan, I thought that was anticlimactic. We started in Kabul, then the adventure in Kandahar and then back to Kabul when that got too tough. It was like the government was trying to figure out how to get out and save face for the last three years. In the end, we left Afghans behind to the Taliban. Our original mission was to secure the population, give them hope and establish a country that could move forward on its own and we let them down. The last interpreter that I had was named Abdul was a great guy. He was a young guy but very committed and I took him under my wing. His brother got killed just by a random rocket attack. He was killed in the bathroom in the FOB. The rocket had a direct hit. I had to break the news because I did not want anyone else to break the news. We brought him in, and he took the news, and then then he got sick. I never saw him again. They put him into the training centre in Kabul at KMTC. So, I went. I saw him. He was. He's part of our team. I kept talking to him like, you know after we left. Here's a guy who's going to be vulnerable. He and his family will be Taliban targets because of the service that he's provided to us. We lost touch, just one of those things and some years later, I got a message that one of our team ran into Abdoul in a movie theatre. Abdoul was actually in Canada. That's a credit to him. I got a hold of him through my buddy. I told my wife that we were going to have company for Christmas. He was in Regina, so I flew them both to our place and we had Christmas together. Abdoul had gotten in through some programs for interpreters. He had a beautiful Canadian wife and had settled in Regina. Quite a culture shock to go from Kabul to Regina. He is Canadian now. I could not be happier that we made those Afghans who had risked so much personally, Canadian citizens. They have lived our nation's ethos and paid for it in blood.

UNCOMFORTABLY NUMB

EVERYONE NEEDS A BREAK.

In a seven-month tour, every soldier was given an allowance to travel back to Canada to visit family. This was known as Home Leave Travel Allowance or HLTA. They could use the same amount of money to travel to another location for their time off. This leave plan was an artifact of six-month peacekeeping UN missions, which did not have the same demands as combat missions. This leave was not optional, regardless of what mission was ongoing or coming up when you had to go. The thought was that the two-week break was good for the soldiers and their families. These breaks or "blocks" were spread out over the tour, so they often came at random times. Some soldiers would go on leave after only a month, while others would be in theatre for several months. The only time soldiers could not go on leave was during the first and last month of the tour.

Often, this left platoons short on personnel, and leaders would need to go on a different leave than their subordinates. It was difficult, as then the leader worried about what was going on in the theatre instead of enjoying the time with family. It is always great to see family, but it can also be disorienting for the soldier. In the era of rapid air travel, soldiers could be in heavy contact, having not showered for days, and within 24 to 48 hours, be back at home with their families.

The minute they arrived, the clock started for them to return to the tour. Often, you were home but not present, with a foot in the present and a foot in the future reality that you would soon return to conflict.

It wasn't the end; it may not even be the halfway point; it was just the next signpost in the routine of moving through time in Afghanistan.

———————

Home Leave Travel Allowance or HLTA was 16 days off at some point during the tour. You could have a free ticket back to Canada, or the government would let you use the money of equal value to go somewhere else in the world. After a particularly violent couple of weeks where we lost two soldiers, I and another section were going on HLTA. I remember driving off to KAF in a convoy, hoping that this ride would not have an IED strike. It seemed that the drive was more stressful when something was on the line. We flew out of KAF and to Dubai. We realized that most of us were headed to Thailand. We're all on the same flight out of Dubai. And most of it, half of them, I guess we're having girlfriends flying in as well from Canada, and we were meeting them in Bangkok, and they were also on the same flight. About Five of us found ourselves at the airport in Thailand waiting for this flight at this time. A salesperson walked by selling beers for about a buck apiece, and this led to multiple rounds of these 1-dollar beers. Sitting in the sun, drinking beer, and letting the guys talk was really good. I just listened and enjoyed their thoughts, and they seemed to download all their angst. I think it was good. By the time the girls got off their plane, we were loaded, arms around each other in bro love...To save our relationships, the party broke up, and we went our separate ways with our respective partners. I didn't see any of them again for the next two and a half weeks and we all came back into Dubai at slightly different times. Once we were down in Spin Boldak, I would do guard shifts with the guys. We always had somebody up in the central tower, stayed up at night and lived vicariously through my soldiers, listening to their stories from Thailand. After about a week back, we started getting shot at again. HLTA was this weird pause, and it was valuable, but it took some time to get back into the mindset of combat after getting this reprieve.

I remember that I went on leave back to Canada and our Sniper Group had yet to have a confirmed kill. We had been in firefights, but no pure sniper work. So, I am back home, I am on leave and out with my wife and at dinner at Sante Fe in Pembroke, Ontario, and I get a call. It is my second in command calling on the satphone (in fact, before they informed the BG CP) that they had just got a guy laying an IED at Twelve fifty meters with a .338 shot. I was happy for the team. But how fucking strange. I am out to dinner with my wife. She asks, "What was that?" I ask if she really wants to know, and she says yes. OK, "The boys just killed a dude". I was excited and smiling, I think I must seem like a psycho. Kind of ruined dinner.

My buddy was going on and on about how he was heading on leave. He was the first one and the rest of us had a long time to wait. I helped him drag his stuff out to the helicopter to start his trip down to Kabul. I'm putting his stuff in, and he won't stop talking about how he will miss the hottest time of year. I was like throwing shit on the chopper, and as I go to shake his hand. I pull him in and say, "I hid five or six rifle rounds somewhere in your luggage. Good luck with airport security and Go fuck yourself and your early leave!" all said with a smile of course. So, he had a layover in Kabul before going on a civilian flight and had to tear his luggage apart six times. There were no rounds, I would never do that, but it served him right for being a prick about leaving.

———————

I deployed on a nine-month deployment 18 days after my son was born. I remember coming back on HLTA seven months into the tour, and he's eight months old. I want to get up and help take care of him. I realize I don't know anything about this kid. I don't know what he eats or actually how to do anything. I was pretty useless. My wife would always get upset because I would feed him food I liked or not use a bowl and just play with him on the floor and throw some crackers around. It was savage! I learned, of course, but I will never get that first 8 months back.

———————

I flew home for HLTA; I got home, it was Easter Sunday. In the airport, we heard something about some casualties, identified as NATO casualties overseas so didn't pay much mind to it. Then we flew into Moncton, we had an apartment there. On the cab ride home, the radio said that there were Canadian soldiers who were killed five; when he got home, we watched the news right away. It changed to six killed and, by this time, had names and pictures. Why now, when I was safe at home on leave? I cried. I bawled. It wasn't just the shock. It wasn't just that you, your friends, died. It was also that it wasn't you. Looking back now, I would not have admitted at the time. There's this loss of innocence to that thought. No matter how prepared you are and how accepting you are of what the scenario is, the fact that they suffered the consequences, the stakes are very real, and you just avoided them by blind luck is also a relief. There is a lot of guilt that gets wrapped up in that. It was a really strange few days. I remember going to the mall the next day and seeing 300 hundred, the movie about Sparta the next day. There's a scene where the captain fights alongside his son. His son does something. He's proud of it, and so is the Dad. He's a man. He's proud. Then he gets killed. I just teared up there, and

I was, you know, breathing heavily and sobbing through the movie. My girlfriend was good. Afterwards, we are walking around the mall, and I see a friend of mine working in sports check, this guy Luke from high school. I remember him and so I stop and talk. I remember him asking how things were. And I was straight up, "like, not great right now. we just had some guys die." He looked at me, a little lost as to what to say, and said he had seen it on the news. I continued, "They're my dudes." That's probably one of the few times in my life where I just stopped and could feel tears coming to my eyes. He was caught short; he had expected me to say everything was fine and make small talk, which I should have. I felt weird and said, "I'm sorry, man, I have to go." And we just walked out. I realized that people at home really didn't connect with the mission or the loss. We were out there dying, and likely, the job at Sports Chek was more real. How could it not be? Being at home then was the worst. I should have been with my brothers. Some people were understanding of that. Other people were completely opposite the spectrum.

I had turned my guns in prior to HLTA, and my roommate and I had mini bottles that his parents had sent and had gotten through the postal service. Super big, no, no. But at this point, we really did not give a fuck. We had a room to ourselves, we did not have any guns, and we were not going to do anyone any harm. Totally worth it to feel human before we went home. So crazy that were trusted to make life-a-death choices daily but not to be trusted to have any drinks. Weird. I remember we watched Superbad and had like two shots of fucking horrible whiskey, and then we flew out the next morning.

I had to go on HLTA, and I had to make the chopper. We loaded up, and all of a sudden, we got smashed by something. I think it was an RPG that didn't detonate and hit underneath the helicopter by one of the guy's feet near me. He flew into the air, and I grabbed him and pulled him back down. Then there was a secondary explosion, which I believe was small arms fire, and that ignited the fuel on the descent. There were 19 people total on the bird, I believe, and crew. We were all sitting in the seats near the front of the Chinook, which was lucky because the fire was in the back. It was the most incredible fucking heat I've ever felt in my life, the bird engulfed by flames in the back. Everybody kind of hit the deck and pulled Kit bags over the top of themselves to get out of the flames that were starting to come at us. I had all of my protective gear on. I only got flash burns from my chin and a lot on my nose, with my vitals all covered. We can feel the bird is going down. When we hit the ground, someone yells for us to get out the back. It is confusing, and they realize we can't get out the back as it's on fire. The side hatches are the way out. The door gunners are trying to get the machine guns off the rockers to free space. We're pushing people out. What do you grab? What do you not grab? I had my go bag with ammo and med supplies. So, it came with me because it was at my feet. As I left, I saw my kit bag mixed in on the floor, I remember thinking, that has everything I'm going on leave with. It has my wallet, my computer, and my BlackBerry like it had everything. And I remember consciously thinking, do I grab this thing? it was like a split-second fucking 'n' NOPE start moving out of the bird! I remember one of the guys couldn't get through the opening because they couldn't get the machine gun quite off the rocker. He was getting hung up and panicking a little. I remember us pushing him out the fucking door, and then we all got on the ground, and the thing started to cook off. Now we are on the ground. We're crawling. We're trying to get over a mud wall to get out of the fire. All the chaff and all the ammo start to cook off, and hundreds if not thousands of rounds, grenades, and explosives could go at any second. So, we crawled for maybe 20, 30 feet, made it over a mud wall, and then everything just fucking went boom. Some locals were coming to the crash, and some were armed; I think we have a few small potshots that came our way, but it is hard to decipher from all the ammo going off. I remember some leaders just spinning out of fucking control, trying to figure out what was going on, these were senior guys that should have known better but were shocked, and it never helps to yell. I wanted to tell them to chill the fuck out. We consolidated in space for a couple of minutes. Almost immediately we start to see other helicopters coming over. The Griffon escorts Apache from Kandahar. Like a warm blanket. No TB would fuck with us while those things are up. It was amazing that no one was killed that day, but the chinook was gone, burned to the ground. I felt very lucky to be alive. The next day I just went on leave. No wallet, no computer, no worries. Crazy day.

I had this funny troop under me, a real character. I had taken him through his basic training and then we ended up on a small team in Afghanistan together. He went on leave in Bali and had a pretty crazy time. He had gotten a tattoo of a hooker on his shoulder when he came back from Bali. We thought this was pretty crazy and gave him a pretty hard time about it. But her name became a type of talisman in the group. So much so that when we had to name a new piece of tactical infrastructure that we were in a " FOB," we tried to name it after her. We got through the necessary initial approvals as this name would go on maps and be official in reports. Then someone in HQ heard that it was the name of a Balinese hooker, and the idea was kyboshed. Proper thing, likely, but it was funny.

It was a pretty good platoon. One thing sticks out of my mind and has always bothered me as I have gotten older. We had strong personalities in the section commanders, and my section and this other section were always fucking with each other, competitive but bordering on animosity. So the next day, I had to leave for HLTA. We just completed this Op that was like 35 days long. It was brutal. But it was time to go on leave. As we are leaving, we circle around the laager to depart. As we were leaving, as we rolled by the section, it was like, "See you later, fuck faces." Then I was off to the Bahamas in Paradise Island, for my HLTA. It was during the NHL playoffs, and I was watching Don Cherry's " Hockey Night in Canada, which announced that some Canadian Soldiers had been killed in Afghanistan. The section that we had a competitive relationship with got hit by an IED, and everyone died or was wounded. That goodbye that I said "Fuck You" was the last time I would ever see them. It always sticks in my mind it was hard. They were guys we were competitive with, but I never wanted them to die. The guys were the same age as me. I had friends that died, and I wasn't there. I hated that they made me go on leave. I hated that I wasn't there, I hated being in the Bahamas and learning about my friends' death on a hockey night in Canada program with a beer in my hand.

I'm leaving for the mid-tour vacation. I'm leaving our strong point to FOB Wilson then I catch the helicopter to KAF. I get back and they explain the routine to me. This is the day I'm handing in my kit. This is the day I'm flying out. I didn't have much time in KAF. I think that was good because I didn't talk to anybody. You know what I mean? I had been living in close quarters for a long time, and a lot of shit had happened, and I really didn't want to talk to KAF people. I had a room to myself. Catch up on sleep. I had a good first cup of coffee. I had the green beans. I finally got on the HERC and am feeling pretty good. We get off and settle into Dubai. On our Chalk, we had one real bear big French dude who looked literally like he could bench press a trailer. We knew him. We hung out together. We shared stories. And he comes back from the gym because he was in there for 3 hours, and he's pissed because the bus downtown has filled up. He didn't know the rules that you have to sign up early. We confirmed it later on that it was most of the people who were posted and lived in Dubai full-time right had taken the spots. He was pretty pissed off as he wanted to buy his family really nice pearls for his wife and girls. So, we had signed up earlier, and when we were out, we pooled our money, bought the pearls that he had wanted and brought them back to him. He was so excited and happy that he could give them when he went home on HLTA. We were like, dude, don't worry about it. A couple of weeks later, when we came back after the HLTA, he talked and said that was the best gift you could give his family. We took back off for KAF, and once we landed, we had to go back through the sausage machine and get briefs like: "What has happened since you've been gone?" We're lining up to go into one of the briefs, and from behind us, this heavy French accent Says, "Ha! BONJOUR fuckers. My family loved the pearls. You sit here and get these briefings; I am going out to see my guys instead of sitting in these fucking briefs." Then he was gone, and he flew out. He immediately went out on patrol with "his guys," and later that afternoon, he got blown up and died. It made me very sad because of the connection we had built. I was really glad we had pitched in for that gift. At least his girls have that.

We came through a very tough period on our tour. We were in contact straight for a couple of weeks and the fight wasn't letting up. The enemy just shifted from shooting at us to trying to kill us with IEDs and suicide bombers. Just as I left, a guy in my company stepped on an IED and was killed. The next day I had to go on my pre-arranged leave. I had organized it before I left; it was supposed to be the highlight of the tour. But now it was different. We were fighting, and I felt guilty leaving right when someone had died in my Company, and my platoon would be short of people. But I left as directed. I went to Thailand by myself for leave. There were four of us. We all went our separate ways once we arrived in Bangkok. And everybody did their own thing. I went down South to find a party and a dive school. At first, it was OK. I mean I did all the things that you are supposed to do on leave. I spent three days learning open water… I partied and did my shit. I drank a lot, I chased women, and it was exactly what Thailand was built for. I wasn't in the headspace. There was this constant guilt and worry in my mind about what was happening in my unit. Goddamn. I did not join the fucking army to go on vacation during a shooting war. I can go on vacation for the rest of my life. I was dark about it, and I started ordering drinks to put away those thoughts and I went into black out drive drunk. I know I went to a bunch of places and did a bunch of things, but I couldn't tell you what. It was a low point; I woke up in a side alley in the garbage pile and there were street dogs licking me and shit. Through my haze, I was just watching the world go by as I lay in a pile of garbage and Thai street dogs licked my face; this sucks. I'm in the greatest place ever to be on vacation, and I don't want to be here. I want to go back to war. That's why I joined. Technically, I had been out of Afghanistan for five days, so I figured that was good enough. I was a bit irrational and internally fucking furious. They made me go on vacation. I want to do my job and be with my team. Join the army, do Afghanistan, so let's do the fucking war. I decided to sneak back into theatre. By orders, you had to be out for your whole leave block. I looked at the calendar and figured out when other leave blocks would be flying back in. I went to Bangkok Airport and booked back to Dubai. Once I landed, I stood in the spot where you are supposed to look for somebody with the Canadian flag and caught the shuttle back to our staging base. I never once had to lie. I mean, who comes back from leave early? If anything, they were having problems with people not wanting to go back to combat after getting a break. I showed up and just talked the talk " blah blah on a different flight, must have been a scheduling problem. Etc etc. Who is going to doubt you? The civilian on a contract that is there to shuttle you to the base? I get into the base and through security, no issues; I go sign for my weapon; the logistics group thought they made a mistake, and it was in the wrong weapons rack as it was for the following week. Then I had to get onto the Herc. These things were packed. They actually bumped someone else because a Battlegroup member would have priority. Now I had my gun, my kit, and a ticket. The next morning, I flew back into theatre. No one was there to meet me when I landed because I was not supposed to be there. I went and found a guy from the transport group and figured out where my rifle company was out in the field. I hitched a ride on a convoy and did not clear in through the arrival group in KAF. When I showed up in the FOB, the Company 2 IC was blown away and didn't know what to do. I had broken so many rules, and he said he did not know whether to charge me for disobeying an order or give me a medal for coming back into theatre. In the end, they decided it was not worth the paperwork, and I got to claim to be one of the only guys that snuck back into theatre (They actually changed the orders and the processes after this to do a better job of tracking) I settled back into my section, I felt like I was in the right spot and we just got on with the job.

HLTA is a double-edged sword. You have to take these 17 days of leave by rule. It is really hard to justify taking one-third of the combat power out of the platoon, and then they go on fighting, that 1/3 extended upwards, and so the BG would, after the first month and until the last month, be on this constant rotation of 1/3 of the org being gone. Think of that for a sports team, let alone a war, I don't think we were ready to adjust our corporate rules for combat and tried to apply UN ideals on what was a fighting war. It caused no end to grief, and people had more anxiety at times being home, particularly leaders because they would check the news first thing every morning to see if anyone died. I was lucky, no one died from my team while I was gone, but I had friends whose units had losses. I am not sure they ever got over the guilt. It was crazy; one day, you are living hard, haven't showered in a month, then back to KAF, shower, change to civvies in Dubai, and then back with family in 24 hours. It was hard to process, and then, just as you normalize at home after 17 days, you head back to the fight and have to go through the trauma of saying goodbye to everyone again. But this time, they know what it means because probably folks have died, and there have been funerals, and kids at your kids' school have lost their Dads. So now, after being home on HLTA, everyone is very aware this may be the last time they see you. I think it sucked. I hated HLTA.

10

BAD DAYS

THE SHOCK OF VIOLENT LOSS IN COMBAT is difficult to understand or explain for anyone who has not experienced it.

It is sudden, it is violent, and you often don't get the chance to say goodbye.

With every death, you may participate in the ramp ceremony, have a short period of grieving and then you'd need to find a way to get psyched back up and get on with the job. You needed to put the team back together, you needed to manage the grief of young Canadian soldiers who may be experiencing death for the first time, and you needed to integrate the replacements into your team.

There is not much time for grief.

That comes later, in quiet moments or after you get home to Canada. For some, it takes years; for others, it takes a lifetime.

When one of your soldiers dies, I think it's good to feel the sadness, the guilt, and the regret; you should carry it. Not to dwell on it and weaken your resolve but to make you sharper, more focused on the job at hand, and a better leader. I remember in the laager that night after my team had taken a couple of losses, I lay in my shell scrape and realized the gravity of commanding. Every decision I make or non-decision, the absence of, like making a call, could have consequences, and I would not necessarily suffer them. It meant that we had to do things the right way, and sometimes the enemy would still be successful, but it did mean that occasionally we would have to do unpopular and hard things. Wear the right protective kit, take difficult routes to avoid IEDs, patrol at all hours to keep the enemy off balance, maintain bounding overwatch, alternate routes and routines to ensure our security, work without light, and ensure proper sleep. All of these things disrupted a soldier's routine and all of these things helped keep soldiers alive. Following the path of least resistance is tempting, but choosing the less popular path can sometimes mean the difference between life and death.

We had a tough day and lost two soldiers killed and two wounded when our strongpoint got hit. The next day, I was walking along and found little charred pieces of our CADPAT uniform, like a Loonie-sized piece. I went down and picked it up. It was a piece of shrapnel that would have killed one of our guys, it had gone through the top part of this vest, missing the plate, basically just punched a hole through it. There was seared CADPAT vest material wrapped around the shrapnel. I thought, what the fuck do I do with this? I took it off to the side of the perimeter, and I just buried it. I didn't want his section to see it. We pulled off the position, and we went up to Wilson. By this point, I went from barely any tactical experience in the battalion to being in a pretty substantial firefight. I lost two killed and four wounded. It was devastating, personally. I took that all on me as a leader. I went into the CP office that we had set up, there was a hallway with stocks of water bottles. I sat down on those water bottles. I did not know what the fuck to do. That's when our Regimental Sergeant Major walked in. He sat down beside me, and said, "You know, you are not the first guy to lose a soldier on this deployment. Appreciate you're not going to be the last." He continued, "Right now, there is a platoon of Soldiers outside, and they're all thinking what they could have done better." "They have to know that that's okay. Take your time and mourn but then they have to see you out there carrying on. Then they will follow you and they will carry on." I was so grateful for his words of mentorship during that time. It was exactly what I needed. He was supportive, and gentle but firm. He understood the role of a junior leader and the requirements of the job. He was also so human about his mentorship. As the Regimental Sergeant Major left me to my thoughts. The acting Sergeant major of the Company arrived. He came over to me. He saw that my gloves were covered in the blood of my soldiers. I hadn't even realized it. Without saying a word, he took my gloves and gave me a new pair of gloves. He quietly went about his business and I felt his presence immensely. Those NCOs saved me and saved my Platoon. They got us back in the fight by being thoughtful and gentle but making sure we knew our job.

We had this guy that was a replacement for our platoon at the last second. He was awesome and a hard worker. He really wanted to be part of it. We were night patrolling, and he volunteered to be the gunner in the vehicle as part of our pick-up team. We are walking back from our operation and linking up with the vehicles. Darkness is turning to light, and it is that light purple sky as the sun is just starting to peak out in the morning; the world is silent; we don't talk on patrol, and the occasional radio message crosses my headset; you focus on your patrol drills, your foot placement, your breathing-all of a sudden there is a massive explosion that cuts the air, and the silence is shattered, the radio explodes with voices seeking answers, the demand for information immediate. We KNOW it means our guys hit something. It can only be our extraction team moving at this time, and no one else is on the road, so I give a quick set of orders and can't raise the vehicle on the radio. Bad news, so we picked up the pace; the first challenge was to enter through the lines of the Patricia Company to get to the location where we could now see smoke rising from. We were running down this wadi, and I realized those troops manning machine guns at the dark buffalo may not know there are friendlies in the area; it is dark, and there has just been a big boom on their flank, so they are likely edgy. We start using the running password yelling, " BLACKHORSE, BLACKHORSE" We turn the corner and run straight into a machine gun position- the gunner does not engage use. He tells me later he was just about to squeeze the trigger when he heard running coming up the Wadi when he heard the Running Password, lucky as shit. We get out of the wadi and hit the road; the vehicle is bent, a tire is on fire and has been thrown thirty feet, and two members of the escort vehicle are out on top and extracting the driver, who was shaken up but is otherwise OK. Hopping up to help with the extraction, we realize the gunner is VSA. A small piece of metal nicked his femoral artery, and he bled out quickly. No time to really think about that now. There was still a threat in the area, we were not sure, and there were reports of the TB looking to come hit the IED site, moving deliberately. The sections spread out and established a perimeter, there were some shots off to the flank from an adjacent wadi system and so we pulled in an Apache and hit it with guns. The section cleared it after, blood trails but no bodies. It was possible to trigger the location, but things began to stabilize. We get the word that QRF is coming to us and that we are not to move off the site, they QRF will not come until it is fully light out because now the route has proven it is IED'd. We medevac the driver off the position settle in and wait for the QRF and IED team to show up. This stage just takes time, and it is necessary but frustrating. It was during this pause that I noted my platoon had changed. Everyone was doing their job, holding security in pairs and staying alert; as the light came up, I gave permission to have a smoke and go to 50 percent in their pairs. I stood there with a senior Sergeant, and he observed, "Look how the troops have changed". They had been in combat for about 2 months at this time and had a number of contacts but also had the unpleasant duty of "cleaning up" a number of IED sites and post-contact situations. As the sun slowly came up, its coppery cold light let me see the body bag of our fallen soldier in the centre of the security perimeter. The burning tire threw a weird flickering effect, and the light soil was stained with fluids from the vehicle and blood. The troops seemed undisturbed, focused on their tasks, moving around the body in a business-like manner, smoking and quietly talking and joking about things only soldiers can understand in these situations. I wondered right at that moment if this was a reflection of our humanity just at this moment or if we were forever changed and had lost something. Able to box up whatever happened to ensure the mission was completed. I am still unsure of the answer, but realized in that moment that all of us, for better or for worse, had been changed.

I'll tell you one other thing that was really fucked up for me. We were in a big contact one day. Multiple casualties, and the enemy was not budging. I was trying to coordinate some movement and reinforce a flank to conduct the assault on the position. The OC was on the higher means I lost the bubble on the number of casualties. We had to try to count them was almost impossible due to the numbers and chaotic reporting. People were reporting 1 casualty 2 or three times. I requested the medevac, set the CCP and established a fucking grid. I called the BN CP for the helicopters and I secured it with my LAV. The SGM was wounded. We were in this sort of interim staging area, tracking all the guys pulling back from the fight with the wounded. I remember the Bison Amb backed in and had some dead bodies in it, from guys that had been killed earlier. I was tracking that more wounded were coming, and I made a mistake. I ordered the guys to get our fallen out of the Amb, as there is more casualties coming. The dead do not get the ambulance; the wounded need it. I then set the snipers to watch the flank, and there were a ton of things going on. Actually, there were no more casualties. I was like fuck, good, no more casualties, but fuck … I had to order the guys to put our fallen back in. That I regret. Hearing all these fucking reports at intervals. Fucking taking those guys out because I thought there were more casualties; they took them out, then they had to pick them up and put them into body bags. In the end it was not necessary, and it was hard on the team. It is hard, and I feel bad. Anyway, it is on me for not being able to track more closely. It is what it is. Fuck.

I was a duty Officer in the BG TOC. I have no real war stories as all the killing we did was remote. But the choices we made directly impacted those teams on the ground. I came in the morning and the Tactical Air Control Party was just getting finished. Due to the cameras and sensors on the jets and UAVs, you could be in the CP, control the aircraft, and authorize strikes remotely. This means that potential collateral damage and/or target confirmation is only as good as the sensors you used. The TACP lead was a CF18 pilot who took no end of grief for being a top gun fly boy slumming with an Infantry Battalion in the land war. But he was good at what he did; he had worked all night, 12-14 hours straight, managing sensors and aircraft to try to kill these guys that he believed were laying IEDs with a UAV known as a " Reaper". The feeds kept going in and out as Bandwidth was a problem and just as he would get to the checklist to drop the bomb the feed would cut out, and he would have to start again from ground zero as you cannot have a break in situational awareness. The lawyer and Commanding Officer are involved directly in these strikes to ensure oversight so the process for taking a life is not an easy one. It can become mechanical, and it should be; there are checks and balances for a reason, but humans are emotional creatures, and he was getting frustrated by the problems. He FELT like this was an IED team, he used professional judgment and experience and was arguing with the CO that we should drop a bomb and kill these guys on the side of the road that were fucking around and seemed to be up to no good. He ends up losing that fight with the CO based on ROE, the CO's low-risk tolerance, and he's super pissed off. He left the TOC for his shift, making it known that we were wrong not to drop. We went through the day and we sent out the PRT from NATHAN SMITH on a patrol. They headed onto the highway, and as they crossed the spot that had been noted the night before, a blast occurred, and a bunch of guys got killed by an IED. Right where the TACP had said it was. I remember I saw the TACP lead that night he came in, I told him the story and he started crying. He felt that it would have been handled differently if he had just argued a little better. He felt like there was zero trust to do the job and that it cost us several Canadians because of risk adversity. The CO wasn't wrong, he followed the rules, and neither was the TACP lead. The level of precision and accountability in war now demands these types of choices. I realized that there are people who do really care about doing the right thing, that it is highly emotive and that choices have real consequences, even for HQ losers who are not "in the fight". As an epilogue, I ran into that pilot 15 years later; it was still the first thing he talked about. Those Canadian lives have weighed on him even though it was not his call.

There was a day that we lost several guys and a couple of them were buddies of mine. We had been in Battle School together, and when we got to the Battalion, they went to a different Company. We lived in the barracks together. We had taken that journey from flat-faced civilian to soldier together, and now they were dead. I became numb. It didn't hit me immediately, the emotion, I don't even remember crying or being upset. When the confirmation of who had died came in, I just remember being emotionless. I think a lot of it has just been driven by the mission because the rage and hurt and anger you actually feel is not helpful to anyone. This is the first time that guys are dying in these numbers in my career. By the end of Afghanistan, over half my section from Battle School would be dead or wounded. I remember the Sergeant came in to talk to us. "just because this happened doesn't mean that anything stops. Stay in the fight." We needed to get after the mission and the assholes that killed them. I remember kind of being at peace with that and then I just started planning for the next patrol.

I went on leave right after I lost three soldiers from my platoon to an IED strike on a road just outside Kandahar City. I made it back in time to be there for the memorial ceremony. The hardest thing was speaking to the families of the individuals and telling them," I'm that guy that sent your young son down that road." Then absorbing their grief, sadness and sometimes anger. You have to own it when you are in command. The families were great, but I still felt terrible. It was not much of a leave period and was hard on my wife. I was focused on the guys that I had lost, which was a constant reminder of the risk we faced and what I was returning to. We were supposed to be reconnecting and relaxing on leave and I spent most of my time with the families of the fallen and the wounded guys that had come back to Canada. Then, in what seemed like a minute I was gone back to Kandahar.

The early days of Afghanistan were very different for the Canadian Forces. It was like no one realized that we were at war and that the tasks in Afghanistan were more important than just other tasks that the forces were trying to accomplish. Sometimes, I felt like the army was at war, but everyone else was business as usual, and even at times, this was kind of a pain to be pulled away from the important work that was ongoing in Ottawa. One of the worst examples of this was not being able to get a C130 for the repatriation of remains when we lost the first guys in

Kabul. We couldn't get an airframe to the theatre because they were doing other training, and they just seemed slow to respond. Like this was just "another" task. I said, "Look, you know, there are people dying out here; the situation is changing from what you are used to." The recognition that the situation had changed was an important thing. There was a lot of frustration. It made me so angry. We had lost friends, and they were not a priority to get them back to Canada. I don't think the Air Force understood the commitment that they signed up for. You can't plan when someone is killed by the enemy. It was like they were trying to figure out how to plan for these tasks. So, you end up arguing with staff about chickenshit rather than being able to deal with the unit and the loss that you have suffered. This particular problem improved over time; sadly, we got better at it as we lost more troops, and there was political pressure to do it promptly. But the point of how we started and our immaturity remains valid. Once the nation puts troops' lives at risk, you have to be on board 100 percent; everything else is subordinated to that effort. It just reflected organizational maturity. Life had changed, and there is a priority, it was the guys in Afghanistan, the CAF took a little while to adjust until they learned the costs. I worry that the farther we get away from that learning, the greater danger we are in of repeating it in the future.

There was a UK NIMROD that crashed in 2006, and we had to sweep the crash site. They asked us to look for anything that looked like electrical components of sensitive equipment, for any personal effects of those killed in the crash, and for any body parts so that they may be returned to the family. As I walked through the wreckage, I noticed little balls of what looked like animal fat. I was looking at little balls of human flesh that were charred and covered with dirt. They were everywhere. I picked up a few electrical components and noticed a small book. I picked up the book and opened it to see what exactly it contained. The first page I turned to was a calendar page, and one of the days read, "Mom's Birthday." I was horrified by the fact that this person who obviously took the time to remember his mom's birthday was now deceased. It was as though I saw his death as the death of a stranger, and now, because I read his day planner, it gave me a human connection to him and forced me to take it personally. The back of the book also contained numerous phone numbers, which made me sick because I knew of his death before any of his loved ones did. It was an awkward feeling and my eyes were opened to how quickly life can be taken from you. They could have been at home with their kids thinking nothing was wrong or grocery shopping for the upcoming week, not knowing their loved one was dead. I placed the book into a bag of personal effects and moved on in our search. We moved past a small wadi or ditch, and when I reached the other side, I noticed something that resembled a body. I went closer, and our Battle Captain was by my side when I got there. We both examined the object but denied that it could be the remains of a person. Then I noticed a seatbelt melted into the waist area, and as the Captain picked up what could be considered one of the individual's arms, we noticed a wristwatch melted into it. After we both looked at each other, he called for a body bag. As cruel and unusual as it may sound, the body was flat and looked like melted plastic resembling overcooked jerky...I don't know how else to describe it. It was only the upper torso, arms, and legs but only above the knees. We treated the individual gently; we ensured the body was placed into a body bag and prepared to be reclaimed by the UK Forces. It was our first experience with the death of friendly elements and, for most of us, our first experience with violent death up close. That type of exposure reminds you how fragile and vulnerable we are.

I think I went to all the ramp ceremonies, except for one or two where like there was an Operation going on. Those were a very powerful experience. I think it's a good thing. We had a rocket attack during one of them. The rocket didn't come close, but it was a reminder that it would be a pretty good target for the enemy. When a soldier died from any country, everyone from the base who's available goes, you know, they put the contingent that's lost their soldier closest to the Herc. If there are other casualties from the incident that are able to attend, they are often there, bandaged and in a wheelchair or on crutches. It's powerful to see the slow procession of the caskets coming in and all nations, a Danish, British, and American mission all attending. There is no way to describe it. It's a super emotional place to see that many people out there in support. Most of the time, we can't even bring that soldier's friends back to Kandahar airfield because there are difficult logistic moves to get people in, and there is the very real threat you will lose more as the TB will target ground convoys if you set a pattern. So they don't get to send their buddy go home. Maybe if they are in the actual unit, but not if they are in another Platoon or Company. You can't take the Battalion out of the field every time you suffer a loss. So many of the people who are close to the fallen never say goodbye and really have to interact with those feelings months later when the mission is over.

We had been out on the operation for a couple of days dismounted. We inserted under the cover of darkness, and as the mission transitioned to the routine of cordon and search the compounds, it was the platoons that were at their busy point, and I needed to find a spot to put the Headquarters that was protected but still near the action. I found this little spot was close to a building; it was a bit of a depression that provided both cover and some concealment should we come across a wandering Taliban patrol. The engineers did a quick search to clear the ground, and we went into all-around defence as we holed up in there. The light was coming, but it was still dark. We had our NVGs on, hoping to be able to transition, taking them off as it started to get light; there was always this point in the day where the NVG was no longer an advantage, but the light was not yet fully up. I could not wear my BEWs with the NVGs, so I went to put on my ballistic eyewear and realized that my dark lenses were in, so I put them on my lap as it was too dark to put them on. Just all the little actions that soldiers do while waiting in a holding area to prepare for the next phase. The sergeant major had to go take a shit. I nodded acknowledgement and was actually focused on wiping the dust off my weapon as we had a few static moments and keeping your weapon clean in the desert is important. The Sergeant Major got up and walked forward with his fire team partner to take his shit. I'm low in the hole, and I am conversing with another guy in a fire position watching our flank; he turns around to talk to me, and I am looking at him right in the face, shifting his position, and he sets off an IED. I didn't hear anything. He was in mid-sentence to me when it went off. I was blown up backwards. My rifle was blown out of my hands there was a massive ball of dust. My first reaction was to try to stand up and try to find my weapon. Every time I tried to stand up, though, I kept falling over and having difficulty breathing. I don't know how long it was, and the best I could do was basically just crawl to a wall. I couldn't find my weapon, and then the medics arrived. One of the medics made her way over to me and the dust was just trying to settle. I can't stand up. I tried to stand up, and it was kind of scary; I didn't know how bad I was hit. I had some shrapnel in my face, embedded in my face and in my right arm, but everything was attached. They thought that maybe I had a collapsed lung from the overpressure, I suppose I was about two meters away from the blast. They checked me out, everything. I didn't really need any bandages, bleeding a little bit out of my face. I couldn't hear anything because my eardrums were blown out. It was pretty clear that I probably had a concussion it was probably about 10 minutes when I started to get a little bit more coherent. I then realised that the solider that set off the device had died and that his fire team partner had bled out, another member of the team had suffered significant injuries and was heading to surgery and my interpreter was killed. I tried to stand up again and I kind of could walk. My equilibrium was kind of coming back and I wanted to stay, but I was not in great shape at that point and the SGM said I should head in to get checked by the hospital. I didn't argue with him too much. I could not really hear anything, everything was moving around me with no sound, like a silent film, It was very, very faint was all I could hear was the radio crackling, I was having a hard time hearing. I can walk on with a bit of help on to the chopper. I finally got back to KAF on the helicopter. They ripped all my clothes off and that sort of stuff. They actually thought I had a broken neck; they were going to try to evacuate me to Germany and but could not risk it if I had a broken neck. I can just sit there and think, that's all I can do, I realise that I am good. I was laid up in the role three for about three days. I had some bleeding in my brain, a concussion, some relatively minor shrapnel wounds, So they decided not to go to Germany. I had to self-notify my wife at home, but could not hear her speak on the phone, it was really hard. They sent me off to go back to the role one and the next Battle group was coming in. It was a bit of an eye opener for the next guy that the guy he was replacing had been wounded and he needed to step in early. I actually managed to convince the team to let me go back into the field. Part of me did not want to go out but it felt it was the right thing to do. It was more just to be with the company. The two guys that were killed were super popular guys within the company and people took it pretty bad. They let me go back and with the stipulation that I couldn't leave Wilson. But I really wanted to see the guys and visit and mourn and So I actually managed to get out of the FOB once and was told that if I did it again, I would be charged! Maybe I should not have done it, but it was good for me. My hearing is still fucked. I was incredibly lucky that day and think every day of those teammates I lost so close to the end of our tour.

We lost guys. We lost a lot of guys. It just it wasn't anyone that I developed a tight bond with. I remember one guy was in a counter IED team that we'd worked with a lot when we found devices on the roads in KC. We were in the city, and the day after we left, they all got killed by a large device. These were guys that I was in the gym with two days prior, talking about workouts. Now they're gone. It's a reflection of our own mortality, right? I would get numb when those things happen, like an absence of feeling. It is sobering. I'll be honest: I didn't experience sadness, but I reflected on the fact that there are people who love that guy in Canada, and his family is never going to see him again. It made me think of my own family, and then I had to shut that down. We had a job to do, so we're going to move on and focus on the now and dial into things we can control and try our hardest not to have our own families experience that.

It was a guy with a wife, two kids, and a young Corporal full of humour. They were killed a few days prior to going on leave by a Taliban RPG. A bunch of the section were wounded. Now we are going to do a ramp ceremony for them. I remember it was emotional, the ramp ceremony and It was it seemed so far removed from the actual trauma. It was hard for us to really quantify what had happened until we went into the back of that Herc, away from the crowd, and said a private goodbye. Just the platoon and our fallen. As we exited, we kind of huddled up. Those who were still left in the platoon and were not wounded attended the ramp ceremony, and I was thinking Fuck, I need to really say something. But what do you say? And nothing was there. It was enough, just enough to be present. I knew right there that there would not be any words of wisdom and that I would go out immediately and needed to get everybody ready to fight again.

Saying goodbye was hard. it sucked. They asked me if I wanted to participate in the ramp ceremony and carry casket and I said, no, I don't. I wouldn't be able to function emotionally and remain stoic enough to get it on the plane. Before the ramp ceremony, we actually got to go to where they keep the caskets, and I had to have a moment with the fallen in that little coroner's office area. These were my friends. The whole section was there; we all had a breakdown, got a good cry in and then went to the ramp ceremony, watching from the sideline. I had another breakdown on the plane, saying goodbye as the loadies were preparing the casket to fly back to Canada. Ya it was tough. I came off the plane, took a little time and then picked up my gun, and we headed back out to the field. I think we were out of the gate before the Herc had even taken off.

We had a really bad day when our medics got hit by an IED. Our fucking ambulance. The medics are good, but they are not trained the same as the infantry, and they sometimes had to come out from KAF to replace other medics, even if they had not done all the field training. We had this one medic show up, she was supposed to work in camp all tour, but there needed to be a replacement for some reason. She gets a quick in brief and shows up in the FOB. On the first day, we headed out to do a resupply run, and we needed to drive in a convoy. She is a vehicle commander of the Ambulance. I had had an argument about the route earlier, saying that it was to dodgy and had been overruled by the bosses. Ten fuckin seconds later, she had deviated off the route and into the moondust that was on the side of the road. We all knew you never drove through fine "moondust" that collected as it would get to ankle deep in some spots, and as the Taliban don't even have to bury IEDs, they can just drop them. They would strap pressure plate IEDs under their man jams, and then as they walked along, they would squat, like they were taking a shit and drop the explosive and then gently sweep the powdery dust over the device. No way for us to stop that. Hundred fifty meters in front of me she goes off the track and BOOM, massive explosion. It knocks my head forward and I immediately fuckin traverse because we're close to compounds and I thought we got hit with SPG 9s because I've been on the receiving end of anti-armour weapons before. I can't see anything dust is everywhere; we are trying to communicate and there is no information. I thought we were ambushed " ambush. Right. Ambush. Right" I am going to "punch" forward to get off the X and I hear on the radio that it was an IED. The dust started to clear, and I could feel the heat. The vehicle is already on fire. I couldn't see the fire, but I could feel the heat…It burnt right down like there was nothing left of it. The Driver died and we were looking for the Crew Commander. We couldn't find her… We were running back to the Lav and saw a combat shirt on the ground. That's her right there in her shirt. Just I mean, it's bad; she was cut in half. This is what is seared into my mind. Her shirt, combat's shirt is open and I don't know what I am looking at, I'm thinking to myself, and here's this woman's spine. Yeah, I don't know if it's because it's a female, and I don't know what it is, but that image is seared into my mind. I can't breathe. I mean, like everything was gone. You know, I mean, like the fact is everything's blown off and here's this little piece of her body, the torso exposed and naked. It shouldn't, but her breasts weirded me out. There's always something that stands out from something terrible. There's some weird detail and that detail gets seared in your head. I immediately felt a need to cover her up. I had lost friends before to IEDs, and for some reason, this was different. It was just so sad. I knew her partner, we had played sports against each other on base. I am not sure what else to say. It was a waste, and I acknowledge that the fact it was a female made a difference. That may make me non-progressive in our modern world, but it was just how I felt. It hit me, not harder, but it impacted me differently.

I went back to KAF after we took a bunch of casualties, and my 2IC was killed. I didn't know how to deal with it at the time. It was surreal. I had good friends in KAF, great people who wanted to support me and know what happened. I roll in, and I see my buddy who has a KAF job, he is awesome and he waves to me as I am coming in, and then it hits me. The NORMALCY hits me and makes me realise it isn't normal, my guys are dead and everyone just seems to be going on about their business. I haven't cried yet. In fact, I gave another leader s shit for crying or tearing up. I Dunno why. Just a fucking Marlboro Man or some shit like that. Total asshole move. I get to the shacks. My good buddy is waiting for me, super big heart, full of support, doing all the right things, and he says, "Bro, you want to talk?" I just fucking slammed the door. I slammed the door on him. A dick move, no hard feelings. He got it, but I still feel terrible about it. I don't know what thing to feel terrible about. My dead friends, slamming the door? The fact I survived? I cried. Because it was the only fucking place I could, in private, alone. I felt that I could just sort of ask for forgiveness from my guys that died. You know. I just sort of tried to process whatever I could. Then I had to take care of my troops. They were angry, they were hurt, and they were mourning; they smashed a fucking door in the shacks. The Garrison Sergeant Major was upset about this fucking door; he didn't get it, yes, the troops shouldn't have done it, but it was like the platoon was a wounded animal that had just had its heart ripped out. That was very tough. We had to get a grip, and so I talked to the most senior NCO and he said that we should do an After-Action Review of the event and how everyone was doing. We called everyone, and everyone showed up, smoking and fucking around, and It's breaking all the fucking rules for the garrison, KAF life that, for the moment, nobody gives a shit about. We talked about it all. We bared our souls and poured out our hurt to each other. Honestly, it was probably the best thing I'd done. I unpacked it out loud with everybody. What I felt we had done right. What I felt I did wrong what I think we need to do when we go back out. Cause the fight is fucking far from over. It was good, man. It was good. We came together and it wasn't like us following the AAR drills. But I think it's part of our doctrine for a reason. You know that process of unpacking whatever you need to get better operationally, and it was beneficial for our mental health. Not that it fucking made anybody better at that point, but it helped us process. I think your ability to process information is important for the soldiers and the team. I would say it was very important to me as a leader. I think everyone just like hearing what happened from all the different perspectives. Everyone tied in and I think it's just digestion of the terrible events that occurred and an opportunity to take that sting out of the hurt and steel ourselves for the next step to go and take it to the enemy. Telling everybody that they were gonna go back out, and we're gonna kill them all. All bullshit, but it helps refocus guys. The mourning, the outpouring of emotion and then the coming together and heading back out into the darkness were probably the most powerful human connections I have ever felt.

I got a cracked rib in an IED strike my LAV was in. In my section, there were three wounded, two seriously. When I was in KAF getting fixed up, the guys were coming out of surgery, and I couldn't go to see them; I thought I let them down. I could not go to the hospital or to the MIR, and I couldn't bear to see them. I thought that they would disown me because I let them down. I had a hard time getting over that feeling. I went back out and did the rest of the tour, and I think I was a good section commander, but it was not until I got home and saw those guys alive and well that they let me know it was all ok and not my fault that I felt a little better. If I am totally honest, I still feel bad. I can't believe how much I push this shit down because I get choked up just thinking about it still. That feeling of responsibility for one of your soldiers being hurt or killed is a real weight.

We got hit hard by a US aircraft, and once the medevacs started, I remember this one soldier; he was holding a friend and his head in his arms and crying. It is hard to see these fucking hard-ticket soldiers cry, man. Teary-eyed, just looking at me, shaking his head. I don't know what to say. Tough. No reason that we got hit by the aircraft's guns. Just bad luck, no one's fault. But so frustrating.

I remember listening on the radio and wanting to be in the fight because that's the company I came from, knowing that so many of my friends were in the shit and were getting injured. It is so strange to listen to a battle on the radio, the updates, and recognize when things are going badly; you hear it in the voices, the sounds of combat in the background. One of my buddies got killed that day. My higher-ups didn't know that we were tight. They can't release the names until the families have been notified. We were out in the field in our fight and there was no ability to get on the Internet and email your buddy in another company to find out what was happening. Everybody thought it was a different soldier that had died. So I got comfortable that was the truth, and I only found out maybe a week, maybe two weeks, later. I was just in my own fight; I didn't even know that he had died. There was a ramp ceremony and everything, and because I was part of another organization, I couldn't go in to say goodbye. We had our own shit to do. Didn't even know. I had to keep it to myself when I learned it was old news. I never got past that. I said goodbye when I got home, and I visited his grave, but it seemed like I missed something.

When one of my best friends died, I had to escort the body home, and I was unprepared. I'd been on patrol the day before, and when I got back in, I found out that he had died. For some reason, they needed someone to identify the body; just part of the process, and that person was me.

They told me to go to the medical tent, and they met me at the front door and brought me, and there he was, just lying on a gurney in a body bag. I went and identified the body, and then they took him up to the reefer. It's all been blurry for me as there's just a lot of shit kind of happening at once. I was asked if I would escort him home, and I offered that another guy should; he decided he wasn't up for it, so I stepped in. The Fallen's wife and my wife were good friends and we had lived close to each other. All the administration started immediately, but Canada was so unprepared. I went up to the Orderly Room., and I signed as a corporal for this fucking $10,000 bag of money for expenses. It was the most ridiculous thing with us on it. In this paper bag! It was to pay for all the costs. I would have to travel like home to Newfoundland and do all these little things to get the body safely back to the family and pay for hotels, food, and all the travel. So I stuffed the paper bag of cash in my backpack, and we started travelling. Before we took off, I found out that the next day. They wanted me to do a eulogy. I did a eulogy for my buddy in front of 2500 people from all these different camps from all the countries on the mission. Of course, that day, it's frigging, hammering snow. All the snow came down from the mountains. And it was insane. I was standing up on this stage and talking to this multinational brigade as a whole, like trying to keep it together. I wrote the eulogy the night before my Field Message Pad, got up there, and eulogized this dude. I don't know if I did it right. I mean, I've never written a eulogy before. After that, we made a procession from there to the airbase.

I said goodbye to my platoon before I left; I wouldn't see them again until Canada. It was so close to the end of the tour. This is how I was going home. I didn't know what I was doing. It was not like what we'd recognized as ramp ceremonies on tours in Kandahar.. some guys carried the casket, so there would have been no drill. There would be no practice. This casket is wrapped in the Canadian flag, but it's like those metal suitcases, and we just had what we had, so the flag was held on by all these different coloured bungee cords around it. Like bright pink, green, and purple, all these crazy ad-hoc chords ensure the flag stays on. So, we get onto the back of the plane, and the Sergeant Major says to me. "Don't leave the side of the body. No matter what, don't leave the body alone. Your post is complete when he is buried." It's all mine. Okay. He's like your date. Your duty is done when the body is in the ground." Then the ramp closed, and it was just me, the escort officer, the loadies and my friend in a casket in the dark of the plane to begin the ride home. Sitting in the plane was unnerving, staring at that casket for the flight. I remember falling asleep, being disoriented, waking up and not realizing where I was, and then focusing on the casket and being brought back into focus. We landed in Dubai and changed into a jet, making me nervous to be apart from the casket. As we approached Canada, CF18 jets were sent up to escort us back through Canadian Airspace. The conversation between the CF18 and our pilot. It was amazing the effort the country was making to welcome us home. They brought us in, we landed, and I had this pillow with his beret, and I was walking around his pillow everywhere, following him. It was a bit of a jug fuck on my part. I formally handed the body off to another escort, and I got 24 hours to sleep and recover before heading to Newfoundland for the funeral. I met the body again. And we flew out. I got off the plane in Newfoundland, and when the body came down, I was following the body as the escort, and all of a sudden, this lady came running out and just started, like laying the fucking slippers to me right on the tarmac. It was unbelievable, it was his sister. They had known that I was bringing the body back, and she was like, how could this have happened? You're supposed to be there to keep an eye on them and all this other stuff. So, it was pretty rough, getting the emotional shit kicked out of you by some girl on the fucking tarmac in Newfoundland. Anyway, I understood, and we are good. I sorted myself out, and we went to the funeral home. It was reinforced to me the orders of "Don't leave this part of the body." So, as the day winds down, it is time to close the funeral home down after visitation. I drag a chair over to sit beside the casket, and they're like, what are you doing? And I'm like, well, I'm sleeping here. They're like, no, you got to go back to the hotel. And I'm like, no, I sleep here beside the body. He's like, well, I don't know if you can. I let him know. Well then, you can stay or arrest me. But this is what I've been told to do; these are my orders. He is not to be alone. So, they just left me in the funeral home. They disabled the motion sensors in the funeral home and set the door alarms. And they showed me where the bathroom was, and they locked me in for the night. I slept on the fucking floor beside the casket. The next day was the ceremony, and I remember everybody leaving at the end of the ceremony. They told me I had to throw the first shovel full of dirt. I don't even know where this came from. But they said to me that after they lowered the casket into the ground. I needed to stay, and I had to throw the first shovelful of dirt onto the casket. And once that was done, my duty was complete as the escort, which I don't know if somebody just made that shit up, but all I remember is like being like this only dude left on this hill, as everybody had left. And so there I am with this, like these funeral home people. You know. I fucking wept. It was just such a release. And I threw this shovel full of dirt on the casket. And I saluted, and I walked away and went home. That was how I finished my first tour. 11 months later, I was back in Afghanistan.

_____*

An A10 is designed to do one thing. Kill things on the ground effectively. It is essentially a flying tank. The craziest day of my life was when we got hit by the A10. We had been in a big fight the day before and taken casualties. We were preparing to go back across and clean out the objective. This time with fire support and preparatory fires, like doctrine. So we are doing confirmatory orders and crushing breakfast and shooting the shit. The fire plan was ramping up, and so all kinds of shit was landing on the Taliban's defensive position. So we're now dropping indirect and all kinds of fucking bombs over there. Seems like the right thing. As a part of the prep, the guys are burning their fucking garbage from the ration packs, normal routine, and we're standing around group behind the LAVs. This thing hits our group as well. Suddenly, dudes started to fall, and I couldn't understand why. I felt like something crazy jumping, and the feel of the earth shaking like something knocked me down. I move like ten feet; I hit the ground. I'm sort of rolling down the hill. I initially thought the Taliban had hit us with effective mortar fire or SPG9s from the other side of the river. I scurry under this fucking LAV. I'm down there for a breath or two and I'm seeing like the red shards rain down everywhere like little explosions. WTF this is an A10. Even in my own panic, I recognize it. I've seen A-10's hitting the other side of the River for the past two days, and I realized we got hit by an A10… I know something is fucked up. I try to run to the Artillery Observers' vehicle. We go to check the fire. Obviously, the FOO almost got killed as well. He has them in check fire. I try to run up higher to see what is going on, and I remember running into this engineer. This dude is like, "…we are all fucked up! "I say, calm down. He's like, "No, this guy I am with is dying." I look at this dude; he looks fine to me. I say this guy's fuckin fine. I was very wrong. He's breathing through a hole in his fucking back. He was bleeding but we just fucking needed to put some pressure on. There were a lot of holes, but they could be treated to sustain life. I recognize that we just killed and hurt our own guys. My brain is not functioning. I realized that I am OK but all of the company leadership is down. I'm the only guy not wounded. So fuckin five to ten minutes have gone by have gone by because of fucking dumb shit. I saved myself, Talked to that panicked dude, and ran the fuck up the hill to confirm check fire with the FOO. As I head down the hill to confirm the leadership and if I am in charge, I recognize that there is a fucking like a sea of blood, a sea of Canadian blood like, what do you do? What do I do? So, I went to the command vehicle, and at this point, I thought everyone else had a narrow miss also. I'm like, SIR! There is no answer, so I say it again: I need to start moving in the right direction. I see him on top of the vehicle, and he says to me, " I have to pack my kit." "What? Why are you packing your kit?" He says again, "I am packing my kit," and then I see it...he has a head wound, and you can see the blood pouring out of his head. "He's totally fucked up." I need to get him treated. I went back to my vehicle and realized that I was in charge. I try to start talking. I can't talk on the radio as I am so emotional. I just watched the company I love destroyed. I can feel it; I am so choked up like I am about to start balling, and I remember this specifically: this seems crazy. But I remember the lessons from Grossmann. I remember feeling, just breathe, just fucking breathe. I breathe like 2 3 times, and then I can settle and push the PTT on the radio and be able to speak to those on the net that are also trying to respond and comprehend what the fuck just happened. I remember guys telling me later that until I spoke, everyone thought we were all dead. That was really hard, I still have a difficult time with that memory of trying to speak at that moment. I remember coming out from the vehicle after I gave a SITREP and started the MEDEVAC. I remember going over to the boss and gently saying, "I'm sorry, Sir, you are all fucked up. I need to take you to the medics. You are hurt, he was bleeding and still talking about needing to pack his kit, we were gentle and let him know his kit would follow. Then I needed the Sergeant Major to help me, but the Sergeant Major was hurt also. We got them to the CCP. I remember going down to see the damage and the troops that were still trying to save life, to get a grip on the scale of the situation, walking, and I don't know where I was going, and I can't remember his name right now, now one of the troops, he was like fucking collapsing, losing his shit, snapping and throwing shit. He was going to hurt himself or someone else, we still had shit to do, I remember grabbing him and tackling him and someone needs to sort this guy out, I grab another fucking sarge, get this fucking dude. The sarge grabbed that dude and calmed him down, and the guys were just so confused and upset, fucking friendly fire, nothing friendly about it. I confirmed with the Battalion CO and HQ that we were suppressing with artillery on the far side of the River, we still had an effective enemy over there while this was going on, and I went down, and I fucking went back to my boat. And I remember the choppers were coming in for MEDEVAC as we had a lot of casualties. We had reported enough that we knew that a chinook was coming in, plus Blackhawks and we were spreading them out. I got word that the Chinook was inbound, and I said over the radio, whatever call sign Chinook is inbound. We're gonna pop purple smoke, and we pop purple smoke, but the fucking enemy popped purple smoke across the river, mimicking what we did, or the rounds coming into support, it blends and shifts the purple smoke that we have popped, making it difficult to determine the location of the PZ. So anyway, this Chinook, an Aussie Chinook. Lands not on our PZ with wounded but actually goes and lands on the enemy side of the River. I was like, OK, everything's going wrong, if we lose that Chinook, it is a really bad day. The Battalion is firing artillery on the far side, where the fucking chopper is landing. The first time I remember screaming over the radio to the Chinook, "You're on the wrong side. Lift off, lift off." I remember screaming that stuff. I remember the helicopter lifting off, and with all this shit going on around him, maybe he did not know the danger he was in. He lifted up and said in a distinctive Australian Accent," So what, you assholes, I made a mistake; calm the fuck down"…great Aussie Character. I was so happy to see that bird and that it did not fall prey to all the fucked up things happening that day. What a fucking day.

One night I had finally put my head down after a long night..not less than 2 minutes after I got my head down, the platoon commander was banging on the door to get me up because the Americans had been hit in their camp, and we have to go help them secure the area and help with their dead. I feel like I was sleepwalking all the way there. I got to stay awake and get ready to go. I have no clue what I am walking into.. As soon as we got there, it was like The Walking Dead. It was dark, but some fires were burning from the explosions, and the Americans were walking around in shock. I think nine were killed. They also had to evacuate a bunch of Pri Alpha wounded. It's pitch black, less the shadows from the fire; I get to the front doors at the gate, and all the tents are all blown up, and there's a big hole in the wall at the back of the camp. These guys are fucked. They had a suicide bomber coming through the back. So, I think one blew the hole in the wall with his vest, and then another guy came in and ran into a tent full of people and blew himself up. One of the Americans was telling one of our guys that the first guy blew a hole in the wall, and the other guy came in; he was calm, lit up a smoke, had a smoke and then just ran into the tent, blew himself up. This guy talking was hurt, I guess, by the initial explosion. He was like lying there by the hole in the wall, his weapon had been jammed in the explosion, and his back and neck were all fucked up. He was frozen; he saw this guy come in later, light up the smoke, run in and then blow himself up. So when we showed up, there was carnage everywhere. It was a crazy scene; my thought was, how do you fight people who are so calm that they light a smoke and then run in to execute their mission and blow themselves up? That is a level of dedication we do not have…It was the first time I wondered if we were going to win.

When we lost our first casualty, I took it pretty hard. We weren't best friends or anything like that, but we were friends. We served a mortar platoon together. We both lived on the north side, married quarters in Petawawa, and we served together mortars. At that point in time, he didn't have a vehicle. I used to pick him up every morning and bring him back and forth to work. We were in rifle company together. The night before he actually went out on that patrol, we were in a mess having some beers again. He was excited to go home because he had a ring. He was gonna propose to his girlfriend, make him make her his fiancee. He was very happy about that. The next morning, a section was short one individual for the patrol. He decided to step up to the plate. It was the last patrol that he ever took. He did not have to volunteer, But it was something that he did. That makes me proud because you know what? He could have said no. Unfortunately, he paid ultimate sacrifice. I remember that morning we were just coming back from a night patrol. I was actually sleep. I heard the booms from a blast. We were on 15 minutes notice to move. You got up dressed. And as soon as my boots were on my feet, somebody was down from the HQ tent and said, hey, you guys are rolling in 10. We ran up to the vehicle. We moved out to the scene. Our job at that point in time was to establish the outer cordon and protect the people dealing with the situation. I remember looking in and seeing the blast site and blankets draped over the casualty. At that point in time, I didn't know who it was. Just that one of my brothers had fallen. You get that little bit of anger that comes in. That was really my first big incident. All the responses started to flow through us. They took away the casualty. And then, of course, a flatbed truck took the blown-up jeep. It wasn't until we were ready to collapse the cordon that I found out who it was. One of the one of the guys working the scene showed up and they told us, you know, like. He says I can't say the name, but he gave us a hint. Yeah, it has the same last name as this individual. And right away, we put two and two together, and it was, well, I'll never forget that. That feeling that came over me. I was very angry. You know, I look back at it. I'm glad that my emotions didn't really take over because all I could think about was that I had a lot of ammo. I could do some damage. I'm glad I didn't get to that point, but I do remember that. I thought, who else is here right now in this crowd? Which one of them knew? Which one is the next suicide bomber? Obviously, training and control kick in, but you do think about it. It was a rough couple of days. We had the ramp ceremony. I was one of the LAVs that escorted his body to the American camp to fly his body home. It was a pretty intense few days. At the same time, you try to remain professional, do your job and not let your emotions get the better of you. I guess it's almost like a protection for soldiers. I think people who continue to do their jobs successfully get through these difficult times. I am unsure if that's a good or bad thing because you learn how to box it very quickly. I completely boxed my feelings of loss, of the loss of the opportunity for him to get married, of us driving to work every day together of the loss of the future friendship. I boxed it all for a long time. I got the job done; maybe that's not the best thing for us.

I hated it when we lost dudes. I didn't want to go to KAF; I wanted to stay in the fight. When I am totally honest, I just became totally obsessed with killing those people those people that hurt our guys. I'm just saying it was my mindset. I never did anything illegal. I just did not want to be pulled back. My mindset wasn't rational. But neither was the situation. I think that if you showed weakness or hesitated, you were going to get people hurt, and we saw that. Afghanistan is not rational. So perhaps I was rational there. I wanted to kill more assholes that were trying to kill me and hurt my friends.

We responded to this massive IED. We lost almost a whole section in the blast. We just caught a glimpse of the wreckage site. The LAV rear ramp weighing thousands of pounds of steel was blown 30 meters, and the spare tire, which is hundreds of pounds, was 35, 40 metres off the side. It launched the Crew Commander out of the turret, completely out of the turret. We had shifted tasks that morning, and that section took our task, and we went to do something else. It was like a double stack of explosives. Just massive. We provided security 24 hours. We couldn't find all the pieces of the vehicle and personnel. I couldn't shake it was supposed to be me. I don't think anybody in our section talked for a good twenty-four hours. No one said a fucking word. Then it was just a voice. The satphone came around. Once we got cleared to call home. We still didn't know everyone who died. We wouldn't find out until we got back to KAF. We all got pulled back into a cab for the ramp ceremony. I knew a number of them well, but one of the guys was like a brother to me. It's tough. I ended up being a pallbearer for him at the ramp ceremony. I was in shock and just wanted to get through it. You have to pull out the casket from the back of an LAV using a certain type of Drill movement; then you have to carry the casket in a slow march to the Hercules aircraft. The actual walk from the LAV to the back of the Herc. Felt like hours was only maybe 10, 15 meters. It just felt like hours rolled through. I feel bad; the casket is getting heavy, but now we've got to do it. I'm not going to fuck this up. I was in a haze, the sound of bagpipes, troops from all these countries lined up saluting the glare of the floodlights, the opening rear ramp of the Herc with a big Canadian flag hanging in the back. The biggest thing I remember is carrying the casket on the Herc, saying my final goodbyes and seeing the door closed. So, I think the one scene when the door closed was hard. Fuck, it is real, it's real. It actually happened. This isn't a dream. He's dead, they are dead. Then you have to go right back. We were back in KAF probably less than 48 hours and we get 24 hours and have to sort of decompress and take it all in. Realise what happened talk about it. We were back at the shacks, and the boys got a hold of one of the guitars from the welfare section, and we sat around smoking cigarettes and playing guitar. Let's go again. That was good. We returned to the field the next morning and got after it again.

———————

I got sent home to recover from a blast injury that I had received from a VBIED that had hit our carrier. I was determined to get back to theatre. I went and stayed with my parents for a week. I remember one morning, I was having coffee at the dinner table with my old man, and the CBC came on and said that NATO had taken a casualty. I was fairly wide-eyed. No surprise there. And by lunchtime, it had been a Canadian casualty. And then, a few hours later, I was in the backyard with my mother, and we were having a cigarette and letting the dogs run around. I told my mother the story about getting blown up, and that this guy in my platoon treated me immediately, I got a little fucked up; it is what it is. Now everything was fine. The guys on the scene took care of me. This one guy in particular who had a lot of medical background when he was a civvie paramedic took real good care of me. We have a moment, and she is doing well as a Mom, supporting me and right at that moment, my younger sister sticks her head out of the back door and says they've released the name_ it's Private _____. It was the guy from my platoon who had just done all the first aid on me when I got fucked up. He had been killed stepping on an IED. I broke down right there. It seemed so unfair. The next week I was back with the Platoon. It was just so strange, I felt good with being with my family, but felt guilty for not being there to help him like he helped me.

———————

One of my best buddies was killed; we were in different companies. I asked to help where I could. When people die in combat, I don't think people understand all the small things that have to happen. Like, you gotta go through all the shit. So you go through the photos, the private photos that are sent to them from their wives or girlfriends. You kind of like you. Hopefully, there's nothing there that is not supposed to be there. You never want to send home what is wrong in their life. Lots of people lead complex lives, and when they die, you don't need all their secrets out. This was not an issue in this case. I was going through all that private stuff, like pictures of their daughter. Like I was really going through a lot of stuff, and it just hit me in waves. What they blew up just destroyed a bunch of lives. Then I went through the personal effects of what goes on in his body, like his wallet, sniper coin, and all that stuff. You really get reacquainted with your friend. In KAF, the Americans do all the work on the body. I don't know if it's embalming, but they put them in the caskets and set up a nice private area. They're like fucking just an emotional wreck. I ask to carry this casket. They let me, and so you stay with the casket until it is time to go. The casket is never alone. So, I was in the back of the LAV and escorting it to the rear of the Herc. Emotional carrying on the plane. The mission doesn't end. You got a job to do, so I am trying to be zero emotion here. It's impossible to think about your friend. I decided that I couldn't let this hang on me, or I knew it would just consume me. So, I put it in the back of my mind. Got back out to the company. But you're fucking pissed. They have killed one of you. Your perspective changes. You're fucking angry, and you want to do something. For me, driving changed. I didn't pull over; I have the 40-ton LAV. Get the fuck out of my way, you fucking get the warning shot, and then you get the shot through the motor. We tried to be nice, and that let you assholes kill us. Not me. Not here.

We were out on patrol one night, going to set up so that the BG could clear this shit little village where the Taliban hung out. As the Talibs learned our tricks, they used to lay IEDs on all the approach routes and then only activate them at night to stop us from gaining the advantage. We learned quickly that you did not take obvious routes and you do not go through gaps in walls that seem too easy. But this one night, we did not follow our SOP. We came to this hole in the wall and were a little behind on our timings. I looked back and told the guy behind me, "I'm going through that gap. We can't go over. That wall is too fucking big. We don't have sledgehammers. We're not gonna pound through it. We're trying to make the best speed. The other patrols were already well ahead of us." We approached the wall; we made a short halt just prior to the gap because that's important. Confirm kind of our surroundings and then. I remember saying to the group, don't step in the hole. Step through the gap. And the very first one through, he led with his right leg. He stepped right through. Then he just moved across. I came up behind him and we did the like the flag drill. I came through, looking in his direction. He turned and looked the other way. The next guy bumped up to me and came through. He Bumped me. I bumped the next guy, and we were through. Now we're moving up the road to secure the bound as the remainder of the det moves through the gap. I was feeling good. I remember, like relaxing my shoulders and bringing my weapon down. And then all of a sudden, I am on my face, and I call to the lead guy because it was a blast, and I don't know where it came from. I don't know, maybe an RPG or something, but there was no sound; my ears were ringing. I feel the guy in front of me in the dark, are you good? He looks at me, I can't really hear him but he says yeah, I am good. So I get up, and I run back, and I put my hand on the guy behind me's back, and I give him a push. Is he good? He says, "I'm good. I'm good." This all happens in seconds, but I am slowly coming back together, and then the sound hits me, this low groan, turning into a scream; we realize that it is coming from the gap we just crossed through. We get to the last man in our patrol, and he's in the fucking gap, and now it is a hole he is right in it. He didn't step through, and he stepped into the hole. I'm like holy fuck. He's screaming it's fuckin head off, I just react. The first thing we do is realize that he's got no fuckin feet. He's got one hanging by a tendon and one we never found. It was just gone. So, we start doing the initial treatment so we get one tourniquet on. Then I get on the radio. I call in the contact. A lot of these things blend together because we put like five fucking tourniquets on him. He just kept bleeding. The first one stayed. The second one broke. The third one is broken. Then we pulled out the American ones with the metal handles because he had big legs. So we're doing this, and the fucking radio is not strong enough so no one can hear us; we can hear convoys checking on the net..their signal was stronger, and we realize no one knows we have been hit. The weirdest thing happens, the Commanding Officer, the Colonel, who was located closest but across the River, comes on and takes the fucking 9 liner. It was insane. Our guy is screaming, and I'm trying to tell him to shut the fuck up; we are in bad guy country, and they are going to come to see what they caught; we can't move him because we are in a grape field, and we need extraction. The shit's happening. Another guy in my patrol got the last tourniquet on finally, and the secondary, we finally got the bleeding stopped. The casualty is complaining about something in the small of his back. I put my hand on the rock that is jammed into his back. He's complaining about a rock and I am leaving it. If it's not the fuckin fact you're missing two feet right now, then I'm leaving that rock. I'm losing my fucking brain because there's a guy here with two missing feet bleeding out, and extraction seems so far away. I am sure that it wasn't but it seemed like forever. I am sitting by him, monitoring vitals and trying to keep him quiet. He was in and out, and we did the nut check for him. That was a thing. Everyone needed the nut check. They were intact and lucky, seeing as the blast went straight up. Any guy would do that for another guy again. Weird moment because I have my red light on to monitor him, check for new bleeds, and watch his face. And I'm over top of his face so he can't look down and see his feet. So, he keeps reaching up, and he keeps flicking or trying to flick my red lens up on my headlamp to make it white light. I say, "We are still in the hurt locker unless we get help soon. It is like 3 dudes in TB country, and you've GOT to stop touching my headlamp! "There is ICOM chatter; the terp says that the TB have heard the screaming and the blast, and they are coming to going to come to check it out." I let the casualty know, "Like we're not okay here, Dude, you need to settle the fuck down." He's like, "The red lights freaking me out. I think it's blood." He is fucked. I try to settle him down. Real gentle. He asks me not to quit. We talk about quitting, Don't be a quitter like you're going to be fine, just talking to him softly, just bullshit stuff; I try to give him updates; he is in and out of consciousness; He starts talking about his mom and shit. Bad stuff... just at that moment, another platoon showed up with a medic, they took over, and the ICOM chatter changed; the TB was not going to fuck with a full platoon; I was so relieved and handed off the casualty. We called in and said that the casualty had been carried off and that we were set to continue our mission. It got scrubbed. That really upset me, not that I wanted to keep walking around in the dark, but the mission had been important enough to have us out there and for my buddy to lose his legs. When a casualty happens, we stop; I am sure there was a good reason, but when I got asked later if we got it done by the dude that took the hit, I would have to tell him we didn't complete the mission. Consciously, I get it; it just burned me. It was kind of a microcosm of the whole Afghanistan action, was any of it necessary?

Ramp ceremonies were difficult. A protocol demands that people of equal rank carry the fallen. That gets harder when they are more senior. When we lost WOs or Sgts that would have meant you need to bring in other platoons off the line to do the ceremony, which means the AOR gets more dangerous and the TB observes you leaving the battlefield after they take one of yours. I remember after we lost some guys of various ranks, we went through a brief rehearsal back in KAF, They assigned who was going to go with who and just directly be involved. It is kind of weird. We've been trying to assess what ranks go with which fallen comrade. And then, in the end, they just said, fuck it. We are not pulling more dudes out of the field and making them drive the roads, and we are going to have the guys in the platoon carry the guys from their platoon regardless of rank. It was an emotional task. When the LAV rolls up to the back of the Herc. I will never forget that sound; It is silent except for the LAV engine. How heavy the casket felt on my shoulder, it was a long walk to the back of the C130 past all the nations lined up to pay their respects, all saluting and the bagpipes playing, but you are just trying to not fuck up the drill, to not stumble to make sure that your buddy has a professional send off because all the cameras are rolling. You are not processing, but all that emotion is there just below the surface because the guy on your shoulder could have been you. You are thinking about losing your friend, and you are also so happy that it isn't you, and then you feel relieved, just a little, and that makes you sadder and a little guilty because that guy that did die is our friend, and how can you be happy to be alive when someone else had to die? It is a confusing time, the easiest thing is to not think about it and shut down those thoughts. The moment it is over, it is time to get back out and get to work. We went and did the ramp ceremony, we said goodbye, and then we went to the Green Bean, got coffee and then rolled out back to the AOR.

I found this story kind of scary, spooky, scary. The RSM was about to leave the camp with the CO; they were getting ready to go. He's leaving out the door. and I say, "Hey RSM, Aren't you going to say goodbye? " He says, "It is not like you will never see me again". Those were his last words. He was killed by an IED 30 minutes later on the Highway. It really made an impression, and after that, I always treated my friends like it was the last time I was going to see them. It took me a long time to get past that. Even at home, not sure my family understood.

I went to Wilson as the duty officer out there to help manage the forward HQ. I found myself a cot and I put it in between the zero-alpha bison with all the radios and a sea can…I thought that would be fairly secure because we were still getting mortared all the time. I worked all night. In the morning, I went to sleep. I remember getting woken up by the assistant Adj who was also doing some of the officer duties. He shook me awake and I was trying to adjust my eyes in the midday sun. As soon as I could start making out what was going on, about 50 meters away soldiers were carrying covered stretchers into the cooler, the cooled sea can where food was packed and meat. They were the remains of four soldiers killed in a suicide attack. So, I slept through that event and then woke up and watched the bodies be put into our food freezer. It was surreal to me. I went to the CP. What's going on? A company just got hit. They had 4 killed, Recce Platoon is on the scene and will secure their area when the company go in for the ramp ceremony. You're going to a Rifle Company as a Platoon commander due to the casualties from the other day. I was trying to process all of that and thankful that I was gonna get a platoon and then realizing that I was only going to the field because of so many guys getting hurt and dying. I had sold my family on this bill of goods that I was not going to ever leave the wire. I managed to send an e-mail saying that my job had changed, but it is what it is. I got on the next convoy back to KAF and then met up with the company and learned to be a leader as a battlefield replacement.

How I dealt with death was very removed from the emotion that is supposed to be present. When you are the radio giving direction, you need to be calm, almost robotic. No emotion so the troops don't panic Particularly when it was someone that was that was close to you or the team… When you heard someone had been killed and you were in the CP, you had to look up the Zap number, you were the only one who knew who had died, then you had to inform the BG and then talk to the dudes doing the recovery. It hard to understand that mix of emotions at play. I just don't know if I could quantify it. I think the ramp ceremonies were really hard. There was this one NCO who had been a good friend and his wife was there as she was also in the BG. That's right. I had signed their statutory declaration for marriage just before the tour. So that was very emotional. They had been "married' for about 6 weeks when he was killed. We just hadn't considered it; we were immature in these areas as we had not suffered a large number of combat losses. Looking back, it was crazy to have had them both there. We sent her home with the body, we lost two for one. I think it's emotional. Anytime you lose someone. And it should be. So, I don't worry about that. I do worry now that I actually forget. I forget stuff. It scares the hell out of me because I'm like, how can I forget these events? It's not a weakness. Maybe it's that I don't want the past. That is why important to kind of commemorate that which has happened and then decide how you're going to move forward from there. So, for death, for me, I think the biggest problem is when you're confronted with a scenario where you think there's a high, high probability that someone's going to die. That manifests itself in a choice as to who's going to die. like most of the time we were reactionary. We reacted to what the enemy did. We were fixed to the situation. So, it's like anything can happen. We can die. So we don't have agency over who lives and who dies. So, you accept it and you accept that people are going to get hurt and wounded. But when we were on the offensive and we're doing some really great stuff really fucking around the enemy. I felt, you know, in control. But what comes with that is decisions about who's going to live and who's going to potentially die. And when that gets narrowed down to a person, well, then you've got to make those choices. Who walks down the road, what vehicle are they in, and who goes on patrol seems easy, each choice represents life or death. It is hard and it is just luck.

———————

We had lost 4 guys and a bunch wounded in quick succession. We were ordered into KAF to do the ramp ceremony, which I had mixed feelings about, but in the end, it was good for the guys and then we get a visit from some senior leaders and, it was basically. "Suck it up, get the fuck back out there". This is coming from people that don't leave the fucking wire! How dare you come in here and tell my team. How dare you. Tell us to suck it up and get the fuck back out there. We know we got to suck it up. I hated the "us and them" shit, I know we all had a job, but when we didn't need false bravado, we needed to say goodbye to our friends and then we would cowboy the fuck up and get after the assholes that did it. This fucking FOBBIT team just pissed me off. After that, I never went back to KAF

———————

I remember after a bad day that we took a bunch of casualties, our boss asked us if we needed to go into KAF for a rest and refit. Every single one of us was like, no. We're out here. We're not going to go in. We looked around at each other, we were in it and it was a bonding moment for us. I remember that night, a reserve corporal in the back of the boat had his iPod out in the field. I remember just all of us kind of huddled around listening to Russell Peters's stand-up comedy I heard that line "like somebody's gonna get hurt real bad". You know, it made us laugh, we had just lost friends and seen guys wounded, but that little skit and being out in the fight together made us feel close.

———————

The IED was the base event for the tour. We had gone into this area. I forget the name of the town, but it was basically right on the Helmand border. We did a cordon and search there probably a week or two weeks prior and we did a search of a compound and found some stuff, but it was just like small-arms. The task was a kind of convoy escort for a huge convoy that was going in to resupply FOB Robinson and the previous day, they were rotating the tasks, and the previous day, another group had done an escort task. We did a combination tunnel and escort method all the way up to FOB Rob and handed it to the Brits. It was like one of those huge jingle truck convoys with 300 trucks and an end. The next day. I was just going to do leaguer security, secure the CP and have a bit of a rest. But then they started losing comms and so they needed to throw us out to set up an RRB on a hill. I didn't realize it at the time that this hill was in proximity to that town where we'd been hit because we'd been like every day we were patrolling. My thought was at the time to go cross country because it was pretty much an open desert. I felt it was pretty unlikely they'd be able to template us if we just went, and I had a habit of not following tracks and going straight cross country. We Were really comfortable kind of moving like just through the desert cross country. The only obstacles were the Kariz systems. Well, they looked like they almost looked like a fire mission had been dropped; they were holes that had been dug down, and they were on their channel, the water underground. And these things go from the mountains down to the agricultural areas for irrigation. They go for fifty or 100 km and are quite deep. And there were small chokepoints to go between these holes. We drove up along the kārīz system and had the option of going through the chokepoint or going like 20, 30 kilometres around this road system. In the interest of time, we had the RRB task and comms were spotty down to get there. So, we crossed it at the choke point. I was the second vehicle. The vehicle, which was a vehicle I normally had in the lead, struck an offset pressure plate IED, where the pressure plate was below the left front wheel and they'd measured it. So, the main charge was right under the troop compartment and it basically was a substantial IED of a triple stack of mines and HME or something. It penetrated the entry of the hole where beneath the troop compartment and just made a mess of the back. The bomb goes off. I get rocked but am down below the turret so protected. Right away, like before I even knew what how bad it was. It was like communicating right away and I actually had a hard time conveying the gravity of it to the Command Post because at that point, like I said, it's been pretty quiet on our tour. It's hard it's hard to convey just how bad it was. My views were obstructed because at that point I had a lot of confidence in my LAV, sergeant, and I was anticipating that I would eventually get into ambushes and I didn't want to have to dismount from the turret under contact… So, we made the decision that I would ride the back, so I didn't, I couldn't see, I didn't see a lot. The first thing was the shock wave. It was like a pretty substantial shockwave. I knew it was big. In my memory, the first view is basically the ramp blown off 30 meters away. You can I couldn't even see into the back to the troop compartment because it basically folded up the floor. So, it was just a mass of like kit and bodies and like just like a mess of equipment. No fire, just a big mess like kit and people. It was hard to describe the scene because I think I wasn't super emotional right away, but I was trying to like I was making a conscious effort to have a very measured speech and not be emotional, I was a Lieutenant on my first tour, in my first contact. I wanted to ensure I was controlled and did the right things. I think it was useful for people. The reaction was really good and we went into autopilot. Once I managed to convey what was going on the CP started throwing stuff at me. Which I what you hope they do. Right away a troop of tanks shows up and sets an outer Cordon in the desert so that we are isolated from any further enemy action. I started pushing anyone coming in. I just pushed them out because I was already right there and right on it My first thought was like secondary devices, and I didn't want a whole bunch of vehicles coming in and setting off more and making it worse. We were already in a pretty bad situation. So, in a sense, I didn't want to put anyone else at risk, so I sent forward my TCCC guy and the medic to get into the wreckage before we got the engineers in. Those guys going in with total disregard for their own safety and then the driver of the LAV, he came out of the smoke and the chaos, we thought everyone was dead and the thing I saw first was this guy coming around to check for survivors with his rifle in the shoulder, still in the fight ready to drop any threat even if he was the last man left. I still get emotional, *he was alive, and he was ready to fight.* I was keeping people out because I didn't know the situation. I brought up, the engineers cleared the path to safe land so that I could get medics in after those two brave dudes that did the first surveys. Six died, and 4 got out with various wounds. The dudes were incredible in the face of that adversity. One thing though, that was hard was right after it happened. There was a guy on a motorcycle speeding away at a high rate of speed. My gunner really wanted to light him up, but there was no PID. It was just as likely that he was just some guy, but that might have been the triggerman. It took a lot of discipline because everyone was so angry and hurt and I had to come on to him pretty hard to stop him from shooting and to keep him from killing him. I'm happy that I did because I'm sure he would have regretted it after. That was an incredibly hard day. Losing a section as a new platoon commander. I still don't know if I ever consider the emotion or just work through the events, like the science of the response is my shield to the emotion of the event. I miss those 6 guys every day.

RANCHO RELAXO

COMBAT IS OFTEN CHARACTERIZED by long periods of boredom interrupted by moments of absolute shocking violence.

In these moments of boredom, you need to figure out ways to entertain yourself, to relax, and to rebuild teams that have been shattered by violence.

You need to check on your teammates' morale and make sure that whatever kept them in the fight, they got some of it.

Reading people was key knowing that for some it was talking to home, for some it was music, others trying to create something gourmet to eat out of issued rations for others it was taking off to find some space or even do a workout.

Practical jokes were a key part of the lives of soldiers.

So was breaking the rules.

Given the nature of combat and the austere conditions, for months soldiers were restricted from drinking and sex - anything fun that would allow you to blow off steam. But as long as there have been young soldiers, there have been people trying to figure out how to break the rules. When they got caught, they paid the price, but for them, the reward was worth the risk.

During the toughest periods, a shower, food, sleep, a feeling of security, or a hot coffee disproportionately positively impacted a soldier's ability to continue fighting.

Our FOB was in Spin Boldak. It was an old French Foreign Legion camp. It was an amazing place to go back to because it was just our spot, it was very secure and made it very relaxed. You had the big wall around the outside and the four guard towers, and then the big guard tower in the middle. There were weird sections of the FOB. You had the old French Foreign Legion tents that we weren't supposed to go in and they were like big canvas tents, circus tents almost. One of them had a bar in it and there was some female underwear pinned to the wall in it, I don't know where they found that. No questions asked, no answers given. Then we had what we called the Rancho Relaxo. Which were the barracks that we were using. It was a brick and mud building with all these tiny cells, it was almost like a prison without any bars. So everybody had a cell to themselves that they put their cot in and their stuff in. It gave everyone privacy and when you came back after the hard days you could decompress and relax. The camp was like a movie set. If I hadn't lived in it I wouldn't have believed it. Rancho Relaxo is in the middle of the Reg desert.

In the FOB we just slept in the open on the crushed stone with Hesco Bastion around it. Under the night sky was routine at that point. The stars were beautiful. I loved nights in Afghanistan (when I wasn't on patrol). It was silent and there was no ambient light. When the moon was out it was bright and unfiltered. Casting its reflected light creating a half light that was pitched with shadows. At times bright when it reflected off the light-coloured gravel or sand of the desert. If I wasn't on security or radio shift, I used to wake up at three, when there was a chill in the air. I would grab the Sat phone, make a coffee, and then head up the hill in MSG on the John Deere gator. I would pull up and overlook the backside of the hill into Panjawaii and call home. No one was around and it provided some peace with nothing going on. Sometimes I would get a whole hour, sitting back in the gator and looking at the stars and speaking to my wife or listening to my kids talk about nothing. It was nice and for some reason, I seemed closer to them at that moment. I was on this hill in Afghanistan, but we were under the same sky and at that moment it was peaceful in both spots. That was my favourite time in Afghanistan. I would get off the phone when I heard the first call for prayer. It was like my alarm to get back into the routine, the sun coming up, shifting the cool grey light of the moon for vibrant reds and oranges that seemed to pull those deep colours from the stone edifices that framed our area of operations: Mahr Ghar, Three tank hill and Masum Ghar framing our area of operations. Another day, had to get ready for patrol, I would descend consciously hoping this was not a bad day for me or my team and I would get back to the top of the hill the next night.

Spunkmeyer muffins were pure morale. They were processed US muffins that came out in cellophane wrappers and were always moist and tasty. The name of these things was a never-ending bullshit session with the troops and no one cared if they were full of preservatives that made them last for weeks in hot temperatures, they were so good. But they were also indestructible. We would play catch with them, kick them like hacky sacks, they seemed to bounce like rubber. I had this one guy in my section who had a contest to see how many Spunkmeyer muffins he could shove in his pants and still do them up. I think it was like 30. When there are no screens, the strangest things will entertain you.

Due to leave and casualties there was one point where there were only twelve of us there from the platoon securing our strong point. So less than half the platoon. I think we went a little feral. That's when the shenanigans started. My section commander and I decided to bleach our hair with peroxide, which didn't go over well with our platoon commander. We had the peroxide because a guy in my section had very stinky feet. OK, so he got a care package sent over with peroxide and a list of like thirty-nine things that peroxide can do, kill the bacteria in the toothbrush, get rid of the stink that's on your feet and of course lighten your hair. You mix 50 percent water, and 50 percent peroxide and spritz your hair for natural highlights. We tried all 39 on the list. Of the thirty-nine things we figured the hair was the only one that would get us in shit. So, we did that for a couple of weeks and the Platoon leadership told us to stop when my black hair was platinum. So, we did- initially- And then everyone left and we didn't have enough firepower to really patrol so we were trapped in the strongpoint, and if you leave soldiers alone with limited supervision. What are they going to do? So, we went back to bleaching our hair. Stupid shit, but it was fun and when they came back and we looked like Slim Shady, we just got a haircut on 0. No harm done. But we were rock stars for a couple of weeks. The Dennis Rodman's of the Battle Group.

I didn't remember feeling tired. But I didn't sleep a lot. I knew over probably was tired. Smoking relaxed me. Started smoking when the fear started. I never acknowledged the fear, but it was ever present, especially once we lost guys in my platoon. Once the fear started, the smoking started. Really interesting because I never I never smoked, and once I felt that fear, smoking became a thing for me, probably a pack every two days. One morning my LAV Sergeant even woke up and he handed me a new smoke and that was it. That was the beginning of a love affair with tobacco and nicotine. I think the guys were also the best way to bring you down after a day. I mean, we lived in this LAV for 7 months. Your home for 10 people in these eight-wheeled steel boxes as the family room, driver hatch as the front bedroom, and a turret penthouse. Everything has a place, food, water, ammunition, personal kit, no space is wasted, and no privacy. Once you start living inside the boat with your crew, that's where the real camaraderie is, the real support. And of course, all the tasty cigarettes.

————————

I had a favourite ration; I ate it as much as I could. It was reminiscent of a poor man's McDonald's McRib thing. I think it was called a pork cutlet or riblet. Some pseudo pork concoction in a cellophane bag full of preservatives and salt. The one shitty thing was that it didn't come with jalapeño cheese. Jalapeño cheese. Like I saw guys get at the fucking fistfights over jalapeño cheese. So it didn't come with that ration. So if I was ever able to exercise enough willpower to save my jalapeño cheese until that particular ration came around again, and some of the bread that came with the breakfast to make a sandwich, that fucking shit was heaven. Pork Riblet, Jalapeno Cheese and break equalled high morale in my book.

————————

Practical jokes. Big thing. In Infantry platoons. Can't take a joke, don't be in the infantry. Fuck 'em if they can't take a joke and joke 'em if they can't take a fuck. But we have one rule. Your bed space is your bed space. Don't mess with a man's bedspace. That's the only place that you can turn around and be yourself and go back to your own home. We were constantly fucking with guys, but don't mess with a dude's bunk space. That shit is serious.

————————

In the COP we had this little TV and DVD player hooked in to the generator. You are living out in a bag guy country and sometimes it is just nice to turn your brain off. We made couches out of old cushions and blankets we found in abandoned buildings. We didn't have many movies, so we watched every Austin Powers about 15 times to the point where we could recite the entire movie. So a lot of the jokes are funny to me now, but make no sense. Black Hawk Down is another one, too. So crazy watching a war movie while fighting in one. Our captain was a reserve captain infantry, but he was Peel Regional Police. He had been on an earlier tour with the PPCLI prior to us a larger prior to us, and he just signed an extension to stay longer until we could get an officer into our team. So he was set in his ways and routines. He was a good guy but he had this one weird habit. He wanted to watch night at the Roxbury before every patrol, because that's what they used to watch before going to the bars downtown in Peel. So it was small thing, makes you feel better, lets watch night at the Roxbury. Repeat, rinse and repeat on those videos. So many bad Austin Powers and Night at the Roxbury quotes. We even used them on the radio as kind of our own code when patrolling. Drove our higher headquarters nuts. YEAAAHH BABY! Do I make you Horny? We were fuckin' weirdos, living on an island in the middle of the Taliban Sea, but I still smile when those movies come on.

Boredom is a thing on tour when things are slow, But you can always count on the team for some levity. I was in the Platoon Headquarters tent, staring at the computer screen, my eyes glazing over at the mountain of paperwork that never seemed to let up. In Kabul, even though we had lost soldiers to enemy action, we weren't "at war yet" and the Army still ran reports on a peacetime schedule. My doldrums were interrupted by the ringing of my telephone that was connected to the observation posts. I lifted the receiver to my ear and Roxanne by the police played on the other end of the line. The voices of one of my sections voices joined Sting's chorus in a duet:

Box Amb,
You don't have to put on the red light
Box Amb,
You don't have to put on the red light"

I fought hard not to break out laughing. It was one of my Section Commanders calling from his observation post in the King's Palace overlooking the camp.

"For you, Sir, anything. Have a good day." He hung up the phone.

A moment later, the phone rang again. The same voice was at the other end of the line, this time without musical accompaniment.

"What is it, Sarge?"

"I'm not wearing any pants, Sir." The line clicked as he hung up.

Just stupid shit, but it keeps you going.

So, we are in the fucking Sea Can accommodations at Kandahar airfield after six months out in the field. We are in the last month of our tour, and we have done a lot of shit. It is time to chill and get ready to go home. I am a Corporal and am in the room with a Master Corporal. We're sitting there and I'm reading a book and we're just chilling out and it is the first time in weeks that no one is tasking us. I hear in the next room a Sergeant, open up the door to the room next to us and grab three guys to go take out the garbage and do a sweep. Pretty fucking standard Shit in a soldier's day. I am not sure why, but it really pissed me off and I didn't want to get tasked, we had just gotten back in and I did not want to get back into garrison chickenshit stuff so soon. It seemed like they had enough guys, I kind of got into my head, and I thought, "Well fuck this. I am just going to hide in this room and not get picked up for this task. "so, I closed the door and locked it. My roommate, a Master Corporal, and future Medal of Valour winner is on board, he nods quietly and we sit quietly and listen to the hallway as the other guys from our platoon are getting lined up and given directions. My buddy that was part of the group selected, knows we are in the room and is pissed we are going to get away chilling escalates by pounding on our door and telling the Sergeant that we are in there. He is pissed that he got picked up and wants us to share the pain. We committed now, no matter what we can't leave this room. We sit there on the other side of the door with our breath held. If the Sergeant figures out a way into our room we are done, so childish, we just fought for six months but this seemed so important. The guy pounding on the door was told to calm down but it gets worse for us and the stakes are elevated. the 3-person task becomes a company clean up and EVERYONE available is going to clean up the company area and do a company garbage sweep. All 130 people. Now this has escalated and we are not just avoiding a Sergeant but the Sergeant Major is involved and he is a scary man, But we are in for a penny, in for a pound. We are going to see this through, and we are like criminals on the other side of this thin door, there are all these people in the halls and at one point I thought they were going to bust down my door. We are sweating bullets. Eventually, the mass left, but we were unsure if there was anyone in the hallway. Me and the Master Corporal collapsed and stayed in the room for 2 hours. Finally, we E and E'd through our window and took all the back routes to the British area of the camp away from all Canadians. We waited to come back later in the evening and just plead ignorance. When they did get back the guys lit us up, my buddy from the original three knew the truth but couldn't prove it. I had been in probably 30 contacts by this point and I think the SGM finding out made me more nervous than the enemy had. In the end, it would have been easier just to do the garbage sweep, but to be honest, I just needed an afternoon off after 7 months. It was too soon to get back to garrison bullshit.

Guys would doze off all the time in the back of the LAV. Seriously crazy but true. The vibration and the darkness of an armoured vehicle are strangely relaxing. You hook your arm through these straps above to stabilize yourself and lay your head on your own bicep. With the movement of the vehicle, the air conditioning would attempt to kick in, providing some relief; the vibration starts, and you are out cold. So, the boys would always take the spare straps that hang from the roof of the carrier and they would hook it onto the NVG mount of a guy's helmet. He would not feel that and it would give a little play but when he woke up and tried to get out his head would snap back and he would fall on his ass. You were always in danger of this happening to you. Someone got it, daily. So funny. We were children.

We had some shenanigans. I am sure there is a statute of limitations. They had a beer call for us one night. Handover to the next group was done. Everyone was allowed "2 beers" and they made us pay for our own beer. After everyone being out for months. So not everyone drank and there was beer left over. We followed the dude at the end of the night who was putting it away. When he left we ended up sneaking over to the sea can where the beer was to drink the rest of our booze. Of course, you know, that starts one case and then two. So, we proceeded to take a couple of cases and then a couple more people showed up on the scene. There goes a couple of cases, and all of a sudden everyone is hanging out in boxer shorts and drinking every fucking drop of alcohol in this trailer. We put all the empties in a blown-up tank hull and the next day whole fuckin Company had a hangover. The OC was not an idiot; no questions came his way, and no one really investigated too closely, and I think it was good for us. The 2 beer rule is stupid.

There was a lot of gambling to pass the time in Kabul. There was a lot of card playing, and we tried to limit it—no more than 20 bucks a night. And yet, guys came back from tour Owing money. Some guys gambled away all of their tour pay. We had to sort out debts at home, and some spouses were not happy.

_____

Then we had this one private in the platoon. He can impersonate anybody but his favourite thing was with Arnold Schwarzenegger. He was really good for morale. He would take your money in poker and do it while acting in a different persona that he was impersonating. The Warrant liked this kid so much due to his humour he moved him to Headquarters and had him do impersonations over the radio in the vehicle! These small things are important for morale.

_____

We had one guy who had brought a tattoo kit with him and I could do tattoos and as I was in charge, I got asked if we could tattoo ourselves and of course, I didn't say no to homegrown tattoos. I went to the pre-med Physician's Assistant, checked it out and made sure we followed the rules to do jailhouse tats. It was it was pretty bad. Lots of bad choices. This one troop told me I could do whatever tattoo I wanted. Back in high school, I used to draw flying Penis' everywhere. That was my signature tag. So, given the choice, I tattoo a flying penis on the back of his calf. He liked it and then he sent a picture to his wife, and she lost it. I was pretty sad to cover over the proud flying penis.

_____

One of the best-planned missions of our time in Kandahar was stealing beer. When we came back into KAF after about 2 months out, we realized that we wouldn't be part of the "two beer per man" issue that those in KAF got for Canada Day or Christmas. Like, we knew that there were all these occasions that all the KAFites were going to get these pints knew we were never going to get them. We figured in a backwards way that we were entitled to the beer we were just missing out on by not being in camp. We basically sat down and talked through it like a mission; We had this little whiteboard drawing of what we would need to consider, and we drew where we would have observation, security and the "assault" force. The first thing was to understand where the target was. There were hundreds of sea cans, and only one had beer. We went and spoke to a clerk that we knew. I started as a joke, but she was happy to chat about it. I asked

"Do you know where this beer is?"

She says, "I 100% know what it is."

Like a kid, I was so excited, and we struck a deal. For the cost of 1 Six pack, we secured confirmation of where the target was. We established two "stalled vehicles" as early warning on the approaches to the target area, then put a guy up in overwatch to get eyes on the sea can. We connected by using our Personal role radios.. When security was set, and there was no movement, we breached through the chain link fence which had a tear in it and brought along some bolt cutters. We were like little kids, but this was all done with complete seriousness, and the mission was on. We got to the Sea can and cracked the lock. I looked in, and man, it was FULL. I was just intending to grab enough so we could each have 2 beers.

My buddy looks at me and says, "I'm not risking my career for four cases of beer." Let's grab 6 or 8. The number of beers made the theft better in some way. So, there we are, piling these things in the back of a little bongo truck that was used around KAF to move things. We had a Ranger blanket. We throw over the top. And drive through KAF with only the Ranger Blanket covering our heist. We went to see the Kitchen Officer and got some ice; pretty ballsy, just a garbage bag of ice. That was it; we were set. Mission complete. Now, we had to consume it safely and get rid of the evidence. It started as just six guys just going to have some beers. As the night moved on, everyone started having a good time. We had all sorts filtering through of all ranks. I think people just needed a break, and we weren't doing anything bad; we were just having a couple of beers, having a shower, and heading back out in the next 48-hour window. The next morning, we were all good, but We had like half a case of beer left. We also had three garbage bags empties. The garbage was proof that, if left unattended, would get us in shit. So, we went to the American SOF compound and asked if they wanted a half case of Canadian beer. Yeah, they were like, "fucking right, we do." So, they took care of the empties and other party garbage. So, they took these 12 cans of beer. We got rid of three garbage bags, and the MPs received some reports but never found anything as we had already headed back out to the field. No doubt it was wrong. Now, as I look back 20 years later, I wouldn't have done it now, but as a twenty-something, out of combat for 48 hours and then heading back in, I don't think I would have changed anything.

I think we certainly changed after we took a lot of losses. We were different at that point. We certainly didn't hesitate to shoot to kill and there was at a certain level of I didn't really fucking care all that much. Like rules and risk aversion were gone, if we needed to make it happen, we could. I didn't care. We were eating rations all the time, and I realized the troops would get some morale from some fresh food. Even if we were out in the field. I went through official channels and got nothing. No BBQs for troops forward, just enough for the folks in KAF. We had to go into KAF one time to refit the LAVs with something and I said, fuck it, man, let's steal some fucking barbecues and bring them out with us. Get the guys some chow. So, we did a little recce on camp and found where there were some BBQs. Maybe they were for contractors or PSP, who knows? They were chained up and we broke in and we stole the barbecues while other guys scavenged meat and chips for our feast downrange. I think it was KBR staff barbecue. So we rolled back to Sperwan Ghar and we had a barbecue. It was a big deal because there were no warm fresh rations at the time. What I did not know was that that same night the Chief of Defence, Rick Hillier was visiting. He came to our BBQ. It was funny because he said, "This isn't so bad isn't so bad, BBQ in the desert!". I should have told him that he was eating off stolen BBQs and scrounged food.

———————

You can't discuss relaxing in the army without recognizing that groups of young (primarily) men in an isolated environment will turn to adult entertainment at some point. There is supposed to be no fraternization; frankly, there is not much opportunity. So doing the scene with a magazine is what is really left to take the edge off. People talk about the army going to digital warfare and high-tech killing in Afghanistan, but I think the biggest digital change to soldiering was how troops consumed their skin mags. There were plenty of magazines going on in Afghanistan, over the decade of rotations those magazines were harder to come by and troops were going digital. It was a digital divide between generations, the Sgts and Majors had magazines and the troops were on their computers and sharing "files". I think that is something that should be studied. I am not even sure if MAXIM or STUFF exists anymore, not that they are porn but they were the magazines were everywhere. I don't know if that "skin mag" culture exists anymore. Glossy pictures of pin-ups hanging up in the Observation Post over your machine gun ammo. Like something out of World War 2. As an Ode to that old pin-up culture, the war artist, Sylvia Picota painted, these pictures of women in combat shirts or just wrapped in the Canadian flag, they were super popular and were given output as postcards and bookmarks to the troops. With the shift in society, I am pretty sure that won't happen again. Anyway, it was seven months of imposed celibacy, and troops needed to release the pressure in some ways.

———————

We were in this position surrounded by Marijuana fields. We had heavy contact for the months of September and October; as we got into November, things slowed down, and my section was fascinated with how we may remove the marijuana fields to avoid letting the enemy get close to our position. As a project in downtime, one of the guys grabbed some spare lumber and made a trebuchet. No shit, a full-sized trebuchet that could fling stuff off the hill we were on into the surrounding area. As if LAVs, M777, and all the guns we had weren't enough, this crazy bastard built a trebuchet. We started practicing with rocks, and when we successfully tried some water bottles, one of the guys in the section suggested we try making Molotov cocktails and that perhaps it would burn down the marijuana plants around us. It was not well thought through, but we gave it a go and successfully tested burning Molotov cocktails in the open area surrounding the hill. The trebuchet bombs landed effectively, flying 100 to 200m outside our perimeter, but the plants did not catch, and once it drew the attention of a senior NCO who saw the routine, he put an end to it and ensured we used our time more productively. Still, it was pretty cool, a working flaming Trebuchet!

It was crazy that the army wanted you to be celibate for 7 months. Think of that in everyday terms. No sex, seven months, no physical intimacy. We were doing these tours every 12 to 18 months. I think it fucked with our mojo. On my second tour, I developed a relationship with a medic who had been out in the FOB with us. Nothing ever happened when we were out in the field. Not only would that be unprofessional, but probably gross, as we didn't shower for weeks on end. When we went back into KAF we would hang out and talk about all the shit that we were doing, She had to work on all the casualties, it was hard work. I was in the infantry and those guys were my friends. We kind of connected as humans. We were both single, both in this situation, but it was not allowed and we could have gotten in big trouble. We would sneak moments alone and sometimes she would sneak us into the bison ambulance or MIR when the door could be locked. I don't regret it. I also don't think we were the only ones doing it. My platoon Commander called it the "Red Cross fever", as many of the medics and docs were female and most of the Infantry was male. He felt that if we did an investigation, this fever would decimate the ranks of the medical and Infantry corps and make us combat ineffective. He was probably right; I can't imagine this was the only war where this kind of thing happened.

No one patrolled on their birthday in our company. The OC didn't anybody dying on their birthday. So, it was like dry humour but important. Your Birthday was a day off. You know, this is just how we deal with things.

––––––––––––

The platoon had to secure the Canadian Embassy in Kabul. The British and Dutch embassies had come under threat, and the Canadian Ambassador's vehicle had been hit by an IED. There was an increased threat that the Canadian Embassy would come under attack. As the three embassies were close to each other, we partnered with the Ghurkas, these awesome UK troops from Nepal. It was a necessary but tough gig. It was long, boring hours, and essentially, we were providing guard duties and deterrence in a pretty secure sector. It was winter in Kabul, and so the weather was shit. It was a change of routine, but it was not an awesome task. The Ambassador, Chris Alexander, was a good guy. He was pretty down to earth, did not want to wear body armour, and wore these big rubber boots when walking around Kabul. Seeing such a civilian approach was a sight when we had to wear all our battle rattle when we left the camp. He was the Ambassador, so what did we know? It was a particularly crap night one night. Cold rain and a stiff wind added to the chill of the altitude. There was no way to stay dry and you got to warm up when not on your shift by hopping in the LAV and hugging the heater. So, we were sitting in there pretty wet and miserable when the back door swung open, and the Ambassador stuck his head into our LAV. He was pretty cheery and asked how we were doing; we exchanged pleasantries, and then he produced this massive Pizza box out of nowhere. Awesome, we had been living on hard rations. It was the weirdest pizza. He told us it was made by a local Kabul joint. There wasn't much cheese; it had peas, goat meat, some type of sauce that was not tomato, corn, and a bunch of other weird stuff. But the crust was awesome, like the local Naan, and it was piping hot. So good for morale. Weird Kabul pizza on a cold night. There is no bad pizza, even weird pizza is good pizza. The Ambassador made our night.

––––––––––––

Sense of Humour should be a principle of war. I appreciated when guys got creative to keep it light. I was a staff weenie in the HQ. At the time it was not all digital and we were still running mapboards in the C.P. at the time. We would have pins with various callsigns marked on them and we would move them around the board indicating where the units are. On one of the other shifts,

I think started reporting about the superweapon. They created a pin that said S.W. Every day they would move this pin all around the board in different spots. At the same time, we had a reserve officer who was very detail-oriented and didn't seem to grasp the battle or what was going on. He became a liaison officer to the regional command hierarchy and was responsible for reporting Battle Group activities. So, he would come in and he would look at the map or he'd get a brief from the duty officers and then he would go and brief at higher headquarters. So, everyone knew what each element was doing. So, he started a briefing at higher headquarters on the "Sierra Whiskey" callsign, which was the imaginary ghost secret weapon pin. We never corrected him or told him what SW stood for and just continued to move that around the map. Lighten the mood a little bit, knowing that this guy was going in and briefing higher headquarters on a call sign that didn't exist anyway. In retrospect, it's very irresponsible. And I hope that we didn't call off fires on a high-value target because they thought that a friendly force was in the area. But at the time it was hilarious. I still have the "SW" pin. Reminds me to confirm all the info that I get briefed.

We were back in KAF for 48 hours. Some maintenance or something. That night there was a knock on my door. My roommate answers as I am out cold. One of my troops is there and says "Wake up the platoon commander there is O Group, the boss needs him for orders." This was not strange, so I pulled myself out of bed and followed one of my Cpls to where the OGrp was, but we weren't heading to the HQ. He told me the orders were just in this room, very hush-hush. So, I follow, we get to the room and he opens it up and there are my troops, drinking beer, some medics that had been out with us were there and seemed pretty close to the troops. Initially, I was confused and then a lightbulb went off. They had scammed some beer, were having an illegal troop party and had invited me to it. It was either a high compliment or super devious because now I was implicated and if I reported it, I would have to charge like my whole platoon. Fuck. Well, I appreciated it either way. So, I dove in, drank a couple of beers, bullshitted about the tour, and we healed a little bit. Things had not been easy. We had been in our first sustained combat, lost friends, faced mortality, and were about to go out and do it again. It seemed that these stupid rules about drinking beer that were designed for the folks who lived in KAF all the time were out of place for us. I am probably justifying the fact that I did the wrong thing, but there was no harm done. We had a good time. No one was hurt, and everyone was ready to go back out 24 hours later. I think it was worth it and it made us a better unit out in the field

Christmas came and we had been out doing an operation. Nothing significant occurred. Christmas Eve went down into Wilson because some V.I.P.s were flying in to see us. We knew the chief of defence staff, General Hillier, was gonna come see us. I remember his helicopter landing and he jumped out. He was instantly recognizable as the chief. Always a happy guy. Good for Morale. And then I remember seeing this brand-new raincoat and I figured it was Some wogs from KAF coming out to do little battlefield tours, and I focused on this guy's haircut. This guy is like the least military person I've ever seen. He was in desperate need of a haircut. I was embittered that this guy coming out to see the soldiers and he looked like that. But there was something off with his uniform also, and it didn't quite fit right, as I look more closely, it's fuck'n Rick Mercer. So that was awesome, Rick Mercer and Rick Hillier! He spent as much time as he had to talk to all the soldiers. They all wanted to talk to him and shake his hands. He picked up on some jokes oriented at the leadership from the troops and started to kind of get the hang of it and did a great job of an impromptu comedy act with various silly things that had occurred in the last couple of weeks. So though that was fun. Then one of our Master Corporals got called up by the Chief of Defence, and "Uncle" Rick, tells this guy that he had met his wife at a spouse's day in Petawawa. She had kissed him on the cheek and asked if the General could pass this on to my husband if you saw him in Kandahar. He kept his word and he went right over and kissed the Master Corporal on the cheek in front of all of us. That made all of our day right there. Merry Christmas with Rick and Rick! Pretty sweet.

So I went on leave, but just after we were attacked by our strongpoint and took some losses. In order to reconstitute, We were sent down to Spin Boldak. In addition, one section plus myself went on leave which was not ideal to put the team back together. So Spin was pretty quiet and the guys did a good job of getting people to recover and get back into the saddle. As a part of this, the Warrant Officer decided to boost morale by allowing Hawaiian shirts to be worn throughout the strong point. Even on duty. So it would be combat pants on the bottom and Hawaiian goodness up to. Like something out of MASH. It was strange but it worked. The guys chilled out a bit, they were ready to get back into the routine after their "vacation" in Spin Boldak. I remember being blown away when I got back, but then realized it was an unconventional effort that was getting the platoon back in shape.

KAF was like grand theft auto. It was a giant base and everything that was spread apart by Kms. Those folks that worked on the base full-time, had bikes or if they were privileged had duty vehicles to get themselves around. We did not have any of it, because we lived out of KAF in the field and only came in for ramp ceremonies when we lost someone or the occasional shower. We were left to hike it around camp and when you only have a couple of hours in, you don't want to waste time. So, We would steal cars, usually senior officers or senior NCOs, we figured out how to hotwire these cars or they left the keys in them so they would always be ready to go…so we would take them and then leave them in other places of the camp, no fucks given because we were gone before we could get caught and would not be back in for months. They would always find their car later, but Fuck'em if they can't take a joke, they got to do Afghanistan in KAF, have Timmies, good food and the gym, so I feel like it evened out.

One of the platoons was pretty, bored and disgruntled with being in the camp so much doing security and a lot of extracurricular stuff. There was a dude from the Hungarian contingent who had a tattoo gun and so would do jailhouse tats in the tent lines. There was a big lineup of guys getting tattoos all the time until the Hungarians got shut down by the medics because of the potential for hepatitis C. Really it just went underground. In the camp, life was really relaxed and where there are multinational contingents there is booze that is not accounted for. Not all Countries are as tea-totalling as Canada. So, the troops would sneak off to the other areas of the camp and have some drinks. I remember one of those nights drinking, the guys said it would be a great idea for multinational confidence if we drove their vehicles. The other guys thought was a great idea. So, with beer in hand, we grabbed an old T64 tank and took it for a rip within the camp lines. Not only were we drunk, not qualified, or any other number of things, but we also did not get caught. That was the most important thing. I always felt like if we didn't drive shit underground, it would be better for everyone. But as a 20-year-old soldier the story, "Remember that time I got drunk and drove a tank in Kabul" is cool.

We had a lot of mice problems in the COP and no entertainment. Where mice are, snakes follow, so we wanted to get rid of the mice and it became an all-out battle. We would set mouse ambushes at night and see how many we could get. We lay out a little food and a shitload of traps and then turn off all the lights and watch with our night vision goggles. all of sudden you hear that snap as the trap catches a rat or a mouse, and another one, and we are cheering like we have just won a hockey game, all of sudden the door opens and the officer flicks on the light to see what was going on. We are all shocked and blinded in our NVGS by the light, he is shocked as there he observes 4 weirdos in NVGS, so many traps, dead mice, and just chaos. "You guys are fucked." That is all he said and left us to it, closing the door behind him.

––––––––––

Some dudes figured out where all the beer was stored. Real being the ingenious types they just started pilfering the beers so they would have a stash. This went on for several fucking weeks. I'm not sure if the civilian managers in the camps just don't do stocktaking regularly or what the deal was or if maybe someone in the PSP side of the house had been skimming off the top in terms of beers, but it got to the point where every bed space within that camp had a flat beer under it. I enjoyed my illegal beer but always wondered why it was never reported because it was hundreds of beers. It was like "too big to fail" maybe and not worth the heartache and investigation. It likely would have made the whole Task Force ineffective as I think everyone would have had to have been charged for having illegal beer. It was nice to have a cold beer though.

––––––––––

We're operating out of KAF at the end of the tour and bored soldiers get in shit. It had been a long tour and we had taken a lot of casualties. There's a flavour of Listerine that looks a lot like rye whiskey, the brown Listerine. So, somebody got a bottle of "Listerine" in a care package, and they were sharing it amongst some of them and two of my soldiers ended up completely like blackout drunk puking all over the place. So, they show up the next morning and they were all fucked up smelling of booze and Sergeant was like well, you're the section 2ic, you're in charge of discipline so, handle it. I figure, cool. You guys were drunk, I didn't get drunk, so look, I need you to go from here, to the CQ compound which was on one side of KAF and then the maintenance compound was on another part of KAF, and then the big QM which is another part of KAF. Probably 6 to 10 km of walking. I need a bushel of rags from QM, like a hay bail size thing of rags, so we can clean up the LAVs to do the handover. So go get me the bushel of rags from

QM. You have 20 minutes. So, they're running across KAF to get this bushel of rags and then they have to run back. So now they're all hungover and they're running in the heat with this bushel of rags to come back. Cool, I need you to go to the maintenance compound and they have the big spools of wire. There's an empty spool of that and the CQ wants it, they're going to turn it into a table so go get that and bring it back here. It is about a hundred pounds and awkward as fuck. They have 20 minutes. They run off to get the thing and now they're rolling this big spool down the road, all the way back and then turn it into the CQ. The CQ didn't want it and the CQ told them to throw it in the dumpster. Then I send them to the big QM for another 20-minute run. They come back and they're all fucked up and I'm like, is all the booze out of you now? Yes, master corporal. Ok, good. Sometimes a charge is not the answer.

We generally patrolled in the morning to sweep the routes for IEDs and there were always a few guys that had to rotate other Guys to stay back to keep security, if they stayed back, it was their job to make breakfast. So, every morning, we get up, give orders, and then roll out, and you come back to bacon and eggs. That was our main routine. We lived in this old Afghan mud compound. My bedroom slash office was a shitty Afghan Hut and the roof of my hut was also the security checkpoint. So this one morning the ceiling to my place opened up and this surprised Afghan that had been standing guard fell through our ceiling and landed on our coffee table. There wasn't much to do other than patrol, improve defences, sleep, and report. When we did have downtime, we had like 2 DVDs and the continuous viewing of Will Farrell's "stepbrothers "movie. It was on continuously up to a point where the guys could recite the entire movie, and everything had a Stepbrother reference. "Haha, that's so funny, last time I heard that joke I laughed so hard I fell off my Dinosaur." I still don't understand why everyone doesn't find Stepbrothers hilarious. I am scarred for life.

I think we just more or less stuck to ourselves when we were back in KAF. In fact, at first, I would try to go back routinely at the start of the tour, and then about halfway through the tour, I would avoid KAF like the plague. I would only go back if I was ordered to. You just felt that sense of not fitting in when you went back. It wasn't an us or them thing. You just had a hard time living like we did, where every step matters and then trying to come to terms with a whole population like an hour away that had never even really seen Afghanistan. When you're out there, the troops would say "Oh, it would be great to get back to KAF and get a pizza" and then we get back to KAF, they'd say, "I can't wait to get back to the FOB and get the fuck out of this place." So, I think we just kept ourselves and did our own thing. When I did have to go back, it was never for more than 24 hours. It just came to be a place that we didn't enjoy and everybody much preferred staying out in the "farm" and doing our own thing within the company. KAF was supposed to be restful and relaxed, but we didn't know the rules and it ended up being stressful. We had these little quirky things that were going on in the company that people just started doing. When we were in Wilson, two of the platoons decided that they were going to form the bicycle gangs and one of them called themselves the "mustachioes", and their logo was Plato's moustache. Funny shit. All these bikes kept popping up in Wilson. I finally asked the sergeant major, where are all these bikes coming from? He told me that when the platoons were returning to KAF, they were stealing bikes, putting them in the LAVs, and bringing them back into the FOB. So, there were like 30 bikes and guys were driving bikes around the FOB after they patrolled and just messing around doing tricks, like the teenagers they were. We had a FOB newspaper called the Wilson Freeholder and a corporal, one of the snipers, was the editor he wrote and people would contribute articles. He wrote a couple of articles about things that he would do, very quirky things like, and try to find out what was the best shitter in the FOB. He had a set of criteria where he'd taken a piss or if you are taking a shit and he would do all these criteria in every shitter and have a score. He determined which one was the best one. Like a yelp rating of the FOB shitters. Every Saturday morning, we get up and guys had like four little mailboxes that he would go around to and deliver before the sun rose. No one escaped his pen. It was hilarious. It was great for morale and though it likely would have been frowned on, the guys could support each other after tough days. I think that even though there were few creature comforts that is why guys liked to chill in the FOB instead of KAF.

———————

I remember my warrant. We've just finished a TIC and were chilling out. He took off his helmet. He was leaning up against a tree like old NCOs do, looking hard as fuck and he was crushed in a butt and a fuckin sniper round hit just above his head. He dropped like a sack of shit. He looked all frazzled and I have never seen him move so fast. It was a single shot, not followed up with any more fire. I remember laughing at him because he fucked up. After all, he took off his helmet while crushing a butt. It was so strange that was funny, he just got lower, lit another butt, and told us to go fuck ourselves.

The difference between Kabul and Kandahar was shocking for downtime. In Kabul, I got so fit. The routine was regular. You did your shift or patrol, you ate great food, you got good sleep and you worked out like a fiend. I was incredibly fit at the end. Kandahar fucked me. Downtime was like sleeping, eating or cleaning your weapon. There was no routine really other than patrolling, seeking out the enemy and fighting. You improved your position or did something that was good for the team. Personal goals were not a thing. The food was hard rations and you were combat fit, but not a beach body. The food was high in salt, sugar and calories. You were stressed all the time. It was so interesting to see the difference between the tours.

There is always downtime, and so the strangest things evolve as important when you have no TV and no way to talk to home and you are living out of a LAV for weeks at a time. One of the boys brought a hacky sack. We would get super serious about keeping it up. Think of soldiers in body armour out in the middle of a desert trying to keep a hacky sack up like kids in a schoolyard. We did the hacky sack for a while and then we get bored, we did stupid competitions Let's just see how far we can throw things with our fucking "off" hands. I have this video of us looking like a bunch of goofballs trying to launch rocks or their left hand. So funny and at the time so good for us, but not sure anyone else would understand, it was nice to just have fun, whatever it was for a couple of minutes.

We are in the field right after a major fight, and the Driver lets me know that he is not feeling very good. feeling very good. Like he's like he's kind of messed up and almost fell over and off the vehicle. You realize he was actually super messed up. We went to the medics and put him on an I.V. drip. He's like pretty messed up. But we drove the LAV back into Kandahar Airfield that day. So, in his up messed up state, he drove us for 40 minutes through Taliban country like, mega messed up. He is sick with something. He goes to ground when we get in, and I take it out to do maintenance as we have been driving them hard for over a month. The next day I'm taking the LAV around by myself, the sausage factory of all the techs, Fire Control Systems, Optics, communications, hull techs…so much technical shit in modern armoured vehicles. You know, just to get the vehicle back up and running again. Then we had a company smoker before returning to the field. And, you know, we're doing the whole, like, the two beer per man thing, but not it's not REALLY two beer per man; it is two beer per man across the company, and there are a lot of guys that don't drink, so I drank theirs. I find I find myself a little drunk at this point. I go back to the shacks to like get smokes. I realize my sick driver is still down and out. He is wrapped in an Arctic sleeping bag in 40-degree Afghan heat. There was a half-eaten burger from the mess hall beside him, and he looked pale and emaciated and really messed up. I'm like, really shit, man. Like, we should actually get you to the role 3 right now. But we can't talk to anyone because we are drunk, so we have to try and be stealthy, or else we will get in trouble. We commandeer this minivan, way too drunk to drive, and we pile him in the back there, take him to the role Three medical centres, and, basically, dump him at the doorstep because we did not want anyone to see how drunk we were and we were driving. We kind of leave him there. The next day, we did our Admin, and the Doctors kept him in for observation, and we acted surprised he was in the hospital. He didn't remember anything. We left, and he joined us in the field a few days later. He's like 15 pounds lighter, but otherwise pretty healthy looking. You know, the colour and come back, and we ask, what happened, man? We all thought that you were not taking your malaria pills, and that's what's wrong with you. But now you're better. He said they never told him what was wrong; he was really, really sick, and then I got better. He was fine for the rest of the tour. So, a year later, we're back in Canada. and he gets called into the MIR (Medical Centre) are like literally a year later. They ran blood work, and the last test they did, just by chance, was for Scorpion venom, and it came up positive! He had been stung by a scorpion that day, and I just didn't know. He still doesn't know that we dumped him like an abandoned baby and ran because we were drunk. At least it all ended well.

We had this troop named Spanky. He had this nickname because he was a chronic masturbator. He was 19 years old, and I think he would sometimes do it 4 or 5 times a day. So, one day he had headed up to the OP at MSG, and he was in there just fucking going to town. The Sergeant Major unknowingly thought he would take this time to visit the OPs in the middle of the day and walk in on Spanky, pants around his ankles, body armour on and helmet "on duty," observing his arcs…. Sergeant Maj lost his mind, and we thought it was pretty funny; we could hear him getting jacked up for jacking off all the way down the hill. But in the end, it was bad for all of us as the Sergeant Major ordered all the porn mags out of the fucking OP.

Working with my interpreters, we had a scheme where I'd trade them a few cans of Rip It Energy drink for fresh kabobs. So, every Wednesday, kabob got these like really good go-to lamb kabobs in a pita or flatbread.

---

56 days, 56 days without a shower. We were pretty stoked to get back in at the end of it. Get back in and get some Burger King or whatever. But I remember being like, pretty well, really busy the first time. I had all that maintenance done on the vehicles and weapons. It was so strange coming from the field and having to put up with KAF bullshit like " wear your hat all the time". You know, get your boots bloused… It's all kind of annoying, and I hated the garrison setting when just on the other side of the wire, things were about business, not bullshit… I remember being stoked the first time I went back into KAF and then a second time, and I don't really care, and then like, you know, the third time, eventually you get in the KAF once a month. Eventually, we're all like, I don't want to go to KAF anymore, just stay in the field where we don't have 'FOBBITS" fucking with us all the time. The green beans and Burger King were not worth the Bullshit.

I think it was halfway through the tour. The Transformers movie had just come out. My LAV Sergeant got a package from his wife, and it was like a full fuckin Bumblebee helmet. So, my LAV Sergeant had this fucking thing out and was wearing it as we were leaving on patrol. He saluted the vehicle with the helmet on and the Major came over the fucking radio. "tell Optimus Prime to put on his proper kit."

Chawl Ghor had one cook. Masum Ghar had a kitchen. So, we cooked our own food pretty much. We go to the Masum Ghar and we get frozen food. We were able to have two big freezers in camp. It was really good food. The cook was he was amazing. All he wanted to do was make sure the guys were fed. Whenever something happened or there was a late patrol, he would make sure there was food. I remember we responded to a chopper being shot down, and we were out there for hours, securing casualties and equipment. We came back at about 2:00 in the morning. When we came back, could smell food. He made chicken cordon blue while we were out on the scene... And we came back. He had chicken cordon blue for everybody. It forced us all to sit down and enjoy the food and talk. I think it was really good for the guys. Food is warmth and morale. That cook was amazing.

We had to establish Laagers or waiting positions out in the desert, no shade, just baking in the hot sun. Some days it was as warm as 55 degrees. We stayed there, and we waited for the Op to start; we called it Operation Camel Spider. Cause the camel spiders chase the shade. We would lay beside the vehicle in the shade until the sun moved, and then we would all move around the vehicle on the clock, trying to stay in the shade and stay as cool as possible. It was crazy. That vehicle was home to 10 guys for 6 months. Operation Camel Spider is funny shit, but that shade made us psychologically feel better, even if it wasn't really any cooler.

There's a picture of me listening to Da Rude's song "Sandstorm" during a sandstorm with these headphones on, dancing out in the mortar pit during that time. I had loaded Sandstorm on my iPod, and as the tour went on and we had sandstorms, I thought, why not? So, one day, it was raining, and then we got a warning of the incoming sandstorm. So, there I am with my stupid little goggles on, my rain poncho on, out there dancing, listening to da rude it was fucking crazy, like literally screaming into the storm. In the end, I had to run into the house because I was about to get blown away. There is a video of this stupidity but the music is in my earphones. It looks like I am crazy, man. Dancing to nothing. Maybe I was a little touched, like something out of a movie, but it was pretty fun.

I had to return to Canada to give a report for the first couple of months on the mission and talk to the incoming guys. It is a whirlwind; still jet lagged, you fly back in your uniform. I got business class for my guys for the first leg. We're sitting in the back row of business class in comes Tom Cochrane Behind him was Rick Mercer. I figure they must be flying over to see the troops because it is Christmas. You know you are never sure when you see a famous person if it is really them, so I give a "talking to Americans bit" as Rick Mercer used to have that on his show about how little the old US of A knew about Canada… Without missing a beat, he immediately starts talking to me. Then he settles in and hangs out with the guys. He's a great guy and Tom Cochrane figured out what was going on and came right back to visit also. His grandfather, if I am not mistaken, was a World War 2 or in Korea pilot. They did photos with us and were just awesome. We all get into Kabul for Christmas. I think it was a big concert. Rick Mercer hosted the whole event, and Tom Cochrane and his band played all their hits. For me, very powerful memories. I hear those Tom Cochrane songs. It brings your head to that one place and time. Both are great Canadians. It felt great to be acknowledged by other Canadians when you are doing a tough thing. Meant the world to us that they came and that they were good dudes

---

I was working in the CQ, and the boys were out on a four-day dismounted Op. Get resupplied by chopper. So, we were doing things like sling loads for water, ammo and in food. There was a Tim Hortons on Camp and I had not handed out the donut coupons for anyone in camp as I was saving them for when the troops came back in. So there were 114 on the op; I used 114 coupons for one hundred fourteen donuts. So, I put it up in the middle of the ammo, where I knew the Platoon WOs would get them. Later, one of the guys tells me in amongst the ammo in the sling load, I saw Tim Horton's boxes, and he thought he was fucking seeing shit. I mean it seemed to come out of nowhere. So that was great morale that the guys out there fighting all day getting to sit down and eat fucking Tim Horton's donuts. I know it is not a big deal, but after I got wounded, I felt like I wanted to contribute somehow, so this was a nice way to let the boys know we were thinking of them. Even in the fight, a little downtime is important to fill up your cup.

I was part of the theatre activation team in Kabul. We had to set up all the camps for the Battle Group and so there was nothing. We lived in these ratty Mod tents with no TV and no radio, so we had to make our own fun on downtime. It was so hot in the summertime, like 55 degrees in the shade. So we started some weird competitions. One of them was we would heat Orange Crush cans on the top of the tent while we were working. The aluminum can was so hot that it would burn your hand when you grabbed it. Have you ever had a hot Orange Crush? It is disgusting. It is warm and sticky and the syrup would congeal inside the can in the extreme heat, and that was the point. It was like a weird eating contest. You had to grab a hot can of Crush, crack it, try and down it, grab a melting chocolate bar, and slide it out of the package into your mouth. I had to do a cycle of the Mars bar and then down a super-hot can of Orange Crush. Whoever could do the most was the winner. There were a lot of sore bellies and some throwing up due to sugar overload. Pretty funny but harmless and good for morale. So, it was like a lot of small things like that. When you have nothing, weird things take on a greater importance.

———————————

We were working 20 hours on patrol and 4 hours for battle procedure and rest. The pace was punishing but necessary during high-intensity periods. I was constantly on the move. Any sleep I got was always interrupted and irregular, as we slept during the day when it was 55 degrees. One day, I returned from orders, and after I did my brief, I said I would grab some kip. The Senior NCOs directed me around the corner near a Texas barrier and there was an Afghan steel frame bed with rope strung out to hold an old mattress. They had found it in a nearby compound while rehearsing and brought it back for me. Around the bed they had arrayed some fans all directed around my bed to cool the area down. I looked at them in disbelief. They smiled and let me know it wasn't because they liked me but because they needed me to have enough sleep to make good choices, so they had set up this area to sleep. I laughed and immediately crashed. It was the best sleep (for about 2 hours) I have ever had!

———————————

We had some beer at the end of the tour. It was mandated only two beers per person. But of course, if there is a way for a Canadian soldier to figure out to get more they will. We had been out in the field for 6 months, so they saw no harm in getting a beer or two extra. The beer was at tables divided by sub-units so you sign your name to a list and get two beers. The guys would go to their own rifle company for their own 2 beers and then rotate to another table to get more. It was just a signing sheet, so they went to every table. The folks doing assurance were civilian PSP and so didn't know who was in a unit or not. But anyway, long story short, with all the extra beer the boys acquired, there was more beer consumed than there should have been. This logistics Captain compiled a big list together and realized that many names were repeated on each list. If she cross-referenced these lists, she would catch a whole bunch of guys that had snuck extra beer. Like it was her defining moment on the tour to get all these guys. So, a buddy of mine, who worked in HQ as a storeman, heard about this investigation, knew the lists were only on paper, and knew where she was keeping them. When she stepped out of the office. He went into the office, took the list, and burned all the nominal rolls. The lists were just a historical record of who had drunk beer, so were not protected. I don't know what happened after, but no one ever got in trouble for an extra beer after 7 months in the combat.

I was at DCO for November 11th, and we're still in contact with the enemy. I prepared a Remembrance Day message that I read on the combat net radio. It was so far from the parades and the dress uniforms. Everyone was dirty, living in holes, and fighting every day. I think the guys liked still taking that moment of remembrance. By that point, I think we were at just over twenty KIA and a couple of hundred wounded on the tour. It was our generation they're our friends now.

We pissed off our Platoon 2IC. I think he hated the Spice Girls, or maybe his kids always listened to them. Anyway, he had some connection to them. I found out that quite a few of the soldiers in our headquarters within the platoon, like all of them, knew pretty much all the words to Spice Girl songs. We would serenade the old 2IC at night, which was probably the gesture that most made me feel at home. Just messing with him in a fun way. The troops were so good, I remember that I came back from my third security shift, and I went to get into my sleeping bag, and it was made up. Someone had made it up to look like a high-end hotel, like a bed with a little mint on a makeshift pillow. That was nice, made me feel connected and accepted. They could have been doing bad things to my bed space.

When we were in Kabul, there was Canex, a little store of stuff from Canada, and you had the drinking mess where you could have 2 beers a day after work was done. I feel like there were more discipline issues in Kabul than later on when we were fighting in Kandahar. Or maybe just different ones. Soldiers will always find themselves in some kind of mischief. Alcohol is the big one. We had this sea container, and I can't remember the name of the beer, but a company sent over a Sea container full of free beer. So, we had beer cards. You have to get your beer card punched every time you have a beer. The PSP staff working the bar would punch cards and sometimes not punch cards if they liked you. It was relatively controlled. They always took the beer from this one sea container and, at the end of the night, returned it to the same container. After a couple of weeks, the troops figured out what sea container it was, and one night they forgot to lock it. When the folks came in the following morning, the sea container was empty and the troops emptied it. There was nothing in there. Cardboard boxes and no cans. The camp's Sergeant Major was not happy. He turned the camp upside down, looking for the beer and the culprits. Launching threats in every direction. No one ever found the beer or the guilty parties. The troops are pretty crafty.

We started moving into the objective areas at night and surprising the Taliban at first light. As the Company was getting ready, I would always have a case of the nerves, and I would really get up for departure at two or three in the morning. I could never sleep. The crew rigged the speakers in the back of the Lav, and he would put on the music, and we would play cards. So, the TAC HQ crew was just sitting there and playing euchre. It became kind of a pre-game ritual for us. Before every company thing it was just my crew at the time. People would be banging on the LAV doors to tell us to turn the music down. It was mindless but seemed to focus us and relax us before we had to go get after it. I will never forget those card games. We lost some of those soldiers, and I always think of them sitting around in the back of a dark LAV playing Euchre and bullshitting.

There were some interesting points of levity. I do remember one instance where they'd come up with a huge decree that no longer was the soldiers going to be able to have energy drinks. There was the Saudi knockoff of Red Bull. It was like a black and silver can with Arabic writing on it. The troops used to call it liquid crack cocaine. This big decree comes out, and there is there's overwhelming disdain from the soldiers. I went to the Doc. I said, What's the deal? And he's like, Well medical opinion is that it is not good for us. They're not sending us any more of it. I said, Okay, well, the troops kind of want it. They like it. It keeps them up. It keeps them focused when they're trying to stay focused on the task at hand. Even if it is bullshit, I would rather not be arguing about it halfway through the tour. He nodded and brought me to a sea can in the yard of the FOB. We had three of these things stacked to the back roof with cans of this Red Bull knockoff. I said, All right, don't tell anyone. And so for the rest of the tour, we were fine. The troops had their drinks and I didn't have to hear about it. I am sure we were wrong medically, but sometimes the psychological effect of something is important, the troops had so little. Don't take away one of the few things they liked. Save the restriction for the next rotation so that you won't miss it.

One day, I got back from an extended recon mission on the outskirts of Kabul, and I could tell someone had been sleeping in my bed. Like Goldilocks and the Three Bears. Apparently, troops were rotating out and had too much beer one night. The PSP manager is trying to shut it down. I guess the MPs show up. The MPs started chasing them. So instead of returning to their tents, no one would get caught while they were drunk. So crashed in our tent to sleep it off. The MPs needed to prove they were drunk, so they just hung out until it was out of their system. They lived in our tent for 48 hours. As they were going home, they had no timings to report. They came to see us as they were leaving and explained all this. I thought it was hilarious but at least make my bed next time. I don't condone it, but it's funny, and I am glad no one got hurt or got caught.

Outside of Kabul, there was this huge lake. We got wind that during the Russian times, the Russians built this kind of chalet on this lake to chill out. We went and scoped it out on a patrol and decided to have a day there instead of doing our patrol route. We ended up with a guy standing guard, and we all stripped down and went swimming. So I can say went swimming in the desert of Afghanistan. It was super sweet, but to be honest, we kind of regretted it after doing it. There were people out there fishing, getting water to boil, and washing, and here we were, just trying to wash off the desert and leaping into the lake and having fun. It felt great to have sun and water on our skin, but probably not the right thing.

We ate jalapeno cheese from the MREs on everything; we had a guy who would collect them from all the garbage across the platoon of any unused packs. It was like liquid orange gold. It made every ration taste better. Creating new concoctions was a platoon pastime. Powdered potatoes in a bag, jalapeno cheese was the answer. Shitty chicken breast, bread and jalapeno cheese to make a sandwich. It was the answer. Until everybody had heartburn and heartburn, the shits or other stomach malady. It is not cheese. I am not sure what it is, like some oil-based paste, but it is spicy and so good. I always wondered what eating MREs for months on end did to our bodies.

We had this bet to see if somebody who drank 10 bottles of water (about 5 Liters) inside the section within an hour to medic wasn't too happy about that. Sometimes, you are just so bored that you work with what you have.

In Kabul, there was downtime. We had a very young section; most guys were between 19 and 23 years old. When we were in the camp, we were always fucking around with each other. Everyone was an equal target. It always seemed to escalate. We tied a guy to a chair and put him in a tower on the perimeter wall. He eventually escaped and plotted his revenge, so the guy leading the first one got duct-taped to his bed. He escaped, and then we all called a truce. Then we turned our attention to this guy who was OCD in our platoon. We would sneak into his bunk space and just change the smallest things. He would not know what was out of place but knew something was wrong and it would drive him crazy. I mean it was all good fun, between the younger guys in the section. We loved each other and all of us are friends 20 years later. But those pranks were good for the morale and the team.

We didn't really have a gym in the beginning while living in the combat outposts. We would slowly steal weights from FOB WILSON. They would steal from KAF and we would steal from them. Seemed fair. They also reported missing showerheads. We had built a shower in the strongpoint. You bring in a bucket of water that you warmed up, and then you kind of sponge bath yourself. Later on, we moved to a 45-gallon drum on a frame to create a gravity-fed shower. We had a tin can at the end of it with a bunch of holes punched into it. I got so annoyed at that. They got a new shower trailer into Wilson. I took the shower heads off in Wilson and took them out to the strong point so I could build a shower out there for us. I acknowledge that it was kind of a dickhead move, but we had a shower.

We had one guy, a Private. He was a great young guy in my platoon. Super good-looking guy, super personable. When the Canadian tour show, known as the CANCON show, came through Kabul, a really hot country singer from the show took a liking to him. It was no surprise, and they hooked up in one of the guard towers. Dudes in overwatch saw movement that seemed out of place, watched the couple head into the guard towers, and watched all the action on thermal. I could have started an investigation for fraternization, but he was a 20-year-old kid who hooked up with a hot rockstar in a warzone. It was a long tour, and we were away from home, and it was all good young person stuff. It was just really, really well nice for him. So, I did not follow discipline protocol. As an addendum, he was sadly killed a year later on our next tour to Kandahar, and so now I am glad that he hooked up with a super-hot French country singer.

These tours were long and, at times, could be boring or could be deadly, and every little thing helped maintain morale. We were helped by having one of the best cooks I've ever met in the Army, and it made a huge difference. He was engaging with the troops when he saw them in line, it was like he knew and monitored the mood in the company. When the company dealt with hard things, he made sure that food was prepared in such a way as to know that he cared and the troops appreciated his flexibility... He was able to manage in such a way that he never ran out of food, which was a challenge out at the far west of Zhari at the end of the supply lines. He broke all the "cook" rules; usually, you go through your steam line, and there are a couple of couple options, but they have to be grouped; spaghetti and garlic bread need to be eaten together, not garlic bread and stew. These are fast and hard rules and seem like a small thing but the fact that he didn't care if you mixed and matched was a huge relief to us. What a small thing, being able to choose your own food blend, but it made a huge difference, and on hard days, it was always nice to have a friendly face waiting to uplift us and who was there as a true support in so many ways. When I think about "contracting" these services and the difference that this particular cook made, it was so valuable, above and beyond the role that is "required" but a role that is needed as a part of any fighting force.

PART IV
RETURNING HOME

EASY IN, HARD OUT

THE LAST FOUR WEEKS OF THE TOUR WERE THE HARDEST.

Fatigue set in, impatience was high, and the countdown to leaving became an obsession.

People who had not been thinking about dying now fixated on it.

Easy In and Hard Out was the soldiers' mantra for this time. This expression was used by soldiers to describe how patrols were executed. The way in was "easy"; you had the initiative, and the Taliban didn't know when or how you would approach. Once you were on the objective, that changed. The initiative shifted to the Taliban, who were observing. There were only limited ways to move, soldiers were tired, and ambushes could be laid by your enemy. This was particularly true during the "witching hour" later in the afternoon when the enemy was most active. "Hard" out described the creation of some type of dilemma for the Taliban; the creation of a hard target required extra emphasis from leaders, minimizing the Taliban's opportunity to strike when we were vulnerable. This tactical lesson used daily over the tour, was applied to the risky period of transition between rotations.

Leadership became a balance of mission, handover, and soldier morale.

The vigilance that had been so present returned in full force. It was a period of anxiety. No one wanted to have the new guys die on your watch, and they didn't want the outgoing guys to die just as they were leaving.

Most promised that once they left this place, they would never come back. Most were wrong, and once they got home, most would find out when—not if—and how soon they were returning.

I think we only had three or four days left in my last tour, we were pushing out from the FOB to secure the routes in and out of the AOR for the BG that was replacing us. It is a tense time; you don't want to lose anyone, and the BG is not fully in tune with the local area; it is a point of transition and so a time when mistakes can be made. The area was not used for anything, no farming, just a patch of Afghan earth that was contested between us and the TB. We only had so many ways out of our FOB and so there was a game of cat and mouse where if we used a route or a spot too often, they would IED it. We would watch the area around our FOFB with patrols and with the LAV thermal sites that can see up to 2800m or so. The terrain has a lot of cover and concealment for elements moving on foot. There are walls and old compounds that were half destroyed from years of fighting in the area creating blind spots and opportunities for the Taliban to lay their devices. We established an observation post at this one spot to ensure that they could not dig IEDs in or ambush us. We did that OP three nights in a row creating a pattern. The very first night that we didn't go out to that OP and shifted location, we decided to watch the old OP location from the LAV. Sure enough, a team of locals moves out to our old spot, and we see them digging in. I jump up into the turret to bring the sites and weapons onto the location. The main gunner jumped up with me. We kicked the two young guys who were on sentry out of the turret out, as I wanted to make sure it was TB, as the locals had permission to work at night when it was not hot, but they were supposed to have lanterns. We had agreed with the local leaders that they would have lanterns, in particular when they wanted to work near roads that were highly contested. I looked through the thermal and there's nothing that indicates the signals we had agreed with the locals on the thermal. We looked through the Image intensifying site and there is there's nothing. I go up to look through my night vision goggles hoping to see a lantern. I couldn't see any light, but they were digging like crazy around where our OP was, an area that has no value to farming. Something is going on there for sure. I call up to the Command Post to initiate an engagement. We need to initiate contact. There's no light. Everything tells me they're digging and are trying to put an IED on our old OP spot. So, I initiated engagement and we fired, I don't know, thirty rounds or so. Hit them with twenty-five mm HEIT right away. I got a message on the radio that more people were approaching the area that I had engaged in and was warned by the Officer who was watching a drone feed that they were trying to come and try to take stuff away. I re-engaged in the area and did not hit anyone. The rounds went high, but it scared off the 5 to 10 guys that approached the area. We departed our location and rolled fast onto the scene. As we were leaving the front gate, the locals had already brought a twelve-year-old boy to the front gate. As I'm looking down two middle-aged men are holding this kid, I push out. Sure enough, we get out there. We can't find bodies. We can't find anything. We found a few men-sized shoes, rags, and blood trails. This was normal as they were very good at getting their dead and wounded out quickly. When I got back to camp the kid that I had seen being carried in as I left to the contact area had already died. He just had a really little hole on the inside of his leg and it had hit one of those arteries in there. He bled out. I realized that it was likely a piece of shrapnel from my firing. There was an investigation. Everything was cleared. It was a good shoot. I saw the footage from the ISR platforms that were overhead, and you can see the TB dragging the bodies away and behind a wall and moving something that looks like a device. But what was a little kid doing out there? Was it just a bad ricochet? I left that country a couple of days later. That's how I left, knowing that I killed a 12-year-old. I know I did everything by the book, but it makes me sick. I'll always remember looking down at the gate with the medic and with some headquarters guys. I remember looking down there and they are holding this kid. That is my last image of Afghanistan and it will never leave me.

We are almost done with our tour, and my buddy, who is our LAV driver, is trying to quit smoking before he gets home. I don't know why the fuck should anyone try and quit smoking cigarettes in Afghanistan? I think he was trying to clean up his act before he got home to his missus in Canada. So he stopped buying cigarettes but was always bumming them off me, in his pretend attempt to quit. I put up with it as a show of support and always gave him a cigarette if he asked. We were located in KAF and doing security on Highway 4. I was in HQ at the time and so did not have as many tasks as the guys in the sections. I was OK with that as it was the last three weeks I was ready to start just chilling out and cruising towards home. This task comes down from the Company and they are short a driver. So they grab my buddy and the asshole says, "I'm driving, I'm not going anywhere without my gunner." So the Sergeant looks at me and says, "Okay, you are going also " I am kind of pissed because I want to chill out and not go outside the wire unless necessary at this point. But we had been a team, been through a bunch of shit and even though I know he was just fucking me around, I know it was important to him to have me there. It is all luck and people get used to what they know. I grudgingly went. So, we depart KAF I am giving him shit on the intercom system about fucking me around and taking me when I could have been at the gym or chilling out, or most importantly could have had the room to myself, blah blah blah… all good shit. Routine, and as we are pulling out onto Highway 4, a car pulls out and smashes into us, and we get blown up by a VBIED. I am rocked by this explosion, luckily, the bomb doesn't in high order, but it is still like you getting your bell rung, like getting smashed in the head and your lungs being sucked of all their oxygen. As I come to, I check in with my buddy who is in the driver's hatch, he is in and out of consciousness, and he kind of rolls the vehicle forward away from the car bomb; he pulls the airbrakes on the LAV. We slam to a stop before rolling off the side of the road. I can't talk to anyone on the ICS; the whole crew is a little fucked up, ears ringing, and some dudes are knocked out. I look at the Crew Commander next to me, he is OK but bleeding from some shrapnel in his hand. I keep trying on the intercom, and finally, I hear my driver speak; he feels fucked up but is OK. We check through the LAV, no fire and so hunker down as the situation isn't over. The driver of the VBIED lived and is now trying to detonate the bomb manually, one of the other LAVs has pulled up and the Crew Commanded laces this guy with like half a belt of 7.62mm, just shredding him so he can't set off the bomb. The immediate danger has passed and so as the counter IED guys are coming up to deal with the bomb and the medics are moving up to check us out, my driver says, " Hey man, Let me have a smoke?", I decide I am not giving him one, for whatever reason I just play the asshole, " I am pretty sure you are trying to quit and I am here to support you, so I will not give you a smoke." He shoots back at me, "we just got fucking blown up. We almost died, just give me a fucking cigarette!" So I lose it a little on him, "Just acknowledge you are not quitting, and I will give you the smoke because if you're gonna have a cigarette every time you almost die in this country, you're never gonna quit." He refused, So I doubled down. "Fine, You go get a cigarette off someone else... I wasn't even supposed to be on this patrol... YOU BROUGHT ME... GO GET A CIGARETTE FROM SOMEONE ELSE!" It is funny now, but at the time, I was pissed, like 2 weeks from going home, and I could have died from a random task I wasn't even supposed to be on. We are still best friends today; both did another tour in Afghanistan and he still only smokes borrowed cigarettes.

Throughout our tour we had a little dog that we called Wilson. It had survived a battle and our unit had found its mother and the rest of the litter dead. This dog was amazing for our morale. It greeted us when we got back from patrol, played when we had some down time, and would snuggle into our sleeping bags as we lay on the crushed gravel of the FOB under the stars. We were not always in FOB Wilson, where the dog was, but whenever we came back, there he was. He was a little puppy and a survivor. It really was good for my team. If I am honest, it was really good for me. I had hardened over the tour and didn't really give a fuck about much and had really just dialled into the job. This dog was like my outlet to something that was good about Afghanistan. As we got to the end of the tour, we joked around about who was going to sneak Wilson into our bags and bring him home to Pet. We knew it couldn't happen, but it was a nice thought. Like saving something innocent from this fucking country. Maybe one good thing. Anyway, the handover with the next battalion started. They came in all fired up and were pretty sure we had done things the wrong way. They didn't say it, but you could tell they didn't believe us and were pretty condescending. Anyway, we handed it off, and part of it was to let them know we looked after this little dog; they were not impressed. Dogs weren't regulation. They were so shiny and clean, so full of being awesome and going to do things right. They had no fucking clue. The new preventative medicine guys decided that the dog did not have shots, could bring disease to the camp, and was a risk. The incoming OC ordered all dogs on the camp shot, including Wilson. I am sure that the regulations were right. By basic human decency, thoughtfulness or just not being assholes, they were wrong. They could have waited until we were gone. I was out on patrol when it happened, but heard it was pretty terrible. My team was upset and angry. It was the worst feeling to leave like that, knowing that the one little piece of goodness that we had, our own people killed it. I hated the Taliban, but at that moment, I hated our system so much more.

We had storage bins in the RG 31. There are two bins over the wheel. We had an IED strike in one of our RGs and when I was doing my post-tour write-ups, every piece of kit that was lost in the platoon was in one of those b. Bins are tiny. So you're telling me there are like six rucksacks, five floppy hats, two pistol mags etc etc... could fill a room with the kit that was lost...but it was all in the right front bin of the RG-31...So funny but no one blinked and I did not really give a fuck

---

Flying out was surreal. We just shuffled onto the tarmac. I was so tired. The minute we were wheels up on our way to Mirage, I was lights out. We landed in Mirage. I could not get enough to eat. I just kept eating especially the yogurt. I ate so much it made me sick. We took off the next day for Cyprus. I was ready to just go home.

In Cyprus, we did this program called "BATTLEMIND." It was a US program that would tell us how to look for indicators that we were not adjusting well to the civilian world. Like if we were driving down the middle of the road, using too much alcohol, or felt the need to be armed all the time. The punchline was always, "If you are exhibiting behaviour X, Y or Z , YOU MIGHT NEED HELP". That line became the troops' punchline whenever someone did something stupid, "You might need help, "in a high-pitched US southern twang. One day, we were walking down the street in town; about a week after getting back, we had gone to get a couple of tattoos and had a beer or two. This car drove by, and there was a double backfire, it sounded exactly like a quick double tap from an AK-47. The two guys I was with and I hit the deck. Two other troops across the street had seen the car and then seen the backfire and our reaction. They were laughing hysterically, and shouted over to us, "HEY! YOU MIGHT NEED HELP!"

On the way home from the tour you stop in Cyprus for decompression. The hotel had this big circular sort of gangway as you walk down from all the floors. We walked into the hotel, just off the plane, not knowing what to expect, and this troop was from another company his guy had been drinking. I think for a long time. We watched this dude run down this ramp 9 floors, down to the main floor, come to the bar, order a drink, butt assed naked, foot up on the rail, like Captain Morgan, and then run back up to the 9th floor with the fucking Sergeant-Major chasing the whole time. Classic. Game on. Time to go home.

HOME AGAIN (FOR NOW)

IT WAS FINALLY OVER, AND TIME TO GO HOME.

Things had changed. Some for better, some for worse.

In many ways, the return was something to savour - back in the warm embrace of loved ones and safety, familiar sights, smells, and food. Soldiers were often surprised at the support of the Canadian population who mobilized to behind the soldiers serving in Afghanistan. Weddings, birthdays, and other milestones that had been kept on hold were now able to be celebrated. Small bases and communities let out a collective sigh of relief. Until the next rotation, they could worry a little less about what was on the news.

For others, the re-deployment back home meant being faced with the realities of loss. The goodbyes that could not be said in theatre happened upon the return.

Families of the fallen felt their loss intensify with the return of the soldiers who should have been their loved ones. Friends of the fallen connected with the families visited grave sites, and, for the first time, took time to mourn. It was a balance and struggle to come to terms with everything that had happened.

However, opportunities for decompression were limited as the machine that is the professional military does not stop. Returning soldiers sometimes often received posting messages, moving their families to new locations almost immediately after returning from a combat tour.

Some even return to receive notification for a return to theatre within the year.

Regardless of the situation, it was time to be home.

Enjoy it, and be ready for the next challenge

When we finished our tour, we flew back to Canada, and when we hit Canadian airspace, we were escorted by two CF18 jets that acknowledged our service, and we could see them through the window. It was pretty cool, as you didn't realize what the narrative had been like in Canada when you were overseas. When we left, the mission in Kandahar was just starting. We landed in Trenton, and we boarded the buses, and we're still in our Desert uniforms fresh out of combat. We're driving up to Petawawa and we stopped at Tweed at Tim Horton's to have our first Tim's Coffee in 7 months. The civilians there stood up and clapped as we walked into Tim Horton's and I never, ever experienced anything like that in Canada. I was more used to not being able to wear my uniform downtown as we went through the decade of darkness and the Somalia Inquiry. You felt like things had changed, you felt appreciated. Tweed left a great impression, and I will never forget how they made me feel that everything we had done was for them, and they appreciated it.

I grew up in a really small town in Newfoundland; I had never been out of the province until I joined the army. Even then, I just went to New Brunswick. Like many young guys, I met a girl and started a family, then went to Afghanistan. That first tour was long and so foreign; the smells were different, the culture was different, and the violence was like something I had never experienced. Not just the fighting with the TB but the violence in the population against each other. They were just violent to their children and to their wives; they were just angry. So, when it was coming to an end, it was hard to believe that I was going home to my wife and my twins, who were less than a year old then and realized that I lost a few months of their early life. I was looking forward to that. I'm looking forward to getting back to my family, you know, and seeing how my kids were and how my wife was holding up. Because that's important. It's not only to soldiers; in my perspective, it is a family's deployment as well. They had to do so much without me. They had to wait, every time there was a death announced and wait and see if it was me. They had to go to memorial services. Kids at school had to talk to kids who had lost their dads. It was hard, I think, at home. I'll never forget the first time when I got off the plane and walked in and I see the twins in the double stroller. My wife waiting there with a smile on her face, and of course, my oldest son. He's there and he's he'd run into me and yell "Dad!" That's an overwhelming feeling. You are all of a sudden surrounded by people who love you, and all that darkness starts to bleed away. I think family helps you bridge back to the real world. When you're deployed like that, and we have our friends that were hurt or killed, when you hit that home station, then your emotions kick in. It was definitely a big lump in your throat. You know, you got to swallow it then and try to, you know, not let your emotions show because it is overpowering. I had to learn to let my emotions show and let that love wash over me. It didn't come naturally after I closed myself off so I wouldn't feel the loss of my friends, feel the fear of not getting home, feel the hate for these people who wanted to take me from my family. I cried a lot, especially when I was holding my kids. I wasn't sad, and I was just releasing all that emotion that had been pent up for 8 months.

I just made it home for my wedding, getting back from Afghanistan on my first tour. My wedding date was already set before we left. When the chalks were issued for departing at the end of the tour, mine was a little late. The day we were supposed to land was when I was supposed to get married. So, I asked if I could go a little bit early. Not easy, given all the planning it takes to get people in and out. They threw me on an admin flight all by myself. I landed in Trenton and drove from Trenton to Toronto. That summer, Toronto had that massive power outage. So spent two days in the Toronto airport, and finally got a flight out, and landed Cape Breton. The guys that were standing at my wedding were just getting back from Afghanistan as well. We had Scarlet (dress) uniforms and hopped in my car, drove to Newfoundland, crossed the ferry, and made it to my wedding with hours to spare. Just barely. The chances of making it from Afghanistan, through a major blackout, to Cape Breton and across on the Ferry in time are almost nil. It seems impossible now, but we made it happen. My speech was pretty much just "I made it."

I got home and was supposed to take a position in the Battalion for some stability. I had been to Afghanistan twice in three years at this point. I had to go away for a wedding, this was before there were cell phones. When I got back from my two weeks, there were a series of messages on my phone answering machine;

"Afternoon, there is a rumour you are posted. Don't worry about it; you are staying." *BEEP!*

"Morning, It seems there is more pressure in the army to post immediately. We are trying to fight it due to your multiple tours. Don't worry about it; we have it." *BEEP!*

"This is the OC. I am sorry, but there is no recourse. You are posted to Wainwright. As it is late in the season, they need you there in three weeks." *BEEP!*

With that, I needed to pack up my pregnant wife, my one-year-old child, and my dog, sell my house and drive across the country to get to Wainwright in time to meet the Army's needs. After being away for 12 months in Afghanistan in the last 36 and away for an additional 7 months for training, the machine needed me somewhere else. We didn't know any better, but this was not good for us or our family. It seemed that if you did everything they asked, they would just keep asking. I got to Wainwright and I took a career course, was around for another 7 months and then deployed out of cycle back to Kandahar for my third tour in four years. It was a crazy time.

The mission goes on. You get home, and it keeps going and you feel like you need to be ready to go again. Things don't stop because guys got killed. I think that's where the detached mindset started for me. I got home, and I was happy but took no joy in things. Nor did I get sad. I just WAS. I became very numb to stuff that should have elicited a normal emotional reaction. We had family members pass. I don't ever remember it ever bothered me. When my wife's parents died, I didn't respond at all. I helped out, but I didn't feel any sense of loss, and I didn't feel for her. I just wanted to move on and did not understand the grieving process. I was just present but absent in the most important ways. Obviously, I cared, but kind of like turning that off just so you could do the job. I made a point of interacting with the wounded or carrying the bodies in the body bag to connect in some way. Nothing. I just couldn't feel it. It didn't have any sort of profound effect on me until we got back to Canada. It was almost kind of like, okay, now I can let my guard down kind of thing. It's like a survival instinct. It's the hardest thing; I think that the more times you do it, the more you withdraw into yourself; it doesn't turn back on when you come home. I think that's the problem.

I had super supportive parents. You know, just everything that you want soldiers to have. Regarding support, I didn't know how lucky I was. Throughout the entirety of my tours, it would not be an exaggeration to say that I received more mail than my entire platoon put together. It was just a big family, my parents were rallying everybody in their town, including people who would not normally support war or anything like that. My Dad instituted the Red Friday thing at his office. It just dawned on me later, like on future deployments, how supportive they were. They were very concerned. Concerned about me and if I had any difficulty transitioning back. I remember we were watching a movie, and it was a really graphic injury that resembled one of the injuries of one of our casualties that had. You know, it like set me off, I buried my head and my fiancée at that point; she just kind of comforted me and put two and two together as to what had occurred. The support was amazing from my family and events like that were super minor. I didn't have any difficulty transitioning back and was eager to get back to work. In fact, the work was something I could focus on and that, with the family support, I think, is what stopped me from focusing on any bad stuff.

I was very busy on my second tour. It was violent, and I never stopped. It took a while to come down from when we got back. My wife told me at one point I was lying in bed, and I was constantly vibrating and never seemed to relax. When I got back, we bought our new house, when we moved into our new house. New baby, new house. We moved into our house four days after our son was born. Stupid. Hindsight is so stupid, but military folks seem to do that kind of stuff all the time. Like we would always package ridiculous things. Return from a combat tour after 7 months away, move, new house and new baby. You tried to adjust to a whole bunch of things, plus coming home from a combat zone. I did get pulled over once when I got back for driving down the middle of the Highway. The Cop was good about it, though. He saw desert camo stuff in the backseat because I still hadn't turned everything back in yet. His first question is, how long have you been back? Three days. He's like, you're back in Canada; drive safe on the correct side of the street. I think that we underestimated the changes required after these tours, and there were hard lessons for us and our families. They just wanted us back and to take up our role and share, but I think we probably needed some time to come down. Hard to balance.

Coming home and coming down is hard. You are used to moving to violence quickly, and when you do, you don't stop. One night this fucking dude is being a douchebag to my sister when we were out at the Pub. I don't remember fucking exactly what happened. I went completely in the black, but I just remember my uncle Pierre fucking dragging me out of the pub, and he's like, what the fuck are you doing? I guess I went so in the black that I fucking grabbed Buddy by the neck. I yelled I'm going to fucking kill you, I had him against the wall, just choking the fuck out of him. I just completely went somewhere else and we get to the car and I think what the fuck man. Like what? Like, what happened? And he's like, Dude, I never seen you like that ever. I went to see someone about anger after that and I never had another incident.

My wife says, hey, someone keeps calling me from the long distance, but won't say anything. When I got home, it happened. It ended up being this soldier in my platoon checking on me by calling my house because I had been badly wounded. Finally, I answered the phone, and I spoke to him. This kid who had saved my life had run 300m into contact and was worried that he had let me down and had forgotten the interpreter that day. He called, and said, "I am so I'm sorry I forgot the interpreter, "he felt so guilty; even though I reassured him that he did amazing that day, he could not shake that he had let me down in some way. It was a really emotional conversation. Afterwards, he was really stuck; he was released from the forces, and he was diagnosed with PTSD. I call him once a month to make sure he is OK. He has had a hard time with that day and some of the other things, you know, because he came close to dying and likely had to kill some enemy while looking after me when I almost died. He gets caught up in what he did on that day. He feels like he failed, and I am here only because of what he did.

When we got home, the army set us up with contracted psychologists to talk through our reintegration and how we were adjusting after a pretty violent tour. It was probably the right idea, but it went wrong. First, they put the psyches n in this old building on base. I think it was condemned and out of the way so you could have privacy, but it was dark and a creepy old warehouse, the lights flickered, and the furniture was old and musty. So, we go into this place and wait for our turn to go in. The first guy goes in, and the door closes, and they are in there for a bit, and when it opens, he is hugging the therapist and telling her it is OK. She shuts the door behind him and takes a moment; he comes out and says to me, "Don't tell her anything." She is not ready for it. "He had told her a story about some kids getting hit by a wayward suicide bomber, and it was tough on her, she had likely been overloaded as we were the 5th platoon to go through, but it was clear to us that what we talked about wasn't normal and that the contracted psyches did not have a good understanding of how to talk to people like us. So, we all went in after that and said fuck all.

When I got home, I thought everything was fine; I seemed OK and was pretty normal; we lived downtown Petawawa by the point. Sometimes the range sound of gunfire would reach, but it did not bother me when I was awake. But one night, I was out cold, sleeping, and was awoken by the LAVs in the distance, and I heard that shooting "bump, bump, bump." I remember waking up and doing that classic thing where you're like looking for shit because every time I heard that sound, we're gonna go do something. It was like this weird, like, oh, I'm home now. However, it was something that I can't quantify kind of changed in me because of the responsiveness like you are ready to go fight. It was hard on my family and hard on me; those sounds increased my heart rate; they made me a bit jumpy, like I had to keep moving, and that sound of the LAVs firing was like the thing that made me respond. It was crazy. I never went and got any help. I focused on breathing and figured out how to not get antsy and angry and go through that transition.

I've been to marriage counselling. She said I changed after deployments. I think I just had less patience with her. Some of her stuff, I think it's something you know, I've gone through a whole a whole rigmarole of marital states, essentially to the point of being separated and getting back together again and some stuff. I would say that every experience changes you. So, it'd be unfair to say that you just spent nine months in the country does not mean you're good or bad, but of course, you've changed, and so has she. It takes a long time to understand that. But she'd bring that up. She'd state, "You're not the person I met. Afghanistan had changed you," Of course, you are not the same person. You have been fighting a war. They have been home alone. It is like meeting someone new. Do I have less patience for bullshit? Potentially. I just did not see the value in day-to-day crap. No one is going to die if some chore list isn't done. It took me a while to recognize that my attitude was not helpful. But I think we needed some training on what it was going to be like going from living in a mud hut, fighting every day to being back at home. I think sometimes I preferred the mud hut.

He was actually the first soldier; there were a number that took their own life since we had been home. It's funny because when I went to the BOI they asked me. I think he was really pushing and trying to indicate that he had PTSD. I said I said I'm not a doctor, I'm not a professional, but I think everyone else has some form of post-traumatic stress. Yeah, well, my point is that it becomes a disorder when they don't how to address it overwhelms them. If you talk about any young adult who goes to a foreign country, surrounded by rules and wires. You can't move without being armed; with your buddies and things blowing up everywhere, you are about to step, and you can start a small war with your own section due to all the arms you have, and you don't have some post-traumatic issue in your life. You're mistaken. But if it becomes a problem it consumes you. It is a disorder. And that's what happens, and some of our guys kill themselves. Was there other stuff that contributed to it? Yeah, it was always something else that compounded it. It may not just be the combat stress; it is compounded by an inability to interact.

I got home and I bought a car and as I was pulling out, the traffic seemed to be moving so fast, I just couldn't merge in. I was staying still at the entrance to the dealership, and it was making me really nervous. I couldn't understand it; I was sweating, my breathing was up, my heart rate was elevated, and I felt threatened. I must have sat there for ten minutes, frozen at the exit of the car dealership, unable to make a decision to move. The salesperson that had helped me noticed this and came out to see what was up and knocked on the window, and I fucking hit my head on the roof. I hit the ceiling in the car. I jumped so high, and I'm fucking reaching for my pistol that is not there. Scared the shit out of me. All I could see was threats everywhere. That was my first real hint that I needed help.

I had a hard problem when I got home from my second combat tour. I had a hard time with short-term memory. It really was frustrating me quite a bit. I don't know why, but I couldn't remember things. You could tell me one thing, and I forget, and it was really, you know, difficult on me, my family, and I did not perform at work that well. I had a senior job, and for some reason, I was just falling off the rails. People would tell me stuff, normally I'm I was pretty good but I wouldn't remember them. I ended up having to kind of learn how to write copious notes. Then, I had to remember to check them every morning. You can have the best notes. And if you don't check them, they're not useful. So it kind of evolved into a system for me to deal with the issue, but it was just a band-aid. I went for help in the mental health system, which was fine. I mean, they offered me several things, like they would give me an electronic planner. So you can have alarms or something. I didn't take that, but I was almost inclined to do it. They really weren't helpful. I found that things have changed at home. My wife was pregnant. There were a lot of changes, not just coming home from Afghanistan. I think my wife used Afghanistan as a default to kind of explain my frustration with life. It was probably a bit of that. Probably a bit of everything. There's so much change when you get home. It is hard to focus and process everything. In the end, the MH folks were good; they didn't help, though, and there were no excuses for not doing career courses. I needed to do French, but I could barely remember shit in English. I needed the course to get promoted. It just made me so angry. I was capable and it just seemed like I had lost something, and I couldn't find it.

I don't remember having nightmares, but I know they did because I would wake up. Soaked head-to-toe. I mentioned to some people that I remember one of my buddies brought this up to me once about night sweats. I was like, oh shit and I eventually heard some other guys talking about the same thing. But what's normal and what's not? It happened three days in a row. I don't remember anything. I don't remember being terrified, but I know it must've been because I was literally soaked. I just rode it out for a couple of months until I adapted and didn't seek help. I didn't want to get on the crazy train and I wanted to stay operational in the army.

REFLECTIONS

IT IS HARD TO QUANTIFY AFGHANISTAN.
We lost.
There is no other conclusion.
Presently, the Taliban are in control of Afghanistan, those brave Afghans who were our partners and trusted us with growing their nation are under threat and have been abandoned by the very nations that had pledged their support and allegiance.
Any reflection on Afghanistan must be shrouded by the cloud of defeat. We can discuss our micro-victories and warm ourselves with the thought of battles won during the period of "these colours don't run," but the reality is that the colours did run when it was no longer politically or economically expedient to continue fighting.

We must face the reality that we lost the war.

———————

I retired from the CAF in October 2023 and as I gathered up 29+ years of military kit to return to clothing stores, I finally unpacked my barrack box from Roto 0. I had opened it only once since returning twenty years ago but had never actually unpacked it. When I lifted the lid, I was greeted with an 8 x 11 picture of my smiling 3 and 5-year-old boys wearing sunglasses with their arms draped around one another—I cried. I cried not just for how much my children have sacrificed so that I could spend a career doing something I loved, but I also cried for all the soldiers who went to Afghanistan—the ones who didn't come back and the ones who will never be the same because of their experiences. I cried because I realized that we, myself included were quick to forget about the true costs of having a professional military. I took the photo off the lid of the barrack box—it is now safely stored in the same padded manila envelope that holds my certificate of service, tucked away on a shelf in the storage room. Maybe I will look at it again in another twenty years.

For me. The mission was never about Afghanistan. Never. The mission was about the platoon, the company, the section. My brothers, my comrades never did I think we're gonna make a difference. I thought we were going to make a difference while we were there. I never once thought that we were gonna change Afghanistan. I went to be with my brothers. Like, that's it. I know it's cliché, but it is the truth.

I stand here in Canada and sometimes I can smell garbage. We lived in a defensive position for months. Fucking burning garbage, burning shit... That certainly sticks with you. It always worms into my mind whenever I smell burning plastic or garbage left out too long. Burning those plastic bottles we drank, that smell sticks. You think of Afghanistan, you think of those terrible smells, it is unfortunate, as it is a physically beautiful country.

People forget how much was going on in the world. It was kind of crazy that Canada had signed up to do a dangerous combat mission in Afghanistan. I always wondered if we became targets in the early days because our government had been kind of wishy-washy on things and other governments pulled out when they took losses. Spain had that train bombing in Madrid in 2003, and they withdrew from Iraq immediately. We replaced the Germans in our AOR in Kabul, and they had had all those casualties on the bus: 4 killed and 29 wounded. They went from a leading role to a supporting role with lots of caveats. The TB and Al Qaida had a good impact on countries that weren't ready to take hits. I always wondered if that was part of it. Like, you know, a strategy to bloody the Canadians, the Dutch and the Danes, these guys would pull out because their nation isn't willing to commit to defeating a determined enemy. They can start to break the coalition a bit at a higher level, cause fissures, through home terrorism or through the killing of deployed soldiers. Every government wants to be re-elected, they really never cared about Afghanistan except in an indirect way. I just wondered why we had so many caveats, especially in Kabul. I assumed it was political so we could stay and be seen to do something without doing anything real. In the end, the enemy strategy worked; we left in 2014 before the other major allies. I mean, we did our part, but the long game of bleeding us and not having the willpower to stay worked for the Taliban. It is interesting that in a war of choice, winning is not necessary; maybe that is why the West has lost so many wars in the last 50 years; our perceived threats aren't real threats. I am just sad because I believed they wanted us to win and now I realize they don't care. I am sad for my friends who were hurt and killed and will never be the same and for their families who lost so much time.

I don't think we were done. I don't think we were done. I think we could have done a little bit more. I get the political side of it and understand it more now than I did then. I think we probably could have done more. I think we did a lot. I was there from day one to almost the last day; there, across 4 rotations, the changes that hit the country were massive. Well, when we first rolled in, you wouldn't see any children out. Schools were just boys. Every woman we saw was covered from head to toe. There was nobody out after dark. There wasn't a lot of anything that even resembled wealth. Later, a lot of cars and houses, I remember seeing toilets for sale because there was a sewer system which did not exist when we came over in 03. Fast forward almost 10 years later, and kids are playing, Girls are going to school, and more women are wearing hijab instead of fully covered. So, they're showing their faces more. They're walking more and shopping more. The airport isn't a base it is something resembling an international airport. With international flights coming in. There's security at the airport. It wasn't great security. It had improved so much that we flew out of Kabul on my last tour instead of by Herc. That one felt weird. You wear all your body armour until you get to the airport and then you fly out without anything. But in general, you felt like you were in a country that was safer than it had been. I think it just required another 10 years. It was a long game.

I think that when the honours and awards come out 6 months or a year after a tour, they are too late to be relevant and usually they get most things wrong. If you know anybody who's won a medal or has seen people who won medals, they know that the reason that medals are won, for the most part, is because something has gone disastrously wrong. There's never a time where, like, everything goes like cleanly, and then you're like, you know what? Medals and tea for everyone that plan worked perfectly. It's because something's become a shit show and somebody has to act abnormally in an abnormal circumstance to be able to right the ship or save a life or do something incredible just to get back to balance. I am glad guys got recognized, but wish we were more honest about it. How are we the only commonwealth country that didn't award a Victoria Cross? Is our bravery less than those of other nations? I think it is Political Bullshit. We lost, so maybe no VCs if you lose.

The outcome of experiencing a lot of violent death young is a realization, as hard as it is that life will end and can end suddenly. It's not minimizing the memory; it's not detaching from, you know, the love that you have for the guys that died. But it's understanding that they signed up the same as I did; it could happen to any of us. We all took that risk, and it's shitty that it was them. There's one thing that stuck with me afterward. Not to be dramatic about this, but the act of Remembrance on Nov 11th. When they say that, it's a big difference between knowing and understanding. "They shall not grow old." You really understand that. My friend who died will be permanently 20. Those guys are permanently that age for the rest of our lives. You can't play the "what if game" What if, like, you know what, if this guy died, this guy lived because the guy who was driving was the secondary driver. The primary driver was Private_____. He died. My buddy _____, who was the secondary driver, I went through battle school with, he lives, and I got to attend his wedding and get to grow up with his kids. It is what it is. You kind of create these alternate histories that can be damaging, and so you need to stay in the now. You can't waste energy and emotion on these things you can't change. It is bad for everyone.

One of the questions is always, in the end, was it worth it? Despite everything. The highs and the lows. I can't imagine my life without my four tours to Afghanistan. Yeah, I mean, I wouldn't understand life like I do, the parameters that I am capable of living within. I wouldn't understand the definition of highs, and I wouldn't understand the definition of lows. It taught me the extremes. I've had the shittiest day of my life in the Army, and I've had the best day of my life there. I am not a victim; I think that the experience allows me to understand life in a different way. It is somehow richer. I can actually feel the joy of having lived when a number of my friends did not. I feel the burden of their bad luck every day, but I try to honour them by pushing and just keep moving forward. Without it? I wouldn't have I wouldn't know the boundaries of the range that I can live in. I am thankful that I am here, and I am also thankful that I know how bad life can be. I think I have grown from it.

This was the first war where everyone had a digital device, there was so much video. I enjoyed the hard rock video montages that were brought back from tours, I did struggle a little bit with kind of the way we would piece these things together. I think it kind of may have changed the way our soldiers look at war. After the hard rock video of things blowing up and troops doing stuff and firing guns, and doing awesome stuff, it says, this video dedicated the memories of those we had lost and then it faded to black with this list of people who were killed. I started to get the sense that we were almost we were living our tours by the number of fatalities as opposed to living our tours by mission. It became almost like "how hard your tour" was. We were casualty-based. You know, I hate to say this, but at one point, I almost felt I was like, why do some people think that we didn't live the same tour that they did? Because we didn't take enough casualties? It was almost as though we hadn't tried hard enough.

I think the "broken veteran narrative" bothered me more than anything when I came back. It wasn't all the stuff that happened, but people back home treating me like more had happened and I needed to be treated like I was sick. No one wants to hear about it. They just want to box you up into the category of damaged. A lot of people make assumptions about things and how you are going to react. The accumulation of a lot of people doing that, asking about PTSD, and treating me like I was sick actually had more of a negative effect. On me than anything else. You notice now that in TV shows, everyone's so messed up if they served in the Sandbox. Like in the 80s, every show had a messed-up Vietnam vet, and now every show has a messed-up Afghan or Iraq vet. It is hard to have pride and be taken seriously when everyone is treating you like you are about to go off like a bomb.

I think you have to remember the good parts when bad things happen to good people. I remember we stopped one day at the Dalla Dam. We were not supposed to stop, but we had not showered in weeks, and it was a sunny, beautiful day. Our section commander said," Right, boys, we have 30 minutes. Let's go get clean and enjoy the water." I'll never forget that day. Everyone unburdened themselves and were like kids in the lake. Cannonballs and floating like we are in Muskoka and not just out of combat. I have this mental picture of a buddy of mine, sitting there in his underwear, a smoke in in his mouth just floating. Just fucking just loving life and having a smoke. Float along. I choose to remember him that way and that day. After we got home, he wasn't that happy, carefree kid anymore, and he killed himself. I choose to remember that great day.

Someone had shaving cream in their kit when we hit an IED and lost some soldiers. The sweet, fresh smell of the shaving cream mixed with the diesel is something stuck in my head. I haven't had it for a while, but sometimes someone will walk by in the morning, and troops will have that shaving cream on. It sets me right back. Craziest little things.

I never told my wife, but I didn't really want to come home from my first tour. I lost three people that were close to me in one day. I lost my Warrant Officer the same day an Afghan I was close to was killed. On the same day, another great ANP officer, Shahkru La, was killed and his best friend, Hamid Agha, also felt the pain as these guys were tight. They patrolled with us all the time. They dressed like us and wanted to be just like us all the time. Hamid was thoughtful when we were up on OP. Often, he just stood there and stared into the horizon at night. He'd come up with tea, and he would just say, this name Mulis Za, something. Which was the guy who took credit for the kills of our friends. So, I started working on it. I don't do revenge. It's not about revenge... maybe it was a bit about revenge. We now had a focus. We got a guy that hurt us, and we're going to get him. We developed informants, and they were sort of developing stuff we found around where he lived. I felt like we were finally winning. We were finding IED caches. Every patrol we went out with, something good was happening. We understood the people in the population way more than when we originally got there. I felt like I was winning when I handed over, like, the bad side of the town wasn't really the bad side of the town and now you had to go further down to get into the bad stuff. We had created space, for ourselves and for the population. Then I had a hand to hand it over. I was just like, man, these guys are gonna start from where I was and have to rebuild and they have to learn all lessons. I did not want to come back. When I did get home, I followed the fight too closely and stayed engaged, like it was still my responsibility. I had a hard time letting go. I never told my wife how I was feeling, about the losses or why I was so focused. It took me a while to understand and talk about it. While I wasn't talking that time was tough on us as a couple.

When you get home, everyone tells you that you're supposed to be sick or you have to be sick. You get really frustrated with that because it's not true. You know what I got? I got in trouble. I walked out on one of the briefings. Those mandatory briefings because the debriefer was hounding me, trying to make me break down and cry. Have something that wasn't there and isn't going to make you feel any better. I also felt like some of the other side guys, in particular, wanted me to reaffirm that I was sick because these things happened. You MUST have PTSD. Well, right now, no. So, what's the right number? How many things need to happen to you to be sick or to still be healthy? Now I'm good. Let's go back to drinking and having a good time. I am fatigued by the wounded veteran shit. It is real but the vast number of people just carried on. The guys that were sick or had a bad experience were just the loudest at times.

I feel like at the time I was angry about a lot of things. I think I think that's a survival mechanism. You express anger and dark humour because it's to shield yourself from the true emotions. Which are things like sadness, grief, and things you don't want to experience. I would say, one of my angry moments, I recognize them for what they were as manifested form something else. I feel like I am good now. But the one part that still angers me is that we thought we were doing what we were told we were doing, and in fact, what we were doing there was not the same thing we were told to accomplish. To think that we were going to go there and that we ever thought that we were going to have a Western democracy in Kandahar was insane. Those making the choices should have known or they should've told us, you know, so we could have done the right thing, whatever that was. Mostly, don't try so hard because we are going to pull out on a timeline instead of when we win. I recognize that that's the only thing I'm left feeling angry about. There's something else there. I think because nobody wanted to fail. Everyone did the best they could. This brings us back to asking, what is success? What success in that environment in Afghanistan? The government defined it a certain way. We failed strategically because we defined it the wrong way and we lost. I mean, when you defined it as a leader, you just want to do right by your soldiers. Bring as many home as you can and do your mission. I mean, that's hard to reconcile, right? It is an impossible metric because it is just luck if everyone comes home or some don't, or some come home missing pieces, you still feel the guilt. I am not sure how to solve that space.

This foreign place. This place was set up to kill you, and you had to kill to survive. Those things were terrible and hard. But there was another side. It had this sense of beauty to it, and I look back on it now. It is like a little bit of our own personal history; we invested so deeply in that country and its people. It was like our home there. That valley, the river, all those villages we spent time in. You know, you might have encountered a kid, a person you helped or talked to somebody. We made a difference at a micro level, in our own time, to individuals and there was enough there to help a corner of the region. You just needed to experience the whole thing because never in my life would I have imagined that I had been on that side of the world, in that environment, helping people that I never would ever in my life have otherwise come in contact with. It was violent, but I believe that I care more now, for my family and for people that come to Canada from war-torn countries. It was the pinnacle of my career as an NCO and maybe the core of my development as a person.

We had hit an IED and had casualties. I was right next to the blast, and the casualties were running around. One of the other guys stopped me and asked if the blood was mine. I was covered in blood, and I was like, fuck. I don't know if that's me or not. Because adrenaline's going so, you can do amazing things. The medics checked me. I was good. The adrenaline died off after the scene was done. I was like, now I'm like, oh, I'm fucking I'm hurt. My head was killing me, and my neck was sore; my balance was off and was just sore all over. They checked me. They put me on some pills and stuff. Then I noticed I was having a lot of pain in my back and neck. I was just hurting. It was the point where I couldn't put my gear on the patrol. So, I went back, and at that point, it was at a point that would normally be a five-minute walk. Took me half an hour. That's what that was weird. I was hobbled. I had all that energy when the adrenaline was going. It didn't feel it. When I woke up the next day, I could confirm that I was all fucked up. It wasn't until a long time later that we started thinking about concussions and my neck being all fucked up. I just felt so bad going and getting checked out because I had not been hit by shrapnel, but my insides were all fucked up; no one realized it back then. The effects of blast and shock were not well understood. I went in for a week or so and then was back out in the shit for the rest of the tour; now, it is hard to explain to doctors why I have all this soreness and constant pain. I hope that I can get treatment. I live with a constant reminder of that day and of Afghanistan.

Up in Kabul we got to see all the old Russian armour which was left behind in the valleys when the Soviets retreated. It's in your back, your minds like, you know, we're patrolling the same areas and could make the same mistakes. We were not the first modern army to be there; the Russians lost, and all this kit stayed behind to remind us; we used to joke that in 20 years, there would be LAVs and RG31s mixed in. It was eerie when Kabul fell to the Taliban, and they had all the MRAPs and HUMVEES that had been left behind. It was like we could see the future.

It was a different feeling, those later tours in Kandahar. It was weird because this counter-insurgency strategy shifted from killing the enemy to protecting the population. The posture changed from 06/07. We didn't go rolling through with our vehicles at platoon strength. We didn't drop the blades and make our own roads. Everything was light infantry, section actions inside of a bigger BG AOR. Instead of 9 Platoon patrols a day, there would be 36 section patrols. Sounds perfect to "surge" amongst the population, but at the section level, sometimes it felt like we didn't have that support of the heavier weaponry, and we were fighting the TB on their terms. It was a different beast, like a knife fight. At times I felt like here I am with six, seven young lads, you know, on their first tour. We had been in the war for a while, and so there had been generational changes, and the army was trying to get folks over that had not been before. The troops had no prior experience. You would head out on patrol and 5 km away would be the command post. We would communicate on these little radios, it always seems so close when you look at a map, but the terrain in Panjawaii, with the tight urban spaces, the wadis in the greenbelt and the grape fields, made you feel alone, and you knew it would take more than an hour for another team to get to you if you got into the shit. I am out with all these kids and I always felt like I had the guys out there out there by myself. You're a Canadian section working against a Taliban section in the bad guys' neighbourhood. They know the locals, they know the terrain, and they could decide, for the most part, when to hit you. That's what I found the move to Counter Insurgency Tactics did. It levelled the playing ground so the TB could gain the local initiative. I don't know the bigger picture. I don't know the strategic picture, just that as a section commander with a dozen young Canadians, you were so alone out on section patrols that you could not use all the resources at your disposal to keep them alive or to defeat the enemy. Maybe it was the right thing, but it made you feel very vulnerable at the lowest level. An average Taliban soldier is not scared of a light or a medium machine gun; they have those. They fear the larger Calibre; it impacts them psychologically. The 25mm from the LAV is a different kettle of fish. When the twenty-five starts going, you can dictate the tactical battle between a section of Canadian Infantry and a section of TB fighters. You're able to break contact and create space; you're able to gain back the initiative and start to manoeuvre on them. When we shifted to smaller section patrols on later tours when the ROE was stricter, the playing field had been levelled, so it was a series of section-on-section actions in the grape fields that were less lethal. You learn pretty quickly that the fighters don't like high explosives or 25mm. They are fine with throwing small arms back and forth. When we came under contact, we would crack out the M72s and volley fire the rockets at the TB positions. That would shock them initially, and then we could look to take the fight to them. This was the reality, as they would invariably get the drop on us in the tight urban terrain and the grape fields. As we didn't have the heavier tools available, we would make ourselves seem bigger than we were with rockets. They don't like that. This would create space and time for the rest of the platoon or QRF to come out to try and hit the TB element. Invariably it was too slow, and they would break away because we were not big enough to fix and manoeuvre when we were by ourselves. I think that it is an important discussion tactically, but really, my memory is feeling alone and having one hand tied behind my back while the weight of those kids' lives was on my shoulders. It was my job, but I learned what "burden of command" meant at the lowest level, and I would never make a subordinate feel like that in the future.

I was a Corporal and machine gunner. I remember that we would listen to the radio in the LAV on the speaker when contacts were happening. It was like listening to a radio program or story, except that the events were real, and you could follow the "game." The worst was when casualties happened. You did not know who it was and were always worried it was one of your friends. I remember this one time the other company was in contact, and I started to get a sense of, oh, this isn't going well. You could hear it in the Company Commander's voice. And I mean, just from a fraternal standpoint, you want to get in there and help your buddies. But you have your own job to do, and here I was. I was in the middle of the worst day of their lives, and I was fucking choking down my fruit cocktail, sitting safe and sound in the back of the LAV as it came over the net, and the casualties grew. You felt so helpless. But here is the thing that matters. The Commander was making a deliberate effort to sound disinterested on the radio. He was calm; you know, there was incredible stress in the firefight, that casualties were happening, and people were hurt and killed. It is something I actually that I took on board from there. He brought a voice of calm in a sea of uncertainty. I always make it a point now when I'm on the radio, regardless of how chaotic something is to sound super fucking disinterested. Because it's contagious, right? You get those guys on the net; they're screaming and yelling, and then they get screaming and yelling responses in return, and everybody gets all fucking amped up. So that was something I took away from that I can throw that one into the toolbox. I never had a chance to tell that major that story. But soldiers need to know that excitement is contagious, but so is being calm.

The knowledge gap between rotations is something I always reflect on. We were killing people. Remotely, with cameras and with bombs that were worth more than their targets. This is what the HQ team was learning about during the handovers. It was such a loss of knowledge every time we rotated. It took 3- 4 months just to learn the system, so you did not make mistakes, and you were judicious with the violence. You are observing a society from 15thousand feet through a camera and then deciding if activity is a threat and then putting a bomb on it. It takes time to learn what is normal. There is a lot of movement out in the farmland of Afghanistan at night because it is so hot during the day. But there are also a lot of IEDs being placed. The two groups look similar. There were always groups that would congregate by the grates that flowed under roads. Initially, we would just confirm that as hostile; why are they up at 3am? It must be bad (and lots of times they were), but sometimes these guys are just accessing their water rights that are controlled by regional and local Tribal elders. They're the lowest level, the peasants in Afghanistan. They get their water rights up two thirty to three thirty am. That's the unwritten rules. We were killing those guys for a long time because why stand near a culvert at 3 am unless you are planting a bomb? Some of them were enemies for sure. But I don't know if we can be 100 percent accountable for all of our rounds. I started my tour dropping bombs and then learning the pattern of life and being far more specific with my understanding. Then the learning happens again every 6 months; the next roto came in and dropped a five-hundred-pound bomb on a tractor as intelligence had indicated that there was a gun system being brought in to shoot down helicopters, and this tractor looked like the profile through the cameras. So they thought it was a mistake, but it wasn't a big deal. We drop a bomb on a tractor, it is a piece of equipment, no one killed, not a big deal, right? WRONG! Then you realize that was the one tractor for all Zhari. One Fucking tractor for all the farmers. There are no spare parts. It's an old Russian tractor. It is simple to use, and the OMLT guys on the ground living in the community let us know this is actually a big deal. It looks like we are punishing the community. In fact, we can kill their people, and they understand that, but if you lose their tractor, that means that their whole community is hurt. This learning cycle was hard on the team in place, on the incoming guys and on the population. The only group the handovers didn't hurt was the Taliban; they got a reprieve because there were new guys in again, and all the old tricks would work for the next 3-4 months, and then it would be time for the next new batch of Canadians. There was lots of good stuff, but the gap, particularly at the headquarters, was difficult, and I am not sure we had it right. Perhaps the HQs should have done a year, and the troops underneath rotated? I don't know; I just think that there was a lot missed, and it didn't help the mission. This is the tyranny of a professional army, I think. In WW2, you stayed until you won. In Afghanistan, you had to return to Canada to take your French course so you could be promoted. I think if we ever fight again, we need to rethink this model.

Kabul seemed more cosmopolitan with a more international flavour. Kabul seemed to be changing in those early days. You know, women wear jeans, shirts, wearing hijabs. There are some beautiful women in that country. I remember speaking to this Afghan official one day when I was out on patrol, and he thought what was going to change that country was going to be women getting an education. And once they had educated women, that country would change.

I knew that we were losing the war between my 2nd and 3rd tours. During my 2nd tour, we were taking the initiative and felt like we owned our space. It was just a feeling I had as I had been a soldier, a section 2IC, and finally a section commander in Afghanistan. As an example, we were on Ghundey Ghar, a desolate hill that controlled access on the western approaches to Kandahar City. The fight was to the west of us. To the east, a normal pattern had developed around the area that had been cleared. We fought and kept pressure on the enemy, we paved roads to encourage commerce and civilian traffic, and it was not in the enemies' best interest to be near Kandahar or around Panjawaii. When I returned a couple of years later, Ghundey Ghar again belonged to the enemy. The Americans had given it up and the fight was around Masum Ghar, where we had been fighting hard a couple of years before. We now had to secure our local area; we were patrolling the bazaar and south of the greenspace with the King's Gardens. We had so much contact that it was obvious that there was an enemy command node command node was close to MSG! As we patrolled off the main road because we would hit the Taliban OPs. They challenged us every time. We couldn't get 200 meters. Even as close as three tank hill, we were in a fight for our lives on my 3rd tour. I think that it was pretty obvious that we were losing, or alternatively, we had stopped trying after the government said that we were not staying until the end. It sucked to go back on multiple rotors, see the advancement, feel the cost in time and blood and then come back the next time, and it was all needing to be done again. I think for the officers it was different, as a lot of the senior guys were one tour types but for the non-commissioned or the guys that started as Lts in Afghanistan and did 2 or 3 tours minimum and so had a memory of the war longer than 6 months.

My biggest regret was that I adopted the hatred of the team that was there before me. They hated, hated everyone. And I took that on when I first got there. It took me months to finally realize that the Afghan people were there just to live. They did not have a choice have a choice in the matter, they weren't necessarily bad, they didn't necessarily hate us, want us dead, or really cared if we were there or not. They just wanted to live. They were caught between us trying to get rid of the Taliban and the Taliban trying to regain power. I found we often blamed the people for everything that happened. As you begin to understand the environment, you realize it's actually not their fault in any way, shape or form. Getting to that compassion level earlier is what you 100 percent need to do, because there is safety in that through safety of the people. I was out and talking to some of them about 9/11, and they didn't even know it had happened. No TV, no radio, desert people with no context. This perspective really surprised me. They told me, "you guys just invaded us." I was set that I were not fighting them, jus the Taliban. They didn't understand why. I explained 9/11, they were pretty surprised and didn't believe me, so I showed them a video of the planes hitting the towers. Then it made sense to them, Pashtun Wali, we were getting revenge on the Taliban because they killed thousands of our people. There was no use trying to explain international politics;

they have a world view, and us getting revenge on the Taliban makes sense. But they let us know every time we killed one of theirs, they needed to get revenge on us, that is Afghanistan, a circle of violence. You start realizing, like, man, they're just people they like us. Canadians would be the same if given a similar situation, and I wish I had come to that conclusion much earlier. It is exhausting to hate.

I don't think we had done reconstitution or a full in-country replacement of units by battlefield replacements due to casualties in a long time, maybe since Korea. I had taken enough casualties in my platoon that we needed to do this. Take in a whole bunch of replacements and integrate them with the original platoon. So, there was a divide between those that had been in the fight and those that had not. It wasn't easy at all. Towards the end of this tour, I was feeling defensive. My 2IC was killed. His replacement came in, and he was a great guy. He had great advice. I remember not being super easy to get along with. I would say, my major mistake was I didn't really think about the building of a new platoon in theatre deliberately. You know what I mean? I didn't put the brain sweat i having replacements coming in. No one could mentor me on this because we hadn't done it before. I didn't think, "what would it be like to lose someone close to me." How do I rebuild a team? How do I think and feel about it? We never talked about it in training and had to learn it after something bad happened. Integration of replacements is going to be difficult. I needed to work on this, and I don't think I did it well. That's the kind that's exactly the kind of thing that no one else will know, you know. I think that's an important point. I just assumed they were going to flow right through, and there was no playbook; there was a lot of emotion. In the end we got the job done, we mourned our losses and built the new team, we got on with the job and stayed in the fight. But I could have been better.

You need to put the effort into orders and make each mission worth it. Too often in training, orders are sluffed off for more time to other things. I realized that when lives are on the line, soldiers want to know that you have put deliberate thought into the action that will occur and that you understand contingencies, and that should the worst thing happen, you have protected their equities. Combat exposes the hierarchy in the army. The social contract between Officers and non-commissioned members. It is a soldier's job to advance towards the enemy and to take the objective, and the Officer's job is to plan and lead. That said, there is psychological support that soldiers deserve when they go into battle. A set of orders clearly articulates the objectives and how that soldier will be cared for if they are injured while carrying out the officer's orders. I felt like giving good orders showed that I cared and understood that they had to walk point and I got to walk slightly behind them; the physical risks may have been similar, but the emotional burden of them being subordinate and under command is different. The mission and their lives are the most valuable thing we have. The lives of Canadian youth are precious; they need to see the effort, and I feel like taking the time to give them good orders is the least we can do as leaders. If there was one thing I would pass on to the next generation of leaders, it is how to respect your soldiers, give them good orders, let them know that you have thought through the problem and if they fall, their lives are not due to carelessness, but due to the harsh realities of combat.

I think there is so much luck involved in surviving in combat. We attach meaning and skill, but in combat there is just so much luck to what happens on any given day. I think about some guys we lost and the survivor's guilt a lot of us hold onto. I think of I think of the morning of the friendly fire incident. So, it's mostly another platoon that got hit. But my call sign, we were there on the side of Masum Ghar and we were kind of left hand of the Company and next to that other platoon. We were all trying to sleep behind the LAVs. It was right after a big fight, and we were getting set to go back over the River to take to the enemy. We were worried about fire from the north of the Arghandab and so took cover behind the steel. That morning, I remember rolling out of my sleeping bag and packing up, climbing into the turret because I was an LAV Gunner and was just firing up the weapon systems for the day. "Turret on, weapons on, auxiliary on and thermals on...all that stuff." All the artillery, the fast air and other LAVs firing was just background noise, it had been going all night. I waited for the thermal to warm up, and as I was popping out of LAV when the A10 came in and strafed across the back of the company the whole position, where everyone had taken cover from Taliban fire. I remember thinking about that. In hindsight, you know, I could very easily been hurt or killed if I hadn't been in the turret at that exact moment. That, to me, just looks like my dumb luck. You know, so many guys got hurt that day and I just so happened to be the LAV gunner. If I'd rolled out of the sleeping bag five minutes later. If I had sat back five minutes earlier and had gotten out of the turret, I would have been hit. Wrong place, wrong time. I think it's just luck. I am not sure I have thought through this completely, but I feel lucky to be here and bad that others aren't. You think about fate a lot after it is over when you are home.

I don't think we, as in the whole mission (NATO Training Mission - Afghanistan or NTM-A), really had a plan. They only took building a training system seriously after fighting in the south had been going on for some time and it became clear that most Western publics would not support another ten years of active operations there. NTM-A leadership was obsessed with metrics and stamping out "corruption," and so were many Canadians. Too late, man. In my view, the Afghan corruption paled to the dishonesty and bad-faith practices of the contractors, who deliberately fostered dependence on them by the Afghans. They sent retired USMC logistics Sergeant Majors to advise on Bde-level operations and all kinds of stuff like that – they had no clue. They created a lot of flashy courses that were largely redundant and undermined our efforts to force the Afghans to fix their sustainment systems rather than hitting their contractor buddies to solve their problems. That's corruption. The unit we took over from had a bad relationship with the contractors, and I tried to turn a new leaf, but sometimes even our sister Regiments are right. It was obvious to Lieutenant-going-on-general that these guys were the systemic problem which we didn't have influence over, as opposed to the petty embezzlement of sporadically paid, ill-equipped Afghans who reflected structural incentives that we didn't have control over. Then again, there are a lot of Lts-going-on-generals and they're usually wrong. Personal patronage is a way of life there (and frankly, in good parts of Canada, too) and usually operated within reasonable boundaries. Making low-level corruption and fancy courses with patches a main effort while we sent under-prepared Afghan kids out to fight in the south and east upset me. It really, really bothered me then and saddens me now knowing that the ANA has taken about 60,000 casualties, and statistically speaking, many of those were genuinely keen kids we trained. Then again, I wasn't near the top, so I might be wrong or have been insufficiently observant enough to discern the plan. I feel like if we do this again, don't privatize war, don't use contractors. It develops the wrong incentives and the wrong goals. If you make a better army, you don't have a job, so you make a complex system and dependency.

Killing someone has different effects on every person. I remember we had Dave Grossman come to talk to us before we went out. He was the guy who did the books "On Killing" and "On Combat." Those circulated around the battalion like wildfire. They were very useful books. A lot of stuff from them held very true. Like my immediate reaction was like once I knew I'd killed in a close firefight, my first reaction was like one of euphoria. Like scoring a goal while playing ball hockey, and you get one in the top corner, you're like, YES. But getting one in the net in a game of ball hockey doesn't kill the goalie. You don't have to look at the goalie lying on the ground bleeding out and be like, look at your friends, and they know you "scored." It shifts from euphoria because you've done your job, survived, and applied the technical skill. You played the game exactly how it was taught, and it worked. You're happy about that. Also, you're happy because you're alive. But then you have to deal with that reality. That guy's dead now. And yeah, it had to happen, but it's still, still fucked up. These emotions conflict with the weird feeling of happiness of surviving. Would you rather be the one lying on the ground bleeding out? When you walk over the top of the bodies, you get to sort of look at them, see them, and realize that's a dude. You know, the Taliban is a title, but that's a fucking dude. Why was he out here? Is he out here because he's a religious fanatic, or are they out here because a fucking bomb that was meant for somebody else dropped through his window and killed his kids. Like you start asking yourself, like, what's this person's fucking story? And that eats at you a little bit, you know? You scored, but you are not sure that you don't want to take that goal back. Fucking confusing.

The younger generation that are in the army often joined because of Afghanistan, but they just missed it. It feels weird to be that guy saying to younger soldiers, "It might not have been what you think, and be glad that you don't have to go kind of thing." It feels kind of weird to say that because we were all like that. We had never experienced war before we deployed. There was that report that came out recently from the US that talked about how Afghanistan knew it was going to be a failure. I took the time to read about Afghanistan a lot. The theme was this has never been winnable. I thought, you know, we should really read about this because this is the quagmire and what we're getting ourselves into. But at the time, you don't think about it. One of the things I personally still have a hard time with is reconciling what we did there and why we went. I don't disagree with the decision to go to Afghanistan. I think we just had to go through this period where, after the war or during the war, we couldn't say anything bad about Afghanistan because it was a slight on the valour of the soldiers. I think as an institution and country, we are still reluctant to admit failure because we're we don't want to insult anyone, and we don't want to hurt the feelings of the families that lost soldiers. I think, to an extent, we need to we need to talk about the things we didn't do well because we learned a lot there. We also learned a lot of bad lessons, some bad lessons tactically. We also did a lot well. But it is like no one can really talk about it. It's hard for us to admit that we lost because I genuinely believe. I look at what was handed over to my Battle Group- an insurgency. And I look at what we handed over to another battle group, which was an insurgency. I don't think we made the place better. I think we kind of played whack-a-mole to a large extent. But that's not the fault of anyone, is it? Counterinsurgency is a long, long burn, and our government didn't see the value; it was a losing proposition, and they didn't stick out. I don't regret my time in Afghanistan, but I wish the government would have told us at the start that they didn't care about winning; I think we would have approached the problem differently.

––––––––––––

When I think about Afghanistan, I feel like I was just lucky not to get seriously hurt or die. It was just not my time to go. I was not even supposed to deploy. I was in the replacement group, and then a friend of mine got in a motorcycle accident, and I got his spot. A year later, after the tour, I was on a Battalion duty shift with a dude that was a sniper on overwatch on a bunch of fights I was in. He thought it was fate as our friend who did not go because of the motorcycle accident. He straight up told me "I thought you were going to die. I thought everything happens for a reason. And I told _____ that the reason he got in a motorcycle accident was because it wasn't his time to time to die. Which implies that I should have died as the replacement. But I'm not dead. And mentally, I don't know; sometimes, I think about it too much. I wasn't the dude who lost his life in Afghanistan. So, I don't know. I mean, I think it's kind of its kind of random. The near misses and talking about fate can fuck with you.

––––––––––––

"Canadian Soldiers Killed in Afghanistan" was the worst message that would run along the bottom of the CTV or CBC newscast. "Names and information to be released once the families have been notified". I was half of a service couple, and we had both deployed. That message would come on and you knew notifications were happening. You wanted to turn off your phone, grab the kids and leave the house. That way, you would not been told that your partner has been killed. It was impossible to get sleep until the names were out. No one had any info due to the communication lockdown from Afghanistan. It was hard. In Petawawa and Gagetown, everyone is connected. It was really hard on families; kids were notified about their parent's death at school, and your kids would find out there. I felt terrible, but I had such a huge relief when I did not get the call. I was so happy, and then angry and then sad. So much loss. You wanted to support your partner and be supported, but it is hard going through it. I hated the news.

It's a beautiful place. I have this amazing picture from Afghanistan. It's one of my wallpaper screens. It's this picture we took on the way to a mission. I remember I snapped it as we drove north up the TK Highway. It's this family of desert nomads. Camels and with carpets and tents strapped to them. There's a family dog there. Everyone's in traditional dress in this picture, the mountains are laid in the background. It looks like something from a thousand years ago. It's amazing. A beautiful sunset set off the vibrant colour of the landscape there. The environment is extreme, and often, these small moments of peace are shattered by violence. Those rare instants of peace stay with you forever and give you hope. They represent the potential Afghanistan holds if it is just given a chance.

It's a little challenging on a philosophical level to say, hey, one of the best experiences of my life was in the middle of a war-torn country where the population was having some of the worst experiences on the globe. What for me was a growth experience because I survived; what about those families that didn't have their family members come home or they came home broken? It left widows, sons and daughters taken from parents, and children left without parents. How do you say this was a positive experience? It really wasn't a negative for me. I give respect to the darker moments, but do not let them colour or overtake the other experiences. This is where I feel conflicted. I feel like I can do anything because I thrived in combat. But feel bad for those that lost.

Did we do something of value for our country? I think we did. In a mission that was not easy. We tried to do right by our country. We tried to complete the mission and tried to give a better life to the Afghans. I believe that. The thing is that even if you could prove to me that we didn't provide a better life to those Afghans, I would tell you that when we served Canada, you can't ask us to do more when the politicians don't really care. We tried our best for Canada despite a poorly conceived mission deemed a failure before it started. Even by trying to do it on the cheap and not being there to win. I think we succeeded in our little corner of Afghanistan during our little part of the war. We can't look at the big picture. It is too painful.

Leaving and going home had an initial euphoria. You just came home, and everything was good with the world. It wasn't till later that you started to see the cracks. It's like coming down off a high. You've just been through something fucking nuts. You survive. You're awesome. Drink beer, party and enjoy being back in Canadian society. Now, you need to calm down and try to get back into your normal routine. Getting into a routine is when it gets awkward. That's when the shit comes out. Even though your family is around you feel alone. You spend all your time on deployment with a group of guys. There's always somebody there, there's always somebody to fucking talk to. There's always somebody to fucking confide in. I remember being in the turret with this one guy night after night. Hundreds of hours were spent talking and scanning the desert through the optics of a 25mm turret. He told me literally about every sexual encounter he'd had in his entire life to the point that he started to repeat himself by the end of the tour. The whole time I am there, I'm just banging my head against the fucking armour of the turret. Just make it fucking stop. I don't want to hear any more about your goddamn sex life. I don't know what you're getting out of this, but I'm getting nothing out of it. Why is it that? Why is this a discussion? There are a lot of military discussions like that, especially young dudes, raging fucking hormones, and three topics; sex, shitting and sports. It is terrible while you are in the country, everyone is in everyone's business, but when you get home, it just stops. You miss that presence, that trust, the fact that you count on each other every day. You do not want the boring discussions, but you miss the closeness, you miss the intimacy of the relationships, it sounds stupid to say that, but that is what it is. The relationships are intimate, then you get home and there is all this space and nothing you do or say seems to matter to anyone else. No one seems to understand you, and you feel alone. I was ready to get back to work after being home for a week; I have never found connections as close. I don't want updates on his sex life, but I love hearing that dude's voice and boring stories. Makes me feel connected.

———

I didn't really understand why Canada was pulling out. I understood that we were taking hits, but that was always the cost and casualties were going down as we got better at fighting the enemy. I was a crew commander for a senior officer and so saw some high-level meetings. We seemed to be making progress. We're building schools, we have polio programs, we are paving roads. We were almost done. I see all this progress being made, yet we're pretty much just gonna wash our hands of it. I feel angry, it really pissed me off. I would especially get angry as we would roll through some of the areas where my buddies had died on previous tours, and now we're just going to fuckin fuck it all off and give it to the A.N.A. or worse, directly back to the Taliban. I knew some progress was going to be lost. It was very stressful; it was really starting to become annoying to me that I still didn't feel that we were completely finished with the mission in Afghanistan. But we were fucking withdrawing. I am not sure I have ever reconciled the loss of my friends, the message that we were supposed to be there to win and then the announcement of the early withdrawal. It is very frustrating.

———————

I have tried to answer a few times if it was all worth it. What about the families of the fallen? Would it be worth it? That's the personal connection. I think if you ask any soldier's family in any war whether their child's death or spouse's death was worth it, what would they say? They would either say that it was worth it because that makes their loss make sense, or they would say, there is nothing worth the loss of their loved one. I focused on a false narrative about what we were there to achieve. I feel now that we were not there to achieve all the goals that we always talked about or that the government talked about because we knew that they were unrealistic. I knew it was unrealistic then; I'm sure those in charge knew that they were unrealistic. Perhaps it is because the stated goals and the national goals had such a big gap. Nationally, we needed to be seen doing something to support our biggest trading partner after saying no to Iraq and we needed to lead in NATO. NATO needed to demonstrate value when there was no existential threat and that it could operate in a pseudo-war setting. It is amazing the alliance did not break up over Afghanistan. But that had nothing to do with what we were trying to do on the ground. It seemed that the operational success was secondary to the metrics of money spent, troops deployed and basking in the warmth of the light of taking a leading role. Was it worth it? Not for you or the individual families that lost a soldier. It never will be. Was it worth it from a national policy perspective? Absolutely. It gave us a small window of opportunity for Canada to sit at a table that is reserved for countries that invest blood and treasure. We did both in Afghanistan, and for a little while that earned some credit from our Allies. I just think we need to be clear on what the definition of "victory" is and why it MAY have been worth it. It definitely wasn't about making Afghanistan better. If it was, we would have stayed.

———————

It was interesting to see how going back into the world was so banal. We got home and did our 2 1/2 days at work in order to "reintegrate". I arrived back home in the middle of winter in New Brunswick and my wife was going back to work. I'm just here by myself, you know. Some of the interesting things I carry from the tour is that I don't like traffic, like confined traffic or traffic jams and the smell of garbage. Makes me retch like every time I smell garbage. I got posted to Toronto and I remember doing my house hunting trip in the middle of rush hour in Toronto, just like a few months before or less about a year before I'd been in Afghanistan. The traffic was just overwhelming I want everybody to get the fuck away from me. Then the smell of garbage, too. I remember one day when a garbage truck had turned over on the side of Shepherd now, and then that smell of that garbage just brought me right back, and I had a hard time dealing with it. It took me a while to get over a kind of sound like a survivor's guilt. I felt kind of guilty in that I didn't feel like we really contributed a whole lot. I was very bitter, upset, and guilty. I remember watching a documentary by Vice called "This is What Winning Looks Like." It was 2015 after we cut and run, watching these Marines down in Helmand, having the same issues we were having years earlier. I realized, at that point, the institutional problems with the Afghans. The issues with ISAF. The issues with the government of Canada's plan, we were in an impossible situation. It wasn't just me. No, it wasn't my fault. It was out of my control. I could empathize with them as our allies carried on the fight and then transfer or absolve myself of that guilt and shame because I realized this was so much bigger than me.

I had a soldier who died under my command; his family thought he was on a shower run, and his vehicle hit the IED. They thought he died going to get a shower. He didn't. He was actually part of my extraction team from a night patrol. They had been told that we hadn't had showered in 40 days and he died shuttling to the shower. It left them wondering about the value of his life. It was not until I got home and visited with the family to let them know the circumstances of how their son died. It shouldn't matter, people died and were hurt doing all sorts of missions, just walking back to the FOB, going on HLTA. I had hit an IED going in for orders. The difference that was made to this family was massive. It mattered to them that he died doing an essential part of the mission, that he was moving into the face of the enemy and that he died like a soldier and not just on a routine drive to get a shower. I am glad that I was able to help them heal a bit, it helped me also. It felt good to see them smile. It changed the picture in my mind from when we were zipping their son up in a bag.

From my personal soldiering point of view, the mission was worthwhile because it allowed me to prove and understand and experience the things that had always been theoretical. I guess the theory lessons of the randomness of combat. It taught me to be a professional and although you can prepare as much as you want for anything, there's this portion or percentage of randomness that's going to happen that's going to affect how things evolve. So professionally, it was definitely rewarding as a professional soldier. From a national perspective. I'm 100 percent convinced and that goes back to how weak we were on fighting the war. There was no national interest and everyone was just rotating through. I think an operational construct was built and we just pounded that round peg into that square hole. We did not match the solution to the problem. We were a solution looking to solve the problem we wanted to. Personally, it was worth it for me, and if I hadn't gone, I would always wonder about not going. I am a soldier and am supposed to fight wars. For the guys who were wounded, perhaps it was less valuable because it changed them forever. However, I think everybody gets changed forever. It's how you deal with it, how you reflect on the change and how you push onto the next challenge.

A few years later, I was milling about with a bunch of battalion officers – this time at a different battalion than I deployed with - for a Remembrance Day ceremony. The CO came over, looked at my campaign star, and said I ought to have a General Service Medal, not GCS because I did Operation Attention instead of combat. I don't fully disagree with him, but it's still a rotten thing to say to someone in front of their peers. It's an instructional story because it shows how much the army as an institution actively didn't care about the mission. I could not help when I joined or what I did in Afghanistan. I was part of the withdrawal and training mission, so what? Lots of people didn't shoot anyone; I hated that shit. I got asked to serve and I did. That should be enough.

Feeling lucky and taking away the good things from the deployments is so important. On the civilian side of things, I find that a lot of my friends, whether they're in their 20s or up to their 50s, especially men, are not validated in a classically macho role or classically masculine role. If they don't feel validated by any of those things, then I find there are a lot of them having these crises of self. I listen to them, and I find I don't have to say I did all these things or rather, my group did all these things. We did accomplish quite a few things, maybe not as much as we had hoped but it wasn't nothing. I don't feel like I need to buy a large truck. I don't need to do all this posturing that a lot of guys do. There's very much richness to my life, not just monetary. But I mean, there's that there's a richness having these experiences combined with regular everyday life and the freedoms that we're allowed here in Canada. Just voting today or going home to see my kids. This is fantastic. And there's not a week, and in most cases, not a day goes by that I don't think about my friends that didn't come home. How it would have been for them with their kids or things with them. Every time I have a milestone, I think of my friends who have kids the same age, and they are not there; they didn't make it back from Afghanistan. I feel validated and so lucky.

By the time we got late in the war. Soldiers needed to sign waivers to go back. This meant they "waived" the mandatory rest time and were willing to go back. Talented NCOs were the hardest and those with specialised skill sets. Counter IED, snipers, and recce were all in high demand. It meant that those doing the hardest jobs were also going back the most. We were dealing with third, fourth and even fifth tour waivers to Afghanistan. When you get to that kind of a point, you're trying to understand if they should really go back again. Effectively, we had to fire seven sergeants during work-up training because they just they weren't they weren't cutting it in. Some we had to remove because they shouldn't go back again. It was for their own good. But some of it was the fact that it's because we were forced to promote quickly as soldiers burnt out, and the rate was not good for the Canadian forces. Some of these guys just weren't competent. So, we had at least three we actually had to remove because they weren't competent. This put incredible pressure on all the units and the leaders that were left in the breach. It meant that people that were not supposed to go, got the call when these guys were cut. I had this one Sergeant. Awesome guy. He already had three combat tours, he had done everything we had asked him, all the courses with all the badges that Infantry soldiers desire. After we had to get rid of dead weight, we came to this guy; he was having Marital issues and had had a couple of hard tours; when he was told he was now going because other people failed, he balked and asked for a pass, this one time. He was not going to sign the waiver, which was his choice. You would think he was one of the guys that had failed us! The senior NCO leadership went up one side of him and down the other. Even going so far as to call him a coward. Then he was forced to come on tour through guilt. It sucked, but if I am honest, I was happy to have him. Later in his career, he flamed out, moral injury and PTSD, I don't doubt it. He was completely used by the organization and tossed when they didn't need him. It was an impossible problem, generating Battle Groups year in and out. I was too young to have done it but even some of the Officers were like that. I had a CO later in my career that had been a 2LT, Captain and Major all outside the wire in Afghanistan. It was a lot to ask, and I am not sure our army is completely recovered from it.

I think I think we fostered a lot of lessons and realizations from the mission. I think we have proven that the way we train NCOs works; we have proven that like we have some of the fucking best leaders and best soldiers. We have proven that the basics work. In that sense, we had received a lot of valuable confirmations. Have we exploited them since we left? I don't think so. So, was it worth it? It's worth it if we learn and build from that. But if we turn into a train to retain (soldiers) organization, then its skin deep. If we turn into that organization that navel gazes and wonders about DEI instead of fighting and winning. We forget these valuable lessons; if we don't respect the level of ability and capability our NCOs have, then I think it was all for nothing. You know, a piece of ground is a piece of ground. Afghanistan is fucking far more complicated than any one country can do to provide security. We were never going to win, and our government didn't care if we did. I don't fucking know. I think I think for us, though, as a regiment as an army, I think we got offered a whole bunch of confirmations, viable shit that you can't figure out in training. As we get farther away, I am sure it happens every war; now we care about haircuts and beards and smoking dope, and we think these things will make better soldiers. Not sure they will, but then again, maybe that isn't what Canada wants from its army. If it is, we better grab onto the lessons we learned, make sure that soldiers go through the required hardships, the team building and the shared risk and understand what we do. We kill on behalf of our government. We are there to try and win. We are not a social experiment. We are tasked to kill the people that the nation believes need to be killed, and one day, maybe sooner than later, we will be asked to defend it, not in a war of choice but one of survival. It will be a shame if all the lessons learned at the cost of the blood of our friends are for nought.

The Army talks about family stuff all the time. But the army wants to post you and to go on courses and even if you are hurt, it WILL impact your career if you don't go, especially at the height of Afghanistan. Make no mistake, it was not "ok to not be OK" and still advance professionally. Reintegration is managed. Almost no one does the questionnaires, honestly, so as to not trip a psych visit, and the Battalion and Army immediately need to keep the machine going, like a tour in war is just another task and then you are shipped off to the next thing. Maybe getting ready for the next tour, maybe a training institution, maybe a career course. So, I like to think that there was nothing wrong with me. We did the usual return routine and talked to people. It would go something like this.

"Hey, how are you feeling?"

Me, "Great. Good. Home in one in piece what could be wrong?"

" That is good to hear, you are cleared without restrictions"

Me, "perfect"

And that was it. I never went to the family integration brief. My wife did as she saw a flyer and went without telling me. She was listening to the dude talking about signs and symptoms of mental health issues. My wife's just checking them all off. When she talked to me about it, I was like And I'm like, no, no, no! It came to a head as I felt pressured by her to seek help and we're pretty close to calling it a day on the marriage. It was tough when she brought that to my attention. You know what? She was right. It's legit. You know, you can't hide it. I'd say the biggest thing I did was just start talking to people and slowly start to address some of the issues. I still kept it under wraps and did not go to Army Psyches. I did not want it on my records. I kept deploying and training. When we got out of Afghanistan, the army improved a lot in that five years with the pressure of deployments off. After the war, it was "let's help you," but for a while, it was grim and just about cost me my marriage.

———————

I look back at all three tours, there's all distinctly different. I don't regret anything from any of them. I think we can feel like we made a difference there. You know, it's funny. I was playing hockey recently and, you know, some of the young guys are asking questions about it. They call me Dad in the dressing room. I'm thirty-nine, they are low thirties or twenties. There really is not that much space between us. I feel like I'm in my mid to late 20s and I spent two years of my life in my twenties in Afghanistan. And another two years training to go. That's right, the best time of your fucking life growing up, and I spent it in or preparing for Afghanistan.

———————

So, the mission made a difference. It's funny because people that think big, they can't see the difference. The first time we got to Panjawaii, there's fucking nothing, and it was a shithole. There are no kids. There are no schools. By the time I went back, two years later, people were out and about the markets were up. I could buy something in the town like it was it was insane. But if the Canadians were there for the first time, they thought that it was violent. For them, it wasn't their fault because they couldn't compare but the level of violence was so far down between 2006 to 2008 to 2010. I just think it's good for us to kind of sometimes keep perspective because we can only talk with the short time we were there. I think that if we had a longer view, we would have seen the improvement.

———————

You know, I don't remember a lot of the details from some of the events. I can't hang on to this stuff. I don't want this to fucking destroy me. I think that's probably one thing that it's kind of helped me nowadays. I don't live in the past. It happened as a part of my life. Did it change me? Yep. I understand changing, I accept who I am. I had no regrets about it. It's OK to be OK, too.

———————

Every time I talk to someone like a civilian friend or family member about Afghanistan they always say, what's stuck out to you? I mean, it was the beauty of Kabul. Not the city itself; it is like a medieval town, but the landscape is breathtaking with the mountain ranges all around. The air was so different. I mean, Poli Charki was a bit cleaner than downtown Kabul. But it was something to wake up in the morning having coffee with like that cool air breeze and the Afghan fucking menthol cigarettes. It's almost detached from the horror show of what humans have done to Afghanistan. It's like untouched terrain, you know, it's just it's raw and wild. The road to Bagram is incredible. There are these giant plateaus. You keep climbing. Then you hit another plateau It's just this wild plain with the tops of the Hindu Kush all around you. It's insane. While there, you don't appreciate the remoteness or the beauty, but later, you realize that you'll never go anywhere in the world like that again.

———————

I go back to my Afghan partner on the question of the value of our mission. My discussions arose because he would always say that he's been alive in Afghanistan for 40 years. And the last 10 years, from 2001 to 2011, were the most peaceful.

He would say "you think this is a war, but no one's raining rockets on us every day like what happened when the warlords were fighting, or the mass killing and fear when the Russians were here. We have structure." "This is peaceful. ISAF has brought stability. It does not look like Canada, but how can it?" And I think that it's a perspective. I thought that was very interesting context. I think sometimes as Canadians, we have been so blessed that we don't understand the success of relative peace. I think about my earlier tours in Yugoslavia. That was a country that had held the Olympics, had everything going for it and it descended into a bloody civil war. We committed and it took us 25 years to see results and in fact there are still forces there. What made everyone think Afghanistan, which was starting well behind Yugoslavia was going to be a shorter commitment. It is generational. We let them down before they had a chance to be successful. Their peace and the opportunity for their young people was in the "too hard box."

Does success in the mission itself garner more questions than answers? By virtue of the fact that it asked more questions and answers, do we have to invest more? I think for the time we were there, we made a difference. I think that in the long term, it's almost like when you look at, you know, there's that old saying, "You have all the watches, but we have all the time." The Taliban just waited for us to leave. Change the mindset of a culture takes roughly three generations. We're not going to invest three generations. Unless you're willing to put a consistent presence there for three generations with the funding and the money and not just deal with the symptoms but the root causes, you are not going to "win."

I don't think I ever really fired my weapon. I got shot at a lot, and we got blown up, but I never fired because I was usually on the radio and other people were doing the shooting. I never had that moment where I had to defend myself or that I would have added more with my rifle rather than my radio. I always wondered if that meant that I was not a real vet. I killed people with bombs and artillery; I risked my life, and I treated casualties. But did not pull the trigger on my rifle.

I think about those guys that didn't make it. I think about this one friend of mine, we were on a patrol near the Arghandab and he stepped in the wrong spot and stepped on an IED. Nothing left. Just mist. The guy walking near him suffered a wound, and we initially thought it was shrapnel, but when they removed it from his hand, it was a bone chip from the guy who had stepped on the IED. That kind of messed with him a little, being wounded by a part of his friend. We were pretty lucky. I just didn't step in the wrong spot. I have to say that that goes back to luck of the draw sometimes. We came very close on a number of occasions. But I am here with my family with all my limbs and others aren't. Who knows why? You just don't know why shit happens the way it does. It's something that you just can't control but you can't help thinking about it. How you choose to live the life you were given is what matters after.

Was it worth it? And did we accomplish anything? I think at the soldier level, definitely worth it. We accomplished things, even if it's the small things. Just working with the Afghans, our mere presence changed the country fundamentally. The countries are fundamentally different. There are people who think about life differently now and have been exposed to us. Our ideas are our views, our values, and our beliefs. I won't say that they adopted them wholesale or any other piece, but the effects have been there. As much as we were affected by our time there, they were affected by our time. Was it worth it? You have to think so. That is the small things that you did where you preserved life in some area, we had a schoolteacher arrested who was fucking with kids. I had an impact on those kids that sexual assault was not Ok. You have to think and act locally. If not, you will drive yourself crazy.

I do think about our national commitment to Afghanistan. You think about what it is that we were trying to do and the cost. You think about that because of the loss of life. I always try to put things into perspective. However, you know, because my wife is very much, I think, an average Canadian who is very unaware of our military history. She feels so terrible about what happened in Afghanistan. She has 158 people and soldiers killed in Afghanistan. You know, I kind of contextualize them and say there were like 60000 kids killed in WW1, just over 20000 killed in World War Two Five hundred and 29 killed in Korea. So, really, this war, a decade long, was pretty cheap, and the majority of our losses were from 2006 to 2010. As a soldier, this is what you sign on for; that possibility is very real. But it's how we're spending those resources and what's the end game? I think there's nothing that really keeps me awake at night other than in the other wars winning wasn't discretionary. It was the expected outcome. Now, war or these wars are not necessary for survival, or we don't really believe that we need to bring democracy to the world so we can quit. I deal with my experiences. But the thing that does keep me awake is how we consider victory as an institution and then what the nation believes in. Those two should be aligned. They weren't in Afghanistan. The soldiers cared. The nation didn't really. If we are ever going to fight again, we have to make sure we have the nation behind us, not in a red Friday way, but in a "demand victory" way. I was idealistic before. I am a cynic now. I think that is what I lost in war.

———————

Sometimes, tactical patience took six months to learn. I always felt like at the end of every one of my six-month tours, I really had a grip on the enemy and terrain. Had we stayed for another six months, then I really could have made a difference. I think the Canadian army pushed a UN tour rotation schedule on a war, and we never gained the advantage of experience in the fight. We should think about that if we ever do it again.

———————

I guess one of the lessons to share here is that all the training that I got did prepare me for Afghanistan. It's just a case of nothing can prepare you for combat. There's no training that actually prepares you. I mean, you get told what it's like. You get told the things that you must do, and then all those lessons are valid. But you still have to see the real thing in order to figure out. It is one thing to do section attacks under control in an open field and it is another to do it at night when you are scared and all you can see is muzzle flashes from a treeline. People have to adapt to that, if they do, they can be a good combat leader, if they cannot make the switch to bringing control to a chaotic situation, they are dangerous.

———————

Fought the demons for a lot of years. You have to learn to try and only control things that are within your influence. I actually reached out and did find help when I needed it. I think it was a mixture of a bunch of things, you know like I was angry. The fact that you know, we lost so many people, so many great men and women. Then the other part that was frustrating for me when I got back to Canada was that there were so many people who had demons that it didn't seem like they were getting the right help. I was angry and of course, when you get angry, it plays on everybody around you. It got to the point where, you know, my wife and my kids were walking on eggshells because they didn't know how dad was going to feel when he came home on a daily basis. So that's when I realized that, hey, something's not right here. We need to look into this. And I'm glad I did because obviously, my family relationship is still there. I'm still married. I still have my kids. They don't hate me. It's important to actually take that step. I felt like a hypocrite for so many years. I was that leader who said to my troops and my subordinates that if you're having problems, go seek help. But I never did. I wanted to I just didn't know how to do it. Finally, I got to the point where I said, OK, enough is enough. I did reach out. And I'm glad I did because I feel that I consider myself a better leader now, knowing that I've hit that road. I did that therapy and I got that help. Now I'm back to a healthy lifestyle.

––––––––––––––––

I struggle with it sometimes, whether it was successful. I wanted to stay. I was really sad that we pulled out. That's what the uncomfortable thing was, I wish we had stayed and continued to improve, or at least stayed until our key allies departed, but not be the first to leave. I guess it must end politically at some point and how to do it right. There may have never been a right way or time, but in the end, the people are the ones who will suffer. I wish we had just stayed. I feel like we gave false hope, and now all those kids who grew up believing that they had an opportunity have been taken away by our betrayal.

––––––––––––––––

The only way for a cost of blood and treasure to be worth it is if we maintained the presence there to see it through. We just gave it all back to them. To me, in my mind, we lost lives for no reason, and if we're going to do that just to abandon it, then we should not have gone in. It'd be different if we were fighting a conventional war, but guerrilla warfare is ugly. I felt good when we pulled out initially, mostly because I was tired, but then to think about it, all these soldiers lost their lives over there. We've just abandoned the country or abandoned all the good that we've done. So that's kind of conflicted me. If we stayed. Yes, we would have lost more lives. But it's difficult. Yeah. I think we're all still a bit conflicted and will likely stay that way for the rest of our lives. We lost, and as soldiers, that runs deep.

––––––––––––––––

I wanted to come in and talk about this to you because, I don't know, killing those guys has been something that I've kept sort of private for a while. Aside from guys who have been there and have close family relations as they know, I don't tell everyone I meet like I don't want anyone to know. I don't necessarily want people to think of me in a certain way, yeah. And you never know how people react to that. This is like. Hi there. I'm so and so... I'm a killer. Do with that, what you do, I guess? Because it's not something you want to define you. It feels like such a big thing to show to people that, in their minds, it will define you. You know, it's a little bit of a central fear and though I have not left the army, sometimes I wonder if I can imagine a job interview. What was an important event in your life? Not many HR folks are ready for that discussion! The biggest thing was when I killed three Taliban soldiers up close that were going to kill me and my friends." I don't remember what I saw through the sites like my mind is a fucking blanket, and I still don't have that to this day. It's taken a lot of time to sort of pull memories back out. I feel like I need to. Like right now, talking about this, I'm a little shaky. Yeah, it's been more than a decade. You know, I had to get help when I got back in because it was pretty fucked up. I deal with it. But yeah, it has been eating me for a while. Like for I'd say for the better part of 10 years, that memory had the best of me. Now I've learned to live with it. I mean, it's still there. I don't think I'm ever going to get rid of it, but I've got ways to deal with it and live with it. One of the reasons to want to tell these stories. So that these lessons don't have to be learned the hard way. You know, somebody, hopefully, some junior leader will read this book, or some private will read this book, and they'll be like, that's something I never thought of.

I am an NCO. A professional soldier with 7 tours overseas. The thing I'm proud of the most, I think is the way the troops performed on patrol. Because not once on that tour did, I have to talk to them about carriage of weapons or spacing. It's like a switch. Not like training in Canada. Every single soldier when they laid it on the line over there. They knew that when I left this gate, it didn't mean I was coming back, and I was going to be ready for whatever was going to happen. That was really good to see. It was amazing to be a part of young Canadians that were so professional. I don't know about all the politics, but I know we knew our shit.

Afghans don't care, they are just fighting to survive. Most of them have been fighting their whole life. They were Mujahedeen or were with the Russians, or they were with the warlords or all three. Some fought with the Taliban to survive and then changed sides after nine eleven. Some are just NATO-trained. The only thing that matters is survival. I don't think we do that because we have never had to live in a lawless society. We saw things as "good" or bad. Us or them. They just saw it as survival.

My biggest lesson was I would just say, like, be calm and be who you are. I think, like, Afghanistan really taught me how to be a calm leader. After experiencing combat and all that being super, super, hyper and such doesn't win in combat. It's just being who you are being nice and calm and relaxed. When the younger soldiers see, you calm. Then they'll be calm. Yeah, I think that was my biggest lesson. Be the calm voice on the radio. When I got back, I had to do my yearlong French course; one of the things I would always get hammered on was sounding like I wasn't excited, or I was very bored doing French. I found the course very stressful; it was necessary for me to be promoted. After I had done 4 tours in Afghanistan the deciding factor for me to be an NCO leader was French. So, I think the system kicked in and it was talking on the radio, just made me calm, almost disinterested. And I think that might fucked me in my yearlong French course because I know when I'm in a high-stress situation, I calm down. And it was one of my points I was brought up was like, it sounds like you're just not excited talking in French. Agreed, I wasn't.

I think part of part of the struggle that people have back home is not having constant support. Overseas your buddies are always around. It's not necessarily the bad days that cause PTSD. It's a lack of the really good days. There is the classic meme of a guy in battle rattle kicking in a door. "This is PTSD, realizing you'll never be this cool again." You know, this is a granule of truth to that, which is you miss that camaraderie, that the singular purpose, waking up, knowing what your mission is, knowing what you have to do. You seem to drift after that and find little purpose where decisions are not life and death, they are all benign. Important but hard to reach the level of what you did at your professional peak.

Hindsight is 20/20, right? When we got home, we posted everyone to their "careers," and they had no one who understood them. The company was torn apart immediately because a professional army needs to post people in and out the next day after getting back from Afghanistan. I was right back in the office early morning to an admin and then finish off around then being a company 2IC, and it was not good. You know what really happened. I think that as fast as guys were reporting in they were sent to new tasks and posts. I think we could've prevented some of the issues that happened because there were a few guys who did kill themselves. Some guys spiralled down the trail because all their leadership and support network was gone. You had good people in their new units who are in there who tried to make sense of it but didn't have the guts to really make the hard calls, the background, and contacts to take care of the people who had just been fighting together for two years.

One of my friends got hit hard by an IED and it wounded him severely. It disfigured his face, so the surgeons had to do total reconstruction, but it would never be the same. I remember sitting there talking to him, and pretending his face was not that bad, and it terrified me, and I realized that it was just random. Just bad luck, between injured or not, dead or not. In the type of war where IEDs are the main weapon, it really does not matter if you are great as a soldier. You can reduce your chances, but you can never, just through skill and dedication, guarantee survival. This is true in a firefight also, but somehow that seems fairer, and gunshot wounds seem less scary than IEDs. After I got out of Afghanistan, I realized that this fear of randomness stayed with me. I developed a fear of flying that started the minute I got on the airplane to leave theatre. I knew it was not rational, I could force myself onto the plane, but inside, I was screaming against getting on. Holy fuck. I was never like this before. I recognized that I changed. I am still not comfortable on planes. I think one of the things that you recognize, the fragility of life there, how in an instant it disappears in very random moments. I get by, but every day, there is this feeling of it ending suddenly. I hide it well; I do my job and take care of my kids and am not a PTSD case. But watching my little kids at the park terrifies me, all I see is how they could hurt themselves, not how much fun they are having. I have not even told my wife. I am on edge quite a bit of the time. I think they call it "hypervigilance." I have to wonder if that just means you are aware of your mortality.

People talk about a stigma around mental health. I've heard guys say things like you go to mental health, they're kicking you out of the army, you know, and it's not true. I mean, I'm still here. I'm still operational. I might need a little bit of extra interview time with the Medical Officer before I deploy, but I'm still good. But I did a lot of stupid shit dealing, trying to deal with shit on my own. With fucking alcohol. I had very poor control over my emotions coming back, I had all sorts of combat stress markers, and they're there plain as fucking day. I just did not want to be broken. You know, as if I don't want that attached to me. I did go in, but I was very resistant to treatment, like things like pharmaceuticals. I remember the MO talking to me like, well, we can prescribe something for this. I'm like, no, I don't want it, crazy people take pills. In hindsight, maybe it would've been a fucking good idea had I have done so. I don't know what the experience of being on that stuff. It had to have been better than me trying to fucking self-medicate with a bottle, you know. I had a lot of shitty fucking experiences; I got in fights, and relationships went to fucking hell, and none of that helps. That's part of the reason I'm here. But I mean, I guess the most important reason I'm here is the pass-on lessons on the lessons like just get fucking help. You know, if somebody reads this book the lesson that they get is don't be afraid to seek help. I mean, if you don't seek help and you behave like a fucking madman, that'll end your career. If you get drunk and rage and fuckin beat your spouse. That ends your career and your life, you know? Just get over the fear and take that step if you need it.

Soldiers have a unique connection. If I don't talk to civvie friends continually, I can't connect in any way. But with the guys I served with we can go years of not talking and pick up like nothing happened and there has been no time lost. You build a relationship with a core group of individuals, spend 24/7/365 with them, and not have them be family. You will know the ins and outs of this guy's life more than probably his family does, and it's just. You don't need to be in constant contact for years. I suppose it sort of makes sense. It's a unique friendship that no one who doesn't live this life will comprehend. So that's a really, really good it's. It's a family, and I find sometimes I am closer to these guys than I am to my own family. You've lived through experiences that no one else will ever understand.

I needed to do something about this. My head space and time was off. I have been going to counselling. I was in pain and was super aggressive. I started seeing a therapist twice a week and stuff. It gave me tools to start to feel like I can deal with what was bothering me. For me the problem is guilt. The guys that died and I wasn't there with them. That's kind of impossible. I lost good friends on some bad days. I always wish I had been there and done more, and we all know we can't be everywhere at once. I would get very angry because you see the general public just going round just living. Daily life and like these people don't have a fucking clue. I didn't want people to forget and I wouldn't want people forget my buddies who died. It made sense in my fucked-up brain, but I was always so angry and guilty. It is getting better, but there are still bad days. When we forget them, we betray them.

When people say, was it worth it? I don't know. People died there, and I think that what we did at the smallest level was worth it; we helped a village or a school or improved someone's life. When you look at the big picture and all that, how much has changed there? Not at all, or is it worse there because everyone's pulled out? I think we were at the point of how much longer we had to stay and what we had to do differently to make a difference. I know that on the first tour, I noticed that difference in Kabul because I think that it was a different place to begin with, more modern compared to Kandahar, which was not interested in changing. I don't know what you could do differently. Like we tried killing everybody. That didn't work. So, we tried doing the rebuilding and all that and that didn't work either. Probably if we had stayed like if we're still there for like forever. I think maybe there are people that don't want to live like us and that has to be OK. But the people in the North that did, well we should have supported them. So in the end we made a difference in our 6 months, but we changed nothing. There are Humvees that are abandoned right next to the Russian BRDMs that were abandoned in the 80s. Afghanistan has no life that isn't conflict. It is what they do. We play hockey, and they fight and beat nations. No changing that ever. Still sucks we lost. I lose sleep over it.

I mean, we were all young guys. We rode that combat wave. I think there was a lot of recruiting back in that day that were just guys who were getting in because there was a fight. You know, they want to join the army to fight. I think a lot of those guys are now out, and they did their three years, they did tours until Afghanistan ended, and then they didn't want to be here anymore. You know, a peacetime army gives differently and rewards differently. I don't know if it is a fact. It's just an observation on Facebook Intel.

I knew he was hurt. He had suffered in the past from surviving an IED blast where his friends were killed. He was like a poster child for how to react. He did physical therapy and mental therapy and was ready to fight again. He fooled all of us. He asked to redeploy to Kandahar and we let him. It was a few months after we got home that I found out he had committed suicide. I always think if there was anything more, I could have done. I don't know, but it makes me sad that the Taliban have killed so many of us after we have gotten home.

I think that it is so strange, Canada chose an ugly war to get involved in, Afghanistan had already been at war for 20 years, our soldiers played hockey and football in their youth, and the kids we were fighting had shot at people since the time they could stand, it was their game, they did not know any different. I felt terrible about killing Afghan youth, what a fucking waste, but it was where our government put us, I wish our foreign policy could have figured out another way, but they didn't and so, in the end, it was our young people, that were going do this for 8 months and return to a peaceful nation, killing their young people that were in it forever. I wonder what is harder psychologically for each side. No doubt Afghans have a harder life, but sometimes I think that Canadian youth seeing the contrast of the realities may be hard, and not having anyone in Canada understand may be harder than living in a society that lives it always. This dissonance between realities is what I think hurts our soldiers after they come home. We needed to kill the people trying to kill us and to be successful, it meant we were killers, but when we got home, we didn't talk about killing, we used antiseptic terms, and it was not polite conversation. If we are going to go to war again we have to figure out to have society aligned and take on their portion of responsibility for what we do. It can't be discussed in hushed tones. You sent us there, you wanted us to kill, and we did now allow it to be discussed in the light and acknowledge its value to society.

These stories have been captured to honour the memory of:

The 158 Canadian soldiers who gave their lives in Afghanistan.

The more than 150 Afghan veterans who have since committed suicide,

The more than 1800 wounded Canadian soldiers who continue to live with the impact of the war.

The more than 5000 homeless veterans living hard across Canada.

And the millions of Afghans abandoned to the Taliban by the West.

ACKNOWLEDGEMENTS

Writing this book has been a long and often emotional journey. I feel a deep responsibility to the subject and the people. My deepest thanks go to the Canadian warriors who bravely shared their stories, reflecting on their experiences in Afghanistan with honesty and courage. Without their trust, this book would not exist, and I am honoured to bring their voices to light.

To Phil and my editors; both from Double Dagger Books and informal, thank you for your keen eyes, guidance, and patience as we shaped these stories together. Thank you for taking a chance on this project.

To my family—Erin, Alexander, and Rachael—thank you for your patience and sacrifice. You've endured my many deployments, the long stretches of absence, and the countless changes that military life has demanded. Your strength and resilience have been a constant reminder of what impressive humans you are-often in spite of the circumstances you find yourselves. I am so grateful and proud of each of you.

Finally to Heather, this journey has been ours as much as mine. We have been inextricably linked regardless of challenge. Your sacrifice and commitment for our family has allowed for all that has occurred. We have faced the strain of separation and the trials that come with distance, yet we've always found a way back. Your steadfast support, even in the hardest moments, have formed my foundation. You supported this work from inception to completion and my deepest thanks to you for walking this difficult path with me. Now, finally, we continue forward with a renewed bond and shared purpose. I am eternally grateful to have you as my partner in life.

This book is not just a collection of stories—it is a testament to the people who have made it possible.

ABOUT THE AUTHOR

Steve MacBeth was born in Moose Jaw, Saskatchewan, and is a a 25-year veteran of the Canadian Armed Forces. He began his career as a soldier in the Princess Patricia's Canadian Light Infantry before being selected to the Officer Corps, where he served with The Royal Canadian Regiment as an Infantry Officer. His deployments include Bosnia, multiple tours in Afghanistan, Latvia, and other small missions. Steve lead at each tactical level on deployments to Afghanistan, including: Rifle Platoon Commander, Reconnaissance Platoon Commander, and Commander of an Afghan Battalion Operational Mentor and Liaison Team. He concluded his Canadian military career as the Commanding Officer of the 1st Battalion, The Royal Canadian Regiment, where he led a multinational battlegroup in Latvia. He has uniquely been awarded national honours from the Governor General of Canada on three seperate occasions; receiving two Meritorious Service Medals for actions during combat tours of duty in Kandahar and the Meritorious Service Cross for his leadership as the Multi-National Battle Group Commander in Latvia. Steve also holds multiple Canadian military national commendations, the Queen's Platinum Jubilee medal for activities supporting Canadian veterans, National Latvian and Slovenian medals of merit.

Following his retirement from the Canadian Forces, Steve continued his service with the New Zealand Defence Force, where he has served as the Deputy Commander of the Queen's Alexandra's Mounted Rifles and is currently the Director of Strategic Concepts for the New Zealand Army. Steve is passionate about veteran's transitions, their stories and volunteers with the Veteran led disaster relief organisation Task Force Kiwi. He resides in Wellington, New Zealand, with his family. In his free time, Steve is trying to learn surf cast fishing and exploring the breathtaking wilderness on the trails of New Zealand.

DOUBLE‡DAGGER

— www.doubledagger.ca —

DOUBLE DAGGER BOOKS is Canada's only military-focused publisher. Conflict and warfare have shaped human history since before we began to record it. The earliest stories that we know of, passed on as oral tradition, speak of war, and more importantly, the essential elements of the human condition that are revealed under its pressure.

We are dedicated to publishing material that, while rooted in conflict, transcend the idea of "war" as merely a genre. Fiction, non-fiction, and stuff that defies categorization, we want to read it all.

Because if you want peace, study war.

www.ingramcontent.com/pod-product-compliance
Lightning Source LLC
Chambersburg PA
CBHW021657120626
46545CB00004B/1282